The First Bilateral Investment Treaties

Nicaraguan Minister of Foreign Affairs Alejandro Montiel and U.S. Ambassador Thomas E. Whelan exchange instruments of ratification for the FCN treaty between the United States and Nicaragua in Managua on April 24, 1958. Minister Montiel is seated and Ambassador Whelan is standing to his right.
SOURCE: Photo by the United States Information Service. This is a reproduction of the original photo which is now housed at the National Archives.

The First Bilateral Investment Treaties

U.S. Postwar Friendship, Commerce, and Navigation Treaties

KENNETH J. VANDEVELDE

OXFORD
UNIVERSITY PRESS

OXFORD
UNIVERSITY PRESS

Oxford University Press is a department of the University of Oxford. It furthers the University's objective of excellence in research, scholarship, and education by publishing worldwide. Oxford is a registered trademark of Oxford University Press in the UK and certain other countries.

Published in the United States of America by Oxford University Press
198 Madison Avenue, New York, NY 10016, United States of America.

Library of Congress Cataloging-in-Publication Data

Names: Vandevelde, Kenneth J., author.
Title: The first bilateral investment treaties : U.S. postwar friendship, commerce, and navigation treaties / Kenneth J. Vandevelde.
Description: New York : Oxford University Press, 2017. | Includes bibliographical references and index.
Identifiers: LCCN 2016047154 | ISBN 9780190679576 ((hardback)
Subjects: LCSH: United States—Foreign relations—Treaties. | Investments, Foreign—Law and legislation—United States. | United States—Commercial treaties. | International and municipal law—United States.
Classification: LCC KF1575 .V37 2017 | DDC 346.73/0922—dc23 LC record available at https://lccn.loc.gov/2016047154

Note to Readers
This publication is designed to provide accurate and authoritative information in regard to the subject matter covered. It is based upon sources believed to be accurate and reliable and is intended to be current as of the time it was written. It is sold with the understanding that the publisher is not engaged in rendering legal, accounting, or other professional services. If legal advice or other expert assistance is required, the services of a competent professional person should be sought. Also, to confirm that the information has not been affected or changed by recent developments, traditional legal research techniques should be used, including checking primary sources where appropriate.

(Based on the Declaration of Principles jointly adopted by a Committee of the American Bar Association and a Committee of Publishers and Associations.)

For Lidia, Jenny, and Shelly

SUMMARY OF CONTENTS

TABLE OF CONTENTS

Introduction

During the final years of the Roosevelt administration, the United States conceived a foreign investment policy that endeavored to project New Deal liberalism onto the world. It launched a new series of friendship, commerce, and navigation (FCN) treaties with a set of investment provisions intended to incorporate that policy into international law. These provisions, particularly as they evolved during the Truman administration, eventually would form the basis for a network of thousands of bilateral investment treaties and regional trade and investment agreements that have established a legal framework for global capitalism.[1] The negotiation of the U.S. postwar FCN treaties, the first bilateral investment treaties in the history of international law, thus is the birthing moment of one of the most important developments in international economic law in the twentieth century. This book tells the story of that moment.

The story in summary form is as follows: In the early 1940s, U.S. policymakers planned the creation of a postwar international economic order designed to avoid the perceived mistakes of the interwar period, including autarkic economic policies and a rigid gold standard, mistakes that they believed had led to economic ruin and then war. To ensure prosperity and thus peace in the postwar era, the United States envisioned a kind of international New Deal, that is, a set of pragmatic, liberal regulatory, fiscal, and monetary policies that, while

1. Extensive discussion of the scope and content of modern bilateral investment treaties may be found in Jeswald Salacuse, *The Law of Investment Treaties* (Oxford: Oxford University Press, 2d edition, 2015); Rudolf Dolzer and Christoph Schreuer, *Principles of International Investment Law* (Oxford: Oxford University Press, 2d edition, 2012); Kenneth J. Vandevelde, *Bilateral Investment Treaties: History, Theory and Interpretation* (New York: Oxford University Press, 2010); Andrew Newcombe and Lluis Paradell, *Law and Practice of Investment Treaties: Standards of Treatment* (Alphen aan den Rijn: Kluwer Law International, 2009); Christopher F. Dugan, Don Wallace Jr., Noah D. Rubins, and Borzu Sabahi, *Investor-State Arbitration* (Oxford: Oxford University Press, 2008); August Reinisch, ed., *Standards of Investment Protection* (Oxford: Oxford University Press, 2008); Surya P. Subedi, *International Investment Law: Reconciling Policy and Principle* (Portland, OR: Hart Publishing, 2008); Campbell McLachlan, Laurence Shore and Matthew Weiniger, *International Investment Arbitration: Substantive Principles* (Oxford: Oxford University Press, 2007).

operating subject to principles of liberal legality, would promote a stable, full employment economy in the United States and abroad. The chief obstacle to a full employment economy in the United States was the manufacturing surplus that the U.S. economy would enjoy when the war ended, which could be eliminated only through exports. Other countries, however, their economies ravaged by the war or still underdeveloped, lacked sufficient dollars to purchase U.S. exports. U.S. prosperity thus necessitated that the United States persuade other countries to open their markets to U.S. goods, while opening its own market to their exports so that other countries could earn the dollars needed to purchase the surplus. Promoting free trade was not a sufficient solution because the export capacity in other countries was insufficient to earn enough dollars to purchase the entire U.S. surplus. Other countries would need to obtain a portion of the necessary dollars from inward foreign investment, both public and private.

U.S. policymakers believed that, to promote international capital movements, U.S. investment abroad must be guaranteed legal protection against adverse host state treatment. At the same time, however, they believed that obtaining the maximum benefit from international capital movements while preserving economic stability necessitated that countries also retain some discretion to regulate foreign investment.

As the war neared its end, the United States proposed a set of multilateral institutions to create the liberal postwar international economic order that it sought. An International Trade Organization (ITO) would facilitate multilateral negotiations to lower trade barriers worldwide. An International Monetary Fund (IMF) would provide stable exchange rates, but with greater flexibility than had the gold standard. An International Bank for Reconstruction and Development (IBRD) would provide public capital to support reconstruction of Europe and economic development in Africa, Asia, and Latin America.

The United States obtained international agreement on the creation of the IMF and IBRD at an international conference at Bretton Woods, New Hampshire, in 1944, a year before the war ended. The proposed ITO, however, was more ambitious, and formal negotiations to create the ITO did not begin until late 1946 and were not completed until early 1948.

Meanwhile, the international business community long had been dissatisfied with the lack of protection for foreign investment under international law. When the United States announced its proposed Charter for the ITO, the business community strongly urged the inclusion of provisions to protect foreign investment, and the U.S. government sought to honor that request. The investment-related provisions proposed by the United States were controversial, with the result that negotiators adopted them, but with modifications. The modifications so weakened the provisions that the U.S. business community believed that they were actually counterproductive, and it turned against the ITO Charter. By this time, the Truman administration, preoccupied with the Cold War and lacking support for the Charter from the business community, abandoned its efforts to obtain congressional approval of the ITO Charter, which was never ratified by the United States and never entered into force.

The end of the war had permitted the United States to resume the negotiation of FCN treaties, which the United States had been negotiating since independence. It had used a hiatus in negotiations during the war to significantly revise the standard draft FCN treaty and, in particular, to include stronger provisions for the protection of foreign investment, especially investment held by corporations.

While the ITO Charter was pending before Congress, U.S. negotiators sought to reconcile the new series of FCN treaties with the ITO Charter by incorporating into the U.S. standard draft FCN treaty additional investment-related provisions, specifically, prohibitions on unreasonable or discriminatory treatment of investment and a guarantee of fair and equitable treatment. Building on the creation of the IMF, they also incorporated into the standard draft treaty new language providing for the transfer of capital and returns. The result was a standard draft treaty more protective of foreign investment than any previous FCN treaty.

As U.S. negotiators crafted the investment-related provisions of the standard draft FCN treaty, they attempted to provide for U.S. investors abroad protections similar to those already enjoyed by foreign investors in the United States under U.S. law, particularly under the principles of U.S. constitutional law. These principles—principles of security, reasonableness, non-discrimination, and due process—were also basic principles of the rule of law, and U.S. negotiators saw the treaties as reflecting both U.S. constitutional principles and the rule of law, concepts that they tended to conflate.

U.S. constitutional and legal principles guided the negotiators' crafting of the treaties' investment-related provisions for at least three reasons. First, the negotiators regarded the FCN treaties as a means of projecting U.S. liberal legality or, in their language, the rule of law, onto the international plane, and the Constitution established the basic principles of that legality. Second, because foreign investors and their investments were protected in the United States by the Constitution, a treaty that failed to include protections similar to those provided by the Constitution would have obtained for U.S. investors abroad less protection than foreign investors received in the United States. Third, the United States did not intend for the treaties to guarantee to foreign investors in the United States greater rights than U.S. investors had in the United States, and thus protections accorded by the treaties should not exceed those already provided by U.S. law, particularly the U.S. Constitution.[2]

The FCN treaties, in at least one respect, did impose obligations beyond basic constitutional or rule of law principles (although not beyond U.S. law and policy), and that was in their provisions that dealt with the movement of capital across borders. These provisions reflected the fact that the treaties were intended to promote not only the rule of law, but also—though to a lesser extent—the system of free enterprise. As the State Department explained during negotiations with France, "the treaty was based on the principle that free market conditions

2. The relationship between the Constitution and the rights granted under the FCN treaties is further discussed in the introduction to Chapter 8.

should govern investment decisions."[3] The treaty provision that the United States most often identified with promoting free enterprise was that which guaranteed to nationals and companies of one party national treatment with respect to engaging in activity for gain and certain non-profit activities in the territory of the other country. Because of widespread concern about the potentially adverse effects of international capital movements, this was the most controversial of the investment provisions, and resistance to it greatly impeded the negotiation of the treaties.

As his 1949 inauguration approached, President Harry Truman sought a memorable theme for his inaugural address. A mid-level State Department official proposed that the United States commit itself to a program of technical assistance for the developing world, an idea that Truman instantly supported because it seemed to be an extension of the New Deal onto the international plane. Truman adopted the proposal as "Point Four" of his inaugural address, although he advocated combining U.S. technical assistance with the promotion of foreign investment, because he recognized the role that foreign investment had played in the economic development of the United States. As the State Department endeavored to create a program to implement Point Four, it began to regard the FCN treaties with their new investment provisions as a key element of the U.S. investment promotion program under Point Four. Meanwhile, Cold War efforts to contain the spread of Soviet influence provided a new rationale for promoting U.S. private investment: the idea that those countries that were the least developed economically were the most susceptible to the appeal of communism. Insofar as it promoted economic development abroad, U.S. private investment would contribute to containment.

The U.S. FCN treaties, which dated back to 1778, traditionally had been concerned with establishing trade and maritime relations, although they generally had included a few provisions for the protection of foreign property. By mid-1949, the State Department had reconceptualized the FCN treaties as investment treaties and the protection of foreign investment had become the primary purpose of the treaties. As the State Department negotiated the postwar FCN treaties, it faced pressure from the business community to negotiate additional treaties and to strengthen further the protection guaranteed by the treaties to U.S. investment. Believing that the treaties represented a mutual acceptance of "right principle" rather than merely a collection of concessions, the State Department rejected the demands of the business community that it use its economic power to coerce other countries to conclude FCN treaties on terms desired by the U.S. government or the U.S. business community.

The election to the presidency of Republican Dwight Eisenhower in 1952 brought continuity, rather than change, to the FCN treaty program. The Eisenhower administration embraced the foreign investment policy developed by the Democratic Roosevelt and Truman administrations and continued to negotiate FCN treaties

3. Despatch dated June 29, 1959, from the U.S. embassy in Paris to the Department of State, NARA, Record Group 59, Department of State File No. 611.514/6-2959.

based on the standard draft treaty developed during those administrations, making only modest evolutionary changes of the type that had occurred throughout the history of the program. Most of the negotiations during the Eisenhower administration merely completed discussions that had begun in the Truman years, although in the late 1950s the Eisenhower administration was able to launch successful negotiations in Southeast Asia, a region previously untouched by the U.S. postwar FCN treaties. The administrations of John F. Kennedy, Lyndon B. Johnson, Richard M. Nixon, and Gerald R. Ford similarly continued to pursue FCN treaty negotiations. By the mid-1960s, the United States had exhausted the number of countries willing to conclude an FCN treaty on the terms desired by the United States, although it continued its efforts to negotiate FCN treaties for another decade.

Meanwhile, at the end of the 1950s, several European countries, led by Germany, had begun successful programs to negotiate bilateral investment treaties (BITs) with developing countries. Several of these European countries, including Germany, had already concluded postwar FCN treaties with the United States. These new European BITs consisted largely of modified versions of the investment-related provisions that had appeared in the U.S. postwar FCN treaties, and they excluded the trade and navigation provisions that had served as the original impetus for the FCN treaties.

In 1977, the Jimmy Carter administration decided to abandon the FCN treaty form and to initiate a new U.S. BIT program. The U.S. BITs were regarded as successors to the FCN treaties and comprised revised versions of the investment-related provisions that had appeared in the FCN treaties and a small number of new provisions that over time had emerged in the European BITs. In 1992, with the conclusion of the North American Free Trade Agreement, the United States began the practice of incorporating into its free trade agreements investment chapters that were based on the language of the U.S. BITs. In so doing, the United States re-embraced the concept of the U.S. postwar FCN treaties—a treaty that provided a comprehensive (though not exhaustive) basis for bilateral economic relations, including the protection of foreign investment. As this manuscript is completed, 70 years after the conclusion of the first U.S. postwar FCN treaty, the investment provisions developed by the Roosevelt and Truman administrations in the U.S. postwar FCN treaties to project New Deal liberalism onto the world remain at the core of U.S. investment treaty practice and, indeed, investment treaty practice worldwide.

ABOUT THIS BOOK

Why This Book Was Written

The idea for this book originated almost 35 years ago. In the early 1980s, I was working in the Office of the Legal Adviser at the Department of State. A series of experiences, dating almost from my first day in the office, brought me to two conclusions: the provisions of the FCN treaties were of growing importance, and we knew too little about them.

The first of these experiences was my work related to the representation of the United States in claims before the Iran-United States Claims Tribunal, which required me to become familiar with the investment-related provisions of the U.S. postwar FCN treaty with Iran and with U.S. foreign investment policy generally. In researching the legal bases for the U.S. claims, I was disappointed at the lack of literature concerning the history and meaning of the investment-related FCN treaty provisions. Next, at the very time that I began my work with the tribunal, the State Department was in the process of developing its model bilateral investment treaty and, because of my work on U.S. investment policy and U.S. investment claims, I was asked to become involved. The U.S. model BIT was based closely on the U.S. postwar FCN treaties and, as we endeavored to understand the potential legal consequences of the new BIT provisions, I again saw the importance of the FCN treaty provisions and lamented the paucity of literature on their history and meaning. Then, in 1984, when Nicaragua submitted a claim against the United States to the International Court of Justice alleging, among other things, violations of the U.S. postwar FCN treaty with Nicaragua, I was asked to join the team representing the United States before the Court. Although the portion of the U.S. memorial for which I eventually assumed primary drafting responsibility was the portion on the Vandenberg reservation, during team meetings we discussed collectively every issue in the case and, once more, I saw the potential importance of the FCN treaties and the inadequacy of the existing literature on those treaties. In 1986, I was asked to lead the team that would represent the United States in the only investment claim ever submitted to the International Court of Justice under a U.S. postwar FCN treaty.[4] Although I declined, for reasons that I no longer recall, once more I saw the significance of both the treaties and the gap in the literature on them. I hoped that one day I would be able to address that insufficiency, at least in part.

My disappointment at the scarcity of materials on the history of the investment-related provisions of the FCN treaties inspired me to want to ensure that the same did not occur with respect to the U.S. BITs. While still working in the Legal Adviser's Office, I began to write the history of the U.S. BIT program—and I have been doing so ever since. I published that history in a series of articles[5] and then, more systematically, in two books. *United States Investment Treaties: Policy and Practice,* published in 1992 by Kluwer Law International, went out of print a few years later. *U.S. International Investment Agreements,* published by Oxford University Press in 2009, replaced it. Because the U.S. BITs drew so heavily upon the investment provisions of the U.S. FCN treaties, both of these books included some discussion of the U.S. FCN treaties. Limitations of time and space, however, prevented me from

4. *Case concerning Elettronica Sicula S.p.A.(ELSI)* (United States v. Italy), 1989 I.C.J. 15.

5. *See, e.g.,* "A Comparison of the 2004 and 1994 U.S. Model BITs: Rebalancing Investor and Host State Interests," in Karl P. Sauvant, ed., *Yearbook on International Investment Law and Policy 2008/2009* (New York: Oxford University Press, 2009); "Of Politics and Markets: The Shifting Ideology of the BITs," 11 *International Tax and Business Lawyer* (now *Berkeley Journal of International Law*) 159 (1993); "U.S. Bilateral Investment Treaties: The Second Wave," 14 *Michigan Journal of International Law* 621 (1993); "The Bilateral Investment Treaty Program of the United States," 21 *Cornell International Law Journal* 201 (1988).

including a fuller treatment of the FCN treaties in either book and, in any event, I had not yet extensively researched the history of the FCN treaties when I wrote those books. I recognized that a more complete history of the U.S. BIT program could be written if more were known about the history of the U.S. FCN treaties and, once again, I regretted the absence of a history of those treaties.

My interest in the U.S. BIT program led me to an interest in the BIT programs of other countries. In the early 1990s, I had begun to write a book on BIT programs worldwide, intended to be the first book on the subject. An unexpected (and unsought) request that I serve as the acting dean of my law school during a search for a permanent dean, which led to an equally unexpected and unsought 11-year stint in the dean's office, forced the postponement of that project, but I provided a revised version of the manuscript already in progress to the United Nations Conference for Trade and Development (UNCTAD), which published that manuscript with numerous revisions as *Bilateral Investment Treaties in the Mid 1990s*. After my successful extrication from the dean's office in 2005, I began work on *U.S. International Investment Agreements*, already mentioned, and *Bilateral Investment Treaties: History, Policy and Interpretation*, published by Oxford University Press in 2010. The latter book surveyed the developments in BIT programs generally from the conclusion of the first German BIT in 1959 through the fiftieth anniversary of that BIT, in 2009. This was the book that I had begun to write in the early 1990s, although intervening events, particularly the commencement of numerous investor-state arbitrations, resulted in a different book than I would have written 15 years earlier. The comparative analysis in that book demonstrated the remarkable uniformity among BITs worldwide and the extent to which they had a common ancestor in the little-studied investment provisions of the U.S. postwar FCN treaties. The analysis made clear that a history of the FCN treaties had become indispensable to achieving an understanding, faithful to history, of not only the U.S. BITs, but the entire global network of BITs and free trade agreements with investment provisions.

The publication of this book completes a trilogy that has been 30 years in the making. It lays the foundation for the other two books with an account of the emergence of a U.S. postwar foreign investment policy that resulted in the transformation of the U.S. FCN treaties into investment treaties, including a description of the legal regime that the investment-related provisions of the FCN treaties were intended to create. *U.S. International Investment Agreements* advances the story by showing how in the 1970s the FCN treaties were succeeded in the United States by the BITs, and explicates the provisions of those BITs. In so doing, it demonstrates the continuity in U.S. foreign investment policy and treaty practice. *Bilateral Investment Treaties: History, Policy and Interpretation* broadens the story to include the network of more than 2,000 BITs worldwide, a network that rests on the foundation laid in the U.S. postwar FCN treaties.

How This Book Was Written

In 2009, having just sent the manuscript for *Bilateral Investment Treaties* to the publisher, I turned my attention to the long-deferred project of unearthing the history of the investment-related provisions of the U.S. postwar FCN treaties, a history that appears in these pages. In September of that year, I commenced graduate study at the University of California, from which I would receive a PhD in history three years later. I had decided prior to commencing my graduate study that a portion of my project on the U.S. postwar FCN treaties would serve as my doctoral dissertation. The dissertation was completed in 2012 and covered only the period through the end of the Truman administration. In writing this book, I have taken the opportunity to add a considerable amount of new material, to revise in places the text that appeared in the dissertation and, in particular, to correct a few minor errors in the dissertation. This Introduction and the first four chapters contain material that appeared in the dissertation, although with some revisions and minor corrections, whereas Chapters 5 through 8 contain much new material. Indeed, all of Chapters 7 and 8 is new. Thus, less than half of the material in this book appeared in the dissertation.

Although in conducting my research I read the existing secondary literature on the FCN treaties and reviewed a diverse array of primary and secondary source materials on U.S. postwar foreign investment policy, some of which is cited in the footnotes, my most productive source was the negotiating history of the FCN treaties and of the Charter of the International Trade Organization, documents that are maintained in the National Archives and Records Administration (NARA) facility in College Park, Maryland. In writing this book, I read some 32,000 pages of that history, a task that stretched over a period of seven years, from 2009 until 2016.

Sadly, as part of the NARA's normal record culling process, many of the relevant records were destroyed before I began my research. An especially lamentable victim of the culling process was the records of the office within the State Department responsible for negotiating the FCN treaties. Thus, a large portion of the records of the Department's internal deliberations with respect to the treaties has been lost and, as a result, we can see the rationale behind particular language in the treaties primarily when it was communicated to an embassy. Further, the State Department changed its record-keeping system rather dramatically in 1964 and few records relating to the FCN treaty program after 1963 appear to have survived.

I was able to read the extant negotiating history of all of the FCN treaties concluded by the United States after the war. I also read thousands of pages of records relating to negotiations that ultimately were not successful or relating to negotiations that were contemplated but that never formally began.

My method was heavily empirical. Although the records included some lamentable gaps, the information was sufficiently abundant that I decided, to the extent possible, to allow those who drafted and negotiated the treaties to tell the story. The result is an account documented by more than 3,200 footnotes, the vast majority of which are to primary sources. In short, I have tried to do little more than to organize and summarize the records in the National Archives, while limiting the extent of my own inferences and interpretations.

The records were riddled with redundancy. U.S. foreign investment policy as reflected in the treaties was unfailingly consistent and the principal negotiators changed little during the course of the program, with the result that the same ideas were reiterated, sometimes in virtually identical terms, over the course of numerous negotiations. Accordingly, I did not attempt to cite exhaustively the records supporting each assertion in this account.

During my years in the Office of the Legal Adviser, because of my work with the U.S. FCN treaties and the U.S. BITs, which included provisions analogous to those in the FCN treaties, I had acquired an understanding of the received wisdom within the State Department concerning the meaning of the various provisions of the FCN treaties. I expected the records to shed new light on that received wisdom, perhaps revealing places where the interpretation of a provision had evolved between 1945, when the first postwar FCN treaty negotiation began, and 1982, when I joined the State Department and BIT negotiations were underway. I found instead that the consistency of interpretation dating from 1945 had survived into the 1980s. Even the negotiating strategy for the BITs was largely unchanged from that of the FCN treaties. The U.S. BITs truly were successors to the U.S. postwar FCN treaties. The U.S. postwar FCN treaties were, just as truly, the first bilateral investment treaties.

Whom I Must Thank

My work on this project benefitted from the kind and capable assistance of many others. I would like to acknowledge my debt to the archivists at the National Archives and Records Administration facilities in Washington, DC, and College Park, Maryland, who were indispensable in guiding me to the relevant records. I must thank two of the archivists in particular. David Langbort provided invaluable advice and information regarding the collection and also assisted me in locating key documents. Rodney Ross very kindly located and retrieved all of the files of the Senate Foreign Relations Committee relating to the postwar FCN treaties and, when I encountered some glitches in the records, came immediately to my assistance, saving me untold hours of work. I must also thank three of the librarians at the Thomas Jefferson School of Law. Marie Templo culled through the Congressional Record and assembled the records of all of the Senate deliberations on the treaties, Lisa Foster assisted me in finding old documents archived on various electronic databases, and Emily Ngo managed to obtain through interlibrary loan every single book that I requested. Dale Stieber, the College Archivist at Occidental College, provided me with images of documents from the John Parke Young papers. Finally, I am grateful for comments on my dissertation to Michael Parrish, who served as my dissertation adviser, and to Richard Feinberg, Mark Hendrickson, David Lake, and Rebecca Plant, who served on my dissertation committee, and grateful as well to Emily Rosenberg, for her tutoring in the literature of international economic history.

What This Book Contains

The remainder of this Introduction addresses two issues. First, it explains how the term “New Deal liberalism” is understood throughout this book. Second, it describes the relationship between New Deal liberalism and U.S. postwar foreign investment policy.

Chapters 1 through 5 provide a continuous narrative concerning the process by which the Roosevelt and Truman administrations during the 1940s developed their postwar foreign investment policy and embodied that policy in a set of investment-related provisions incorporated into the U.S. postwar FCN treaties. The effect was to reconceptualize treaties formerly concerned primarily with trade and navigation as the first bilateral investment treaties. This process was largely completed by 1949. These chapters address the question of what the Roosevelt and Truman administrations were seeking to accomplish when they drafted the investment-related provisions of the U.S. postwar FCN treaties and transformed those treaties into the first bilateral investment treaties. These chapters include a discussion of the negotiation of the first of the U.S. postwar FCN treaties, those with China, Italy, Colombia, Uruguay, and Ireland: the negotiations in which the United States determined the substance of nearly all of the investment-related provisions of the treaties.

Chapters 6 and 7 provide an account of the negotiation of the FCN treaties in the years following their reconceptualization as bilateral investment treaties. These chapters examine the considerations that led other countries to undertake successful FCN treaty negotiations with the United States, the strategies employed by the United States to bring those negotiations to a successful conclusion, the chief objections that other countries raised to the conclusion of an FCN treaty, the kinds of concessions that the United States was willing to make to meet those objections, and the kinds of concessions that it was not willing to make. The purpose of these chapters is to show U.S. foreign investment policy and U.S. negotiating strategy in operation.

The account in these two chapters focuses primarily on the negotiation of the investment-related provisions of the treaties. In some cases, the account addresses other issues, such as those related to trade or freedom of religion, particularly in cases where those other issues threatened to prevent the successful conclusion or entry into force of a treaty. These chapters, however, do not chronicle in any systematic way issues not directly related to investment protection. Nor do they provide a comprehensive summary of the investment-related provisions of any specific treaty or a complete description of all of the departures from the standard draft treaty that appear in any concluded treaty. These chapters are concerned with the process of negotiating the investment-related provisions of the treaties rather than the legal consequences of each individual treaty.

Chapter 8 explicates the meaning of the investment-related provisions of the FCN treaties, as reflected in the negotiating history. Chapter 8 thus demonstrates how the foreign investment policy developed by the Roosevelt and Truman administrations in the 1940s found concrete expression in the provisions of the U.S. postwar FCN treaties. The standard draft FCN treaty evolved continuously throughout the duration of the program. Considerations of space precluded any attempt to trace in detail each of the changes to the standard draft treaty. Rather, the 1955 standard draft treaty was used as the exemplar. The standard draft treaty had reached its mature form by the end of the Truman administration, but the choice of a later draft as the exemplar facilitated the discussion of a very few changes that occurred during the mid-1950s. Although I have attempted in Chapter 8 to summarize the results of my research on the meaning of specific treaty provisions, particular treaty provisions are also discussed in the accounts of the individual treaty negotiations that appear in earlier chapters, and these accounts may contain bits of explanatory information that are not repeated in Chapter 8.

The appendix contains excerpts from the 1955 standard draft U.S. postwar FCN treaty.

NEW DEAL LIBERALISM

Economic Liberalism

Although the FCN treaties were instruments of foreign economic policy, U.S. government officials during the Truman administration drew analogies between U.S. foreign economic policy and the liberal domestic economic policies of Franklin Roosevelt's New Deal. Truman himself formulated portions of his foreign economic policy with explicit reference to the domestic policies of the New Deal.

Roosevelt's New Deal endeavored to end the Great Depression and to reform the U.S. economy to prevent a recurrence of the economic panics that had occurred intermittently for more than a century. The policies employed to these ends changed, and, particularly in the beginning, could be contradictory. The New Deal's legislative program over time reflected a shift from policies of restricting supply to policies of stimulating demand,[6] from policies of organizing cartels to policies of restoring competition,[7] and from policies of economic nationalism to policies of liberal internationalism.[8]

Most historians now regard the New Deal as a pragmatic collection of experiments.[9] The New Deal rejected economic orthodoxies constructed around

6. Ellis W. Hawley, *The New Deal and the Problem of Monopoly: A Study in Economic Ambivalence* (Princeton, NJ: Princeton University Press, 1966); Alan Brinkley, *The End of Reform: New Deal Liberalism in Recession and War* (New York: Alfred A. Knopf, 1995).

7. Michael A. Bernstein, *A Perilous Progress: Economists and Public Purpose in Twentieth-Century America* (Princeton, NJ: Princeton University Press, 2001), page 76; Kenneth S. Davis, *FDR: The New Deal Years, 1933–1937: A History* (New York: Random House, 1986), pages 233–235.

8. Robert Dallek, *Franklin Roosevelt and American Foreign Policy, 1932-1945* (New York: Oxford University Press, 1979), page 38; Lloyd C. Gardner, *Economic Aspects of New Deal Diplomacy* (Madison: University of Wisconsin Press, 1964), pages 3–4.

9. Michael Bernstein, for example, writes, "It was in fact this willingness to experiment . . . that in large part animated the New Deal itself." Bernstein, *A Perilous Progress*, page 74. Kenneth S. Davis similarly argues that the New Deal mind was "a composite or conglomerate, a mixture and mingling of mental tendencies and points of view that differed from one another to the point, often enough, of direct contradiction." Davis, *FDR*, page 233. Elizabeth Borgwardt refers to the "pragmatic and polyglot New Deal idiom." Elizabeth Borgwardt, *A New Deal for the World: America's Vision for Human Rights* (Cambridge, MA: Harvard University Press, 2005).

rationalist models of economic behavior in favor of a more empirical approach to policymaking.[10] For example, the early New Deal experimented with a planning model, whereas the later New Deal turned to vigorous antitrust enforcement.[11] Early attempts to end the Depression by controlled production yielded to a later policy of promoting consumption through the creation of a welfare state and through Keynesian countercyclical spending.[12] The United States shifted from a producer-oriented to a consumer-oriented economy.[13]

Postwar New Deal liberals "praised the New Deal for having solved the problems of capitalism without altering the structure of capitalism; for having used the state to save the economy without intruding the state too far into the economy."[14] The state's role was "to compensate for capitalism's inevitable flaws and omissions without interfering very much with its internal workings."[15]

Several programmatic elements of New Deal liberalism in its mature form are especially relevant to the development of U.S. foreign investment policy. Although they remained committed to a system of free enterprise, when the market failed to generate full employment, New Deal liberals willingly embraced state capitalism, as reflected in programs such as the Reconstruction Finance Corporation, the Tennessee Valley Authority, the Rural Electrification Administration, and

The characterization of the New Deal as a pragmatic collection of sometimes contradictory policies appeared early in the literature. *See, e.g.,* C. Herman Pritchett, *The Roosevelt Court: A Study in Judicial Politics and Values, 1937–1947* (New York: MacMillan, 1948), page 265.

10. The emergence of an empirical, pragmatic mode of policymaking in the early years of the twentieth century is wonderfully sketched in Louis Menand, *The Metaphysical Club: A Story of Ideas in America* (New York: Farrer, Straus and Giroux, 2001) and in Edward A. Purcell, *The Crisis of Democratic Theory: Scientific Naturalism and the Problem of Value* (Lexington: University Press of Kentucky, 1973). The connection between this mode of policymaking and Keynesian economics is described in Robert Skidelsky, *Keynes: The Return of the Master* (New York: Public Affairs, 2009). The connection to postwar developmental assistance programs modeled after the state capitalism of the New Deal, such as the International Bank for Reconstruction and Development, the Marshall Plan, and Truman's Point Four program, is drawn in Michael E. Lathan, *Modernization as Ideology: American Social Science and "Nation Building" in the Kennedy Era* (Chapel Hill: University of North Carolina Press, 2000). Pragmatism had emerged in the United States during the Progressive era, and many of Roosevelt's advisors were products of that era. Alonzo Hamby, *For the Survival of Democracy: Franklin Roosevelt and the World Crisis of the 1930s* (New York: Free Press, 2004), page 204.

11. Hawley, *The New Deal and the Problem of Monopoly*; Alan Brinkley, *The End of Reform: New Deal Liberalism in Recession and War* (New York: Alfred A. Knopf, 1995).

12. Hawley, *The New Deal and the Problem of Monopoly;* Brinkley, *The End of Reform.* On Roosevelt's gradual conversion to countercyclical spending, *see* Kenneth S. Davis, *FDR: Into the Storm, 1937–1940: A History* (New York: Random House, 1993), especially pages 536–537.

13. Kathleen G. Donohue, *Freedom from Want: American Liberalism and the Idea of the Consumer* (Baltimore: Johns Hopkins University Press, 2003).

14. Hawley, *The New Deal and the Problem of Monopoly,* page 266.

15. Ibid., page 269.

numerous public works projects.[16] By promoting economic development, these kinds of projects stimulated consumption and thus employment.

New Deal liberals also embraced regulation as a means of addressing market failure. For example, labor laws addressed market failure in the form of unequal bargaining power, but also served to promote consumption.[17] Antitrust laws addressed market failure in the form of anticompetitive business practices.

The pragmatism and empiricism of the New Deal were evident in its foreign economic policy.[18] Roosevelt's initial approaches to foreign economic policy were contradictory and included some experiments with economic nationalism.[19] Roosevelt soon adopted, however, the free trade policies of Secretary of State Cordell Hull and publicly embraced the view that "a full and permanent domestic recovery" depended upon an increase in U.S. exports.[20] The critical turning point was Roosevelt's 1934 decision to seek passage of the Reciprocal Trade Agreements Act, legislation that gave the executive unprecedented authority to negotiate tariff reductions with other countries without the need to obtain congressional

16. Jordan A. Schwartz, *The New Dealers: Power Politics in the Age of Roosevelt* (New York: Alfred A. Knopf, 1993); Jason Scott Smith argues that Truman's Point Four program of developmental assistance was a legacy of New Deal state capitalism. Jason Scott Smith, *Building New Deal Liberalism: The Political Economy of Public Works, 1933–1956* (New York: Cambridge University Press, 2006), pages 248–249.

17. Steve Fraser, "The 'Labor Question,'" in Steve Fraser and Gary Gerstle, eds., *The Rise and Fall of the New Deal Order 1930–1980* (Princeton, NJ: Princeton University Press, 1989).

18. Lloyd C. Gardner has argued to the contrary, asserting that "[t]he domestic pragmatism of the New Deal was not repeated in foreign policy matters, though there were tactical shifts from time to time." Gardner, *Economic Aspects,* page 20. Gardner's account does not address FCN treaties except very briefly.

19. Patricia Clavin writes in detail about a particular instance of economic nationalist behavior, Roosevelt's decision to torpedo the 1933 World Economic Conference by refusing to agree to a currency stabilization plan, thereby leaving the United States free to allow further devaluation of the dollar. Patricia Clavin, *The Failure of Economic Diplomacy: Britain, Germany, France and the United States, 1931–1936* (New York: St. Martin's Press, 1996). Other accounts of Roosevelt's early economic nationalism include Alfred E., Eckes Jr., *A Search for Solvency: Bretton Woods and the International Monetary System, 1941–1971* (Austin: University of Texas Press, 1975), pages 20–24; John M. Rothgeb Jr., *U.S. Trade Policy: Balancing Economic Dreams and Political Realities* (Washington, DC: Congressional Quarterly Press, 2001), pages 40–42; Robert A. Pollard, *Economic Security and the Origins of the Cold War, 1945–1950* (New York: Columbia University Press, 1985), page 7; Diane B. Kunz, *Butter and Guns: America's Cold War Economic Diplomacy* (New York: The Free Press, 1997), page 11; Dallek, *Franklin Roosevelt,* pages 35–77; Jeffrey Frieden, "Sectoral Conflict and U.S. Foreign Economic Policy, 1914–1940," in G. John Ikenberry, David A. Lake, and Michael Mastanduno, eds., *The State and American Foreign Policy* (Ithaca, NY: Cornell University Press, 1988); and Stephan Haggard, "The Institutional Foundations of Hegemony: Explaining the Reciprocal Trade Agreements Act of 1934," in Ikenberry et al., *The State and American Foreign Policy.*

20. Edward S. Kaplan, *American Trade Policy, 1923–1995* (Westport, CT: Greenwood Press, 1996), page 46.

approval of each reduction.[21] Able to guarantee that the United States would meet its commitments to tariff reductions, the State Department after passage of the act possessed the bargaining leverage necessary to persuade other countries to lower their tariffs and to open their markets to American exports. Lowered U.S. tariff barriers would enable other countries to earn the dollars needed to purchase U.S. exports.[22] After 1934, the New Deal embraced liberal internationalism.

Truman's succession to the presidency upon the death of Franklin Roosevelt in April 1945 in no way diminished the administration's commitment to the New Deal.[23] Truman as president "proposed a liberal program to extend the New Deal."[24] Indeed, only four days after the surrender of Japan, Truman forwarded a message to Congress outlining his domestic program, a list of 21 New Deal programs that had not yet been enacted.[25] In January 1949, having just won re-election, Truman announced in his State of the Union address that "every segment of our population and every individual has a right to expect from his government a fair deal."[26] Truman's Fair Deal programs, however, consisted largely of the same New Deal measures that he had proposed in 1945[27] and, in fact, Truman had not intended to designate the phrase "fair deal" as a sobriquet for his policies.[28]

Truman continued to regard his administration as an extension of the New Deal. In his final State of the Union address, delivered on January 7, 1953, Truman reviewed the accomplishments of his eight years in the White House. He did so by

21. The administration's rationale for this legislation was described by Harry Hawkins, who had primary responsibility for the negotiation of trade agreements during the 1930s, in Harry C. Hawkins and Janet L. Norwood, "The Legislative Basis of United States Commercial Policy," in William B. Kelly Jr., *Studies in United States Commercial Policy* (Chapel Hill: University of North Carolina Press, 1963). The process of legislative enactment is described in Robert A. Pastor, *Congress and the Politics of U.S. Foreign Economic Policy, 1929–1976* (Berkeley: University of California Press, 1980) and Kaplan, *American Trade Policy,* pages 43–65.

22. Gardner, *Economic Aspects,* page 39.

23. Patrick Hearden argues that the same was true with respect to foreign policy. He writes, "The foreign policy of the United States did not undergo any fundamental change when Roosevelt died and Truman moved into the White House. . . . [T]he basic ideas that had been institutionalized in the State Department continued to guide the conduct of U.S. diplomacy." Patrick J. Hearden, *Architects of Globalism: Building a New World Order during World War II* (Fayetteville: University of Arkansas Press, 2002), page 314.

24. Robert H. Ferrell, *Harry S. Truman* (Washington, DC: Congressional Quarterly Press, 2003), page 4. *See also* Robert J. Donovan, *Conflict and Crisis: The Presidency of Harry S. Truman, 1945–1949* (New York: W. W. Norton, 1977), pages 30, 118.

25. Ferrell, *Harry S. Truman,* page 115.

26. Harry S. Truman, State of the Union Message, January 5, 1949, *quoted in* ibid., page 115.

27. Ferrell, *Harry S. Truman,* page 115.

28. Robert J. Donovan, *Tumultuous Years: The Presidency of Harry S. Truman, 1949–1953* (New York: W. W. Norton, 1982), page 23.

posing, and then answering, some of the questions he faced at the end of the war. With respect to domestic policy, he said,

> Now let me turn to another question we faced at the war's end. Would we take up again, and carry forward, the great projects of social welfare—so badly needed, so long overdue—that the New Deal had introduced into our national life? Would our government continue to have a heart for the people, or was the progress of the New Deal to be halted in the aftermath of war as decisively as the progress of Woodrow Wilson's New Freedom had been halted after the First World War?[29]

Similarly, in his final annual Economic Report, made to Congress on January 15, 1953, Truman elaborated upon what had been his philosophy. He explained that "[i]t is the duty of government to help improve the environment in which private enterprise works. . . . [T]he government should place principal reliance upon the careful use of fiscal and credit policy, along with the well established regulatory and protective programs."[30] The role of the government was to supervise the market through regulatory, fiscal, and monetary policies.

Legal Liberalism

As New Deal liberals experimented with various forms of market regulation and state capitalism, they recognized that the U.S. Constitution imposed constraints on the measures that they could employ. The relationship between the state and the market in the United States is structured by the U.S. Constitution, principally through four clauses: the contract clause, the takings clause, the due process clause, and the equal protection clause. Each of these clauses embodies norms that not only establish a particular relationship between the state and the market, but are central to the American understanding of the rule of law.

The contract clause was the first of these clauses to appear in the Constitution. The clause, set forth at Article I, section 10, provides that "[n]o State shall . . . pass any . . . Law impairing the Obligation of Contracts. . . ." The framers of the Constitution intended the contract clause to protect the security of rights created through contract. They included the clause primarily to prevent states from enacting debtor relief laws, although the language of the clause was broad enough to apply to a much wider range of circumstances.[31] Early decisions of the

29. Harry S. Truman, State of the Union Message, January 7, 1953, *quoted in* Louis W. Koenig, *The Truman Administration: Its Principles and Practice* (New York: New York University Press, 1956), page 255.

30. Truman's economic report, dated January 15, 1953, may be found in Koenig, *The Truman Administration,* page 197.

31. James W. Ely Jr., *The Guardian of Every Other Right: A Constitutional History of Property Rights* (New York: Oxford University Press, 1992), page 45; Douglas W. Kmiec and John O. Malone, "The Contract Clause: A Return to the Original Understanding," 14 *Hastings Constitutional Law*

Supreme Court read the clause expansively in order to protect the security of investment.[32]

The Great Depression awakened the Supreme Court to the impact of private contracts on the public sphere. In its 1934 decision in *Home Building & Loan v. Blaisdell,*[33] the Supreme Court upheld a Minnesota law that imposed a moratorium on mortgage foreclosures, a clear interference with the creditors' right to receive timely payments on loans and thus, seemingly, a law impairing the obligation of contract. The Court explained, however, that

> there has been a growing appreciation of public needs and of the necessity of finding ground for a rational compromise between individual rights and public welfare. . . . Where, in earlier days, it was thought that only the concerns of individuals or of classes were involved, and that those of the State itself were touched only remotely, it has later been found that the fundamental interests of the State are directly affected, and that the question is no longer merely that of one party to a contract as against another, but of the use of reasonable means to safeguard the economic structure upon which the good of all depends.[34]

The Supreme Court thus held that the contract clause permitted the state to impair the obligation of contract as long as the impairment, in effect, was a reasonable means of furthering the state's legitimate aims. That is, the state's regulation of contractual obligations and thus its interference with contractual entitlements was subject only to a norm of reasonableness. Further, under the reserved powers doctrine, dating back to the nineteenth century, contracts by the state in derogation of its reserved powers—the police power and the power of eminent domain—could be abrogated by the state without violation of the clause.[35]

The adoption of the Fifth Amendment to the Constitution in 1791 incorporated into the Constitution a second protection for the security of entitlements, the takings clause. That clause provides: "nor shall private property be taken for public use, without just compensation." Although the Supreme Court initially held that the clause applied only to the federal government,[36] by the end of the nineteenth century the Court had held that the adoption of the Fourteenth Amendment had resulted in the application of the takings clause to the states.[37] The language of the clause seems to address the situation where the state seizes property, but the

Quarterly 525 (1987); Steven R. Boyd, "The Contract Clause and the Evolution of American Federalism, 1789–1815," 44 *William and Mary Quarterly* 529 (1987).

32. The classic examples are *Fletcher v. Peck,* 10 U.S. 87 (1810) and *Dartmouth College v. Woodward,* 17 U.S. (4 Wheat.) 518 (1819).

33. 290 U.S. 398 (1934).

34. Ibid. at 442.

35. *See Stone v. Mississippi,* 101 U.S. 814 (1880); *West River Bridge Co. v. Dix,* 47 U.S. 507 (1848).

36. *Barron v. City of Baltimore,* 32 U.S. 243 (1833).

37. *Chicago, Burlington & Quincy R.R. v. City of Chicago,* 166 U.S. 226 (1897).

Supreme Court held in 1922 that a mere regulatory act that "goes too far" could also be considered a taking of property that requires payment of compensation.[38] Thus, the takings clause imposes an outer limit on the extent of state regulatory power. Left unclear by the Court in that decision was precisely how far the regulation must go before it would constitute a compensable taking.

The adoption of the Fifth Amendment also incorporated into the Constitution a third protection for property rights, the due process clause. The due process clause provides: "nor shall any person . . . be deprived of life, liberty, or property, without due process of law. . . ." The adoption of the Fourteenth Amendment imposed a similar restriction on the states. The Supreme Court held in 1856 that the phrase "due process of law" includes those procedural rights existing in the common law and statute law of England.[39] At a minimum, this requires notice and an opportunity to be heard.[40]

By the middle of the nineteenth century, members of the Supreme Court had begun to suggest that the due process clause imposed a substantive restriction on legislative enactments,[41] more specifically, a requirement that legislative action be a reasonable exercise of the state's regulatory power.[42] Although initially the Court used this clause to invalidate social reform legislation, most famously a maximum-hour law in *Lochner v. New York*,[43] in the 1930s the Court adopted a more deferential stance, holding that only the wholly arbitrary legislative act would violate the norm of reasonableness.[44] This shift reflected the same pragmatism and empiricism that underlay the New Deal's economic policy. Justice Oliver Wendell Holmes Jr. had complained in a dissenting opinion in *Lochner* that the Court's opinion invalidating the maximum-hour law had rested on "an economic theory which a large part of the country does not entertain."[45] The Fourteenth

38. *Pennsylvania Coal v. Mahon*, 260 U.S. 393, 415 (1922).

39. *Murray's Lessee v. Hoboken Land & Improvement Co.*, 59 U.S. 272 (1856).

40. *Hagar v. Reclamation District*, 111 U.S. 701, 708 (1884); *Hurtado v. California*, 110 U.S. 516, 534 (1884).

41. The history is traced in John V. Orth, *Due Process of Law: A Brief History* (Lawrence: University Press of Kansas, 2003).

42. *Allgeyer v. Louisiana*, 165 U.S. 578 (1897).

43. 198 U.S. 45 (1905). The Court held that a law prohibiting the employment of bakers in excess of 60 hours a week was not a reasonable health measure and therefore violated the due process clause.

44. *United States v. Carolene Products Co.*, 304 U.S. 144 (1938); *West Coast Hotel Co. v. Parrish*, 300 U.S. 379 (1937). Several scholars have argued that the extent of the shift has been overstated, and that the Supreme Court used the doctrine of substantive due process to invalidate legislation before 1937 far less often than is normally believed. *See, e.g.*, Michael J. Phillips, *The* Lochner *Court, Myth and Reality: Substantive Due Process from the 1890s to the 1930s* (Westport, CT: Praeger, 2001). No one denies, however, that, at least where economic regulations were concerned, the Supreme Court by the end of the 1930s invalidated only the wholly arbitrary law.

45. *Lochner v. New York*, 198 U.S. 45, 75 (Holmes, J., dissenting).

Amendment, he argued, did not "enact Mr. Herbert Spencer's Social Statics."[46] Put another way, the Constitution did not require a policy of laissez-faire. Rather, it permitted the legislature the discretion to experiment with interventionist economic policies. As the Court would note in 1940, echoing Holmes's comment in his *Lochner* dissent, in assessing the constitutionality of state action, "It is equally immaterial that such state action may run counter to the economic wisdom either of Adam Smith or of J. Maynard Keynes."[47]

The Fourteenth Amendment also prohibits any state from denying "to any person within its jurisdiction the equal protection of the laws," a prohibition that the Supreme Court in the 1950s would begin to apply to the federal government through the due process clause of the Fifth Amendment.[48] Although the Court initially suggested that this clause prohibited only race discrimination,[49] it soon was adjudicating the consistency of other kinds of legislative classification with the clause[50] and generally allowing them as long as they were reasonable.[51]

Although this development threatened to collapse the norm of non-discrimination into the norm of reasonableness, the Supreme Court would hold in 1944 that certain discriminations, particularly those involving race, would be subject to the "most rigid scrutiny."[52] Indeed, as early as 1886, the Supreme Court had invalidated ordinances that were based on "hostility to the race and nationality" of the Chinese subjects to whom the ordinances applied.[53] Thus, the norm of non-discrimination retains some independent content. It indicates that certain kinds of discriminations are suspect and cannot be justified merely on a showing of reasonableness. Further, even apart from the concept of suspect classifications, the principle of non-discrimination represented by the equal protection clause requires a different inquiry than the norm of reasonableness represented by the doctrine of substantive due process. The doctrine of substantive due process requires that a state's infringement of liberty or property rights be reasonable, whereas the doctrine of equal protection requires that the state's different treatment of persons be reasonable. A state in theory might have a reasonable justification for regulating a particular activity (and thus would satisfy the norm of reasonableness under the doctrine of substantive due process), but might not have a reasonable justification for regulating a particular activity when some but

46. Ibid.

47. *Osborn v. Ozlin,* 310 U.S. 53, 62 (1940).

48. *Bolling v. Sharpe,* 347 U.S. 497 (1954).

49. *Slaughterhouse Cases,* 83 U.S. 36 (1873).

50. *See, e.g., Munn v. Illinois,* 94 U.S. 113 (1877) and *Missouri v. Lewis,* 101 U.S. 22 (1880).

51. David P. Currie, *The Constitution in the Supreme Court: The Second Century, 1888–1986* (Chicago: The University of Chicago Press, 1994), page 136. Among these decisions are *Barbier v. Connolly,* 113 U.S. 27 (1885) and *Soon Hing v. Crowley,* 1134 U.S. 703 (1885).

52. *Korematsu v. United States,* 323 U.S. 214 (1944).

53. *Yick Wo v. Hopkins,* 118 U.S. 356, 374 (1886).

not other persons engage in the activity (and thus would not satisfy the norm of non-discrimination).[54]

In short, by the 1940s, U.S. constitutional law imposed norms of security, reasonableness, non-discrimination, and procedural due process on the state in its regulation of economic activity. In applying these norms, the Court embraced a pragmatic and empirical philosophy under which it would permit the state to experiment with different forms of economic organization and to intrude upon the private sector as long as the regulations met these basic norms. As I have argued elsewhere, these norms—along with the norm of transparency—are elements of the rule of law, which is founded upon a "government of laws and not of men."[55]

New Deal liberalism thus comprised affirmative and negative dimensions. The state had an affirmative obligation to regulate the economy to ensure full employment and to correct market failures. At the same time, it must operate within basic rule of law constraints imposed by the Constitution.

NEW DEAL LIBERALISM IN U.S. FOREIGN INVESTMENT POLICY

From the inception of the postwar FCN treaty program, the State Department regarded the treaties as instruments of New Deal liberalism. For example, according to a 1946 State Department publication, the modern FCN treaty program was "designed to provide a legal framework, based on liberal principles and adapted to modern conditions affecting international intercourse, for mutually advantageous

54. For example, in *Lawrence v. Texas,* 539 U.S. 558 (2003), Justice Sandra Day O'Connor wrote a separate opinion in which she contended that Texas had a reasonable basis for enacting a law prohibiting sodomy, but not a reasonable basis for enacting a law that prohibited sodomy only between same-sex couples.

55. Kenneth J. Vandevelde, "A Unified Theory of Fair and Equitable Treatment," 43 *New York University Journal of International Law and Politics* 43 (2010). The meaning of the "rule of law" is highly contested, and the literature on the subject grows rapidly, which only exacerbates the profusion of definitions. Useful surveys of the debate may be found in Jeremy Waldron, "The Concept and Rule of Law," 43 *Georgia Law Review* 1 (2008) and Brian Z. Tamanaha, "The History and Elements of the Rule of Law, Washington University in St. Louis Legal Studies Research Paper No. 12-02-07 (February 2012). My definition of the rule of law is a relatively minimalist one, intended to include elements that most theorists would agree are embraced within the concept of the rule of law, even if they would include others. It is rooted in a liberal legal tradition that draws on the work of A.V. Dicey, Lon Fuller, and Joseph Raz. *See* A. V. Dicey, *An Introduction to the Law of the Constitution* (New York: MacMillan, 1959); Lon Fuller, *The Morality of Law* (New Haven, CT: Yale University Press, 1969); and Joseph Raz, *The Authority of Law* (Oxford: Oxford University Press, 1979). My purpose here, in any event, is not to defend my definition of the rule of law, which, as already noted, I have done elsewhere. Rather, my argument is that my definition encapsulates the core constitutional principles that U.S. postwar FCN treaty negotiators incorporated into the treaties, and repeated references to the rule of law by treaty negotiators indicate that they believed that the principles of the treaties were rule of law, as well as constitutional, principles.

relations between two countries over a long period of time."[56] President Truman, in transmitting the FCN treaty with Italy to the Senate on April 14, 1948, observed that the treaty confirmed the determination of the two countries to apply "the liberal principles that are fundamental to the democratic way of life."[57] Similar statements referring to the FCN treaties as instruments of liberalism appeared repeatedly not only in the Truman administration, but in subsequent administrations as well.[58] For example, in submitting the FCN treaty with Japan to President Eisenhower in 1953, the State Department observed that the treaty "expresses the common faith of the two countries in liberal principles."[59] In 1961, during the first weeks of the new Kennedy administration, Ambassador William A. M. Burden observed at the signing of the FCN treaty with Belgium that the treaty helped "to establish more firmly the liberal standards regarding navigation and establishment which we now both practice, and it should thus be of benefit . . . in gaining a wider respect for those standards throughout the world."[60]

Thus, the FCN treaties were one part of the effort by the Roosevelt and Truman administrations to project New Deal liberalism onto the international plane. Those administrations sought through an array of means to use both state capitalism and regulated private markets to promote full employment at home and abroad. At the same time, they sought to ensure through treaty negotiations that the regulation of capital, particularly by foreign governments, would conform to basic rule of law principles, most notably those reflected in U.S. constitutional law.

56. Memorandum by Vernon G. Setser headed "Status of Commercial Treaty Program," dated November 5, 1946, NARA, Record Group 59, Department of State File No. 711.002/11-546.

57. Message from the President of the United States, *reprinted in Treaty of Friendship, Commerce and Navigation with the Italian Republic*, Executive E, 80th Cong. 2d Sess. (1948), pages 1–2.

58. *See, e.g.*, Letter dated January 12, 1950, from the Secretary of State to the President, *reprinted in Treaty of Friendship, Commerce and Economic Development with the Oriental Republic of Uruguay*, Executive D, 81st Cong. 1st Sess. (1950), page 2; Undated letter from the Secretary of State to the President, *reprinted in Treaty of Friendship, Commerce, and Navigation with Colombia*, 82nd Cong. 2d Sess. (1951), page 2; Letter dated June 17, 1955, from the Acting Secretary of State to the President, *reprinted in Treaty of Friendship, Commerce, and Navigation between the United States of America and the Republic of Haiti, with Protocol and Exchange of Notes*, Executive H, 84th Cong. 1st Sess. (1955), page 2; Telegram dated January 14, 1955, from the Department of State to the U.S. embassy in Karachi, NARA, Record Group 59, Department of State File No. 611.90D4/1-1455; Letter dated March 6, 1956, from the Acting Secretary of State to the President, *reprinted in Treaty of Friendship, Commerce and Navigation with the Republic of Nicaragua, and a Protocol Relating Thereto*, Executive G, 84th Cong. 2d Sess. (1956), page 2; Statement of Assistant Secretary of State Thorsten Kalijarvi, *reprinted in Treaty of Friendship, Commerce and Navigation between the United States of America and the Republic of Korea*, Exec. Rept. No. 5, 85th Cong. 1st Sess. (1957), page 6; Press Release headed "Signature of Treaty of Friendship and Commerce between the United States and Pakistan," dated November 12, 1959, NARA, Record Group 46, Box 42, Folder No. SEN86B-B8.

59. Memorandum dated June 22, 1953, from the Secretary of State to the President, NARA, Record Group 59, Department of State File No. 611.944/6-2253.

60. Despatch dated February 23, 1961, from the U.S. embassy in Brussels to the Department of State, NARA, Record Group 59, Department of State File No. 611.554/2-2361.

U.S. officials spoke often about constitutional principles or the rule of law, although at times they treated the two as almost synonymous. For example, Truman himself delivered a speech on September 17, 1951, the anniversary of the signing of the Constitution, in which he noted that the Constitution expresses "the higher principles of political life: that all men have certain inalienable rights, that guarantees are set up to provide for the welfare of the people, and that the rule of law stands above government and citizen alike."[61] Thus, Truman continued, under the Constitution, "the rule of law is made supreme."[62] Yet, Truman also emphasized that the Constitution posed no barrier to the economic policies of New Deal liberalism. "We have," he noted, "been able to make the necessary reforms without overthrowing the ancient guarantees of our liberty."[63]

In some instances, policy statements emphasized the treaties as a means of promoting the rule of law. For example, Democratic senator Elbert D. Thomas of Utah, in describing the FCN treaty program during Senate consideration of the FCN treaty with Uruguay in 1950, explained, "I know the idea of the United States is to teach respect for law, so that wherever our citizens go they will be protected by the laws of the land. The whole essence of this treaty is to bring to the attention of the world those theories of ours which are to protect the individual wherever he goes. We want all nations to respect the rights of the individual."[64]

Similarly, Thorsten Kalijarvi, a deputy assistant secretary of state for economic affairs, when testifying before the Senate in support of the FCN treaties with Iran, the Netherlands, and Nicaragua, expressed the belief that these treaties could make "at least a modest contribution to the development of the rule of law and of fair treatment of the foreigner and his enterprise. . . ."[65] Deputy Assistant Secretary of State W. T. M. Beale, when testifying in support of the treaty with the sultanate of Muscat and Oman, explained that, like the 16 other U.S. postwar FCN treaties previously concluded by the United States, the treaty promised to make "a significant contribution to strengthening the rule of law in dealings between nations."[66]

Although they did not engage in extended public discussion of the subject, those involved in setting foreign investment policy through the negotiation of FCN treaties were acutely aware of the limitations on state regulation imposed by constitutional principles. They regarded the FCN treaties as charters that conferred

61. "The Constitution—A Means of Correcting Injustices in Human Society," *Department of State Bulletin*, Vol. 25, No. 636, October 1, 1951, page 528.

62. Ibid., page 529.

63. Ibid., page 530.

64. 96 *Congressional Record* 12087 (1950).

65. Statement of Thorsten v. Karlijarvi, *Commercial Treaty with Iran, Nicaragua and The Netherlands*, Hearing Before the Committee on Foreign Relations, 84th Congress, 2d Sess. (1956).

66. Statement of W. T. M. Beale Before the Senate Committee on Foreign Relations, April 7, 1959, NARA, Record Group 46, Box 41, File No. SEN86B-B7.

on U.S. investors certain basic rule of law protections analogous to those that foreign investors in the United States already enjoyed under U.S. law, most notably U.S. constitutional law.

For example, the State Department's letter transmitting the treaty with Ireland to the president in 1950 noted that the treaty "is designed to provide a comprehensive, integrated legal framework within which general economic relations between the two countries may develop in harmony with modern economic conditions. As an essential part of this framework, it defines in broad and liberal terms the fundamental rights and privileges which nationals and enterprises of each country enjoy in the other"[67] Five years later, the State Department's press release announcing signature of the treaty with Pakistan used identical language.[68] In testifying before the Senate Foreign Relations Committee on behalf of the FCN treaties with Uruguay and Ireland on May 4, 1950, Assistant Secretary of State Willard Thorp observed that "[a] treaty of this kind is, in effect, a 'bill of rights' for the nationals of one country in their dealings with the government, nationals and enterprises of the other."[69] Democratic senator John Sparkman of Alabama, during hearings on a group of FCN treaties in 1952, quoted a State Department publication that described the treaties as "a charter of the American citizen's rights when he is in a foreign country. They assure him for the most part the fundamental personal liberties that he enjoys in this country."[70] In favorably recommending several FCN treaties to the Senate in 1953, the Senate Foreign Relations Committee explained that the treaties "ensure for American citizens abroad many of the fundamental personal liberties that they enjoy in this country."[71] Deputy Assistant Secretary of State Harold F. Linder, testifying in support of several FCN treaties pending before the Senate in 1952, explained that the FCN treaty "aims at establishing the rule of law in our everyday relations with the country concerned. . . ."[72]

As they drafted this "bill of rights" aimed at "establishing the rule of law," the key architects of U.S. foreign investment policy at the inception of the U.S. postwar FCN treaty program were fully conscious of U.S. constitutional norms that structured the relationship between the state and the market. For example,

67. *Department of State Bulletin,* Vol. 22, No. 555, February 20, 1950, page 297.

68. Telegram dated January 14, 1955, from the Department of State to the U.S. embassy in Karachi, NARA, Record Group 59, Department of State File No. 611.90D4/1-1455.

69. *Department of State Bulletin,* Vol. 22, No. 568, May 22, 1950, page 811.

70. *Commercial Treaties,* Hearing Before a Subcommittee of the Committee on Foreign Relations, 82d Cong. 2d Sess. (1952), page 1.

71. *Treaties of Friendship, Commerce and Navigation,* Exec. Rept. No. 5, 83rd Cong. 1st Sess. (1953), page 2.

72. *Commercial Treaties,* Hearing Before a Subcommittee of the Committee on Foreign Relations, 82d Cong. 2d Sess. (1952), page 3; *Department of State Bulletin,* Vol. 26, No. 675, June 2, 1952, pages 881–882.

Robert Wilson, a principal FCN treaty negotiator during the early years of the Truman administration, after leaving the Department wrote about a "Fourteenth Amendment psychology" that prevailed during the New Deal that prompted the United States to project U.S. constitutional norms onto the plane of international law.[73] Wilson in another setting observed that "believing strongly in the rule of law in their domestic affairs, [U.S.] policy makers have not unnaturally thought internationally in terms of legality . . . ."[74] Clair Wilcox, who served as Director of the Office of International Trade Policy (which oversaw FCN treaty negotiations) during the early years of the Truman administration, authored a book on business regulation entitled *Public Policies toward Business.*[75] The book's second chapter, "The Framework of Control," consisted largely of an extended discussion of U.S. constitutional principles that structure government regulation of business. Wilcox explained that the purpose of the chapter was to identify "the limitations imposed by law" upon the government's exercise of the methods for controlling business.[76] After discussing principles relating to the allocation of power within a government—federalism and separation of powers—Wilcox turned to limitations on the power of government to regulate business, specifically, the requirements of procedural due process, substantive due process, equal protection of the laws, and payment of compensation for expropriation. He urged the reader to memorize these provisions of the Constitution "for it is upon them that the system of law that governs the public control of business in the United States is based."[77] Wilcox observed that the requirements of substantive due process and equal protection were, ultimately, protections against arbitrary government action.[78] He also cited the prohibition on impairment of contracts, but noted that this applied only to action by state governments,[79] not the federal government. He observed that the Constitution "interposed no obstacles to public ownership."[80] The government was permitted to "socialize an existing private business whose owners do not wish to sell," although the taking must be for a public use and just compensation must be paid.[81] Thus, Wilcox had

73. Robert R. Wilson, *United States Commercial Treaties and International Law* (New Orleans, LA: Hauser Press, 1960), page 98.

74. Robert R. Wilson, *The International Law Standard in Treaties of the United States* (Cambridge, MA: Harvard University Press, 1953), page 24.

75. Clair Wilcox, *Public Policies toward Business* (Chicago: Richard D. Irwin, 1955).

76. Ibid., page 23.

77. Ibid., page 36.

78. Ibid., pages 43–47.

79. The Supreme Court has held, however, that contracts are property rights that are protected by the takings clause against repudiation by the state without just compensation. *See Lynch v. United States*, 292 U.S. 571 (1934).

80. Wilcox, *Public Policies*, page 48

81. Ibid.

identified four principles imposed by the U.S. Constitution, those of procedural due process, reasonableness, non-discrimination, and security, and he saw those principles as establishing a framework for the regulation of business activity. John Parke Young, the chairman of the Foreign Investment Policy Committee during the Truman years, would later write his own book, in which he characterized the world as divided "politically and economically into two opposing campus, one based on Western concepts of constitutional organization, economic life, and personal freedom, and the other on Marxian and neo-Marxian political and economic organization and concepts."[82] Young too identified the constitutional framework for state regulation as a defining feature of the U.S. economic system.

The State Department often invoked the Constitution explicitly as the basis for FCN treaty norms. For example, after it signed its FCN treaty with Israel in 1951, the Truman administration issued a press release explaining that the treaty "formally endorses standards regarding the protection of persons and their property and interests which reflect enlightened constitutional and legal principles."[83] Press releases issued by the Truman administration on the occasion of the signature of other FCN treaties similarly referred to the treaties as formally endorsing "enlightened" constitutional and legal principles.[84]

This understanding of the treaties continued beyond the end of the Truman administration. When the United States signed its FCN treaty with Japan, the Eisenhower administration issued a press release in which it explained that the treaty "formally endorses standards regarding the protection of persons, their property, and interest that reflect the most enlightened constitutional principles."[85] When the United States concluded its FCN treaty with the Republic of Korea in 1956, the State Department issued a press release stating that these provisions "reflect liberal and enlightened legal and constitutional principles."[86] Ambassador Walter Dowling's comments at the signing ceremony similarly noted that the treaty "formally endorses standards regarding the protection of persons, their property and interests that reflect liberal and enlightened legal and

82. John Parke Young, *The International Economy* (New York: Ronald Press, 4th edition, 1963), page 4.

83. Press release headed "U.S., Israel Sign Treaty of Friendship, Commerce, and Navigation," dated August 23, 1951, *Department of State Bulletin*, Vol. 25, No. 636, September 3, 1951, page 382.

84. *See, e.g.*, press release headed "Treaty of Friendship, Commerce and Navigation with Colombia Signed," dated April 26, 1951, *Department of State Bulletin*, Vol. 24, No.618, May 7, 1951, page 746; Press release headed "Friendship Treaty with Denmark," dated October 1, 1951, *Department of State Bulletin*, Vol. 25, No.641, October 8, 1951, pages 575–576.

85. Press release headed "Treaty of Friendship, Commerce, and Navigation with Japan," dated April 2, 1953, *Department of State Bulletin*, Vol. 28, No.720, April 13, 1953, page 531.

86. Instruction dated October 31, 1956, from the Department of State to the U.S. embassy in Seoul, NARA, Record Group 59, Department of State File No. 611.95B4/10-3156.

constitutional principles."[87] The press release announcing signature of the FCN treaty with France in 1959 explained that the treaty, which was limited largely to the investment provisions, reflected "enlightened legal and constitutional principles."[88] A 1955 report of the National Advisory Council[89] on the investment provisions of the FCN treaties observed that by means of these provisions "the enlightened concept of the status of the alien embodied in the United States Constitution and laws is given salutary influence beyond the borders of this country."[90]

The State Department also invoked the Constitution as the basis for treaty norms when it submitted the FCN treaties to the president. For example, the State Department's letter submitting the FCN treaty with Japan to the president explained that the treaty "expresses the common faith of the two countries in liberal principles . . . ." The letter then elaborated upon the nature of these liberal principles. It explained that the treaty "formally endorses standards regarding the protection of persons and their property and interests that reflect the most enlightened constitutional principles" while recognizing "the need for special attention to the problem of stimulating the flow of private capital investment."[91] The Department routinely used similar language when submitting other postwar FCN treaties to the president.[92]

87. Despatch dated November 29, 1956, from the U.S. embassy in Seoul to the Department of State, NARA, Record Group 59, Department of State File No. 611.95B4/11-2956.

88. Press Release headed "Signing of Convention of Establishment between the United States of America and France," dated November 25, 1959, NARA, Record Group 46, Box 40, Folder No.SEN86B-B3.

89. The National Advisory Council was an interagency group formed to coordinate U.S. policy on international monetary and financial affairs. The origin and functions of the National Advisory Council are described in Chapter 5.

90. NAC Staff Document No. 740, Program for Obtaining Treaty Assurances to Protect United States Citizens and Property and Promote United States Private Investment in Foreign Countries, NARA, Record Group 353, Records Relating to the Council on Foreign Economic Policy 1955–1961, Box 4, Folder marked "Investment in Underdeveloped countries CFEP 511 (Folder 2)."

91. Letter dated June 22, 1953, from the Secretary of State to the President, NARA, Record Group 59, Department of State File No. 611.944/6-2253.

92. *See, e.g.,* Letter dated May 4, 1955, from the Secretary of State to the President submitting the treaty with Germany, *reprinted in Treaty of Friendship, Commerce, and Navigation with the Federal Republic of Germany*, Executive E, 84th Cong. 1st Sess. (1955), page 2; Letter dated June 17, 1955, from the Secretary of State to the President submitting the treaty with Haiti, NARA, Record Group 46, Box 37, Folder No.SEN84B-B6; Letter dated March 6, 1956, from the Acting Secretary of State to the President submitting the treaty with Nicaragua, *reprinted in Treaty of Friendship, Commerce, and Navigation with the Republic of Nicaragua, and a Protocol Relating Thereto*, Executive G, 84th Cong. 2d Sess. (1956), page 2; Letter dated February 4, 1957, from the Secretary of State to the President submitting the treaty with Korea, *reprinted in Treaty of Friendship, Commerce and Navigation between the United States of America and the Republic of Korea*, Executive D, 85th Cong. 1st Sess. (1957), page 2.

State Department officials were quite conscious that they were projecting U.S. constitutional and legal principles onto the world.[93] As Michael Hunt has argued, the United States set out to create a new postwar order in which "American institutions would provide the model." [94] During the Truman years, the State Department often noted that U.S. foreign economic policy prescriptions were "based on our own experience."[95] As the Department explained in 1952, "Our foreign economic policies attempt to translate what we have learned into international terms."[96] That understanding of the treaty continued in the Eisenhower administration. In describing the national treatment provision of the treaty, the State Department noted in 1955 that "[t]his paragraph expresses the liberal policy toward alien investment that has been followed in general by the United States throughout its history, and which has contributed significantly to the economic development of this country"[97] Herman Walker, a principal U.S. FCN treaty negotiator, observed in 1956 that "to the great benefit of its own economic growth, [the United States] embodied in its legal system principles favorable to foreign capital; now through treaty negotiations it seeks to project similar principles onto the international plane . . . ."[98] Secretary of State Christian Herter observed, at the signing of the FCN treaty with Pakistan in 1959, that "[w]e are

93. Emily Rosenberg has argued that America's quest to spread its norms and institutions to other lands began well before the New Deal, as early as 1890. Emily S. Rosenberg, *Spreading the American Dream: American Economic and Cultural Expansion, 1890–1945* (New York: Hill and Wang, 1982). Rosenberg focuses on the spread of a constellation of American economic policies and institutions that she terms "liberal developmentalism," and she concentrates on the decades before the Truman administration.

Elizabeth Borgwardt similarly argues that Roosevelt sought to "internationalize the New Deal," Borgwardt, *A New Deal for the World,* page 3, although, apart from two chapters on the Bretton Woods conference, she addresses primarily U.S. efforts to promote human rights rather than foreign economic policy. Further, to the extent that she does discuss foreign economic policy in those two chapters, she is concerned primarily with economic assistance and Roosevelt's idea of freedom from want, whereas my concern is the state as promoter and regulator of private economic activity. Nevertheless, the parallels in our accounts are striking. She also sees U.S. postwar foreign policy as an attempt to avoid the mistakes of the interwar years, and she contends that U.S. negotiators pursued a postwar order in which "ideas about democracy, rights and constitutionalism . . . had a distinctly American flavor," ibid., page 15, a contention that parallels my claim that the FCN treaties represented an attempt to promote the U.S. concept of liberal legality as reflected in U.S. constitutional norms.

94. Michael H. Hunt, *Ideology and U.S. Foreign Policy* (New Haven, CT: Yale University Press, 1987), page 160.

95. Department of State, *Our Foreign Policy, 1952*, Department of State Publication 4466, (Washington, DC: Government Printing Office, 1952), page 47.

96. Ibid.

97. Instruction dated April 5, 1955, from the Department of State to the U.S. embassy in Seoul, NARA, Record Group 59, Department of State File No. 611.95B4/2-2855.

98. Herman Walker Jr., "Treaties for the Encouragement and Protection of Foreign Investment: Present United States Practice," 5 *The American Journal of Comparative Law* 229 (1956).

convinced that the application in our relations with other nations of such rules of conduct as those expressed in our treaties contributed substantially to our country's growth, and facilitated our obtaining from abroad essential components of economic development."[99]

Consistent with this view, the State Department sometimes described the FCN treaties as a means of educating other governments concerning the policies that they should adopt with respect to foreign investment. For example, during negotiations in 1950 with India, the Department observed that "Indian economic policy is in many respects at the present time in a formative stage. The standard treaty rules applicable to established enterprises, if in force in India, would serve to guide the development of India's domestic policy along lines in accord with U.S. foreign policy objectives. Our refusal to make a treaty would have the effect of restricting our opportunity to influence the development of India's policies."[100] Three years later, the Department noted that discussions of an FCN treaty with Indonesia "could have much educational value and possibly a worthwhile influence on any unilateral policy statement the Indonesian government may issue."[101] Two years later, a report of the National Advisory Council noted that the "[t]he negotiation of such a treaty is a valuable educational process, and a country presently unwilling to accept the liberal treaty principles may come by degrees to a clear conception of the worth of what this Government is proposing."[102] More generally, the Department noted in 1949 that it had widely distributed its proposed standard draft FCN treaty "partly in recognition of the possibility that a long period of education might prove beneficial in some of the economically underdeveloped countries."[103]

The negotiation of the U.S. postwar FCN treaties was a mechanism through which the United States exported New Deal liberalism, particularly its liberal legal culture, to the rest of the world.[104] The "enlightened constitutional principles" of

99. Remarks on the Occasion of the Signing of the Treaty of Friendship and Commerce between the United States and Pakistan on November 12, 1959, Washington, DC, NARA, Record Group 46, File No.SEN86B-B8.

100. Memorandum headed "Negotiation of Treaty of Friendship, Commerce and Navigation with India," dated September 11, 1950, NARA, Record Group 59, Department of State File No. 611.914/9-1150.

101. Airgram dated June 24, 1953, from the Department of State to the U.S. embassy in Jakarta, NARA, Record Group 59, Department of State File No. 611.004/5-2153.

102. NAC Staff Document No. 740, "Program for Obtaining Treaty Assurances to Protect United States Citizens and Property and Promote United States Private Investment in Foreign Countries," NARA, Record Group 353, Records Relating to the Council on Foreign Economic Policy 1955–1961, Box 4, Folder marked "Investment in Underdeveloped Countries CFEP 511 (Folder 2)."

103. *Current Economic Developments,* May 2, 1949, page 1, NARA, Record Group 59, Department of State Lot Files.

104. Robert R. Wilson, *The International Law Standard in Treaties of the United States* (Cambridge, MA: Harvard University Press, 1953), pages 4, 24. The diplomatic historian John Basset Moore argued that a "conception of legality" had always formed a part of U.S. diplomacy. John Basset Moore, *The Principles of American Diplomacy* (New York: Harper and Brothers, 1918), page 424.

New Deal liberalism were reflected most vividly in the investment-related provisions of the treaties. These provisions eventually would provide the model for a global network of thousands of bilateral treaties for the promotion and protection of foreign investment. The contemporary law of foreign investment traces its origins to the first bilateral investment treaties, the set of U.S. postwar FCN treaties that were initiated, and reconceived as investment treaties, in the years of the New Deal and the Fair Deal.

1

U.S. Postwar Foreign Investment Policy

Long before the bombing of Pearl Harbor, the Roosevelt administration was engaged in planning the postwar international economic order.[1] As administration officials contemplated this new order, their chief concern was to avoid the mistakes in international economic policy that had contributed to the two great scourges that would dominate the 1930s and 1940s: the economic scourge of the Great Depression and the political-military scourge of the Second World War.[2] As Assistant Secretary of State Will Clayton, described by *Newsweek* as "the principal architect of American postwar foreign economic policy,"[3] explained in 1946, "There are only two economic roads open to us. One leads backwards to the tragic mistakes all of us made following the first World War. The other leads forward to peace and prosperity."[4] This would continue to be a theme of U.S. postwar foreign policy. President Truman would tell the American Legion in 1949 that "[t]he free nations are determined to avoid the mistakes of the past."[5]

1. The Roosevelt administration's early postwar planning is described in Harley A. Notter, *Postwar Foreign Policy Preparation, 1939–1945* (Washington, DC: Government Printing Office, 1950). As the title of his book implies, Notter traces the beginning of the postwar planning process back to 1939.

2. The Roosevelt administration had studied the mistakes of interwar economic policy so extensively in the 1930s that, when the postwar planning process began, the administration had a more clearly defined sense of its postwar economic goals than of its postwar political or territorial goals. Ibid., page 23.

3. *Newsweek,* October 27, 1947, "Good-By, Mr. Clayton."

4. Quoted in William L. Garwood Jr., *Will Clayton: Economic Statesman* (Washington, DC: The American Studies Center, 1981), page vi.

5. Harry S. Truman, "New Problems in World Prosperity," August 29, 1949, *reprinted in* Department of State, *A New Era in World Affairs: Selected Speeches and Statements of President Truman, January 20 to August 29, 1949,* Department of State Publication 3653 (Washington, DC: Government Printing Office, 1949), page 52.

U.S. foreign economic policy in the postwar era was to be based on "enlightened self-interest."[6] Such self-interest included "the maintenance of international security" to avoid another world war and the attainment within the United States of "the maximum of economic benefits for all of the people" to avoid another Great Depression.[7]

As U.S. troops battled in Europe, Africa, and the Pacific, State Department officials, who had primary responsibility for planning the postwar international economic order,[8] focused particularly on the avoidance of war. The avoidance of war, however, required a prosperous global economy. The Department noted in 1943 that "the past few decades" had demonstrated that "international political stability cannot be hoped for except against a backdrop of reasonably good economic conditions. Countries suffering from economic instability and distress have been fertile ground for the seeds of aggression and for ideas threatening the safety of the world."[9] Roosevelt told Congress in March 1945, "We know that we cannot succeed in building a peaceful world unless we build an economically healthy world."[10] Thus, U.S. government officials concluded, raising the standard of living[11] in other countries would promote peace.[12]

The end of the war brought no change in this perspective. Secretary of State Edward R. Stettinius explained on August 21, 1945, that "[p]eace and prosperity are the twin goals of America's post-war effort."[13] Similarly, in May 1946, Assistant Secretary Clayton, in a speech before the U.S. Chamber of Commerce, proclaimed that the fundamental objective of U.S. foreign policy was to preserve the peace. Peace, however, was most likely when every country enjoined a rising

6. Memorandum in Reply to the President's Letter of April 9, 1943, NARA, Record Group 43, International Trade Files, Box 37, Folder marked "Foreign Investment Policy (I)."

7. Ibid.

8. Patrick J. Hearden, *Architects of Globalism: Building a New World Order during World War II* (Fayetteville: University of Arkansas Press, 2002), page xi.

9. Memorandum in Reply to the President's Letter of April 9, 1943, NARA, Record Group 43, International Trade Files, Box 37, Folder marked "Foreign Investment Policy (I)."

10. *New York Times,* March 27, 1945, page 36. Roosevelt's belief that peace and prosperity were mutually dependent preceded his election to the presidency. Robert Dallek, *Franklin Roosevelt and American Foreign Policy, 1932–1945* (New York: Oxford University Press, 1979), page 20.

11. Victoria de Grazia has shown how, in the late 1920s, the notion of a "standard of living," particularly the American standard of living, became especially in Europe the measure of national prosperity. Victoria de Grazia, *Irresistible Empire: America's Advance through Twentieth-Century Europe* (Cambridge, MA: Harvard University Press, 2005). American policy statements in the 1940s consistently treated a rising standard of living as the goal of economic policy. Roosevelt in his 1944 State of the Union address promised "the establishment of an American standard of living higher than ever before known." Dallek, *Franklin Roosevelt,* page 444.

12. Letter dated November 20, 1943, from Secretary of State Cordell Hull to President Franklin D. Roosevelt, NARA, Record Group 43, International Trade Files, Box 37, Folder marked "Foreign Investment Policy (I)".

13. *Department of State Bulletin,* Vol. 13, No. 322, August 26, 1945, page 279.

standard of living.[14] Article 55 of the United Nations Charter, signed in June 1945, reflected the widespread understanding of the link between higher standards of living and world peace when it declared that "[w]ith a view to the creation of conditions of stability and well-being which are necessary for peaceful and friendly relations among nations . . . the United Nations shall promote . . . higher standards of living, full employment, and conditions of economic and social progress and development."[15]

Congress was in accord. A 1945 report by a special House of Representatives committee on postwar economic planning noted, "Almost all post-war policies, whether international or domestic, economic or political, will have two general aims: (1) the establishment and maintenance of peaceful conditions, and (2) the provision of a high and expanding level of income and employment both at home and abroad."[16]

The view that the United States must act to ensure full employment and a rising standard of living was essentially a projection of the New Deal onto the international economy.[17] The New Deal had arisen as a response to the Great Depression, the first of the two great scourges of the 1930s and 1940s. As discussed in the Introduction, the early years of New Deal economic policy had been marked by pragmatism, the willingness to experiment with a variety of sometimes inconsistent approaches in order to bring recovery. By the 1940s, with the war having brought full recovery, the central tenet of New Deal liberalism was that the government was responsible for maintaining a full employment economy, in particular through countercyclical spending policies, in accordance with Keynesian economic theory. Spending might involve consumption expenditures, but it might also include public investment.

PROMOTING GLOBAL FULL EMPLOYMENT

In seeking to achieve full employment and a rising standard of living around the world, the Roosevelt administration initially focused its postwar international economic planning on trade policy and on monetary policy. Trade was the central concern of foreign economic policy in the early 1940s. As Leo Pasvolsky, who served as Special Assistant to Secretary of State Cordell Hull during the war and who was extremely close to Hull,[18] explained in 1942, international trade "is by far

14. Address by Assistant Secretary of State Will Clayton before the U.S. Chamber of Commerce, May 2, 1946, NARA, Record Group 59, Department of State File No. 611.0031/5-146.

15. Charter of the United Nations, signed June 26, 1945, Article 55, 59 Stat. 1031, T.S. No. 93.

16. *Post-War Economic Policy and Planning*, Sixth Report of the House Special Committee on Post-War Economic Policy and Planning, House Report No. 541, 79th Congress, 1st Sess., May 8, 1945, page 8.

17. As Elizabeth Borgwardt writes, Roosevelt "attempted to project an activist regulatory state onto the wider world stage." Elizabeth Borgwardt, *A New Deal for the World: America's Vision for Human Rights* (Cambridge, MA: Harvard University Press, 2005), page 70.

18. John Parke Young Oral History, Harry S. Truman Library.

the most important of international economic relationships and is, in fact, basic to all others."[19]

Roosevelt had been elected only two years after the enactment of the notorious Smoot-Hawley tariff of 1930. That act had raised U.S. tariffs to their highest level since the Civil War, triggered a trade war, and resulted in a 60 percent reduction in world trade between 1929 and 1932.[20] U.S. exports had fallen by 70 percent.[21] Cordell Hull, an ardent free trader, argued that reversing the decline in export trade would contribute importantly to recovery.[22] As early as 1934, at Hull's urging, Congress approved the Reciprocal Trade Agreements Act, which gave the executive branch unprecedented discretion for a period of three years to negotiate treaties to reduce tariffs by as much as 50 percent without further congressional approval.[23] The United States would offer to lower its tariffs in exchange for a reduction of trade barriers by other countries, thereby opening foreign markets to U.S. goods and promoting economic recovery.[24] The administration regarded the act as "a New Deal for our foreign trade."[25]

The outbreak of war only strengthened the Roosevelt administration's commitment to free trade. U.S. policymakers believed that the war was in part a result of the protectionist policies of the interwar years[26] and that free trade would promote peace. Secretary Hull observed that "it is a fact that war did not break out between the United States and any country with which we had been able to negotiate a trade agreement. It is also a fact that, with very few exceptions, the

19. Leo Pasvolsky, "The Problem of Economic Peace after War," *State Department Bulletin*, Vol. 6, No. 141, March 7, 1942, page 211.

20. Thomas W. Zeiler, *Free Trade Free World: The Advent of GATT* (Chapel Hill: University of North Carolina Press, 1999), page 7; Robert A. Pastor, *Congress and the Politics of U.S. Foreign Economic Policy, 1929–1975* (Berkeley: University of California Press, 1980), page 79.

21. John M. Rothgeb Jr., *U.S. Trade Policy: Balancing Economic Dreams and Political Realities* (Washington, DC: Congressional Quarterly Press, 2001), page 38.

22. Rondo Cameron, *A Concise Economic History of the World* (New York: Oxford University Press, 3rd ed., 1997), pages 370–371.

23. A contemporary account of the enactment of the legislation may be found in Frances Bowes Sayre, *The Way Forward: The American Trade Agreements Program* (New York: MacMillan, 1939), pages 54–59. Sayre served as assistant secretary of state during the Roosevelt administration. A more recent account may be found in Rothgeb, *U.S. Trade Policy*, pages 43–46.

24. David A. Lake, *Power, Protection, and Free Trade: International Sources of US Commercial Strategy 1887—1939* (Ithaca, NY: Cornell University Press, 1989), page 204. Lake argues that the act was "a tactical and pragmatic response" to retaliation precipitated by the Smoot-Hawley tariff two years before. Ibid.

25. October 1941 address by Undersecretary of State Sumner Welles to the National Foreign Trade Convention, *Department of State Bulletin*, Vol. 5, No. 120, October 11, 1941, page. 268.

26. On interwar protectionism, *see* Alfred E. Eckes Jr., *A Search for Solvency* (Austin: University of Texas Press, 1975), pages 20–22.

countries with which we signed trade agreements joined together in resisting the Axis. The political line-up followed the economic line-up."[27]

International monetary policy prior to Roosevelt's election had been structured around the gold standard.[28] Under the gold standard, countries fixed the value of their currencies in relation to gold and pledged to redeem their currencies with gold. Accordingly, each unit of currency was the equivalent of a fixed amount of gold and could be exchanged for the gold equivalent. Because every currency on the gold standard had a fixed value in relation to gold, every such currency also had a fixed value in relation to every other such currency. Currencies could be readily exchanged with no risk of loss attributable to changes in exchange rates. This system thus promoted stable exchange rates between currencies as well as capital mobility. Stable exchange rates promoted international trade by eliminating the risk that the exchange rate would change between the time when the parties agreed to a transaction and payment was made.

In September 1931, Great Britain, deprived of reparation payments from a financially precarious Germany, had abandoned the gold standard in order to obtain flexibility to devalue the pound and thereby lower the price of British goods in international markets and increase its exports. Other countries soon followed Britain's example, enabling them to engage in competitive devaluations, and, by April 1932, 41 countries effectively were off the gold standard.[29] A major problem arising from the gold standard was that much of the foreign investment of the 1920s had been portfolio investment that moved easily between countries.[30] If a country during the Depression lowered interest rates to spur recovery, capital would flee in search of higher returns. Capital flight would drain the country of gold, fueling deflation, which would be ruinous to debtors with fixed payment obligations and deepen the Depression. If the same country raised interest rates to attract capital and thus restore its gold reserves, the higher interest rates would increase the cost of investment and stall economic recovery. Thus, those countries that remained on the gold standard the longest generally suffered the most during the Depression.[31]

27. Cordell Hull, *Memoirs of Cordell Hull*, Vol. I (New York: MacMillan, 1948), page 365.

28. Harold James, *International Monetary Cooperation since Bretton Woods* (Washington, DC: International Monetary Fund, 1996), pages 14–17.

29. Mira Wilkins, *The Maturing of Multinational Enterprise: American Business Abroad from 1914 to 1970* (Cambridge, MA: Harvard University Press, 1974), page 169.

30. Robert A. Pollard, *Economic Security and the Origins of the Cold War, 1945–1950* (New York: Columbia University Press, 1985), page 26.

31. Economic historians still debate the causes of the Great Depression, but few appear to doubt that the gold standard was an aggravating factor. The contribution of the gold standard to the Great Depression is discussed in detail in Barry Eichengreen, *Golden Fetters: The Gold Standard and the Great Depression, 1919–1939* (New York: Oxford University Press, 1992). For other accounts of the adverse impact of the gold standard on recovery, *see* Charles P. Kindleberger, *The World in Depression, 1929–1935* (Berkeley: University of California Press, Revised and Enlarged

Although the State Department had primary responsibility for foreign trade policy, the Treasury Department had primary responsibility for monetary policy. As early as 1941, Harry Dexter White, an assistant to Secretary of the Treasury Henry Morgenthau,[32] and John Maynard Keynes, an advisor to the British Treasury, began to exchange proposals for a system that would replace the gold standard after the war.[33] White's proposal was entitled "A New Deal in International Economics."[34]

Keynes and White believed that two defining features of the gold standard—rigid exchange rates and capital mobility—had aggravated the economic consequences of the Great Depression.[35] Indeed, Keynes believed that "capital flight had been the major international interwar problem."[36] He also believed that "control of capital movements, both inward and outward, should be a permanent feature of the post-war system."[37] White independently had come to believe that international capital flows must be regulated. He had written in his doctoral dissertation that "some measure of the intelligent control of the volume and direction of foreign investments is desirable."[38] White and Keynes, however, meant to regulate, not halt, international capital movements.[39]

Edition, 1986) and Ben S. Bernanke, *Essays on the Great Depression* (Princeton, NJ: Princeton University Press, 2000).

32. Morgenthau told his staff that White was to be treated as if he held the status of assistant secretary and that White was responsible for all matters within the Treasury that bore on foreign relations, although White was never formally appointed to the position of assistant secretary. David Rees, *Harry Dexter White: A Study in Paradox* (New York: Coward, McCann and Geoghegan, 1973), pages 131–132.

33. Alan P. Dobson, *The Politics of the Anglo-American Economic Special Relationship, 1940–1987* (New York: St. Martin's Press, 1988), pages 48–59.

34. Garwood, *Will Clayton*, page 21.

35. Harold James argues that, by the early 1940s, a "consensus" had emerged among economists that the short-term capital flows of the 1920s and 1930s were an important contributing factor to the severity of the Great Depression. James, *International Monetary Cooperation*, pages 37–38.

36. Ibid., page 38. Keynes's thought during this period is exhaustively described in Robert Skidelsky, *John Maynard Keynes: Fighting for Britain, 1937–1946* (London: MacMillan, 1946).

37. Eckes , *A Search for Solvency*, page 68. According to Robert Skidelsky, Keynes believed that "[n]othing is more certain than that the movement of capital funds must be regulated." Skidelsky, *John Maynard Keynes*, page 205.

38. Harry Dexter White, *The French International Accounts: 1880–1913* (Cambridge, MA: Harvard University Press, 1933), pages 311–312. White's doubts about the desirability of free capital movements dated from his work on his doctoral dissertation. Eckes, *Search for Solvency*, page 46. The context of White's dissertation is sketched in Rees, *Harry Dexter White*, pages 33–36. *See also* James M. Boughton, "Why White, Not Keynes? Inventing the Postwar International Monetary System," IMF Working Paper, WP/02/52 (Washington, DC: International Monetary Fund, 2002), page 10.

39. Boughton, *Why White, Not Keynes?*, page 10.

The views of White and Keynes prevailed in Washington and London and, by the end of the war, the State Department acknowledged that a return to rigid exchange rates and "complete freedom of international capital movements" was "neither feasible nor desirable."[40] The Roosevelt administration sought an international economic order designed to *promote* free trade, but to *regulate* capital movements.[41]

In July 1944, the United Nations Monetary and Financial Conference met at the Mount Washington Hotel in Bretton Woods, New Hampshire, and adopted a plan, based predominantly on White's proposals, that was intended to address both the problems of rigid exchange rates and free capital movements.[42] Under that plan, the U.S. dollar would have a fixed value expressed in terms of gold and all other currencies would have a fixed value expressed in terms either of gold or the U.S. dollar. As it would happen, members other than the United States would choose to fix the value of their currencies in relation to the U.S. dollar. The Bretton Woods conference created the International Monetary Fund (IMF), which lent money to governments that needed financing to maintain the value of their currencies against short-term pressures, such as in the case of a temporary decrease in exports. If a country found that its currency was fundamentally under- or overvalued, then with the approval of the IMF the country could modify the exchange rate. This system would stabilize exchange rates, while permitting greater flexibility than had the gold standard.

The plan adopted at Bretton Woods also contemplated that countries would be permitted to limit capital mobility. Article VI(3) of the IMF Articles of Agreement explicitly authorized members to impose exchange controls with respect to the transfer of capital. That is, members were permitted to prohibit a foreign investor from withdrawing capital from the host country.

The treatment of currency transfers for capital transactions differed from the treatment of currency transfers for current transactions, that is, transactions related to trade. Article VIII of the IMF Articles of Agreement prohibited members from imposing exchange controls on current transactions, as opposed to capital transactions, except with the approval of the IMF. Exchange controls had functioned during the interwar years as a means of controlling imports (by limiting access to foreign currencies needed to purchase imports). One goal of the IMF Articles of Agreement was to foreclose that possibility, at least over time, by ensuring the availability of foreign currencies (often referred to as "foreign exchange") for trade transactions. In other words, the IMF agreement sought to promote free trade in goods, but not the free mobility of capital.

40. "Questions and Answers on Foreign Economic Problems and Policies," attachment to *Current Economic Developments*, July 9, 1945, NARA, Record Group 59, Department of State Lot Files. White's doubts about the desirability of free capital movements dated from his work on his doctoral dissertation. Eckes, *Search for Solvency*, page 46.

41. Pollard, *Economic Security*, page 26.

42. On the Bretton Woods conference generally, *see* James, *International Monetary Cooperation*, and Eckes, *Search for Solvency*.

In the period immediately after the war, most countries had serious foreign exchange shortages and thus convertibility of their currency even for current transactions was difficult for most countries to achieve. In fact, at the end of the war, only the U.S. dollar was freely convertible.[43] Accordingly, Article XIV of the IMF Articles of Agreement allowed members to defer their acceptance of the Article VIII obligation with regard to current transactions during a transitional period.

As the war drew to a close, memories of the Great Depression haunted Americans.[44] U.S. policymakers feared that the end of the war, rather than bringing the full employment and the rising standards of living sought by U.S. foreign economic policy, would plunge the United States back into another Great Depression,[45] a fear shared by many other countries.[46]

The problem was overproduction (or its correlate, underconsumption). In 1940, 45 million Americans had been employed. By 1943, as a result of increased production for the war, the American workforce had grown to 60 million. Although some of these workers, such as women "return[ing] to their homes,"[47] would leave the workforce at the end of the war, the avoidance of serious economic and social problems after the war would necessitate the continued employment of some 56 to 57 million people, or about 30 percent more than were employed at the beginning of the war.[48] To keep this substantially larger number of people employed would require the production of far more goods and services than the American people could consume. Thus, the Roosevelt administration believed, the only way to avoid a serious economic crisis was to create an export market for surplus U.S. goods and services. As James F. Byrnes, then the director of War Mobilization, wrote in January 1945, "We must export goods if we are to provide jobs for all of our workers."[49] Indeed, exports were twice as important to the U.S. economy at the end of the war as they were at the beginning.[50]

43. Eckes, *Search for Solvency*, page 226.

44. Robert J. Donovan, *Conflict and Crisis: The Presidency of Harry S. Truman, 1945–1949* (New York: W. W. Norton, 1977), pages 107–108. Donovan notes that some 10 million people had been unemployed as recently as 1939.

45. Alan Lawson, *A Commonwealth of Hope: The New Deal Response to Crisis* (Baltimore: The Johns Hopkins University Press, 2006), page 238. Lawson describes a "widespread expectation" that the depression would return once the "artificial prosperity" induced by war ended.

46. Economic Report to the President, *Department of State Bulletin*, Vol. 16, No. 394, January 19, 1947, page 126.

47. Memorandum in Reply to the President's Letter of April 9, 1943, NARA, Record Group 43, International Trade Files, Box 37, Folder marked "Foreign Investment Policy (I)."

48. Ibid.

49. *New York Times*, January 2, 1945, p. 12.

50. Jeffrey A. Frieden, *Global Capitalism: Its Fall and Rise in the Twentieth Century* (New York: W.W. Norton, 2006), page 262.

Creating an export market for the U.S. surplus, in turn, necessitated the lowering of trade barriers in other countries. As already noted, the promotion of liberalized trade had been Roosevelt administration policy since the adoption of the Reciprocal Trade Agreements Act in 1934. The reduction of trade barriers through bilateral negotiations with one country at a time, however, was a slow process. By 1943, the United States and Great Britain were engaged in extensive discussions about the creation of an international trade organization that would facilitate multilateral negotiations for the reduction of trade barriers.[51] Under that process, a country would lower trade barriers to all participants in the multilateral process simultaneously.

THE ROLE OF INTERNATIONAL INVESTMENT

Simply reducing legal barriers to trade, however, was not enough to create an export market for the U.S. surplus. Other countries would not be able to purchase U.S. exports unless they had access to U.S. dollars.[52]

Lowering U.S. trade barriers would address that problem to some extent because it would allow other countries to sell their goods to the United States and thereby earn dollars needed to purchase U.S. exports. The productive capacity in other countries, however, was sufficiently small that these countries would not be able to sell enough to the United States in the foreseeable future to acquire all of the dollars needed to purchase the entire U.S. surplus. For example, in 1947, U.S. exports totaled $19 billion, whereas U.S. imports equaled only $8 billion, giving the United States an $11 billion trade surplus.[53] For other countries to purchase that surplus, they would need to acquire $11 billion from some source other than exports to the United States. One source from which they could obtain access to U.S. dollars was outward U.S. investment. U.S. investors had invested abroad since colonial times, but the amounts were small until the 1890s, at which point outward investment began to grow rapidly. World War I, in particular, had stimulated U.S. outward investment, especially outside Europe in areas where European businesses previously had been dominant, and by the end of the war the United States, for the first time, was a creditor nation.[54] The war years had also witnessed U.S. legislative enactments to encourage outward foreign investment, including the approval in 1918 of foreign tax credits and the enactment in 1919 of the Edge Act, which authorized the creation of federally chartered corporations to engage in international banking.[55] U.S. outward investment continued to grow

51. These are described in Richard N. Gardner, *Sterling-Dollar Diplomacy in Current Perspective: The Origins and the Prospects of Our International Economic Order* (New York: Columbia University Press, 1980), pages 101–109.

52. Memorandum in Reply to the President's Letter of April 9, 1943, NARA, Record Group 43, International Trade Files, Box 37, Folder marked "Foreign Investment Policy (I)".

53. Ibid., page 11.

54. Wilkins, *Maturing of Multinational Enterprise,* pages 8, 29.

55. Ibid., page 50.

in the 1920s, more than doubling between 1919 and 1929.[56] By 1929, outward private investment had grown from less than $1 billion in 1897 to more than $15 billion,[57] an amount that was about evenly divided between direct and portfolio investment.[58] By the late 1920s, many U.S. foreign investors had become multinational companies.[59] The Great Depression, however, sharply reduced the amount of U.S. private foreign investment after 1929, and by 1940 U.S. outward investment still had not returned to 1929 levels.[60]

At the end of the war, U.S. policymakers recognized that U.S. capital was available and could be profitably employed abroad. As a 1945 House of Representatives report on postwar planning noted, following the war, the United States would have an "enormous" surplus of capital[61] and returns on investment would be higher abroad than in the United States because of the relative scarcity of capital in many foreign countries.[62]

Further, outward U.S. investment could benefit both the United States and the capital importing country. As the same House report observed, "After the war, extensive foreign investments by the United States will have important benefits both to the United States and to the rest of the world. The scarcity of capital in undeveloped regions and in countries devastated by the war will provide a large opportunity for American investments. If loans are made on a productive basis, both the lending nation and the borrowing nations will benefit from the resulting industrial expansion."[63] The benefit to the United States would come from increased exports made possible by the money invested abroad and from higher returns on the investments. Other countries would benefit from industrial development. Further, the diversification of their economies would insulate them to some extent from the impact of fluctuations in commodity prices.

The administration concurred in the value of international investment flows. The Executive Committee on Economic Foreign Policy (ECEFP), an interdepartmental group that Roosevelt appointed in April 1944 as the primary planning

56. Cleona Lewis, *America's Stake in International Investment* (Washington, DC: The Brookings Institution, 1938), page 425.

57. Ibid.

58. Ibid., page 426. Direct investment is investment that is made for the purpose of controlling the enterprise in which the investment is made, such as majority stock ownership in a company. Portfolio investment is investment that is made for the purpose of earning a return or diversifying risk, but not controlling the enterprise in which the investment is made, such as in the case of stock ownership too small in amount to be controlling or bonds purchased from an enterprise.

59. Wilkins, *Maturing of Multinational Enterprise,* page 138.

60. Ibid., pages 182, 205.

61. *Post-war Economic Policy and Planning,* Sixth Report of the House Special Committee on Post-War Economic Policy and Planning, House Report No. 541, 79th Congress, 1st Sess., May 8, 1945, page 19.

62. Ibid.

63. Ibid., page 2.

and coordinating group for foreign economic policy,[64] believed that a properly conceived program of foreign investment would be "of substantial benefit" to the United States. It would contribute to employment and a high level of national income. It would provide an outlet for surplus equipment and excess capacity, thereby facilitating the adjustment to a peacetime economy. It would restore European productivity and international trade and promote international security.[65] The State Department noted that, as a result of increased efficiency in the capital importing countries, outward U.S. foreign investment would allow the United States to acquire imports at a reduced cost.[66]

Thus, the administration recognized that prosperity in the United States was dependent upon prosperity in the rest of the world. As Assistant Secretary of State Will Clayton explained in a May 1946 address before the American Chamber of Commerce, "It is essential that American capital, private and public both, make a major contribution over a long time to the increase of production and wealth in many countries. This is true, both because we are able to do it (and almost the only country that is) and because the peace and well-being of the world demand it. We cannot long continue to enjoy great wealth and prosperity, with most of the rest of the world lying prostrate from the war."[67]

The American business community understood this as well. For example, the Final Declaration of the 1946 National Foreign Trade Convention, an annual meeting of U.S. business executives, proclaimed that "[t]he economic well-being of the United States is bound up inextricably with the economic well-being of the world as a whole."[68]

Private investment in some cases could be supplemented by public investment. Here, the administration drew upon the New Deal's experience with public capital formation.[69] The Bretton Woods conference created an International Bank for Reconstruction and Development (IBRD). The bank would provide public capital for the reconstruction of Europe and the development of economically

64. The origins of the ECEFP are described in Notter, *Postwar Foreign Policy Preparation,* pages 218–219.

65. Executive Committee on Economic Foreign Policy, Memorandum headed "Subcommittee on Foreign Investment Policy," dated June 26, 1945, NARA, Record Group 43, International Trade Files, Box 38, Folder marked "FIP Documents."

66. Memorandum in Reply to the President's Letter of April 9, 1943, NARA, Record Group 43, International Trade Files, Box 37, Folder marked "Foreign Investment Policy (I)."

67. Address by Assistant Secretary of State Will Clayton before the U.S. Chamber of Commerce, May 2, 1946, NARA, Record Group 59, Department of State File No. 611.0031/5-146.

68. National Foreign Trade Council, *Draft Final Declaration of the Thirty-Third National Foreign Trade Convention, 1946,* page 4, NARA, Record Group 59, Department of State File No. 611.0031/11-1446.

69. On the importance of state capitalism to the New Deal, *see* Jordan A. Schwartz, *The New Dealers: Power Politics in the Age of Roosevelt* (New York: Alfred A. Knopf, 1993) and Jason Scott Smith, *Building New Deal Liberalism: The Political Economy of Public Works, 1933–1956* (New York: Cambridge University Press, 2006).

underdeveloped countries. Such a bank was necessary because private investors were reluctant to invest in public works projects, such as railroads and ports, that would not generate a return for a long period of time.[70] The bank could finance public works projects that were necessary to attract private capital but that would be difficult to finance through private investment. Thus, the bank acted as a supplement to private investment, leaving to private investment the primary role in promoting capital formation abroad.[71]

THE NEED TO PROMOTE AND REGULATE INTERNATIONAL INVESTMENT

Two important problems, however, attended efforts to promote outward private foreign investment. First, as State Department officials openly acknowledged, international investment in the past had not always operated to the benefit of the capital importing country.[72] New Deal liberals recognized that private sector activity has public consequences, and believed that these public consequences justified the regulation of private activity.[73] Governments would need to regulate international investment flows to ensure that they operated to the benefit of both the capital exporting and the capital importing countries.

Much of the discussion in the mid-1940s focused on the problem of avoiding the undesirable consequences of foreign investment. In attempting to anticipate some of these consequences, the State Department looked particularly to the experience of British investment from 1815 to 1914 and again during the 1920s.[74] The State Department found that the behavior of British investors largely had been guided by profit considerations, and that such investment had not always contributed as much as it might have to the economic development of the host country. For example, the benefits of increased productivity sometimes were not widely diffused, the local economies failed to develop in a balanced way, and local entrepreneurship was restricted. Similarly, other commentators noted that much of the international lending in Europe during the 1920s provided new capital in the short run, but drained the economies of foreign exchange in the long run as the amount of money paid to foreign lenders in principal and interest exceeded

70. Frieden, *Global Capitalism,* at 258.

71. David A. Baldwin, *Economic Development and American Foreign Policy, 1943–1962* (Chicago: University of Chicago Press, 1966), page 22.

72. Memorandum in Reply to the President's Letter of April 9, 1943, NARA, Record Group 43, International Trade Files, Box 37, Folder marked "Foreign Investment Policy (I)." Economist Cleona Lewis in a widely cited study made the same observation. Cleona Lewis, *The United States and Foreign Investment* (Washington, DC: The Brookings Institution, 1948), page 1.

73. Note in this regard the discussion of *Home Building & Loan v. Blaisdell* in the Introduction.

74. Memorandum headed "British Foreign Investment Experience," dated May 24, 1943, NARA, Record Group 43, International Trade Files, Box 37, Folder marked "Foreign Investment Policy (I)."

the original loan amount.[75] The Department noted that "[s]ome of these obstacles to development might have been eliminated by a considered investment policy" that took account of factors other than prospective profits.[76]

Apart from the specific case of British foreign investment, State Department policymakers saw that a variety of other problems sometimes occurred.[77] For example, a foreign investor might have established an investment in a host country, following which the host country raised tariff barriers to protect the investment against competition. The investment thus may have failed to lower consumer prices in the host country, while the capital exporting country may have lost an export market. Loans to foreign countries were sometimes used in ways that failed to increase productivity, leaving the host country with an increased debt service that was not offset by a higher income. Further, if the debt was denominated in U.S. dollars, then any depreciation in the currency of the borrower would result in an even greater burden of debt service. Foreign investors tended to abandon countries precisely when their economies were faltering, thereby aggravating the impact of a recession.

Outward foreign investment could adversely affect the political relations between the capital exporting and capital importing countries.[78] Foreign investors sometimes had acted in such a way as to raise claims of exploitation or interference in local affairs. Outward foreign investment also could imperil relations with countries where nationalism was on the rise. As the State Department told Franklin Roosevelt in 1943, it was necessary to "so organiz[e] the flow of investment funds that they shall not in themselves become a source of international economic friction."[79]

For these reasons, the State Department believed, the United States must adopt safeguards to secure the maximum benefit from foreign investment and the minimum detriment. The United States government "must recognize its responsibilities over the entire range of foreign investment."[80] In best Keynesian fashion, the United States should encourage countercyclical flows of investment to smooth the effects of booms and depressions. Investment should take the form of equity rather than debt denominated in foreign currency. Cartels and monopolies should be controlled, adequate labor standards should be encouraged, and agreements should be concluded to ensure non-discriminatory treatment of foreign

75. Sir Arthur Salter, *Foreign Investment* (Princeton, NJ: Princeton University Press, 1951), pages 19, 25, and 34.

76. Memorandum headed "British Foreign Investment Experience," dated May 24, 1943, NARA, Record Group 43, International Trade Files, Box 37, Folder marked "Foreign Investment Policy (I)."

77. Memorandum in Reply to the President's Letter of April 9, 1943, NARA, Record Group 43, International Trade Files, Box 37, Folder marked "Foreign Investment Policy (I)."

78. Ibid.

79. Ibid.

80. Ibid.

investment. Adequate machinery should be developed for collaboration between the United States government and U.S. foreign investors.

State Department officials even contemplated the creation of an international organization to regulate private investment flows. In December 1943, John Parke Young, an economist in the State Department's Division of Financial and Monetary Affairs, circulated a proposal for a United Nations Investment Board that would complement the proposed agency that eventually would be known as the International Bank for Reconstruction and Development.[81] The proposed board was to serve a number of purposes, the first of which was to ensure that capital exported "is not for undesirable purposes, especially from the standpoint of international security and economic stability."[82] This included the discouragement of excessive borrowing and speculation.[83] The board would also "facilitate and encourage" foreign investment if it was "legitimate foreign investment for desirable purposes."[84]

Although the proposal for a U.N. Investment Board was abandoned, the Roosevelt administration recognized that the United States would have a responsibility to regulate capital movements. For example, a June 1944 memorandum transmitting the ECEFP's recommendations to Roosevelt explained that U.S. foreign economic policy included "the elimination of unnecessary obstacles to the flow of private foreign investment and the regulation of private foreign investment to the extent necessary to eliminate abuses detrimental to international relations."[85]

As suggested by the ECEFP's memorandum, the second problem that attended efforts to promote outward foreign investment was that private investors were often reluctant to invest abroad because the risks could be high and the returns in the past had been disappointing. U.S. foreign direct investors in some cases, particularly in the mining and petroleum industries, had enjoyed "spectacular gains."[86] Investments in manufacturing had grown steadily, largely through

81. John Parke Young Oral History, Harry S. Truman Library; Memorandum headed "A United Nations Investment Board," dated December 7, 1943, NARA, Record Group 43, International Trade Files, Box 37, Folder marked "Foreign Investment Policy (I)."

82. Ibid.

83. Economist James Meade, who would win the Nobel Prize in Economics in 1977 for his work on the theory of international trade and capital movements, argued in 1940 that "short-term speculative movements of capital serve no useful purpose." J. E. Meade, *The Economic Basis of a Durable Peace* (New York: Oxford University Press, 1940), page 110. He also acknowledged, however, that in some cases "legitimate investments" might be difficult to distinguish from purely speculative ones. Ibid.

84. Memorandum headed "A United Nations Investment Board," dated December 7, 1943, NARA, Record Group 43, International Trade Files, Box 37, Folder marked "Foreign Investment Policy (I)."

85. The original memorandum may be found at NARA, Record Group 59, Department of State File No. 611.0031 Executive Committee/826. Excerpts appear in *Foreign Relations of the United States*, Vol. II (Washington, DC: Government Printing Office, 1967), pages 44–45.

86. Lewis, *America's Stake*, page 427.

the reinvestment of earnings. Portfolio investors, by contrast, had fared poorly, earning a lower return on average from foreign investment than they would have received by investing in U.S. government bonds.[87]

The poor performance of these investments was attributable in part to increasingly autarkic foreign economic policies of the 1920s and 1930s, when countries embraced high tariffs, prohibitions on inward foreign investment, and controls on currency transfers, and in part to more recent events, including a global depression and a world war.[88] Harry Dexter White had noted during the planning for the IBRD that private capital "has suffered too many losses. It has been too severely discouraged by depreciating currencies, exchange controls and defaulting governments, to justify the hope that investors will lend large sums to a foreign country."[89]

In the postwar era, policymakers believed that the single greatest deterrent to foreign investment was the risk of currency exchange controls.[90] Countries with insufficient reserves of foreign currency, which after the war included virtually all countries except the United States, typically prohibited private parties from exchanging local currency for foreign currency so that foreign currency reserves could be used to purchase necessary imports, such as fuel or food. A foreign investor who earned profits in the local currency could be prevented by exchange controls from transferring those profits into the investor's own currency and repatriating them for use in the investor's home country. Similarly, if the foreign investor chose to liquidate an investment, exchange controls could prevent the investor from obtaining the foreign currency needed to repatriate the liquidation proceeds. A potential investor who knew that capital invested in another country could not be repatriated and could not generate a return usable outside the host country would be unlikely to invest in that country.

The postwar era featured other nonbusiness risks to foreign investment.[91] The greatest of these was the risk of expropriation.[92] Other risks included

87. Ibid., page 436.

88. Executive Committee on Economic Foreign Policy, Memorandum headed "Subcommittee on Foreign Investment Policy," dated June 26, 1945, NARA, Record Group 43, International Trade Files, Box 38, Folder marked "FIP Documents."

89. Eckes, *Search for Solvency,* page 52.

90. Transcript of Proceedings, Meeting of Economic Consultants on Point Four Program, dated April 8, 1949, page 81, NARA, Record Group 59, Department of State File No. 800.50T.A./4-849.

91. Deputy Assistant Secretary of State Harold Linder referred to these nonbusiness risks as "grave hazards" to foreign investment and mentioned, in particular, inequitable tax laws, expropriation, employment controls, special favors to state-owned enterprises, exchange controls, and other discriminations against foreign capital. *Commercial Treaties,* Hearing Before a Subcommittee of the Committee on Foreign Relations, 82d Cong. 2d Sess. (1952), page 4. The impediments to foreign investment are discussed in greater detail in Chapter 6 in the section headed "Refusal to Correlate Treaties with Increased Investment."

92. Transcript of Proceedings, Meeting of Economic Consultants on Point Four Program, dated April 8, 1949, page 81, NARA, Record Group 59, Department of State File No. 800.50T.A./4-849.

physical destruction from war or civil disturbance and harm from discriminatory legislation.[93]

Policymakers believed that reviving private investment flows necessitated government action to minimize these risks.[94] The government action most desired by investors was the conclusion of treaties to create a favorable legal environment for investment.[95]

United States policy at the end of the war thus was to promote and to regulate international investment flows. As will be seen in the remainder of this chapter, however, the attempt to develop that policy at a greater level of detail resulted in a gradual recognition of the impracticality of regulating outward foreign investment. Thus, the trend in U.S. policy during the mid-1940s was toward a gradual abandonment of proposals to regulate outward foreign investment, which was accompanied, as shown in Chapters 2 through 5, by increased efforts to develop treaty provisions to protect such investment. The United States recognized that foreign investment must be regulated, but that task must fall to host countries acting through domestic legislation, albeit subject to certain restrictions imposed by treaty provisions negotiated to protect foreign investment.

DEVELOPING A FOREIGN INVESTMENT POLICY

As the war drew to a close, the ECEFP decided that its policy of both promoting and regulating outward investment required greater elaboration. On July 10, 1945, it created a Foreign Investment Policy Committee to prepare a formal statement of U.S. foreign investment policy.[96] The State Department had been under pressure for several years to produce a foreign investment policy and Franklin Roosevelt, who died only weeks before the Committee came into existence, had been especially interested in the development of such a policy.[97] As the United States began to encourage private foreign investment, a formal government policy was desirable to provide guidance to officials responsible for that encouragement.[98]

93. Ibid.

94. Executive Committee on Economic Foreign Policy, Memorandum headed "Subcommittee on Foreign Investment Policy" and dated June 26, 1945, NARA, Record Group 43, International Trade Files, Box 38, Folder marked "FIP Documents."

95. Transcript of Proceedings, Meeting of Economic Consultants on Point Four Program, dated April 8, 1949, page 112, NARA, Record Group 59, Department of State File No. 800.50T. A./4-849.

96. Memorandum from Committee on Foreign Investment Policy to the Executive Committee on Economic Foreign Policy, dated July 8, 1946, NARA, Record Group 43, International Trade Files, Box 38, Folder marked "FIP Documents."

97. Memorandum to Will Clayton dated June 17, 1946. NARA, Record Group 43, International Trade Files, Box 38, Folder marked "FIP Documents."

98. Executive Committee on Economic Foreign Policy, Memorandum headed "Subcommittee on Foreign Investment Policy," dated June 26, 1945, NARA, Record Group 43, International Trade Files, Box 38, Folder marked "FIP Documents."

The Committee would comprise representatives of the Departments of State, Treasury, Commerce, and Labor; the Federal Reserve Board; the Securities and Exchange Commission; and the Export-Import Bank.[99] Almost immediately, it began to consider ways in which the U.S. government might control investment flows to ensure that they promoted productivity without damaging the foreign relations of the United States.[100]

Even before the Committee undertook to draft a formal statement of U.S. foreign investment policy, others within the federal government were already deliberating about discrete aspects of the problem of how best to regulate capital movements. The State Department's Division of Financial and Monetary Affairs, for example, had produced a policy statement on the subject in 1944.[101] According to that policy statement, such investment should genuinely improve the productive capacity of the host state and generate enough foreign exchange to pay for the returns on the investment, so that it did not result in a net foreign exchange loss for the host country. Foreign investment should not be protected by tariffs or other trade restrictions, which were *prima facie* evidence that the investment was not an efficient one. Foreign investments should avoid a monopolistic or privileged position and should adopt adequate labor standards, defined as those comparable to the most advanced standards practiced by similar enterprises in the country. Equity investment was preferable to debt investment because it permitted greater flexibility to the host country and was safer and more lucrative for the investor. Local participation in the investment was often desirable, particularly where nationalistic sentiment was strong. Foreign investment should not conflict with local mores and should be consistent with the general foreign policy of the United States.

A study prepared by the ECEFP in January 1945 urged that foreign investors take account of the foreign exchange position of the host country.[102] According to the study, the Departments of Commerce and State should use their good offices to dissuade investors from making investments inconsistent with the foreign economic policy of the United States. In deciding whether to make representations on behalf of U.S. investors, the State Department should consider the consistency of the investment with U.S. policy and the ethical character of the investor's business practices. The United States should discourage efforts by U.S. investors to gain monopolistic or other special privileges. To the extent feasible, investments should be undertaken in cooperation with local investors.

99. Memorandum to Will Clayton dated June 17, 1946. NARA, Record Group 43, International Trade Files, Box 38, Folder marked "FIP Documents."

100. Foreign Investment Policy Committee Minutes, February 21, 1946, NARA, Record Group 43, International Trade Files, Box 37, Folder marked "FIP Agenda & Lists."

101. Department of State Division of Financial and Monetary Affairs, "Considerations Affecting Private Direct Investment in Foreign Countries," July 26, 1944, NARA, Record Group 43, International Trade Files, Box 38, Folder marked "FIP Docs. 1–4."

102. Executive Committee on Economic Foreign Policy, Memorandum headed "Investment of United States Public and Private Funds in Latin America," dated January 2, 1945, NARA, State Department File No. 611.0031Executive Committee/1-1545.

Despite their belief that foreign investment should be controlled to ensure that it benefited home and host countries, U.S. government agencies recognized the limitations in their own ability to evaluate the impact of specific investments.[103] During discussions within the Foreign Investment Policy Committee, for example, the Department of Commerce noted the lack of information sufficient to make the necessary judgments, whereas the State Department feared that a requirement of advance approval would disadvantage U.S. investors competing with foreign investors of countries that imposed no such requirement.[104] The State Department argued that the U.S. government should use the force of public opinion to discourage investments that threatened economic stability or the foreign relations of the United States, but not undertake to prohibit them through criminal penalties.[105] The Department might also threaten to deny diplomatic protection to investments made contrary to its wishes.[106] Even those modest efforts, however, raised the potential problem that, if the Department were to review proposed investments, it would be blamed, wrongly or rightly, for any adverse consequences of foreign investments that it approved.[107]

By April 1946, the Foreign Investment Policy Committee under the leadership of John Parke Young, who by then was the associate chief of the State Department's Division on Investment and Economic Development, had produced a draft of a U.S. foreign investment policy. The draft stated that investment flows would expand production and trade, resulting in greater prosperity and international security.[108] It noted that the U.S. desire for a liberal, multilateral, non-discriminatory trade regime could not be easily achieved unless U.S. capital was available to other countries. At the same time, barriers to trade would limit the capacity of countries to service their inward foreign investment and would interfere with the benefits of investment. Liberal trade and international capital movements thus were mutually dependent. The primary emphasis, however, still was on promoting international trade. The Committee regarded outward investment as important principally because it provided a means of financing exports.

Under the draft policy, the United States expressed a preference for private investment over government loans, but anticipated that such loans would be

103. Foreign Investment Policy Committee Minutes, January 7, 1946, NARA, Record Group 43, International Trade Files, Box 37, Folder marked "FIP Agenda & Lists."

104. Foreign Investment Policy Committee Minutes, February 21, 1946, NARA, Record Group 43, International Trade Files, Box 37, Folder marked "FIP Agenda & Lists."

105. Ibid.

106. Foreign Investment Policy Committee Minutes, January 7, 1946, NARA, Record Group 43, International Trade Files, Box 37, Folder marked "FIP Agenda & Lists."

107. Foreign Investment Policy Committee Minutes, February 21, 1946, NARA, Record Group 43, International Trade Files, Box 37, Folder marked "FIP Agenda & Lists."

108. "United States Foreign Investment Policy," Working Paper dated April 3, 1946, NARA, Record Group 43, International Trade Files, Box 38, Folder marked "FIP Docs 1–4."

necessary at times to supplement private investment.[109] For that reason, a large portion of the policy addressed U.S. lending policy. When public lending was necessary, the United States preferred that it occur through the IBRD.

The policy statement observed that the flow of investment, although desirable, must be regulated by the government rather than left entirely to market forces, so as to ensure economic development while mitigating the effects of economic fluctuations.[110] The United States encouraged private investment abroad, provided that it was adapted to local conditions, could survive without undue government assistance, and was consistent with the foreign policy of the United States.[111] The policy described various forms of undesirable foreign investment, including investment under terms that were likely to become the subject of public resentment or to be otherwise detrimental to U.S. foreign relations. Thus, investment should not receive special tax concessions, except perhaps for "an initial short period of time," or exclusive concessions unless essential to the nature of the undertaking.[112] It should provide opportunities for the participation of local capital and management. Investment should be in the form of equities rather than loans with fixed payment obligations. Interest rates should be reasonable and amortization schedules should take account of economic circumstances. The United States expressed its desire that U.S. investors inform the government when they contemplated the establishment of new investments or the expansion of existing investments whenever "substantial sums" were involved.[113]

The Committee also examined the problem of promoting private investment flows. The ECEFP had noted the previous year that the promotion of private investment would require legal protections. As it had observed, "If United States investors are to commit their funds to undertakings abroad, they must have from those Governments the assurance of nondiscriminatory and just treatment."[114]

Despite the call for government regulation of the flow of capital, the draft policy criticized restrictions on inward investment as undesirable deterrents to investment.[115] It recommended intergovernmental cooperation to facilitate the flow of private investment, such as measures to eliminate exchange controls, to promote exchange stability, and to establish investment practices conducive to healthy private investment. The policy called for national treatment of foreign

109. Ibid.

110. Ibid.

111. "United States Foreign Investment Policy," Working Paper dated April 16, 1946, NARA, Record Group 43, International Trade Files, Box 38, Folder marked "FIP Docs 1–4."

112. Ibid.

113. Ibid.

114. Executive Committee on Foreign Economic Policy, Memorandum headed "Investment of United States Public and Private Funds in Latin America," dated January 2, 1945, NARA, Record Group 59, State Department File No. 611.0031Executive Committee/1-1545.

115. "United States Foreign Investment Policy," Working Paper dated April 16, 1946, NARA, Record Group 43, International Trade Files, Box 38, Folder marked "FIP Docs 1–4."

investment, except when contrary to "the fundamental principles of public interest," and for intergovernmental agreements to assure non-discrimination.[116] It sought payment of adequate and effective compensation without undue delay when foreign investment was expropriated and noted that, where U.S. investors in a dispute with the host country were unable to obtain "adequate consideration," the U.S. government might make representations on behalf of the investors.[117] The policy thus embraced norms of access, non-discrimination, and security.

By May, the policy cited a higher "standard of living" as an element of the prosperity that foreign investment would promote. It called for intergovernmental cooperation to ensure "just and equitable treatment" for private investment.[118] In June, the committee amended the draft policy to include, among undesirable forms of investment, those that engaged in monopolistic practices or exploited labor.[119]

None of these executive branch policy statements emphasized the conclusion of FCN treaties as a means to promote outward foreign investment, although they did speak of obtaining legal protections. Policymakers in the mid-1940s did not yet regard FCN treaties as among the principal instruments for promoting outward investment.

Neither did Congress at that time associate FCN treaties in any important way with the promotion of outward investment. The 1945 House report on postwar planning made several recommendations to encourage "the free flow of investment funds abroad."[120] First among these was the establishment of the IBRD "as soon as practicable."[121] The principal advantage of the bank was its ability to finance long-term developmental projects, thereby raising the standard of living throughout the world.[122] Three other recommendations appeared, including increased funding for the Export-Import Bank, repeal of the Johnson Act[123] (which prohibited U.S. investors from making private loans to countries in default on past debt, including the United Kingdom and France), and the settlement of Lend Lease Act obligations. Notably, the negotiation of FCN treaties to promote foreign investment was not among the recommendations.

116. Ibid.

117. Ibid.

118. "United States Foreign Investment Policy," Working Paper dated May 3, 1946, NARA, Record Group 43, International Trade Files, Box 38, Folder marked "FIP Docs 1–4."

119. "United States Foreign Investment Policy," Working Paper dated June 10, 1946, NARA, Record Group 43, International Trade Files, Box 38, Folder marked "FIP Docs 1–4."

120. *Post-war Economic Policy and Planning*, Sixth Report of the House Special Committee on Post-War Economic Policy and Planning, House Report No. 541, 79th Congress, 1st Sess., May 8, 1945, page 2.

121. Ibid.

122. Ibid., page 25.

123. 48 Stat. 574.

As the federal government pondered the development of a foreign investment policy, the U.S. business community sought to influence the direction of that policy. The most influential U.S. business organization with respect to foreign investment policy was the National Foreign Trade Council (NFTC), which held an annual meeting of business executives known as the National Foreign Trade Convention. These conventions produced declarations regarding U.S. foreign economic policy that reflected the perspective of major actors in the business community. Like the U.S. government, much of the American business community in the mid-1940s saw the purpose of U.S. foreign economic policy as primarily to promote international trade. To the extent that these annual declarations addressed investment, not surprisingly, they focused far more on the problem of creating conditions conducive to international investment flows than on the problem of controlling the undesirable effects of foreign investment.

The Final Declaration of the convention's meeting in 1946 contained a section detailing "A Proposed Foreign Economic Policy for the United States."[124] The declaration began by proclaiming that the purpose of U.S. foreign economic policy was "to fortify and implement our established foreign policy, and to encourage, in the process, the development of an optimum flow of international trade." [125] Next, the declaration stated that "our foreign economic policy is dedicated to the attainment and maintenance of an international trading system. . . ."[126] Only after two pages of discussion of the benefits of free trade did the declaration address the promotion of foreign investment. Even at that point, however, the declaration observed that "attainment of the high level of foreign trade . . . demands that the flow of physical goods and services internationally be supplemented by a free and unrestricted flow of capital and earnings."[127] In other words, the promotion of foreign investment was a means to promote international trade. U.S. outward investment by raising the standard of living in other countries would create a market for U.S. exports and provide other countries with dollars with which to purchase U.S. exports.

Although U.S. government policy statements on foreign investment policy in the mid-1940s rarely mentioned FCN treaties, the business representatives at the National Foreign Trade Convention believed that the promotion of outward investment necessitated the conclusion of FCN treaties. As its 1946 final declaration proclaimed,

> If the productivity of other lands is to be rapidly expanded, thus increasing the benefits to be derived from an exchange of our products for theirs, encouragement must be given to the projection abroad of private American capital,

124. National Foreign Trade Council, *Draft Final Declaration of the Thirty-Third National Foreign Trade Convention, 1946*, page 3, NARA, Record Group 59, Department of State File No. 611.0031/11-1446.

125. Ibid.

126. Ibid.

127. Ibid.

> either as loans, or as direct investments supported by the necessary management and techniques. Our foreign economic policy will seek, through the medium of treaties of friendship and commerce or by other means legitimately available, to secure the protection of such capital investments against expropriation without adequate, prompt and effective compensation, and against discrimination in any form. It will insist, specifically, upon the protection of proprietary rights; upon provision to the enterprises represented of equal opportunity to compete with local enterprises, without regard to the participation or non-participation in such American enterprises of local capital; upon avoidance of international double taxation and other unfair or discriminatory tax practices; and upon granting to American citizens the right to travel, sojourn, trade and work within foreign countries—all on the basis of full reciprocity vis-à-vis the country concerned.[128]

The National Foreign Trade Convention wanted FCN treaties that guaranteed access, non-discrimination, and security.

In February 1947, Britain formally notified the United States that it no longer could provide financial assistance to Greece and Turkey.[129] Greece was engaged in a civil war that could have resulted in victory for communist forces, while Turkey was struggling to prevent the Soviet Union from gaining control over the Dardanelles. In March, President Truman announced the Truman Doctrine, under which the United States would provide assistance to free peoples resisting subjugation, and asked Congress to approve economic assistance to Greece and Turkey, a request that Congress granted in May.[130]

As Congress was approving funding for Greece and Turkey, Assistant Secretary Will Clayton returned from several weeks in Europe, where he had been attending the International Trade Organization negotiations, discussed in Chapter 3, and reported that the wartime destruction throughout the entire continent was far worse than the United States had believed.[131] As Secretary of State Dean Acheson recalled, Clayton presented "a dark and frightening picture."[132] General Dwight D. Eisenhower, who had served as supreme commander of the Allied forces in Europe during the war, concurred with Clayton's bleak assessment.[133]

On June 5, 1947, Secretary of State George C. Marshall delivered a commencement address at Harvard, where he proposed a massive program of economic

128. Ibid.

129. Pollard, *Search for Solvency,* page 119. U.S. postwar aid to Europe and the Marshall Plan are described in Diane B. Kunz, *Butter and Guns: America's Cold War Economic Diplomacy* (New York: Free Press, 1997), pages 29–56.

130. The emergence of the Truman Doctrine is described in Pollard, *Search for Solvency,* pages 107–132.

131. Garwood, *Will Clayton,* page 59.

132. Ibid., page 60.

133. Rothgeb, *U.S. Trade Policy,* page 86.

assistance for reconstruction in Europe. Such a program would prevent an economic disaster in Europe, enable Europe to continue to purchase U.S. exports, and help to prevent a recession in the United States.[134]

The 1946 election had given control of Congress to the Republicans, who were opposed to the statist programs of the New Deal. To overcome congressional resistance to increased spending, the Truman administration increasingly justified its foreign assistance requests as necessary to contain Soviet expansionism.[135] The rhetoric of promoting peace and prosperity that dominated policy pronouncement during the years of the Second World War gave way to the rhetoric of winning the Cold War.

Anti-communism had been all but absent from the declaration of the 1946 National Foreign Trade Convention. A year later, however, the convention had begun to justify policies of free trade and free capital movements by reference to the Cold War. The 1947 declaration began with a statement headed "America's Stake in the World." That statement explained that "the nations of the world are confronted with a choice between two opposing economic courses."[136] The statement described the first course as "the course of economic freedom, with its reliance upon free, private, competitive enterprise as the mainspring of accomplishment and progress, and its recognition of the dignity and worth of the individual as inherent in political democracy and in the spiritual concept of freedom itself."[137] This was the course to which the United States was committed. The second course, according to the statement, was "the course of economic regimentation, with its invitation, under socialism, to the materialist concept that the individual is the servant of the State and a cog in the collectivist machine, and its subversion not only of economic freedom but of political freedom as well."[138] The declaration went on to say that communism posed a great threat to American security and to the integrity of American institutions. It found that the appeal of communism in certain countries was "no accident."[139] Rather, wherever poverty existed, "the appeal of collectivist security will be compelling."[140] The solution to the communist threat was to create a system that would enhance world productivity.

To this end, the declaration specified a program of action that called for subsistence relief, public investment in areas where private capital could not be attracted, and the encouragement of private capital. Only after articulating these proposals did the declaration call for the promotion of free trade. Thus, between 1946 and 1947, the

134. Kunz, *Butter and Guns*, page 35.

135. Ibid., pages 37–47.

136. National Foreign Trade Council, *Final Declaration of the Thirty-Fourth National Foreign Trade Convention, 1947*, page 6, NARA, Record Group 59, Department of State File No. 611.0031/10-2747.

137. Ibid.

138. Ibid.

139. Ibid.

140. Ibid. page 7.

business community began to shift its defense of outward foreign investment from treating it as a means of promoting trade to regarding it as a means of economic development, which in turn was necessary to halt the spread of communism.

By 1948, the National Foreign Trade Convention was characterizing its policy statements as a defense of capitalism. Its declaration that year began with a statement headed "Private Enterprise Is the World's Best Hope." The opening paragraph of the statement celebrated American freedom embodied in free political institutions and the free enterprise system. The second paragraph turned immediately to the importance of capital. It said that "[t]he right to acquire and own property is inherent in the free enterprise concept; and it is through the process of capital formation, based upon private ownership, profits and saving, that the dynamic potentialities of free enterprise find release and consummation. The process of capital formation underlies all industry and trade in our industrial civilization and it constitutes the mechanism through which private enterprise must function."[141] Thus, capital formation, which in 1946 was a way of stimulating trade, by 1948 had become the foundation of the American economic system.

As the National Foreign Trade Convention developed increasingly elaborate defenses of capitalism, it acknowledged the right of governments to regulate international capital movements. Not even the American business community advocated a policy of laissez-faire.[142] The 1948 declaration undertook to dispel "popular misconceptions which exist concerning capital and its function in our complex economy."[143] The declaration explained that the private enterprise system "must be imbued with the public interest."[144] That is, "it cannot countenance that unbridled license which is the abuse of freedom."[145] Thus, the American free enterprise system "is not pure laissez-faire, since it operates within a framework which combines enlightened self-discipline with a substantial measure of intelligent and purposive regulation by government."[146] Legislation to promote the general welfare and to assure public order and safety, to eliminate unfair business practices or to regulate natural monopolies, all were consistent with the free enterprise system. Private enterprise, however, "cannot willingly accede to arbitrary governmental intervention in the processes of production, investment,

141. National Foreign Trade Council, *Final Declaration of the Thirty-Fifth National Foreign Trade Convention, 1948*, page 6, NARA, Record Group 59, Department of State File No. 611.0031/11-2948.

142. The process by which major corporate leaders gradually accommodated themselves to the New Deal's regulatory state is traced in Kim McQuaid, *Big Business and Presidential Power from FDR to Reagan* (New York: William Morrow, 1982). *See also* Kim McQuaid, *Uneasy Partners: Big Business in American Politics, 1945–1990* (Baltimore: Johns Hopkins University Press, 1994).

143. National Foreign Trade Council, *Final Declaration of the Thirty-Fifth National Foreign Trade Convention, 1948*, page 6, NARA, Record Group 59, Department of State File No. 611.0031/11-2948.

144. Ibid., page 7.

145. Ibid.

146. Ibid.

and trade."[147] In short, the government must regulate the capital market, although subject to the basic norm of reasonableness.

The 1948 declaration included a series of recommendations. The first was the preservation and expansion of private enterprise. That is, the first goal of the business community was to project the American system of liberal capitalism onto the rest of the world. The second recommendation was the promotion of foreign trade, whereas the third was the encouragement of private investment abroad. The declaration commended the efforts of the State Department to "modernize and expand" the network of FCN treaties.[148] The declaration stated that the convention was "impressed by the substantial improvements" over earlier FCN treaties that could be found in a recently concluded FCN treaty with Italy, and recommended that the treaty be utilized as a model for future FCN negotiations. [149] It also recommended that the FCN program be pursued "with vigor."[150]

Meanwhile, John Parke Young's Foreign Investment Committee continued to work on its own foreign investment policy. By August 1947, the policy had been renamed the United States Foreign Credit and Investment Policy. The August 1947 draft of the policy indicated that the U.S. government had become less sanguine about its ability to direct investment flows to mitigate the effects of economic fluctuations, and called for doing so "in so far as practical."[151] A year later, when President Truman signed the policy, it would call for mitigating economic fluctuations when mitigating measures were "consistent with other major domestic and international objectives."[152] Embracing the new Cold War rhetoric, the August 1947 draft policy statement touted foreign investment as a means of promoting "fundamental freedoms" as well as prosperity and international security.[153]

By the spring of 1947, as will be seen in Chapter 3, the business community had persuaded the State Department to draft a code of protection for foreign investment for inclusion in the charter of the proposed International Trade Organization. Reflecting the work on the code, the August 1947 draft policy called for a more detailed list of measures to promote investment. The detailed list included the negotiation of FCN treaties, the negotiation of treaties to prevent

147. Ibid.

148. Ibid., page 18.

149. Ibid.

150. Ibid.

151. "United States Foreign Credit and Investment Policy," August 15, 1947, NARA, Record Group 43, International Trade Files, Box 38, Folder marked "FIP Docs 1–4."

152. "United States Foreign Credit and Investment Policy," August 11, 1948, NARA, Record Group 43, International Trade Files, Box 38, Folder marked "FIP Docs 1–4."

153. "United States Foreign Credit and Investment Policy," August 15, 1947, NARA, Record Group 43, International Trade Files, Box 38, Folder marked "FIP Docs 1–4."

double taxation, and "agreements looking toward the elimination of impediments to fair, equitable and nondiscriminatory treatment of foreign capital."[154] As this suggests, the State Department had not yet decided that FCN treaties would be the primary instrument by which the United States would obtain treaty protection for foreign investment. In a separate paragraph, the policy also called for "the establishment of standards of fair practice with respect to the treatment accorded private international investment."[155]

The 1947 draft omitted the description of undesirable forms of investment, instead identifying the desirable attributes of investment. These included an adequate opportunity for the participation of local capital and management, an economically desirable purpose, flexible terms of repayment, reasonable rates of interest, and appropriately long amortization periods. A year later, the policy would add an additional criterion, that the investment was "adequately complemented by the providing of skills and technology where appropriate."[156]

By March 1948, the protection of foreign investment had become a much more significant concern of the policy, and the policy was becoming increasingly specific about the nature of the investment-related provisions that the United States should seek. In the section stating the willingness of the U.S. government to make representations on behalf of U.S. investors involved in disputes with the host country, the policy specifically identified situations where a U.S. investor was "subject to arbitrary or unreasonable action" as a circumstance when the State Department might assist the investor.[157]

At the same time, the policy stated that the U.S. government would assume no responsibility for protecting private investments that had features described in previous drafts as undesirable. These included investment made under terms likely to become the subject of reasonable public resentment in either country or to injure U.S. foreign relations, such as those where the investor received special tax exemptions or exclusive concessions, those involving anticompetitive behavior, or those that exploited labor. It also would assume no responsibility for protecting private investments that were concealed from the State Department or were made against the advice of the Department.

By May 1948, however, the Foreign Investment Policy Committee had reconsidered the idea of declaring certain investments, even if inconsistent with U.S. policy, outside the protection of the State Department.[158] The draft policy no longer disclaimed any responsibility for protecting undesirable investments. The May draft stated merely that the U.S. government discouraged such investment.

154. Ibid.

155. Ibid.

156. "United States Foreign Credit and Investment Policy," March 9, 1948, NARA, Record Group 43, International Trade Files, Box 38, Folder marked "FIP Docs 1–4."

157. Ibid.

158. "United States Foreign Credit and Investment Policy," May 7, 1948, NARA, Record Group 43, International Trade Files, Box 38, Folder marked "FIP Docs 1–4."

In June, the years of effort to develop a foreign investment policy culminated in the adoption of the policy by the ECEFP.[159] That committee declared that U.S. foreign investment policy was intended "to facilitate the expansion of production and trade, to raise standards of living, and to foster economic and social progress and development."[160] The report addressed both U.S. government loans and credits and U.S. policies to promote private foreign investment.

The report asserted that "to promote good international relations," private investment should adhere to certain principles. It should "1) be made in a manner consistent with the best interest of both the supplying and recipient countries; 2) provide an adequate opportunity for the voluntary participation of capital and management of the country where the investment takes place; 3) be adequately complemented by furnishing skills and technology where appropriate; 4) be on an equity basis where appropriate; and, when on a loan basis, should provide for reasonable rates of interest and amortization."[161] Further, the report noted that the United States government "discourages private investments the terms of which are likely to give rise to reasonable public resentment in either country or occasion unfriendly relations" between the United States and the other country.[162]

The report suggested a number of measures that the United States should take in order to facilitate and encourage outward foreign investment flows. The second item on the list was negotiating FCN treaties, treaties to prevent double taxation of foreign earned income, and "agreements looking toward the assurance of fair, equitable and nondiscriminatory treatment of foreign capital."[163] That is, the report seemed to contemplate that the United States would negotiate bilateral investment treaties that would complement the more traditional FCN treaties.

Other recommended measures included providing information on investment opportunities abroad, selling to private investors foreign obligations owned by the U.S. Export-Import Bank (ExIm Bank), guaranteeing through ExIm Bank private credits extended by U.S. lenders, ensuring foreign exchange convertibility, reducing U.S. taxation on foreign earned income, and promoting international economic conditions conducive to foreign investment, such as the elimination of restrictions on trade, investment, and currency exchange.[164]

The report also identified measures that other governments should take. These included facilitating private investment "for purposes economically suited to the area," according "fair and nondiscriminatory treatment" to foreign investment, and imposing "no unreasonable barriers to the transfer of capital and earnings."[165]

159. *Current Economic Developments*, June 7, 1948, page 2, NARA, Record Group 59, Department of State Lot Files.

160. Ibid.

161. Ibid., page 4.

162. Ibid.

163. Ibid., page 3.

164. Ibid.

165. Ibid., page 4.

The report noted that, in this connection, the United States favored the "establishment of standards of fair practice with respect to the treatment and conduct of private international investment."[166]

Thus, by 1948, the State Department knew that it wanted to obtain increased treaty protection for foreign investment, that is, to conclude treaties that would guarantee "fair, equitable and nondiscriminatory treatment" of foreign investment. More specifically, its foreign investment policy called for national treatment of foreign investment; prompt, adequate, and effective compensation for expropriated property; and a prohibition on exchange controls, and it opposed "arbitrary or unreasonable" treatment of foreign investment. The Department had not yet decided, however, that FCN treaties would be the primary instrument for obtaining the protection sought by its foreign investment policy. The process by which the FCN treaties became the first bilateral investment treaties begins with the launching of the U.S. postwar FCN treaty series, which is the subject of Chapter 2.

166. Ibid., page 3.

2

Launching the U.S. Postwar FCN Treaty Program

The negotiation of FCN treaties dates from the very founding of the republic. The War of Independence severed the legal ties between the United States of America and the British Empire and placed the new nation outside the imperial trading system. Aware that the United States would need new trading partners to purchase its surplus commodities and to provide it with manufactured goods, the Continental Congress in 1776 authorized the preparation of a model FCN treaty for use in negotiations with the major European powers.[1] In July of that year, it adopted a Declaration of Independence in order to provide a legal basis for other nations to treat with the new republic.[2] The earliest FCN treaties thus were intended to obtain recognition of U.S. independence and to establish trade and maritime relations with the powers of Europe.[3]

The first FCN treaty was signed with France in 1778,[4] on the same day that the United States concluded its treaty of alliance with that country.[5] The FCN treaty was signed first and thus it became the first treaty concluded in the history of the United States.[6] During the War of Independence, the United States also

1. The early history of the FCN treaties is sketched in Doron S. Ben-Atar, *The Origins of Jeffersonian Commercial Policy and Diplomacy* (New York: St. Martin's Press, 1993).

2. David Armitage, *The Declaration of Independence: A Global History* (Cambridge, MA: Harvard University Press, 2007), pages 35–36.

3. Department of State, Office of Public Affairs, *Commercial Treaty Program of the United States* (Washington, DC: Government Printing Office, 1952), NARA, Record Group 59, Department of State File No. 611.004/3-453.

4. February 6, 1778, 8 Stat. 12, T.S. No. 83.

5. Department of State, Office of Public Affairs, *Commercial Treaty Program of the United States* (Washington, DC: Government Printing Office, 1952), NARA, Record Group 59, Department of State File No. 611.004/3-453.

6. John Bassett Moore, *The Principles of American Diplomacy* (New York: Harper and Brothers, 1918), page 12.

concluded FCN treaties with the Netherlands in 1782[7] and with Sweden in 1783.[8] Following the end of the war, Congress established a commission comprising John Adams, Benjamin Franklin, and Thomas Jefferson to negotiate additional FCN treaties. From 1778 until the second term of the Truman administration, the United States would negotiate some 130 such treaties.[9]

Although the initial series of FCN treaties was directed at establishing U.S. relations with Europe, during the antebellum period the United States undertook to negotiate FCN treaties with the newly independent Latin American countries.[10] FCN treaties concluded before the Civil War, however, were not limited to Europe and Latin America. For example, a leading object of Caleb Cushing's mission to China in 1844 was to conclude an FCN treaty with that country.[11] In the first half of the nineteenth century, the United States placed particular importance on the navigation provisions of the treaties, which gained access to foreign ports for U.S. vessels and which protected the right of U.S. vessels to engage in neutral trade with belligerent countries.[12]

In the years following the Civil War, the pace of negotiations slowed. Industrialization in the United States reduced the need to import manufactured goods, while the construction of a transcontinental railroad allowed U.S. producers to concentrate on serving a large domestic market. The United States maintained high tariffs to protect American industry against foreign competition and de-emphasized the promotion of international trade. After World War I, however, the growing U.S. industrial surplus created a need for new markets. Thus, after that war, trade emerged as by far the most important element of the FCN treaties.[13] By the mid-1920s, the United States was engaged in highly productive

7. Treaty of Amity and Commerce, United States-Netherlands, signed October 8, 1782, 8 Stat. 32, T.S. No. 249.

8. Treaty of Amity and Commerce, United States-Sweden, signed April 3, 1783, 8 Stat. 60, T.S. No. 346.

9. Herman Walker Jr., "Provisions on Companies in United States Commercial Treaties," 50 *American Journal of International Law* 373, 374 n. 4 (1956). According to Walker, this estimate was published by the Department of State in 1952. For a brief survey of U.S. FCN treaty practice, *see* Eric V. Youngquist, "United States Commercial Treaties: Their Role in Foreign Economic Policy," 2 *Studies in Law and Economic Development* 72 (1967).

10. Memorandum from Winthrop Brown dated February 13, 1950, NARA, Record Group 59, Department of State File No. 611.004/3-850.

11. Department of State, Office of Public Affairs, *Commercial Treaty Program of the United States* (Washington, DC: Government Printing Office, 1952), NARA, Record Group 59, Department of State File No. 611.004/3-453.

12. Ibid. On the navigation provisions generally, *see* Don C. Piper, "Navigation Provisions in the United States Commercial Treaties," 11 *American Journal of Comparative Law* 184 (1962); Harry C. Hawkins, *Commercial Treaties & Agreements: Principles & Practice* (New York: Rinehart, 1951), pages 34–44.

13. Department of State, Office of Public Affairs, *Commercial Treaty Program of the United States* (Washington, DC: Government Printing Office, 1952), NARA, Record Group 59, Department of State File No. 611.004/3-453.

negotiations with several countries in Central America and Europe. It concluded FCN treaties with Germany[14] in 1923, Estonia[15] in 1925, El Salvador[16] in 1926, Honduras[17] in 1927, and Austria,[18] Latvia,[19] and Norway[20] in 1928. The Great Depression and the embrace of autarkic economic policies throughout the world created an inhospitable environment for negotiations[21] and no further treaties were concluded until the mid-1930s. Ultimately, 12 treaties were concluded during the interwar period.[22]

With the trade provisions growing in importance, the United States during the 1920s incorporated into the treaties a clause requiring unconditional most-favored-nation (MFN) treatment with respect to trade.[23] An unconditional MFN treatment clause requires a country to extend to the other treaty party treatment that is at least as favorable as the treatment that the country extends to any other country. Thus, if an importing country lowers the tariff on a particular product imported from a particular exporting country, it must lower the tariff on that same product imported from any other exporting country to which it has promised unconditional MFN treatment. The clause that had appeared in prior treaties was a reciprocal MFN treatment clause. Under that clause, a country was obligated to extend MFN treatment to other treaty parties only if they reciprocated toward that country. An unconditional MFN treatment clause thus leads to a more rapid liberalization of trade because all trade concessions made by a country

14. Treaty of Friendship, Commerce and Consular Rights, United States-Germany, December 8, 1923, 44 Stat. 2132, T.S. No. 725. The treaty with Germany formed the model for those concluded over the ensuing 15 years.

15. Treaty of Friendship, Commerce and Consular Rights, United States-Estonia, signed December 23, 1925, 44 Stat. 2379, T.S. No. 736.

16. Treaty of Friendship, Commerce and Consular Rights, United States-El Salvador, signed February 22, 1926, 46 Stat. 2817, T.S. No. 827.

17. Treaty of Friendship, Commerce and Consular Rights, United States-Honduras, signed December 7, 1927, 45 Stat. 2618, T.S. No. 764.

18. Treaty of Friendship, Commerce and Consular Rights, United States-Austria, signed June 19, 1928, 47 Stat. 1876, T.S. No. 838.

19. Treaty of Friendship, Commerce and Consular Rights, United States-Latvia, signed April 20, 1928, 45 Stat. 2641, T.S. No. 765.

20. Treaty of Friendship, Commerce and Consular Rights, United States-Norway, signed June 5, 1928, 47 Stat. 2135, T.S. No. 852.

21. These policies are described in more detail in Jeffrey A. Frieden, *Global Capitalism: Its Fall and Rise in the Twentieth Century* (New York: W.W. Norton, 2006).

22. *Commercial Treaties,* Hearing Before a Subcommittee of the Committee on Foreign Relations, 82d Cong. 2d Sess. (1952), page 3.

23. The history and rationale of this change are described in William B. Kelly Jr., "Antecedents of Present Commercial Policy," in William B. Kelly, Jr., ed., *Studies in United States Commercial Policy* (Chapel Hill: University of North Carolina Press, 1963).

are immediately generalized to all treaty parties with which that country has an unconditional MFN treatment obligation, even if those parties do not provide the same concession in return.[24]

The FCN treaties were not sufficient in themselves to open markets to U.S. exports because they did not reduce tariffs, instead promising only nondiscriminatory treatment. Most of the FCN treaty provisions addressed other aspects of trade, such as the treatment of merchants in the territory of the host state.

Because tariffs were taxes and could be reduced only by an act of Congress, efforts by the State Department to negotiate reductions in tariffs were impeded by the Department's inability to ensure that Congress would enact legislation to implement any reductions to which the United States might agree during negotiations.[25] To remedy this situation, in 1934, Secretary of State Cordell Hull persuaded Congress to enact the Reciprocal Trade Agreements Act (RTAA), which authorized the State Department to conclude treaties that reduced tariffs by as much as 50 percent without further approval from Congress. Although the State Department continued to conclude FCN treaties, much of its effort shifted to the negotiation of trade agreements under the 1934 legislation. In the three years after the RTAA was enacted, the State Department concluded 15 trade agreements under the act.[26] By contrast, it concluded only three FCN treaties during the entirety of the Roosevelt Administration—with Finland[27] in 1934, Siam (now Thailand)[28] in 1937, and Liberia[29] in 1938.

World War II reduced commercial affairs "to a bare minimum,"[30] and the United States suspended the negotiation of FCN treaties during the war years, even when negotiations were already in progress. For example, the negotiation of an FCN treaty with India ended abruptly when the State Department received a

24. As Lloyd Gardner notes, the United States sought more rapid liberalization of trade because its enhanced productive capacity following World War I demanded larger export markets. Lloyd C. Gardner, *Economic Aspects of New Deal Diplomacy* (Madison: University of Wisconsin Press, 1964), page 40.

25. David A. Lake, *Power, Protection, and Free Trade: International Sources of US Commercial Strategy 1887–1939* (Ithaca, NY: Cornell University Press, 1989), page 204.

26. John M. Rothgeb Jr., *U.S. Trade Policy: Balancing Economic Dreams and Political Realities* (Washington, DC: Congressional Quarterly Press 2001), page 47.

27. Treaty of Friendship, Commerce and Consular Rights, United States-Finland, signed February 13, 1934, 49 Stat. 2659, T.S. No. 868.

28. Treaty of Friendship, Commerce and Navigation, United States-Siam, signed November 13, 1937, 53 Stat. 1731, T.S. No. 940.

29. Treaty of Friendship, Commerce and Navigation, United States-Liberia, signed August 8, 1938, 54 Stat. 1739, T.S. No. 956.

30. Dean Acheson, *Present at the Creation: My Years in the State Department* (New York: W. W. Norton, 1969), page 17.

message from the Indian attorney general stating that it was "wiser, in view of the changed situation in India, to defer the conclusion of the negotiations until conditions are more settled."[31]

INAUGURATION OF THE U.S. POSTWAR FCN TREATY PROGRAM

In 1944, anticipating the imminent end to the war, the Roosevelt administration launched a program to extend and modernize the U.S. FCN treaty program.[32] At that time, some 29 FCN treaties were still in force, the oldest of which was an 1815 treaty with the United Kingdom.[33] More than half of these existing FCN treaties had been concluded in the nineteenth century[34] and most of those had been concluded before 1860.[35]

The State Department intended Cordell Hull's trade agreements to lower barriers that impeded trade between nations. The FCN treaties, by contrast, dealt "largely with the rights of persons and corporations and with instrumentalities by means of which the flow of goods and services is carried on."[36] In a sense, whereas trade agreements operated principally at the border to lower barriers to entry for goods, the FCN treaties operated to a large extent behind the border. They addressed the legal climate that would exist within the host country for traders and vessels from abroad.

The business community strongly supported this new initiative and, after the end of World War II, was impatient for the United States to begin concluding FCN treaties with other countries. At its annual meeting in Atlantic City, in late April and early May 1946, the United States Chamber of Commerce adopted a resolution "that the Department of State be urged to negotiate [FCN] treaties with countries with which we have substantial commercial relationships and that negotiations to modernize existing treaties of friendship and commerce be

31. The message is quoted in Acheson, ibid., at pages 17–18.

32. *Current Economic Developments,* January 21, 1946, page 9, NARA, Record Group 59, Department of State Lot Files.

33. Airgram dated November 17, 1954, from the Department of State to the U.S. embassy in Cairo, NARA, Record Group 59, Department of State File No. 611.004/11-1754.

34. *Current Economic Developments,* January 21, 1946, page 9, NARA, Record Group 59, Department of State Lot Files.

35. Treaties concluded before 1860 and still in force in the mid-twentieth century included those with Argentina (1853), Bolivia (1858), Brunei (1850), Colombia (1846), Costa Rica (1851), Denmark (1826), Morocco (1836), Muscat-Zanzibar (1833), Paraguay (1859), Switzerland (1850), and United Kingdom (1851).

36. Memorandum by Vernon G. Setser headed "Status of Commercial Treaty Program," dated November 5, 1946, NARA, Record Group 59, Department of State File No. 711.002/11-546.

instituted without delay."[37] The National Foreign Trade Convention, meeting in New York the following November, "urge[d] that the negotiation of treaties of friendship and commerce with other nations be pursued vigorously, so that our commercial treaty structure, which has fallen into obsolescence, may be rapidly brought to the point where the needs of American foreign trade and investment can be effectively served."[38] According to its president, Charles Carroll, the National Foreign Trade Council (NFTC) believed that the conclusion of FCN treaties was of the "utmost importance" to U.S. foreign economic policy.[39]

In 1944, when the Roosevelt administration inaugurated the postwar FCN treaty program, the organizational structure of the State Department reflected both the importance of trade to U.S. foreign economic policy and the traditionally peripheral importance of investment protection to the FCN treaty program. U.S. foreign economic policy was the responsibility of the Office of Economic Affairs, headed by Harry Hawkins, whom Cordell Hull regarded as the man primarily responsible for the negotiation of the reciprocal trade agreements.[40] Hawkins's position as director of the office suggests the importance of the trade agreements to the Department. Hawkins reported directly to Dean Acheson, who at that time was assistant secretary of state for economic affairs. The Office of Economic Affairs comprised three divisions. One of these, the Division of Commercial Policy, bore primary responsibility for negotiating FCN treaties and trade agreements under the RTAA. A separate division, the Division of Financial and Monetary Affairs, bore responsibility for U.S. foreign investment policy. That is, investment policy was the responsibility of a different division than that which negotiated the FCN treaties. The Office also included a Commodities Division.

Changes in senior personnel would occur before the end of the year, just as FCN treaty negotiations were beginning, although none of these changes would result in an important change in policy. In December 1944, Acheson left the economic affairs bureau and assumed responsibility for legislative affairs. He was replaced by Will Clayton, who would serve as assistant secretary of state and then undersecretary of state until 1947.

Clayton, like Hull, was a strong proponent of free trade.[41] In urging that Roosevelt approve the appointment of Clayton, Roosevelt's advisor Harry

37. Letter from the Chamber of Commerce to the Department of State, dated June 12, 1946, NARA, Record Group 59, Department of State File No. 711.002/6-1246.

38. National Foreign Trade Council, *Draft Final Declaration of the Thirty-Third National Foreign Trade Convention*, 1946, page 10, NARA, Record Group 59, State Department File No. 611.0031/11-1446.

39. Charles Carroll, "Comments on the Suggested Charter for an International Trade Organization," November 6, 1946, NARA, Record Group 43, International Trade Files, Box 60, File marked "National Foreign Trade Council—Carroll Rpt."

40. Cordell Hull, *The Memoirs of Cordell Hull* (New York: Macmillan, 1948), page 366.

41. The leading biography of Will Clayton is Gregory A. Fossedal, *Our Finest Hour: Will Clayton, the Marshall Plan and the Triumph of Democracy* (Stanford, CA: Hoover Institution Press,

Hopkins told Roosevelt that Clayton's views were identical to Hull's.[42] Born on a cotton farm in Tupelo, Mississippi, in 1880, Clayton had quit school at the age of 13 to drive a laundry wagon. He taught himself shorthand and then became a court reporter. At the age of 15, he left home to work for a St. Louis cotton merchant, who soon moved, along with Clayton, to New York. In 1902, Clayton married a young woman from Kentucky, Sue Vaughn, who was also being courted by a local prosecutor named Alben Barkley, a future congressman, senator, and vice president under Harry Truman. The marriage would have important consequences for Clayton's career.

At the age of 24, Clayton left the cotton trading firm at which he had worked for the past eight years and, in partnership with two members of his wife's family, founded his own cotton trading firm with an investment of $3,000 apiece. Cotton was the largest U.S. export at the time, and thus Clayton gained considerable experience with foreign purchasers. Clayton's company became one of the first cotton brokerage firms to establish offices overseas, and eventually would have offices in Europe, Asia, Latin America, and the Middle East. A quarter of a century after Clayton and his partners founded the firm, it had annual sales in excess of $200,000,000. Clayton himself became known as "King Cotton" and he was featured on the cover of *Time* magazine on August 17, 1936.

Clayton left his company in 1940 to join the New Deal as a deputy to Nelson Rockefeller, who was serving as coordinator of Inter-American Affairs. He moved from there to the Reconstruction Finance Corporation, then to the Department of Commerce, and then to the Office of War Mobilization, until Secretary of State Edward Stettinius appointed him assistant secretary in December 1944. In August 1946, just prior to the launching of the ITO Charter negotiations, Sue Clayton, suspected by some of being mentally ill, in part because of her habit of insulting and badgering Will Clayton in public,[43] insisted that Clayton resign so that they could return to their home in Houston. Clayton submitted his resignation to Dean Acheson, who by then was the secretary of state and who thought that the problem might well have been that Sue Clayton believed that Will Clayton was underappreciated. Accordingly, Acheson created the position of undersecretary of state for economic affairs for Clayton in the hope that the promotion would induce Mrs. Clayton to change her mind. The ploy worked for a time and Clayton would remain at the State Department until October of the following year.

1993). Also useful is William L. Garwood Jr., *Will Clayton: Economic Statesman* (Washington, DC: American Studies Center, 1979). The latter was written by Clayton's grandson and tends toward the hagiographic. My sketch of Clayton draws on these two accounts, except where a different source is cited.

42. Patrick J. Hearden, *Architects of Globalism: Building a New World Order during World War II* (Fayetteville: University of Arkansas Press, 2002), page 49.

43. Willard Thorp Oral History, Harry S. Truman Library. Gregory Fossedal attributes Sue Clayton's "extreme emotional volatility" to her arteriosclerosis. Fossedal, *Our Finest Hour*, page 279.

Clayton's experience as an exporter convinced him that American prosperity depended upon opening world markets to American products. He was not, however, a proponent of laissez-faire economics.[44] He believed that the government had a responsibility to "regulate the excesses of the economy" as well as to take care of the poor.[45] Like Cordell Hull, Clayton saw international trade as the central concern of foreign economic policy. He had seemingly little interest in international capital movements or foreign investment policy.

Harry Hawkins, meanwhile, was offered a post as economic counselor in London and was succeeded as director of the Office of Economic Affairs in July 1945 by Clair Wilcox, an economics professor on leave from Swarthmore College. Wilcox had gained national attention in 1930 by sending to President Herbert Hoover a letter enclosing a petition signed by more than a thousand economists opposing the Smoot-Hawley tariff.[46] Clayton and Wilcox presented a pair of sharply contrasting figures. Clayton was the self-taught southern businessman who had dropped out of school at the age of 13, whereas Wilcox was a northern career academic with a PhD in economics from the University of Pennsylvania. These two quite different men shared, however, a strong commitment to free trade as a matter of principle.[47] During Wilcox's tenure, the Office of Economic Affairs would be renamed the Office of International Trade Policy, reflecting the centrality of trade in U.S. foreign economic policy at that time.

The same month that Wilcox assumed his duties, Winthrop Brown, a Yale-educated lawyer who had joined the administration in 1941 to work in the Lend Lease program, assumed responsibilities as chief of the Commercial Policy Division. Brown, too, "was smitten by free trade fervor."[48] His own involvement in U.S. foreign economic policy over the next three years would center on tariff negotiations. In short, none of the top policymakers in the offices that oversaw the negotiation of FCN treaties was particularly interested in investment policy.

None of these personnel changes resulted in any immediate, discernible alteration in FCN treaty policy. The personnel changes, however, put in place the men in charge of commercial treaty policy during the years when the State Department would launch the postwar FCN treaty program.

44. Garwood, *Will Clayton,* page 12. Fossedal quotes a speech that Clayton gave in Augusta, Georgia, in 1928 in which he said, "I do not belong to the laissez-faire school, whose philosophy will not permit acceptance of any government regulation. I am sorry to say that business . . . has not always shown itself competent or willing to put its house in order." Fossedal, *Our Finest Hour,* page 40. Clayton nevertheless did believe that the New Deal had been too interventionist, and he supported Roosevelt in 1940 largely because of Roosevelt's international trade policy.

45. Garwood, *Will Clayton,* page 12.

46. Michael A. Bernstein, *A Perilous Progress: Economists and Public Purpose in Twentieth Century America* (Princeton, NJ: Princeton University Press, 2001), page 1.

47. Historian Thomas Zeiler calls Wilcox "a free trade idealist" with a "vision of free trade universalism." Thomas W. Zeiler, *Free Trade, Free World: The Advent of GATT* (Chapel Hill: University of North Carolina Press, 1999), pages 56–57.

48. Ibid., page 76.

By September 1944, the Division of Commercial Policy had completed the preparation of a preliminary draft of a new model FCN treaty for use in negotiations.[49] The substantive articles of the treaty fell into four categories: (1) establishment, (2) trade, (3) navigation, and (4) general and miscellaneous.

Establishment provisions addressed the right of nationals and companies of one party to the treaty to enter the territory of the other party and to engage in various activities there. These provisions guaranteed various rights including freedom of worship, exemption from compulsory military service, access to courts, the right to compensation for expropriated property, and freedom from unreasonable searches and seizures.

None of the provisions expressly mentioned investment. Nevertheless, a few of the establishment provisions did have the effect of promoting or protecting foreign investment. These provisions included those that guaranteed to individuals the right to enter the territory of the host state, the right of corporations to be organized within that territory, the right of both individuals and corporations to engage in activities there, and their right to the protection of their property and to access to courts.

The most important innovation in the proposed postwar standard draft FCN treaty was its guarantee of rights to corporations.[50] Corporations had scarcely been mentioned in FCN treaties prior to 1911, when the United States concluded an FCN treaty with Japan. Earlier treaties conferred rights on "nationals," a term that generally referred to natural persons and not to corporations.[51] The treaty with Japan guaranteed to corporations the right to appear in courts.[52] Twelve years later, the U.S. FCN treaty with Germany granted to corporations the right to have their juridical status recognized.[53] These provisions, however, did not guarantee to corporations the right to engage in any particular business activity. Rather, their ability to do so was governed entirely by the domestic law of the host state.

In general, companies were protected by the U.S. postwar FCN treaties only if they had the nationality of one of the parties. These treaties deemed a company to have the nationality of the country where it was incorporated. Each party,

49. Proposed Articles for Use in Drafting Treaties of Friendship, Commerce and Navigation with Particular Countries (September 1944), NARA, Record Group 59, Department of State File No. 711.002/9-44.

50. Herman Walker Jr., "Provisions on Companies in United States Commercial Treaties," 50 *American Journal of International Law* 373 (1956). *See also* the discussion of companies in Chapter 8.

51. Hawkins, *Commercial Treaties*, page 4; Walker, "Provisions on Companies in United States Commercial Treaties."

52. Treaty of Commerce and Navigation, United States-Japan, signed February 21, 1911, Article VII, 37 Stat. 1504, T.S. No. 558.

53. Treaty of Friendship, Commerce and Consular Rights, United States-Germany, signed December 8, 1923, Article XII, 44 Stat. 2132, T.S. No. 725.

however, reserved the right to deny treaty benefits to any company organized under the laws of the other party if nationals of a third country controlled the company.

Although all of the provisions relating to the rights of individuals and companies in the territory of the host state were sometimes described as establishment provisions, the specific right to enter as a natural person or to be legally constituted as a legal person and to engage in activities in the territory of the host state would often be described as the "right of establishment." This right of establishment could be distinguished from other provisions of the treaty that protected property after establishment. The right of establishment provided access (generally on a non-discriminatory basis), whereas the property protection provisions guaranteed non-discriminatory treatment, security of property rights, and due process.

The trade provisions included those relating to import or export duties, import or export quotas, the internal taxation of imports, exchange controls, the granting of public contracts, and the operation of state trading enterprises. Although the provision on exchange controls was situated among the trade provisions of the treaty, it also applied to certain transfers related to investments. Later in the decade, as the FCN treaties were reconceptualized as investment treaties, the State Department would revise the exchange controls provision so that it emphasized the protection of the right to make certain transfers related to an investment, and the provision would be resituated at the end of the establishment provisions, rather than among the trade provisions.

The navigation provisions granted a right of vessels of one party to enter the ports of the other party and to be free of discriminatory port charges or other discriminatory treatment. They also provided for assistance to vessels in times of distress.[54]

The general provisions called for perpetual peace and friendship between the two parties, language that generally was considered a formality,[55] and provided for the resolution of disputes concerning the treaty before the International Court of Justice. The latter provision marked the first time that the United States had agreed in its commercial treaties to the compulsory jurisdiction of an international court over treaty disputes prior to the occurrence of the disputes.[56] The general provisions also included exceptions "to allow necessary freedom of action in national emergencies and to keep the treaty in harmony with the programs of the specialized agencies of the United Nations, such as the International Monetary Fund."[57]

54. On the navigation provisions generally, *see* Piper, "Navigation Provisions."

55. Hawkins, *Commercial Treaties*, page 2.

56. Robert R. Wilson, *United States Commercial Treaties and International Law* (New Orleans: Hauser Press, 1960), page 23.

57. Memorandum by Vernon G. Setser headed "Status of Commercial Treaty Program," dated November 5, 1946, NARA, Record Group 59, Department of State File No. 711.002/11-546.

PREPARING A STANDARD DRAFT TREATY

The standard draft FCN treaty was a long and complex document. At the inception of the postwar treaty program, the standard draft treaty had an estimated length of 10,300 words.[58] An October 1946 memorandum written by Herman Walker, an adviser on commercial treaties in the Division of Commercial Policy, with a doctorate in economics from Duke University,[59] noted that the standard draft treaty was perceived to be "too verbose and tedious."[60] On the whole, Walker observed, "it is a forbidding document to read appreciatively."[61] Some of its provisions were "quite difficult to follow."[62]

Walker blamed the problem in part on the nature of a legal document and in part on "the multiplicity of outside drafting contributions that perforce entered the picture."[63] Indeed, the drafters had consulted approximately 33 government agencies with respect to various aspects of the standard draft treaty.[64] The State Department, which had primary responsibility for drafting and negotiating FCN treaties, consulted with other government agencies with respect to provisions that would affect the work of those agencies, and it consulted with the Commerce Department with respect to the entire treaty.[65]

Walker hoped to improve the style of the treaty. The FCN treaties were intended to endure for years to come and constituted, in Walker's mind, "an enterprise deserving finesse in language as well as excellence in substance."[66] Shortening the

58. Memorandum by Herman Walker headed "Shortening the Present Draft Treaty of Friendship, Commerce and Navigation," dated October 15, 1946, NARA, Record Group 59, Department of State Lot Files, Walter Hollis Papers, Folder marked "Investment Treaties."

59. "Herman Walker, 83, Professor and U.S. Foreign Officer, Dies," *New York Times*, May 13, 1994.

60. Memorandum by Herman Walker headed "Shortening the Present Draft Treaty of Friendship, Commerce and Navigation," dated October 15, 1946, NARA, Record Group 59, Department of State Lot Files, Walter Hollis Papers, Folder marked "Investment Treaties."

61. Ibid.

62. Ibid.

63. Ibid.

64. Memorandum dated September 30, 1959, from John A. Calhoun to Brigadier General A. J. Goodpaster, NARA, Record Group 59, Department of State File No. 611.514/9-3059. *See also* Memorandum by Charles Bevans headed "Signing of a Treaty of Friendship, Commerce and Navigation with Israel," dated August 22, 1951, NARA, Record Group 59, Department of State File No. 611.84A4/8-2251.

65. Memorandum of Conversation headed "Consultation with Other Government Agencies and with Business Interests in Connection with the Negotiation of Treaties of Friendship, Commerce and Navigation," dated June 29, 1948, NARA, Record Group 59, Department of State File No. 711.002/6-2948.

66. Memorandum by Herman Walker headed "Shortening the Present Draft Treaty of Friendship, Commerce and Navigation," dated October 15, 1946, NARA, Record Group 59, Lot Files, Walter Hollis Papers, Folder marked "Investment Treaties."

draft would "speed up its readability, and increase the ease with which it can be comprehended."[67] It would enhance the treaty's prestige, render it less suspect to officials of other countries, decrease the difficulty of translation, and save costs in producing copies. Walker believed that any proposal to modify the language would face two obstacles, however: inherent resistance to change and the fear of having to repeat the laborious interagency clearance process. Thus, Walker proposed to modify the language only in ways that were purely stylistic.

Walker estimated that four stylistic clichés accounted for about 1,075 of the more than 10,000 words. These clichés included, for example, references to "the High Contracting Parties" rather than simply "the parties." He proposed to eliminate these clichés and to streamline the language in other ways that largely eliminated surplus or redundant language.[68]

Despite Walker's efforts, however, a year later the model treaty still was "widely criticized for its length and complexity."[69] Experience had shown that extensive revisions were so time-consuming that they foreclosed proposing new treaty negotiations within any reasonable period. Accordingly, the Department decided to proceed with the draft as shortened by Walker's stylistic revisions, dealing with the most serious substantive defects as they became evident.

Following the conclusion of the treaty with Italy in February 1948, only two years after Walker's effort, the standard draft was "completely recast."[70] Walker explained a decade later that the revision was "in the interest of compactness, greater clarity and legal sufficiency, and completeness of content."[71] As discussed in Chapter 5, this revision accompanied the transformation of the FCN treaties from treaties concerned primarily with trade and navigation to investment treaties. The revision that occurred in 1948–1949 was the last comprehensive one and thereafter the standard draft treaty was regarded as largely settled in form and content.

Another reason for the length and complexity of the treaty was that, as new problems arose affecting U.S. economic interests abroad, those seeking to address the problems sought inclusion of new language in the FCN treaties for that purpose. In 1951, three years after the treaty had been completely recast, Assistant Legal Adviser Stanley Metzger noted that "[t]here is a constant stream of proposals to remedy this, that or the other special evil."[72] Indeed, Metzger believed that

67. Ibid.

68. Ibid.

69. Memorandum dated March 28, 1947, from Vernon G. Setzer to Seymour J. Rubin, NARA, Record Group 59, Department of State Lot Files, Walter Hollis Papers, Folder Marked "Investment Treaties."

70. Herman Walker Jr., "Modern Treaties of Friendship, Commerce and Navigation," 42 *Minnesota Law Review* 805, 807 (1958).

71. Ibid.

72. Memorandum of Conversation headed "Addition to FCN Treaties of Provision on Government-Owned Patents," dated November 21, 1951, NARA, Record Group 59, Department of State File No. 611.944/11-2151.

the standard draft treaty was already "overloaded" and "now burdened close to the breaking point."[73] Accordingly, it was "necessary to maintain guard lest the treaty become overloaded to the point of rendering it even less negotiable than it already [was] and of frustrating its major design and purpose."[74]

Despite Metzger's admonition, the pressure to modify the treaty, including its investment provisions, continued. Indeed, a National Advisory Council report noted in December 1955 that

> [e]fforts are constantly underway in the Department of State to perfect the investment provisions of the basic FCN treaty proposals. Consultations with business groups and with officers of other Federal agencies are frequent. Ideas that develop in the course of practical experience in negotiation are constantly being checked and developed. [75]

The Department's ability to modify the provisions was limited, however. Walker had noted in 1946 the constraints imposed by inherent resistance to change and the burdens of the interagency clearance process. The 1955 National Advisory Council report described other impediments to the further revision of the treaty:

> There are always, however, two invariable controlling factors that limit experimentation in the field of treaty provisions: (1) United States laws and policies, and (2) practical negotiating considerations. . . . [T]here seems to be no possibility of negotiating treaties of this type upon any other basis that that of substantial mutuality. This means that no treaty provision can be more advanced in promoting private investment than the generality of U.S. laws and policies . . . On the other hand, . . . [i]f real progress is to be made through the treaty provisions, the provisions must not be so severe as to be unacceptable to other countries.[76]

Thus, despite the continuing desire to improve the treaty, revisions made to the standard draft after the major recasting of 1948–1949 were relatively minor, at least in substance.

73. Ibid.

74. Ibid.

75. NAC Staff Document No. 740, Program for Obtaining Treaty Assurances to Protect United States Citizens and Property and Promote United States Private Investment in Foreign Countries, NARA, Record Group 353, Records Relating to the Council on Foreign Economic Policy 1955–1961, Box 4, Folder marked "Investment in Underdeveloped Countries CFEP 511 (Folder 2)."

76. Ibid.

THE INFLUENCE OF THE AMERICAN BUSINESS COMMUNITY

From the moment that it launched its new treaty series, the State Department sought to collaborate with business groups to ensure that the new FCN treaties took account of the needs of the American business community.[77] It worked regularly with a small number of organizations, such as the NFTC, the National Association of Manufacturers (NAM), and the Chamber of Commerce. The Department consulted with special frequency with the NFTC,[78] which represented some of the largest companies in the United States,[79] but was regarded by the State Department as having "a broadly representative membership and an active treaty committee that has shown an uncommonly continuous and conscientious interest in the treaties."[80] As a State Department official observed in an internal memorandum written during negotiations in 1950 with India, "We are anxious, if possible, to have the good will of the NFTC in connection with the Indian treaty, because the NFTC is the principal business group interested generally in the treaty program, and the one which takes pains to communicate its views to the Senate concerning any treaty we send up" to the Senate for advice and consent to ratification.[81] Consultations with the NFTC, in fact, were routine and involved casual conversations as well as formal discussions. The Department would ask business representatives for their opinion of potential changes in treaty language, and generally offered to show copies of proposed treaty drafts to those who were interested.[82] As Willard Thorp described the process in a 1952

77. Letter from the National Foreign Trade Council to Secretary of State James Byrnes, dated July 10, 1945, NARA, Record Group 59, Department of State File No. 611.031/7-1045; Memorandum by Willard Thorp, headed "Consultation with Businessmen Regarding Treaties of Friendship, Commerce and Navigation," dated January 14, 1952, NARA, Record Group 59, Department of State File No. 611.964/1-1452.

78. The NFTC had established a committee of "well qualified" persons to study FCN treaty-related matters, and the Department therefore valued the NFTC's advice. Memorandum of Conversation headed "Consultation with Other Government Agencies and with Business Interests in Connection with the Negotiation of Treaties of Friendship, Commerce and Navigation," dated June 29, 1948, NARA, Record Group 59, Department of State File No. 711.002/6-2948.

79. The Board of Directors of the NFTC included representatives of Bethlehem Steel, Pan American Airways, Socony-Vacuum Oil Company, Firestone Tire and Rubber, Chase National Bank, General Motors, Goodyear Tire and Rubber, Coca Cola, Caterpillar Tractor, Otis Elevator, General Electric, Johnson and Johnson, International Harvester, United Fruit Company, Standard Oil, Chrysler Motors, DuPont, Kodak, Armour, Wrigley, Ford, IT&T, Montgomery Ward, Westinghouse, Pillsbury, IBM, and McGraw-Hill.

80. Memorandum by Willard Thorp headed "Consultation with Businessmen Regarding Treaties of Friendship, Commerce and Navigation," dated January 14, 1952, NARA, Record Group 59, Department of State File No. 611.964/1-1452.

81. Memorandum headed "Screening Problem in the Projected FCN Treaty with India," dated October 31, 1950, NARA, Record Group 59, Department of State File No. 611.914/11-250.

82. Memorandum of Conversation headed "Consultation with Businessmen Regarding Treaties of Friendship, Commerce and Navigation," dated February 24, 1950, prepared by Vernon G. Setser, NARA, Record Group 59, Department of State File No. 611.004/2-2450.

memorandum, "The practice which we now follow is rather informal and flexible, so as to foster an atmosphere of friendly, unceremonious give-and-take concerning an enterprise of mutual interest."[83] Thus, "[i]nterested businessmen are kept informed, though through no fixed procedure, of our general plans and prospects; we have taken pains to make them realize that they are always most welcome to write or come in, if they have anything on their minds; and when some special problem arises in connection with the treaty program generally or a specific negotiation in particular, we try to get in touch with them about it."[84] Keeping the business community informed about the existence of negotiations with a particular country also provided an opportunity for the State Department to learn about "special problems" of which it should be aware during negotiations.[85]

Although the State Department had consulted "extensively" with the NFTC during the preparation of the standard draft treaty, by January 1952, when Thorp wrote his memorandum, the draft had achieved a "crystallized, definitely approved form" as a result of the 1948–1949 recasting, and thus the Department no longer had as many occasions to solicit the advice of the NFTC as it had in the past.[86] Indeed, the Department feared that continuous solicitation of advice from the business community, once the content of the standard draft treaty was largely settled, might appear to invite a reconsideration of settled policy, an appearance that the Department wished to avoid.[87]

The State Department did not actively seek broad involvement by the business community beyond this small number of organizations, for at least three reasons. First, although wanting the treaties to address the needs of the business community, the Department recognized that the interests of the business community did not entirely coincide with those of the U.S. government[88] and feared that too much involvement by business groups would stimulate organized political pressure to alter the terms of the treaties in ways that were inconsistent with U.S. government policy.[89] Second, the State Department believed that the Commerce

83. Memorandum by Willard Thorp dated January 14, 1952, NARA, Record Group 59, Department of State File No. 611.964/1-1452.

84. Ibid.

85. Ibid.

86. Ibid.

87. Ibid.

88. Mira Wilkins has noted that "there was by no means an exact coincidence between U.S. government policies and the desires of international businesses—although often such approaches did coincide." Mira Wilkins, *The Maturing of Multilateral Enterprise: American Business Abroad from 1914 to 1970* (Cambridge, MA: Harvard University Press, 1974), page 286. She cited, for example, congressional passage in 1949 of the Export Control Act, which authorized the president to prohibit exports where necessary to national security. Ibid., page 287. The disjunction between U.S. policy and the interests of the business community is further discussed in Chapter 6 in the section on the refusal of the United States to coerce other countries to negotiate an FCN treaty.

89. Memorandum of Conversation headed "Consultation with Other Government Agencies and with Business Interests in Connection with the Negotiation of Treaties of Friendship,

Department and the U.S. missions abroad were in continuous contact with the business community and could provide the Department with much of the needed information about the problems and recommendations of the business community.[90] Third, State Department officials believed that giving business groups a greater opportunity to influence U.S. policy was unjustified unless other groups interested in foreign relations were also consulted.[91]

Following the signature of a treaty, business groups could influence the content of the treaty only by either opposing Senate advice and consent to ratification of the entire treaty, in effect surrendering all the benefits of the treaty, or by persuading the Senate to attach a reservation to the treaty, which would have the effect of modifying the treaty only if the other party accepted the reservation, and which risked the loss of all treaty benefits because the other party's refusal to accept the reservation could prevent the treaty from entering into force.[92] In the case of the treaties with China, Ireland, and Ethiopia, some American business groups did oppose Senate advice and consent, although they were unsuccessful.[93] In the case of the treaty with Haiti, organized Protestant groups, rather than business groups, actively opposed the treaty, resulting in its eventual withdrawal, and the treaty never entered into force.[94] In two instances, particular interest groups succeeded in persuading the Senate to attach a reservation to a treaty. During Senate consideration of the treaty with China, a group of publishers and authors persuaded the Senate to attach a reservation to the treaty with respect to the provision on copyright protection of translations.[95] During Senate consideration of a group of treaties in 1952–1953, the organized bar persuaded the Senate to attach to each of the treaties a reservation with respect to the practice of professions.[96] In both cases, the interest groups had a very narrow interest in the treaties and apparently were willing to sacrifice the treaties, if necessary, in pursuit of that narrow interest. All reservations were accepted by the other treaty parties and the treaties entered into force with the reservations.

Commerce and Navigation," dated June 29, 1948, NARA, Record Group 59, Department of State File No. 711.002/6-2948.

90. Ibid.

91. Memorandum dated August 29, 1950, from Vernon Setser to John M. Leddy, NARA, Record Group 59, Department of State File No. 611.914/8-2950.

92. A summary of the international law of treaty reservations appears in Ian Sinclair, *The Vienna Convention on the Law of Treaties* (Manchester, UK: Manchester University Press, 1984).

93. Business opposition to the treaty with China is described in more detail later in this chapter. Business opposition to the treaties with Ireland and Ethiopia is described in more detail in Chapters 5 and 6, respectively.

94. Protestant opposition to the treaty with Haiti is described in more detail in Chapter 7.

95. This reservation is described in more detail later in this chapter.

96. These reservations are described in more detail in Chapter 6 in the section headed "Senate Advice and Consent to Ratification 1952–1953."

Although the State Department wished to address the needs of the business community in ways that were consistent with U.S. policy, it did not want to enable business groups to dictate the substance of the FCN treaties, and it sometimes rejected proposals by the business community.[97] In particular, as discussed more extensively in Chapter 6, the State Department generally refused to coerce other countries to conclude an FCN treaty or to agree to provisions more favorable to U.S. investors, despite demands from business groups that it do so.

For example, the NFTC sought to use U.S. economic power to obtain treaty guarantees of national treatment for American businesses.[98] A guarantee of national treatment is a guarantee that a country will treat foreign nationals or companies no less favorably than it treats its own nationals or companies in similar circumstances. The United States market was one of the most protected markets in the world,[99] and the NFTC knew that other countries were willing to negotiate trade agreements with the United States in order to lower U.S. trade barriers.[100] In July 1945, the NFTC proposed that the State Department condition the conclusion of a reciprocal trade agreement on the conclusion of an FCN treaty with a national treatment guarantee.[101] That is, under the NFTC proposal, other countries would be able to gain greater access to the protected U.S. market only by concluding an FCN treaty (as well as a trade agreement) with the United States.

As was often the case when U.S. business interests tried to persuade the State Department to use its bargaining leverage to obtain more favorable FCN treaty provisions, the Department refused to accede to the NFTC proposal. Willard Thorp, the deputy assistant secretary of state for economic affairs, replied that the Reciprocal Trade Agreements Act authorized the executive branch to negotiate treaties that lowered U.S. tariffs in exchange for reciprocal reductions in tariffs by other countries. As the Department interpreted this legislation, Congress meant for U.S. tariff reductions to be used solely for the purpose of opening foreign markets to U.S. goods and not for other purposes, however desirable the achievement of those other purposes might be. Thorp also noted that the circumstances surrounding treaty negotiations with each country varied too much for the United States to adopt a single policy, such as that proposed by the NFTC, for all countries. The Department nevertheless was concerned not to damage relations

97. For example, the discussion later in this chapter of the negotiation of the FCN treaty with China describes an instance in which the State Department refused entreaties by the China-America Council on Commerce and Industry that the United States demand from China national treatment with respect to the acquisition of real property.

98. Letter from the National Foreign Trade Council to Secretary of State James Byrnes, dated July 10, 1945, NARA, Record Group 59, Department of State File No. 611.031/7-1045.

99. *Post-War Economic Policy and Planning*, Sixth Report of the House Special Committee on Post-War Economic Policy and Planning, House Report No. 541, 79th Congress, 1st Sess., May 8, 1945, page 35.

100. Ibid.

101. Letter from the National Foreign Trade Council to Secretary of State James Byrnes, dated July 10, 1945, NARA, Record Group 59, Department of State File No. 611.031/7-1045.

with the NFTC. After the Department rejected the NFTC proposal, Assistant Secretary Will Clayton sent a further response in which he invited NFTC officials to have lunch with him at the Metropolitan Club.[102]

The State Department also rejected proposals by business groups that the federal government use its power to conclude treaties to preempt state laws that impeded efforts to obtain protection for U.S. business overseas.[103] Various state laws discriminated against foreign investors in different ways. For example, 13 states did not allow foreign ownership of real property.[104] These state laws enabled other countries to refuse to grant national treatment to U.S. investors on the ground that the United States itself discriminated against foreign investors. The NFTC proposed in 1946 that the State Department negotiate treaties that would preempt these conflicting state laws, or ask Congress to enact federal legislation that would have the same effect.[105] The State Department again declined to agree to the NFTC proposal. Woodbury Willoughby, the associate chief of the Division of Commercial Policy, responded by offering merely to discuss the proposal with NFTC representatives.[106]

In 1949, the State Department rejected recommendations by the Commerce Department's Business Advisory Council to strengthen the FCN treaties because those recommendations would have resulted in granting foreign investors greater rights than those accorded under the U.S. Constitution.[107] In 1950, the NFTC urged the U.S. government to deny public capital to developing countries because the receipt of public capital would diminish the incentive for these countries to conclude FCN treaties in order to attract private capital.[108] The State Department declined to follow the NFTC's advice in that case as well.

NEGOTIATING THE FIRST POSTWAR FCN TREATY: CHINA

The conflict between the interests of the American business community and U.S. government policy became apparent publicly at the very inception of the U.S.

102. Letter dated October 4, 1945, from Will Clayton to E. P. Thomas, NARA, Record Group 59, Department of State File No.611.0031/9-1245.

103. Under the supremacy clause of the U.S. Constitution, Article VI, clause 2, treaties are the supreme law of the land and prevail over inconsistent state laws. *See United States v. Belmont,* 301 U.S. 324 (1937); *United States v. Pink,* 315 U.S. 203 (1942).

104. Letter dated March 25, 1946, from the National Foreign Trade Council to Secretary of State James Byrnes, NARA, Record Group 59, Department of State File No. 611.0031/3-2546.

105. Ibid.

106. Letter dated April 18, 1946, from Woodbury Willoughby to E. P. Thomas, NARA, Record Group 59, Department of State File No. 611.0031/3-2546.

107. This discussion is described below in the section on the negotiation of the FCN treaty with Colombia.

108. Robert F. Loree, *Position of the National Foreign Trade Council with respect to the Havana Charter for an International Trade Organization* (New York: National Foreign Trade Council, 1950), page 49.

postwar FCN treaty program. The first negotiation of a U.S. postwar FCN treaty occurred with China, in part because the two countries already had agreed during the war that such a negotiation would occur promptly, but also in part because the State Department believed that China could be a huge export market for surplus U.S. goods.[109]

Chinese-American economic relations after the 1840s had been governed by a treaty system based on the doctrine of extraterritoriality. Under that doctrine, many foreign nationals in China, including Americans, were exempted from the application of Chinese law.[110] In 1943, however, the United States, at that time allied with China against Japan and seeking for China a broader role in the postwar world order, concluded with China a treaty in which the United States agreed to surrender its extraterritorial rights.[111] Because U.S. commercial relationships with China in the past had been based on extraterritoriality, the relinquishment of extraterritorial rights by the United States rendered many existing treaty provisions essentially meaningless.[112] If the United States and China were to continue to structure their economic relations through an FCN treaty, they must negotiate a new treaty. Accordingly, Article VII of the 1943 treaty provided that the two countries would "enter into negotiations for the conclusion of a comprehensive modern treaty of friendship, commerce, navigation, and consular rights, upon the request of either Government or in any case within 6 months after the cessation of the hostilities in the war against the common enemies."[113]

Discussions between U.S. and Chinese officials concerning the negotiation of a new FCN treaty in fact were already in progress by 1943.[114] In March 1944, the State Department reported to the U.S. embassy in Chongqing (Chungking)

109. Gardner, *Economic Aspects,* page 248.

110. The prewar system of extraterritoriality in China is described in John King Fairbank, *The United States and China* (Cambridge, MA: Harvard University Press, 4th edition, 1983), pages 163–171.

111. Treaty for the Relinquishment of Extraterritorial Rights in China and the Regulation of Related Matters, 57 Stat. 767, T.S. No. 984, 6 Bev. 739, *reprinted in* 37 *American Journal of International Law Supplement* 65 (1943). The long process by which extraterritoriality was ended in China is described in Wesley R. Fishel, *The End of Extra-territoriality in China* (Berkeley: University of California Press, 1952).

112. Statement of Thomas C. Blaisdell, Director, Office of International Trade, U.S. Department of Commerce, *Friendship, Commerce, and Navigation with China,* Hearing Before a Subcommittee of the Committee on Foreign Relations, United States Senate, 80th Cong. 2d Sess. (1948), page 36.

113. Treaty between the United States of America and the Republic of China for the Relinquishment of Extraterritorial Rights in China and the Regulation of Related Matters, *signed* January 11, 1943, 57 Stat. Pt. 2, 771. *See* Memorandum of Conversation dated July 9, 1945, NARA, Record Group 59, Department of State File No. 611.9331/7-945.

114. Telegram dated March 8, 1944, from the Department of State to the U.S. embassy in China, NARA, Record Group 59, State Department File No. 711.932/11, *reprinted in* Department of

that the Department was in the process of drafting the language of a proposed treaty, but that certain articles were posing difficult problems, particularly those relating to the acquisition of land and the rights of corporations.[115] In drafting the proposed treaty, U.S. officials were soliciting the views of "representative business organizations" with respect to treaty coverage.[116] Ambassador Clarence E. Gauss replied that Chinese attitudes regarding potential treaty provisions had not yet "crystallized," and he recommended that a draft of a proposed commercial treaty be given to China as soon as possible while Chinese policy was still fluid.[117]

A week later, on April 15, Ambassador Gauss reported to the State Department that he had learned that China was drafting a treaty for proposal to the United States. He again urged that the Department complete its draft quickly.[118] As it happened, he need not have worried. Two days later, the embassy reported on the contents of the proposed Chinese treaty. The Chinese draft appeared in a number of respects to be based on existing U.S. FCN treaties, including the treaties with Liberia[119] and Thailand.[120] Indeed, it appeared that the Chinese government had drafted the treaty in English and then translated it into Chinese.[121] On April 22, the State Department sent a proposed draft to the embassy for comments. Revisions on the draft then continued until early the following year.[122]

State, *Foreign Relations of the United States*, Vol. VI (Washington, DC: Government Printing Office 1967), pages 1009–1011.

115. Ibid.

116. Statement of Charles E. Bohlen, Counselor, Department of State, *Friendship, Commerce, and Navigation with China*, Hearing Before a Subcommittee of the Committee on Foreign Relations, United States Senate, 80th Cong. 2d Sess. (1948), page 4.

117. Telegram dated April 8, 1944, from the U.S. embassy in China to the Department of State, NARA, Record Group 59, Department of State File No. 711.932/12, *reprinted in* Department of State, *Foreign Relations of the United States*, Vol. VI (Washington, DC: Government Printing Office 1967), pages 1011–1014.

118. Telegram dated April 15, 1944, from the U.S. embassy in China to the Department of State, NARA, Record Group 59, Department of State File No. 711.932/10, *reprinted in* Department of State, *Foreign Relations of the United States*, Vol. VI (Washington, DC: Government Printing Office 1967), page 1015.

119. Treaty of Friendship, Commerce and Navigation, United States-Liberia, August 8, 1938, 54 Stat. 1739, T.S. No. 956.

120. Treaty of Friendship, Commerce and Navigation, United States-Siam, November 13, 1937, 53 Stat. 1731, T.S. No. 940, 11 Bev. 1016.

121. Telegram dated April 17, 1944, from the U.S. embassy in China to the Department of State, NARA, Record Group 59, Department of State File No. 711.932/4-1744, *reprinted in* Department of State, *Foreign Relations of the United States*, Vol. VI (Washington, DC: Government Printing Office 1967), pages 1015–1018.

122. Telegram dated February 16, 1945, from the Department of State to the U.S. embassy in China, NARA, Record Group 59, Department of State File No. 711.932/2-1645, *reprinted in* Department of State, *Foreign Relations of the United States*, Vol. VII (Washington, DC: Government Printing Office 1969), pages 1258–1259.

The United States finally commenced its first negotiation under the new FCN treaty program on April 2, 1945, when U.S. embassy officials in Chongqing presented a proposed draft FCN treaty to the Chinese government.[123] In June, the Chinese government appointed Dr. Kan Lee, the commercial counselor to the Chinese embassy, to begin treaty discussions with the United States.[124] Dr. Lee discussed the treaty with State Department officials in Washington until July 9, after which he returned to China for consultations with the appropriate Chinese ministries.[125]

By the time it presented the draft treaty to China, the State Department had spent more than a year attempting to craft a proposed treaty that was appropriate for China's circumstances. The Department proposed the new treaty some four months before Japan surrendered to the United States and 101 years after Caleb Cushing had extracted extraterritorial rights from the Chinese in the first FCN treaty between China and the United States.

The proposed treaty was based on the last FCN treaty concluded by the United States before the war, the 1938 U.S. FCN treaty with Liberia that the Chinese government had also used as a basis for its proposed treaty text.[126] The State Department "discreetly" emphasized to Chinese officials the importance of concluding the treaty expeditiously, but also recognized that "undue pressure" could undermine the U.S. bargaining position.[127]

The proposed treaty consisted of 30 articles, one of which effected the termination of nine prior treaties between China and the United States,[128] including those establishing extraterritorial rights for the United States in China. Much of the treaty dealt with matters of trade. For example, the treaty guaranteed non-discriminatory treatment with respect to trade[129] and non-discriminatory treatment by state trading companies.[130] No fewer than five articles conferred on each party various navigation rights with respect to the other party.[131]

123. Memorandum of Conversation dated April, 20, 1946, NARA, Record Group 59, Department of State File No. 611.9331/4-2045; *Current Economic Developments,* January 1, 1946, page 9, NARA, Record Group 59, Department of State Lot Files.

124. Letter dated June 13, 1945, from the Chinese Minister of Foreign Affairs to Will Clayton, NARA, Record Group 59, Department of State File No. 711.932/6-1345.

125. Letter dated November 30, 1945, to General George C. Marshall, NARA, Record Group 59, Department of State 711.932/11-3045.

126. Memorandum of Conversation dated April, 20, 1946, NARA, Record Group 59, Department of State File No. 611.9331/4-2045.

127. *Current Economic Developments,* September 17, 1945, NARA, Record Group 59, Department of State Lot Files.

128. Draft Treaty of Friendship, Commerce and Navigation between the United States of America and the Republic of China, Article XXIX, NARA, Record Group 59, Department of State File No. 771.932/1-1845.

129. Ibid., Article XVI.

130. Ibid., Article XX.

131. Ibid., Articles XXI through XXV.

Several articles that are direct antecedents to contemporary investment treaty provisions appeared in the proposed FCN treaty with China. Regarding the norm of access, Article II required each party to provide nationals of each party with national and MFN treatment with respect to the right to engage in commercial, manufacturing, scientific, educational, religious, and philanthropic activities. Article III extended similar rights to corporations, an innovation in U.S. treaty practice. Before the war, such rights generally had been limited to individuals,[132] although some prewar FCN treaties had required that the host country recognize the juridical status of corporations and grant them free access to the courts of law.[133] Some FCN treaties concluded prior to the war also had guaranteed national and MFN treatment with respect to the right to organize corporations.[134] The proposed treaty with China, in addition, granted to nationals and companies of a party the right to employ agents or employees of their choice, regardless of nationality.[135]

Regarding the norm of security, Article VI(1) required each party to provide the most constant protection and security to property owned by nationals of the other party, a provision under which the host state must exercise due diligence to protect foreign investment.[136] The same provision also guaranteed "in this respect the full protection and security required by international law." The FCN treaties of the late 1930s had included a similar provision.[137] Article VI(2) prohibited a party from taking property owned by nationals or companies of the other party except in accordance with due process and upon prompt payment of just and effective compensation.[138] In the late 1930s, U.S. FCN treaties had required that takings be in accordance with due process and upon payment of just compensation.[139]

132. *See, e.g.,* Treaty of Friendship, Commerce and Navigation between the United States of America and the Republic of Liberia, August 8, 1938, Article I, 54 Stat. 1739, T.S. No. 956, 9 Bevans 595. The treaty did grant corporations MFN treatment with respect to the right to explore and exploit mineral resources. The treatment of corporations in treaties prior to the war is further discussed in Chapter 8 in the section on companies.

133. Draft Treaty of Friendship, Commerce and Navigation between the United States of America and the Republic of China, Article XVII, NARA, Record Group 59, Department of State File No. 771.932/1-1845.

134. Ibid., Article XVIII.

135. Ibid., Articles II(2) and III(3).

136. The early history and meaning of this provision is traced in Robert R. Wilson, "Property-Protection Provisions in United States Commercial Treaties," 45 *American Journal of International Law* 83 (1951).

137. *See, e.g.,* Treaty of Friendship, Commerce and Navigation between the United States of America and the Republic of Liberia, August 8, 1938, Article I, 54 Stat. 1739, T.S. No. 956, 9 Bevans 595.

138. The early history of the expropriation provision is traced in Wilson, "Property-Protection Provisions."

139. Ibid.

Thus, the explicit reference to the promptness of payment and the effectiveness of compensation (meaning that the compensation must be paid in a form usable to the recipient, such as in a freely convertible currency) constituted an innovation. By way of elaborating upon the requirement of effective compensation, Article VI(2) required that, if compensation were not paid in the currency of the country of which the owner was a national or company, the owner would have the right to transfer the compensation "without restraint or interference" into the currency of the owner's choice at any time within three years of payment, language that was "specifically designed" to discourage expropriation.[140]

Article XIX provided limited protection against the imposition of currency exchange controls, regulations that can prevent an investor from transferring capital or earnings from the host country to the investor's home country and thus effectively deprive the investor of their use. In particular, that article required each party to provide "fair and equitable treatment" as well as national and MFN treatment with respect to the transfer of profits, dividends, interests, and of other funds. Article XIX also required that each party administer any exchange controls so as not to influence to the disadvantage of the other party the competitive relationships between the nationals, corporations, and associations of the other party and the nationals, corporations, and associations of any third country, language based in part on Article IV(2) of the 1942 trade agreement with Mexico.[141] The placement of the article on exchange controls among the articles on trade reflects the fact that in 1945 that article was perceived as related primarily to trade.

Regarding the norm of due process, Article VI(4) guaranteed to nationals and companies "freedom of access" to the courts of justice and national and MFN treatment with respect to such access. The prewar FCN treaties also had guaranteed freedom of access to the courts for both nationals and companies.[142] Article XXVIII required that disputes concerning the interpretation or application of the treaty be submitted to judicial or arbitral settlement, a provision that had no counterpart in the FCN treaties of the late 1930s. Thus, the proposed treaty made provision for recourse to both local courts and international tribunals.

The proposed treaty did not incorporate a general requirement of non-discrimination. As the foregoing summary shows, however, the proposed treaty

140. Memorandum of Conversation headed "Exchange Control Provisions in Commercial Treaties," dated July 13, 1946, NARA, Record Group 43, International Trade Files, Box 61, Folder marked "Nationalization"; Memorandum of Conversation headed "Provisions in Commercial Treaties for Withdrawal of Compensation in Case of Expropriation of Property," dated December 17, 1946, NARA, Record Group 59, Department of State File No. 711.932/12-1746.

141. Memorandum to the Embassy at Chungking for Use in Negotiating Treaty of Friendship, Commerce and Navigation, NARA, Record Group 59, Department of State File No. 711.932/2-1645.

142. The early history of the judicial access provision in U.S. FCN treaty practice is traced in Robert R. Wilson, "Access-to-Courts Provisions in United States Commercial Treaties," 47 *American Journal of International Law*, 20 (1953).

did require national and MFN treatment with respect to engaging in a large number of activities and with respect to a variety of other matters.

The political demands of a wartime alliance had demolished the old order applicable to foreign businesses operating in China. The U.S. business community desperately sought through the FCN treaty negotiations a new order that would preserve American privileges as much as possible, including extraterritorial rights. Viola Smith, an official at the Far East-America Council of Commerce and Industry, would comment in late 1946, following signature of the treaty, that she was "black and blue from battling businessmen in China who have not yet realized that extraterritoriality was a thing of the past."[143] If they were not to be exempt from Chinese law, as they had been under the regime of extraterritoriality, U.S. business interests wanted Chinese law to conform to American norms.

Accordingly, the U.S. business community in China was deeply interested in the progress of the negotiations. On April 24, 1945, about three weeks after the draft treaty was provided to Chinese officials, State Department officials met with representatives of the China-America Council on Commerce and Industry, which represented about 300 U.S. companies in China.[144] These business representatives told the State Department that it was "highly desirable that a new commercial treaty should be concluded prior to the resumption of normal trade relations anticipated for the post-war period."[145] They inquired as to whether a draft treaty had been given to the Chinese government. On May 9, the China-America Council sent a letter to the secretary of state averring that "[n]o one development, save possibly V-Day, would encourage the American business community so much as an announcement that a new commercial treaty had been concluded . . . ."[146] In August, a representative of the Washington office of the China-America Council met with State Department officials to urge conclusion of a treaty "at the earliest possible date."[147]

During the April 24 meeting, the China-America Council representatives expressed special interest in a provision on the acquisition of real property. Chinese law forbade foreign ownership of land unless the right was granted by treaty. Other countries had treaty rights in that regard, but the United States

143. Memorandum of Conversation headed "Commercial Treaty with China," dated December 10, 1946, NARA, Record Group 59, Department of State File No. 711.932/12-1046.

144. These companies included Bristol Meyers, B.F. Goodrich, Firestone, Goodyear, Alcoa, Boeing, Coca Cola, IT&T, Standard Oil, Marine Midland, Pepsi Cola, International Harvester, Union Pacific Railroad, General Electric, Chase Bank, Reynolds, Socony-Vacuum Oil (which later became Mobil Oil Company), Time, Kodak, and Pan American Airways.

145. Memorandum of Conversation dated April 30, 1945, NARA, Record Group 59, Department of State File No. 611.9331/4-3045.

146. Letter dated May 9, 1945, from the China-America Council on Commerce and Industry to the Secretary of State, NARA, Record Group 59, Department of State File No. 711.932/5-945.

147. Memorandum headed "Draft Treaty of Friendship, Commerce and Navigation with China," dated August 21, 1945, NARA, Record Group 59, Department of State File No. 711.932/8-2145.

had not obtained such rights for U.S. nationals.[148] In a letter to the secretary of state dated September 28, 1945, the China-America Council asserted that securing a right for U.S. nationals to purchase real property on the same basis as Chinese nationals was "highly essential" to the future of American business in China.[149]

The State Department, however, declined to support the position of the Council. Assistant Secretary of State Will Clayton explained to the Council that many American states restricted alien ownership of land and, for this reason, the United States did not believe that it could demand a right for all Americans in China to acquire real property.[150] The most that the United States could demand was national treatment for nationals and companies from states that allowed foreign ownership of land.

The American business community continued to pressure the State Department with respect to the proposed treaty with China. On April 5, 1946, General George C. Marshall, then serving as a U.S. envoy to China, received a report on Chinese-American commercial relations jointly authored by the China-America Council on Commerce and Trade and the NFTC. The memorandum set forth a series of points that the two organizations regarded as "fundamental for the establishment of a healthy trade with China and the encouragement of maximum investment of American capital in China."[151] The first point listed in the memorandum was "China-America Treaty of Commerce and Amity." More specifically, the memorandum argued that "[a] healthy economic climate must be provided for the maximum development of two-way trade between America and China. The most effective results can be attained only by the fullest enlistment of free enterprise with Government encouragement. *A modern treaty of commerce and amity on a most-favored-nation basis should be consummated immediately between the United States and China.*"[152] The memorandum characterized the FCN treaty as "the cornerstone upon which the foundation of our trade will be laid," and asserted that the treaty "must be concluded before the resumption of normal trade relations can take place."[153] The memorandum noted that the two organizations "would like to know the current status of the Chinese-American negotiations regarding

148. China-America Council on Commerce and Industry, Memorandum on Real Property Rights of Americans in China and of Chinese in America, NARA, Record Group 59, Department of State File No. 611.9331/ 6-1845.

149. Letter dated September 28, 1945, from Blackwell Smith to the Secretary of State, NARA, Record Group 59, Department of State File No. 611.9331/9-2845.

150. Letter dated November 8, 1945, from Assistant Secretary of State William L. Clayton to Blackwell Smith, NARA, Record Group 59, Department of State File No. 611.9331/9-2845.

151. Memorandum presented April 5, 1946, to General George C. Marshall regarding Chinese-American commercial and fiscal relations, NARA, Record Group 59, Department of State File No. 611.9331/2-1346.

152. Ibid.(emphasis in original).

153. Ibid.

this treaty."[154] After observing that a tax convention "should also be concluded," the memorandum said that the two organizations "would like to know too, what opportunity, if any, will be afforded business for examining the proposals with a view to ascertaining the suitability of both the treaty and convention (as referred to above) to commercial requirements."[155]

The preeminent position of the FCN treaty in the memorandum from two major business organizations demonstrates the paramount importance placed by the business community on the conclusion of such a treaty with China. The passage regarding the treaty appears as the first listed point on the first page of the seven-page memorandum. The sentence regarding the FCN treaty is the only underscored sentence in the memorandum. The memorandum concluded by calling for free enterprise with "[g]overnment encouragement."[156] U.S. business interests were not advocating a policy of laissez-faire.

In February 1946, following Dr. Kan Lee's consultations in China, the United States and China began a series of negotiations that continued until August, when the parties reached agreement on all issues of substance. China commenced the negotiations by presenting a counterdraft that followed the order of the U.S. draft, but with a number of changes.[157] The Chinese negotiators explained that their counterdraft was confidential and asked that it not be shown to any other government.[158]

Chinese officials explained that, in proposing the changes, the Chinese government needed to take account of its relations with other countries as well as with the United States; that China was in the early stages of industrialization and needed "reasonable protection of one form or another"; and that, because China and the United States were at different stages of economic development, some of the provisions of the U.S. draft would not be to the equal advantage of both parties.[159] The U.S. negotiators replied that "it would be unlikely that [the] parties to any treaty would be exactly equal in their capacity to enjoy treaty rights" and that, if China wished to attract American capital, it would be "important that there be a condition of confidence . . . ."[160] The counterdraft revealed that China was reluctant to agree to any provision that would require changes to existing law, that would make commitments that might later be sought by other foreigners whose economic presence and penetration would be troubling to China, or

154. Ibid.

155. Ibid.

156. Ibid.

157. Telegram dated February 6, 1946, from the U.S. embassy in Chongqing to the Department of State, NARA, Record Group 59, Department of State File No. 711.932/2-646.

158. Telegram dated February 18, 1946, from the U.S. embassy in Chongqing to the Department of State, NARA, Record Group 59, Department of State File No. 711.932/2-1846.

159. Ibid.

160. Telegram dated February 15, 1946, from the U.S. embassy in Chongqing to the Department of State, NARA, Record Group 59, Department of State File No. 711.932/2-1546.

that would constrain China's freedom to make economic policy.[161] Thus, China's counterdraft raised several difficult investment-related issues.

First, China objected to the treaty provision that granted national treatment to companies with respect to engaging in certain gainful and nonprofit activities because the provision was not completely reciprocal. Specifically, Article III(3) of the U.S. draft defined national treatment by the individual states of the United States as the treatment that such states provided to out-of-state (as opposed to in-state) U.S. companies. China, however, was required to provide U.S. companies treatment as favorable as that provided to any Chinese company. The U.S. negotiators responded that this asymmetry was unavoidable because of the nature of the U.S. federal system.[162] They also noted that to treat Chinese companies as favorably as companies chartered under the laws of the regulating state would result in treating Chinese companies more favorably than companies from the other 47 states, and said that, in actual practice, out-of-state companies were not disabled from operating on a national basis.[163] The Chinese negotiators understood the reason for the provision, but noted that a lack of mutuality existed nonetheless.[164]

Second, China wished to reserve its power to deny national treatment to U.S. companies in all sectors because of the "uncertainties" of their situation and in consideration of the unequal treatment of Chinese companies in the United States.[165] U.S. negotiators replied that, without a treaty guarantee of national treatment, U.S. investors might be less willing to invest.[166]

Third, China objected in particular to granting U.S. companies national treatment with respect to engaging in financial activities because U.S. law at that time did not allow the operation of out-of-state banks, and thus Chinese banks would not be able to enjoy the same treatment in the United States that U.S. banks

161. Telegram dated February 18, 1946, from the U.S. embassy in Chongqing to the Department of State, NARA, Record Group 59, Department of State File No. 711.932/2-1846.

162. Memorandum of Conversation dated July 9, 1945, NARA, Record Group 59, Department of State File No. 611.9331/7-745.

163. Memorandum headed "The Proposed Sino-American Treaty of Friendship, Commerce and Navigation," dated February 14, 1946, NARA, Record Group 59, Department of State File No. 711.932/12-2046.

164. Memorandum of Conversation dated July 9, 1945, NARA, Record Group 59, Department of State File No. 611.9331/7-745.

165. Telegram dated February 26, 1946, from the U.S. embassy in Chongqing to the Department of State, NARA, Record Group 59, Department of State File No. 711.932/2-2646. *See also* Memorandum headed "The Proposed Sino-American Treaty of Friendship, Commerce and Navigation," dated February 14, 1946, and NARA, Record Group 59, Department of State File No. 711.932/12-2046; Memorandum headed "The Proposed Sino-American Treaty of Friendship, Commerce and Navigation," dated February 21, 1946, NARA, Record Group 59, Department of State File No. 711.932/12-2046.

166. Memorandum headed "The Proposed Sino-American Treaty of Friendship, Commerce and Navigation," dated February 21, 1946, NARA, Record Group 59, Department of State File No. 711.932/12-2046.

received.[167] It also wished to exclude financial activities from the right of national treatment to be accorded to nationals of the other party, fearing that such a right might be construed to imply a right to organize banking companies.[168] China wanted to reserve as well its power to exclude foreigners from direct participation in mining activities.[169]

Ultimately, the United States yielded on the issue of national treatment. The final treaty language, at Article III, subordinated to local law the right of companies to engage in business activities in China. In other words, China could deny national treatment to U.S. companies merely by enacting legislation to that effect. In addition, the treaty, at Article II(2), excluded financial activities from the list of activities with respect to which nationals were entitled to national treatment and, under Article V, only MFN treatment was granted with respect to the exploration for, and exploitation of, mineral resources.

Fourth, China proposed the deletion of the language permitting free transferability of compensation for expropriation.[170] The Chinese negotiations explained that the provision would create an inequality because Chinese property owners would not have a similar right, that the amounts involved might be large, and that, in light of the unstable exchange rate in China, the government was reluctant to make a treaty commitment in this regard.[171] The U.S. negotiators replied that takings presumably would be exceptional, that in such cases the deprivation of property would be involuntary, and that the absence of such an assurance might deter U.S. investment in China.[172] The parties agreed to a compromise that reserved to each party the prerogative to provide foreign exchange in the currency of the expropriated owner's country in reasonable installments over a period not to exceed three years.[173]

Fifth, China objected to a provision in Article VIII granting to U.S. nationals and companies national treatment with respect to the right to acquire real property in China, provided that those nationals or companies were domiciled or constituted

167. Telegram dated February 26, 1946, from the U.S. embassy in Chongqing to the Department of State, NARA, Record Group 59, Department of State File No. 711.932/2-2646.

168. Memorandum headed "The Proposed Sino-American Treaty of Friendship, Commerce and Navigation," dated February 9, 1946, NARA, Record Group 59, Department of State File No. 711.932/12-2046; Telegram dated March 9, 1946, from the U.S. embassy in Chongqing to the Department of State, NARA, Record Group 59, Department of State File No. 711.932/3-946.

169. Memorandum headed "The Proposed Sino-American Treaty of Friendship, Commerce and Navigation," dated March 28, 1946, NARA, Record Group 59, Department of State File No. 711.932/12-2046; Memorandum headed "The Proposed Sino-American Treaty of Friendship, Commerce and Navigation," dated February 21, 1946, NARA, Record Group 59, Department of State File No. 711.932/12-2046.

170. Memorandum headed "The Proposed Sino-American Treaty of Friendship, Commerce and Navigation," dated February 9, 1946, NARA, Record Group 59, Department of State File No. 711.932/12-2046.

171. Ibid.

172. Ibid.

173. China FCN treaty, Article VI(2).

in a state that permitted Chinese nationals and companies to acquire real property. The Chinese negotiators were aware of state laws in the United States that discriminated against foreign nationals with respect to the acquisition of real property, and the State Department informed them that the federal government would not be willing to use the treaty to preempt such state laws.[174] They expressed the concern that, if Americans were permitted to acquire Chinese real property, the depreciated Chinese currency would allow Americans to purchase so much land that relations between the two countries might be damaged.[175] They also noted that, if the United States received national treatment, other countries would expect it at as well.[176] The Chinese negotiators would agree to MFN treatment with respect to the acquisition of real property, saying that they did not object to U.S. laws restricting alien land ownership as long as those laws did not treat the Chinese less favorably than nationals of other countries.[177] Ultimately, the parties agreed that MFN treatment would apply,[178] except in the case of states that did not permit Chinese nationals or companies to acquire real property. U.S. nationals or companies domiciled or constituted in such states would receive only reciprocal treatment.[179]

Sixth, the Chinese negotiators also objected to Article IX, which protected intellectual property rights.[180] Dr. Kan Lee, the commercial counselor to the Chinese embassy, had told State Department officials at a June 22, 1945, meeting that copyright laws conflicted with the goal of cultural exchange. He suggested that "the best way for the United States to make information available to China [was] to permit Chinese to translate American books freely."[181] Because it believed that allowing unrestricted translations was "essential" to making available to the Chinese people literary and scientific material from around the world,[182]

174. Telegram dated March 13, 1946, from the U.S. embassy in Chongqing to the Department of State, NARA, Record Group 59, Department of State File No. 711.932/3-1346; Memorandum headed "The Proposed Sino-American Treaty of Friendship, Commerce and Navigation," dated March 4, 1946, NARA, Record Group 59, Department of State File No. 711.93212-2046.

175. Memorandum of Conversation dated June 25, 1945, NARA, Record Group 59, Department of State File No. 611.9331/6-2645.

176. Memorandum headed "The Proposed Sino-American Treaty of Friendship, Commerce and Navigation," dated February 14, 1946, NARA, Record Group 59, Department of State File No. 711.932/12-2046.

177. Ibid.

178. China FCN treaty, Article VIII(1).

179. Ibid.

180. Memorandum headed "The Proposed Sino-American Treaty of Friendship, Commerce and Navigation," dated February 7, 1946, NARA, Record Group 59, Department of State File No. 711.932/12-2046.

181. Memorandum of Conversation dated June 22, 1945, NARA, Record Group 59, Department of State File No. 611.9331/6-2245. *See also* letter dated May 13, 1948, from Winthrop Brown to John W. Vandercook, NARA, Record Group 59, Department of State File No. 711.932/4-2948.

182. Letter dated June 21, 1948 from Woodbury Willoughby to George P. Brett, NARA, Record Group 59, Department of State File No. 711.932/6-2148.

China insisted in all of its treaty negotiations that any writing, once translated into Chinese, be exempted from treaty protection.[183] The Chinese negotiators noted the greater difficulty of translating an English work into Chinese than into another Western language and argued that sales of a Chinese edition might actually increase sales of the English edition.[184] They also argued that Chinese translations do not compete with the original works in English.[185] The State Department capitulated on this point by agreeing to a provision in the protocol that exempted translations from copyright protection.[186] The Department noted that the treaty nevertheless conferred on American authors national treatment with respect to copyright and otherwise extended "a large new measure of protection" to copyrighted works.[187]

Seventh, China sought language granting MFN treatment with respect to immigration.[188] U.S. negotiators responded that the practical effect would have been to grant Chinese immigrants greater immigration rights than those possessed by British immigrants and rights equivalent to those enjoyed by immigrants from Western Hemisphere countries, which were not subject to country quotas under U.S. immigration laws.[189] The Chinese negotiators responded that they did not expect greater rights than those enjoyed by Europeans or rights equivalent to those enjoyed by nationals of Western Hemisphere countries, but that they wanted to ensure that U.S. immigration laws as applied to Chinese nationals would not be based on race or color.[190] After the State Department had consulted with members of the Senate, U.S. negotiators reported that Senate leaders had "indicated conclusively" that a treaty containing the language sought by China would not be approved.[191] U.S. negotiators observed that U.S. immigration

183. Statement of Winthrop Brown, *Friendship, Commerce, and Navigation with China*, Hearing Before a Subcommittee of the Committee on Foreign Relations, United States Senate, 80th Cong. 2d Sess. (1948), page 16.

184. Telegram dated March 14, 1946, from the U.S. embassy in Chongqing to the Department of State, NARA, Record Group 59, Department of State File No. 711.932/3-1446.

185. Memorandum headed "The Proposed Sino-American Treaty of Friendship, Commerce and Navigation," dated February 7, 1946, NARA, Record Group 59, Department of State File No. 711.932/12-2046.

186. China FCN treaty, Protocol, Paragraph 5(c).

187. Letter dated June 21, 1948, from Woodbury Willoughby to George P. Brett, NARA, Record Group 59, Department of State File No. 711.932/6-2148.

188. Memorandum of Conversation headed "The Proposed Sino-American Treaty of Friendship, Commerce and Navigation," dated February 20, 1946, NARA, Record Group 59, Department of State File No. 911.932/12-2046.

189. Ibid.

190. Ibid.

191. Memorandum of Conversation headed "The Proposed Sino-American Treaty of Friendship, Commerce and Navigation," dated June 6, 1946, NARA, Record Group 59, Department of State File No. 911.932/12-2046.

laws reflected a general policy and were not applicable to China alone. Late in the negotiations, China withdrew its proposal on immigration.[192]

Finally, China wished to remove a sentence from Article XV that stated explicitly that commercial provisions requiring MFN treatment referred to unconditional MFN treatment.[193] Although the Chinese negotiators explained that they accorded unconditional MFN treatment in practice, the Legislative Yuan would not permit the conclusion of a treaty that bargained away its discretion in this regard. Thus, the treaty could not contain an explicit reference to unconditional MFN treatment, although the Chinese negotiators understood that the United States intended the MFN treatment provisions to be unconditional.[194] The United States yielded and the explicit reference to unconditional MFN treatment was deleted.[195]

The two parties signed the treaty on November 4, 1946.[196] Five days later, the Legislative Yuan approved it.[197] The treaty had been submitted to the Yuan quickly because the election of a new Yuan was imminent and the Chinese foreign minister "gravely doubted" that the new Yuan would approve the treaty, given growing sentiment against the United States and against the Chinese government.[198] Two days later, on November 11, 1946, President Jiang Jieshi (Chiang Kai-shek) conferred his approval.[199]

Signature of the treaty was announced on the front page of the *New York Times*. The *Times* story reported an acknowledgment by State Department officials that, in light

192. Memorandum of Conversation headed "The Proposed Sino-American Treaty of Friendship, Commerce and Navigation," dated August 14, 1946, NARA, Record Group 59, Department of State File No. 911.932/12-2046.

193. Memorandum headed "The Proposed Sino-American Treaty of Friendship, Commerce and Navigation," dated February 9, 1946, NARA, Record Group 59, Department of State File No. 911.932/12-2046; Memorandum headed "The Proposed Sino-American Treaty of Friendship, Commerce and Navigation," dated March 13, 1946, NARA, Record Group 59, Department of State File No. 911.932/12-2046.

194. Memorandum headed "The Proposed Sino-American Treaty of Friendship, Commerce and Navigation," dated March 25, 1946, NARA, Record Group 59, Department of State File No. 911.932/12-2046.

195. Memorandum headed "The Proposed Sino-American Treaty of Friendship, Commerce and Navigation," dated June 27, 1946, NARA, Record Group 59, Department of State File No. 911.932/12-2046.

196. Treaty of Friendship, Commerce and Navigation, with protocol, entered into force, November 30, 1948, 63 Stat. 1299, TIAS 1871, 6 Bevans 761, 25 UNTS 69.

197. Statement of Charles E. Bohlen, Counselor, Department of State, *Friendship, Commerce, and Navigation with China*, Hearing Before a Subcommittee of the Committee on Foreign Relations, United States Senate, 80th Cong. 2d Sess. (1948), page 4.

198. Telegram dated June 25, 1948, from the Department of State to the U.S. embassy in Nanking, NARA, Record Group 59, Department of State File No. 711.932/6-2548.

199. Statement of Charles E. Bohlen, Counselor, Department of State, *Friendship, Commerce, and Navigation with China*, Hearing Before a Subcommittee of the Committee on Foreign Relations, United States Senate, 80th Cong. 2d Sess. (1948), page 4.

of the civil strife in China, many of the rights for American business "might largely exist only on paper, rather than in practice, for some time."[200] The story also included denials by State Department officials that the treaty was intended to strengthen Jiang's government in its civil war with communist forces. The Soviet press, by contrast, characterized the treaty as a "document consolidating the economic domination of the United States in China for long years" and charged that the United States had signed the treaty to demonstrate support for Jiang's government.[201]

The Chinese press widely criticized the treaty as unequal because Chinese nationals and companies were not in a position to take advantage of the opportunities provided by the treaty in the United States to the same extent that Americans could take advantage of the opportunities in China.[202] For example, the treaty gave China navigation rights in the United States, but China lacked ships to utilize those rights.[203] Some newspapers criticized the secrecy of the negotiations.[204] Many newspapers expressed concern about China's ability to compete with American goods and capital.[205] A Chongqing city council member likened the treaty to "a sheep inviting a wolf to come in and live with it on a basis of reciprocity and equality."[206] A rumor held that the signing of the treaty was facilitated by the presence of U.S troops in China.[207]

The Chinese government responded with a statement defending the treaty. The statement argued that the treaty was necessary to replace existing unequal treaties still in force, that China needed to grant non-discriminatory treatment to foreigners whose countries granted non-discriminatory treatment to Chinese nationals, particularly if China wished to attract foreign investment and technical experts for industrialization and reconstruction, and that the treaty had adequate safeguards to protect Chinese interests.[208]

The U.S. business community initially applauded this first achievement of the postwar FCN treaty program. The National Foreign Trade Convention, meeting in New York City between November 11 and 13, 1946, issued a final

200. "U.S.-China Treaty of 'Mutual' Trade and Amity Signed," *New York Times*, November 4, 1946, page 1.

201. "U.S.-China Pact Scored," *New York Times*, December 9, 1946, page 3.

202. Telegram dated November 15, 1946, from the U.S. embassy in Nanking to the Department of State, NARA, Record Group 59, Department of State File No. 711.932/11-1546.

203. Telegram dated November 16, 1946, from the U.S. consulate in Chongqing to the Department of State, NARA, Record Group 59, Department of State File No. 711.932/11-1646.

204. Telegram dated November 15, 1946, from the U.S. embassy in Nanking to the Department of State, NARA, Record Group 59, Department of State File No. 711.932/11-1546.

205. Ibid.

206. Telegram dated November 16, 1946, from the U.S. consulate in Chongqing to the Department of State, NARA, Record Group 59, Department of State File No. 711.932/11-1646.

207. Ibid.

208. Telegram dated November 19, 1946, from the U.S. embassy in Nanking to the Department of State, NARA, Record Group 59, Department of State Lot Files, Walter Hollis Papers.

declaration that "welcome[d] the evidence of the Government's intention to modernize and expand our existing commercial treaty structure afforded by the signing" of the FCN treaty with China.[209] Charles Carroll, chairman of the NFTC, noted "wholehearted satisfaction" with the announcement of the conclusion of the FCN treaty with China.[210] He called for the conclusion of FCN treaties "with as many nations as are agreeable, substantially earlier than 1948," which meant, in effect, the following year.[211] The NFTC Subcommittee on Treaties recommended that the NFTC express its satisfaction with the treaty and commend the State Department for concluding it.[212] The Subcommittee noted in particular that the treaty was "more complete" than any previous FCN treaty, and that approval by the State Department and the Chinese legislative assembly of any additional improvements was doubtful.[213] The NFTC Board of Directors unanimously approved the recommendation on January 16, 1947, and urged early ratification of the treaty.[214] On January 24, the China-America Council notified Will Clayton that its Legislative Committee had endorsed the treaty as well, and commended the State Department for its perseverance in concluding the treaty.[215] Viola Smith, a representative of the Far East-America Council of Commerce and Industry, told State Department officials that she was "amazed" that the State Department had been able to conclude such a treaty. [216]

Soon, however, the business community began to turn against the treaty because many believed that the United States had conceded too much to China. The first criticism of the treaty came from an official at the Commerce Department. At a meeting with the NFTC on November 30, 1946, less than a month after the treaty was concluded, the head of the China legal section in the Commerce Department complained "to everyone he could talk to" that the State Department had disregarded the recommendations of the Commerce Department in negotiating the treaty, that the treaty did not meet the needs of

209. National Foreign Trade Council, *Draft Final Declaration of the Thirty-Third National Foreign Trade Convention*, 1946, page 10, NARA, Record Group 59, State Department File No. 611.0031/11-1446.

210. Ibid.

211. Ibid.

212. Report to the Board of Directors on the Treaty of Friendship, Commerce and Navigation between the United States and the Republic of China, January 16, 1947, NARA, Record Group 59, Department of State File No. 711.932/1-1747.

213. Ibid.

214. Letter dated January 17, 1947, from E. P. Thomas to Will Clayton, NARA, Record Group 59, Department of State File No. 711.932/1-1747.

215. Letter dated January 24, 1947, from Arthur B. Foye to Will Clayton, NARA, Record Group 59, Department of State File No. 711.932/1-2447.

216. Memorandum of Conversation headed "Commercial Treaty with China," dated December 10, 1946, NARA, Record Group 59, Department of State File No. 711.932/12-1046.

American business interests in China, and that the NFTC would be disappointed in the treaty.[217]

By January, although conceding that the China treaty was a "great improvement" over past FCN treaties concluded by the United States, NFTC representatives were expressing disappointment regarding the limited rights for U.S. companies to engage in business activities in China. They recommended that the United States make use of "all bargaining power available to it" to obtain for U.S. companies the same right to conduct business in China that the treaty gave to individuals. In particular, they suggested that loans from the United States to China be used as bargaining leverage to improve company rights.[218]

In fact, the United States already had considered the relationship between foreign assistance and the conclusion of the FCN treaty with China. In December 1945, as the United States and China were commencing negotiations, the Chinese government had requested a $2 billion credit to be made available over a three-year period, including an immediate credit of $560 million.[219] In response, the U.S. Export-Import Bank (ExIm Bank) announced that it was prepared to offer China several loans, each worth tens of millions of dollars. Further, the ExIm Bank loans could be made available immediately upon the recommendation of U.S. envoy General George C. Marshall. The Department believed, however, that loans for reconstruction and industrial development in China (as opposed to the ExIm Bank loans) should be "preceded by appropriate Chinese actions or assurances," including the adoption of a satisfactory plan for currency stabilization, provision for the transfer of funds at a reasonable rate, and the conclusion of an FCN treaty.[220] The numerous concessions subsequently made by the United States to conclude the treaty with China demonstrate that the State Department's position was not that reconstruction and development loans should be used to coerce China to conclude a treaty on the terms sought by the U.S. government.[221] Rather, it appears that the Department's position was that the United States should not provide reconstruction and industrial development loans to China unless China adopted the kinds of trade, monetary, and foreign investment policies that the

217. Ibid.

218. Memorandum of Conversation dated January 6, 1947, NARA, Record Group 59, Department of State File No. 611.9331/1-647.

219. *Current Economic Developments,* December 29, 1945, pages 1–2, NARA, Record Group 59, Department of State Lot Files.

220. Ibid.

221. E. F. Penrose argues that U.S. postwar policy generally was that "financial aid should not be used as a weapon to force concessions on commercial policy" but that financial assistance could be effective only in a world shaped by liberal trade principles. E. F. Penrose, *Economic Planning for the Peace* (Princeton, NJ: Princeton University Press, 1953), pages 208–209. This certainly appears to be true with respect to the FCN treaties. As will be seen in Chapter 3, however, the United States did use financial assistance to pressure Britain to dismantle its imperial preference system.

United States believed were necessary for the economic development that the loans were intended to promote. Without such policies, the Department believed, the loans would not have their intended effect and the money would be wasted. Indeed, many in the U.S. government were skeptical about the efficacy of any financial assistance to China. As noted below, President Truman himself likened providing financial assistance to Jiang's government with "pouring sand down a rat hole."[222]

Professor Simei Qing has written that, in March 1946, about three months after China requested the loans, "[t]he American [FCN treaty] negotiators recommended using a U.S. government loan as a bargaining chip to bring the [Chinese] government to terms."[223] In support of this finding, she cited a March 8, 1946, note from Willard Thorp, then deputy assistant secretary of state for economic affairs, to Emilio G. Collado, the director of the Office of Financial and Development Policy, and John Carter Vincent, the director of the Office of Far Eastern Affairs. In that note, Thorp observed that

> [w]hile progress has been made in the negotiation of the commercial treaty with China, there remain some important points on which agreement has not been reached. I do not think that we should specifically link the commercial treaty with the proposed loan in preliminary loan discussions. I believe, however, that before making any definitive commitment with respect to the loan we should reexamine the situation carefully to determine whether it is reasonably certain that a satisfactory treaty will be concluded and, if not, whether bargaining power of the loan should be utilized in this connection.[224]

Thus, as of March 1946, when Thorp wrote his note, no decision had been made to link any of the proposed loans with the conclusion of the treaty. Moreover, Thorp was not recommending that this be done, but suggesting that such linkage be discussed as a possibility, if it appeared that a satisfactory treaty would not be obtained. Professor Qing also cited a March 14, 1946, briefing memorandum drafted by Woodbury Willoughby, the associate chief of the Division of Commercial Policy, to Secretary of State James F. Byrnes and Under Secretary Dean Acheson, explaining the status of the FCN treaty negotiations with China in preparation for their imminent meeting with General Marshall, who was visiting Washington from China. In that briefing memorandum, Willoughby

222. Arnold A. Offner, *Another Such Victory: President Truman and the Cold War, 1945–1953* (Stanford, CA: Stanford University Press, 2002), page 307. Professor Lanxin Xiang argues that the "central element" of U.S. policy in China after the war was "the judgment that Chiang's regime was a bottomless pit . . . ." Lanxin Xiang, *Recasting the Imperial Far East: Britain and American in China, 1945–1950* (Armonk, NY: M. E. Sharpe, 1995), page 109.

223. Simei Qing, *From Allies to Enemies: Visions of Modernity, Identity, and U.S.-China Diplomacy, 1945–1960* (Cambridge, MA: Harvard University Press, 2007), page 50.

224. Professor Qing very graciously provided me with an electronic image of the March 8, 1946, note, which she found in the National Archives. The face of the document does not indicate where in the archives it was filed.

reminded Byrnes and Acheson that departmental policy was that certain loans should be preceded by various actions by China, one of which was the conclusion of an FCN treaty. Willoughby then quoted Thorp's note to Collado and Vincent, without comment.[225]

No further reference to any loan appears in the negotiating history of the treaty.[226] Although the negotiations were conducted by the U.S. embassy, none of the State Department's instructions to the embassy regarding the treaty mention a loan, nor do any of the minutes of the negotiations themselves mention a loan. The March 8, 1946, note from Thorp indicates that no linkage between a loan and the treaty had been established as of that time. As described above, the United States made major concessions that enabled the conclusion of the negotiations in August, only five months after Thorp wrote his note. The record contains nothing

225. Professor Qing very graciously provided me with an electronic image of the March 14, 1946, briefing memorandum, which she found in the National Archives. The face of the document does not indicate where in the archives it was filed.

226. In her first account of the negotiations, published in 1998, Professor Qing wrote that, after March 1946, "the State Department began to push the Chinese Government to come to terms in the treaty negotiations through the bargaining power of the U.S. Government loan." Simei Qing, "Visions of Free Trade and U.S.-China Commercial Treaty Negotiations, 1945–1960," in Xiaobing Li and Hongshan Li, eds., *China and the United States: A New Cold War History* (Lanham, MD: University Press of America, 1998), page 138. She added that, after May 1946, "State Department officials continued to use the leverage of a U.S. Government loan to force the hands of the Nationalist Government in the treaty negotiation. Firmly believing in the justice of free trade and free economy, they were determined to bring the Chinese to the American terms." Ibid., page 140. Her account, however, did not contain any citations to the negotiating history to document these findings, and my research similarly found no record indicating that any loan played a role in the negotiations. She concluded that "the Chiang Kai-shek Government finally bowed to the pressures of the U.S. loan." Ibid. In support of this conclusion, she cited a document written in Chinese (which I have not seen and would not be able to read) that she located in an archive in Nanjing. In any event, nine years later, Professor Qing published a revised account of the negotiations. In her revised account, she omitted all of the statements quoted in this note. *See* Simei Qing, *From Allies to Enemies: Visions of Modernity, Identity, and U.S.-China Diplomacy, 1945–1960* (Cambridge, MA: Harvard University Press, 2007), pages 49–51. Rather her revised account contained a sentence stating that U.S. negotiators recommended use of a loan as bargaining power, followed immediately by a sentence stating that the treaty was signed on November 8, 1946. Ibid., pages 50–51. The revised account of the negotiations thus does not assert that the recommendation was adopted, that a loan was used to pressure the Chinese government, or that China's decision to sign the treaty resulted from such pressure. As described in the text, U.S. negotiators never recommended use of the loan as bargaining power, although Willard Thorp suggested that, under certain circumstances, the possibility of doing so should be discussed. There is no evidence that the possibility was later discussed, and no evidence that the loan was mentioned to the embassy officials conducting the negotiations or to the Chinese negotiators. Although the negotiating history includes numerous English language newspaper editorials published in China criticizing the treaty, none of these claimed that the United States used a loan to pressure China to conclude the treaty.

Professor Lanxin Xiang has written that China signed its FCN treaty "[u]nder heavy U.S. pressure." Xiang, *Recasting the Imperial Far East*, page 100. Professor Xiang did not elaborate upon the nature of the pressure or cite any evidence for his finding. In particular, he did not refer to any loan as an element of the negotiation.

to indicate that the discussion regarding the possible use of the loan as a bargaining chip that Thorp had suggested should occur, if a satisfactory treaty could not be obtained, ever did occur.

As the treaty awaited hearings in the Senate, the U.S. business community continued to complain about the failure of the State Department to use its economic leverage to force China to make additional concessions. An official of the NFTC reported in January 1948 that the Council at that point was undecided as to the position that it would take with respect to the China treaty. The NFTC believed it "possible that we might use the prospective aid program as bargaining power to obtain further concessions on some points."[227]

A committee formed by the American Chamber of Commerce of Shanghai to review the treaty recommended that the treaty not be ratified, claiming that "American business in China would be better off without the 1946 treaty than with it."[228] The Chamber particularly objected to the provision that abrogated prior agreements between the United States and China dating from the era of extraterritoriality. The Shanghai Chamber of Commerce in effect was attempting to preserve the old regime to the extent possible, believing it preferable to that promised by the new treaty.

After the Shanghai Chamber of Commerce voiced its opposition, the Tianjin (Tientsin) Chamber of Commerce formed a special committee to review the treaty, and that committee similarly recommended against ratification.[229] The American consul in Tianjin believed that the recommendation of the committee was "fairly representative of the views of the American business community in Tientsin as a whole."[230] The Tianjin Chamber decried the fact that since 1946 the Chinese government had imposed "strangling" controls on foreign trade, and that Chinese in the United States were treated much better than Americans in China.[231] It argued that the United States would be in a better position to protect American interests in China if it were not bound by the provisions of the proposed treaty.

According to the Tianjin Chamber, the treaty would produce several ill effects. First, it would abrogate existing treaties that conferred "substantial rights" on

227. Memorandum of Conversation dated January 21, 1948, NARA, Record Group 59, Department of State File No. 611.9331/1-2148.

228. Memorandum dated March 22, 1948, NARA, Record Group 59, Department of State File No. 611.9331/3-2248; Letter dated February 27, 1948, from the Committee to Study the Sino-American Treaty to the Board of Directors, American Chamber of Commerce, Shanghai, NARA, Record Group 59, Department of State File No. 711.932/2-2748; Letter dated March 5, 1948, from the American Chamber of Commerce, Shanghai, to Senator Arthur H, Vandenberg, NARA, Record Group 59, Department of State File No. 711.932/3-1148.

229. Letter dated May 5, 1948, from American Consul General Frederick W. Hinke to U.S. Ambassador J. Leighton Stuart, NARA, Record Group 59, Department of State File No. 611.9331/5-548.

230. Ibid.

231. Ibid.

Americans in China. Second, it would create a false impression that the problems of U.S. businesses in China had been remedied. Finally, it would likely preempt the negotiation of a better treaty at a later time. Thus, the Chamber contended that the treaty should not be ratified and that the State Department should defer the conclusion of any commercial agreement "until such time as the two nations concerned can offer each other something approaching equality of treatment."[232] The Chamber suggested that the United States use its impending aid to China as bargaining leverage to obtain a more favorable treaty from China.[233]

In March 1948, the Far East-America Council of Commerce and Industry reported to the State Department that considerable dissension existed within the organization, with some supporting the position taken by the business community in Shanghai and others supporting the treaty.[234] The NFTC continued to question its own earlier expressions of support for the treaty.[235]

The State Department itself appeared to lack enthusiasm for the treaty. Although the treaty was transmitted to the Senate in March 1947, only a few months after it had been signed in November 1946, the Senate took no action on the treaty before the session ended, apparently because of a lack of interest from the State Department. In December, members of the Senate Foreign Relations Committee told the Congressional Affairs staff of the State Department that they were "a little miffed with the Department over its failure strongly to support" the treaty during the session.[236] Indeed, a few months after the treaty entered into force, State Department officials acknowledged that the treaty represented an early effort, and that the United States probably would not again conclude a treaty in that form.[237] The treaty with China had included too many "serious compromises,"[238]

232. Ibid. *See also* Airgram dated April 28, 1948, from the American Chamber of Commerce of Tientsin, NARA, Record Group 59, Department of State File No. 711.932/4-2848; "Memorandum Submitted by the American Chamber of Commerce of Tientsin, China, to Show That the Pending Treaty of Friendship, Commerce and Navigation, Between America and China, Will Not Lead to Equitable or Satisfactory Business Relations between the Two Countries," NARA, Record Group 59, Department of State File No. 711.932/5-448.

233. Airgram dated April 28, 1948, from the American Chamber of Commerce of Tientsin, NARA, Record Group 59, Department of State File No. 711.932/4-2848.

234. Memorandum of Conversation headed "Views of Shanghai Business Community on Senate Approval of the Treaty of Friendship, Commerce and Navigation with China," dated March 31, 1948, NARA, Record Group 59, Department of State File No. 711.932/3-3148.

235. Ibid.

236. Memorandum headed "Treaty of Friendship with China," dated December 23, 1947, NARA, Record Group 59, Department of State File No. 711.932/12-2347.

237. Memorandum of Conversations, headed "Proposed Treaty of Friendship, Commerce and Navigation between the United States and India," dated August 23 and 24, 1949, NARA, Record Group 59, Department of State File No. 711.452/9-2149.

238. Telegram dated September 8, 1948, from the Department of State to the U.S. mission in Cairo, NARA, Record Group 59, Department of State File No. 711.832/4-2148.

and for that reason had been much criticized.[239] The Department considered the treaty with Italy, signed in February 1948, to be more representative of the type of treaty that it would be willing to conclude in the future.[240]

The Senate Foreign Relations Committee held hearings on the treaty on April 26, 1948. By that time, the division within the business community concerning whether to demand that the United States threaten to withhold loans in order to coerce China to conclude a more favorable treaty had prevented both the NFTC and the Far East-America Council of Commerce and Industry from taking a final position on whether the Senate should approve the treaty. [241] Both organizations declined invitations to testify at the hearings.[242]

At the hearings, Bruce Smith, the former president of the Shanghai Chamber of Commerce, testified in opposition to the treaty.[243] He proposed that the United States renegotiate the treaty, and renewed the business community's suggestion that the United States use its financial assistance to China as leverage to obtain a treaty guaranteeing greater rights for Americans in China. The Tianjin Chamber of Commerce sent a written statement in opposition to the treaty, arguing that it would eliminate valuable extraterritorial rights for Americans and prevent the negotiation of a treaty that would provide more robust protections.[244] The Shanghai Chamber of Commerce also sent a written statement contending that U.S. nationals in China received more favorable treatment under the old treaties with China than under the new treaty, and that the United States should not relinquish its extraterritorial privileges.[245]

Opposition to the treaty came as well from Maud Russell, the executive director of the Committee for a Democratic Far Eastern Policy, an advocacy group whose board of directors included Paul Robeson, an internationally acclaimed

239. Telegram dated August 5, 1948, from the Department of State to the U.S. embassy in Manila, NARA, Record Group 59, Department of State File No. 711.962/8-348.

240. Memorandum of Conversations, headed "Proposed Treaty of Friendship, Commerce and Navigation between the United States and India," dated August 23 and 24, 1949, NARA, Record Group 59, Department of State File No. 711.452/9-2149; Telegram dated September 8, 1948, from the Department of State to the U.S. mission in Cairo, NARA, Record Group 59, Department of State File No. 711.832/4-2148.

241. Telegram dated February 16, 1948, from the Department of State to the U.S. embassy in Nanking, NARA, Record Group 59, Department of State File No. 611.9331/2-1048.

242. Telegram dated April 21, 1948, from E. L. Behr Jr., to the Clerk of the Senate Foreign Relations Committee, NARA, Record Group 46, File No. SEN80B-B5; Telegram dated April 24, 1948, from Arthur B. Foye to the clerk of the Senate Foreign Relations Committee, NARA, Record Group 46, File No. SEN80B-B5.

243. Statement of Bruce Smith, *Friendship, Commerce, and Navigation with China,* Hearing Before a Subcommittee of the Committee on Foreign Relations, United States Senate, 80th Cong. 2d Sess. (1948), pages 70–75.

244. Statement by H. Hodes, President, American Chamber of Commerce Tientsin, NARA, Record Group 46, File No. SEN80B-B5.

245. Letter dated March 5, 1947, from C. V. Schelke to Senator Arthur H. Vandenburg, NARA, Record Group 46, File No. SEN80B-B5.

singer and actor, and Edgar Snow, an American journalist who had been the first Western reporter to interview Mao Zedong. Its members also included in the 1940s future president Ronald Reagan as well as other performers, such as Gregory Peck, Edward G. Robinson, Leonard Bernstein, and Artie Shaw. An April 1946 Committee fundraiser in New York was publicly endorsed by a number of celebrities, including Reagan, Peck, Robinson, and Shaw.[246] Russell opposed ratification of the treaty because it had been concluded with Jiang Jieshi's government, which she characterized as corrupt and undemocratic,[247] a characterization not inconsistent with the views of the Truman administration.[248]

Appearing in opposition to a portion of the treaty was William Sloane, a representative of the American Book Publishers Council. Sloane complained that the intellectual property protection provision of the treaty did not require payment of a royalty to an author for translations of his or her work.[249] Prior to the hearing, the Senate Foreign Relations Committee had received numerous statements in opposition to that provision from various publishers, such as McGraw-Hill, Simon and Schuster, W. W. Norton and Company, Random House, Harper and Brothers, Bobbs Merrill, Alfred A. Knopf, Pocket Books, Harcourt Brace and Company, Ginn and Company, the MacMillan Company, G. P. Putnam's Sons, Rinehart and Company, and John Wiley and Sons; from several colleges and universities, including Harvard University, the University of California, Northwestern University, the University of Texas, the University of Minnesota, and Smith College; from noted authors, including Arthur M. Schlesinger, Charles and Mary Beard, Lillian Hellman, John Hersey, Moss Hart, Agnes Slight Turnbull, and Russel Crouse; and from a variety of other organizations, including the Modern Language Association, William Morrow and Company, the Authors Guild, and *Look* magazine.

No business organizations appeared in support of the treaty, although the treaty was endorsed by Alfred Kohlberg, on behalf of the America-China

246. Karen Garner, *Precious Fire: Maud Russell and the Chinese Revolution* (Amherst: University of Massachusetts Press, 2003), page 190.

247. Statement of Maud Russell, *Friendship, Commerce, and Navigation with China,* Hearing Before a Subcommittee of the Committee on Foreign Relations, United States Senate, 80th Cong. 2d Sess. (1948), pages 52–65.

248. Truman "regarded Jiang's regime as the world's 'rottenest,' comprising 'grafters and crooks,' and he likened giving aid to China to 'pouring sand in a rat hole.'" Arnold A. Offner, *Another Such Victory: President Truman and the Cold War, 1945–1953* (Stanford, CA: Stanford University Press, 2002), page 307. This view predated the Truman administration. Roosevelt's secretary of the treasury, Henry Morgenthau, in 1944 referred to Jiang's regime as "just a bunch of crooks." Robert Dallek, *Franklin Roosevelt and American Foreign Policy, 1932–1945* (New York: Oxford University Press, 1979), page 486. Yet, Truman continued to support the Jiang regime because, as Cold War tensions increased, he did not want to negotiate with Mao's Chinese Communist Party. Offner, *Another Such Victory,* pages 344–345.

249. Statement of William Sloane, *Friendship, Commerce, and Navigation with China,* Hearing Before a Subcommittee of the Committee on Foreign Relations, United States Senate, 80th Cong. 2d Sess. (1948), page 66. The objectionable provision was Paragraph 5(c) of the protocol, added at China's insistence.

Policy Association, an advocacy group headed by Clare Boothe Luce, a former Republican congresswoman and the wife of Henry Luce, the publisher of *Time* magazine. The Association's members included former Harvard Law School dean Roscoe Pound, who had learned Chinese at the age of 76 and was serving as an advisor to Jiang.[250] Kohlberg, an importer of Chinese lace, regarded himself as an expert on communist subversion, and later worked covertly with Senator Joseph McCarthy to discredit critics of Jiang's government.[251] He urged that the treaty be approved as a demonstration of support for Jiang in his battle against communist forces.[252] Kohlberg argued that opposition to the treaty was led by communists, although under questioning he conceded that the American Chamber of Commerce in Shanghai was not a communist organization but was "purely and truly American."[253] He went on to note, however, that the Committee for a Democratic Far Eastern Policy had been cited as a communist front by the House Committee on Un-American Activities.[254]

Despite opposition from the U.S. business community in China and ambivalence from the NFTC, the Senate Committee on Foreign Relations voted to report the treaty favorably to the Senate on May 25.[255] The Senate approved the treaty on June 2 by a voice vote.[256] In approving the treaty, however, the Senate included in the resolution of ratification a reservation stating that the United States "does not accept" Paragraph 5(c) of the protocol, the paragraph that exempted translations from copyright protection.[257] Further, the United States understood that copyright protection would be governed by the 1903 Treaty as to Commercial Relations between the United States and China. The 1903 treaty was one of the treaties from the era of extraterritoriality terminated by Article XXIX of the new FCN treaty. The State Department believed that the 1903 treaty did not "afford any substantial protection" with respect to translations.[258] Nevertheless, the

250. "Roscoe Pound Dies at 93, Revitalized Legal System," *Harvard Crimson*, July 3, 1964.

251. Stanley I. Kutler, *The American Inquisition: Justice and Injustice in the Cold War* (New York: Hill and Wang, 1982), page 187.

252. Statement of Alfred Kohlberg, *Friendship, Commerce, and Navigation with China*, Hearing Before a Subcommittee of the Committee on Foreign Relations, United States Senate, 80th Cong. 2d Sess. (1948), pages 46–48.

253. Ibid., page 49.

254. Ibid., page 51. Ronald Reagan would later deny membership in any organizations deemed subversive, a denial that, in light of his membership in the council, was incorrect and that could have been prosecuted as a felony. *See* Seth Rosenfeld, "Secret FBI Files Reveal Covert Activities at UC/ Bureau's Campus Operations Involved Reagan, CIA," *San Francisco Chronicle*, June 9, 2002.

255. *Treaty of Friendship, Commerce and Navigation with China*, Exec. Rept. No. 8, 80th Cong. 2d Sess. (1948), page 8. *See also* 94 *Congressional Record* 6484 (1948).

256. 94 *Congressional Record* 6928 (1948).

257. Ibid.

258. Telegram dated May 27, 1948, from the Department of State to the U.S. embassy in Nanking, NARA, Record Group 59, Department of State File No. 711.932/5-2748.

effect of the reservation was to establish the standard of protection under the 1903 treaty, such as it was, as the standard of protection for translations under the new treaty.[259] The State Department feared that, in view of anti-American and anti-Chinese government "agitation" in China, the Chinese legislative assembly would reject the treaty if resubmitted with the reservation.[260] The Chinese government concluded, however, that submission of the reservation to the Yuan would be necessary,[261] although that did not occur before the Yuan adjourned.[262] When the Yuan reconvened, the embassy's pessimism proved unwarranted and the Yuan approved the reservation on October 31.[263] The embassy urged an immediate exchange of the instruments of ratification because it believed that the "fall of [the] government within [a] matter of days [was] very possible."[264]

The parties exchanged instruments of ratification on November 30, 1948,[265] which brought the treaty into force on that date, slightly more than two years after the treaty had been signed. The ensuing months would witness decisive military victories by the People's Liberation Army and, on October 1, 1949, 11 months after the exchange of ratifications, Mao Zedong would proclaim the founding of the People's Republic of China. Two months later, barely more than a year after the exchange, Jiang and his remaining forces fled to the island of Taiwan.

NEGOTIATING AN FCN TREATY WITH ITALY

The first European country with which successful FCN treaty negotiations commenced was Italy. In December 1945, Secretary of State James Byrnes exchanged notes with the Italian ambassador committing the two countries to the negotiation of an FCN treaty as soon as possible.[266] A year passed, however, before the State Department completed its draft of a proposed treaty with Italy.

259. Telegram dated October 12, 1948, from the Department of State to the U.S. embassy in Nanking, NARA, Record Group 59, Department of State File No. 711.932/9-1448.

260. Telegram dated June 25, 1948, from the Department of State to the U.S. embassy in Nanking, NARA, Record Group 59, Department of State File No. 711.932/6-2548.

261. Telegram dated July 14, 1948, from the U.S. embassy in Nanking to the Department of State, NARA, Record Group 59, Department of State File No. 711.932/7-1448.

262. Telegram dated July 28, 1948, from the U.S. embassy in Nanking to the Department of State, NARA, Record Group 59, Department of State File No. 711.932/7-2848.

263. Telegram dated October 31, 1948, from the U.S. embassy in Nanking to the Department of State, NARA, Record Group 59, Department of State File No. 711.932/10-3148.

264. Ibid.

265. Telegram dated November 30, 1948, from the U.S. embassy in Nanking to the Department of State, NARA, Record Group 59, Department of State File No. 711.932/11-2048.

266. Memorandum of Conversation headed "Proposed Commercial Treaty with Italy," dated June 4, 1947, and NARA, Record Group 59, Department of State Lot Files, Walter Hollis Papers, Folder marked "Italy."

In January 1947, the State Department forwarded a draft treaty to the U.S. mission in Rome for comments.[267] The mission responded by expressing concern that Italy could not abide by the MFN requirement with respect to exchange controls.[268] Nevertheless, in April, the Department sent to the embassy for transmission to the Italian government copies of a draft treaty that included such a requirement.[269] The Department indicated that the draft was still subject to revision and that the United States reserved the right to propose changes to the draft at a later time. In September, the Department proposed several changes to the draft.[270] Days later, having finally achieved a draft treaty with which it was satisfied, the State Department commenced negotiations with Italy.[271]

The proposed FCN treaty with Italy differed from that with China in that Article II(3) guaranteed to companies, and not just to individuals as in the treaty with China, national and MFN treatment with respect to engaging in certain activities for gain. In effect, U.S. companies would have a right to invest in most sectors of the Italian economy where investment by Italian or foreign companies was permitted.

The most difficult issue that arose during negotiations involved Italy's objection to language under which the exchange rate for expropriation compensation would be that on the date of expropriation rather than that on the date of payment.[272] Italy proposed that the transferability of expropriation proceeds depend upon whether the investment was made in dollars or lire and that the exchange rate be the most favorable rate applicable to capital transfers on the date of application for transfer.[273] The United States objected that the Italian proposal to differentiate among investments would necessitate a complex inquiry to determine the nature of the original investment and would lead to disputes.[274] Further, the United States wished to ensure that the expropriated investor did not bear the risk

267. Despatch dated January 21, 1947, from the Department of State to the U.S. mission in Rome, NARA, Record Group 59, Department of State File No. 711.652/1-2147.

268. Telegram dated March 25, 1947, from the U.S. mission in Rome to the Department of State, NARA, Record Group 59, Department of State File No. 711.652/3-2447.

269. Memorandum of Transmittal dated April 17, 1947, NARA, Record Group 59, Department of State File No. 711.652/4-1747.

270. Despatch dated September 5, 1947, from the Department of State to the U.S. mission in Rome, NARA, Record Group 59, Department of State File No. 711.652/9-547.

271. Telegram dated September 16, 1947, from the U.S. mission in Rome to the Department of State, NARA, Record Group 59, Department of State File No. 711.652/9-1647.

272. Telegram dated September 24, 1947, from the U.S. embassy in Rome to the Department of State, NARA, Record Group 59, Department of State File No. 711.652/9-2047. Using the rate on the date of expropriation is more favorable to the investor because the investor avoids the risk of adverse changes in the exchange rate between the date of the expropriation and the date of payment.

273. Telegram dated October 11, 1947, from the U.S. embassy in Rome to the Department of State, NARA, Record Group 59, Department of State File No. 711.652/10-947.

274. Telegram dated October 24, 1947, from the Department of State to the U.S. embassy in Rome, NARA, Record Group 59, Department of State File No. 711.652/10-947.

of currency depreciation and thus objected to using the exchange rate on the date of application rather than the date of expropriation. Finally, it wanted the "prevailing" rate of exchange to apply, rather than the rate prescribed for capital transfers.[275] Italy ultimately agreed to the exchange rate on the date of expropriation, but insisted on differentiating between investments made in dollars and those made in lire.[276] The United States acquiesced and proposed language, ultimately accepted by Italy, under which, in the event of exchange difficulties that necessitated restrictions on the withdrawal of expropriation compensation, Italy would be permitted to give priority to the withdrawal of compensation for the expropriation of investments made before December 8, 1934, when exchange controls were implemented and to certain other classes of investments.[277] The United States also proposed that, in the event that multiple exchange rates were in force, the rate to be used would be one that would permit the recipient of the compensation to realize the full economic value of the compensation in U.S. dollars.[278] After a lengthy discussion, Italy accepted the U.S. proposal on the exchange rate.[279] The parties incorporated their agreement regarding differentiated transfers and the exchange rate into an additional protocol.[280] As will be seen in Chapter 6, Italy later would conclude that the weakened language in the exchange controls provision had discouraged U.S. investors from investing in Italy, and would request the negotiation of a supplemental agreement strengthening the provision.

The treaty with Italy was the first to include a new "competitive equality" provision under which economic advantages, such as subsidies and taxes, extended by a party to public enterprises engaged in trading and manufacturing in competition with private enterprises of the other party must also be extended to such private enterprises.[281] It included as well new language requiring a party to pay compensation for indirectly held interests in property that it expropriated.[282]

The negotiations were completed in December, just a little more than three months after they began, and the parties signed the treaty on February 2, 1948.[283] The results of the negotiations pleased everyone. The Italian government

275. Ibid.

276. Telegram dated November 20, 1947, from the U.S. embassy in Rome to the Department of State, NARA, Record Group 59, Department of State File No. 711.652/11-2047.

277. Telegram dated December 5, 1947, from the Department of State to the U.S. embassy in Rome, NARA, Record Group 59, Department of State File No. 711.652/11-2047.

278. Ibid.

279. Telegram dated December 24, 1947, from the U.S. embassy in Rome to the Department of State, NARA, Record Group 59, Department of State File No. 711.652/12-2447.

280. Italy FCN treaty, Additional Protocol, Paragraphs 5 and 6.

281. Italy FCN treaty, Protocol, Paragraph 2.

282. Italy FCN treaty, Protocol, Paragraph 1.

283. Treaty of Friendship, Commerce and Navigation, with protocol, additional protocol and exchange of notes, entered into force July 26, 1949, 63 Stat. 2255, TIAS 1965, 9 Bevans 261, 79 UNTS 171.

congratulated itself on the concessions that it had obtained from the United States, particularly regarding trade. The State Department haled the FCN with Italy as "the most liberal and comprehensive treaty of this type that the US has ever negotiated"[284] and noted that, more so than the treaty with China, it reflected the kind of the instrument desired by the United States, both because the language included various "perfecting modifications and additions" and because it contained "fewer serious compromises."[285] The NFTC regarded the Italian FCN as "by far" the best FCN treaty ever negotiated.[286] It enthusiastically endorsed ratification because the treaty included a right of national treatment with respect to the establishment of investment by U.S. companies. The FCN treaty with Italy became the first U.S. FCN treaty in which corporate and individual investors would have parity of treatment on all important investment-related matters.

The Senate Foreign Relations Committee held hearings on the FCN treaty with Italy on April 30, 1948.[287] The administration sent a significant delegation to testify. Appearing on behalf of the State Department were Assistant Secretary of State for Economic Affairs Willard Thorp, Chief of the Division of Commercial Policy (and Acting Deputy Director of the Office of International Trade Policy) Winthrop G. Brown, Chief of the Division of Southern European Affairs Walworth Barbour, and Acting Assistant Chief of the Division of Commercial Policy Vernon G. Setser. Appearing on behalf of the Commerce Department was Assistant Secretary of Commerce for International Trade Thomas C. Blaisdell Jr. One other witness appeared, Richard M. Egan, who was foreign sales manager of the Great Lakes Carbon Corporation of New York, a company that had done between 5 and 6 million dollars' worth of business in Italy.[288] Egan testified that the treaty was "very satisfactory for the American businessman" and complimented the U.S. government for having concluded a treaty as satisfactory as the treaty with Italy.[289] Asked by the Committee Chair whether he had any criticisms of the treaty, he replied, "None, Senator."[290] On May 25, 1948, the Committee recommended that the Senate advise and consent to ratification.[291]

284. *Current Economic Developments,* January 5, 1948, page 7, NARA, Record Group 59, Department of State Lot Files.

285. Telegram dated September 8, 1948, from the Department of State to the U.S. mission in Cairo, NARA, Record Group 59, Department of State File No. 711.832/4-2148.

286. Letter dated June 1, 1950, from National Foreign Trade Council president E. P. Thomas to Senator Arthur H. Vandenberg, NARA, Record Group 59, Department of State File No. 611.004/5-350.

287. *Proposed Treaty of Friendship, Commerce, and Navigation between the United States and the Italian Republic,* Hearing Before the Committee on Foreign Relations, 80th Cong. 2d Sess. (1948).

288. Ibid., page 28.

289. Ibid.

290. Ibid.

291. *Treaty of Friendship, Commerce and Navigation with the Italian Republic,* Exec. Rept. No. 6, 80th Cong. 2d Sess. (1948), page 7.

During Senate deliberations on the treaty, Democratic senator J. Howard McGrath of Rhode Island asked how the treaty affected the concord between Italy and the Vatican. Democratic senator Elbert D. Thomas of Utah, who chaired the subcommittee that had considered the treaty, replied that the concord "would in no sense affect this treaty."[292] Senator McGrath then asked how the treaty dealt with matters of religion. Senator Thomas replied that the treaty provided Americans in Italy with the same religious freedom that Italians received in the United States.[293] Senator McGrath questioned the appropriateness of including a provision on religious freedom in a commercial treaty, observed that Italy had never denied religious freedom to Americans, and said that, if the United States was going to embark upon negotiating FCN treaties with a provision on religion, then a similar provision should be included in every FCN treaty in the future.[294] Senator Thomas replied that the provision on religion had been included in the treaty because the peace treaty with Italy called for the negotiation of an FCN treaty with provisions on individual rights, such as freedom of religion and freedom of information, but that he anticipated that such provisions would appear in all future FCN treaties.[295] Following that exchange, the Senate, on June 2, 1948, gave advice and consent to ratification by a voice vote.

PROPOSING AN FCN TREATY WITH THE SOVIET UNION

In the days immediately following the end of the war, the State Department encouraged commercial relations with its wartime ally, the Soviet Union, envisioning a vast market for U.S. exports.[296] In October 1945, for example, Robert G. Hooker, the assistant chief of the State Department's Division of East European Affairs, told Lewis H. Brown, the president of Johns-Manville Corporation, that the Department was "anxious to give assistance" to plans by American companies to develop trade relations with the Soviet Union. Hooker advised Brown regarding the best way to proceed in order to avoid "delay and difficulties."[297] That same month, the Department sent a memorandum to the U.S. mission in Moscow stating that the State and Commerce Departments were "interested in the problem of developing commercial relations" between American businesses and Soviet commercial organizations.[298] The two departments were coordinating joint efforts to advise American businesses on the commercial policies and procedures followed

292. 94 *Congressional Record* 6935 (1948).

293. Ibid., page 6936.

294. Ibid.

295. Ibid.

296. Hearden, *Architects of Globalism*, pages 84–89; Gardner, *Economic Access*, pages 313–314.

297. Letter from Robert G. Hooker to Lewis H. Brown dated October 11, 1945, NARA, Record Group 59, Department of State File No. 611.6131/10-1145.

298. Memorandum dated October 11, 1945, concerning the commercial and economic program of the United States in relation to the U.S.S.R., NARA, Record Group 59, Department of State File No. 611.6131/10-1145.

by Soviet economic organs.[299] During the war, Roosevelt had been convinced that the United States should extend a large postwar reconstruction loan to the Soviet Union, which could be used to purchase U.S. exports, although by 1945 Roosevelt had concluded that the loan must be conditioned upon Soviet cooperation with U.S. postwar foreign policy.[300]

Even before the war ended, the State Department had begun to contemplate the negotiation of an FCN treaty with the Soviet Union. Between May 19, 1945, and March 6, 1946, a team of State Department officials that included representatives of the Division of Commercial Policy and the Office of the Legal Adviser met some 42 times to develop a special draft of an FCN treaty that would be suitable for conclusion with a communist country.[301] This project in particular evidences the State Department's understanding of the FCN treaties as essentially a reflection of the rule of law rather than a doctrinaire prescription for a particular set of economic policies. Although the standard draft FCN treaty unquestionably promoted a system of free enterprise, the United States was prepared to conclude an FCN treaty with a country, such as the Soviet Union, that had abolished the free enterprise system, provided that the country was willing to accept certain rule of law principles.

In drafting the proposed treaty, these officials were prepared to accommodate many of the differences between the Soviet and the American economies. For example, they observed that national treatment with respect to engaging in various commercial and manufacturing enterprises, the provision of the treaty that the State Department most associated with the promotion of free enterprise, would give U.S. companies only "nominal" access to the Soviet economy, and that the value of a national treatment obligation would be "virtually nil," given that Soviet citizens did not enjoy the right to engage in private enterprise.[302] They recognized that no possibility existed that U.S. companies would receive the same treatment as Soviet state enterprises, noting that the Soviet Union imposed the death penalty for theft from a state enterprise.[303] Similarly, they were prepared to accept that the right of U.S. nationals to enter and to travel within the Soviet Union

299. Ibid.

300. Randall B. Woods and Howard Jones, *Dawning of the Cold War: The United States' Quest for Order* (Athens: University of Georgia Press, 1991), pages 26–29. Woods and Jones argue that, by the end of the war, Roosevelt and Truman were more interested in using the loan to extract political concessions than to open markets to U.S. exports. Ibid., pages 60–61.

301. Memorandum headed "The Forty-Second Meeting to Consider a Tentative Draft Treaty of Friendship, Commerce and Navigation between the United States and the U.S.S.R. Held March 6, 1946," NARA, Record Group 59, Department of State File No. 711.612.

302. Memorandum headed "The Third Meeting to Consider a Tentative Draft Treaty of Friendship, Commerce and Navigation between the United States and the U.S.S.R. Held May 24, 1945," NARA, Record Group 59, Department of State File No. 711.612.

303. Memorandum headed "The Eleventh Meeting to Consider a Tentative Draft Treaty of Friendship, Commerce and Navigation between the United States and the U.S.S.R. Held August 7, 1945," NARA, Record Group 59, Department of State File No. 711.612.

would be curtailed.[304] They did, however, retain in their draft those provisions that guaranteed to U.S. nationals protection in accordance with international law and, in particular, a right to compensation in the event of an expropriation of U.S.-owned property.[305] In short, they expected the Soviet Union to grant U.S. property security under the rule of law, but acknowledged that access to the Soviet economy would be greatly restricted. By October 1945, the State Department could report internally that "considerable study" had been given to the preparation of a proposed FCN treaty with the Soviet Union, and that "many changes" had been made in the standard draft language to accommodate the absence of free enterprise in that country.[306]

On February 21, 1946, the United States delivered a diplomatic note to the Soviet Union proposing that the two countries begin the negotiation of a $1 billion credit from the United States to the Soviet Union "as soon as possible."[307] The U.S.S.R. had requested such a credit in August of the prior year. The United States also suggested that the discussions cover a number of other topics, including the negotiation of an FCN treaty.[308]

A few days later, John N. Hazard, an expert on Soviet law serving as an adviser on state trading and government monopolies in the Division of Commercial Policy, met with Fedor Orekhov, the First Secretary of the Soviet embassy, to discuss a U.S. proposal for an international trade organization. Hazard told Orekhov that the United States was "pleased" that the Soviet Union would be participating in the preliminary conference to establish the entity.[309] Hazard also told Orekhov that the proposed FCN treaty between the United States and the Soviet Union would be "very desirable" for both countries because it would "establish rules and avoid misunderstandings."[310] The meeting ended on a "most cordial" note.[311] Orekhov asked Hazard for advice on how to research U.S. economic agreements,

304. Memorandum headed "The Third Meeting to Consider a Tentative Draft Treaty of Friendship, Commerce and Navigation between the United States and the U.S.S.R. Held May 24, 1945," NARA, Record Group 59, Department of State File No. 711.612

305. Memorandum headed "The Eighth Meeting to Consider a Tentative Draft Treaty of Friendship, Commerce and Navigation between the United States and the U.S.S.R. Held June 28, 1945," NARA, Record Group 59, Department of State File No. 711.612.

306. Memorandum dated October 11, 1945, concerning the commercial and economic program of the United States in relation to the U.S.S.R., NARA, Record Group 59, Department of State File No. 611.6131/10-1145.

307. *Current Economic Developments,* March 25, 1946, NARA, Record Group 59, Department of State Lot Files.

308. Ibid.

309. Memorandum of Conversation dated February 26, 1946, between John N. Hazard and Fedor Orekhov regarding Commercial Relations with the USSR, NARA, Record Group 59, Department of State File No. 611/6131/2-2646. As discussed in Chapter 3, the Soviet Union ultimately would decline to participate in the ITO negotiations.

310. Ibid.

311. Ibid.

which Hazard agreed to provide, and offered to lend Hazard books on the Soviet system for the purpose of making photostatic copies.

Hazard returned to the embassy on March 12 to deliver copies of U.S. commercial treaties, for which Orekhov was "very grateful."[312] Orkekhov commented that the restoration of commercial relations between the United States and the Soviet Union was "very important," and said that he was sorry about the delays in re-establishing them.[313] Orekhov mentioned the shortages in the U.S.S.R. of housing and steel and described how a friend from Minsk recently had told Orekhov that residents there, having no building materials, were constructing earthen huts in which to live. He again offered to lend books from his library to Hazard. On March 15, the Soviet Union sent a diplomatic note to the United States agreeing that the two countries should commence the negotiation of an FCN treaty.[314]

The Cold War, however, soon overtook the proposed FCN treaty. On February 22, three weeks before Hazard's second visit to Orekhov, George F. Kennan, the interim American charge d'affairés in Moscow, sent his famous "long telegram" from Moscow warning of Soviet expansionist intentions. On March 5, a week before Hazard's second visit, Winston Churchill delivered his speech in Fulton, Missouri, warning that an "iron curtain" had descended over Europe.

On March 13, the day after Hazard's second meeting with Orekhov, Hazard sent a letter to Kennan in Moscow enclosing a copy of the proposed FCN treaty on which the Division of Commercial Policy and the Office of the Legal Adviser had been laboring for nearly a year. Hazard explained that the Department had "done its best to suit the conventional form of the treaty to Soviet conditions."[315] As a result, the Department had introduced into the draft "numerous departures" from the language of the standard draft U.S. FCN treaty.[316] Hazard solicited Kennan's suggestions with respect to additional ways in which the treaty could be made more effective, and indicated that the proposed treaty would be circulated to other agencies of the U.S. government for comment. The embassy sent a telegram to the Department on April 4 urging that it not submit the draft treaty to the Soviet Union for negotiation until Kennan's response was received.[317]

Kennan's response, soon received by diplomatic pouch, was devastating. He began with an attempt to soften the blow that would follow. Kennan explained

312. Memorandum of Conversation dated March 12, 1946, between John N. Hazard and Fedor Orekhov, NARA, Record Group 59, Department of State File No. 611.6131/3-1246.

313. Ibid.

314. *Current Economic Developments,* April 22, 1946, NARA, Record Group 59, Department of State Lot Files.

315. Letter dated March 13, 1946, from John N. Hazard to George F. Kennan, NARA, Record Group 59, Department of State File No. 611.6131/3-1346.

316. Ibid.

317. Telegram dated April 4, 1946, from the U.S. embassy in Moscow to the Department of State, NARA, Record Group 59, Department of State File No. 711.612/4-446.

that he had read the proposed draft "with as much care as a very hectic period here will permit."[318] He acknowledged that "a great deal of work and of careful thought" went into the proposed treaty and that "the persons who worked on this made a genuine and loyal effort to combine our traditional treaty procedures with the peculiar situation existing in the U.S.S.R."[319]

Then Kennan delivered the punch. "I have to tell you," he wrote, "(and I hope you will forgive my frankness) that I consider it quite useless to attempt to negotiate an agreement of this nature with the Russians and I am afraid that the entire approach to it in Washington must have rested on an imperfect understanding of Russian realities as we know them today."[320] Kennan added that he did not have the time to go into details, but that he would adduce a few points in support of his general reaction to the proposed treaty.

Kennan's first point was directed at the very nature of the FCN treaty as a treaty to promote the rule of law. "Russia is not," Kennan explained, "a Rechtsstaat. The relationships between its citizens and the State are governed only in minor degree by legal norms and rights. Of far greater importance is the sheer administrative will of the executive authority, even in minor matters."[321]

Further, the arbitrary nature of Soviet administration was even more apparent in the government's dealings with aliens. As Kennan explained, "If this is true with respect to relationships between Soviet citizens and the State, it is far more true with respect to residence and activities of foreigners in Russia. Questions involving residence and activities of foreigners rest, I should say, 100 percent on the arbitrary will of the administrative authorities. There is no Soviet law which is worth the paper it is written on in so far as it bears on foreigners in the Soviet Union."[322] In short, the Soviet Union was not a nation constructed on the principle of the rule of law. A treaty intended to promote the rule of law within the Soviet Union was doomed to fail.

Kennan argued that the effect of the treaty would be to "give to the Russians a legal basis for claiming as a treaty right many privileges in the United States which they now enjoy simply by custom and by the good will of our Government."[323] As a result, he contended, "We would be in a much better position vis-à-vis the Russians if we had it in our power to extend or withdraw these privileges at will, depending on treatment we are getting here."[324]

318. Letter dated April 3, 1946, from George F. Kennan to John N. Hazard, NARA, Record Group 59, Department of State File No. 611.6131/3-1346.

319. Ibid.

320. Ibid.

321. Ibid.

322. Ibid.

323. Ibid. A Princeton-trained diplomat, but not a lawyer, Kennan appears to have been unaware that many of the rights that the treaty would have granted to Soviet companies in the United States were already guaranteed to them by the U.S. Constitution and could not be withdrawn at will.

324. Ibid.

Kennan believed that the Soviet authorities had no intention of allowing "more than a handful of private Americans to live in this country for years to come."[325] Thus, even to the extent that Americans in the Soviet Union benefited from a treaty provision, the number of beneficiaries would be small and "the practical significance would be negligible."[326] He concluded by noting, as many others had before him, that the U.S. draft was "long, legalistic, [and] obscure in wording."[327] He added that "[i]t would take the Russians weeks to translate it, months to study it and years to understand it."[328]

Even as Kennan was denouncing in confidential internal communications the very idea of an FCN treaty with the Soviet Union, the two countries ostensibly were moving toward the negotiation of such a treaty. On April 18, the United States sent the Soviet Union a note proposing a schedule for the negotiation of the FCN treaty and other agreements, including the extension of the $1 billion credit.[329] In May, the Soviet government responded that it was prepared to commence the negotiations.[330]

Meanwhile, on May 10, Hazard responded to Kennan. Hazard characterized Kennan's pessimism about the usefulness of the treaty as "disheartening."[331] Yet, he acknowledged the power of Kennan's concern about the absence in the Soviet Union of the particular conception of the rule of law reflected in the U.S. FCN treaties. "I would be the first to agree with you," wrote Hazard, "that the U.S.S.R. is not a 'Rechsstaat'. Those who have followed events in the field of municipal or international law, as you and I have, can hardly take heart in the trend toward negation of all the Anglo-Saxon jurists have held sacred for years."[332] Hazard, however, did not share Kennan's pessimism about the future prospects for the rule of law in the Soviet Union. Hazard believed that "if our relations with the Soviet Union are made the subject of written rules, it is not too much to anticipate that these rules will become eventually a charter, even though they may be violated at frequent intervals during the early months."[333] Hazard went on to comment that many of the protections guaranteed by the treaty already were extended to Soviet citizens as a matter of right by the U.S. Constitution. He said

325. Ibid.

326. Ibid.

327. Ibid.

328. Ibid.

329. *Current Economic Developments,* May 27, 1946, NARA, Record Group 59, Department of State Lot Files.

330. Ibid.

331. Letter dated May 10, 1946, from John N. Hazard to George F. Kennan, NARA, Record Group 59, Department of State File No. 611.6131/5-1046.

332. Ibid.

333. Ibid.

that he looked forward to having Kennan in Washington in the near future "so that we may proceed with the necessary revisions in the draft."[334]

Kennan's reply appears to have ended any further work within the State Department on an FCN treaty with the Soviet Union. Five days after Hazard sent his reply to Kennan, the Department's U.S.S.R. Committee circulated Kennan's message and Hazard's reply in anticipation of a discussion about the desirability of concluding such a treaty.[335] If any further discussions regarding such a treaty occurred, no record of them has survived in the negotiating history in the National Archives. On June 15, the U.S. embassy in Moscow sent a telegram to the State Department endorsing Kennan's views in their entirety.[336] At the end of the summer, Hazard would leave the State Department for a post at Columbia University teaching Soviet law, where he would remain for the rest of his career.

In July, Democratic congressman Jerry Voorhis of California wrote a letter to Undersecretary of State Dean Acheson enclosing his remarks from the *Congressional Record*, in which he had urged the Department to negotiate an FCN treaty with the Soviet Union.[337] Acheson replied on August 1, stating that such a treaty would be "most desirable" and informing Voorhis, "for [his] confidential information," that the Department had been in the process of preparing such a treaty for more than a year.[338] Voorhis also wrote to Clair Wilcox, the director of the Office of International Trade Policy.[339] Wilcox explained that the State Department had "given a great deal of thought to the problem of negotiating" an FCN treaty with the Soviet Union.[340] Then, without further elaboration, Wilcox told Voorhis, "If you should at any time wish to discuss this matter with officers of the Department I shall be happy to arrange a meeting."[341] If the Department had still been engaged in any activity related to the negotiation of such a treaty, Wilcox presumably would have mentioned it. Instead, he responded with a polite offer to arrange a meeting at some unspecified time in the future, should Voorhis wish to take the initiative to request it. The clear inference is that the Department

334. Ibid.

335. Memorandum dated May 15, 1946, from William Adams Brown Jr., to the Department of State U.S.S.R. Committee, NARA, Record Group 59, Department of State File No. 611.6131/3-1346.

336. Telegram dated June 15, 1946, from the U.S. embassy in Moscow to the Department of State, NARA, Record Group 59, Department of State File No. 611.612/6-1546.

337. Letter dated July 20, 1946, from Congressman Jerry Voorhis to Undersecretary of State Dean Acheson, NARA, Record Group 59, Department of State File No. 611.6131/7-2046.

338. Letter dated August 1, 1946, from Undersecretary of State Dean Acheson to Congressman Jerry Voorhis, NARA, Record Group 59, Department of State File No. 611.6131/7-2046.

339. Letter dated July 20, 1946, from Congressman Jerry Voorhis to Clair Wilcox, NARA, Record Group 59, Department of State File No. 611.6131/7-2046.

340. Letter dated July 31, 1945, from Clair Wilcox to Congressman Jerry Voorhis, NARA, Record Group 59, Department of State File No. 611.6131/7-2046.

341. Ibid.

by then had abandoned the project, but Wilcox sought not to antagonize Voorhis unnecessarily and chose not to tell him that no further progress was anticipated.

Voorhis replied to Acheson on August 5, expressing his pleasure at knowing that the Department was studying the matter of an FCN treaty with the Soviet Union. He added that he wished that he were not compelled to leave for California right away so that he could take advantage of Acheson's offer to discuss the treaty.[342] Voorhis seems not to have pursued the matter further and, three months later, he was defeated for re-election by a little known Navy veteran named Richard Milhous Nixon.

342. Letter dated August 5, 1946, from Congressman Jerry Voorhis to Undersecretary of State Dean Acheson, NARA, Record Group 59, Department of State File No. 611.6131/8-546.

3

Seeking a Multilateral Treaty on Investment

The International Trade Organization

Prior to the end of the Second World War, the U.S. government believed that the principal problems of the international economy revolved around trade and monetary policy, although policymakers knew that after the war they would also face the temporary problem of European reconstruction. As discussed in Chapter 1, the 1944 Bretton Woods conference addressed the problem of monetary policy through the establishment of the International Monetary Fund and the problem of European reconstruction through the creation of the International Bank for Reconstruction and Development.

The United States intended to address the problem of international trade through a third multilateral institution, an international trade organization. Months before formally entering the war, the United States was already publicly linking postwar economic prosperity with liberalized trade. For example, the Atlantic Charter, adopted by the United States and the United Kingdom on August 12, 1941, declared that these two countries would "endeavor, with due respect for their existing obligations, to further the enjoyment by all states, great or small, victor or vanquished, of access, on equal terms, to the trade and to the raw materials of the world which are needed for their economic prosperity."[1]

The Atlantic Charter was not a free trade manifesto. In 1932, the United Kingdom had established its imperial preference system, which provided for special trade preferences within the British Empire while imposing barriers to trade with countries outside the empire. A major goal of U.S. foreign trade policy after 1932 was to dismantle that system.[2] The reference to "due respect for . . . existing

1. The negotiations with respect to this language are described in Alan P. Dobson, *The Politics of the Anglo-American Economic Special Relationship, 1940–1987* (New York: St. Martin's Press, 1988), pages 25–31; Robert Dallek, *Franklin Roosevelt and American Foreign Policy, 1932–1945* (New York: Oxford University Press, 1979), pages 281–284; and Lloyd C. Gardner, *Economic Aspects of New Deal Diplomacy* (Madison: University of Wisconsin Press, 1964), pages 275–280.

2. John M. Rothgeb Jr., *U.S. Trade Policy: Balancing Economic Dreams and Political Realities* (Washington, DC: Congressional Quarterly Press, 2001), pages 66–68.

obligations" was a concession to the United Kingdom, which hoped to maintain the imperial preference system after the war.[3] Roosevelt, always the pragmatist, accepted the idea that compromises with respect to trade liberalization would be necessary.[4] The Atlantic Charter nevertheless did call for liberalized trade, and the destruction of the British system remained a primary objective of U.S. postwar trade policy.[5]

The United States continued to pressure the British, particularly during the negotiation of the agreement governing the operation of the Lend-Lease program, under which the United States provided military assistance to Britain. When the two countries signed the agreement in February 1942, Article VII stated that the terms and conditions of the assistance

> shall not be such as to burden commerce between the two countries, but to promote mutually advantageous relations between them and the betterment of world-wide economic relations. To that end, they shall include provisions for agreed action by the United States and the United Kingdom, open to participation by all other countries of like mind, directed to the expansion, by appropriate international and domestic measures, of production, employment, and the exchange and consumption of goods, which are the material foundations of the liberty and welfare of all peoples; to the elimination of all forms of discriminatory treatment in international commerce, and to the reduction of tariffs and other trade barriers. . . .[6]

The Lend-Lease agreement seemed to commit the United Kingdom to the eventual end of the imperial preference system[7] and to the creation of an international regime to promote trade liberalization, a commitment that the United States wanted in exchange for its assistance during the war.[8] During the course of the

3. Patrick J. Hearden, *Architects of Globalism: Building a New World Order during World War II* (Fayetteville: University of Arkansas Press, 2002), pages 31–32.

4. Thomas W. Zeiler, *Free Trade, Free World: The Advent of GATT* (Chapel Hill: University of North Carolina Press, 1999), page 26

5. Rothgeb, *U.S. Trade Policy,* pages 66–68.

6. Clair Wilcox, *A Charter for World Trade* (New York: MacMillan, 1949), page 38.

7. Despite the language of Article VII, Roosevelt sent a private letter to Churchill in which he assured Churchill that the United States was not asking Britain for "a commitment in advance" to abolish the imperial preference system, and that Article VII contained no such commitment. Dobson, *Politics,* page 33.

8. Patrick Hearden argues that the Treasury Department wanted to require Great Britain after the war to repay the United States with natural resources, such as rubber and tin. The State Department, however, did not wish to impose repayment requirements that might impede

war, the United States entered into similar lend-lease agreements with more than 30 countries, including most members of the United Nations.[9]

Secretary of State Cordell Hull had been calling for the creation of an "international trade agreement congress" since at least 1916, when he was a congressman from Tennessee.[10] In 1942, an interagency committee led by Hull's State Department began work on a formal proposal for an International Trade Organization to promote multilateral trade negotiations.[11] The committee included representatives of the Departments of State, Treasury, Commerce, Justice, Agriculture, and Labor, and the Tariff Commission, and was chaired by the assistant secretary of state for Economic Affairs, first Myron Taylor, then Dean Acheson, and then Will Clayton.[12]

In September 1943, the United States and the United Kingdom began "informal exploratory conversations at the expert level" regarding the implementation of Article VII of the Lend-Lease Agreement,[13] discussions known as "Article VII conversations." That same month, even before the discussions with the British began, the United States extended a similar invitation to its wartime ally, the Soviet Union.[14] In October, the United States submitted a formal proposal to the Soviet Union, but no discussions ever occurred.[15] The Soviet Union believed that the developed countries sought free trade so that they could dominate overseas markets, and that the development of Eastern Europe required a protected market.[16] In 1944, the United States began conversations with Canada.[17]

British recovery, and sought instead to trade military assistance for a British commitment to dismantle the imperial preference system. Hearden, *Architects of Globalism,* pages 29–30.

9. Memorandum dated October 11, 1945, concerning the commercial and economic program of the United States in relation to the U.S.S.R., NARA, Record Group 59, Department of State File No. 611.6131/10-1145.

10. Statement of Clair Wilcox, *International Trade Organization,* Hearings Before the Committee on Finance, United States Senate, 80th Cong. 1st Sess., Parts 1 and 2 (1947), pages 42–43.

11. Ibid., page 44.

12. Ibid.

13. Memorandum dated October 11, 1945, concerning the commercial and economic program of the United States in relation to the U.S.S.R., NARA, Record Group 59, Department of State File No. 611.6131/10-1145; Statement of Clair Wilcox, *International Trade Organization,* Hearings Before the Committee on Finance, United States Senate, 80th Cong. 1st Sess., Parts 1 and 2 (1947), page 52.

14. Memorandum dated October 11, 1945, concerning the commercial and economic program of the United States in relation to the U.S.S.R., NARA, Record Group 59, Department of State File No. 611.6131/10-1145.

15. Ibid.

16. E. F. Penrose, *Economic Planning for the Peace* (Princeton, NJ: Princeton University Press, 1953), page 112.

17. Wilcox, *Charter,* page 38.

The trade discussions between the United States and the United Kingdom progressed much more slowly than their discussions leading to the postwar Bretton Woods system. The United States remained committed to the system of bilateral trade negotiations authorized by the Reciprocal Trade Agreements Act, in part because it feared the difficulties of obtaining congressional approval of anything more ambitious, and thus initially exercised caution in the development of a proposal for a multilateral trading regime. The United Kingdom, by contrast, was willing to abandon its imperial preference system only in exchange for a multilateral reduction in trade barriers, in order to ensure that it would find sufficient new markets for its exports, particularly in the developing world, to replace those that would be lost when the preference system was abolished.[18] By 1943, however, the British government had become the principal cause of delay.[19] The British cabinet was deeply concerned that nothing it could expect to gain from the International Trade Organization negotiations would be sufficient to offset the loss to its export trade attributable to the abandonment of the imperial preference system. Further, the United States wanted to prohibit quantitative restrictions on trade, and the British cabinet believed that the United Kingdom needed to retain the discretion to impose such restrictions in the event of a balance of payments crisis. As a result, discussions between the two countries halted from late 1943 until early 1945, well after the conclusion of the Bretton Woods conference.[20]

THE PROPOSAL FOR AN INTERNATIONAL TRADE ORGANIZATION

By July 1945, the United States and the United Kingdom had prepared a formal "Proposal to Establish an International Trade Organization."[21] The proposed International Trade Organization (ITO) would address five concerns: the relaxation of trade barriers, the maintenance of full employment, the elimination of private restrictive business practices, the regulation of international commodity agreements (which in effect were cartel agreements negotiated by sovereign nations), and the establishment of an international organization to discuss trade problems.

The promotion of full employment, of course, was the quintessential goal of New Deal economic policy, and the liberalization of trade and the regulation of restrictive business practices were long-standing New Deal policies. The

18. Penrose, *Economic Planning*, pages 87–103, 107.

19. Ibid., page 104.

20. Richard N. Gardner, *Sterling-Dollar Diplomacy in Current Perspective: The Origins and the Prospects of Our International Economic Order* (New York: Columbia University Press, 1980), page 145.

21. Memorandum dated October 11, 1945, concerning the commercial and economic program of the United States in relation to the U.S.S.R., NARA, Record Group 59, Department of State File No. 611.6131/10-1145.

proposed ITO Charter reflected a projection of the New Deal onto the international economy.

The State Department forwarded the proposal to President Truman on September 7, 1945.[22] No part of the memorandum to the president referred to investment promotion or protection. Four days after receiving the State Department's memorandum, Truman approved the proposal.[23]

The two governments did not immediately publish their proposal. In late August 1945, Truman had abruptly cancelled U.S. assistance to Britain under the Lend-Lease program, the rationale being that Germany's surrender had ended the military action that justified the program. The sudden loss of assistance threatened Britain with financial disaster. In September, John Maynard Keynes led a British delegation to the United States to settle accounts under Lend-Lease and to request new assistance to take the place of the Lend-Lease program. The negotiations were exceedingly difficult, with the parties trapped between American public opinion, which with the end of the war opposed any further U.S. assistance to Europe, and British public opinion, which held that Britain's extraordinary sacrifices during the war to defeat a common enemy justified further assistance.[24] After several weeks, the two countries agreed that the United States would forgive the United Kingdom's obligation to repay some $20 billion in Lend-Lease assistance and would extend to the United Kingdom a $3.75 billion interest-bearing loan.[25] To convey the impression that the United States had obtained something in exchange for the Lend-Lease settlement and the loan, specifically, U.K. support for the creation of the ITO, the State Department delayed announcement of agreement on the ITO proposal until the financial negotiations were completed. The impression conveyed was not entirely false. Clayton had told the British that the United States could not extend any further assistance without a promise that the United Kingdom would participate in establishing the ITO and ratify the Bretton Woods agreements.[26]

In December 1945, with the financial negotiations between the two countries completed, the United States published the ITO proposal under a new name, *Proposals for Expansion of World Trade and Employment*.[27] As this indicates,

22. Memorandum dated September 7, 1945, from Dean Acheson to the President, NARA, Record Group 59, Department of State File No. 611.0031/9-1145.

23. Memorandum dated October 11, 1945, concerning the commercial and economic program of the United States in relation to the U.S.S.R., NARA, Record Group 59, Department of State File No. 611.6131/10-1145.

24. Gardner, *Sterling-Dollar Diplomacy*, page 188.

25. Ibid., page 208.

26. Ibid., page 191.

27. Department of State, *Suggested Charter for an International Trade Organization of the United Nations* (Washington, DC: Government Printing Office, 1946), page III; William Diebold Jr., *The End of the I.T.O.* (Princeton, NJ: Princeton University, 1952), page 3; *Current Economic Developments*, November 17, 1947, page 13, NARA, Record Group 59, Department of State Lot Files.

U.S. policy was to advocate trade liberalization as a means to full employment. Internal State Department documents described the purpose of the ITO as being to "reduce trade barriers and promote employment."[28] The proposed name for the conference to create the ITO was the "International Conference on Trade and Employment."[29]

Copies of the proposal were sent to every country in the world.[30] Although the United States sponsored the proposal, the British government announced that it was in "full agreement on all important points" with the proposal.[31] Between October 1945 and December 1946, Belgium, Czechoslovakia, France, Greece, the Netherlands, Poland, and Turkey also endorsed the proposal.[32]

Hoping to include the Soviet Union in the organization, the United States and the United Kingdom included provisions to establish non-discriminatory trade between free market economies and state trading economies.[33] Trade on the basis of "commercial considerations" would be treated as the equivalent of trade on the basis of the most-favored-nation.[34] As a substitute for reduced tariffs, state trading economies would agree to purchase a certain quantity of imports.[35] This reflected the same pragmatism that prompted the State Department to consider negotiating an FCN treaty with the Soviet Union in 1945 and early 1946.

Following publication of its proposal, the United States invited 15 countries—Australia, Belgium, Brazil, Canada, China, Cuba, Czechoslovakia, France, India, Luxembourg, the Netherlands, New Zealand, South Africa, the U.S.S.R., and the United Kingdom—to attend a preparatory meeting to draft a proposed Charter for the ITO.[36] The countries were chosen because of their "commercial

28. *Current Economic Developments,* October 7, page 1, NARA, Record Group 59, Department of State Lot Files.

29. *Current Economic Developments,* July 9, 1945, page 3, NARA, Record Group 59, Department of State Lot Files; *Current Economic Developments,* October 7, page 1, NARA, Record Group 59, Department of State Lot Files.

30. Wilcox, *Charter,* page 40.

31. Joint Statement by the United States and the United Kingdom, December 6, 1945, *reprinted in Anglo-American Financial and Commercial Agreements,* Department of State Publication 2439, Commercial Policy Series 80 (Washington, DC: Government Printing Office, 1945).

32. Wilcox, *Charter,* page 39.

33. Memorandum dated October 11, 1945, concerning the commercial and economic program of the United States in relation to the U.S.S.R., NARA, Record Group 59, Department of State File No. 611.6131/10-1145.

34. Ibid.

35. Ibid.

36. *Official Report of the United States Delegation to the United Nations Conference on Trade and Employment, Havana, Cuba,* NARA, Record Group 43, International Trade Files, Box 148, Folder marked "Official Report of the United States Delegation to the United Nations Conference on Trade and Employment, Havana, Cuba."

importance and diverse economic systems."[37] All of the countries except the Soviet Union accepted.[38]

At the behest of the United States, the United Nations Economic and Social Council, at its first meeting on February 18, 1946, adopted a resolution whereby it decided to sponsor the proposed conference.[39] The Council also formed a 19-nation preparatory committee to prepare the draft Charter.[40] The preparatory committee comprised the United States, the 15 countries invited by the United States, and Chile, Lebanon, and Norway.

In September 1946, the United States published a draft Charter as a basis for public discussion.[41] Article I(3) identified one of the Charter's purposes as being "[t]o encourage and assist the industrial and general economic development of Member countries, particularly those still in the early stages of industrial development."[42] Internal State Department documents also identified the promotion of the economic development of member nations as one of the purposes of the Charter.[43] The protection or promotion of foreign investment, however, was not cited in internal State Department reports as one of the Charter's purposes[44] nor was it included as a purpose in Article 1 of the proposed Charter. Rather, the Charter would promote economic development primarily by increasing world trade.

Most provisions of the Charter dealt with free and non-discriminatory international trade, including limitations on subsidies and prohibitions on discriminatory practices by state trading enterprises and on anticompetitive business practices. Article 23 of the proposed Charter prohibited exchange controls on trade transactions, but allowed them with respect to capital transfers,[45] an approach that was consistent with that of the IMF Articles of Agreement.

37. Zeiler, *Free Trade, Free World,* page 61.

38. The U.S.S.R.'s official reason for refusing to participate in the work of the committee was that the Soviet Union "had not found it possible to devote sufficient preliminary study to the important questions" to be discussed. Department of State, *Draft Charter for the International Trade Organization of the United Nations,* Department of State Publication 2927, Commercial Policy Series 106 (Washington, DC: Government Printing Office, 1947), page 6.

39. *Current Economic Development,* November 17, 1947, page 13, NARA, Record Group 59, Department of State Lot Files; Department of State, *Suggested Charter for an International Trade Organization of the United Nations* (Washington, DC: Government Printing Office, 1946), page III.

40. Ibid., page 13.

41. Department of State, *Suggested Charter for an International Trade Organization of the United Nations* (Washington, DC: Government Printing Office, 1946).

42. Ibid., page 1.

43. *Current Economic Developments,* July 29, 1946, page 15, NARA, Record Group 59, Department of State Lot Files.

44. Ibid.

45. Ibid., page 17; *Current Economic Developments,* July 23, 1945, page 3, NARA, Record Group 59, Department of State Lot Files; *Current Economic Developments,* July 29, 1946, page 17, NARA, Record Group 59, Department of State Lot Files.

The proposed Charter also included a dispute resolution mechanism. Article 76 provided that questions regarding the interpretation of the Charter would be referred to an executive board and then to a conference of the members. Justiciable issues arising out of a ruling of the conference could be referred to the International Court of Justice.

The proposed Charter did include a reference to investment protection. Under Article 50, one of the functions of the ITO was "[t]o make recommendations for international agreements designed to improve the bases of trade and to assure just and equitable treatment for the enterprises, skills, capital, arts and technology brought from one country to another, including agreements on the treatment of foreign nationals and enterprises, on the treatment of commercial travelers, on commercial arbitration, and on the avoidance of double taxation." This provision of the Charter was based on the evolving language of the U.S. policy statement on investment, discussed in Chapter 1, which by this time already called for intergovernmental cooperation to ensure just and equitable treatment for private investment.

THE LONDON PREPARATORY CONFERENCE

The Preparatory Committee met for the first time in London from October 15 to November 26, 1946, using the United States' suggested Charter as the principal basis for discussion.[46] The Committee adopted a draft Charter consisting of 74 articles.

At the opening of the London conference "a considerable number of countries emphasized their interest in industrialization and other aspects of economic development, indicated that in their view the provisions in the Draft Charter were inadequate to meet the needs of under-developed countries, and asked that the provisional agenda be modified to allow full discussion of this subject."[47] These "under-developed countries," led by Australia, India, Brazil, and Chile,[48] believed that provisions on economic development were a "necessary and proper" part of the Charter.[49] The United States recognized that developed countries were the most lucrative markets for U.S. exports and that the wealth created when a country developed economically, through trade, would be shared with other countries.[50]

46. Department of State, *Charter for the International Trade Organization of the United Nations* (Washington, DC: Government Printing Office, 1947), page I.

47. Official Report of the United States Delegation to the First Meeting of the Preparatory Committee for the International Conference on Trade and Employment, London, England, October 15, 1946, *reprinted as* Exhibit IV-D in *International Trade Organization*, Hearings Before the Committee on Finance, United States Senate, 80th Congress, First Session, on Trade Agreements System and Proposed International Trade Organization Charter, Part 2 (Washington, DC: Government Printing Office, 1947), page 909.

48. Gardner, *Sterling-Dollar Diplomacy*, page 365.

49. Statement of Under Secretary William Clayton, *International Trade Organization*, Hearings Before the Committee on Finance, United States Senate, 80th Congress, First Session, on Trade Agreements System and Proposed International Trade Organization Charter, Part 1 (Washington, DC: Government Printing Office, 1947), page 4.

50. Ibid., pages 5–6.

Thus, the promotion of economic development abroad was in the economic interest of the United States.

At the suggestion of the United States,[51] the London conference established a Joint Committee on Industrial Development, which decided that the Charter should be expanded to include a chapter on economic development.[52] Discussions within the Joint Committee stressed that economic development required "adequate supplies of capital funds, materials, equipment, advanced technology, trained workers, and managerial skill."[53] Further, "unless capital funds [were] available it may often be impossible to obtain the various other facilities in question."[54] The Joint Committee recognized that developing countries usually would need to obtain these facilities from abroad, and thus delegations from developing countries formulated the problem of development as "securing agreement that such facilities would be obtainable from other countries on as favorable terms as possible."[55] Developing countries at London expressed the view that developed countries had an obligation to make capital available for economic development in accordance with the development policy of the capital importing country, including local participation in management and local retention of an adequate share of the returns.[56]

The Joint Committee also recognized that the Charter must consider as well the interests of the countries supplying the facilities. Accordingly, the Joint Committee approved a text that recognized the "reciprocal obligations" of countries providing and countries receiving assistance.[57]

The text recognizing these reciprocal obligations comprised two articles, Article 11 and Article 12. Under Article 11, the members undertook "to promote the continuing industrial and general economic development of their respective

51. Wilcox, *Charter*, page 42.

52. Official Report of the United States Delegation to the First Meeting of the Preparatory Committee for the International Conference on Trade and Employment, London, England, October 15, 1946, *reprinted as* Exhibit IV-D in *International Trade Organization*, Hearings Before the Committee on Finance, United States Senate, 80th Congress, First Session, on Trade Agreements System and Proposed International Trade Organization Charter, Part 2 (Washington, DC: Government Printing Office, 1947), page 909.

53. Ibid.

54. Ibid.

55. Ibid., page 910.

56. Memorandum by John Parke Young headed "An International Investment Code: Proposals Likely to be Advanced by Underdeveloped Countries," dated April 8, 1947, NARA, Record Group 43, International Trade Files, Box 55, Folder marked "Investment."

57. Official Report of the United States Delegation to the First Meeting of the Preparatory Committee for the International Conference on Trade and Employment, London, England, October 15, 1946, *reprinted as* Exhibit IV-D in *International Trade Organization*, Hearings Before the Committee on Finance, United States Senate, 80th Congress, First Session, on Trade Agreements System and Proposed International Trade Organization Charter, Part 2 (Washington, DC: Government Printing Office, 1947), page 910.

countries. . . ."[58] Further, under Article 12, the members recognized that "progressive economic development is dependent upon the availability of adequate supplies of: (a) capital funds; and (b) materials, equipment, advanced technology, trained workers and managerial skill."[59] Accordingly, the members agreed "to impose no unreasonable impediments that would prevent other Members from obtaining access to facilities required for their economic development."[60] This language was balanced by a provision that host states would take no "unreasonable action injurious" to the interests of members, business entities, or persons supplying them with facilities for their development.[61] Further, upon receipt of a complaint of a violation of these obligations, the organization was authorized to request the members concerned to consult regarding the complaint and to lend its good offices toward that end.[62]

The language was the result of a compromise.[63] Developing countries sought language that would impose on developed countries an obligation to provide resources to countries in the process of development.[64] The United States replied that the facilities necessary for development should be obtained through trade and that the Charter provision should do no more than prohibit members from imposing unreasonable impediments on private sellers willing to trade with developing countries.

The London conference thus took three important steps with respect to capital movements. First, it linked economic development to the provision of foreign capital. Second, it imposed obligations regarding international capital movements on both capital exporting and capital importing states. Third, it adopted a principle of "reasonableness" to govern the extent of those obligations. That is, capital exporting countries were obligated to impose no unreasonable impediments to capital movements, while capital importing countries were obligated not

58. Department of State, *Charter for the International Trade Organization of the United Nations* (Washington, DC: Government Printing Office, 1947), page 4.

59. Ibid., Article 12(1).

60. Ibid., Article 12(2).

61. Ibid.

62. Article 12(5).

63. Statement of Clair Wilcox, *International Trade Organization,* Hearings Before the Committee on Finance, United States Senate, 80th Congress, First Session, on Trade Agreements System and Proposed International Trade Organization Charter, Part 1 (Washington, DC: Government Printing Office, 1947), page 143. *See also* Memorandum dated December 18, 1946, and headed "Chapter on Economic Development in ITO London Draft Charter," NARA, Record Group 43, International Trade Files, Box 61, Folder marked "National Foreign Trade Council—Carroll Report."

64. Cleona Lewis, an economist at the Brookings Institution who specialized in international investment, reported that the ITO Charter negotiations featured a proposal for a provision "making it a crime for any nation to discourage investors from sending their capital abroad, even to a country whose history shows expropriation of foreign property without compensation." Cleona Lewis, *The United States and Foreign Investment Problems* (Washington, DC: The Brookings Institution, 1948), page 264.

to take unreasonable action injurious to investment. In addition, the London conference retained the language authorizing the ITO to recommend agreements for the "just and equitable treatment" of investment.

The London conference marked the high point of U.S. influence with respect to the investment-related provisions of the ITO Charter. The negotiation of the Charter would continue through two more major conferences over a period of more than a year, but, at least with respect to investment policy, the United States would accomplish little more than it had already accomplished by the end of the London conference. The draft Charter that emerged from London had adopted the term "just and equitable treatment" as a descriptor of the type of treatment that foreign investment should receive, and had prohibited "unreasonable" action injurious to investment.

The London Preparatory Committee appointed a drafting committee, which met at the United Nations headquarters, then located at Lake Success, New York, from January 20 to February 15, 1947. The committee held 29 meetings to edit the draft Charter produced in London.[65] The Soviet Union was a member of the committee, but declined to attend.[66] Colombia and Mexico, which were not members, sent observers.[67]

THE PROPOSAL FOR AN INVESTMENT CODE

In February and March of 1947, the ECEFP held hearings on the ITO Charter in seven cities around the country "to afford all interested persons and groups an opportunity to present their views on the proposed Charter as a whole or on any part of it."[68] More than 240 witnesses testified, of which the great majority supported the Charter.[69] Witnesses included major business organizations such as the NFTC, the National Association of Manufacturers (NAM), the United States Chamber of Commerce, and the United States Associates of the International Chamber of Commerce (ICC).[70] Only 16 witnesses expressed opposition to the Charter, although more than 60 witnesses suggested improvements.

65. Department of State, *Charter for the International Trade Organization of the United Nations* (Washington, DC: Government Printing Office, 1947), page 5.

66. Report of the Drafting Committee of the Preparatory Committee of the United Nations Conference on Trade and Employment, NARA, Record Group 43, International Trade Files, Box 123, Folder marked "E/PC/T/34."

67. Ibid.

68. Report on Informal Hearings on Proposed Charter for an International Trade Organization, Exhibit V, *International Trade Organization,* Hearings Before the Committee on Finance, United States Senate, 80th Congress, First Session, on Trade Agreements System and Proposed International Trade Organization Charter, Part 1 (Washington, DC: Government Printing Office, 1947), page 917. The seven cities were Boston, Chicago, Denver, New Orleans, New York, San Francisco, and Washington, DC.

69. Ibid., page 936; *Current Economic Developments,* March 31, 1947, page 15, NARA, Record Group 59, Department of State Lot Files.

70. Wilcox, *Charter,* page 44.

The 1946 elections had brought the Republican Party to power in Congress. Republican senator Eugene Millikin of Colorado, the new chairman of the Senate Finance Committee, decided that the Committee should hold its own hearings on the proposed ITO Charter. The Senate Finance Committee conducted extensive hearings over a period from March 20 to April 3, 1947.[71]

As Will Clayton himself acknowledged in October 1946, American investors long had complained that the U.S. government did not give them "adequate political backing" with respect to the protection of their overseas investments.[72] Clayton noted that the United States traditionally had insisted upon payment of compensation for expropriation, but otherwise largely had left American investors to rely upon their own "initiative and enterprise."[73] Business groups lamented that the State Department refused to "use muscle" against foreign governments that defaulted on their loans, and yearned for the days when the marines would seize the customs houses of countries in default on their loans from foreign lenders.[74] In short, mere reliance upon diplomatic representation by the State Department had not provided sufficient protection, in the view of the U.S. investor community.[75]

By early 1947, when the ECEFP conducted its hearings, U.S. business groups already were on record as supporting the creation of an international legal regime for the protection of foreign investment. As noted in Chapter 2, the negotiation of the first FCN treaty with China had occurred amid strong expressions of support from the NFTC and the Chamber of Commerce for the negotiation of FCN treaties with as many nations as feasible. The business community's desire for stronger legal protection for foreign investment predated the inauguration of the postwar

71. Official Report of the United States Delegation to the United Nations Conference on Trade and Employment, Havana, Cuba, page 4, NARA, Record Group 43, International Trade Files, Box 148, Folder marked "Official Report of the United States Delegation to the United Nations Conference on Trade and Employment, Havana, Cuba."

72. "American Holdings Abroad Now Vital, Clayton Declares," *New York Times*, October 26, 1946. Lanxin Xiang has noted that American businessmen in the Far East in particular lamented the inadequacy of the support they received from the State Department. Lanxin Xiang, *Recasting the Imperial Far East: Britain and America in China, 1945–1950* (London: M. E. Sharpe, 1995), page 30.

73. Ibid.

74. David A. Baldwin, *Economic Development and American Foreign Policy, 1943–1962* (Chicago: University of Chicago Press, 1966), page 55.

75. An extended discussion of efforts by the State Department to protect U.S. foreign investment against expropriation and bond defaults in the early twentieth century may be found in Lewis, *United States and Foreign Investment Problems*, pages 220–227. Lewis found that the United States generally intervened only in cases where a foreign government discriminated against the entry of U.S. investment, "grossly violated" the rights of U.S. investors, expropriated U.S. investment, or discriminated against U.S. bondholders. She concluded that these efforts had "not always given the protection required to prevent real losses on existing investments, but to some extent they have encouraged new investments abroad." Ibid., page 279. U.S. government efforts to protect foreign investors in the raw materials sector are discussed in Stephen D. Krasner, *Defending the National Interest: Raw Materials Investment and U.S. Foreign Policy* (Princeton, NJ: Princeton University Press, 1978). Krasner concludes that "American policy-makers have consistently placed general

FCN treaty program, however. For example, on January 5, 1940, the NFTC had sent a letter to the State Department requesting that the FCN treaties be strengthened in ways useful to investors. Specifically, the NFTC had requested that the treaties guarantee that U.S. companies receive national treatment with respect to the protection of their property, require that compensation for expropriation be prompt and effective, and provide for arbitration of any dispute under the treaty.[76] That is, the NFTC wanted provisions that reflected norms of non-discrimination, security, and due process. The NFTC also requested that the treaties clarify that the protection for U.S.-owned property extended to local companies in which U.S. investors owned a controlling interest. The State Department replied by noting that U.S. FCN treaty provisions protecting property abroad extended to all property in the host state of whatever character, that the United States already had arbitration treaties in force with many countries, and that the Department was already considering the addition of the requirements of promptness and effectiveness to the provision on expropriation.[77]

So intent was the American business community on promoting international legal protection for investment that, following the announcement of the U.S. proposal for an international trade organization, the NAM and the Chamber of Commerce recommended the creation of a fourth international organization to deal with international investment.[78] The NFTC, by contrast, believed that FCN treaties could provide the necessary protection. It urged the negotiation of FCN treaties with "as many nations as are agreeable," with particular emphasis on those regions where U.S. foreign investment already existed or where such investments would be mutually advantageous.[79] Indeed, the NFTC's initial response to the ITO Charter was that the Charter should not be accepted as a substitute for the expansion of the FCN treaty program.[80]

Business groups soon realized, however, that the ITO Charter provided another means by which foreign investment could obtain legal protection. In December

foreign policy aims above security of supply. . . ." (148) In other words, "Nationalized companies have not been able to use state power for their own ends." (149) He attributes this to divisions within the business community prompted by fears that intervention on behalf of one injured investor will invite retaliation against other investors, and to the fact that decisions regarding a U.S. response typically are within the purview of the executive branch, which is less subject than Congress to the importuning of a particular investor. (149–150).

76. Letter dated January 5, 1940, from the National Foreign Trade Council to Secretary of State Cordell Hull, NARA, Record Group 59, Department of State File No. 711.002/60.

77. Letter dated February 1, 1940, from Assistant Secretary Henry F. Grady to the National Foreign Trade Council, NARA, Record Group 59, Department of State File No. 711.002/60.

78. Foreign Investment Policy Committee Minutes, July 11, 1946, NARA, Record Group 43, International Trade Files, Box 37, Folder marked "FIP Agenda & Lists."

79. Charles Carroll, "Comments on the Suggested Charter for an International Trade Organization," November 6, 1946, NARA, Record Group 43, International Trade Files, Box 60, File marked "National Foreign Trade Council—Carroll Rpt."

80. Ibid.

1946, two months before the hearings began, the ICC, at its annual meeting in Paris, adopted a resolution calling upon the negotiators of the ITO Charter to include a section on capital movements that would provide for the development of a code of "fair" practice with respect to foreign investment.[81]

When the ECEFP held its hearings in February and March of 1947, various business groups, particularly the NFTC, the NAM, and the United States Associates of the ICC, recommended amendment of the Charter to include provisions for the protection of foreign investment.[82] The proposal by U.S. business groups to inject investment-related matters into the ITO negotiations reflected more than a simple desire to use any available opportunity to gain legal protection for U.S. investments abroad. The NFTC in particular long had been concerned that the best bargaining leverage that the United States possessed for strengthening the position of U.S. investors abroad was the offer to lower U.S. trade barriers. When the ITO negotiations began, the NFTC expressed the concern that the lowering of trade barriers by the United States in the ITO negotiations would deplete U.S. bargaining power.[83] Any concessions with respect to the protection of investment that the United States did not obtain in exchange for its lowering of tariffs might not ever be obtained. Initially, the NFTC hoped that the United States would offer some concessions outside the multilateral framework so that they could be used in bilateral negotiations to protect investment. An alternative tactic was to bring investment matters into the ITO negotiations, thereby permitting U.S. negotiators to use the bargaining power represented by the offer to lower trade barriers to obtain better protection for U.S. foreign investment.

The hearings caused the Truman administration to reconsider an initial decision to avoid any further discussion of investment in the ITO Charter.[84] The NFTC, NAM, and U.S. Associates of the ICC pressured Will Clayton and Willard Thorp to include investment protection provisions in the ITO Charter, particularly provisions to create a commission within the ITO charged with protecting foreign investment, with the result that both men began to take a "strong personal interest" in the matter.[85] These groups told Clayton and Thorp that they would "'swallow' all other provisions" of the Charter and would "strongly support the ITO Charter *in toto*" in Congress if investment protection provisions

81. Letter dated January 31, 1947, from Arvid L. Frank to Clair Wilcox, NARA, Record Group 43, International Trade Files, Box 136, Folder marked "Trade (Geneva) Investment."

82. *Current Economic Developments,* March 31, 1947, page 15, NARA, Record Group 59, Department of State Lot Files.

83. Letter dated March 26, 1946, from National Foreign Trade Council president E.P. Thomas to Assistant Secretary of State Will Clayton, NARA, Record Group 59, Department of State File No. 611.0031/3-2646.

84. Memorandum by Edmund H. Kellogg dated April 2, 1947, and headed "Establishment of a Fourth Commission in ITO concerned with Economic Development and Protection of U.S. Investments Abroad," NARA, Record Group 43, International Trade Files, Box 41, Folder marked "ITO—General (1)."

85. Ibid.

were included.[86] The pressure led Clair Wilcox to declare as well that he "strongly favored" creating an investment protection commission in the ITO.[87]

In early April, the ICC released a lengthy report on the draft ITO Charter.[88] The ICC criticized the prohibition in Article 12 on "unreasonable" action on the grounds that the term "unreasonable" was too vague and provided a basis for justifying host state action. That is, rather than seeing Article 12 as introducing a new norm of investment protection that improved the position of foreign investors, the ICC regarded the reasonableness principle as providing a shelter for host state regulatory action that met the "vague" norm of reasonableness.[89] The report was not entirely critical. For example, the ICC welcomed the role of the ITO in dispute settlement. The ICC again recommended that the ITO adopt a code of fair practice with respect to private foreign investment.

DRAFTING AN INVESTMENT CODE

Following the February and March hearings, in which U.S. business interests called for the insertion of investment-related provisions into the ITO Charter, a working group within the State Department began to discuss the kinds of provisions that might be included.[90] The effort came at the behest of the business community, which wanted a code that would create opportunities for the establishment of foreign investment and would protect existing investment.

The project fell under the leadership of John Parke Young. Young in the spring of 1947 was a 51-year-old economist with a PhD from Princeton. He had taught economics at Occidental College for 15 years and then joined the administration in 1941. Young had represented the United States at conferences leading to the establishment of the IMF and the IBRD. In March 1944, he had been appointed assistant chief of the State Department's Division of Financial and Monetary Affairs, which was responsible for foreign investment policy. A year later, the division was renamed the Division for Economic Development and Young held the titles of associate chief of the Division and Advisor on Investment. Young would remain at the State Department until 1965, the year he turned 70. He was the author of a successful economics textbook, *The International Economy,* the first edition of which was published in 1942, with subsequent editions published at least until 1963. Young thus brought to the task the benefit of a broad understanding of international economics and the approach of a systemic thinker.

86. Ibid.

87. Ibid.

88. Report from the International Chamber of Commerce, dated April 14, 1947, NARA, Record Group 43, International Trade Files, Box 123, Folder marked "E/PC/T/35 to 125."

89. Ibid.

90. Memorandum headed "Investment Provisions for ITO Charter," dated April 25, 1947, from Joseph D. Coppock to Clair Wilcox, NARA, Record Group 43, International Trade Files, Box 136, Folder marked "Trade (Geneva) Investment."

On March 28, 1947, Young circulated a proposed outline of an investment code.[91] Young's responsibilities at that time included chairing the Foreign Investment Policy Committee established by the ECEFP in July 1945, and Young's outline followed closely the committee's notion of foreign investment policy, which was that the United States should promote outward investment, but only if it was desirable from a developmental perspective. The outline did not attempt to provide the language of the code itself, but rather it described the kinds of provisions that should be included.

A plurality of its provisions sought to eliminate barriers to capital movements and to protect investment once established. The proposal called for free entry of capital, except where "the national interest is paramount"; national and MFN treatment of investment, again subject to limited exceptions in the national interest; payment of prompt, adequate, and effective compensation for expropriation; free transfer of funds, except in cases of extreme scarcity of foreign exchange; settlement of loan defaults; sharing of "investment information"; third party settlement of investment disputes; and the negotiation of FCN and double taxation treaties. It also would prohibit local participation requirements (i.e., host country laws requiring foreign investors to permit local investors to acquire an interest in the investment), again except where the national interest was paramount, and unfair competition by state enterprises. Young's farsighted proposal thus embraced principles of access, non-discrimination, security, due process, and transparency. Reflecting the novelty of the reasonableness principle in foreign investment policy, Young's proposal did not include a general obligation of reasonable treatment, notwithstanding that a reasonableness standard was already in the London draft of the ITO Charter.

Several provisions would have regulated international capital movements in the public interest. Young's proposal called for preventing anticompetitive practices and discouraging investments that required tariff protection or subsidies to be competitive. It stated that foreign investors should provide opportunities for local participation in the investment.

The proposed code also addressed the conduct of capital exporting states. It provided that states should impose no obstacles to the export of capital goods, except in the case of temporary scarcities, and should prevent anticompetitive practices. The responsibility of capital exporting states thus was largely to facilitate the operation of the market, by removing state-imposed capital export controls and preventing monopolistic practices.

Finally, Young's proposed code addressed the behavior of foreign investors. It provided that they should refrain from participation in local political affairs, and should observe the laws of the host country.

On April 18, Young and two other members of the working group, Woodbury Willoughby and Herman Walker, met at the Federal Reserve Bank of New York with some 20 representatives of seven groups representing the interests of foreign investors, to discuss the prospect of including investment provisions in

91. Memorandum from John Parke Young headed "Investment Code," dated March 28, 1947, NARA, Record Group 43, International Trade Files, Box 136, Folder marked "Trade (Geneva) Investment."

the Charter.[92] The business groups represented were the American Bankers Association, the Chamber of Commerce, the Foreign Bondholders Protective Council, the Investment Bankers Association of America, the NAM, the NFTC, and the U.S. Associates of the International Chamber of Commerce. The meeting thus included representatives of major direct and portfolio investors.

All three State Department representatives were professional economists. Young's PhD was from Princeton, Walker had a PhD from Duke and a master's degree from Harvard, and Willoughby earned his PhD from Johns Hopkins. Yet, the three men brought to the meeting not an argument about the economics of foreign investment, but an assessment of the harsh political realities of seeking an investment code.

Young opened the meeting by explaining that the State Department had given "considerable thought" to some kind of international agreement on investment principles and in particular to the idea of including an investment section in the ITO Charter.[93] He then gave the floor to Walker and Willoughby, who would deliver some sobering truths. Walker argued that developing countries sought foreign capital, but wanted it on their own terms and would not sign a treaty with the assurances desired by the United States unless the treaty was "full of escape clauses."[94] Willoughby contended that any kind of treaty that emerged from a multilateral meeting would be based on the "least common denominator" and would be so weak as to be unsatisfactory. The existence of such a multilateral treaty would render more difficult the task of negotiating bilateral treaties with stronger protection. Finally, he said, the United States would not have sufficient bargaining power at the next preparatory conference, to be held in Geneva, to obtain investment provisions that other countries did not want. Young tried to end the Department's presentation with a mildly positive comment. He explained that, although the Department "was impressed with the difficulties," it nevertheless was desirous of doing what it could under the circumstances.[95]

The business representatives, for their part, sought to stiffen the spines of the three economists. The first business representative to speak was Warren Pierson of the U.S. Associates of the International Chamber of Commerce, who raised the question of obtaining national treatment for American investors overseas.[96] Pierson's question, however, failed to have its intended effect. The attendees generally acknowledged that the United States did not itself provide unqualified national treatment and, therefore, was not in a position to demand it from other countries. The ensuing discussion nevertheless gave several business

92. Memorandum of Conversation, headed "Foreign Investment Policy—Meeting with Business Groups at the Federal Reserve Bank of New York, April 18, 1947," dated April 23, 1947, NARA, Record Group 43, International Trade Files, Box 136, Folder marked "Trade (Geneva) Investment."

93. Ibid.

94. Ibid.

95. Ibid.

96. Ibid.

representatives the opportunity to criticize the State Department for failing to do enough to assist American investors abroad. Young, again trying to maintain a positive atmosphere, replied that the Department stood ready to assist investors whenever they were unable through their own efforts to obtain "fair" treatment.[97]

Several business representatives also challenged Willoughby's claim that the United States would not have sufficient bargaining power at Geneva to obtain a satisfactory investment code. W. W. Cumberland of the NAM argued that the United States could use its lending power as leverage to obtain a satisfactory code. He said that the United States should withhold all capital from countries that refused to promise fair treatment for foreign investment. The group as a whole shared this sentiment.[98] As would happen repeatedly during the Truman administration, the U.S. business community urged that the State Department use U.S. economic power to coerce other countries to conclude an agreement committing them to the protection of foreign investment.

Asked how the United States should proceed if agreement on acceptable principles proved impossible, the business representatives said that, as a last resort, the United States should agree to the formation of a commission that would prepare model agreements for future bilateral negotiations. The group again suggested that the State Department perhaps failed to recognize how much bargaining power it really had. The meeting closed with a suggestion by the State Department representatives that the business groups establish a committee to draft the provisions that they wanted included in the Charter.[99]

Following the meeting, Young's working group completed its proposed draft, which it forwarded to Clair Wilcox, the deputy head of the U.S. delegation in Geneva, on April 25.[100] The proposed draft called for national and MFN treatment with respect to the right to establish investment, although it contemplated exceptions in the national interest; payment of prompt, adequate, and effective compensation for expropriation; consultations with respect to loan defaults; and free transfer of payments except in times of scarcity of foreign exchange. It would discourage unfair competition by state enterprises, local participation requirements, and any other practices that would "increase unduly the burdens" on foreign investment. It proposed a role for the ITO in resolving disputes between investors and host countries. It also allowed each member to file with the ITO a statement of the treatment that it intended to afford investment, in effect allowing each member to declare that it would provide more favorable treatment than required by the Charter. Thus, the draft sought to promote norms of access, non-discrimination, security, due process, transparency, and, if "undue" meant "unreasonable," reasonableness.

97. Ibid.

98. Ibid.

99. Ibid.

100. Memorandum from Joseph D. Coppock to Clair Wilcox headed "Investment Provisions for ITO Charter," dated April 25, 1947, NARA, Record Group 43, International Trade Files, Box 136, Folder marked "Trade (Geneva) Investment."

The draft code also called for the regulation of international investment flows by both capital importing and capital exporting countries. Under the draft code, all members would agree to discourage investment that would result in unfair economic or political advantages, that would lower or impede the progressive development of labor standards, or that would give rise to anticompetitive practices.

The draft sent to Wilcox on April 25 was substantively quite similar to that proposed by Young four weeks before, although slightly less ambitious. Some of the provisions imposing obligations on host states were softened so that mandatory language became precatory. The obligations that the earlier draft imposed on investors disappeared as did the obligation on capital exporting states to remove export controls. In short, the April 25 draft weakened, to some degree, the obligations imposed on everyone. Yet, in some respects it was stronger. It imposed a new general prohibition on "undue" burdens on foreign investment, and sought to prevent the lowering of labor standards. Further, the novel concept of a statement describing the treatment that each member intended to afford foreign investment in some respects addressed the weakened nature of some of the investment protection provisions, while increasing transparency.

In the same memorandum in which the working group transmitted its proposed code, the group reported to Wilcox that, despite the effort expended in developing the code, the members had "serious misgivings" about the entire project.[101] The group noted that the U.S. business community wanted both increased business opportunities abroad and greater protection for foreign investment. The business community believed that the State Department had not given U.S. foreign investors sufficient assistance in the past. Business leaders were prepared to see such assistance provided through bilateral treaties, multilateral treaties or otherwise, but they wanted more than they believed that they were receiving through the U.S. FCN treaty program, diplomacy, or economic policies.

The working group believed, however, that it would be impossible at Geneva to negotiate detailed provisions to protect foreign investment. As the group explained to Wilcox, "It would mean all of the complications of the China [FCN] Treaty negotiations multiplied by the number of countries present."[102] Even if a multilateral convention could be negotiated, the result would "almost certainly" provide less protection than customary law[103] or existing treaties.[104] Developing countries likely would demand an assurance that they would receive investment in exchange for concessions with regard to investment protection, and the United

101. Ibid.

102. Ibid. *See also* Memorandum dated April 7, 1947, from Joseph Coppock to Paul Nitze, NARA, Record Group 43, International Trade Files, Box 55, Folder marked "Investment."

103. Under international law, nations are bound by certain rules of law that originate not in treaties, but in the customary practice of states. Such rules must reflect a general and consistent practice in which states engage under a sense of legal obligation. Ian Brownlie, *Principles of Public International Law* (New York: Oxford University Press, 7th edition, 2008), page 6.

104. Memorandum from Joseph D. Coppock to Clair Wilcox headed "Investment Provisions for ITO Charter," dated April 25, 1947, NARA, Record Group 43, International Trade Files, Box 136, Folder marked "Trade (Geneva) Investment."

States was not in a position to promise that private investment would be forthcoming. Further, countries might be unwilling to grant in the ITO Charter concessions regarding foreign investment protection that they could offer the United States in exchange for something of value in bilateral negotiations.

The United States might attempt to avoid detailed provisions that provided low standards of protection by proposing language in the form of vague, general principles. Such language, however, would likely be useless. Thus, the working group believed, the best approach was simply to include in the Charter language providing for the negotiation of investment treaties in the future, an idea already included in the London draft.[105] Another alternative favored by the working group was to treat the ITO as a body for resolving investment disputes between the investor and the host state.

The working group also feared that any attempt to propose investment-related provisions would be characterized as an act of imperialist capitalism. A resulting anti-imperialist backlash could threaten the negotiation of the entire Charter. Injecting investment into the Charter might taint it in the mind of the American public, which was suspicious of U.S. multinational companies.

State Department policymakers recognized that developing countries would not be concerned merely about U.S. multinationals, but about the entire American free enterprise system. In a memorandum dated April 16, 1947, Woodbury Willoughby feared that developing countries would regard a proposed investment code as an American attempt to impose its economic system on them.[106] In light of this possible problem, Willoughby believed that the United States should not use its limited bargaining power at Geneva in a futile attempt to obtain more than it had already obtained in London.

PROPOSING AN INVESTMENT CODE IN GENEVA

The Preparatory Committee met again in Geneva from April 10 to August 22, 1947. By the time that the State Department representatives met with the business groups at the Federal Reserve Bank in New York, Will Clayton, who was heading the U.S. ITO delegation, was already in Geneva.

On May 1, the State Department sent a telegram to Clayton in Geneva to report on the New York meeting and to inform the Geneva delegation that the Department was considering the inclusion of an investment section in the Charter, a draft of which in fact the Department had already sent to Clair Wilcox,[107]

105. *See also* Memorandum dated April 7, 1947, from E. C. Carlson to Woodbury Willoughby, NARA, Record Group 43, International Trade Files, Box 55, Folder marked "Investment."

106. Memorandum from Woodbury Willoughby to Ness, headed "Some Problems Relating to Article on Investment for Inclusion in the ITO Charter," dated April 16, 1947, NARA, Record Group 43, International Trade Files, Box 55, Folder marked "Investment."

107. Telegram dated May 1, 1947, from the Department of State to the U.S. delegation in Geneva, NARA, Record Group 43, International Trade Files, Box 134, Folder marked "ITO (Geneva) Conference—From May 1, 1947 to June 1, 1947."

although it appears that Wilcox had not yet received it. The State Department reported that the business representatives "strongly" desired inclusion of "certain basic investment principles."[108] At the same time, the Department perceived numerous obstacles to the inclusion of an investment section, including "shortness of time, [the] attitude of underdeveloped and nationalistic countries whose conception of [an] investment code differs from that of US business groups, [the] possibility of final provisions['] being watered down and full of escape clauses due [to the] weak US bargaining position thereby perhaps prejudicing further bilateral negotiations, [and the] possibility [that] other countries will be critical [of a] US attempt to obtain protection for capitalist investments."[109] The Department also thought, however, that an investment section would yield "important advantages if feasible."[110] The Department told Clayton that the business representatives with whom it had met quoted him as assuring them that he would endeavor to include investment provisions in the Charter, and asked Clayton for confirmation.[111]

Five days later, on May 6, the same business groups that had met with State Department officials at the Federal Reserve Bank in New York asked the Department to relay a message to Clayton reaffirming the support of these groups for investment provisions in the ITO Charter. "We feel," said the business groups, "that the drafting and adopting of an international code of principles to govern foreign investment is an urgent and practicable object."[112] The business groups favored inclusion in the Geneva draft of either an investment code or an authorization for a commission to draft an investment code in the future. They also wanted the Charter to proclaim that the encouragement of foreign investment was one of its purposes.

Two days later, at the May 8 meeting of the U.S. delegation in Geneva, Clair Wilcox reported on the May 6 telegram received from the State Department relaying the business groups' call for an investment code. Wilcox noted the "restrained nature" of the communication.[113] These business groups were willing to give the U.S. delegation latitude in deciding whether to seek detailed investment provisions in the Charter or merely an agreement on general principles coupled with a commitment to form a commission that would develop an investment code later.

The delegation wanted to respond favorably to the wishes of the investor community, but that community had not expressed its expectations clearly. Herman Walker, who was not in Geneva but who had met with the business representatives

108. Ibid.

109. Ibid.

110. Ibid.

111. Ibid.

112. Telegram dated May 6, 1947, from the Department of State to the U.S. delegation in Geneva, NARA, Record Group 43, International Trade Files, Box 134, Folder marked "ITO (Geneva) Conference—From May 1, 1947 to June 1, 1947."

113. Second Meeting of the U.N. Preparatory Committee for the International Conference on Trade and Development Geneva, Minutes of Delegation Meeting, May 8, 1947, NARA, Record

at the Federal Reserve Bank in New York, believed that business interests were using the ITO Charter negotiations as an opportunity to pressure the State Department to adopt a stronger policy in favor of protecting foreign investment, and did not necessarily expect the Department to succeed in persuading the Geneva conference to incorporate an investment code into the Charter.[114]

At a delegation meeting in Geneva, Wilcox speculated that the indefiniteness in the position of the business groups reflected the fact that they had been unable to agree among themselves on the best strategy. After some discussion about how to proceed, Winthrop Brown, the Yale-educated lawyer who was then serving as the chief of the Division of Commercial Policy and who was the chief negotiator for the United States in Geneva on trade, suggested that the delegation attempt to obtain an investment code in Geneva, but if that effort should fail the delegation could "fall back on a commission."[115] John Walker Evans, a Commerce Department official sent to Geneva to work on the trade negotiations, observed that the first alternative might be feasible. With momentum in the delegation moving toward adoption of Brown's suggestion, Harry Hawkins, the former director of the Office of Economic Affairs, then serving as an economic advisor to the U.S. embassy in London, proposed that the delegation cable Washington immediately and ask for a draft by June 1 from the private groups of the kind of code that they wanted.

Following the meeting, the U.S. delegation notified the Department that it would endeavor to include investment provisions in the Charter, if they were received by early June.[116] The delegation said that, even if it was not possible to include investment provisions in the Charter, it could urge inclusion of investment-related language in the Charter's statement of purposes and a provision establishing a commission. The Geneva delegation thus had embraced the more ambitious goal of obtaining provisions in the Charter itself, rather than seeking only to obtain agreement on a commission to draft a code in the future.

The following day, Clair Wilcox reported that he had received the State Department working group's latest draft of a proposed investment code. He also

Group 43, International Trade Files, Box 133, Folder marked "Minutes U.S. Delegation (Geneva 1947) April–June 20, 1947."

114. Walker's view was recorded in undated handwritten notes taken by State Department attorney Walter Hollis at a meeting on the ITO Charter. The notes may be found in NARA, Record Group 59, Department of State Lot Files, Walter Hollis Papers, Folder marked "Walter Hollis Notes."

115. Second Meeting of the U.N. Preparatory Committee for the International Conference on Trade and Development Geneva, Minutes of Delegation Meeting, May 8, 1947, NARA, Record Group 43, International Trade Files, Box 133, Folder marked "Minutes U.S. Delegation (Geneva 1947) April–June 20, 1947."

116. Telegram dated May 8, 1947, from the U.S. delegation in Geneva to the Department of State, NARA, Record Group 43, International Trade Files, Box 134, Folder marked "ITO (Geneva) Conference—From May 1, 1947 to June 1, 1947."

noted that the draft was accompanied by "long arguments" as to why it should not be used.[117]

Despite the doubts expressed by the State Department working group and the ambivalence of business groups concerning the best strategy, the Geneva delegation adhered to its decision of the day before to propose a detailed provision on investment protection. The men responsible for the decision—men such as Clayton, Wilcox, Hawkins, Brown, and Evans—were all men whose primary interest and experience lay in the field of international trade, rather than international investment. Those primarily responsible for, and experienced in, foreign investment policy—such as the members of Young's working group—had advised against any attempt to incorporate an investment code into the ITO Charter, but the senior officials serving on the Geneva delegation, wanting to ensure business support for the ITO Charter and to honor the commitment that Clayton had made to business representatives to seek an investment code, ignored the advice of those in Washington working on investment policy. They believed that there would be little harm in at least making a proposal and then gauging the reaction. Not having yet received a formally approved policy from the Department[118] and facing a deadline for submission of amendments to the draft Charter, the Geneva delegation decided to prepare its own proposal.[119]

By May 20, the U.S. delegation had drafted its proposal.[120] The delegation's proposal was much shorter than the more elaborate code drafted by Young's working group. It added two important substantive provisions to the Charter, both in Article 12. First, it required members to grant to nationals and companies of the other members national treatment with respect to the opportunity to establish investment and with respect to the treatment of investment once established, subject to the right of the host state to make exceptions where "essential national interests" so required, provided that the exceptions were notified to the ITO.[121] In any event, members must accord MFN treatment to the nationals and companies of the other members. Second, it required members to pay prompt, adequate, and effective compensation for the expropriation of property.[122] These requirements

117. Second Meeting of the U.N. Preparatory Committee for the International Conference on Trade and Development Geneva, Minutes of Delegation Meeting, May 9, 1947, NARA, Record Group 43, International Trade Files, Box 133, Folder marked "Minutes U.S. Delegation (Geneva 1947) April–June 20, 1947."

118. The draft sent to Clair Wilcox on April 25 was the product of John Parke Young's working group, but had not yet been approved by the ECEFP.

119. Memorandum dated June 16, 1947, from John Parke Young to Will Clayton, NARA, Record Group 43, International Trade Files, Box 38, Folder marked "FIP Documents."

120. Second Meeting of the U.N. Preparatory Committee for the International Conference on Trade and Development Geneva, Minutes of Delegation Meeting, May 20, 1947, NARA, Record Group 43, International Trade Files, Box 133, Folder marked "Minutes U.S. Delegation (Geneva 1947) April–June 20, 1947."

121. U.S. Proposal dated May 22, 1947, NARA, Record Group 43, International Trade Files, Box 55, Folder marked "ITO–Investment (2)."

122. Ibid.

of non-discrimination and compensation for expropriation were the protections most desired by the business community.

The Geneva delegation's proposal also placed greater emphasis on the concept of fair and equitable treatment as a way of describing the general nature of the treatment that foreign investment should receive. It would have added to the statement of the ITO's purposes in Article 1 the encouragement of "the international flow of capital for productive investment through measures designed to ensure fair and equitable treatment of the legitimate interests of investors."[123] The London draft (as edited in New York), at Article 61, had authorized the ITO to recommend and promote international agreements on measures designed to ensure "just and equitable" treatment for the enterprise, skills, capital, arts, and technology brought from one member country to another. The U.S. proposal moved this language to Article 12, where it would appear with the other investment protection provisions, and added a specific reference to the future elaboration of a code on investment principles as one of the kinds of agreements that the ITO was authorized to recommend and promote.

The U.S. proposal would have made other changes as well. For example, to promote transparency, it would have added a new paragraph to Article 12 authorizing members to file with the ITO a statement of any conditions, requirements, or restrictions relating to the treatment or establishment of investment by nationals or companies of other members. The Charter would prohibit a member from acting inconsistently with any such statement, although a member could amend its statement. To execute the various responsibilities of the organization relating to investment, the U.S. proposal would have amended Article 72 to authorize the establishment of a commission on economic development and international investment.

Wilcox suggested a "comprehensive lobbying" campaign to build support among other delegations for the U.S. proposal.[124] He recommended, in particular, a series of lunches with members of other delegations. He said that he would meet with the delegates from the United Kingdom, Canada, Belgium, the Netherlands, and India. Wilcox expected the first four delegations to be among the strongest supporters of the U.S. proposal and India to be one of the harshest critics, and thus these were the most important meetings. Wilcox suggested a schedule whereby different pairs of U.S. delegates would hold separate lunches with the delegates from Australia, Brazil, Chile, China, and Cuba.

Two days later, Wilcox reported on his lunch with the U.K., Canadian, Belgian and Dutch delegations. He said that the U.S. proposal had been greeted with "enthusiasm" and that some delegates suggested that the U.S. proposal did not go far enough.[125] Although the minutes of the meeting do not identify those

123. Ibid.

124. Second Meeting of the U.N. Preparatory Committee for the International Conference on Trade and Development Geneva, Minutes of Delegation Meeting, May 20, 1947, NARA, Record Group 43, International Trade Files, Box 133, Folder marked "Minutes U.S. Delegation (Geneva 1947) April–June 20, 1947."

125. Ibid.

delegates, presumably they were the Belgian and Dutch ones. As time would show, those two delegations along with that of the United States were the delegations most sympathetic to the protection of foreign investment. Wilcox, in any event, acknowledged that the U.S. proposal "might run into more difficulties" with other delegations.[126] The lunches later in the week with other delegations would provide some indication of the general sentiment.

By May 27, the deadline to submit amendments to Chapter IV, the chapter on economic development where the U.S. investment provision would appear, had passed. Wilcox noted at the delegation meeting that morning that a large number of amendments had been submitted by various delegations. Chapter IV was scheduled for discussion at a meeting of Commission A that morning. Harry Hawkins suggested that Wilcox open the meeting with a statement on behalf of the proposal on investment. John Walker Evans warned that this would simply provide a target for opponents. After some discussion, the delegation decided to adopt Hawkins's suggestion.

At the first meeting of Commission A, the United States faced the delicate task of reorienting the discussion of economic development that had occurred in London toward a discussion of investor protection. Consideration of Chapter IV began at the May 27 meeting when the first two speakers, the delegates of Cuba and Czechoslovakia, inquired about the U.S. proposal.[127] Wilcox explained that, although economic development could be promoted through international financial institutions and public and private loans, the United States believed that the flow of direct investment capital that had been interrupted by the war should be renewed. The minimum rules required to encourage private foreign investment were non-discrimination and compensation for expropriation. Responding to a concern expressed by the delegate from Czechoslovakia, Wilcox denied that the U.S. proposal would require any country to accept foreign investment that it did not want.

The immediate reaction to the proposal was favorable. Delegates from a variety of countries—including Australia, Belgium, Brazil, Chile, China, France, and the Netherlands—expressed support for the proposal, while reserving the right to suggest amendments. The delegate from India, however, urged the United States not to press its proposal at this time. He argued that it could completely alter the nature of the Charter and render its acceptance more difficult. The delegate from Czechoslovakia argued that capital investment could not be treated the same way as trade in goods, and that rules regarding investment must be different from those relating to trade. Wilcox replied that, in light of the sympathy for the U.S. proposal expressed by the other delegates, the United States did not think that acceding to India's request would be appropriate. The commission referred

126. Ibid.

127. United Nations Conference on Trade and Development, Commission A, Summary Record of First Meeting, held on Tuesday, 27 May 1947, NARA, Record Group 43, International Trade Files, Box 123, Folder marked "E/PC/T/A/SR/1 to 43."

the U.S. amendments to a subcommittee consisting of Australia, Brazil, Chile, France, India, the United Kingdom, and the United States.[128]

At a general staff meeting the following day, Wilcox reported that his extemporaneous speech on behalf of the proposed investment provision at the Commission meeting the previous day had received "extraordinary support" from Australia, Belgium, Brazil, Chile, China, Cuba, France, and the Netherlands.[129] He believed that this reflected the success of the lunches held by the U.S. delegation the previous week to build support for the proposal. The British and Canadian delegations had remained silent at the Commission meeting, but Wilcox thought that their silence was fortunate because it helped to avoid criticism that the U.S. proposal was "a put up job by the industrialist countries."[130] He anticipated that both delegations would support the proposal, as would those from New Zealand and South Africa.

Wilcox had been surprised, however, that the delegation from India had attacked the U.S. proposal "vigorously," referring to the ITO Charter as a "banker's Charter," complaining that the United States had introduced the proposal without adequate preliminary consideration, and requesting that the United States withdraw the proposal.[131] Wilcox had left his lunch with the Indian delegation the previous week with the impression that the Indian delegation was "not particularly opposed" to the proposal.[132]

On the second day of Commission A's meeting, May 28, New Zealand defied Wilcox's optimistic prediction by expressing strong opposition to the U.S. proposal, arguing that it upset the balance of the Charter and that the language was both too general and too specific.[133] The delegate from India took the floor to suggest that the Charter must be revised to impose greater obligations on member states.[134] He said that the facilities needed for rapid economic development were not equally available to every country and, therefore, the Charter should make some arrangement for a sharing of such facilities on "fair and reasonable" terms.[135] The Indian delegation told the U.S. delegation that the Indians had been "caught

128. Ibid.

129. Second Meeting of the U.N. Preparatory Committee for the International Conference on Trade and Development Geneva, Minutes of General Staff Meeting, May 28, 1947, NARA, Record Group 43, International Trade Files, Box 133, Folder marked "Minutes U.S. Delegation (Geneva 1947) April–June 20, 1947."

130. Ibid.

131. Ibid.

132. Ibid.

133. Ibid.

134. United Nations Conference on Trade and Development, Commission A, Summary Record of Third Meeting, held on Wednesday, 28 May 1947, NARA, Record Group 43, International Trade Files, Box 123, Folder marked "E/PC/T/A/SR/1 to 43."

135. Ibid.

napping" on the investment provisions, implying that they were now awake and vigilant.[136] The Cuban delegate later that day proposed redrafting the U.S. language so that foreign investment would not be placed in a better position than domestic investment.[137]

AMENDING THE U.S. PROPOSAL IN GENEVA

Meanwhile, on May 27, the very day on which Commission A began its discussion of the U.S. proposal, the ECEFP finally approved the proposed investment code on which John Parke Young's working group had been laboring since March. The approved proposal would have made extensive changes to the London draft of the ITO Charter (as edited in New York).[138]

First, it would have added new language to Article 9, which in the revised London draft merely recognized the importance of economic development. The new language stated that economic development would be promoted by an increase in international investment, that capital should be available on reasonable terms and conditions, that it should be invested for productive purposes economically suited to the area and in a manner consistent with the best interests of both the capital exporting and the capital importing countries, and that it should be accorded fair and equitable treatment.

The proposal would have added to Article 12 several protections for investment beyond those in the London draft. The proposed new language would have required the payment of prompt, adequate, and effective compensation for expropriation, and MFN treatment with respect to the establishment and operation of an investment. The first requirement, relating to expropriation compensation, was substantively identical to the language proposed by the Geneva delegation. The second requirement, relating to MFN treatment, was weaker than the language proposed by the Geneva delegation, which also called for national treatment.

The ECEFP-approved proposal included protections with no counterpart in the Geneva delegation's proposal. The proposal would have guaranteed the right to transfer earnings from investment and a moderate amount for amortization of loans, except as permitted by the IMF Articles of Agreement. It would have required the parties, in the event of a loan default, to negotiate with a view toward arriving at a fair and non-discriminatory settlement of the loan obligations.

136. Second Meeting of the U.N. Preparatory Committee for the International Conference on Trade and Development Geneva, Minutes of Delegation, TAC and Charter Working Group Meeting, May 29, 1947, NARA, Record Group 43, International Trade Files, Box 133, Folder marked "Minutes U.S. Delegation (Geneva 1947) April–June 20, 1947."

137. United Nations Conference on Trade and Development, Commission A, Summary Record of Fourth Meeting, held on Wednesday, 28 May 1947, NARA, Record Group 43, International Trade Files, Box 123, Folder marked "E/PC/T/A/SR/1 to 43."

138. "Revision of Chapter IV of the ITO Charter" as approved by the ECEFP on May 27, 1947, NARA, Record Group 43, International Trade Files, Box 38, Folder marked "FIP Documents" and Box 14, Folder marked "Chapter IV, Articles 9 through 13."

Finally, it would have authorized any member to submit a dispute related to investment to the organization, which would utilize its good offices in an effort to resolve the dispute.

The proposal approved by the ECEFP also included provisions intended to diminish some of the potential undesirable effects of investment. One provision stated that members and their investors should avoid "misuse of investment," which meant the employment of investment in a manner that would result in unfair political or economic advantage or harm to the member receiving the investment or to the relations among members; that would lower prevailing wages or labor standards or impede the progressive improvement of wages and working standards; that would give rise to anticompetitive conditions; or that would constitute interference in the political affairs of other members. Another provision stated that the managers of foreign investment should provide adequate and effective opportunities for the participation of local capital and management. These provisions were phrased in precatory rather than mandatory language.

Finally, the ECEFP-approved proposal would have authorized the ITO to promote international agreements designed to achieve several purposes. These included ensuring just and equitable treatment of investment, avoiding double taxation, permitting the freest possible flow of capital and returns, and guaranteeing national treatment for investment.

Just as it was completing work on its proposed language, the State Department received word from the Geneva delegation that the latter had already submitted its own proposal in order to meet the May 27 deadline. John Parke Young complained that the Geneva delegation had never informed the Department of the deadline.[139] Indeed, as noted above, the Geneva delegation had sent the Department a telegram on May 8 asking that any recommendations regarding the content of an investment code be sent to Geneva by early June, which was too late to meet the deadline in Geneva. In any event, the Geneva delegation's proposal met with "considerable disapproval" in Washington.[140] The various agencies involved in preparing the ECEFP-approved policy objected both to the substance of the Geneva delegation's proposal and to the process by which it had been prepared, that is, by the Geneva delegation without consulting any of the agencies in Washington.

A further problem arose from the fact that, at the April 18 meeting with business representatives at the Federal Reserve Bank in New York, Young and his colleagues had solicited suggestions from the business groups concerning the content of any investment provisions to be proposed by the Department, and had given these groups a deadline of June 1 to submit their suggestions. Most of these groups had submitted suggestions, only to learn that the Geneva delegation

139. Memorandum dated June 16, 1947, from John Parke Young to Will Clayton, NARA, Record Group 43, International Trade Files, Box 38, Folder marked "FIP Documents."

140. Ibid.

had already submitted its proposal on behalf of the United States, a fact that was embarrassing to the Department.[141]

Meanwhile, contemporaneously with the ECEFP's review of the language proposed by Young's working group, the Committee on Foreign Investment Policy chaired by Young had been reviewing the language proposed by the Geneva delegation. On June 11, the State Department sent a telegram to the Geneva delegation lamenting the delegation's "considerable departure in fundamental policy" from the language approved by the ECEFP.[142] The telegram began by noting the numerous omissions from the ECEFP- approved policy. The telegram also identified objections to two provisions in the Geneva delegation's language.

First, the Geneva delegation had drafted language guaranteeing national treatment, except when contrary to essential national interests. The State Department observed that the United States itself could not abide by this guarantee inasmuch as it had enacted laws that denied national treatment to foreign investment, and that such laws could not be defended under the essential national interest exception, without a strained interpretation of the exception, which the Department did not wish to encourage. The Department noted that its proposal had addressed national treatment through the language proposed for inclusion in Article 9 calling for fair and equitable treatment.[143] The Department also noted that even the MFN treatment obligation in the Geneva proposal was too absolute.

Second, the Department questioned the "efficacy" of the language in the Geneva delegation's proposal permitting members to submit to the ITO a statement of their laws relating to foreign investment, from which no departures would be permitted.[144] The Department contended that the difficulty of identifying all such laws would discourage most countries from utilizing this procedure. Even those countries that attempted to comply likely would find that they had omitted some laws and that investors would feel misled when they discovered that the host country sought to enforce laws not included in the statement submitted to the ITO.

The Geneva delegation replied that it would modify its proposal to take account of the concerns about its non-discrimination provision and the provision for filing statements of investment policy.[145] Regarding the other provisions of the ECEFP-approved policy, the Geneva delegation told the Department that it had consulted with other delegations and that any attempt to introduce these other provisions would meet strong opposition that might result in the loss of all investment-related provisions.

141. Ibid.

142. Telegram dated June 11, 1947, from the Department of State to the U.S. delegation in Geneva, NARA, Record Group 43, International Trade Files, Box 14, Folder marked "Chapter IV Articles 9 through 13."

143. Ibid.

144. Ibid.

145. Telegram dated July 10, 1947, from the U.S. delegation in Geneva to the Department of State, NARA, Record Group 43, International Trade Files, Box 14, Folder marked "Chapter IV, Articles 9 through 13."

Meanwhile, although the State Department was displeased with the terms of the Geneva delegation's proposal, the business community was delighted. The delegation's proposal, unlike the ECEFP-approved one, was limited to protecting the rights of investors, and it offered strong protection that went beyond even U.S. law. In June, Clair Wilcox traveled to Montreux to attend an ICC Convention.[146] He spoke with several U.S. business representatives, including a representative of the NAM. The NAM representative said that U.S. business interests were "thoroughly pleased" with the positions taken by the United States at the Geneva conference. The representative said that the United States could "count on the full and vigorous support" of business representatives in obtaining congressional support of the Charter.

In mid-July, in response to the State Department's objections, the U.S. delegation submitted amendments to its own proposal. By this time, the delegation had been joined by Seymour J. ("Sy") Rubin, the 34-year-old assistant legal adviser for economic affairs, who was then not quite 10 years out of Harvard Law School, where he had been one of Felix Frankfurter's protégés.[147] Rubin was a late addition to the delegation and was serving as the delegation's legal counsel. Upon his arrival, Rubin was assigned primary responsibility for the negotiation of the investment-related provisions of the Charter, while the more senior members of the delegation continued to concern themselves principally with trade. Before enrolling at Harvard Law School, Rubin had attended the University of Michigan, where he was a member of the university's wrestling team, an experience that may have presaged the metaphorical hand-to-hand combat in which he would soon engage with the Indian delegation over the proposed investment provisions of the Charter.

One change embodied in the U.S. July amendments to its May proposal was that the prohibition in Article 12(a) on unreasonable action injurious to the rights of foreign nationals and their investment conduct was modified so that it became a prohibition on "unfair and inequitable" action. Rubin explained to the other delegations that the change was in the nature of a clarification. He believed that the terms "unfair" and "inequitable" had "a broader and more precise connotation."[148] In other words, fair and equitable treatment included reasonable treatment, but went beyond merely reasonable treatment. The change had the effect of placing more emphasis, as the Department seemed to wish, on the concept of fair and equitable treatment.

After objections from Australia and India to the word "inequitable," the U.S. delegation suggested that "unfair and inequitable" become "unfair and

146. Second Meeting of the U.N. Preparatory Committee for the International Conference on Trade and Development Geneva, Minutes of the General Staff Meeting, June 12, 1947, NARA, Record Group 43, International Trade Files, Box 133, Folder marked "Minutes U.S. Delegation (Geneva 1947) April–June 20, 1947."

147. A brief biographical sketch of Sy Rubin's early years appears in Bennett Boskey, "Seymour J. Rubin—Some of the Origins," 4 *American University International Law Review* 1245 (1995).

148. Minutes of Delegation Meeting, July 17, 1947, NARA, Record Group 43, International Trade Files, Box 133, Folder marked "Minutes—U.S. Delegation (Geneva 1947) April–June 20, 1947."

unreasonable."[149] The objection to "inequitable" was that it suggested the Anglo-American system of equity jurisprudence, which did not exist in civil law countries.[150] The U.S. delegation noted that the term "equitable" was already in the proposed language calling for the conclusion of agreements providing for just and equitable treatment of investment, but that argument was unavailing.[151] In any event, Rubin did not believe that the change was of much substance.[152]

A second change would have required national and MFN treatment with respect to the right to establish investment, "except as otherwise deemed necessary in the national interest." Once investment was established, the change would have required each member to provide national and MFN treatment, except for limitations or conditions existing at the time the investment was made or at the time the Charter entered into force. This exception addressed objections by India that it was about to gain its independence, after which it wished to adopt measures that would promote Indian investment in India and end the period of British domination of the Indian economy.[153] The language of the national and MFN treatment provision also made explicit that the provision prohibited placing "more onerous" burdens on covered investment, but did not require the host country to extend subsidies or other benefits to covered investment.[154]

NEGOTIATING THE U.S. PROPOSAL IN GENEVA

By the time the United States submitted its amended proposal in July, work on the U.S. proposal had shifted to the subcommittee level, where the proposal led to a "prolonged debate."[155] The United States faced much difficulty with Article 12 because many countries believed that its purpose was to impose an American conception of economic organization on the rest of the world.[156]

149. Ibid.

150. Letter dated August 5, 1947 from Seymour Rubin to Walter S. Surrey, NARA, Record Group 59, Department of State Lot Files, Walter Hollis Papers, Folder marked "Walter Hollis Notes."

151. Ibid.

152. Ibid.

153. Minutes of Delegation Meeting, July 17, 1947, NARA, Record Group 43, International Trade Files, Box 133, Folder marked "Minutes—U.S. Delegation (Geneva 1947) April–June 20, 1947."

154. Minutes of Delegation Meeting, July 19, 1947. NARA, Record Group 43, International Trade Files, Box 133, Folder marked "Minutes—U.S. Delegation (Geneva 1947) April–June 20, 1947."

155. Wilcox, *Charter,* page 146.

156. Meeting of the American Delegation to the Havana ITO Conference, November 18, 1947, 10:15 am to 12:25 pm, pages E-1-E-2, NARA, Record Group 43, International Trade Files, Box 147, Folder marked "Trade—Briefing Sessions—Habana."

The principal U.S. representative on the subcommittee, Sy Rubin, later recounted that "We had vey [very] tough going in the subcommittee at first. We got almost no support. We were attacked viciously on the grounds that the proposals came too late, that the Delegations had no investment experts here, that they distorted the 'balance' of the Charter by magnifying only one aspect of economic development, etc."[157]

Within the subcommittee, India and Australia led the attack against the U.S. proposal, with support from the British. Only Brazil strongly supported the United States, with France offering modest support. Chile remained neutral.

Rubin was able to persuade the subcommittee that it needed to analyze the proposal line by line before voting on it. He believed that the delegates ultimately approved a modified version of the U.S. proposal because they did not want the time invested in reviewing it to have been for naught.[158]

The substance of the proposal was negotiated by Rubin and the Indian delegate, and was driven by India's desire to gain control over the Indian economy. Rubin believed that the United States could hardly argue that India under no circumstances could do so, and thus the goal became to place "safeguards" around the process. Rubin did not believe that it was possible to get much more than the United States had achieved.[159]

The subcommittee rewrote the chapter on economic development to include the investment protection provisions sought by the U.S. delegation, but in a substantially modified form. The obligations with respect to foreign investment contained in the London draft (as edited in New York) were largely retained in the Geneva draft in Article 11 with minor changes. The prohibition on the imposition of unreasonable impediments that would prevent a member from obtaining facilities for their economic development was recast in Article 11(1) as a prohibition on "unreasonable or unjustifiable impediments" that would prevent another member from obtaining facilities for development "on equitable terms." Similarly, the prohibition on "unreasonable action injurious" to the interest of other members, business entities, or persons providing facilities for development became in Article 11(2) a prohibition on "unreasonable or unjustifiable action . . . injurious to the rights or interests of nationals of other Members in the enterprise, skills, capital, arts or technology which they have supplied." The requirement of reasonableness introduced in London thus survived.

Article 12 was headed "International Investment for Economic Development." Article 12(1) recognized that "development would be facilitated if Members were to afford, for international investments acceptable to them, reasonable opportunities upon equitable terms to the nationals of other Members and security for existing and future investments." Accordingly, the members "agree[d] to provide, consistent with the limitations recognized as necessary in this Article, the widest

157. Letter dated August 5, 1947 from Seymour Rubin to Walter S. Surrey, NARA, Record Group 59, Department of State Lot Files, Walter Hollis Papers, Folder marked "Walter Hollis Notes."

158. Ibid.

159. Ibid.

opportunities for investment and the greatest security for existing and future investment." Article 12(1), in other words, included vaguely worded commitments to access and security.

Article 12(2), which was destined to become one of the most controversial provisions of the entire Charter, set forth two more specific obligations, one relating to non-discrimination against foreign capital and one relating to the security of foreign capital. These were the successors to the non-discrimination and expropriation provisions of the U.S. delegation's original proposal submitted in May. The non-discrimination obligation prohibited the imposition of requirements on foreign investment that were "appreciably more onerous" than those imposed "in similar circumstances" upon nationals of the host state or nationals of any third state.[160] That is, foreign investment was entitled to national and MFN treatment. Article 12, however, recognized important exceptions to the non-discrimination obligation. These included requirements in force at the time the Charter came into force or at the time the investment was made, whichever was later; requirements in force at the time of any substantial addition to the investment or change in the nature of the business based upon the investment; reasonable measures to ensure participation by local investors in the expansion of foreign investment; and reasonable measures to transfer ownership of foreign investment to local investors. In effect, the exceptions allowed the host state to preserve existing discriminatory measures and to adopt new discriminatory measures prior to the establishment of an investment. They also permitted discriminatory expropriation programs.[161]

The obligation relating to security required that the host state pay "just compensation" for the expropriation of foreign investment, regardless of whether the expropriated property was transferred to local investors, was taken into public ownership, or was placed under public management or occupation.[162] Because of concerns about the requirement of effectiveness, the United States was unable to obtain agreement to include an explicit requirement of prompt, adequate, and effective compensation.[163] Many countries lacked sufficient dollars to make payment in a convertible currency. Even the British and the French were concerned that dollar shortages could preclude them from engaging in nationalization programs, such as the nationalization of the British railway system, if they were required to make prompt payment in dollars.[164] Further, Rubin conceded that nationalization in some instances could

160. Article 12(2)(a).

161. Ibid.

162. Articles 12(2)(a)(iv) and 12(2)(b). The former related to transfers to private ownership, and the latter related to transfers to public ownership, occupation, or management.

163. Meeting of the American Delegation to the Havana ITO Conference, November 18, 1947, 10:15 am to 12:25 pm, page D-14, NARA, Record Group 43, International Trade Files, Box 147, Folder marked "Trade—Briefing Sessions—Habana."

164. Letter from Seymour Rubin to Walter S. Surrey, date July 16, 1947, NARA, Record Group 59, Department of State Lot Files, Walter Hollis Papers, Folder marked "Walter Hollis Notes."

lead to an improvement in a country's balance of payments.[165] Ultimately, the United States accepted language calling for "just" compensation, the term used in the U.S. Constitution and in U.S. FCN treaties. Rubin believed that the requirement of "just" compensation implicitly required some degree of transferability.[166]

The requirement of just compensation was critical because it provided the only security against expropriation. An explanatory note to Article 12(2) stated that the requirement of just compensation did not apply where the property was taken because of a violation of law or pursuant to the terms of a treaty of peace or another international agreement related to the conclusion of the war. The note further explained that, where just compensation required payment of currency, payment in local currency would satisfy the obligation. This language responded to the argument that a dollar shortage should not preclude a country from exercising its sovereign right to expropriate.[167] Further, the transferability of the payment into another currency would be determined in accordance with the host country's general foreign exchange policy maintained in a manner consistent with the IMF Articles of Agreement. The IMF articles, as has been seen, allowed members to restrict capital transfers without IMF approval.

The investment-related provisions of the Charter constituted only one small part of the negotiations in Geneva. Indeed, the ITO Charter itself was only a part of the Geneva negotiations. At its first meeting in London in the autumn of 1946, the Preparatory Committee had agreed that the creation of the ITO "would be facilitated if concrete action were taken by the principal trading nations to enter into reciprocal negotiations directed to the substantial reduction of tariffs and to the elimination of preferences on a mutually advantageous basis."[168] Secretary of State James Byrnes wanted the tariff negotiations delayed until the Geneva conference so that they would not become an issue in the 1946 elections.[169] Thus, even while they were negotiating the draft ITO Charter, the governments represented at the Geneva conference commenced the negotiation of trade concessions that were to be incorporated, along with appropriate provisions of the draft ITO Charter, into a separate General Agreement on Tariffs and Trade (GATT)[170] that would implement immediate reductions in trade barriers even before the

165. Ibid.

166. Ibid.

167. Meeting of the American Delegation to the Havana ITO Conference, November 18, 1947, 10:15 am to 12:25 pm, page D-13, NARA, Record Group 43, International Trade Files, Box 147, Folder marked "Trade—Briefing Sessions—Habana."

168. Department of State, *Draft Charter for the International Trade Organization of the United Nations*, Department of State Publication 2927, Commercial Policy Series 106 (Washington, DC: Government Printing Office, 1947), page 70.

169. Zeiler, *Free Trade, Free World*, page 63.

170. Ibid., page 161.

ITO Charter entered into force.[171] The GATT negotiations ended successfully, and 23 countries signed the agreement.[172]

THE COLD WAR COMES TO GENEVA

The drafting of the ITO Charter required that the United States weigh its foreign economic policy against other aspects of its foreign policy. The Second World War had demonstrated the extent of U.S. dependence on critical raw materials from abroad,[173] and the War and Navy Departments were concerned that ITO Charter commitments to free trade could interfere with measures that the military might wish to take in order to ensure the availability of natural resources needed for defense purposes. They also wanted to ensure that trade commitments would not prevent efforts by the United States to halt the shipment of fissionable materials and military technology to the Soviet Union.[174]

Article 32 of the suggested Charter proposed by the United States in September 1946 had set forth a number of exceptions to Chapter IV of the Charter, which was the chapter on trade. That article provided,

> Nothing in Chapter IV of this Charter shall be construed to prevent the adoption or enforcement by any Member of measures . . .
>
> d. relating to the traffic in arms, ammunition and implements of war and to such traffic in other goods and materials as is carried on for the purpose of supplying a military establishment;
>
> e. in time of war or other emergency in international relations, relating to the protection of the essential security interests of a Member; . . . . [or]
>
> h. undertaken in pursuance of obligations under the United Nation Charter for the maintenance or restoration of international peace and security.

Article 49 included a similar exception for the chapter on commodity agreements. It stated that none of the provisions of that chapter shall be "interpreted as applying to agreements relating to fissionable materials; to the traffic in arms, ammunition and implements of war and to such traffic in other goods and materials as is carried on for the purpose of supplying a military establishment; or, in

171. Although not a member of the Preparatory Committee, Syria participated in the GATT negotiations because it was a member of a customs union with Lebanon, which was a member of the Committee. Department of State, *Draft Charter for the International Trade Organization of the United Nations*, Department of State Publication 2927, Commercial Policy Series 106 (Washington, DC: Government Printing Office, 1947), page 6.

172. Diebold, *End of the I.T.O.*, page 27.

173. Robert A. Pollard, *Economic Security and the Origins of the Cold War, 1945–1950* (New York: Columbia University Press, 1985), page 21.

174. Zeiler, *Free Trade, Free World*, pages 64–65.

time of war or other emergency in international relations, to the protection of the essential security interests of a Member."

The national security exception became a matter of serious contention within the U.S. delegation at Geneva. At a delegation meeting on May 30, 1947, Captain W. B. Thorp, the Navy Department's representative on the delegation, expressed the concern that the chapter on international commodity agreements would prevent the United States from entering into international commodity agreements needed to supply materials for military use. Thorp wanted a broader exception to the commodities chapter for actions taken in pursuit of national security. Clair Wilcox countered that "such an exception would be unquestionably used as a means of evading responsibilities. . . ."[175] He added that "most of the countries present would be entirely happy if they could find a means of evading the responsibilities which they may have to assume here." [176]

By early June 1947, nearly two months after the Geneva conference began, Wilcox had decided that at least some of the exceptions to the commercial policy chapter, including the national security exception, should be revised to apply to all obligations under the charter.[177] A member of the U.S. delegation, Edmund H. Kellogg, a Harvard-educated lawyer who had reached the rank of major in the U.S. Army Air Force during the war and then joined the foreign service after the war,[178] prepared draft language for a general exception for measures necessary to protect national security. The proposed language provided that "[n]othing in this Charter shall be construed to prevent the adoption or enforcement by any Member of any measure which it may deem necessary" relating to fissionable materials, traffic in arms, traffic in any goods to supply a military establishment, relating to the protection of the member's "essential security interest" in time of war or other emergency in international relations, or undertaken pursuant to obligations under the U.N. Charter for the maintenance or restoration of international peace and security.[179]

175. Second Meeting of the U.N. Preparatory Committee for the International Conference on Trade and Development Geneva, Minutes of Delegation, TAC and Charter Working Group Meeting, May 30, 1947, NARA, Record Group 43, International Trade Files, Box 133, Folder marked "Minutes U.S. Delegation (Geneva 1947) April–June 20, 1947."

176. Ibid.

177. Second Meeting of the U.N. Preparatory Committee for the International Conference on Trade and Development Geneva, Minutes of the General Staff Meeting, June 4, 1947, NARA, Record Group 43, International Trade Files, Box 133, Folder marked "Minutes U.S. Delegation (Geneva 1947) April–June 20, 1947."

178. "Edmund H. Kellogg, Professor Emeritus and Diplomat, 81," *New York Times*, April 14, 1993.

179. Second Meeting of the U.N. Preparatory Committee for the International Conference on Trade and Development Geneva, Minutes of Staff Meeting of Entire Delegation, July 2, NARA, Record Group 43, International Trade Files, Box 133, Folder marked "Minutes U.S. Delegation (Geneva 1947) April–June 20, 1947."

On June 16, after seeing Kellogg's draft of a general national security exception, Howard H. Neff, the War Department's representative on the delegation, and Captain Thorp sent Wilcox a memorandum arguing that Kellogg's language was not adequate to protect U.S. national security interests.[180] In particular, the United States needed the sole discretion to enter into intergovernmental commodity agreements that would ensure the availability of copper, lead, zinc, petroleum, and lumber products, critical materials that the United States did not produce in sufficient abundance. They also wanted latitude for the United States to protect the market for synthetic rubber.

At its July 2 meeting, the U.S. delegation considered a proposal by Howard Neff to revise Edmund Kellogg's language.[181] Neff's proposal added a qualifying phrase at the beginning that read "without limiting the generality of any other exception or qualification." It reformulated the reference to "any measure" as a reference to "any measure or agreement" so that the exception would apply to international commodity agreements explicitly. It qualified the reference to supplying a military establishment with the additional phrase "directly or indirectly." The addition of the phrase was intended to render the language of the exception consistent with the language of a measure pending before Congress, the Munitions Control Act, which authorized various export controls. Neff's draft also deleted the word "essential" from the phrase "essential security interests." The deletion of the word "essential" similarly was intended to render the language of the exception consistent with the pending legislation. Finally, Neff's draft added a specific exception for the supplying of information if to do so would be contrary to a member's national security. Neff wished to ensure that the ITO Charter would not require the United States to disclose information that could compromise national security, such as certain defense production processes.

Neff's proposed draft provoked "considerable discussion."[182] Many members of the delegation questioned the need for the changes. Because of the legal importance of the exception, Wilcox asked Rubin to study Neff's draft carefully and to submit a report to the delegation with respect to the questions raised at the meeting. Rubin responded by preparing a new draft of the national security exception, which the delegation considered at its July 4 meeting.[183]

180. Memorandum from Howard H. Neff and Captain W. B. Thorp to Clair Wilcox, dated June 16, 1947, NARA, Record Group 43, International Trade Files, Box 133, Folder marked "Minutes U.S. Delegation (Geneva 1947) April–June 20, 1947."

181. Second Meeting of the U.N. Preparatory Committee for the International Conference on Trade and Development Geneva, Minutes of Staff Meeting of Entire Delegation, July 2, NARA, Record Group 43, International Trade Files, Box 133, Folder marked "Minutes U.S. Delegation (Geneva 1947) April–June 20, 1947."

182. Ibid.

183. Second Meeting of the U.N. Preparatory Committee for the International Conference on Trade and Development Geneva, Minutes of Delegation Meeting, July 4, NARA, Record Group 43, International Trade Files, Box 133, Folder marked "Minutes U.S. Delegation (Geneva 1947) April–June 20, 1947."

Rubin effectively decided against Neff on nearly every point. He did retain the new language on furnishing information. Rubin, however, omitted Neff's introductory qualifying phrase and the reference to "directly or indirectly," while restoring the word "essential." He left in the reference to agreements, but offered his opinion that the word was unnecessary. This led to an extended discussion of whether the word "measure" included an agreement, with Rubin, Robert Terrill, and John M. Leddy all insisting that it did, whereas Neff argued that it did not. At Rubin's suggestion, the delegation compromised by using the term "any action" in lieu of "any measure or agreement."

The delegation then turned to the most contentious issue raised by Neff's proposal. Kellogg's proposed language had applied to "any measure which [a Member] may deem necessary" relating to various enumerated topics, such as fissionable materials or a national emergency. The implication was that each member had sole discretion to determine whether a measure it took was necessary, but not whether it related to one of the enumerated topics. Neff's draft had deleted the quoted language, but added a new paragraph stating that each member shall have "independent power of interpretation" of the language of the exception and that the provisions of Article 86 relating to disputes concerning the interpretation or application of the Charter would not apply to the national security exception. Neff's revision made quite explicit that any invocation of the national security exception by a party was conclusive and not reviewable in any respect.

Rubin apparently disliked the new paragraph that Neff drafted, but he did not restore the original language either. Instead, he drafted new language under which the Charter did not preclude any action "which [a Member] may consider to be necessary and to relate to" the various enumerated topics, such as fissionable materials, traffic in arms, or an emergency in international relations. The change from the original language was subtle, but Rubin, Neff, and Wilcox all recognized what was at stake. Under the new language, the member could determine both whether the measure was necessary and whether it related to the enumerated topics, and these determinations would not be subject to review in any respect. A member could avoid any Charter obligation by a mere unilateral invocation of its essential security interests.

Wilcox asked that the words "and to relate to" be replaced with the original phrase "relating to." The purpose of Wilcox's proposal was to indicate that the determination to be made by a member was whether a measure it adopted was necessary, and not whether the measure related to the enumerated topics. That is, the ITO could determine that a measure adopted under the national security exception violated the Charter because the measure did not relate to any of the enumerated topics. Rubin then reported that he had favored the same language that Wilcox was proposing, but that Neff had objected "vigorously" to the change.[184] Neff argued that the phrase "and to relate to" in Rubin's draft made clear that the United States "may take unilateral action."[185]

184. Ibid.

185. Ibid.

John Evans, John M. Leddy, and Robert Terrill concurred "strongly" with Wilcox that Neff's preferred language should be deleted.[186] As the minutes of the meeting explained, "They argued that such a provision destroyed the efficacy of the entire Charter."[187] The most important consideration was not the scope of action left to the United States by the Charter. Rather, the most important consideration was that "[p]roviding the means for unilateral action will surely be abused by some countries."[188] As they noted, "Under Mr. Neff's language any country could, under the pretext of national security, take any measure whatsoever it might wish in complete disregard of all provisions of the Charter."[189] Leddy argued "that it would be far better to abandon all work on the Charter" than to place a provision in it that would, "under the simple pretext that the action was taken to protect the national security of the particular country, provide a legal escape from compliance with the provisions of the Charter."[190]

Neff stood his ground. He replied that "when matters of national security are involved the US must be given a free hand to make whatever decisions may be necessary without challenge by the ITO."[191]

Other members of the delegation contended, however, that as a practical matter the United States simply did not need a right to engage in unfettered unilateral action. Both John Walker Evans and Winthrop Brown, for example, argued that the United States would be such an important member of the organization that the ITO would have no choice but to decide in favor of the United States in any case where the United States had a *bona fide* national security claim. Oscar Ryder, the chairman of the U.S. Tariff Commission and one of the members of the working group negotiating trade issues, agreed that "as a practical matter no injury could possibly come to the US by ITO intervention to determine whether the measures introduced by the US in a particular instance were in fact taken in the interest of national security."[192] Wilcox added that "he did not think that the ITO would ever become an international forum to discuss national security interests."[193]

Following this discussion, Wilcox called for a vote on his proposal. Ten members of the delegation, counting Wilcox, favored the change that he had proposed. Only three members favored the language sought by Neff. Neff asked that the record show clearly his dissent to the delegation's decision.

The discussion and its resolution indicate unambiguously that the U.S. delegation rejected the idea that the any member of the ITO, including the United

186. Ibid.

187. Ibid.

188. Ibid.

189. Ibid.

190. Ibid.

191. Ibid.

192. Ibid.

193. Ibid.

States, should have a right to take nonreviewable action under the national security exception. The delegation recognized that to permit any member to be the sole judge of its own claim to an exception would render the Charter legally meaningless. As Leddy argued, no charter at all would be better than one that appeared to bind countries but that did not.

Neff understood the significance of his defeat. On July 10, he sent a memorandum to the rest of the U.S. delegation noting that the language approved by the delegation did not confer upon a member the power to decide "with finality" whether any action that it took related to any of the enumerated topics, such as fissionable materials or traffic in arms.[194] He concluded that "[t]he content therefore of the exceptions does not fall within the power of any individual Member to determine but rests solely within the general power to interpret otherwise conferred by the Charter."[195] He noted that the U.S. delegation's choice of this language "would seem to indicate that there is *not* the intent to reserve full power of unilateral interpretation."[196] Neff went on to lament the deletion of the phrase "directly or indirectly" and the inclusion of the word "essential." He continued to be concerned that these changes rendered the language of the Charter inconsistent with pending legislation in Congress. He observed that "[t]he exclusion of these words is all the more important because the interpretation of the content of the security exceptions is not reserved to the country taking action."[197]

The next day, Captain Thorp circulated a memorandum supporting Neff's position. He argued that a security exception "subject to definition or interpretation in any way by the ITO is certainly not satisfactory from a national security standpoint."[198] Responding to the argument that the language preferred by Neff would be subject to abuse, Thorp noted that "[i]f the Members of the ITO do not intend to follow the spirit as well as the letter of the ITO Charter, there might as well not be a Charter." He did add that he did "not feel too strongly" about the phrase "directly or indirectly" or the word "essential." He thought that the phrase was implied and that any security interest was essential.

On July 14, Rubin circulated a response to Neff's memorandum. He began by agreeing with Captain Thorp regarding the phrases "directly or indirectly" and "essential." Turning to Neff's proposal to add the words "which it may consider to relate to," Rubin agreed with Neff that the addition of such language "would

194. Second Meeting of the U.N. Preparatory Committee for the International Conference on Trade and Development Geneva, Memorandum from Howard H. Neff dated July 10, 1947, Record Group 43, International Trade Files, Box 133, Folder marked "Minutes U.S. Delegation (Geneva 1947) April–June 20, 1947."

195. Ibid.

196. Ibid.(emphasis in original).

197. Ibid.

198. Second Meeting of the U.N. Preparatory Committee for the International Conference on Trade and Development Geneva, Memorandum from Captain W. B. Thorp to the Chairman of the Delegation, dated July 11, 1947, Record Group 43, International Trade Files, Box 133, Folder marked "Minutes U.S. Delegation (Geneva 1947) April–June 20, 1947."

make it perfectly clear that any Member had the unilateral power to decide that any action which it proposed to take did relate to the matters contained in the lettered paragraphs. This would make unchallengeable by the Organization or any other Member a justification, however far-fetched, of any action on this basis." By contrast, the language approved by the delegation "limit[ed] the scope of the unilateral interpretation portion of the security exception." Rubin observed that the hearings before the Senate Finance Committee did not "indicate a desire on the part of the Committee that the Charter should in effect be negated by such a broad and unilateral exception that any action, no matter how little related to security, would be immune even from question." Rubin concluded that the phrasing desired by Neff "would in fact make the Charter in terms an illusory document."[199] He further noted an exception phrased as Neff wished would be invoked by other countries, rather than by the United States, and that the United States could justify any security measures that it contemplated under the language approved by the U.S. delegation.

The language approved by the U.S. delegation was forwarded to the Subcommittee on Chapter VIII. On July 24, the Subcommittee on Chapter VIII sought the comments of Commission A on the U.S. proposal for a new Article 94 with general exceptions to the Charter.[200] The essential security interests exception was discussed and no objection was raised, except for a minor clarification of the language on fissionable materials.

In early August, U.S. Secretary of War Kenneth Royall traveled to Geneva, where he met for lunch with Clair Wilcox, Winthrop Brown, and Howard Neff. During the lunch, the four men discussed in detail the security exception, including Neff's proposed amendments. Although Secretary Royall showed "considerable interest" in the subject, he did not insist upon Neff's amendments[201] and no further action was taken with respect to them. The principle that no country would be the sole judge of whether measures it took were justified by the security exception had been accepted at the highest level of the U.S. military.

The State Department's understanding of the essential security interests exception in the ITO Charter remained unchanged. For example, written answers prepared by the State Department in response to questions about the Charter posed by the Senate Finance Committee confirmed that a member's discretion under the essential security interests exception related only to the necessity of

199. Second Meeting of the U.N. Preparatory Committee for the International Conference on Trade and Development Geneva, Memorandum from Seymour J. Rubin dated July 14, 1947, Record Group 43, International Trade Files, Box 133, Folder marked "Minutes U.S. Delegation (Geneva 1947) April–June 20, 1947."

200. United Nations Conference on Trade and Development, Commission A, Summary Record of Thirty-Third Meeting, held on Thursday, 24 July 1947, NARA, Record Group 43, International Trade Files, Box 123, Folder marked "E/PC/T/A/SR/1 to 43."

201. Excerpt of minutes of meeting attached to letter dated August 5, 1947, from Clair Wilcox to Robert Schaetzel, NARA, Record Group 43, International Trade Files, Box 133, Folder marked "Minutes—U.S. Delegation (Geneva 1947), July 31–August 25, 1947."

the action, not to the other elements of the exception. In response to the question, "Are there any limits to the security exception?" the State Department drafted a response that read, "Yes, since the action taken by a Member under Paragraph 1(b) must relate to fissionable materials, the supply of a military establishment, or be taken in time of war or other international emergency."[202] A follow-up question asked, "Could such arrangements as are made under the exception be reviewed by the ITO or the Court?" The State Department responded, "The necessity for the action is not subject to review; the relationship of such action to the subjects referred to is subject to review."[203]

Similarly, a February 1949 internal State Department briefing paper explained that, under the exception, "a member . . . may take any action which it considers necessary for its essential security interests. Discretion is thus left in the hands of the member concerned, the only qualification being that the member taking action under this Article which is contested by another Member must prove to the satisfaction of the Organization that the action relates to fissionable material, to traffic in arms, ammunition or implements of war or traffic in other goods for the supply of a military establishment, or is taken in time of war or other military emergency."[204]

The inauguration of a Republican president in 1953 had no effect on the U.S. interpretation. A memorandum drafted in the Trade Agreements Division of the State Department in 1955 addressed the issue of whether the Trade Agreements Extension Act of 1955, which required adjusting imports to levels that would not threaten national security, could be justified under the essential security interests exception of the GATT, which was based upon the language of the ITO Charter. The memorandum observed that the exception gave each GATT contracting party "full discretion" to determine whether the action was necessary for the protection of its essential security interests.[205] The memorandum further observed, however, that action taken under the act would have to satisfy one of the additional objective criteria in the GATT exception, most likely those applying to measures relating to traffic destined for a military establishment or those taken in time of war or other emergency in international relations. As the United States understood when it drafted the language of the exception in Geneva, each party had sole discretion to determine the necessity of a measure, but the measure's

202. Memorandum headed "Questions Asked in Senate Finance Committee," NARA, Record Group 43, International Trade Files, Box 18, Folder marked "Chapter IX."

203. Ibid.

204. Excerpt from State Department ITO briefing book drafted by Edmund H. Kellogg, attached to memorandum by Edmund H. Kellogg to Mr. Burns dated February 15, 1949, and headed "Amendments to Your Copy of My Material on Chapter IX," NARA, Record Group 43, International Trade Files, Box 18, Folder marked "Chapter IX."

205. Memorandum headed "Consistency of Trade Agreements Act National Security Clause with GATT," dated May 24, 1955, NARA, Record Group 59, Department of State Lot Files, Walter Hollis Papers, Folder marked "National Security Amendment."

consistency with the other elements of the exception was subject to review. Thus, no party was sole judge of whether its actions fell within the exception.

The concern about abuse of the exception that led the U.S. delegation in Geneva to ensure that a party's invocation of the exception be reviewable also persisted. For example, in 1957, during the U.S. government's consideration of whether to invoke the national security exception of the GATT to justify discriminatory import duties on crude petroleum, an internal State Department memorandum noted that the exception had not been invoked on the basis of an emergency in international relations during such crises as the Berlin airlift, the Korean War, and the closing of the Suez Canal. The memorandum further observed that invocation by the United States to justify its oil import policy would enable other countries to invoke the exception to the detriment of the United States in the future.[206]

Neff's concern that the Charter would constrain U.S. freedom of action with respect to national security also led him to propose an amendment to the Charter's prohibition on "unreasonable impediments" to outward investment. More specifically, he proposed that the language be amended to allow any impediment "required by national security or other national necessity." Wilcox replied that "it was utterly inconceivable that any country would be willing to agree that national security considerations were 'unreasonable.'"[207] He argued that the requirement of reasonableness gave the United States even broader latitude than the national security exception, noting that the United States maintained export controls for protectionist reasons that could be justified as reasonable, but not necessary to U.S. national security. One member of the delegation observed that the United States had fought hard in London to obtain a prohibition on unreasonable action and, if the delegation now recommended that the language be changed, a "Pandora's box" of issues would be opened throughout the Charter. Sympathetic with Neff's concern, Captain Thorp suggested that the phrase "contrary to the public interest" be substituted for "unreasonable."[208] Ultimately, however, no other member of the delegation shared the concerns of Neff and Thorp about the term "unreasonable," and the delegation voted to leave the existing language unchanged.

Neff's proposal regarding the national security exception was nothing less than an assault on the Charter as an instrument of the rule of law. In the name of national security, Neff sought to create an exception that would allow the United States to exempt itself from any obligation of the Charter at any time in its

206. Unsigned memorandum headed "Most-Favored-Nation Commitments of the United States in Relation to Possible Differential Duties on Crude Petroleum," dated December 10, 1957, NARA, Record Group 59, Department of State Lot Files, Walter Hollis Papers, Folder marked "National Security Amendment."

207. Second Meeting of the U.N. Preparatory Committee for the International Conference on Trade and Development Geneva, Minutes of Delegation Meeting, May 22, 1947, NARA, Record Group 43, International Trade Files, Box 133, Folder marked "Minutes U.S. Delegation (Geneva 1947) April–June 20, 1947."

208. Ibid.

sole discretion. The exception in effect would have negated the provisions of the Charter as binding rules. Every member of the delegation understood what was at stake. An exception created for the United States would have been equally available to any other member. The Charter would have lost its force as law.

The State Department in the years of the Truman administration was seeking to create an international economic order governed by notions of liberal legality. Neff's proposal challenged that policy and, for that reason, no issue during the entire course of negotiation over the ITO Charter was more controversial within the U.S. delegation than Neff's proposal. Neff staged a challenge to the rule of law, and the rule of law won.

4

Abandoning the International Trade Organization

The results of the Geneva conference were disastrous. The United States had proposed the inclusion of investment-related provisions at the behest of the U.S. investor community, but U.S. investors were so dissatisfied with the language on non-discrimination and expropriation in Article 12(2) that they threatened to oppose the entire Charter if Article 12(2) remained in it.[1]

The NFTC believed that Article 12 allowed too many exceptions to the requirements of national and MFN treatment, its provisions with respect to requirements that local investors be permitted to participate in the expansion of foreign investment or that ownership of foreign investment be transferred to local investors were objectionable in principle, and the obligation to pay just compensation for expropriation was not defined clearly enough.[2] It argued that Article 12 would not promote investment, but would prejudice the United States in its attempt to conclude bilateral treaties for the protection of foreign investment.[3] The NAM criticized the draft not only because it gave "undue emphasis" to the right of a country to expropriate, but because it permitted payment of compensation in local currency.[4] Orville Harden, the vice president of the Standard Oil Company, sent Will Clayton a letter written by Standard Oil's counsel, George Koegler, expressing concern that Article

1. Memorandum by Seymour Rubin and Harry Hawkins headed "Investment Clauses in Geneva Draft Charter," dated November 21, 1947, NARA, Record Group 43, International Trade Files, Box 14, Folder marked "Chapter III."

2. Letter dated December 18, 1947, from NFTC president E. P. Thomas to Assistant Secretary of State Will Clayton, NARA, Record Group 43, International Trade Files, Box 147, Folder marked "Trade—Correspondence, General—Havana."

3. Ibid.

4. Department of State Briefing Memorandum dated May 1, 1949, NARA, Record Group 43, International Trade Files, Box 14, Folder marked "Chapter III."

12(2) prohibited only treatment that was "appreciably more onerous"[5] than national treatment, and allowed payment of expropriation compensation in local currency.[6]

Even some within the State Department were troubled by the compromises. John Parke Young later recalled that he was "shocked" when he learned that the U.S. delegation had agreed to language, not approved in Washington, allowing payment of compensation in local currency.[7]

DEVISING A STRATEGY FOR THE HAVANA CONFERENCE

After their return to the United States, the members of the Geneva delegation realized that the investment-related provisions drafted in Geneva were unacceptable. In November, Sy Rubin and Harry Hawkins prepared a memorandum reviewing the alternatives available to the United States with respect to Article 12.[8] One alternative was to reopen the discussion of Article 12(2) at the final conference, to be held in Havana, with the goal of obtaining the inclusion of language on expropriation similar to that in the U.S.-China FCN treaty. The problem was that Article 12(2) was "the result of extensive and often heated discussions on a subject which excited as much controversy as anything else in the Charter, and on which the U.S. delegation had few allies."[9] No countries other than Belgium and the Netherlands appeared likely to support an effort to strengthen Article 12(2).

A second alternative was to delete Article 12(2) in its entirety. This would eliminate much of the opposition of the U.S. investor community to the Charter. Further, Article 12(2), Hawkins and Rubin conceded, did establish a bad precedent that would hinder efforts to obtain better language in bilateral negotiations. Deletion of that provision would eliminate the bad precedent.

Although the arguments for seeking deletion of Article 12(2) were strong, ultimately, Rubin and Hawkins recommended a third course, which was to seek to replace Article 12(2) with new language calling upon the parties to negotiate bilateral treaties for the protection of foreign investment. This would neutralize the opposition of the investor community, as well as eliminate the bad precedent, and might salvage something of value for the protection of foreign investment. They hoped that such language would enable the United States to achieve a better treaty bilaterally than it could obtain through the multilateral forum, and would strengthen the ability of the United States to conclude more FCN treaties. The

5. Letter from George Koegler to Eugene Thomas dated October 24, 1947, NARA, Record Group 43, International Trade Files, Box 14, Folder marked "Chapter III."

6. Letter from Orville Harden to Will Clayton dated November 21, 1947, NARA, Record Group 43, International Trade Files, Box 14, Folder marked "Chapter III."

7. John Parke Young Oral History, Harry S. Truman Library.

8. Memorandum by Seymour Rubin and Harry Hawkins headed "Investment Clauses in Geneva Draft Charter," dated November 21, 1947, NARA, Record Group 43, International Trade Files, Box 14, Folder marked "Chapter III."

9. Ibid.

members of the U.S. delegation drawn from the business community, including representatives of the NFTC, the NAM, and the United States Chamber of Commerce, concurred with this approach.[10]

Eight days after Rubin and Hawkins proposed their amendment, Will Clayton replied to Orville Harden's letter, informing him that the U.S. delegation was in agreement with Harden's position on Article 12(2) and would be submitting an amendment to the article.[11] On January 5, Clair Wilcox wrote to NFTC president Eugene Thomas, reported on the proposed amendment to Article 12(2), and assured him that the U.S. delegation had "given its complete, unanimous, and vigorous support" to the position taken by the NFTC and other business groups in the United States.[12] Wilcox told Thomas that the United States would "continue to fight for the sort of investment provisions which the Council seeks. . . ."[13]

THE HAVANA CONFERENCE

Fifty-six nations participated in the Conference on International Trade and Employment, which convened in Havana on November 21. Most of these countries had not been invited to participate in the preparatory meetings, and thus the Havana conference was their first opportunity to shape the ITO Charter.[14]

Winthrop Brown, the chief of the Commercial Policy Division and the lead U.S. negotiator for tariff reductions in Geneva, recalled the "anguish" of the Havana conference.[15] It was "long and dreary," and by the time of the conference the U.S. delegation was "fed up" with rehashing a subject on which it already had worked for a very long time.[16] Further, the delegation sensed that the top officials in Washington had lost interest in the negotiations, to a large extent because

10. Susan Ariel Aaronson, *For the People, But Not by the People: A History of the International Trade Organization* (unpublished PhD diss., 1993), page 160.

11. Letter from Will Clayton to Orville Harden dated November 29, 1947, NARA, Record Group 43, International Trade Files, Box 14, Folder marked "Chapter III."

12. Letter from Clair Wilcox to Eugene Thomas dated January 3, 1948, NARA, Record Group 43, International Trade Files, Box 14, Folder marked "Chapter III."

13. Ibid.

14. Some countries that were not members of the Preparatory Committee had sent to earlier sessions of the conference observers who were permitted to express their views. Colombia, Denmark, Mexico, Peru, Poland, and Syria sent observers to the first session, while those same countries, as well as Afghanistan, Argentina, Ecuador, Egypt, Greece, Iran, Saudi Arabia, Siam, Sweden, Turkey, Uruguay, Venezuela, and Yugoslavia sent observers to the second session. Colombia and Mexico sent observers to the meeting of the drafting committee in New York. Department of State, *Draft Charter for the International Trade Organization of the United Nations*, Department of State Publication 2927, Commercial Policy Series 106 (Washington, DC: Government Printing Office, 1947), page 6.

15. Winthrop Brown Oral History, Harry S. Truman Library.

16. Ibid.

the conclusion of the GATT had resulted in the tariff reductions that the United States hoped to achieve through the ITO. Although he continued to serve as the head of the U.S. delegation, Will Clayton had resigned as undersecretary prior to the commencement of the Havana Conference, symbolizing the extent to which the time of the ITO had passed.

Some of the delegations from other countries openly questioned whether the conference would accomplish anything useful. For example, at one point during the conference, the Afghan delegation invited Clair Wilcox to dinner. Wilcox was uncertain about the purpose of the meal, which was sumptuous. Finally, after the brandy had been served, the head of the delegation turned to Wilcox and said, "Mr. Wilcox, may I ask you a question?"

Wilcox replied, "Why, of course."

The Afghan delegate then asked, "Why are we here?"[17]

The conference opened with a "chorus of denunciation" in which developing countries argued that the Geneva draft favored the interests of industrialized nations and would not promote economic development.[18] The criticisms were not directed only at the investment provisions. Developing countries objected that the draft prepared in Geneva prohibited quantitative restrictions on trade, which they wished to maintain, and that the Charter "should insure development as well as promote trade."[19] Participants proposed some 602 amendments to the Charter, of which 432 were regarded as "antithetic to the essential purposes of the charter."[20] Even the countries that had participated in the Geneva conference offered 166 amendments to the Charter.[21] The organizers anticipated that the conference would last for seven weeks, but it continued for slightly more than four months.

At Havana, the delegates expressed widespread agreement that the problem of economic development constituted "the key problem," the solution of which would facilitate the resolution of other issues before the conference.[22] A number of delegates said that any provisions on investment must protect the interests of host states as well as the interests of foreign investors. Most delegates agreed that developing countries understood the value of foreign investment for economic

17. Ibid.

18. Clair Wilcox, *A Charter for World Trade* (New York: The MacMillan Company, 1949), page 47.

19. *Current Economic Developments*, December 27, 1947, page 1, NARA, Record Group 59, Department of State Lot Files.

20. *The International Trade Organization: Key to Expanding World Trade and Employment*, Department of State Publication 3882, Commercial Policy Series 130 (Washington, DC: Government Printing Office, 1950), page 7.

21. Ibid.

22. United Nations Conference on Trade and Employment, Press Release ITO C.2/1, 1 December 1947, NARA, Record Group 43, International Trade Files, Box 139, Folder marked "ITO/C.2/."

development, although some noted that foreign investment sometimes impeded development. Guatemala, for example, argued that sudden inflows of foreign investment could be inflationary.[23] Some expressed skepticism about too much reliance on foreign investment. Many delegates announced that they would be submitting proposed amendments to Chapter III, which in the Geneva draft of the Charter was the chapter on economic development.

The Havana Conference referred Chapter III to the "Second Committee." In the Second Committee, there was little support for an unqualified right of national treatment for foreign investment. Early in the discussion of Article 12, the Australian delegate argued that every state needed to reserve the right to deny national treatment in some cases, and even Rubin, speaking on behalf of the United States, agreed.[24]

Much of the discussion concerned the U.S. proposal to replace Article 12(2) with language calling for the negotiation of bilateral treaties. Delegates expressed a wide variety of reactions with little consensus.

Some countries supported the U.S. proposal to replace Article 12(2). For example, Costa Rica supported the U.S. position on the ground that the language of Article 12(2) might alarm prospective investors, defeating the purpose of Article 12.[25] The ICC representative agreed and argued that deletion of Article 12 would be preferable to its retention in its current form.[26] Liberia reached the same result, for somewhat different reasons. The Liberian delegate believed that, given the diversity of investment policies in different countries and the varied forms of investment, the adoption of detailed rules such as those set forth in Article 12(2) simply was not feasible. Rather, the Charter should merely adopt general language calling for "equity and fair play" as in Article 11.[27] Liberia also believed that the ITO was venturing too deeply into investment matters. It should not supervise investment matters or resolve disputes, but focus on promoting information exchange.

23. United Nations Conference on Trade and Employment, Second Committee: Economic Development, Summary Record of Twelfth Meeting, 22 December 1947, NARA, Record Group 43, International Trade Files, Box 141, Folder marked "U.N. Conf. on Trade & Employment Havana Nov. 1947–Mar. 1946."

24. United Nations Conference on Trade and Employment, Press Release ITO/C.2/7, 16 December 1947, NARA, Record Group 43, International Trade Files, Box 139, Folder marked "ITO/C.2/."

25. United Nations Conference on Trade and Employment, Second Committee: Economic Development, Summary Record of Twelfth Meeting, 22 December 1947, NARA, Record Group 43, International Trade Files, Box 141, Folder marked "U.N. Conf. on Trade & Employment Havana Nov. 1947–Mar. 1946."

26. United Nations Conference on Trade and Employment, Second Committee: Economic Development, Summary Record of Thirteenth Meeting, 23 December 1947, NARA, Record Group 43, International Trade Files, Box 141, Folder marked "U.N. Conf. on Trade & Employment Havana Nov. 1947–Mar. 1946."

27. Ibid.

Other countries opposed the U.S. proposal for language on bilateral negotiations, although they did not always agree on the reasons for their opposition. Chile argued that bilateral negotiations would favor the interests of the more powerful country.[28] Argentina agreed.[29] The Netherlands, by contrast, feared that bilateral negotiations would result in too many different approaches, thereby undermining the MFN treatment principle.[30] Perhaps to avoid this result, the United Kingdom believed that the Charter should set forth the principles on which any bilateral agreements would be based.[31]

Several countries, including Ceylon, Uruguay, and Venezuela, argued that the conference should delete Article 12(2) in its entirety.[32] Burma and India went even farther and proposed deleting all of Article 12 on the ground that the purpose of Chapter III was economic development and that investor protection was adequately addressed by Article 11, which prohibited unreasonable or unjustifiable action injurious to investment and authorized the ITO to recommend further international agreements to assure just and equitable treatment for capital.[33]

Other countries argued that Article 12 or at least Article 12(2) must be retained. Sweden contended that Article 12 was necessary to provide security to investors and that the elimination of Article 12 would disserve the interests of capital importing countries.[34] China argued that deletion of Article 12(2) would leave the matters covered by that paragraph uncertain.[35]

28. United Nations Conference on Trade and Employment, Second Committee: Economic Development, Summary Record of Twelfth Meeting, 22 December 1947, NARA, Record Group 43, International Trade Files, Box 141, Folder marked "U.N. Conf. on Trade & Employment Havana Nov. 1947–Mar. 1946."

29. United Nations Conference on Trade and Employment, Second Committee: Economic Development, Summary Record of Thirteenth Meeting, 23 December 1947, NARA, Record Group 43, International Trade Files, Box 141, Folder marked "U.N. Conf. on Trade & Employment Havana Nov. 1947–Mar. 1946."

30. United Nations Conference on Trade and Employment, Second Committee: Economic Development, Summary Record of Twelfth Meeting, 22 December 1947, NARA, Record Group 43, International Trade Files, Box 141, Folder marked "U.N. Conf. on Trade & Employment Havana Nov. 1947–Mar. 1946."

31. Ibid.

32. United Nations Conference on Trade and Employment, Document entitled "Second Committee: Economic Development," Doc. E/CONF.2/C.2/9, 8 December 1947, NARA, Record Group 43, International Trade Files, Box 140, Folder marked "Second Committee."

33. Ibid.; United Nations Conference on Trade and Employment, Second Committee: Economic Development, Summary Record of Twelfth Meeting, 22 December 1947, NARA, Record Group 43, International Trade Files, Box 141, Folder marked "U.N. Conf. on Trade & Employment Havana Nov. 1947–Mar. 1946."

34. United Nations Conference on Trade and Employment, Second Committee: Economic Development, Summary Record of Thirteenth Meeting, 23 December 1947, NARA, Record Group 43, International Trade Files, Box 141, Folder marked "U.N. Conf. on Trade & Employment Havana Nov. 1947–Mar. 1946."

35. Ibid.

Mexico proposed that Article 12(2) be replaced with new language embodying the Calvo Doctrine.[36] The Calvo Doctrine, named for nineteenth-century Argentine jurist Carlos Calvo, held that foreign nationals or companies were not entitled under international law to treatment any more favorable than that accorded to local nationals and companies.[37] The United States immediately expressed opposition to the Mexican proposal.[38]

Some countries offered criticisms of Article 12 that were different from those offered by the United States. For example, Venezuela found the reference to "widest" opportunity to invest and "greatest" security for investment too vague.[39] Pakistan proposed amending the sentence to remove the superlatives on the ground that they implied that foreign investment might receive treatment superior to that received by domestic investment.[40] Mexico proposed deleting the sentence in its entirety.[41]

Indeed, the delegates proposed so many amendments to the chapter on economic development that the conference formed two different subcommittees to review them. On December 11, the conference created a Joint Subcommittee on Articles 9 through 11.[42] The Joint Subcommittee would have little impact on the evolution of the investment-related provisions.

On December 23, the conference referred the highly controversial Article 12 to a separate subcommittee, known as Subcommittee B.[43] This Subcommittee consisted of Australia, Brazil, Canada, Ceylon, Czechoslovakia, Egypt, India,

36. Ibid.

37. The Calvo Doctrine has been explicated in Donald Shea, *The Calvo Clause: A Problem of Inter-American and International Law and Diplomacy* (Minneapolis: University of Minnesota Press, 1955).

38. United Nations Conference on Trade and Employment, Second Committee: Economic Development, Summary Record of Thirteenth Meeting, 23 December 1947, NARA, Record Group 43, International Trade Files, Box 141, Folder marked "U.N. Conf. on Trade & Employment Havana Nov. 1947–Mar. 1946."

39. United Nations Conference on Trade and Employment, Second Committee: Economic Development, Summary Record of Twelfth Meeting, 22 December 1947, NARA, Record Group 43, International Trade Files, Box 141, Folder marked "U.N. Conf. on Trade & Employment Havana Nov. 1947–Mar. 1946."

40. United Nations Conference on Trade and Employment, Second Committee: Economic Development, Summary Record of Thirteenth Meeting, 23 December 1947, NARA, Record Group 43, International Trade Files, Box 141, Folder marked "U.N. Conf. on Trade & Employment Havana Nov. 1947–Mar. 1946."

41. Ibid.

42. United Nations Conference on Trade and Employment, Press Release ITO/C.2/4, 11 December 1947, NARA, Record Group 43, International Trade Files, Box 139, Folder marked "ITO/C.2/."

43. United Nations Conference on Trade and Employment, Press Release ITO/C.2/11, 23 December 1947, NARA, Record Group 43, International Trade Files, Box 139, Folder marked "ITO/C.2/."

Mexico, the Netherlands, New Zealand, Sweden, United Kingdom, the United States, and Venezuela.[44]

When Subcommittee B held its initial meeting, Rubin explained that the United States wished to replace Article 12(2) with new language. The United States justified its proposed amendment by asserting that the existing language of that provision was "cloudy and difficult."[45] In particular, the exceptions to national and MFN treatment were such as to "obscure and overshadow" the rule.[46] Accordingly, the United States was proposing a simple statement under which members, if requested, would proceed with the negotiation of a bilateral agreement giving effect to the provisions of Article 12(1). The provisions of Article 12(1) had been those under which each party agreed to provide the "widest opportunity" to invest and the "greatest security" for existing and future investment. The new language proposed by the United States provided that "each member shall, upon the request of any other member, enter into and carry out with such other member negotiations directed to giving effect to the provisions of paragraph 1 of this article."[47] The United States argued that this new language would solve the interpretive difficulties of the existing language and would provide an unambiguous means of putting into effect the principles of Article 12(1).[48]

Even with the proposed revision, the language of Article 12 remained controversial. In particular, the references in Article 12(1) to the "widest opportunity" for new investment and the reference to the "greatest security" for existing investment continued to be the subject of dispute, in part because their meaning was uncertain.[49] The Indian delegate stressed the importance of protecting the interests of the capital importing country, prompting Rubin to remind the Subcommittee that the host country has sovereignty over foreign investment in its territory, which provided the best means by which to protect its interests.[50]

44. Official Report of the United States Delegation to the United Nations Conference on Trade and Employment, Havana, Cuba, page 13, NARA, Record Group 43, International Trade Files, Box 148, Folder marked "Official Report of the United States Delegation to the United Nations Conference on Trade and Employment, Havana, Cuba."

45. Amendment Proposed by Delegation of the United States of America, USD/12, dated November 27, 1949, NARA, Record Group 43, International Trade Files, Box 14, Folder marked "Chapter III."

46. Ibid.

47. United Nations Conference on Trade and Employment, Press Release ITO/C.2/13, 29 December 1947, NARA, Record Group 43, International Trade Files, Box 139, Folder marked "ITO/C.2/."

48. United Nations Conference on Trade and Employment, Second Committee: Economic Development, Doc. E/CONF.2/C.2/9, 8 December 1947, NARA, Record Group 43, International Trade Files, Box 140, Folder marked "Second Committee."

49. United Nations Conference on Trade and Employment, Press Release ITO/C.2/19, 15 January 1948, NARA, Record Group 43, International Trade Files, Box 139, Folder marked "ITO/C.2/."

50. Ibid.

Subcommittee B met a total of seven times.[51] By January 22, the Subcommittee had reached unanimous agreement on a new draft of Article 12.[52] The chair of the Subcommittee emphasized the diversity of views on the Subcommittee and the fact that unanimity had been reached only as the result of a spirit of compromise.[53]

The United States achieved its goal in the Subcommittee of replacing Article 12(2) with language in which the members undertook to enter into bilateral negotiations upon the request of another member "if mutually acceptable."[54] As the language explicitly acknowledged, the ITO Charter could not compel the members to reach agreement, and thus this provision did not guarantee that a bilateral treaty would be concluded. To further promote the negotiation of future agreements, Article 11 of the Charter authorized the ITO to "make recommendations for and promote bilateral or multilateral agreements on measures designed . . . to assure just and equitable treatment for the enterprise, skills, capital, arts and technology brought from one Member country to another."[55] This latter provision was based on language that had appeared in the suggested Charter proposed by the United States in September 1946 and that had been retained in subsequent drafts.

At the same time, the United States failed to exclude entirely language that would be troubling for investors. Indeed, the Subcommittee adopted other changes to Article 12 that actually weakened the language adopted in Geneva. For example, the Subcommittee changed the language calling for the "widest opportunity" for investment to language calling for "reasonable opportunities for investments acceptable" to the host country. The Subcommittee changed the language guaranteeing the "greatest security" to investment to language guaranteeing "adequate security" for investment. The U.S. proposal to delete Article 12(2) had resulted in the elimination of any explicit reference to compensation for expropriation, although new language specified that each party had the right "to prescribe and give effect on just terms to requirements as to the ownership of existing and future investment," language that, Rubin believed, recognized implicitly an obligation of just compensation.[56] In addition, the requirement of

51. United Nations Conference on Trade and Employment, Report of Sub-Committee B on Article 12—International Investment for Economic Development, Record Group 43, International Trade Files, Box 141, Folder marked "U.N. Conf. on Trade & Employment Havana Nov. 1947–Mar. 1948."

52. United Nations Conference on Trade and Employment, Press Release ITO/C.2/20, 22 January 1948, NARA, Record Group 43, International Trade Files, Box 139, Folder marked "ITO/C.2/."

53. United Nations Conference on Trade and Employment, Second Committee: Economic Development, Summary Record of Seventeenth Meeting, 26 January 1948, NARA, Record Group 43, International Trade Files, Box 141, Folder marked "U.N. Conf. on Trade & Employment Havana Nov. 1947–Mar. 1946."

54. Article 12(2)(b).

55. Article 11(2)(a)(i).

56. Department of State Briefing Memorandum dated May 1, 1949, NARA, Record Group 43, International Trade Files, Box 14, Folder marked "Chapter III."

"adequate security" presumably addressed that issue to some degree as well. The requirement of non-discrimination that had appeared in the deleted version of Article 12(2) survived in the form of a much weaker obligation "to give due regard to the desirability of avoiding discrimination as between foreign investments."[57]

Before Subcommittee B completed its discussion of Article 12, Wallace Phillips, a representative of the ICC, took the floor to say that the Chamber opposed Article 12 as currently drafted because the Chamber believed that it would discourage foreign investment. He said that the deletion of Article 12 in its entirety would be preferable to a version that would be prejudicial to the revival of international capital movements. He added that the ICC wished to make clear that foreign investment was entitled at least to national treatment.[58]

Rubin told the Committee that the new Article 12 was not all that the United States wanted, but it was a "workable and worthwhile addition" to the Charter.[59] At the same time, however, Rubin said that the United States would support an effort to strengthen the language.[60] Belgium, the Netherlands, and Switzerland all called for stronger language.

Belgium proposed an amendment, supported by the United States, to strengthen the non-discrimination language.[61] The Belgian amendment would have replaced the language requiring the members to give "due regard to the desirability of avoiding discrimination as between foreign investments" with language prohibiting "all unjustifiable discrimination" between foreign and domestic investors. The amendment was defeated, however, with numerous delegates noting that the Subcommittee language was a compromise and that the amendment would upset the balance reached through the compromise. On January 30, the Committee approved Article 12 without the non-discrimination guarantee sought by Belgium, the United States, and the ICC.[62]

57. Article 12(2)(a)(ii).

58. United Nations Conference on Trade and Employment, Press Release ITO/C.2/22, 28 January 1948, NARA, Record Group 43, International Trade Files, Box 139, Folder marked "ITO/C.2/."

59. United Nations Conference on Trade and Employment, Second Committee: Economic Development, Summary Record of Eighteenth Meeting, 29 January 1948, NARA, Record Group 43, International Trade Files, Box 141, Folder marked "U.N. Conf. on Trade & Employment Havana Nov. 1947–Mar. 1946."

60. United Nations Conference on Trade and Employment, Second Committee: Economic Development, Summary Record of Seventeenth Meeting, 26 January 1948, NARA, Record Group 43, International Trade Files, Box 141, Folder marked "U.N. Conf. on Trade & Employment Havana Nov. 1947–Mar. 1946."

61. United Nations Conference on Trade and Employment, Press Release ITO/C.2/22, 28 January 1948, NARA, Record Group 43, International Trade Files, Box 139, Folder marked "ITO/C.2/."

62. United Nations Conference on Trade and Employment, Press Release ITO/C.2/23, 30 January 1948, NARA, Record Group 43, International Trade Files, Box 139, Folder marked "ITO/C.2/."

On February 16, the recommendation of the Joint Subcommittee on Articles 9 through 11 came before the full Committee. The Joint Subcommittee had held some 27 meetings on those three articles.[63]

The Joint Subcommittee had discussed the meaning of "unjustifiable" and "unreasonable." It had agreed that the fact that the host state provided national treatment to covered investment was evidence that the treatment was not unreasonable or unjustifiable. It also agreed, however, that national treatment would not be sufficient to constitute justifiable or reasonable treatment. In other words, the Subcommittee had acknowledged that the norms of reasonableness and non-discrimination had independent content. Finally, it had agreed that the terms "unreasonable" and "unjustifiable" should be interpreted in light of other provisions of the Charter, particularly Article 12.[64]

The Committee approved Article 11, except paragraph 4, which provided that the term "nationals" as used in Articles 11 and 12 comprised natural and legal persons.[65] A number of delegations had expressed concern that this language would create complications with respect to provisions of their constitutions or other domestic laws that referred to nationality. The Committee decided to delete the language in order to avoid those difficulties, but the deletion was not intended to affect the interpretation of the term "nationals" as embracing corporate entities as well as individuals. Further, the issue of the nationality of legal entities was not implicated by the paragraph or by its deletion.[66]

During the debate on Article 11, the Burmese delegation proposed an amendment that would have eliminated the prohibition on unreasonable or unjustifiable action injurious to investment and substituted a prohibition on discriminatory treatment, explaining that the existing language gave foreign investment more protection than national investment.[67] Burma

63. United Nations Conference on Trade and Employment, Report of Joint Sub-Committee of Committees II and VI on Articles 9, 10, and 11, Record Group 43, International Trade Files, Box 141, Folder marked "U.N. Conf. on Trade & Employment Havana Nov. 1947–Mar. 1948."

64. United Nations Conference on Trade and Employment, Draft Report of Joint Sub-Committee of Committees II and VI on Articles 9, 10, and 11, dated 3 February 1948, NARA, Record Group 43, International Trade Files, Box 141, File marked "U.N. Conf. on Trade & Employment, Havana, Nov. 1947–Mar. 1948."

65. United Nations Conference on Trade and Employment, Press Release ITO/C.2/24, 16 February 1948, NARA, Record Group 43, International Trade Files, Box 139, Folder marked "ITO/C.2/."

66. United Nations Conference on Trade and Employment, Second Committee: Economic Development, Doc. E/CONF.2/C.2/39, 20 February 1948, NARA, Record Group 43, International Trade Files, Box 140, Folder marked "Second Committee"; United Nations Conference on Trade and Employment, Reports of Committees and Principal Sub-Committees, page 25, September 1948, NARA, Record Group 43, International Trade Files, Box 148, Folder marked "Havana Conference: Reports of Committees and Principal Subcommittees."

67. United Nations Conference on Trade and Employment, Second Committee: Economic Development, Doc. E/CONF.2/C.2/9, 8 December 1947, NARA, Record Group 43, International Trade Files, Box 140, Folder marked "Second Committee."

understood that the norm of reasonableness was distinct from the norm of non-discrimination and wanted to ensure that the Charter embraced only the latter. The Burmese amendment, however, was not adopted.

The Conference considered a number of proposals to impose affirmative obligations on developed countries to assist developing countries in acquiring various facilities for economic development. For example, Mexico proposed the creation of a permanent Economic Development Commission to address that issue.[68] Chile proposed an amendment to Article 11 that would have required all members to notify other members of a shortage of consumer goods, to consult with members having a substantial interest in the importation of such goods in order to reserve an essential minimum supply for them, and to prevent speculation in consumer goods of vital importance to other members.[69] Costa Rica proposed that profits and dividends be taxable only by the host state.[70] Colombia proposed an entirely new article that would have authorized regional organizations to provide technical assistance to developing countries and to coordinate tax systems to ensure that income from investment could be taxed only in the host country.[71] None of these proposals was adopted, however.

On March 24, 1948, 53 nations signed the Final Act, which constituted the Charter of the International Trade Organization.[72] Argentina and Poland declined to sign because they were dissatisfied with the Charter. Turkey signed later.[73]

Meanwhile, as the process of negotiating the very controversial Article 12 had neared the end, Rubin prepared a memorandum seeking to evaluate the results of the Havana Conference. He believed that the deletion of Article 12(2) as drafted in Geneva had been of "utmost importance."[74] That language had reserved too many rights for host countries with respect to investment. The right of non-discriminatory treatment had been qualified by numerous exceptions. The requirement of "just" compensation was to have been evaluated from the point of view of the payer, suggesting that poor countries owed a lesser standard of compensation than rich countries. Payment could have been made in local currency. The deletion of Article 12(2) even provided an argument that the

68. Ibid.

69. Ibid.

70. Ibid.

71. Ibid.

72. Official Report of the United States Delegation to the United Nations Conference on Trade and Employment, Havana, Cuba, page 23, November 1948, NARA, Record Group 43, International Trade Files, Box 148, Folder marked "Official Report of the United States Delegation to the United Nations Conference on Trade and Employment, Havana, Cuba."

73. Ibid.

74. Memorandum by Seymour J. Rubin dated January 23, 1948, NARA, Record Group 43, International Trade Files, Box 14, Folder marked "Chapter III."

interpretation of "just compensation" as allowing payment in local currency was incorrect.[75]

With regard to lessons for the future, Rubin believed that any treaty must leave countries with "almost unlimited discretion" with respect to the right to establish investment, because of policies that the United States and other countries had adopted that limited the right of establishment and that these countries were unlikely to abandon.[76] Further, the U.S. delegation had determined that highly specific language with respect to expropriation, such as might be found in a bilateral treaty, was "impossible" to negotiate in a 60-nation, multilateral conference that was principally concerned with other matters.[77]

Rubin recognized that the new language adopted in Havana, although an improvement over the Geneva language, still would likely raise concerns. The U.S. delegation was especially troubled by references to taking ownership of property "on just terms." The problem was partly psychological because even the U.S. Constitution recognized the sovereign's power to expropriate with just compensation, and thus the U.S. delegation could hardly object to the Charter's recognition of such a power. Nevertheless, the footnote on local currency in the Geneva draft had raised sensitivity about the issue of expropriation and thus business groups would be particularly alert to the treatment of expropriation in the Havana Charter, which seemed to emphasize the host state's power.[78]

At the same time, however, Rubin noted that the Havana Charter did represent an improvement in the international investment regime insofar as it permitted certain issues relating to investment to be submitted to the dispute resolution mechanism of the Charter, including ultimately to the International Court of Justice, rather than merely to diplomatic representation, which in the past had been the only remedy for "unfair" treatment. For this reason, Article 12 provided American investors with an "improved status" with respect to their investments.[79] Further, the provision authorizing each member to call upon other members to negotiate bilateral treaties might well prove to be a "substantial help" to the United States in its efforts to negotiate FCN treaties. Rubin believed, on balance, that Article 12 was a "useful addition" to the Charter and that it gave an "important additional measure of security" to foreign investment.[80]

Rubin thus regarded the availability of binding dispute resolution as the most important accomplishment of the ITO Charter negotiation process with respect

75. Ibid.

76. Ibid.

77. Ibid.

78. Ibid.

79. Ibid.

80. Ibid.

to investment. Rubin's memorandum also reflected the continuing use of the concept of "fairness" as a way of characterizing the appropriate climate for foreign investment. Interestingly, Rubin did not draw particular attention to the principle of reasonableness that had been introduced in London and that had survived Geneva and Havana, although that may have been because he was evaluating the Havana Conference, and the establishment of the reasonableness principle had occurred well before Havana.

In later discussions, Rubin would continue to refer to fairness and would occasionally advert to the reasonableness principle. For example, in a talk that he delivered in October 1948, Rubin contended that a capital exporting country "looks chiefly for guarantees of fair treatment," and then moments later noted that the "best guarantee of continued foreign investment . . . is a reasonable and justifiable measure of security for the foreign private investor."[81] In his October talk, Rubin saw fairness as the overarching concept in a favorable investment climate, and linked this to norms of reasonableness and security.

In a speech that he delivered the following month, Rubin conceded that Article 12 was not "a ringing declaration of the rights of and security to be afforded to private foreign investors."[82] Much of Article 12 was phrased in terms of the powers of the capital importing country. Yet, Article 12 did have certain "compelling virtues."[83] The language on "just terms" was "not too far" from that of the Fifth Amendment to the U.S. Constitution.[84] The Charter recognized the importance of security to private investment. It contemplated further bilateral negotiations. The prohibition on "unjustifiable and unreasonable action" injurious to investment was "also a substantial guarantee of fair treatment."[85] Once again, Rubin treated "fairness" as a general term for the character of a favorable investment climate and suggested that fairness embraced the norm of reasonableness. Throughout his talk, he continued to refer to the treatment desired as "fair" treatment. He turned to the dispute resolution procedures of the Charter and argued that the Charter coupled "an agreement to give fair treatment" with an "agreed procedure" for resolving disputes with respect to such treatment.

The official report of the U.S. delegation concluded that the investment provision gave "the United States a basis for obtaining new commercial treaties and to safeguard investors against unfair treatment by complaining to the ITO that benefits of the Charter are being nullified or impaired."[86] Overall, the

81. Seymour J. Rubin, "Private Foreign Investment—The ITO Charter and the Bogota Economic Agreement," American Foreign Law Association, Proceedings No. 31, November 1948.

82. Ibid.

83. Ibid.

84. Ibid.

85. Ibid.

86. Official Report of the United States Delegation to the United Nations Conference on Trade and Employment, Havana, Cuba, page 27, November 1948, NARA, Record Group 43, International Trade Files, Box 148, Folder marked "Official Report of the United States Delegation to the United Nations Conference on Trade and Employment, Havana, Cuba."

delegation claimed, the accomplishments at the Havana Conference were "truly remarkable."[87]

THE AFTERMATH OF THE HAVANA CONFERENCE

Despite the efforts of the U.S. delegation to the Havana Conference to improve the language of the Geneva draft, the business community remained hostile to the investment provisions of the ITO Charter.[88] For example, in November 1949, at a meeting of the President's Committee on Financing Foreign Trade, an advisory group that included representatives of companies such as Chase National Bank, Bank of America, Westinghouse, U.S. Steel, and John Deere, several members of that Committee expressed the view that "ratification of the ITO Charter would render foreign investment impossible because of the investment provisions it contains."[89]

Although the NFTC, the NAM, and the Chamber of Commerce had representatives on the U.S. delegation at Havana, all three organizations opposed the Charter. The NFTC attacked the Havana Charter as worse than no charter at all. It argued that Article 12 "not only affords no protection for foreign investments of the United States but it would leave them with less protection than they now enjoy."[90] According to the NFTC, the prohibition on unreasonable treatment was not specific enough,[91] the provision calling for the negotiation of agreements ensuring just and equitable treatment for investment imposed no real obligation,[92] the requirement of "due regard" for avoiding discriminatory treatment offered too little reassurance,[93] and the dispute resolution provision did not commit the host country to binding arbitration of disputes concerning an investment.[94] Further, the NFTC believed that Article 12 would undermine U.S. efforts to negotiate stronger bilateral treaties for investment protection.[95]

87. Ibid., page 29.

88. Aaronson, *For the People,* page 164.

89. Memorandum headed "Meeting of the President's Committee on Financing Held at Mr. Aldrich's Office," dated November 28, 1949, NARA, Record Group 56, Subject Files of the Assistant Secretary of the NAC, Box 1.

90. *International Trade Organization,* Hearings Before the Committee on Finance, United States Senate, 80th Cong. 1st Session, Parts 1 and 2 (Washington, DC: Government Printing Office, 1947), page 200.

91. Robert F. Loree, *Position of the National Foreign Trade Council with Respect to the Havana Charter for an International Trade Organization* (New York: National Foreign Trade Council, 1950), page 53.

92. Ibid., pages 53–54.

93. Ibid., page 59.

94. Ibid., page 56.

95. Ibid., page 60.

The NAM also opposed the Charter, with the investment article providing one of the principal justifications for its opposition.[96] Acceptance of the modest protections in the Charter, according to the NAM, would impede efforts to strengthen the investment climate abroad, particularly those to protect investors against injurious conduct that passed the test of reasonableness.[97] That is, whereas the NFTC believed that the norm of reasonableness was too vague, the NAM went further and argued that the norm of reasonableness was intrinsically insufficient.

Although it conceded that the Havana Charter was an improvement over the Geneva draft, the ICC argued that the Charter did not provide foreign investors with "the kind of assurance they need in order to venture into foreign countries without fear of arbitrary governmental action."[98] The Charter failed to require just compensation for expropriation or to prohibit discrimination against foreign investment.

Critics even argued that the dispute resolution procedures, which Rubin saw as the single most important accomplishment with respect to investment in the Charter, disadvantaged U.S. investors because, without them, the United States could "throw [its] full weight against a country that expropriates."[99] The State Department noted in response that, in fact, it had tried to protect U.S. investors through diplomatic means "for a long time."[100] Despite U.S. efforts, however, "a long history of cases" existed where U.S. investors had received no compensation or inadequate compensation for expropriation.[101] In short, the State Department believed that investors failed to understand that the Charter provided them with more protection than could the Department through the exercise of diplomacy.

More generally, business groups saw the ITO Charter as a retreat from the original U.S. proposal and worried that the processes to be established by the Charter would result in further retreats.[102] This was particularly the case because each member would have a single vote within the ITO, and thus the United States, it was argued, would be outvoted by developing countries or those that favored objectionable policies. In the view of the investor community, concessions made by the United States would bind it, but other countries would invoke

96. William Diebold Jr., *The End of the I.T.O.* (Princeton, NJ: Princeton University Press, 1952), page 19.

97. Ibid., page 18.

98. International Chamber of Commerce, "Basic Criticisms of the Havana Charter," September 15, 1948, NARA, Record Group 43, International Trade Files, Box 147, Folder marked "Havana Conference—Basic Criticisms of the Havana Charter."

99. Department of State Briefing Memorandum dated May 1, 1949, NARA, Record Group 43, International Trade Files, Box 14, Folder marked "Chapter III."

100. Ibid.

101. Ibid.

102. Diebold, *End of the I.T.O.*, page 19.

various exceptions or escape clauses to avoid their own obligations so that the ITO Charter would represent a one-sided deal.

Woodbury Willoughby, by this time the chief of the Division of Commercial Policy, scheduled a meeting with the NFTC in November 1948 as part of an effort to build support for the Charter. An internal briefing memorandum written to assist him in his preparation for the meeting stressed two principal advantages of the ITO Charter. First, the Charter for the first time had subjected host state treatment of foreign investment to the "rule of reason." The memorandum identified three places where the rule of reason appeared: the provision in Article 12(1)(c)(iii) stating that a member of the ITO had the right to "prescribe and give effect on just terms" requirements with respect to ownership of investment, the provision in Article 12(1)(c)(iv) stating that a member of the ITO had the right to "prescribe and give effect to other reasonable requirements" with respect to investment, and the prohibition in Article 11(1)(b) on unreasonable or unjustifiable action injurious to the rights or interests of nationals of other members in their enterprise, skills, capital, arts, or technology. The memorandum further noted that these provisions created a basis on which to obtain payment of just compensation for expropriation.

The State Department believed that Articles 11 and 12 "require[d] fair treatment for foreign investments and facilities and [were] in conformity with the practice and the constitutional requirements of the U.S."[103] Thus, the Department saw the concept of fair treatment as a general term that embraced the entire corpus of investment-related obligations under the Charter, and it argued that these obligations were consistent with U.S. constitutional requirements. The Department noted, in particular, the parallel between "just terms" and the Fifth Amendment's requirement of "just compensation."

Second, the Charter had introduced binding, third-party dispute resolution.[104] The memorandum rejected the claim by opponents of the Charter that the Charter would preclude diplomatic protection with respect to a claim. Articles 41 and 93(1), for example, provided for consultations between the parties. The Charter facilitated negotiations by providing an agreed set of rights and obligations to which appeal could be made during diplomatic representations. In the event that consultations were unsuccessful, the dispute could be submitted to the dispute resolution provisions of the ITO, where again the Charter included rights and obligations that would form the basis for the complaint and where the United States could argued its case "without incurring, at least to the same degree, the charge of using its political and economic power to gain the decision it wants irrespective of the merits of the case."[105] The memorandum acknowledged that the ITO procedures could be slow, but that would depend upon how they were

103. Department of State Briefing Memorandum dated May 1, 1949, NARA, Record Group 43, International Trade Files, Box 14, Folder marked "Chapter III."

104. Memorandum dated November 8, 1948, from Weiss to Woodbury Willoughby, NARA, Record Group 43, International Trade Files, Box 14, Folder marked "Chapter III."

105. Ibid.

implemented in the future. The United States could use its influence to encourage expeditious procedures. In any event, the procedures should be shaped in order to ensure both speed and justice

The State Department understood that the investment provisions of Article 12 had placed the entire Charter in jeopardy, and sought to de-emphasize them. When Secretary of State Dean Acheson testified on behalf of the ITO Charter before the House Foreign Affairs Committee in 1950, his prepared statement, which was some 400 lines long, devoted only about 5 lines to the provisions on investment protection.[106] Public relations materials published by the State Department to build support for approval of the ITO Charter generally omitted any reference to the promotion or protection of U.S. foreign investment.[107]

The investment provisions were not the only cause for criticism by business groups. Some business interests opposed the Charter because they believed that, in light of its many exceptions and escape clauses, it would contribute too little to the liberalization of trade.[108] For example, they feared that exceptions for balance of payments difficulties would tend to perpetuate exchange controls and import quotas.[109] They also were concerned that the United States would make tariff concessions and receive too little in return.[110] Other business interests opposed the Charter because it could result in the reduction or elimination of U.S. trade restrictions that benefited them.[111] In short, free traders and protectionists alike joined in opposition to the Charter, the former because the Charter was said to be too weak and the latter because it was said to be too strong.

The ITO Charter did enjoy support from some interest groups. Labor and farm groups generally supported the Charter, as did many professional economists and civic organizations. Because of various compromises in the Charter, however, this support often lacked enthusiasm.[112]

Opposition to the Charter was sometimes ideological. Some businesses objected in principle to the idea, reflected in the Charter, that governments are

106. Testimony by the Honorable Dean Acheson, Secretary of State, Before the House Committee on Foreign Affairs, In Support of United States Acceptance of Membership in the International Trade Organization, NARA, Record Group 43, International Trade Files, Box 55, Folder marked "International Trade Organization (5)."

107. Examples include *World Trade and the United States*, Department of State Publication 3492, Commercial Policy Series 119 (Washington, DC: Government Printing Office, 1949) and *The International Trade Organization: Key to Expanding World Trade and Employment*, Department of State Publication 3882, Commercial Policy Series 130 (Washington, DC: Government Printing Office, 1950).

108. Diebold, *End of the I.T.O.*, pages 14–16; Thomas W. Zeiler, *Free Trade, Free World: The Advent of GATT* (Chapel Hill: University of North Carolina Press, 1999), pages 148–149.

109. Diebold, *End of the I.T.O.*, page 16.

110. Zeiler, *Free Trade, Free World*, page 148.

111. Diebold, *End of the I.T.O.*, page 23.

112. Ibid., page 10.

responsible for maintaining full employment, an idea that they rightly associated with the New Deal.[113] The Charter, in their view, was another step toward statism and socialism. Some opposed the Charter because they believed that it infringed upon U.S. sovereignty or required an unconstitutional delegation of federal power to an international body, a position supported to some extent by the American Bar Association.[114] Others criticized it on separation-of-powers grounds, believing that it institutionalized executive control over trade.[115]

Some even raised the question whether the ITO Charter coincided with communist doctrine, insofar as it called for future agreements giving "due regard" to the needs of each member.[116] As early as 1947, opponents of the ITO Charter had tried to link the ITO with communist subversion, a tactic that dissuaded some from publicly supporting the Charter.[117] The allegations were ironic, given that the Soviet Union refused to attend the Havana Conference and opposed the ITO Charter. Charter supporters attempted to use Soviet opposition to their advantage, arguing that by promoting trade the Charter would strengthen the free world in its struggle against communism.[118] In language reflecting the symbolic warfare between proponents and opponents and the need to identify the Charter with traditional American values, the State Department argued that the Charter called for "a 'Yankee swap' (a far cry from Communist doctrine)."[119]

In any event, the Soviet Union's refusal to participate in the ITO Charter negotiations undermined the argument that trade would promote peace.[120] By 1948, Americans regarded the Soviet Union as the chief threat to peace, and the Soviet Union's abstention from the ITO Charter negotiations meant that the ITO likely would not be a means for linking the two potential belligerents with bonds of mutually beneficial trade. If anything, the ITO merely provided other countries with a platform from which to denounce the United States.

In addition to bolstering ideological objections to the ITO Charter, the Cold War changed U.S. foreign policy priorities in ways adverse to the Charter. The U.S. delegation to the Havana Conference returned just as Congress was approving the European Recovery Plan, often referred to as the Marshall Plan.[121] Secretary

113. Ibid., page 17; Zeiler, *Free Trade, Free World*, page 150.

114. Diebold, *End of the I.T.O.*, page 23; Zeiler, *Free Trade, Free World*, page 148.

115. Zeiler, *Free Trade, Free World*, page 148.

116. Department of State Briefing Memorandum dated May 1, 1949, NARA, Record Group 43, International Trade Files, Box 14, Folder marked "Chapter III."

117. Aaronson, *For the People*, page 140.

118. Zeiler, *Free Trade, Free World*, page 158.

119. Ibid.

120. John M. Rothgeb Jr., *U.S. Trade Policy: Balancing Economic Dreams and Political Realities* (Washington, DC: Congressional Quarterly Press, 2001), page 77.

121. The debate regarding the Marshall Plan is described in Charles L. Mee Jr., *The Marshall Plan: The Launching of Pax Americana* (New York: Simon and Schuster, 1984), pages 225–245,

George C. Marshall and Undersecretary Robert Lovett did not wish to devote attention to long-term initiatives such as the ITO Charter that might dilute public support for immediate financial assistance to Europe.[122] The Marshall Plan also diminished business support for the Charter because many business groups had begun to believe that the stimulus to European reconstruction promised by that plan had eliminated the need for the ITO.[123] Following approval of the Marshall Plan, Congress turned its attention to other measures related to the Cold War, such as approval of the North Atlantic Treaty Organization and the Mutual Defense Assistance Program.[124]

Congressional inattention to the Charter also stemmed from the State Department's inept congressional relations. Prior to the Havana Conference, the State Department had declined to include congressional representatives in its delegation to the ITO preparatory conferences, thereby missing an opportunity to build support for the Charter within Congress.[125] When two senators and two congressmen were invited to Havana, the two senators declined, an indication of congressional indifference.[126]

Critical personnel changes undermined support for the Charter within the executive branch. Will Clayton, the head of the U.S. delegation and a highly visible and charismatic figure, had resigned as Undersecretary of State in October 1947, a month before the Havana Conference began, in order to spend more time with his ailing wife, although he had agreed to participate in the Havana Conference.[127] Clair Wilcox, the deputy head of the U.S. delegation, resigned after the conference from sheer exhaustion[128] and returned to the economics department at Swarthmore, where he immediately started work on a book explaining the Charter and urging its ratification, a book that he would publish in 1949.[129] With Clayton and Wilcox both gone, the State Department had lost the ITO Charter's most influential and knowledgeable advocates. At the same time, Dean Acheson, who would become Truman's secretary of state in January 1949, unlike Cordell Hull and Will Clayton, was not a strong proponent of free trade. In his

and Diane B. Kunz, *Butter and Guns: America's Cold War Economic Diplomacy* (New York: Free Press, 1997), pages 29–56.

122. Aaronson, *For the People*, page 156.

123. Telegram dated July 25, 1947, from the Department of State to the U.S. delegation in Geneva, NARA, Record Group 43, International Trade Files, Box 134, Folder marked "ITO Geneva Conference (chron) from July 1, 1947"; Zeiler, *Free Trade, Free World*, page 153.

124. Diebold, *End of the I.T.O.*, page 6.

125. Aaronson, *For the People*, page 119.

126. Ibid., page 158; Rothgeb, *U.S. Trade Policy*, page 75.

127. William L. Garwood Jr., *Will Clayton: Economic Statesman* (Washington, DC: American Studies Center, 1979), page 74.

128. John M. Leddy Oral History, Harry S. Truman Library.

129. Wilcox, *Charter*.

mind, foreign economic policy should serve national security, and thus the ITO Charter simply was of less importance than NATO and foreign aid for defense.[130] Without Clayton or Wilcox, Acheson lacked an influential advisor to keep the ITO Charter on his agenda.

To the extent that trade liberalization remained an administration priority, the ITO Charter was eclipsed by other instruments of trade policy. In the period immediately after the end of the Havana Conference, State Department officials wrestled with the question whether to give priority to approval of the ITO Charter or renewal of Cordell Hull's Reciprocal Trade Agreements Act, finally deciding to seek renewal of the trade act and to defer consideration of the ITO Charter until the next year.

Even more devastating was the parallel negotiation of the GATT[131] during the Geneva Conference. The participants in the Geneva Conference, as of 1947, were responsible for 70 percent of world trade.[132] The GATT, which entered into force on January 1, 1948, during the Havana Conference, covered about half of all world trade.[133] Thus, increasingly, it appeared that much of the desired trade liberalization could be achieved through the GATT, which weakened the argument for the necessity of an ITO. Indeed, by July 1948, the State Department had decided that those countries that participated in the Havana Conference but that were not parties to the GATT should be invited to accede to the GATT, and that a second round of tariff negotiations should be scheduled "at an early date with as large a number of countries as possible."[134] In April 1949, just as Truman was transmitting the ITO Charter to Congress, the GATT parties held a second round of negotiations in Annecy, a round in which 34 nations participated and that continued until August.[135] The resulting agreements covered 80 percent of world trade.[136]

Finally, ratification of the Charter was subject to election year politics. Delaying submission of the Charter to Congress until 1949 would remove it as an issue in Truman's re-election campaign and, if the Democrats regained control of Congress, allow its consideration by a more sympathetic legislative body.[137]

130. Zeiler, *Free Trade, Free World*, page 154.

131. General Agreement on Tariffs and Trade, October 30, 1947, TIAS No. 1700.

132. *Draft Charter for the International Trade Organization of the United Nations*, Department of State Publication 2927, Commercial Policy Series 106 (Washington, DC: Government Printing Office, 1947), page 6.

133. *World Trade and the United States*, Department of State Publication 3492, Commercial Policy Series 119 (Washington, DC: Government Printing Office, 1949).

134. *Current Economic Developments*, July 6, 1948, page 5, NARA, Record Group 59, Department of State Lot Files.

135. Zeiler, *Free Trade, Free World*, page 170.

136. Ibid., page 176.

137. Zeiler, *Free Trade, Free World*, page 153.

Truman at last submitted the ITO Charter to Congress on April, 18, 1949.[138] Congress delayed action, however, while it debated another renewal of the Reciprocal Trade Agreements Act, which had been renewed for only one year in 1948. The House had approved the renewal in February, but the Senate did not do so until September.[139] Truman continued to give priority to renewal of the Marshall Plan and approval of military assistance.[140]

The House Foreign Affairs Committee did not hold hearings on the ITO Charter until April 19, 1950, slightly more than two years after the Havana Conference ended. The committee chair, Democratic congressman John Kee of West Virginia, believed that the Charter could not pass the House.[141] Thus, the Committee never issued a report and the Charter was never brought to the House for debate.[142] Rather, members of the president's own party kept the Charter in the Committee. The Senate never even held hearings, in part because Democratic senator Tom Connally of Texas, the chairman of the Senate Foreign Relations Committee, believed that Truman would be "embarrassed" by the "indifference" of members of his party toward the ITO.[143]

The allegations of Republican senator Joseph McCarthy of Wisconsin, beginning in February 1950, that communists had infiltrated the State Department created additional problems for two reasons.[144] First, it increased the political cost of being associated with any program linked to socialism or even statism.[145] Second, McCarthy's theatrics distracted the Senate. For example, Senator Connally, in noting the failure of his Committee to hold hearings on the Charter, explained that "five of our members are on the sub-committee handling the charges made by Senator McCarthy."[146]

The outbreak of the Korean War in June 1950 struck the death blow. First, it further focused congressional attention on defense-related matters.[147] Second, it only heightened opposition to anything associated with socialism or statism.[148]

During the November 1950 midterm elections, Republicans gained 28 seats in the House and 5 seats in the Senate, diminishing the support that Truman

138. Aaronson, *For the People,* page 186; Zeiler, *Free Trade, Free World,* page 156.

139. Aaronson, *For the People,* page 205.

140. Zeiler, *Free Trade, Free World,* page 157.

141. Ibid., page 160.

142. Diebold, *End of the I.T.O.,* page 6.

143. Zeiler, *Free Trade, Free World,* page 160.

144. McCarthy's accusations are described in David M. Oshinsky, *A Conspiracy So Immense: The World of Joe McCarthy* (New York: Free Press, 1983).

145. Zeiler, *Free Trade,* page 159.

146. Aaronson, *For the People,* page 223.

147. Zeiler, *Free Trade, Free World,* page 161.

148. Ibid., page 159.

could expect for his legislative agenda in 1951.[149] Accordingly, at a cabinet meeting on November 21, as Chinese forces were driving into South Korea, Secretary of State Dean Acheson recommended that the administration abandon the ITO proposal[150] and pursue its trade agenda through the GATT, which at that moment was holding its third round of trade negotiations in Torquay.

In December 1950, the State Department issued a press release announcing that Truman had decided that the proposed ITO Charter would not be resubmitted to Congress during the current session.[151] The following year, Secretary Acheson finally acknowledged publicly that the Charter would never be resubmitted to Congress.[152] That same year, several other governments also withdrew the Charter from their own parliaments, explaining that the ITO would serve no purpose if the United States refused to join.[153] The decade-long effort to create the ITO had ended in failure.

Meanwhile, so controversial had the ITO Charter become that the State Department decided to remove references to the ITO Charter from those FCN treaties then under negotiation.[154] The Department believed that eliminating references to the Charter would reduce the possibility that Senate advice and consent to the ratification of the FCN treaties would become enmeshed in the controversy regarding the ITO Charter.[155]

The GATT originally was expected to be a temporary agreement that would be displaced within three years by the ITO Charter.[156] When the GATT parties realized that the ITO Charter would not come into force as anticipated, they maintained the GATT in force indefinitely.[157]

Although the effort to create an international trade organization ended in failure, it had major consequences for the evolution of U.S. foreign investment

149. Aaronson, *For the People*, page 123.

150. Ibid., page 224.

151. *Department of State Bulletin*, Vol. 23, No. 598, December 18, 1950, page 977.

152. Diebold, *End of the I.T.O.*, page 24.

153. Ibid., page 25.

154. *See, e.g.*, Telegram dated July 6, 1951, from the Department of State to the U.S. legation in Beirut, NARA, Record Group 59, Department of State File No. 611.83A4/6-1251; Despatch dated February 8, 1952, from the Department of State to the U.S. embassy in New Delhi, NARA, Record Group 59, Department of State File No. 611.914/2-852; Telegram dated June 18, 1952, from the Department of State to the U.S. embassy in Cairo, NARA, Record Group 59, Department of State File No. 611.744/6-1852.

155. Airgram dated February 8, 1951, from the Department of State to the U.S. embassy in Copenhagen, NARA, Record Group 59, Department of State File No. 611.594/1-251. *See also* Telegram dated June 18, 1952, from the Department of State to the U.S. embassy in Cairo, NARA, Record Group 59, Department of State File No. 611.744/6-1852.

156. Diebold, *End of the I.T.O.*, page 28.

157. Ibid.

policy. First, the hearings on the Charter provided a forum in which the U.S. business community could pressure the U.S. government to seek treaty provisions to strengthen the protection of international investment. Second, that pressure prompted the U.S. government to consider at length the kinds of provisions that should appear in an investment treaty. Third, the ITO negotiations demonstrated the impossibility of negotiating investment-related provisions acceptable to the U.S. business community in a multilateral forum, and thus the need to incorporate any such provisions in bilateral treaties, whether FCN treaties or new bilateral treaties dedicated solely to investment protection. Fourth, the negotiations led to efforts, described in Chapter 5, to incorporate at least some of the investment-related provisions developed for the ITO Charter into the U.S. FCN treaties, thus permanently transforming those treaties. Fifth, the negotiations introduced a new norm of reasonableness into the regime of international investment law and, in particular, into the U.S. FCN treaties. Sixth, it led to the formulation of a general prohibition on discriminatory treatment, apart from more specific requirements of national and MFN treatment. Seventh, although the concept of fair and equitable treatment previously had appeared in U.S. investment policy statements and in provisions of the FCN treaties addressing specific problems, the ITO Charter negotiations incorporated the concept for the first time in a proposed treaty as a descriptor of the general investment climate that the United States sought to create, although the term used in the final language of the Charter was "just and equitable."

5

The FCN Treaties Become Investment Treaties

As his 1949 inauguration approached, President Harry S. Truman, an avid reader of U.S. history, wanted to deliver a memorable speech, like Washington's farewell address, that would enhance his stature.[1] The problem was that his speech lacked a memorable idea or theme.

The solution to Truman's problem would come from a mid-level State Department official named Benjamin H. Hardy. Hardy had served in Latin America as a naval officer during the war, when he had concluded that U.S. foreign policy should place greater emphasis on improving living conditions around the world rather than cultivating the support of elites.[2] After the war, he worked as a speechwriter in the State Department's Office of Public Affairs. In August 1948, he told the office director, Francis Russell, that the United States should develop a program of technical assistance for developing countries, an idea that he formalized in a memorandum in November. A native of Georgia, where he had seen how new technology could transform an economy, Hardy saw his proposal as an application of the New Deal to less-developed countries.[3]

The idea of U.S. technical assistance to developing countries was not entirely new. In 1940, Nelson Rockefeller had expressed a concern to Franklin Roosevelt that the Nazis were gaining influence in Latin America, after which Roosevelt appointed Rockefeller to a new position as coordinator of Inter-American affairs. The Rockefeller Foundation already was involved in programs of technical assistance in Latin America[4] and, in 1942, the Roosevelt administration established

1. Thomas G. Paterson, "Foreign Aid under Wraps: The Point Four Program," 56 *The Wisconsin Magazine of History* 119 (1972).

2. Ken Hechler, *Working with Truman: A Personal Memoir of the White House Years* (New York: G. P. Putnam's Sons, 1982), pages 115–116.

3. Clark Clifford, *Counsel to the President* (New York: Random House, 1991), page 149.

4. Sergei Y. Shenin, *The United States and the Third World: The Origins of Postwar Relations and the Point Four Program* (Huntington, NY: Nova Publishers, 1999), page 162.

the Institute of Inter-American Affairs, headed by Rockefeller, to provide government-funded assistance.

Russell forwarded Hardy's suggestion to other officials in the Department, but these officials believed that it would never be funded. With Secretary of State George Marshall hospitalized for kidney surgery (and on the verge of resigning), Acting Secretary of State Robert Lovett requested that Russell assist him in developing ideas for Truman's inaugural address. Russell suggested to Hardy that he prepare a draft incorporating his technical assistance proposal. Russell forwarded Hardy's draft to Lovett, who rejected it with a notation that read, "Francis, I am not sure this is a good idea, but I am quite sure that it's not appropriate for an inaugural address."[5]

Undeterred, Hardy boldly telephoned Truman's speechwriter, George Elsey, whom he knew only from some telephone conversations, to request a meeting.[6] Believing that Hardy was calling on behalf of the State Department, Elsey agreed to the meeting. After Hardy explained his proposal, Elsey realized "instantly" that Hardy's proposal was the idea for which he had been searching.[7] Clark Clifford, Truman's special assistant, later explained the reason that Hardy's proposal had found its way into Truman's inaugural address: "While we had a speech in search of an idea, Hardy had an idea in search of a speech."[8]

To avoid any retribution against Hardy for communicating with the White House outside of the normal channels, Elsey asked the State Department to include a technical assistance program in its recommendations for the inaugural address. No reply came from the Department. After several days, Hardy brought another draft to Elsey, saying that Lovett had refused to send it to the White House. Lovett believed that the proposal had "insufficient preparation and analysis."[9]

When Truman read the first draft of his address, which included Hardy's proposal, he saw the proposal as a New Deal program. More particularly, he analogized the proposal to the Tennessee Valley Authority, which had brought prosperity to the Southeast, and to the educational programs of the Department of Agriculture.[10] Truman also was aware, as a student of history, that economic development in the United States had been financed during the nineteenth century by

5. Hechler, *Working with Truman*, page 116.

6. Clifford, *Counsel to the President*, page 249.

7. Paterson, *Foreign Aid under Wraps*, page 121.

8. Ibid., page 250.

9. Hechler, *Working with Truman*, page 117.

10. Ibid. page 118. Jason Scott Smith argues that Point Four was also a legacy of the public works programs of the New Deal. Jason Scott Smith, *Building New Deal Liberalism: The Political Economy of Public Works, 1933–1956* (New York: Cambridge University Press, 2006), pages 248–249.

foreign investment.[11] Truman later explained, "It seemed to me that if we could encourage stabilized governments in underdeveloped countries in Africa, South America, and Asia, we could encourage the use for the development of those areas of some of the capital which had accumulated in the United States."[12] Truman recognized, however, that promoting international capital movements would require, as State Department policymakers repeatedly had recognized, both extending legal protection to foreign investment and ensuring that foreign investment contributed to economic development. As he wrote, "If the investment of capital from the United States could be protected and not confiscated, and if we could persuade the capitalists that they were not working in foreign countries to exploit them but to develop them, it would be to the mutual benefit of everybody concerned."[13]

The benefit to the United States, in Truman's mind, was that prosperity would enable developing countries to purchase American exports.[14] This, of course, was the very benefit of foreign investment that U.S. policymakers had been citing at least since the early 1940s, when they were planning the postwar economic order. At the same time, Truman believed, such a program would demonstrate the tangible benefits of the American way of life and thereby thwart the expansion of communism,[15] particularly in developing countries. As this indicates and as was seen in Chapter 1, the Cold War had added a further justification for promoting outward U.S. investment. The notion, prevalent at the beginning of the decade, that foreign investment would foster prosperity and peace had evolved, by the end of the decade, into the notion that foreign investment would foster prosperity and victory in the Cold War.

Thus, as the process of drafting Truman's address progressed, Hardy's proposal of technical assistance became coupled with the idea of promoting private investment. The White House sent the final draft of the speech to the State Department two days before the inauguration and, again, Lovett objected to the Hardy proposal. Dean Acheson, who would serve as secretary of state in Truman's second administration, liked the speech, however, and the proposal remained despite Lovett's objections.[16]

TRUMAN PROPOSES THE POINT FOUR PROGRAM

January 20, 1949, was a cold, but almost cloudless, day. A little after noon, under a brilliant sun, Truman ascended "the most monumental and costly inaugural stand

11. Harry S. Truman, *Memoirs by Harry S. Truman, Volume II, Years of Trial and Hope* (Garden City, NJ: Doubleday, 1956), page 231.

12. Ibid.

13. Ibid.

14. Ibid., pages 232–233.

15. Ibid.

16. Clifford, *Counsel to the President,* pages 250–251.

ever seen up to that time,"[17] constructed with funds generously appropriated by the Republican Eightieth Congress with the expectation that the man standing atop the platform would be named Thomas E. Dewey, not Harry S. Truman. At 1:29 pm, having taken the oath of office and kissed the Bible, Truman turned to the crowd of more than a million people and delivered the first inaugural address ever televised, an address devoted entirely to the foreign policy of the United States.

He explained that his foreign policy would "emphasize four major courses of action." The first of these four points was to support the United Nations, the second was to continue the program for "world economic recovery," and the third was to "strengthen freedom-loving nations against the dangers of aggression." American foreign policy, in other words, would continue to include the promotion of economic prosperity and victory in the Cold War. None of that was new, and that part of his address would soon be forgotten.

Truman next turned to the innovative idea for which his inaugural address long would be remembered: a new way of achieving economic prosperity and victory in the Cold War. He announced his adoption of Ben Hardy's proposal, a proposal that soon was known universally as "Point Four." In Truman's words, "Fourth, we must embark on a bold new program for making the benefits of our scientific advancement and industrial progress available for the improvement and growth of underdeveloped areas."[18]

Truman began his discussion of Point Four with an explanation of the circumstances that necessitated the program: "More than half the people of the world are living in conditions approaching misery. Their food is inadequate. They are victims of disease. Their economic life is primitive and stagnant. Their poverty is a handicap and a threat both to them and to more prosperous areas. . . ."[19]

Next, he explained the reason that the burden of addressing world poverty fell to the United States: "The United States is pre-eminent among nations in the development of industrial and scientific techniques. The material resources which we can afford to use for the assistance of other peoples are limited. But our imponderable resources in technical knowledge are constantly growing and are inexhaustible."[20]

Truman then restated his proposal, but this time he added a second component. Technical assistance must be accompanied by increased private investment: "I believe that we should make available to peace-loving peoples the benefits of our store of technical knowledge in order to help them realize their

17. Robert J. Donovan, *Tumultuous Years: The Presidency of Harry S. Truman, 1949–1953* (New York: W. W. Norton, 1982), pages 20–21.

18. Harry S. Truman, "The Faith of the American People: The Inaugural Address," January 20, 1949, *reprinted in* Department of State, *A New Era in World Affairs: Selected Speeches and Statements of President Truman, January 20 to August 29, 1949,* Department of State Publication 3653 (Washington, DC: Government Printing Office, 1949), page 6.

19. Ibid.

20. Ibid., page 7.

aspirations for a better life. And, in cooperation with other nations, we should foster capital investment in areas needing development. With the cooperation of business, private capital, agriculture, and labor in this country, this program can greatly increase the industrial activity in other nations and can raise substantially their standards of living."[21]

The State Department long had acknowledged in its foreign investment policy statements that foreign investment did not always serve the interests of capital importing countries, a fact that Truman understood as well.[22] He was aware that much foreign investment in developing countries was a product of colonialism, and he envisioned a form of development that would yield self-sufficiency, not a new kind of foreign domination.[23] Thus, he explained, the United States must promote the interests of the host countries as well as those of the foreign investors: "Such new economic developments must be devised and controlled to benefit the peoples of the areas in which they are established. Guarantees to the investors must be balanced by guarantees in the interest of the people whose resources and whose labor go into these developments. The old imperialism—exploitation for foreign profit—has no place in our plans. What we envisage is a program of development based on the concepts of democratic fair-dealing."[24]

Truman had announced his "Fair Deal" legislative proposals in his annual State of the Union address, delivered to Congress only 15 days before. Through his reference to "development based on the concepts of democratic fair-dealing," Truman explicitly linked the principles of his foreign policy with those underlying his domestic policy.

Perhaps anticipating Republican objections to an extension of the Fair Deal abroad, Truman emphasized that his Point Four proposal served the economic interests of the United States as well as those of the developing countries: "All countries, including our own, will greatly benefit from a constructive program for the better use of the world's human and natural resources. Experience shows that our commerce with other countries expands as they progress industrially and economically."[25]

Truman wanted as well to sound an idealistic note, to link Point Four to aspirations greater than merely the economic self-interests of the United States: "Only by helping the least fortunate of its members to help themselves can the human family achieve the decent, satisfying life that is the right of all people. Democracy alone can supply the vitalizing force to stir the peoples of the world into triumphant action, not only against their human oppressors, but also against their ancient enemies—hunger, misery, and despair."[26]

21. Ibid.

22. Truman, *Memoirs,* page 232.

23. Ibid.

24. Truman, "Inaugural Address," pages 7–8.

25. Ibid., page 8.

26. Ibid.

Truman's announcement of the Point Four program was received with "immense and sustained" applause.[27] The *Washington Post* reported on the speech under the headline "Truman Proposes 'Fair Deal' Plan for the World."[28]

Clark Clifford later explained that the proposal for assistance to developing countries had been included as the final of four points precisely so that it would provide a climax following the recitation of familiar policies. "You go through the dog acts and acrobats on up to the headline, and that's the last act of the evening. That's why it was made Point 4."[29]

Point Four represented a significant departure in U.S. foreign economic policy. It was the first substantial U.S. bilateral program directed at economic development in other countries.[30] The United States had provided aid to Europe under the Marshall Plan for purposes of reconstruction, that is, for rebuilding economies devastated by the war. Point Four, however, was aimed not at European countries adjacent to the Iron Curtain, but at developing countries, many of which were newly freed from colonialism. Walt W. Rostow has argued that Truman's inaugural address "constituted a turning point in Western policy."[31]

Secretary of State Acheson claimed that Point Four was more than just another instrument of the Cold War policy of containment, explaining that "the program has a much more enduring and fundamental purpose than [containment], and we should be carrying it forward even if there were no Soviet threat."[32] Truman too had linked Point Four to goals beyond winning the Cold War. He sought through technical assistance and private investment to bring economic development to the entire world. It would project the New Deal, through its direct successor the Fair Deal, onto the international plane and contribute to higher standards of living worldwide.

Soviet commentators took a different view. They regarded Point Four as a means of expanding capitalist penetration of developing countries, focusing less on the technical assistance aspects than on its stimulation of private investment, which they regarded as a form of neocolonialism.[33]

Truman's assertion that Point Four would not constitute a new form of colonial domination apparently represented a sincere belief. The day after his inauguration, Truman told the cabinet that the work of Point Four would be done principally

27. David McCullough, *Truman* (New York: Simon and Schuster, 1992), page 731.

28. *The Washington Post*, January 21, 1949, page 1.

29. Clark Clifford Oral History, Harry S. Truman Library; Thomas G. Paterson, *Meeting the Communist Threat: Truman to Reagan* (New York: Oxford University Press, 1988), page 147.

30. W. W. Rostow, *Theories of Economic Growth from David Hume to the Present* (New York: Oxford University Press, 1990), page 376.

31. Ibid.

32. Department of State, *What Is Point Four? Address by the Secretary of State*, Department of State Publication 4487 (Washington, DC: Government Printing Office, 1952), page 6.

33. Shenin, *United States and the Third World*, page 172.

through private enterprise. He explained, however, that "[t]he private concerns would be required to give assurances that they would not exploit the foreign country into which they went, but would operate to the benefit of that country."[34] The interdepartmental Foreign Investment Policy Committee, as shown in Chapter 1, had been working for years on a policy that embraced precisely that idea.

Because the Point Four program had originated as the inspiration of a mid-level speech writer and did not enjoy much support from the State Department leadership, the Department prior to Truman's inauguration had not developed any plans for implementing the Point Four proposal. After the address, Acheson insisted that the State Department have responsibility for the administration of the program,[35] but then largely ignored it. Willard Thorp, who served as the assistant secretary of state for economic affairs following Will Clayton's elevation to undersecretary, recalled that "nobody upstairs paid much attention" to Point Four.[36]

CREATING A POINT FOUR PROGRAM

Developing a policy to implement Point Four would fall to mid-level officials within the federal government, who searched for programs that would add content to Truman's new policy. In February, the State Department convened an interagency group called the Advisory Committee on Technical Assistance (ACTA) to develop a more specific proposal to implement Point Four. ACTA prepared a document entitled "Objectives and Nature of the Point IV Program,"[37] which the ECEFP adopted on March 1.[38] The president approved the policy on April 21.[39]

The ACTA policy on Point Four began by recapitulating the goals of U.S. foreign economic policy, particularly foreign investment policy. The first goal was "contributing to domestic economic stability and productivity."[40] The document noted that exports were necessary to prevent a contraction in the U.S. economy, but that the United States was not importing enough to allow other countries to pay for U.S. exports. Outward capital investment would provide other countries with the dollars that they needed to pay for U.S. exports. More generally, outward

34. Robert A. Pollard, *Economic Security and the Origins of the Cold War, 1945–1960* (New York: Columbia University Press, 1985), page 206.

35. Clifford, *Counsel to the President*, page 252.

36. Willard Thorp Oral History, Harry S. Truman Library.

37. Department of State, *Foreign Relations of the United States, 1949*, Vol. 1 (Washington, DC: Government Printing Office, 1976), page 763.

38. Memorandum headed "Objectives and Nature of the Point IV Program," approved March 1, 1949, NARA, Record Group 59, Department of State File No. 800.50T.A./5-349.

39. Department of State Circular Telegram headed "Planning the 'Point Four' Program," May, 1949, NARA, Record Group 59, Department of State File No. 800.50T.A./5-349.

40. Memorandum headed "Objectives and Nature of the Point IV Program," approved March 1, 1949, NARA, Record Group 59, Department of State File No. 800.50T.A./5-349.

investment would "achiev[e] a better balance in the world economy" by increasing productivity everywhere.[41] Increased productivity in "underdeveloped areas" would benefit those areas as well as the rest of the world.[42] It would enable developing countries to buy manufactured goods from Europe and the United States, thereby increasing employment in developed countries, while also giving developed countries access to lower cost goods produced by more productive developing countries.

Point Four would contribute as well to U.S. victory in the Cold War. It would strengthen U.S. national security by creating goodwill with developing countries and strengthening "freedom loving" nations.[43] In this way, the appeal of communist subversion would be reduced, while U.S. allies in the Cold War would become more effective.[44] Increasing prosperity everywhere would promote peace, as the energies of peoples were channeled toward constructive activity.

These goals were little different from those articulated at the end of the war: using foreign investment to promote prosperity and peace, except that the promotion of peace now included defeating communism in addition to eliminating the economic hardship that had led to war in the past.

The ACTA document observed that it was "particularly important" that countries conclude bilateral or multilateral agreements to encourage international investment flows.[45] The document did not specifically refer to FCN treaties, but very quickly State Department officials would decide that FCN treaties could fulfill the need identified by the policy statement.

Business groups believed that the negotiation of an investment treaty was the single most important thing that the government could do to promote and protect foreign investment,[46] and strongly supported the negotiation of FCN treaties as an element of the Point Four program.[47] In a pamphlet published in December 1949 concerning the program, the New York Chamber of Commerce called for the negotiation of bilateral treaties to protect U.S. investment abroad.[48] Writing to the chair of the Senate Committee on Foreign Relations about FCN treaties in

41. Ibid.

42. Ibid.

43. Ibid.

44. As several historians have argued, Point Four was a way of extending containment to the developing world. *See, e.g.*, David A. Baldwin, *Economic Development and American Foreign Policy, 1943–62* (Chicago: University of Chicago Press, 1966), page 74.

45. Memorandum headed "Objectives and Nature of the Point IV Program," approved March 1, 1949, NARA, Record Group 59, Department of State File No. 800.50T.A./5-349.

46. Transcript of Proceedings, Meeting of Economic Consultants on Point Four Program, April 8, 1949, page 109, NARA, Record Group 59, Department of State File No. 800.50T.A./4-859.

47. Baldwin, *Economic Development*, page 104.

48. Chamber of Commerce of the State of New York, *The Point 4 Program* (December 1949), *reprinted in* Walter M. Daniels, *The Point Four Program* (New York: H. W. Wilson, 1951), pages 125–128.

1950, the president of the NFTC observed that "[c]onsideration of measures to implement President Truman's Point IV Program has given greater emphasis to the need for this type of diplomatic arrangement. We need scarcely add that we are greatly in favor of the accelerated program of negotiating treaties of friendship, commerce and navigation initiated by the State Department."[49] The U.S. Chamber of Commerce went farther and argued that the provision of assistance to foreign countries should be conditioned upon their concluding agreements guaranteeing "fair treatment" for U.S. investment.[50] Once again, elements of the business community sought to use economic leverage to pressure other countries to conclude FCN treaties with the United States.

The State Department almost immediately began to refer to FCN treaties as treaties intended to promote foreign investment. For example, during a press conference held on July 13, 1949, Secretary Acheson explained that the FCN treaty between Italy and the United States was "designed to stimulate a mutually advantageous flow of capital and technology which is in line with basic objectives of [the] Point Four program."[51] An internal State Department memorandum drafted by a member of the Division of Commercial Policy a few months later noted that "[t]his Government is now actively promoting the investment of private American capital in foreign countries through the projected Point Four program, treaties of friendship, commerce and navigation and other measures."[52]

Indeed, the Department of State soon regarded the protection of foreign investment as the primary function of the FCN treaties. By February 1950, Winthrop Brown, who had succeeded Clair Wilcox as the Director of the Office of International Trade Policy, could say that "the predominant (but not the only) interest of this Government in seeking to negotiate [FCN treaties] lies in the contribution which they can make in promoting economic development by the creation of a climate favorable to the flow of private capital into foreign investments, and thus increasing standards of living everywhere. The treaty program is being developed with a view to its forming an integral and important part of the Point IV program."[53] An internal State Department report written in March 1950 explained, "During the past several months there has been evidence of a broader general understanding of the functions of treaties of friendship, commerce and navigation. Clarifications of policy with respect to the Point Four program and

49. Letter dated March 6, 1950, from Eugene P. Thomas to Senator Tom Connally, NARA, Record Group 59, Department of State File No. 611.334/2-2350.

50. Chamber of Commerce of the United States, *What the Chamber Stands for in World Affairs, reprinted in* Daniels, *Point Four Program,* pages 63–66.

51. Telegram dated July 13, 1949, from the Department of State to the U.S. mission in Rome, NARA, Record Group 59, Department of State File No. 711.652/7-1349.

52. Memorandum by Charles H. Sullivan headed "Entry of Foreign Investors into the United States under Treaties of Friendship, Commerce and Navigation," dated November 23, 1949, NARA, Record Group 59, Department of State File No. 611.004/5-350.

53. Memorandum dated February 13, 1950, from Winthrop Brown to Sheldon Mills, NARA, Record Group 59, Department of State File No. 611.004/3-850.

the signing of the treaties with Ireland and Uruguay have tended to focus attention upon the role of these treaties in promoting the investment of private capital in foreign countries and thus in furthering one of the major objectives of Point Four."[54] Similarly, the State Department explained to the U.S. embassy in Cairo the same month that "[a] major interest of this Government at present in seeking to negotiate treaties of this type lies in the contribution which they make to the creation of a climate favorable to the flow of American private capital into foreign investments. The treaty program is being developed with a view to its forming an integral and important part of the Point IV program."[55] When transmitting a proposed FCN treaty to the U.S. ambassador to Ethiopia in July 1950, the State Department explained that "[t]he enclosed draft, as the Uruguay treaty and others of the sort, is quite relevant to the Point IV program and constitutes an important element in the realization of Point IV objectives, inasmuch as such treaties are calculated to establish a 'climate' of conditions conducive to the flow of investment capital."[56] A September 1950 memorandum regarding negotiations with India noted that "[a]t the present time, the major interest in the treaty program derives from the utility of the treaties in establishing and formalizing conditions favorable to a flow of foreign investments for the economic development of under-developed areas."[57] A September 1950 State Department press release described the FCN treaty between Ireland and the United States as "an example of the type of treaty the United States is seeking to negotiate with many countries with the object of encouraging the flow of investment capital, expanding world trade and stimulating productive economic intercourse generally.[58] In October, the Department described the promotion of private investment as "currently the major emphasis of the [FCN] treaty program."[59]

Even provisions of the FCN treaties guaranteeing noneconomic rights were reconceived as investment-related. As the March 1950 internal State Department report explained, "Concurrently, there has been growing appreciation of the value of those provisions in commercial treaties which provide assurances respecting

54. Memorandum headed "Present Status of Program for Negotiating Treaties of Friendship, Commerce and Navigation," dated March 10, 1950, NARA, Record Group 59, Department of State File No. 611.004/3-2250.

55. Telegram dated March 9, 1950, from the Department of State to the U.S. embassy in Cairo, NARA, Record Group 59, Department of State File No. 711.832/3-950.

56. Letter dated July 18, 1950, from Willard Thorp to Ambassador George Merrill, NARA, Record Group 59, Department of State File No. 611.654/6-1550.

57. Memorandum headed "Negotiation of Treaty of Friendship, Commerce and Navigation with India," dated September 11, 1950, NARA, Record Group 59, Department of State File No. 611.914/9-1150.

58. Department of State Press Release No. 959, September 15, 1950, *reprinted in Department of State Bulletin,* Vol. 13, No. 587, October 2, 1950, pages 550–551.

59. *Current Economic Developments,* October 23, 1950, NARA, Record Group 59, Department of State Lot Files.

fundamental personal rights and of the way in which such provisions contribute to the development of a favorable climate for investment. . . . [P]rivate business interests are particularly aware of the importance of assurances of this kind and of their direct relation to actual business operations abroad."[60]

More than two years after Truman's inaugural address, the State Department's new understanding of the FCN treaties had not changed. A December 29, 1951, memorandum from Assistant Secretary for Economic Affairs Willard Thorp regarding a group of FCN treaties negotiated during 1951 referred to those treaties as part of a "program of extending and modernizing the treaty protection of American citizens, corporations, capital, trade and shipping abroad, with special emphasis on establishing conditions favorable to private investment."[61] During testimony in 1952 in support of several FCN treaties pending before the Senate, Deputy Assistant Secretary of State Harold F. Linder explained that "[p]erhaps the most important respect in which the current treaties differ from those of the twenties and thirties is in the greatly increased emphasis on the encouragement of American private investment abroad, by the expansion and strengthening of provisions relating to the protection of the investor and his interests."[62]

Congress saw the FCN treaties similarly. When it enacted the Mutual Security Act of 1952,[63] Congress inserted a new section 516(d) into the Mutual Security Act of 1951 directing the State Department to "accelerate a program of negotiating treaties of commerce and trade," and noted specifically that the treaties "shall include provisions to encourage and facilitate the flow of private investment to countries participating in programs under this Act."[64]

The State Department's reconceptualization of the FCN treaties as investment treaties continued beyond the change of administration and political party that occurred with the 1953 inauguration of Republican president Dwight D. Eisenhower. In a telegram dated November 5, 1954, sent to the American embassies in Brussels, The Hague, and Luxembourg, the State Department explained that the trade provisions of the FCNs were of "quite secondary importance."[65] Rather, it noted, "The major present emphasis and purpose of the FCN

60. Memorandum headed "Present Status of Program for Negotiating Treaties of Friendship, Commerce and Navigation," dated March 10, 1950, NARA, Record Group 59, Department of State File No. 611.004/3-2250.

61. Memorandum dated December 29, 1951, from Willard Thorp to the Office of Congressional Relations, NARA, Record Group 59, Department of State File No. 611.004/12-2951.

62. *Commercial Treaties*, Hearing Before a Subcommittee of the Committee on Foreign Relations, 82nd Cong. 2d Sess. (1952), page 1

63. 66 Stat. 141.

64. 66 Stat. 146. For the State Department's report to its embassies on this legislation, *see* Department of State Circular Airgram dated August 6, 1953, NARA, Record Group 59, Department of State File No. 611.004/8-653.

65. Instruction dated November 5, 1954, from the Department of State to the U.S. embassy in Brussels, NARA, Record Group 59, Department of State File No. 611.554/11-554.

treaty lies in its establishment and investment provisions."[66] Further, "[t]he main current incentive to negotiate such a treaty, aside from the political and traditionalist incentive, is to lay the foundation for increased foreign investment."[67] The following month, the U.S. embassy in Belgium informed Belgian diplomats that the United States "considered the most important feature of the Treaty to be its provisions for improving the investment climate with respect to relations between the two countries."[68] When testifying before the Senate in July 1956 in support of the FCN treaties with Iran, the Netherlands, and Nicaragua, Deputy Assistant Secretary of State Thorsten Kalijarvi explained that "the principal immediate incentive in the negotiation of these treaties is the desire to help create conditions favorable to foreign private investment. . . ."[69] The following month, during negotiations with Korea, the State Department informed its embassy in Seoul that the "[p]urpose of [the] treaty is [to] promote investment."[70] At the commencement of negotiations with the sultanate of Muscat and Oman, an internal State Department memorandum sent to the lead U.S. negotiator in April 1957 observed that many considered the creation of favorable conditions for capital investment to be "the most important single objective of treaties of this kind."[71]

Congress continued to agree about the importance of using FCN treaties to promote outward foreign investment. In 1954, Congress enacted section 413 of the Mutual Security Act of 1954, which provided that the president "shall accelerate a program for negotiating treaties of commerce and trade . . . which shall include provisions to encourage and facilitate the flow of private investment to, and its equitable treatment in, nations participating in programs under this Act." [72]

Other countries conceptualized the FCN treaties the same way, and came to regard the chief reason for concluding an FCN treaty to be not the creation of trade or navigation rights, but the promotion of foreign investment. For example, in 1950, officials of the Bank of Mexico asked for a copy of the standard draft U.S.

66. Ibid.

67. Ibid.

68. Memorandum of Conversation dated November 30, 1954, NARA, Record Group 59, Department of State File No. 511.554/12-454.

69. *Commercial Treaties with Iran, Nicaragua and the Netherlands*, Hearing Before the Committee on Foreign Relations, 84th Cong. 2d Sess. (1956).

70. Telegram dated August 3, 1956, from the Department of State to the U.S. embassy in Seoul, NARA, Record Group 59, Department of State File No. 611.95B4/8-356.

71. Memorandum headed "Summary of Provisions of Draft Treaty of Amity and Economic Relations," enclosure to Instruction dated April 17, 1957, from the Department of State to the U.S. Consulate General in Dhahran, NARA, Record Group 59, Department of State File No. 611.86E1/4-1757.

72. Public Law 665, 83rd Congress, 1st Session.

FCN treaty and explained that they were particularly interested in the provisions for the protection of foreign investment and the Point IV program.[73]

During negotiations with Argentina that same year, the chief Argentine negotiator noted that the FCN treaty was "primarily to afford protection to American investment in Argentina," and for that reason treaty provisions should be "as well defined and as specific as possible," because guarantees that were too "elastic" would not satisfy investors.[74]

Similarly, the State Department reported to its embassy in Brussels that, during a visit to Washington by a Belgian official, the Department had cited the value of an FCN treaty for creating a "'climate' conducive to investment."[75] That prompted the Belgian embassy in Washington to express interest in concluding such a treaty.[76] Less than a month later, a Belgian official in the Ministry of Trade told a U.S. embassy official that he agreed with the U.S. government that the promotion of foreign investment was the main purpose of an FCN treaty and that Belgium was "favourably disposed" to negotiate such a treaty in the near future.[77] As will be seen in Chapters 6 and 7, several countries that ultimately concluded FCN treaties with the United States, such as Belgium, France, Israel, and Nicaragua, made clear that their decision to negotiate an FCN treaty was motivated by their desire to attract U.S. investment.

CONTEMPLATING A NEW INVESTMENT TREATY

Although by late 1949 the State Department had decided that the FCN treaty would serve as the bilateral investment treaty contemplated by the Point Four program, in the days following Truman's inaugural address, as has been noted, the Department contemplated the development of an entirely new treaty for that purpose.[78] The task of developing such a treaty fell to John Parke Young's Committee on Foreign Investment Policy.[79]

73. Memorandum dated March 8, 1950, from Harvey R. Wellman, NARA, Record Group 59, Department of State File No. 611.004-3-850.

74. Memorandum of Conversation headed "Discussion of FCN Treaty with Argentines," dated April 18, 1950, NARA, Record Group 59, Department of State File No. 611.354/4-1850.

75. Instruction dated November 5, 1954, from the Department of State to the U.S. embassy in Brussels, NARA, Record Group 59, Department of State File No. 611.554/11-554.

76. Ibid.

77. Memorandum of Conversation dated November 30, 1954, NARA, Record Group 59, Department of State File No. 511.554/12-454.

78. Transcript of Proceedings, Meeting of Economic Consultants on Point Four Program, April 8, 1949, page 79, NARA, Record Group 59, Department of State File No. 800.50T.A./4-859.

79. Report of the NAC-ECEFP Joint Committee on Foreign Investment Policy, June 7, 1949, NARA, Record Group 43, International Trade Files, Box 38, Folder marked "Foreign Investment Policy—General."

In drafting a new bilateral investment treaty, the Committee sought commitments that would be strong enough to encourage investment, that would have a reasonable prospect of acceptance by other countries, that would be consistent with U.S. law and acceptable to Congress, and that would be considered "fair and reasonable" by both parties. In June 1949, the Committee recommended the drafting of a treaty under five main headings: equitable treatment, reasonable freedom to operate and manage an enterprise, compensation for expropriation, withdrawal of funds, and taxation.

Meanwhile, as Young's committee worked on the proposed treaty, the question of how to stimulate outward foreign investment became the subject of interagency discussions among officials responsible for monetary policy. The Bretton Woods Agreement Act, which Congress enacted in 1945, had established a National Advisory Council on International Monetary and Financial Problems (NAC) to coordinate U.S. policy on international monetary and financial affairs.[80] The NAC included representatives of the Departments of Treasury, State, and Commerce as well as the board of governors of the Federal Reserve Bank, the Export-Import Bank, the Economic Cooperation Administration, the Securities and Exchange Commission, and the International Bank for Reconstruction and Development. Only weeks after the president's announcement of Point Four, Undersecretary of State James E. Webb asked the NAC to make recommendations concerning measures that the federal government might take to encourage international investment flows.[81]

On June 8, the NAC recommended three sets of measures to promote foreign investment: the creation of an experimental investment guarantee program, the conclusion of "appropriate investment treaties," and the enactment of tax incentives for outward foreign investment.[82] Less than a week later, on June 14, the NAC recommended to the State Department a proposed outline for the negotiation of treaties to provide protection for foreign investment, an outline that essentially adopted the recommendations of Young's committee. Like the Committee recommendations, the NAC outline called for treaty provisions under five headings: equitable treatment, reasonable freedom to operate and manage an enterprise, compensation for expropriation, withdrawal of funds, and taxation.[83]

80. 59 Stat. 512. *See* "Objectives of International Foreign Policy," Message of the President to the Congress, March 1, 1946, *Department of State Bulletin*, Vol. 14, No. 349, March 10, 1936, page 380.

81. Memorandum from the Under Secretary of State to the Chairman of the National Advisory Council, March 1, 1949, NARA, Record Group 59, NAC Subject Files, Lot File 60D137, *reprinted in Foreign Relations of the United States, 1949*, Vol. 1 (Washington, DC: Government Printing Office, 1976), page 773.

82. National Advisory Council, Action No. 333, June 8, 1949, NARA, Record Group 56, Subject Files of the Assistant Secretary of the NAC, Box 1.

83. National Advisory Council, Action No. 334, June 14, 1949, NARA, Record Group 56, Subject Files of the Assistant Secretary of the NAC, Box 1.

Under the heading of "equitable treatment," the NAC outline of treaty provisions stated that "United States investors shall at all times be accorded non-discriminatory, reasonable, fair and equitable treatment." As the language indicates, the United States was using the heading of "equitable treatment" to embrace a set of principles that included non-discrimination and reasonableness. Discussions in other documents of the role of investment treaties in Point Four also used the term "fair treatment" as a descriptor of the general level of treatment sought.[84] In amplification of the requirement of non-discrimination, the outline called for national treatment with respect to the right to engage in economic activities, except in certain reserved sectors of the economy, where MFN treatment would be required.[85] Under the heading relating to the freedom to operate and control an enterprise, the outline called for a right of investors to engage employees of their choice, regardless of nationality. Under the heading relating to expropriation, the outline provided that property shall not be taken for a public purpose except upon prompt payment of just compensation. Adequate provision for payment of compensation shall be made prior to the expropriation, and payment shall be made in the currency of the investor or in a convertible currency.[86]

As would be expected given the mandate of the NAC, the largest section of the outline dealt with the withdrawal of funds. The NAC believed that, as a result of postwar conditions, the inconvertibility of currencies had become the chief obstacle to the flow of international capital, and thus took a special interest in the problem of exchange controls.

At the same time, however, State Department officials recognized that some countries needed to restrict currency transfers. As John Parke Young later wrote, "The end of the war in 1945 found production and trade seriously dislocated, and widespread imbalance in international payments and receipts. . . . Under such conditions exchange control was essential to prevent severe exchange depreciation, speculation, and additional hardship for large masses of people dependent upon imports."[87]

Yet, State Department officials also believed that exchange controls should be temporary. As Young later explained, the fact that exchange controls were needed demonstrated that a country's volume of exports was too small, a problem that exchange controls would not solve. Exchange controls, moreover, tended to promote inefficient industries, redistribute income, create windfall gains, and discourage investment. Exchange controls could be useful while a state undertook

84. *See, e.g.*, Executive Committee on Economic Foreign Policy, "Objectives and Nature of the Point IV Program," page 4, March 1, 1949, NARA, Record Group 56, Subject Files of the Assistant Secretary of the NAC, Box 1.

85. National Advisory Council, Action No. 334, June 14, 1949, NARA, Record Group 56, Subject Files of the Assistant Secretary of the NAC, Box 1.

86. Ibid.

87. John Parke Young, *The International Economy* (New York: Ronald Press, 4th ed. 1963), page 408.

"remedial measures" to address its underlying problem, such as the disruption of production during the war, and to prevent capital flight during a crisis, but they should be avoided when possible and should be permitted eventually to disappear.[88]

Young's Foreign Investment Policy Committee had given much attention to the problem of withdrawals and had already drafted a new article on withdrawal of funds for inclusion in U.S. FCN treaties.[89] The Committee wished to provide investors with a right to withdraw from the host country their earnings, any compensation for expropriation, and the amount of their capital invested. It also wished to ensure that the withdrawal was not compromised by an unfavorable exchange rate. The Committee recognized, however, that shortages of foreign exchange in many countries precluded an absolute commitment in that regard and that some kind of escape clause would be necessary. The Committee sought an escape clause that would "retain a reasonable degree of protection for the investor while being sufficiently flexible to meet changing economic circumstances and to be acceptable to the foreign country."[90]

The NAC's outline again adopted the recommendation of the Foreign Investment Policy Committee. The outline called for a right of national and MFN treatment with respect to the international transfer of payments.[91] Further, nationals and companies of one party were to be guaranteed the right to transfer freely in the currency of that party both capital and earnings from the territory of the other party. The rate of exchange was to be that approved by the IMF for such transactions or, in the absence of an approved rate, a rate that was just and reasonable.

The outline of provisions included an escape clause applicable to periods of "exchange stringency."[92] It permitted exchange restrictions necessary to assure the availability of foreign exchange for goods and services essential to the health and welfare of the people of the host country or approved by the IMF. In the event that a party applied exchange restrictions, that party must within a period of three months in consultation with the other party make reasonable provisions for such withdrawals "as may be feasible," giving consideration to special needs for other transactions. Such provisions must be reviewed at intervals of not more than 12 months. In general, any restrictions could not be administered so as to disadvantage the competitive position of capital covered by the treaty relative to capital of any third country.

88. Ibid., page 414.

89. Memorandum headed "Report of the Joint NAC-ECEFP Committee on FCN Financial Clauses," dated March 22, 1949, NARA, Record Group 43, International Trade Files, Box 38, Folder marked "Foreign Investment Policy—General."

90. Ibid.

91. National Advisory Council, Action No. 334, June 14, 1949, NARA, Record Group 56, Subject Files of the Assistant Secretary of the NAC, Box 1.

92. Ibid.

Finally, under the heading of taxation, the NAC outline called for national and MFN treatment with respect to matters of taxation. It also provided that, where income was earned in two or more countries, income taxes shall be apportioned among the countries.[93]

The NAC's proposed investment treaty would exclude from treaty obligations any measures necessary to protect a party's essential security interests. Absent from the proposed treaty was the language of the ITO Charter authorizing each country to determine for itself the necessity of a measure.[94]

The State Department never adopted for use the model treaty envisioned by John Parke Young's committee and the NAC. As will be seen below, after the Havana Conference the State Department had begun to strengthen the investment provisions of the FCN treaties. By June 1949, when Young's committee completed its work on the proposed model bilateral investment treaty, much of what was in the model treaty had already been incorporated into the standard draft FCN treaty, in some cases years before and in other cases only recently. Young's committee and the NAC devoted considerable attention in 1949 to modifying the treaty provisions on exchange controls and, as will be seen below, the State Department would immediately propose the incorporation of those modifications into the FCN treaties under negotiation. These modifications of the exchange controls provision of the FCN treaties would be the chief legacy of the work of Young's committee on a model bilateral investment treaty.

The record suggests several reasons for the U.S. decision to continue to negotiate FCN treaties, rather than to replace them with treaties limited solely to the protection of foreign investment. First, history favored the use of the treaties. As Herman Walker explained, "The FCN treaty-type became the chosen instrument presumably because it afforded a ready-made framework into which the desired provisions could conveniently be fitted, and because past experience had demonstrated its negotiability. The diplomatic *desiderata* of precedent and tested practicability favored it."[95] Walker also noted that FCN treaties were regarded as an appropriate vehicle for the protection of investment because of "their historical concern with establishment matters. Familiar elements in them stood ready to be amplified and reconditioned to meet contemporary needs and circumstances."[96] The FCN treaty series held an honored place in American diplomacy. It had been launched by the Continental Congress contemporaneously with the adoption of the Declaration of Independence, and it had served American foreign economic policy for more than 170 years, proving itself endlessly adaptable to changing circumstances. The needs that emerged at the end

93. Ibid.

94. Ibid.

95. Herman Walker Jr., "Treaties for the Encouragement and Protection of Foreign Investment: Present United States Practice," 5 *American Journal of Comparative Law* 229 (1956).

96. Herman Walker Jr., "Modern Treaties of Friendship, Commerce and Navigation," 42 *Minnesota Law Review* 805, 806 (1958).

of the war—to protect U.S. investment abroad, to extend treaty protection to corporations, and to address increased state involvement in economic affairs—were merely the latest in a long line of needs that the treaties had been adapted to address in the past. The State Department had every reason to believe that the treaties were suited to serve these postwar needs as well. Linking the postwar treaties to a successful treaty series that dated back to the founding era also served to legitimate the new treaties and any innovations that they might contain. Those responsible for negotiating the treaties could not be expected to abandon easily so much tradition and proven success in favor of an untested innovation.

Second, the United States believed that FCN treaty provisions that addressed matters other than investment, such as trade or the personal rights of individuals residing in the host country, contributed to the creation of a better investment climate.[97] For example, such provisions offered greater security for individuals who needed to reside abroad to operate an investment, and they facilitated trade that might be necessary for the successful operation of the investment. A treaty that addressed investment in isolation would have created a less favorable environment in which to establish and operate foreign investment. Thus, the State Department told its embassy in New Delhi in 1949 that it was "persuaded that the development of private investment is aided not only by legal assurances immediately directed at major investment problems (such as expropriation, taxation and exchange), but also by assurances of less immediate relevance (such as security for the person, property rights, settlement of disputes, treatment of shipping and importation, etc.) as well as the existence of equitable attitudes generally toward the treatment of Americans and their legitimate interests. Private investment cannot be expected to expand adequately unless the country concerned is favorably disposed to the various aspects of equitable policy contained in a fairly comprehensive treaty such as that under reference."[98] Herman Walker writing in his personal capacity in 1956 argued that an FCN treaty "as a whole" is an investment treaty. A specialized investment agreement "would be to that extent unrealistic and inadequate." [99] Indeed, Walker also questioned the justification for protecting only persons classified as investors and suggested that an individual engaged in sales should be protected as well. At the same time, investors were interested in treaty provisions beyond those intended to protect the investment, such as those protecting fundamental personal rights, like freedom of conscience and humane treatment from police officers and jailors. He questioned whether an investor could be considered properly protected unless such traditional FCN treaty rights were assured. Walker also noted the links between investment provisions and trade and navigation provisions. Those engaged in trade and shipping must make capital outlays, while investors usually

97. This conception of the U.S. postwar FCN treaties is discussed further in Chapter 8.

98. Airgram A-252 dated July 27, 1949, from the Department of State to the U.S. embassy in New Delhi, NARA, Record Group 59, Department of State File No. 711.52/7-1949.

99. Walker , "Treaties for the Encouragement and Protection of Foreign Investment," page 244.

have an interest in importing equipment and supplies and in using maritime transportation.[100]

Third, the business community itself seemed to prefer the continued use of FCN treaties. Illustrative of that support is a conversation between Woodbury Willoughby, the chief of the Division of Commercial Policy, and Charles R. Carroll on March 3, 1949, only weeks after Truman's inaugural address and at the very moment that the State Department was deliberating over the creation of a dedicated investment treaty. Carroll was the chair of the NFTC's Law Committee and the general counsel to General Motors for overseas operations. Carroll initially telephoned Willoughby to express concern that the State Department was shifting emphasis from FCN treaty negotiations to trade agreement negotiations.[101] Carroll regarded FCN treaties as more important than bilateral trade agreements. Carroll also "wished to know what was the significance of the new phrase 'investment treaty' that he had recently heard."[102] Willoughby reassured Carroll that the Department was not losing interest in the FCN treaty program and that, in fact, the program fit very well into President Truman's Point Four program because "these treaties are the traditional instruments designed to create a favorable environment for foreign investment."[103] He explained that the term "investment treaty" referred to "an attempt to develop what is essentially an establishment treaty."[104] Willoughby said that the Department hoped to prepare a treaty that might be easier to negotiate than an FCN treaty, while containing stronger investment-related provisions.[105] Carroll replied that the FCN treaty should be retained as is, rather than placing the investment provisions into a separate treaty.[106] The Department of Commerce also endorsed the continued negotiation of FCN treaties to protect foreign investment, rather than the development of a separate investment treaty.[107] Although business groups periodically recommended small modifications to the FCN treaties, sometimes successfully and sometimes not, the change that they most desired was an increase in the number of such treaties in force. Shifting attention to the development of a new treaty could delay the conclusion of additional treaties, and any such new treaty might not be as favorable to business interests, all things considered, as the existing standard FCN treaty. Any new protections sought by business groups could

100. Ibid.

101. Memorandum of Conversation between Charles R. Carroll and Woodbury Willoughby, dated March 3, 1949, NARA, Record Group 59, Department of State File No. 711.002/3-349.

102. Ibid.

103. Ibid.

104. Ibid.

105. Ibid.

106. Ibid.

107. Letter dated August 12, 1949, from Clarence I. Blau to Winthrop Brown, NARA, Record Group 59, Department of State File No. 711.002/8-1249.

be incorporated into the existing standard draft treaty without the need to create an entirely new treaty series.

Although, as indicated above, some within the State Department believed that a treaty limited to investment might be easier to negotiate, others disagreed. Herman Walker wrote in 1956 that an FCN treaty "has an accordion-like quality. It can be of variable scope; and, so long as it contains the basic investment-interest content, it can be shortened or lengthened to suit the desires and needs of each country. That none of the treaties so far signed actually has been pared down to its investment hard-core, or anywhere near so, evidently signifies that countries willing to entertain the subject are very apt to choose to do so in the framework of a comprehensive settlement of their relations with the United States."[108] Walker noted that, although the United States, in concluding FCN treaties, was motivated primarily by investment considerations, other countries sometimes attached greater importance to other provisions. In the case of a country having little capital to export, treaties addressing only the legal rights of investors could "appear on their face to constitute a lopsided bargain unless balanced by rights utilizable in actual practice by that country's own citizens."[109] Walker cited as examples the rights of individuals to obtain treaty trader visas, to engage in "the common occupations," and to receive workers' compensation.[110] President Eisenhower's Commission on Foreign Economic Policy concluded in its 1954 report that the United States had little reason to prefer a treaty limited to investment over an FCN treaty. The Commission observed that, "if it were possible to reach agreement on investment provisions but not on others, it would be desirable to go ahead with a separate treaty. However, the experience in general is that it is the investment provisions that are the most difficult to reach agreement on, and that it is these negotiations that delay the conclusion of the rest of the treaty rather than vice versa."[111]

After 1949, the State Department does not appear to have seriously considered the idea of negotiating a new series of treaties dedicated exclusively to investment protection until the 1970s, when it launched the U.S. BIT program. Indeed, as early as August 1949, when India raised the possibility of concluding a treaty limited to foreign investment, the State Department decided that it was unwilling to negotiate such a treaty as a substitute for an FCN treaty.[112] In 1956, the slow pace of FCN treaty negotiations would prompt the NFTC to ask the State Department whether "a new type of treaty limited entirely to provisions for the protection of

108. Walker, "Treaties for the Encouragement and Protection of Foreign Investment," page 243.

109. Ibid., page 244.

110. Ibid.

111. *Quoted in* Robert R. Wilson, *United States Commercial Treaties and International Law* (New Orleans, LA: Hauser Press, 1960), page 21.

112. Memorandum of Conversations headed "Proposed Treaty of Friendship, Commerce and Navigation between the United States and India," dated August 23 and 24, 1949, NARA, Record Group 59, Department of State File No. 711.452/9-2149.

investments might not prove more effective and easier to negotiate than the general treaty of friendship, commerce and navigation."[113] The NFTC was concerned about nationalization programs, such as had recently occurred in the Suez, and wanted to see a more active treaty program. Vernon Setser, by then the chief of the Economic Treaties Branch of the Commercial Policy Staff, the office responsible for negotiating FCN treaties following a 1951 reorganization, responded that the State Department would not object to further exploration of such a proposal, and noted that the idea had been considered in the past. He observed, however, that the State Department had long adopted the policy of deleting the trade or navigation provisions if it appeared that these provisions were "hindering seriously" the conclusion of a treaty with "good investment provisions."[114] In fact, Setser maintained, in some cases the other provisions had facilitated the conclusion of the treaty as a whole. The discussion ended inconclusively, with members of the NFTC declining to express a general preference for a "limited" investment treaty.[115] The NFTC strongly desired the conclusion of more bilateral investment treaties, but was not yet persuaded that a treaty limited solely to investment was preferable to an FCN treaty with the kinds of investment provisions that had been incorporated into the U.S. treaties.

POINT FOUR ASSISTANCE AND FCN TREATIES

While the executive branch deliberated over the substance of its investment treaty provisions, Democratic congressman John Kee of West Virginia, the chairman of the House Committee on Foreign Affairs, introduced on July 12, 1949, the International Technical Cooperation Act of 1949[116] to implement the Point Four program. Many Republicans, led by Republican senator Robert Taft of Ohio, opposed Point Four because they regarded it as an extension abroad of New Deal programs such as the Works Progress Administration.[117]

As Republican opposition to a Point Four program mounted, Republican congressman Christian Herter of Massachusetts introduced, on August 17, an alternative bill: the Foreign Economic Development Act of 1949.[118] Herter was sympathetic with the Point Four program, but believed that Congress would

113. Memorandum of Conversation headed "NFTC Committee Review of Comment upon FCN Treaty Program," dated November 9, 1956, NARA, Record Group 59, Department of State File No. 611.004/11-959.

114. Ibid. For example, as discussed in Chapter 6, in the section on U.S. bargaining power, the trade or navigation provisions were deleted from FCN treaties with Belgium, France, Luxembourg and Pakistan.

115. Ibid.

116. H.R. 5615.

117. Thomas G. Paterson, *Meeting the Communist Threat: Truman to Reagan* (New York: Oxford University Press, 1988), page 152; Shenin, *United States and the Third World,* page 50.

118. H.R. 6026.

approve it only with certain compromises. Among the provisions in Herter's legislation was language conditioning the receipt of technical assistance upon the conclusion of a treaty guaranteeing that U.S. investment would receive fair and equitable treatment, just compensation in the event of expropriation, the convertibility of profits, and protection against discriminatory taxes and double taxation.[119] Herter acknowledged during floor debate that his legislation "was a hastily drafted composite" of views expressed by the NFTC and the U.S. Chamber of Commerce.[120] Herter's bill offered in essence an alternative vision of Point Four, one in which the program consisted of limited technical assistance and the negotiation of FCN treaties as a condition of receiving that assistance.

One notable feature of Kee's legislation was a proposed investment guarantee program, under which new U.S. private investment would be guaranteed against certain risks, such as expropriation, exchange controls, and physical destruction during hostilities.[121] Truman believed that insurance was necessary because developing countries might simply be unable to prevent certain losses for foreign investors, particularly those arising out of internal or international hostilities.[122]

The NFTC denounced investment guarantees as "wrong in principle."[123] Such guarantees, the NFTC contended, would shift the responsibility for protecting investment from the host country to the United States and would tend to involve the U.S. government in approving and disapproving investments.[124] The NAM believed that investment guarantee programs removed the incentive for developing countries "to correct errors of financial and economic policy."[125] The business community argued that the best form of guarantee for an investment was not an insurance program, but the negotiation of FCN treaties.[126] The problem from the business community's perspective, however, was that the United States had encountered considerable resistance from other countries with which it sought to conclude FCN treaties.[127] Conditioning Point Four assistance on the conclusion of an FCN treaty, as required by the Herter bill, would provide a means for overcoming that resistance.

The Truman administration opposed the use of foreign assistance as a means of coercing other countries to sign FCN treaties,[128] and received support even

119. Willard Thorp Oral History, Harry S. Truman Library.

120. 96 *Congressional Record* 4111 (1950).

121. Shenin, *United States and the Third World,* pages 47–48.

122. *New York Times,* June 25, 1949; Shenin, *United States and the Third World,* page 42.

123. Shenin, *United States and the Third World,* page 50.

124. Ibid., pages 50–51.

125. Baldwin, *Economic Development,* page 104.

126. Shenin, *United States and the Third World,* page 28.

127. Ibid.

128. In opposing Herter's compromise version, Truman received a great deal of support from Christian groups, who regarded Point Four as a humanitarian program consistent with their

from some Republicans. For example, Republican congressman Jacob Javits of New York argued that "making treaties a condition of giving aid would be tying a string to technical know-how which the Communists would make big propaganda about, charging that we are trying to do something for American capital before we do anything for anybody in the world."[129] State Department officials hoped to pre-empt enactment of legislation conditioning technical assistance on the conclusion of an FCN treaty by concluding more FCN treaties with strong investment protection provisions.[130]

To gain congressional support for Point Four, Truman emphasized the benefits of Point Four to the U.S. economy. Increased development in Africa, Asia, and Latin America, he argued, would create a market for U.S. exports.[131] Truman also characterized Point Four as a containment measure.[132]

The bill that finally emerged from Congress and that Truman signed into law on June 5, 1950, the Act for International Development,[133] omitted the language conditioning aid upon the conclusion of an FCN treaty. The bill did include a finding that "capital investment can make the maximum contribution to economic development only . . . where there is confidence of fair and reasonable treatment and due respect for the legitimate interests of the peoples of the countries to which the assistance is given and in which the investment is made . . . ."[134]

The legislation reflected the State Department's long-standing view that foreign investment must benefit both the investor and the host state. Regarding the interests of the host state, the legislation said that "this involves confidence on the part of the people of the underdeveloped areas that investors will conserve as well as develop local resources, will bear a fair share of local taxes and observe local laws, and will provide adequate wages and working conditions for local labor."[135] Regarding the interests of the investor, the legislation noted that this "involves confidence on the part of investors, through intergovernmental agreements or otherwise, that they will not be deprived of their

own values. They saw Point Four as "a twentieth-century missionary vehicle for both democracy and Christianity." Shenin, *United States and the Third World,* page 165.

129. Committee on Foreign Affairs, *Hearings on Act for International Development, H.R. 5615,* page 202, *quoted in* Shenin, *United States and the Third World,* page 47.

130. Memorandum dated April 11, 1949, from Assistant Legal Adviser Stanley D. Metzger to Michael H. Cardozo, NARA, Record Group 59, Department of State File No. 711.8311/10-2449.

131. Robert Packenham, *Liberal America and the Third World: Political Development Ideas in Foreign Aid and Social Science* (Princeton, NJ: Princeton University Press, 1973), pages 44–45; Shenin, *United States and the Third World,* page 50.

132. "Truman Message Asks $45,000,000 for Point 4 Fund," *New York Times,* June 25, 1949; Shenin, *United States and the Third World,* page 41.

133. Public Law 81-535, Title IV, 64 Stat. 204.

134. Ibid., Section 402(c).

135. Ibid.

property without prompt, adequate and effective compensation; that they will be given reasonable opportunity to remit their earnings and withdraw their capital; that they will have reasonable freedom to manage, operate, and control their enterprises; that they will enjoy security in the protection of their persons and property, including industrial and intellectual property, and nondiscriminatory treatment in taxation and in the conduct of their business affairs."[136]

NEGOTIATING AN FCN TREATY WITH COLOMBIA

In the months following the conclusion of the Havana Conference, the Truman administration, not yet knowing that the ITO Charter would never enter into force, had begun to consider including in its FCN treaties investment-related provisions that would harmonize the treaties with the Charter.[137] Although the United States had sought in Havana to eliminate the exception-riddled non-discrimination and security provisions adopted in Geneva, the provisions that introduced into the Charter the concept of just and equitable treatment and the principle of reasonableness had represented a genuine accomplishment, and these had survived the Geneva and Havana Conferences.

By mid-1948, the State Department was in search of opportunities to insert provisions harmonizing the FCN treaties with the ITO Charter into an FCN treaty under active negotiation. Thus, even before Truman's announcement of Point Four and the reconceptualization of the FCN treaties as investment treaties, the State Department was bolstering the investment protection provisions of those treaties as part of the harmonization process. In the early months of 1949, when the State Department went in search of instruments to advance Point Four through the promotion of private investment, the FCN treaties would already include much of what they needed to serve that function.

The first opportunity to harmonize an FCN treaty with the results of the ITO negotiations came during negotiations with Colombia. The U.S. business community in Colombia long had sought an FCN treaty between the United States and Colombia to replace an existing 1846 treaty between the two countries. In fact, the State Department had prepared a proposed draft treaty for negotiation with Colombia in 1940.[138] As has been noted, however, the United States had suspended FCN treaty negotiations during the war.

136. Ibid.

137. Robert Wilson, one of the principal FCN treaty negotiators, wrote in 1949 about the efforts of the State Department to reconcile the FCN treaty provisions with the ITO Charter provisions, although he was referring specifically to the trade provisions rather than the investment provisions. Robert R. Wilson, "Postwar Commercial Treaties of the United States," 43 *American Journal of International Law* 281, 282 (1949).

138. Despatch dated December 19, 1940, from the Department of State to the U.S. embassy in Bogota, NARA, Record Group 59, Department of State Lot Files, Walter Hollis Papers.

U.S. investors sought an FCN treaty with Colombia in particular because the Colombian Constitution allowed expropriation without compensation,[139] and thus foreign investors in Colombia felt especially vulnerable.[140] In addition, following the war, Colombia held limited reserves of foreign exchange. Accordingly, the U.S. business community was also concerned about its ability to transfer funds out of Colombia.[141]

As the war drew to a close and the United States inaugurated its postwar FCN treaty program, the State Department began to contemplate once more the negotiation of a new FCN treaty with Colombia. When the U.S. ambassador to Colombia visited Washington in November 1945, State Department officials inquired about the possibility of negotiating a treaty.[142] The ambassador informed the Department that the time for negotiating a treaty was not propitious. First, anti-American sentiment in Colombia was high, as a result of wartime price controls on coffee. Second, the Colombian political situation was unstable.

The U.S. business community continued to pressure the Department for a new treaty. Only a couple of months after the ambassador's visit, the Colombian-American Chamber of Commerce adopted a resolution urging the Department to initiate the negotiation of a new FCN treaty with Colombia.[143]

The prospects for a treaty only deteriorated, however. The proposal for the creation of an ITO aroused protectionist sentiment in Colombia, with many Colombians fearing that free trade would allow stronger countries to dominate Colombia. The Colombian government began to consider not only opposing the creation of the ITO, but terminating the existing FCN treaty with the United States because it contained provisions on trade that were suggestive of the controversial ITO Charter.[144]

139. Article 30 of the Colombian Constitution, after stating that in general expropriation required payment of indemnification, further provided: "Nevertheless, the Legislature, for reasons of justice, may determine the cases in which there is not ground for indemnification, by a favorable vote of an absolute majority of the members of each Chamber." Seymour J. Rubin, *Private Foreign Investment: Legal and Economic Realities* (Baltimore: Johns Hopkins Press, 1956), page 14.

140. Letter dated July 30, 1948, from Mitchell Carroll to Secretary of State George C. Marshall, NARA, Record Group 59, Department of State File No. 711.212/7-3048.

141. Memorandum of Conversation dated March 2, 1949, NARA, Record Group 59, Department of State File No. 711.212/3-249.

142. Memorandum of Conversation dated November 30, 1945, NARA, Record Group 59, Department of State File No. 611.2131/11-3045.

143. Letter dated January 23, 1946, from the Colombia-American Chamber of Commerce to the Secretary of State, NARA, Record Group 59, Department of State File No. 611.2131/1-2346.

144. Letter dated September 26, 1947, from the U.S. embassy in Bogota to the Department of State, NARA, Record Group 59, Department of State File No. 611.2131/9-2647; Letter dated October 17, 1947, from the U.S. embassy in Bogota to the Department of State, NARA, Record Group 59, Department of State File No. 611.2131/10-1747.

By the summer of 1948, the Havana Conference had ended, removing a major impediment to the negotiation of an FCN treaty between Colombia and the United States. The State Department again proposed the negotiation of a modern FCN treaty with Colombia, a proposal that met a favorable reaction from the Colombian foreign minister.[145] In August, the Department transmitted a proposed treaty to the U.S. ambassador in Bogota for his review, but noted that additional investment-related provisions likely would be included.[146] Meanwhile, American businesses in Colombia, particularly Pan America Airways and companies in the petroleum industry, were showing "considerable interest" in the proposed negotiation.[147]

The United States presented a draft treaty to the Colombian embassy on October 14, 1948, but alerted the Colombian government that the United States still was reviewing the text and might make further changes to its own proposal.[148] The proposed draft, dated October 11, 1948, included the investment-related provisions that had appeared in the FCN treaty with Italy and that were discussed in Chapter 2. It also included, however, a new Article V, headed "Promotion of Investment," as well as a new Article VIII on currency transfers.[149] The text proposed to Colombia was similar to drafts already presented to the Netherlands and Belgium earlier that year, although neither of those countries had been prepared to commence negotiations.

These new articles signaled the beginning of a transformation in the investment protection provisions of the FCN treaties. They reflected the work of John Parke Young's Foreign Investment Policy Committee and the impact of the ITO Charter negotiations.

First, the new article on investment promotion required each party to accord "equitable treatment" to the "capital" of nationals and companies of the other party.[150] Dating back to the first postwar treaty with China, U.S. FCN treaties had sometimes required "fair and equitable" treatment with respect to some specific activity, such as with respect to the imposition of exchange controls, purchases by state trading companies, or the awarding of contracts and concessions.[151]

145. Telegram dated July 29, 1948, from the Department of State to the U.S. embassy in Bogota, NARA, Record Group 59, Department of State File No. 711.212/7-2948.

146. Despatch dated August 5, 1948, from the Department of State to the U.S. embassy in Bogota, NARA, Record Group 59, Department of State File No. 711.212/7-1648.

147. Despatch dated September 28, 1948, from the U.S. embassy in Bogota to the Department of State, NARA, Record Group 59, Department of State File No. 711.212/9-2848.

148. Despatch dated October 15, 1948, from the Department of State to the U.S. embassy in Bogota, NARA, Record Group 59, Department of State File No. 711.212/9-248.

149. Draft Treaty of Friendship, Commerce and Navigation Between the United States of America and the Republic of Colombia, October 11, 1948, NARA, Record Group 59, Department of State File No. 711.212/9-248.

150. Ibid.

151. Illustrative of these provisions are Articles XIX (exchange controls) and XX (state trading companies and awarding of contracts and concessions) of the U.S.-China FCN Treaty.

Even before the conclusion of the treaty with China, the United States had used the concept of "fair" or "equitable" treatment to refer to the kind of treatment it desired for foreign investment. For example, the ECEFP in January 1945 had called for "nondiscriminatory and just" treatment.[152] By May 1946, the Foreign Investment Policy Committee's draft foreign investment policy statement was proposing "just and equitable" treatment of investment and, by August 1947, the Committee's statement had adopted instead the phrase "fair, equitable and non-discriminatory" treatment of investment.[153] During the negotiation of the ITO Charter, the United States had proposed that the ITO recommend the negotiation of treaties for the "just and equitable" treatment of investment, and both the investment code drafted by the Foreign Investment Policy Committee and the investment proposal drafted by the Geneva delegation had called for "fair and equitable treatment" of investment.[154] Thus, for more than two years the State Department had been using the phrases "just and equitable treatment" and "fair and equitable treatment" as general descriptors of the type of investment climate that it sought. The new investment promotion provision, however, represented the first time that the United States sought to use in an FCN treaty the phrase "equitable treatment" as a way of describing the overall investment climate that should exist. Notably, the article referred to the treatment of capital, as opposed to "property," the term previously used in FCN treaties to refer to protected interests, including investment. This reflected the influence of the ITO Charter negotiations, where the term "capital" was used.

Second, the new article prohibited "unjustified, unreasonable or discriminatory measures that would impair the legally acquired rights or interests" of investors of the other party in the enterprises that they had established or in the capital, skills, arts, or technology that they had supplied.[155] This represented another innovation in U.S. treaty practice. The foreign investment policy statement adopted by the ECEFP in June 1948 had identified "arbitrary or unreasonable" treatment as a situation in which the United States might intervene to assist a U.S. investor. With the proposal of the new investment promotion article, the United States was seeking for the first time to incorporate the norm of reasonableness explicitly into the investment protection provisions of an FCN treaty. Host state action could violate the treaty if it was arbitrary, much in the way that arbitrary regulations could violate the due process clause of the U.S. Constitution. The incorporation of the norm of reasonableness was inspired by the ITO Charter, which had prohibited unreasonable action injurious to the rights or interests of investors.

152. *See* Chapter 1.

153. *See* ibid.

154. *See* Chapter 3.

155. Draft Treaty of Friendship, Commerce and Navigation Between the United States of America and the Republic of Colombia, October 11, 1948, Article V, NARA, Record Group 59, Department of State File No. 711.212/9-248.

The article also introduced a general prohibition on discriminatory treatment, analogous to the equal protection clause of the U.S. Constitution. FCN treaties in the past had required national or MFN treatment with respect to particular activities, but had never prohibited all forms of unreasonable discrimination injurious to investment. The ECEFP as early as January 1945 had called for "nondiscriminatory and just" treatment of foreign investment.[156] The Foreign Investment Policy Committee, as early as August 1947, had included language in its draft policy calling for "fair, equitable and nondiscriminatory" treatment of foreign investment[157] and thus U.S. policymakers had contemplated a general prohibition on discrimination for some time. The United States during the ITO Charter negotiations in Geneva had supported a Belgian proposal to include a general prohibition on discriminatory treatment in the ITO Charter, but the proposal had failed.[158] The language of the new investment promotion article reflected continued U.S. support for the idea of a general prohibition on discriminatory treatment.

The article introduced as well a general prohibition on unjustified treatment, but this language soon vanished from the U.S. standard draft treaty language and did not appear in any of the signed treaties. It essentially was redundant of the requirements of reasonableness and non-discrimination.

Like the ITO Charter, the new article addressed state-imposed impediments to the free flow of capital. It provided that neither party shall deny "appropriate opportunities and facilities" for the investment of capital by nationals or companies of the other party.[159] Additionally, it prohibited either party from "unreasonably or unjustifiably imped[ing]" nationals or companies of the other party from obtaining on equitable terms the capital, skills and technology it needed for economic development.[160] The first of these sentences would be removed from the standard draft treaty by 1950, and the second would be removed by 1953.

A new article on withdrawals guaranteed to nationals and companies of either party the right to withdraw freely from the territory of the other party earnings and reasonable amounts of capital.[161] An escape clause allowed either party, in periods of exchange stringency, to depart from this obligation to the extent necessary to give preference to transfers related to imports essential to the health and welfare of its people and to service its external debt and other international contractual obligations.[162] In the event that a party departed from its obligation

156. *See* Chapter 1.

157. *See* ibid.

158. *See* Chapter 3.

159. Draft Treaty of Friendship, Commerce and Navigation Between the United States of America and the Republic of Colombia, October 11, 1948, Article V, NARA, Record Group 59, Department of State File No. 711.212/9-248 Article V.

160. Ibid.

161. Ibid., Article VIII(1).

162. Ibid., Article VIII(2).

of free transfer, it was required to provide the other party an opportunity for consultation with respect to a schedule or other arrangements for the withdrawals that had not been freely permitted.[163] The general provision on exchange controls used in earlier treaties remained, and it required national and MFN treatment with respect to any such controls.[164] The inclusion of two separate provisions relating to transfer of funds was an interim solution, however, that never found its way into any of the FCN treaties that entered into force. Rather, the principle of free transferability subject to restrictions during periods of foreign exchange stringency that appeared in the proposed FCN treaty with Colombia would be incorporated into the long-standing provision on exchange controls, resulting in a single provision that provided for non-discrimination with respect to transfers and that limited the parties' discretion to impose exchange controls.[165]

As it would happen, neither of these new articles would appear in its original form in the treaty text signed by the parties. The new article on investment promotion would be divided, with the equitable treatment standard placed in a new Article I and the remainder placed in the article on protection of property. The new article on withdrawals would be merged into the standard article on exchange controls.

Finally, the preamble to the treaty was modified to reflect the reconceptualization of the FCN treaties as investment treaties. The preambles to the treaties with China and Italy had not mentioned investment, although they had mentioned the commercial purposes of the treaties. The preamble to the treaty with Italy, for example, had proclaimed that the parties were "desirous . . . of promoting closer intercourse between their respective territories through provisions responsive to the spiritual, cultural, economic and commercial aspirations of their peoples." The preamble to the treaty proposed to Colombia stated that the parties were "desirous . . . of encouraging closer economic and cultural relations between their peoples," and then had declared that the parties were "cognizant of the contributions which may be made toward these ends by arrangements encouraging mutually beneficial investments, promoting mutually advantageous commercial intercourse, and otherwise establishing mutual rights and privileges. . . ." For the first time, a reference to investment appeared in the preamble of a U.S. FCN treaty and the reference to "mutually beneficial investments" preceded the reference to "mutually advantageous commercial intercourse."

The U.S. business community watched the negotiations closely. In early March 1949, for example, a representative of the NFTC, Mitchell B. Carroll, met with several State Department officials to discuss the status of the treaty.[166] Although

163. Ibid.

164. Ibid., Article XVIII.

165. *See, e.g.,* Greece FCN treaty, Article XV; Israel FCN treaty, Article XII; Denmark FCN treaty, Article XII.

166. Memorandum of Conversation dated March 2, 1949, NARA, Record Group 59, Department of State File No. 711.212/3-249.

four months had passed since it had provided its proposed draft to the Colombian government, the Department was still studying and revising the investment-related provisions of the treaty. At the meeting, Carroll stressed the importance of being able to repatriate compensation for expropriation and sought strong treaty protection in that regard. He argued that countries with insufficient foreign exchange to allow transfer of expropriation compensation should not expropriate. One of the State Department officials present at the meeting, Sheldon Mills, doubted, however, that Colombia would agree not to expropriate unless it had sufficient foreign exchange reserves to allow transfer of compensation. John Parke Young noted that there was "little point in tying a country down to transfer requirements which we know in advance cannot be fulfilled if economic conditions take an adverse turn."[167] Accordingly, the United States must be prepared to agree to "a certain amount of flexibility."[168] Carroll concluded the discussion by asking for a report on the progress of the FCN treaty program worldwide. Young said that the Department was "pushing them actively," but that officials of other countries could not "get too far ahead of public opinion."[169]

The State Department also sought the views of the Business Advisory Council, affiliated with the Department of Commerce, on the investment-related provisions of the FCN treaties.[170] The Council recommended strengthening the provisions in various respects, but the Office of the Legal Adviser responded by noting the inconsistency of the proposals with U.S. constitutional principles.[171] Department officials observed that treaty provisions were mutual, meaning that adopting the proposed revisions would require the United States to extend protection beyond that required by the U.S. Constitution.[172] None of the proposed revisions was adopted.

As State Department officials were discussing treaty protections with U.S. business representatives, Colombia was focusing on a different aspect of international capital movements—the problem of double taxation. On March 9, 1949, a week after State Department officials met with Carroll, the U.S. ambassador met with

167. Ibid.

168. Ibid.

169. Ibid.

170. Memorandum by Herman Walker Jr., headed "Further Possible Provisions in Standard Draft of Treaty of Friendship, Commerce and Navigation (or Economic Development)," dated October 12, 1949, NARA, Record Group 59, Department of State Lot Files, Walter Hollis Papers, Folder marked "Commercial Treaties."

171. Memorandum dated November 15, 1949, from Stanley Metzger to Michael Cardozo, NARA, Record Group 59, Department of State Lot Files, Walter Hollis Papers, Folder marked "Commercial Treaties."

172. Memorandum by Herman Walker Jr., headed "Further Possible Provisions in Standard Draft of Treaty of Friendship, Commerce and Navigation (or Economic Development)," dated October 12, 1949, NARA, Record Group 59, Department of State Lot Files, Walter Hollis Papers, Folder marked "Commercial Treaties."

the Colombian foreign minister to discuss the treaty. The foreign minister said that Colombia would have "no important objections" to the treaty, but wished to add a provision to prevent the double taxation of investment.[173] The ambassador replied that the United States preferred to address problems of double taxation in a separate treaty.[174]

By April, the Colombian government had decided that the conclusion of an FCN treaty with the United States must be conditioned upon the conclusion of a double taxation treaty, perhaps at the same time.[175] The United States was still considering its tax policy with respect to foreign investment and was not yet prepared to negotiate a tax treaty with Colombia.[176] By October, the Colombian government had decided that it would not negotiate an FCN treaty until after a double taxation treaty was concluded.[177] At the end of that month, a team traveled from Washington to Bogota and successfully concluded the double taxation treaty negotiations.[178]

FCN treaty discussions resumed the following June.[179] A problem that quickly emerged was that Colombia wished to replace language in the U.S. standard draft treaty with language based on Article 25 of the Economic Agreement of Bogota, which required national treatment with respect to expropriation and payment of fair compensation in a prompt, adequate, and effective manner. The United States, however, believed that this formulation was not as clear as the language of the U.S. standard draft treaty and successfully resisted its inclusion.[180] Although the disagreement might be interpreted as an attempt by Colombia to weaken the provision, more likely it reflected Colombia's desire to use language that it had already accepted in another instrument. Indeed, later in the month, when a

173. Telegram dated March 9, 1949, from the U.S. embassy in Bogota to the Department of State, NARA, Record Group 59, Department of State File No. 711.212/3-949.

174. Ibid.

175. Telegram dated April 27, 1949, from the U.S. embassy in Bogota to the Department of State, NARA, Record Group 59, Department of State File No. 711.212/4-2749.

176. Telegram dated May 17, 1949, from the Department of State to the U.S. embassy in Bogota, NARA, Record Group 59, Department of State File No. 711.212/4-2749.

177. Memorandum of Conversation dated October 7, 1949, NARA, Record Group 59, Department of State File No. 711.212/10-749.

178. Airgram dated October 21, 1949, from the Department of State to the U.S. embassy in Bogota, NARA, Record Group 59, Department of State File No. 711.212/10-2149; Despatch dated December 5, 1949, from the U.S. embassy in Bogota to the Department of State, NARA, Record Group 59, Department of State File No. 711.212/12-549.

179. Memorandum of Conversation headed "Negotiation of Treaty of Friendship, Commerce and Navigation with Colombia: First Meeting," dated June 6, 1950, NARA, Record Group 59, Department of State File No. 611.214/6-650.

180. Memorandum of Conversation headed "Negotiation of Treaty of Friendship, Commerce and Navigation with Colombia: Fourth Meeting," dated June 14, 1950, NARA, Record Group 59, Department of State File No. 611.214/6-1450.

representative of the United Fruit Company in a conversation with a Colombian government official criticized the expropriation provision of the standard draft FCN treaty because it lacked explicit assurances with respect to the withdrawal of expropriation compensation, the Colombian government requested that such assurances be added.[181] U.S. negotiators noted that the assurances appeared in the article on exchange controls and agreed, at the suggestion of the Colombian negotiators, that the language be moved to the expropriation provision.

By August, the major remaining issue was one related to trade. Colombia sought a "substantial concession" from the United States with respect to trade in return for the commitments that Colombia had made to the United States in the investment provisions.[182] Specifically, Colombia wanted a commitment that it would receive unqualified MFN treatment with respect to customs matters for a period of 10 years, an apparent attempt to ensure duty-free treatment for coffee. The United States was unwilling to make such a concession outside of the GATT framework. The United States countered with a proposal that the MFN treatment obligation remain unchanged, but be made terminable with one year's notice, and that an exception to the treaty for GATT and ITO commitments be deleted, a proposal that Colombia accepted subject to some additional conditions,[183] which the United States accepted.[184]

While the two parties resolved the details of the U.S. concession on trade, they continued to address other issues as well. The United States amended its own proposal relating to exchange controls, prompting Colombia to offer a counterproposal under which Colombia, although it did not have exchange controls at the time, in the future could grant a preference to imported capital over capital borrowed locally with respect to outward transfers.[185] The United States objected that such a distinction would be too difficult to administer in the case of investments financed with both imported and locally borrowed capital, that the Colombian counterproposal would be unattractive to foreign investors, and that such a provision was unnecessary because the U.S. proposal gave Colombia ample protection

181. Memorandum of Conversation headed "Negotiation of Treaty of Friendship, Commerce and Navigation with Colombia: Ninth Meeting," dated June 29, 1950, NARA, Record Group 59, Department of State File No. 611.214/6-2950.

182. Memorandum of Conversation headed "Negotiation of Treaty of Friendship, Commerce and Navigation with Colombia: M-F-N Clause and Preferences," dated September 13, 1950, NARA, Record Group 59, Department of State File No. 611.214/9-1350.

183. Memorandum by Vernon Setser headed "Formula on Unconditional MFN Treatment for Discussion with Colombia Ambassador," dated August 17, 1950, NARA, Record Group 59, Department of State File No. 611.214/8-1750.

184. Memorandum of Conversation headed "Negotiation of Treaty of Friendship, Commerce and Navigation with Colombia: Twenty-First Meeting," dated April 12, 1951, NARA, Record Group 59, Department of State File No. 611.214/4-1251.

185. Ibid.; Memorandum of Conversation headed "Negotiation of Treaty of Friendship, Commerce and Navigation with Colombia: Twenty-Second Meeting," dated April 13, 1951, NARA, Record Group 59, Department of State File No. 611.214/4-1351.

insofar as it required Colombia to make only reasonable provision for withdrawals.[186] The Colombian delegation asked whether during periods of exchange stringency it could give priority to imported capital with respect to withdrawals, and the U.S. delegation replied in the affirmative, provided that such priority was not unreasonable, leading the Colombian delegation to accept the U.S. language.

The treaty was signed by the secretary of state and the Colombian ambassador on April 26, 1951. Within the United States government, the treaty was regarded as "[i]n many respects . . . the best treaty of this type" yet concluded by the United States and "much better" than the United States had expected to obtain when the negotiations began.[187] The treaty was "basically" the same as that negotiated with Uruguay, discussed below, but with fewer qualifications.[188] The NFTC urged Senate advice and consent to the treaty and commended the State Department for concluding the treaty.[189]

As the treaty lay before the Senate, however, a serious difficulty arose. The Colombian government feared that one of the MFN treatment provisions would prevent Colombia from according special privileges to the Vatican on religious matters under the Concordat of 1887 between Colombia and the Vatican.[190] State Department officials responded that the United States did not consider the Vatican to be a third country within the meaning of the MFN treatment provision and that the United States therefore would not demand equal treatment with the Vatican under this provision.[191] The Office of the Legal Adviser questioned this rationale internally on the ground that President Truman had been seeking to confirm an ambassador to the Vatican and to recognize the Vatican, with the result that agreements entered into by the Vatican would be treaties subject to the MFN treatment obligation.[192] The Legal Adviser's Office would concur in the assurances sought by the Colombian government only if the officers who negotiated the treaty actually considered during the negotiation that the MFN treatment provision would not extend to the Concordat of 1887.[193] In any event, the assurances offered by the United States proved inadequate. The Catholic Church

186. Memorandum of Conversation headed "Negotiation of Treaty of Friendship, Commerce and Navigation with Colombia: Twenty-First Meeting," dated April 12, 1951, NARA, Record Group 59, Department of State File No. 611.214/4-1251.

187. *Current Economic Developments*, April 23, 1951, page 6, NARA, Record Group 59, Department of State Lot Files.

188. Ibid.

189. Letter dated October 9, 1951, from Robert F. Loree to Senator Tom Connally, NARA, Record Group 59, Department of State File No. 611.214/10-1051.

190. Memorandum of Conversation headed "FCN Treaty with Colombia," dated April 9, 1952, NARA, Record Group 59, Department of State File No. 611.214/4-952.

191. Ibid.

192. Memorandum dated April 11, 1952, from Charles Bevans to Vernon Setser, NARA, Record Group 59, Department of State File No. 611.214/4-1152.

193. Ibid.

in Colombia was intensely opposed to Colombian ratification of the treaty as long as it included provisions on religious matters,[194] which Catholic officials feared would open the door to the spread of "Protestant propaganda."[195] This opposition rendered Colombian ratification politically impossible.[196] The Colombian ambassador suggested that all clauses addressing religious matters be deleted, but the State Department replied that to do so would prompt opposition from Protestant groups in the United States equal to Catholic opposition to the treaty in Colombia.[197]

Because the Senate was preparing to consider several pending FCN treaties together, including the treaty with Colombia, the State Department needed to make a prompt decision with respect to whether to seek Senate advice and consent to ratification.[198] Accordingly, on April 20, 1953, the Department notified the Colombian embassy that it had decided to withdraw the treaty from the Senate in light of Colombia's inability to ratify it.[199] On June 23, 1953, the president requested that the Senate return the treaty, a request to which Senate gave unanimous consent on June 30.[200]

NEGOTIATING AN FCN TREATY WITH URUGUAY

Meanwhile, during the period when the Colombian negotiations were stalled over the problem of double taxation, the State Department's attention shifted to negotiations with Uruguay. In July 1948, U.S. embassy personnel in Montevideo had suggested to officials of the Uruguayan Ministries of Foreign Affairs and Finance the possibility of negotiating an FCN treaty between the United States and Uruguay. These officials responded with "eager interest."[201]

The Department was "pleased" at the response, but wanted to be certain that Uruguay's conception of the treaty was in accord with the U.S. conception.[202] The

194. Memorandum of Conversation headed "FCN Treaty with Colombia," dated November 26, 1952, NARA, Record Group 59, Department of State File No. 611.214/11-2652.

195. Despatch dated August 11, 1953, from the U.S. embassy in Colombia to the Department of State, NARA, Record Group 59, Department of State File No. 611.214/4-1153.

196. Memorandum of Conversation headed "FCN Treaty with Colombia," dated November 26, 1952, NARA, Record Group 59, Department of State File No. 611.214/11-2652.

197. Ibid.

198. Memorandum of Conversation headed "FCN Treaty with Colombia," dated April 20, 1953, NARA, Record Group 59, Department of State File No. 611.214/4-2053.

199. Ibid.

200. 99 *Congressional Record* 7675 (1953).

201. Telegram dated July 30, 1948, from the U.S. embassy in Montevideo to the Department of State, NARA, Record Group 59, Department of State File No. 711.332/7-3048.

202. Telegram dated August 6, 1948, from the Department of State to the U.S. embassy in Montevideo, NARA, Record Group 59, Department of State File No. 711.332/7-3048.

Department transmitted copies of the recently signed FCN treaty with Italy to illustrate the type of treaty that the United States wanted to conclude. At the same time, however, the Department alerted the embassy to the fact that it had revised the standard draft treaty since the completion of the negotiations with Italy. The Department told the embassy that it would forward the draft to be proposed to Colombia as soon as it was completed, and anticipated that this draft would likely form the basis for negotiations with Uruguay as well.[203]

When the text of the treaty with Italy arrived, the embassy complained that it was too technical and legalistic and suggested that a simpler draft would be more likely to lead to a successful negotiation.[204] The Department responded that the technical legal issues of the treaty must eventually be addressed and, if Uruguay was not prepared to address them, the Department would prefer to know that before it invested time in a futile negotiation.[205]

The embassy's fears proved unfounded, however. When the embassy presented the sample draft to the Uruguayan finance minister on September 23, he indicated that the treaty would be approved because it did not require anything that was not already part of Uruguayan law and practice.[206] In October, the director of economic and commercial affairs at the Ministry of Foreign Affairs told the embassy that Uruguay could sign the proposed treaty with only "minor" changes, primarily for domestic political reasons.[207] Uruguayan officials said that they would need to insist upon some changes to demonstrate to the political opposition that the government had not simply accepted the American proposal.[208] Such changes might include ones to the language on expropriation compensation, the language on access to mining rights, and the language granting the right to practice law.

On October 28, the Department forwarded to the U.S. embassy in Montevideo the draft that it had proposed to Colombia. The Department noted that the draft contained new language on the subject of "encouragement and protection of investments" that had not appeared in any prior draft sent to the embassy.[209] This language included the new investment provision, which appeared at Article V, as

203. Ibid.

204. Telegram dated August 18, 1948, from the U.S. embassy in Montevideo to the Department of State, NARA, Record Group 59, Department of State File No. 711.332/8-1848.

205. Telegram dated August 30, 1948, from the Department of State to the U.S. embassy in Montevideo, NARA, Record Group 59, Department of State File No. 711.332/8-1848.

206. Despatch dated October 5, 1948, from the U.S. embassy in Montevideo to the Department of State, NARA, Record Group 59, Department of State File No. 711.332/10-548.

207. Despatch dated October 22, 1948, from the U.S. embassy in Montevideo to the Department of State, NARA, Record Group 59, Department of State File No. 711.332/10-2248.

208. Ibid.

209. Airgram dated October 28, 1948, from the Department of State to the U.S. embassy in Montevideo, NARA, Record Group 59, Department of State File No. 711.332/10-2248.

well as the new language on exchange controls and the new preambular language referring to "arrangements encouraging mutually beneficial investments."

On November 9, the Department reported to the embassy that it was preparing a draft tailored to Uruguay. The draft for Uruguay would be similar to the one for Colombia, except for changes to the provision on currency transfers, which the Department was still in the process of revising.[210]

On January 6, 1949, the Department transmitted its proposed draft for negotiations with Uruguay.[211] The Department alerted the embassy that the draft was still subject to revision and that the Department might suggest changes to its own draft, particularly to the provision on withdrawal of funds.[212]

The investment provisions in the draft for Uruguay differed from those in the draft for Colombia in a few respects. The general prohibitions on unreasonable or discriminatory treatment remained, but the prohibition on "unjustified" treatment disappeared, presumably because it was redundant of the other two. Similarly, the language in the draft for Colombia prohibiting either party from unreasonably or unjustifiably impeding either party from obtaining on equitable terms the capital, skills, and technology that it needed for its economic development omitted the reference to unjustifiable impediments and prohibited only unreasonable ones.

Although Uruguay raised a number of concerns, most of them posed no serious difficulty. By early March, the negotiations had come to a halt over a single issue: withdrawal of funds.[213] The problem was that the United States government itself was not satisfied with the language in the proposed treaty that it had given to Uruguay and was still attempting to draft a provision acceptable to all U.S. agencies.[214] As noted above, the NAC would not approve treaty language on exchange controls until some three months later. The Department finally decided to propose language that would be used only in the treaty with Uruguay and to consult further with the business community before selecting language for inclusion in the standard draft treaty.[215]

On March 9, the Department forwarded its proposed language,[216] which was based on the recommendations of John Parke Young's Foreign Investment

210. Airgram dated November 9, 1948, from the Department of State to the U.S. embassy in Montevideo, NARA, Record Group 59, Department of State File No. 711.332/10-2248.

211. Airgram dated January 6, 1949, from the Department of State to the U.S. embassy in Montevideo, NARA, Record Group 59, Department of State File No. 711.332/1-649.

212. Ibid.

213. Telegram dated March 9, 1949, from the U.S. embassy in Montevideo to the Department of State, NARA, Record Group 59, Department of State File No. 711.3321/3-949.

214. Memorandum to the File dated February 24, 1949, NARA, Record Group 59, Department of State File No. 711.332/2-1049.

215. Memorandum of Conversation headed "FCN Treaties—Special Provision on Withdrawal of Earnings," dated March 8, 1949, NARA, Record Group 59, Department of State File No. 711.332/3-849.

216. Telegram dated March 9, 1949, from the Department of State to the U.S. embassy in Montevideo, NARA, Record Group 59, Department of State File No. 711.332/3-949.

Policy Committee, although the Committee's recommendations had not yet been approved by the NAC. The new language was similar to, but stronger than, that which had appeared in the draft proposed to Colombia. It provided that, in the event that exchange controls were imposed during periods of exchange rate stringency, the host state was required within three months to make reasonable provision for withdrawals of returns on the investment as well as withdrawals of such capital as may be feasible, "giving consideration to special needs for other transactions."[217]

The Uruguayan government immediately accepted the new provision. Two days after the State Department proposed the new provision, on March 11, the two countries reached agreement on the final text of the treaty.[218]

That same day, the Uruguayan government notified the State Department that it wished to announce publicly that negotiations had begun so as to avoid claims that Uruguay had accepted a treaty dictated by Washington without negotiations.[219] The State Department agreed to the announcement.[220] The U.S. embassy urged the Department to approve the text quickly because the political circumstances in Uruguay were favorable for ratification at that moment and because the chief Uruguayan negotiator was leaving the country by the end of the month and his absence could delay ratification for several months.[221] Over the next few weeks, the two governments worked out various technical details, such as stylistic corrections and reconciliations of the original English text and the Spanish translation.

The treaty with Uruguay had been completed only a few weeks after Truman's announcement of the Point Four program. Although the link between Point Four and the FCN treaties would favor the negotiation of the treaties in some instances, in the case of Uruguay the link provided ammunition for the treaty's opponents. On May 6, 1949, the *Wall Street Journal* published an article referring to the FCN treaty with Uruguay as a "pilot" for the Point Four program.[222] Until the *Wall Street Journal* article appeared, the Uruguayan press, apart from one communist newspaper, had been content merely to report the existence of the negotiations and to withhold comment until the actual text of the treaty was made public.[223]

217. Ibid.

218. Telegram dated March 11, 1949, from the U.S. embassy in Montevideo to the Department of State, NARA, Record Group 59, Department of State File No. 711.332/3-1149.

219. Ibid.

220. Telegram dated March 14, 1949, from the Department of State to the U.S. embassy in Montevideo, NARA, Record Group 59, Department of State File No. 711.332/3-1149.

221. Telegram dated March 11, 1949, from the U.S. embassy in Montevideo to the Department of State, NARA, Record Group 59, Department of State File No. 711.332/3-1149.

222. Telegram dated May 19, 1949, from the U.S. embassy in Montevideo to the Department of State, NARA, Record Group 59, Department of State File No. 711.332/5-1949.

223. Ibid.

The *Wall Street Journal* article triggered an immediate adverse reaction from several Uruguayan newspapers, which denounced efforts by the United States to treat Uruguay as a "guinea pig" for the program and warned that the treaty would open the door to "Yankee trusts" that would crush local industry.[224] The principal Uruguayan negotiator expressed apprehension to U.S. embassy personnel about the potential effect of the adverse commentary on Uruguay's ability to conclude the negotiations successfully. Uruguayan officials feared that the treaty would be portrayed as another "imperialist tentacle."[225]

The criticism eventually subsided, at least for a time. The treaty was signed on November 23, 1949, after which coverage of the treaty in the Uruguayan press was "slight," except for two newspapers, one leftist and the other communist, both of which opposed the treaty.[226]

President Truman transmitted the Uruguay treaty to the Senate in January of the following year[227] and the Committee on Foreign Relations scheduled hearings on the treaty for May 4. As the treaty lay before the Senate, the Uruguayan press renewed its interest in the treaty. Initially, the press coverage was favorable and several newspapers published editorials in support of the treaty.[228] By April, however, the tone of press coverage had changed and newspapers that formerly were supportive had begun to question the desirability of the treaty.[229] This time the opposition proved fatal. The Uruguayan government never ratified the treaty and it never entered into force.

NEGOTIATING AN FCN TREATY WITH IRELAND

The first FCN treaty with the new investment provisions that would enter into force was that concluded with Ireland. The foundation for the successful negotiation was laid in March 1948, when the State Department transmitted a proposed FCN treaty to the U.S. legation in Dublin and authorized legation officials to approach the Irish government to ascertain its interest in negotiating a treaty.[230] The Department alerted the legation to the fact that the treaty still was under

224. Ibid.

225. Memorandum dated June 9, 1949, by R. K. Oakley, NARA, Record Group 59, Department of State File No. 711.332/6-949.

226. Despatch dated December 30, 1949, from the U.S. embassy in Montevideo to the Department of State, NARA, Record Group 59, Department of State File No. 611.334/2-350.

227. *Treaty of Friendship, Commerce and Economic Development with the Oriental Republic of Uruguay*, Executive D, 81st Cong. 1st Sess. (1950).

228. Despatch dated March 10, 1950, from the U.S. embassy in Montevideo to the Department of State, NARA, Record Group 59, Department of State File No. 611.334/3-1050.

229. Despatch dated April 5, 1950, from the U.S. embassy in Montevideo to the Department of State, NARA, Record Group 59, Department of State File No. 611.334/4-550.

230. Message dated March 5, 1948, from the Department of State to the U.S. legation in Dublin, NARA, Record Group 59, Department of State File No. 711.41D2/1-1248.

review and that the United States might wish to modify the proposed treaty in the future.[231]

After studying the proposed treaty, Irish officials met with U.S. negotiators at the U.S. legation over a period of several days in May. Those meetings revealed that the principal issue was likely to be the conflict between the national treatment provision of the treaty and the Irish Control of Manufactures Act, which required that 51 percent of any industrial enterprise in Ireland be owned by Irish nationals, and thus was inconsistent with the national treatment provisions of the treaty.[232] The legislation addressed a problem that had arisen in the past when British companies established Irish subsidiaries, which the British parents would close when financial circumstances in Britain so warranted.[233] The Irish officials believed that these decisions were made without regard to the consequences for Ireland and thus wished to avoid foreign control of Irish manufacturing enterprises. They asserted that they were not concerned that U.S. investors would act similarly to the British investors.[234] In fact, they were not confident that significant U.S. investment would come to Ireland.[235] Rather, their concern was that, if the United States gained national treatment with respect to the right to establish manufacturing enterprises, Ireland would have no choice but to grant the same treatment to the United Kingdom, which would defeat the purpose of the Irish legislation[236] and lead to British domination of the Irish economy.[237] Ironically, the prime minister confided to the U.S. embassy that the legislation was "humbug"[238] because the British already had found ways to circumvent it and that he wanted it repealed. The political opposition, however, was charging that the government was too committed to free trade and insufficiently supportive of Irish industry, and thus the government was reluctant to

231. Ibid.

232. Memorandum of Conversation dated March 20, 1948, NARA, Record Group 59, Department of State File No. 711.41D2/5-2448.

233. Memorandum of Conversation dated October 21, 1948, NARA, Record Group 59, Department of State File No. 711.41D2/10-2848.

234. Ibid.

235. Airgram dated December 17, 1948, from the U.S. legation in Dublin to the Department of State, NARA, Record Group 59, Department of State File No. 711.41D2/12-1748; Memorandum of Conversation dated October 21, 1948, NARA, Record Group 59, Department of State File No. 711.41D2/10-2848.

236. Ibid.; Memorandum of Conversation dated October 21, 1948, NARA, Record Group 59, Department of State File No. 711.41D2/10-2848.

237. Airgram dated October 21, 1948, from the U.S. legation in Dublin to the Department of State, NARA, Record Group 59, Department of State File No. 711.41D/10-2148.

238. Airgram dated October 28, 1948, from the U.S. legation in Dublin to the Department of State, NARA, Record Group 59, Department of State File No. 711.41D2/10-2848; Airgram dated December 17, 1948, from the U.S. legation in Dublin to the Department of State, NARA, Record Group 59, Department of State File No. 711.41D2/12-1748.

lend credence to the charges by publicly proposing repeal of the legislation.[239] If the Irish government had some assurance that U.S. investors would invest in Ireland, granting U.S. investors rights of entry would be less difficult. History, however, suggested that U.S. investors were unlikely to show sufficient interest.[240] The Irish government similarly feared British purchase of residential real estate, which would drive up prices in the residential real estate market.[241] Irish officials also faced difficulty accepting commitments regarding exchange controls, given that Ireland was a member of the sterling bloc and thus not in control of its currency reserves.[242]

The issue of national treatment proved so difficult in the Irish negotiations, as well as in discussions with France and the Netherlands occurring during that time, that by November Herman Walker, one of the Department's principal treaty negotiators, questioned whether the Department should abandon the national treatment provision entirely.[243] Ultimately, he recommended instead that the Department agree to transitional exceptions tailored to each country.

The two parties commenced formal negotiations on October 6 and continued them until October 24.[244] By December only three important issues remained, one of which related to the Control of Manufactures Act.[245] The others related to exchange controls and the acquisition of real property. In the case of real property, the problem was that the obligation of national treatment conflicted with an Irish stamp tax that applied to all conveyances and that responded to heavy British purchases of Irish real property.[246]

By late January 1949, the Irish foreign minister had suggested that negotiations relating to the Control of Manufactures Act be suspended but that negotiations on

239. Ibid.

240. Ibid.

241. Ibid.

242. The sterling bloc was an arrangement under which Britain purchased food from other members of the empire, which then used the receipts to purchase manufactured goods from Britain. This trade was financed through pound sterling accounts that could not be converted to dollars. Thomas W. Zeiler, *Free Trade, Free World: The Advent of GATT* (Chapel Hill: University of North Carolina Press, 1999), page 22; Harold James, *International Monetary Cooperation since Bretton Woods* (Washington, DC: International Monetary Fund, 1996), page 90.

243. Telegram dated November 23, 1948, from the U.S. embassy in Paris to the Department of State, NARA, Record Group 59, Department of State File No. 711.41D2/11-2348.

244. Airgram dated December 23, 1948, from the Department of State to the U.S. embassy in London, NARA, Record Group 59, State Department File No. 711.41D2/12-2348.

245. Ibid.

246. Telegram dated December 5, 1949, from the U.S. legation in Dublin to the Department of State, NARA, 711.41D/12-549; Airgram dated December 23, 1948, from the Department of State to the U.S. embassy in London, NARA, Record Group 59, State Department File No. 711.41D2/12-2348.

the remaining issues continue.[247] The State Department broke the impasse, however, on March 22, when it notified its legation in Dublin that the United States had decided to compromise. The United States would agree to an exception for the Control of Manufactures Act for a period of four years.[248] The Irish government had indicated that it would provide favorable consideration to U.S. investors who wished to establish enterprises in Ireland.[249] If, after four years, the United States believed that Ireland had departed in an unjustifiable manner from the principle of national treatment, then the United States would have the right to terminate the treaty on 90 days' notice.[250] In exchange for this concession, the United States sought Ireland's agreement to the new investment protection provision that had appeared in the treaties with Colombia and Uruguay.[251] The new provision included a requirement that property receive "equitable treatment" and prohibited unreasonable or discriminatory measures that would impair property rights.[252]

The same date, the United States proposed new language to address the problem of exchange controls. The language was broadly similar to that which had been proposed in the negotiations with Colombia and Uruguay. It allowed either party to depart from the obligation of national and MFN treatment during times of foreign exchange stringency, while also requiring that any exchange controls imposed make "reasonable provision" for withdrawal of expropriation compensation, of earnings, and of capital, and that the party imposing them provide an opportunity for consultations with the other party.[253] The Department explained that the term "reasonable" took account of "all points of view including [the] realities [of the] Irish exchange situation, and allow[ed] priorities for such things as needful imports and maintaining financial solvency."[254] The Irish government nevertheless sought language in the minutes of interpretation that would clarify the meaning of "reasonable provision"[255] Ultimately, the parties agreed upon

247. Airgram dated January 20, 1949, from the U.S. legation in Dublin to the Department of State, NARA, Record Group 59, Department of State File No. 711.41D2/1-2049.

248. Airgram dated March 22, 1949, from the Department of State to the U.S. legation in Dublin, NARA, Record Group 59, Department of State File No. 711.41D2/1-2049.

249. *Treaty of Friendship, Commerce, and Navigation with Ireland, with Protocol Relating Thereto*, Exec. Rept. No. 8, 81st Cong. 2d Sess. (1950), pages 2–3.

250. Ibid. *See also* Ireland FCN treaty, Article VI(4) and Minutes of Interpretation *Ad Article VI, paragraph 4*.

251. Airgram dated March 22, 1949, from the Department of State to the U.S. legation in Dublin, NARA, Record Group 59, Department of State File No. 711.41D2/1-2049.

252. Ireland FCN treaty, Article V.

253. Ibid., Article XVII and Protocol, Paragraph 8.

254. Telegram dated October 18, 1949, from the Department of State to the U.S. legation in Dublin, NARA, Record Group 59, Department of State File No. 711.41D2/10-1849.

255. Telegram dated December 9, 1949, from the U.S. legation in Dublin to the Department of State, NARA, Record Group 59, Department of State File No. 711.41D2/12-949.

language that specified that "reasonable provision" allowed either party during periods of exchange stringency to apply exchange restrictions necessary to assure the availability of foreign exchange for purchases essential to the health and welfare of its people, and also allowed consideration to be given to special needs for other exchange transactions,[256] essentially the language that had been used in the texts of the treaties with Colombia and Uruguay.

The proposal by the United States with respect to national treatment proved acceptable to Ireland. The United States also compromised on the right of national treatment with respect to the acquisition and disposal of real property.[257] With agreement reached as well on the exchange controls provision, the two countries signed the treaty on January 21, 1950.[258]

SENATE ADVICE AND CONSENT TO RATIFICATION 1950

The Senate Foreign Relations Committee held hearings on the FCN treaties with Uruguay and Ireland in executive session on May 4, 1950.[259] Assistant Secretary of State for Economic Affairs Willard Thorp and Director of the Office of International Trade Policy Winthrop Brown testified on behalf of the State Department. No public witness asked to be heard.

The treaty with Uruguay received strong support from the business community. The National Association of Manufacturers commended the State Department for negotiating the treaty and hailed the treaty as "a model for countries desiring to benefit from American private enterprise under the Point 4 program"[260] and a model for future FCN treaties.[261] Anderson, Clayton & Co., Will Clayton's cotton trading firm, sent the Committee a letter that "thoroughly endorse[d]" the treaty and praised the new approach to investment protection reflected in it.[262] The NFTC urged "prompt ratification of the treaty as in the

256. Ireland FCN treaty, Minutes of Interpretation, *Ad Article XVII, paragraph 5.*

257. *See* Ireland FCN treaty, Article VII(3). Acquisition of real property was subject to local law, except that the parties shall be permitted to "possess and occupy" real property incidental to the enjoyment of rights secured by the treaty. The provision for national treatment with respect to the disposition of real property was omitted entirely.

258. Treaty of Friendship, Commerce and Navigation with Protocol, entered into force September 14, 1950, 1 UST 785, TIAS 2155, 206 UNTS 269.

259. Senate Committee on Foreign Relations, Transcript of Executive Session dated May 4, 1950, NARA, Record Group 46, File No. SEN81B-B7.

260. Unsigned note to Francis [Wilcox] dated April 28, 1950, NARA, Record Group 46, File No. SEN81B-B13.

261. Resolution on the United States-Uruguay Treaty adopted by the International Relations Committee and Advisory Group, National Association of Manufacturers, February 14, 1950, NARA, Record Group 46, File No. SEN81B-B13.

262. Letter dated January 27, 1950, from S. M. McAshan Jr., to Senator Tom Connally, NARA, Record Group 46, File No. SEN81B-B13.

best interests of American business enterprises engaged in business in Uruguay," although it did criticize certain aspects of the treaty, including among others the absence of provisions granting entry of technical personnel and guaranteeing to covered property protection no less favorable than that required by international law.[263] More generally, the NFTC added that it was "greatly in favor of the accelerated program of negotiating treaties of friendship, commerce and navigation initiated by the State Department."[264] On May 16, the Committee voted to report the treaty with Uruguay favorably to the Senate.[265]

The Committee temporarily delayed action on the treaty with Ireland to allow the NFTC time to submit comments on it. Three weeks later, the NFTC notified the Committee that it was unable to recommend advice and consent to ratification of the treaty with Ireland because the treaty offered insufficient assurances. The NFTC's strongest objections were to the departure from national treatment to accommodate the Control of Manufactures Act, a provision of the protocol excluding mining from MFN treatment, and a provision on entry for traders that the NFTC believed was not strong enough.[266] The first of these was the most serious objection.[267] The NFTC also wanted a right of entry for technical personnel, which the treaty did not guarantee because U.S. immigration laws would not have allowed the United States to offer such a right. It objected as well to the new investment clause appearing in the treaties with Ireland and Uruguay. It believed that the requirement of "equitable" treatment and the prohibition on "unreasonable" measures, which it noted were based on Article 12 of the ITO Charter, were "ambiguous" and added little to the assurances contained elsewhere in the treaty.[268] It recommended that these provisions be omitted from future treaties. This was yet another recommendation from the business community with respect to the FCN treaties that the State Department would reject. The NFTC also objected to the provision requiring that exchange controls make only "reasonable" provision for withdrawals by investors.[269]

The State Department insisted that the treaty was the best that could be obtained and, in deference to that position, the NFTC refrained from opposing

263. Letter dated March 6, 1950, from E. P. Thomas to Senator Tom Connally, NARA, Record Group 46, File No. SEN81B-B13.

264. Ibid.

265. *Treaty of Friendship, Commerce and Economic Development with the Oriental Republic of Uruguay*, Exec. Rept. No. 5, 81st Cong. 2d Sess. (1950), page 2.

266. Letter dated May 24, 1950, from Austin T. Foster to R. F. Loree, NARA, Record Group 46, File No. SEN81B-B7.

267. Telegram dated May 12, 1950, from E. P. Thomas to Senator Tom Connally, NARA, Record Group 46, File No. SEN81B-B7.

268. Letter dated May 24, 1950, from Austin T. Foster to R. F. Loree, NARA, Record Group 46, File No. SEN81B-B7.

269. Ibid.

the treaty.[270] The NFTC nevertheless complained that the inability of the State Department to secure more satisfactory treaties would have a "substantial adverse effect" on the expansion of U.S. investment abroad.[271] On June 23, 1950, having received the comments of the NFTC, the Senate Foreign Relations Committee voted to report the treaty favorably to the Senate.[272]

Despite the concerns of the NFTC, on July 6, 1950, the Senate gave advice and consent to ratification to the treaty with Ireland by a voice vote.[273] The treaty with Uruguay was brought to the floor on the same date. Republican senator Forrest C. Donnell of Missouri, however, requested that consideration be postponed because he had not been aware that the treaty was scheduled for consideration and had not had an opportunity to read it.[274] Meanwhile, Republican senator Guy Cordon of Oregon asked why the word "Oriental" appeared in the name of the Oriental Republic of Uruguay. Democratic senator Dennis Chavez of New Mexico explained that the term originated in colonial times to distinguish the region from the area around Buenos Aires to the west.[275] The treaty was brought before the Senate a second time on August 9, at which time Senator Donnell asked whether the treaty would interfere with state laws requiring incorporators to be residents of the state or U.S. citizens. Democratic senator Elbert D. Thomas of Utah responded that the state laws would prevail. Senator Donnell expressed doubt that Senator Thomas was correct, but did not challenge the assertion further. Senator Donnell also asked a series of questions relating to the operation of the competitive equality provision, which Senator Thomas answered. Following this exchange, the Senate gave advice and consent to ratification of the treaty by a voice vote.[276] As noted above, however, by this time opposition to the treaty had arisen in Uruguay, and Uruguay would never ratify the treaty.

Despite the disappointing failure to bring the treaties with Colombia and Uruguay into force, the negotiations in 1948 and 1949 of the treaties with Colombia, Uruguay, and Ireland had provided an opportunity for the United States to develop a new standard draft FCN treaty that had been reconceived as an investment treaty. This new investment treaty included guarantees of national and MFN treatment, of most constant protection and security, of judicial access, and of just compensation for expropriation and the provision for adjudication of

270. Letter dated May 25, 1950, from E. P. Thomas to Senator Tom Connally, NARA, Record Group 46, File No. SEN81B-B7.

271. Ibid.

272. *Treaty of Friendship, Commerce and Navigation with Ireland, with Protocol Relating Thereto*, Exec. Rept. No. 8, 81st Cong. 2d Sess. (1950), page 1.

273. 96 *Congressional Record* 9715 (1950).

274. 96 *Congressional Record* 9710 (1950).

275. Ibid.

276. 96 *Congressional Record* 12087–12088 (1950); Telegram dated August 9, 1950, from the Department of State to the U.S. embassy in Montevideo, NARA, Record Group 59, Department of State File No. 611.334/8-950.

treaty disputes before the International Court of Justice as had the treaty with Italy, but included new provisions guaranteeing equitable treatment of investment, prohibiting unreasonable measures that impaired investment, proscribing discriminatory measures that impaired investment, and providing a more robust right to transfer capital and earnings.

A series of negotiations that commenced in 1950 would provide the State Department with additional opportunities to refine some of the language, but by this time the substantive content of the new investment treaty was largely settled. Modest revisions would occur in future years,[277] and the negotiations with Ethiopia would prompt the Department to develop a short draft for use with certain less-developed countries, but there would be no further reconceptualizations of the standard draft treaty. By early 1950, with the substantive content of the standard draft treaty largely settled, the task that lay ahead for the United States was to persuade other countries to negotiate and to conclude an FCN treaty, which by then was understood to be a bilateral investment treaty.

277. Perhaps the most important subsequent revision that occurred, beginning with the treaty with Israel, was the recasting of the national treatment provision so that it applied to engaging in all gainful activity, except for that in specified reserved sectors. Prior to that, the provision guaranteed national treatment with respect to engaging in certain broad categories of gainful activity. Other noteworthy revisions included the insertion, after 1952, of the provision for treaty investor visas and the omission, after 1953, of the right of national treatment with respect to engaging in the professions.

6

Negotiating the First Bilateral Investment Treaties

The Truman Years

The State Department intended, following World War II, to negotiate a network of FCN treaties that would spread principles of American liberal legality everywhere. It sought to negotiate FCN treaties on as wide a basis as possible[1] and was willing to negotiate with any friendly, "like-minded" country.[2] As the National Advisory Council would note in December 1955, "the Department of State has not attempted to be highly selective in proposing treaty negotiations. Instead, seeking the widest treaty network possible, it has approached every country with which negotiations appeared at all feasible with a view to negotiating a satisfactory treaty. As a consequence, in addition to the treaties signed, inconclusive negotiations or exploratory discussions have been held with a considerable number of other countries."[3]

At first, it appeared that progress might be rapid. By the end of 1946, the United States had signed an FCN treaty with China, was in the final stages of

1. Memorandum from the Undersecretary of State to the Acting Secretary, headed "Request for Delegation of General Authorization to Commence Negotiation of Treaties of Friendship, Commerce and Navigation with Other Countries," dated February 6, 1959, NARA, Record Group 59, Department of State File No. 611.004/2-659.

2. Ibid.; Circular Airgram dated December 28, 1950, from the Department of State to certain diplomatic and consular officers, NARA, Record Group 59, Department of State File No. 611.84A4/12-2850; Memorandum by Willard Thorp headed "Consultation with Businessmen Regarding Treaties of Friendship, Commerce and Navigation," dated January 14, 1952, NARA, Record Group 59, Department of State File No. 611.964/1-1452. *See also* letter dated November 16, 1958, from Assistant Legal Adviser Charles I. Bevans to James P. White, NARA, Record Group 59, Department of State File No. 611.004/10-1658.

3. NAC Staff Document No. 740, Program for Obtaining Treaty Assurances to Protect United States Citizens and Property and Promote United States Private Investment in Foreign Countries, December, 1955, NARA, Record Group 353, Records Relating to the Council on Foreign Economic Policy 1955–1961, Box 4, Folder marked "Investment in Underdeveloped Countries CFEP 511 (Folder 2)."

negotiations with Lebanon, and was preparing to negotiate with 15 other countries: Afghanistan, Australia, Austria, Brazil, Canada, Chile, Cuba, Egypt, France, Greece, Iran, Italy, Philippines, United Kingdom, and the U.S.S.R.[4]

The United States found, however, that progress in concluding treaties was slow. The State Department did not conclude a single FCN treaty in 1947, a year dominated by the ITO Charter negotiations. During the first several months of 1948, with the ITO Charter negotiations completed, the State Department returned to the FCN treaty program with renewed vigor.[5] It signed a treaty with Italy in February and began negotiations with Australia, France, and Ireland. It sent draft treaties to another seven countries: Belgium, Iran, India, Netherlands, New Zealand, Pakistan, and South Africa. The Department also began to plan negotiations with Colombia and Uruguay.

Despite the renewed vigor, however, progress remained slow.[6] By May 1949, the Department had sent draft treaties to three more countries (Costa Rica, Ecuador, and Luxembourg), but was in negotiations with only one, Uruguay. Four years after the end of the war in Europe, the United States still had concluded only two FCN treaties, with China and with Italy.

By March 1950, the State Department had sent draft treaties to eight more countries (Denmark, Israel, Paraguay, Peru, Portugal, Spain, Sweden, and Syria), and was preparing to send a treaty to a ninth country, Argentina. These additional discussions meant that the United States had inaugurated inconclusive treaty discussions with 31 countries in Europe, Asia, Africa, and South America.[7] By this time, the State Department had held discussions with Afghanistan, Argentina, Australia, Belgium, Brazil, Chile, Colombia, Costa Rica, Cuba, Denmark, Ecuador, Egypt, France, Greece, India, Iran, Israel, Lebanon, Luxembourg, the Netherlands, New Zealand, Pakistan, Paraguay, Peru, Philippines, Portugal, Spain, Sweden, Syria, South Africa, and the United Kingdom. As of March 1950, however, treaties had been signed only with China, Italy, Uruguay, and Ireland.

U.S. NEGOTIATING STRATEGY

Seeking a Charter of Liberal Principles

The United States saw the FCN treaty as a charter of liberal legal principles, not a catalog of concessions. As will be seen in the discussion of the negotiation of

4. *Current Economic Developments,* January 20, 1947, NARA, Record Group 59, Department of State Lot Files.

5. *Current Economic Developments,* August 23, 1948, NARA, Record Group 59, Department of State Lot Files.

6. *Current Economic Developments,* May 2, 1949, NARA, Record Group 59, Department of State Lot Files.

7. Memorandum headed "Present Status of Program for Negotiating Treaties of Friendship, Commerce and Navigation," dated March 10, 1950, NARA, Record Group 59, Department of State File No. 611.004/3-2250.

individual treaties, the United States often agreed to the deletion or modification of a provision in a proposed treaty when it believed that the other country was unwilling to agree to the principle at stake, but it rarely did so in exchange for a concession from the other party.[8] Rather, each provision was negotiated on the basis of its own merits.

Thus, State Department officials noted in 1950 that "[t]reaties of this type never have been and cannot be negotiated like boundary treaties or trade agreements on the basis of give-and-take bargaining. When the United States proposes a treaty of friendship, commerce and navigation to a foreign government, it is simply proposing that the two governments define the general principles governing their policies affecting alien enterprises."[9] Or, as the State Department explained in 1954, "the process of negotiation is in no way a bargaining over concessions, but rather a mutual search for right principle to which both countries are willing to subscribe in the interest of each, and a joint formulation of rules which the two countries wish to declare, on a fully equal, friendly and reciprocal basis, as governing their relationship toward one another."[10] Herman Walker, a principal FCN treaty negotiator, reiterated this understanding of the treaties in 1958, when he observed, writing in his private capacity, that FCN treaties "do not entail bargaining for concessions. Rather they deal with matters of right principle, to which both signatories are willing to subscribe formally,"[11] a sentiment shared by

8. The discussion of the negotiation of the FCN treaty with Ireland in Chapter 5 includes an arguable exception to this statement. During that negotiation, the United States offered to accept a limitation on national treatment if Ireland would agree to include a new "investment clause" that the State Department had recently drafted and that was being incorporated into the standard draft treaty at the time. The negotiating history contains no indication, however, that Ireland had any objection to the new investment clause. Thus, this does not appear to be a situation in which the two parties exchanged concessions. Because the new investment clause prohibited certain discriminatory conduct, the State Department may have seen the new clause as merely a way of moderating the concession that it was making.

Similarly, the discussion in Chapter 7 of the negotiation of the FCN treaty with Korea indicates that the United States offered to include in the protocol a paragraph sought by Korea that permitted screening of investment for balance of payments reasons if Korea would accept the language originally proposed by the United States relating to the right of establishment. Korea countered that it would accept the language proposed by the United States if the United States would agree to a memorandum interpreting the protocol paragraph proposed by Korea. In this discussion, the United States and Korea were not trading concessions on unrelated matters, but essentially sculpting the scope of the right of establishment.

9. Memorandum headed "Negotiation of Treaty of Friendship, Commerce and Navigation with India," dated September 11, 1950, NARA, Record Group 59, Department of State File No. 611.914/9-1150.

10. Instruction dated December 14, 1954, from the Department of State to the U.S. embassy in Brussels, NARA, Record Group 59, Department of State File No. 611.554/12-454.

11. Herman Walker Jr., "The Post-war Commercial Treaty Program of the United States," 73 *Political Science Quarterly* 57, 78 (1958).

Robert Wilson, another principal FCN treaty negotiator.[12] Walker observed on another occasion the same year that "[b]eing occupied with essential principles of equity and fair treatment, their negotiation does not provide an arena for the trading of concessions or the bargaining for an array of tangible *quid pro quos*."[13] The treaties, in short, established a charter of "broad general principles under which economic relations between the United States and various other countries are conducted."[14]

These broad liberal principles might have varying application, depending upon the circumstances of the other country, but the goal was an agreement on principles, not the extraction of maximum gains. As President Truman would tell Congress in 1949, when negotiating FCN treaties, "we do not, of course, ask privileges for American capital greater than those . . . we ourselves grant in this country."[15]

Thus, the United States did not regard signature of an FCN treaty as a favor to the United States, but a recognition that the treaty was mutually beneficial.[16] The Department repeatedly emphasized that the FCN treaties benefitted both parties.[17] For example, in submitting the treaty with Uruguay to President Truman, Secretary of State Dean Acheson explained that the treaty created a legal framework within which business relations "may, through liberal principles, develop effectively and to the mutual advantage of the two countries."[18] Similarly, in transmitting the treaty with Colombia to President Truman the following year,

12. Robert R. Wilson, *United States Commercial Treaties and International Law* (New Orleans, LA: Hauser Press, 1960), page 322.

13. Herman Walker Jr., "Modern Treaties of Friendship, Commerce and Navigation," 42 *Minnesota Law Review* 805, 809–810 (1958).

14. Memorandum by Charles H. Sullivan headed "Entry of Foreign Investors into the United States under Treaties of Friendship, Commerce and Navigation," dated November 23, 1949, NARA, Record Group 59, Department of State File No. 611.004/5-350.

15. Harry S. Truman, "The Point 4 Program: Aid to Underdeveloped Areas," June 24, 1949, *reprinted* in Department of State, *A New Era in World Affairs: Selected Speeches and Statements of President Truman, January 20 to August 29, 1949,* Department of State Publication 3653 (Washington, DC: Government Printing Office, 1949), page 32.

16. Letter dated January 19, 1954, from Weir M. Brown to Jack C. Corbett, NARA, Record Group 59, Department of State File No. 611.62A4/1-1954.

17. *See, e.g.,* letter dated February 27, 1950, from the Secretary of State to the President, *reprinted in Treaty of Friendship, Commerce, and Navigation with Ireland, with Protocol Relating Thereto,* Executive H, 81st Cong. 2d Sess. (1950), page 2; Letter dated January 29, 1952, from the Secretary of State to the President, *reprinted in Treaty of Friendship, Commerce, and Navigation with the Kingdom of Greece,* Executive J, 82nd Cong. 2d Sess. (1952), page 2; Letter dated January 10, 1952, from the Secretary of State to the President, *reprinted in Treaty of Amity and Economic Relations with Ethiopia,* Executive F, 82nd Cong. 2d Sess. (1952), page 2.

18. Letter dated January 12, 1950, from the Secretary of State to the President, *reprinted in Treaty of Friendship, Commerce, and Economic Development with the Oriental Republic of Uruguay,* Executive D, 81st Cong. 2d Sess. (1950), page 2.

Secretary Acheson observed that the treaty, "formulated in accordance with liberal principles, creates a legal framework within which business, trade, and cultural relations between the United States and Colombia may develop effectively and to the mutual advantage of the two countries."[19]

Indeed, the preambles to both of these treaties included language that was incorporated into the standard draft treaty as well and that referred to the FCN treaties as "arrangements encouraging mutually beneficial investments, promoting mutually advantageous commercial intercourse, and otherwise establishing mutual rights and privileges . . . ."

Pragmatic Attitude

Like New Deal liberalism generally, FCN treaty policy was pragmatic, rather than doctrinaire. That is, the United States did not believe that every treaty party must sign the same agreement, and it was prepared to adapt each treaty to the circumstances of the other country with which it was negotiating.[20] The State Department recognized that "different conditions, different human attitudes, and different basic political, economic and social policies in various countries made adjustments necessary."[21]

Although the United States had prepared a standard draft treaty on which to base negotiations, that draft was not "a model which should be rigidly and inflexibly followed."[22] As the State Department explained to its embassy during negotiations with the Netherlands, the standard draft treaty was a basis for discussion, not a "take it or leave it document."[23] In some instances, the State Department agreed to negotiate on the basis of a counterdraft prepared by the other party.

Thus, State Department officials explained in a 1945 internal memorandum, written in preparation for negotiations with Brazil, that "[t]he Brazilian Government should not, of course, be given the impression that it is expected to sign a treaty formula as drafted by the United States. On the contrary, it should be invited to comment fully and freely and to submit its own draft for consideration

19. Undated letter from the Secretary of State to the President, *reprinted in Treaty of Friendship, Commerce, and Navigation with Colombia*, Executive M, 82nd Cong. 2d Sess. (1951), page 2.

20. Memorandum headed "Draft Treaty of Friendship, Commerce and Navigation Presented to the Chinese Government on April 2, 1945," dated May 24, 1945, NARA, Record Group 59, Department of State File No. 911.932/5-2445.

21. Memorandum of Conversation headed "Review of the Status of the FCN Treaty Program and Particularly the Indian Project with Especial Reference to the Problem of the Screening of Investments," dated September 26, 1950, NARA, Record Group 59, Department of State File No. 611.914/9-2650.

22. Memorandum of Conversation dated June 20, 1945, NARA, Record Group 59, Department of State File. No. 611.9331/6-2045.

23. Airgram dated August 8, 1952, from the Department of State to the U.S. embassy in The Hague, NARA, Record Group 59, Department of State File No. 611.564/6-1952.

by this Government if it deems desirable."[24] Similarly, when it transmitted a proposed draft treaty with Uruguay to its embassy in Montevideo in 1948, the State Department informed the embassy that the draft was "intended merely to serve as a basis for negotiations, and counter-proposals by the Uruguayans [would] be welcomed, and [would] receive the sympathetic consideration of the Department."[25]

As the State Department explained during negotiations with Germany in July 1953, "In proposing its draft, of course, the Department is by no means suggesting a rigid document that it expects to be signed as presented. It is a starting-point draft from which, through negotiation and exchanges of views, a mutually satisfactory instrument can be ultimately developed."[26] It reiterated the same point a few months later, noting that "the Department's standard draft is a starting-point for developing a negotiation and an ultimately agreed text, rather than a final and inflexible proposal. And, while the draft is believed to be well-considered and realistically pitched to the situation of foreign countries, a purpose of a negotiation is to discover what if any adjustments need to be made in it to fit it to the special circumstances and requirements of a particular country."[27] Problems with a particular provision should not disrupt exploratory discussions.[28]

In sending a message to its embassies in March 1953 emphasizing the importance of the FCN treaties, the State Department observed that "there may be a variety of ways whereby the treaty can be adapted to local situations without violation to its basic principles."[29] The Department noted in the same message that it would even consider negotiating a treaty relating principally to establishment and investment, rather than a standard FCN treaty, as it would later do in the case of France. This would remain the Department's approach throughout the years of the FCN treaty program. For example, in 1954, in response to an expression of concern by a Belgian official that the United States might have negotiated a better treaty with Germany than it would with Belgium, the Department of State sent a telegram to its embassy in Brussels explaining the U.S. negotiating posture. The

24. Memorandum headed "First Meeting to Consider a Tentative Draft Treaty of Friendship, Commerce and Navigation between the United States and Brazil Held October 31, 1945," NARA, Record Group 59, Department of State File No. 711.322/4-2346.

25. Airgram dated November 9, 1948, from the Department of State to the U.S. embassy in Montevideo, NARA, Record Group 59, Department of State File No. 711.332/10-2248.

26. Airgram A-164 dated July 28, 1953, from the Department of State to the U.S. High Commissioner in Bonn, NARA, Record Group 59, Department of State File No. 611.62A4/6-2653.

27. Instruction dated November 16, 1953, from the Department of State to the U.S. High Commissioner in Bonn, NARA, Record Group 59, Department of State File No. 611.62A4/11-1653.

28. Ibid.

29. Circular Airgram headed "FCN Treaty Program of the United States," dated March 4, 1953, NARA, Record Group 59, Department of State File No. 611.004/3-453. For example, as discussed below, in preparation for negotiations with Ethiopia, the Department in 1950 had prepared an alternative, shorter draft tailored for use with less developed countries.

telegram noted initially that every FCN treaty negotiated by the United States to date, that is, by December 1954, differed from the U.S. standard draft treaty, although all FCNs were alike in "scope, orientation and fundamental content."[30] Thus, in a decade of negotiations, no country had agreed to the standard draft treaty as proposed. Further, no two FCNs were alike. Rather, "[e]ach country negotiates in light of its own circumstances and requirements and its conception of a proper and useful treaty. . . ."[31] Because each treaty was tailored to the needs of the other party, the United States generally resisted proposals to use a treaty negotiated with one country as a model for negotiations with another country,[32] although, in fact, other countries sometimes were keen to ensure that the treaty that they negotiated would not be perceived as less favorable than the treaty of some other country in particular.[33]

The Department's pragmatism had limits, however. The Department believed that treaty negotiations would be feasible only if the two countries had "substantial agreement" on the "basic treaty philosophy."[34] As the State Department explained during negotiations in 1950 with Israel, although there was "room for considerable revision and adjustment" in the treaty language, the treaty contained "a hard core of principle" that the State Department regarded as indispensable.[35] Winthrop Brown observed that same year that "[i]f a treaty is to be of any value [with regard to promoting investment and raising standards of living], it must contain effective provisions. A watered-down agreement that fails to come to grips with reality is worse than useless, because it tends to give a stamp of official approval to conditions and practices which obstruct the achievement of the announced purposes of the agreement."[36] The State Department believed that FCN treaties "must provide as a minimum for assurances of national treatment for U.S. enterprises located in the other country and for prompt, just and effective compensation

30. Instruction dated December 14, 1954, from the Department of State to the U.S. embassy in Brussels, NARA, Record Group 59, Department of State File No. 611.554/12-454.

31. Ibid.

32. Ibid. As described in Chapter 7, the United States and Luxembourg did agree to use the treaty with Belgium as the basis for their negotiation.

33. *See, e.g.,* Instruction dated December 14, 1954, from the Department of State to the U.S. embassy in Brussels, NARA, Record Group 59, Department of State File No. 611.554/12-454.

34. Airgram dated June 16, 1950, from the Department of State to the U.S. embassy in Greece, NARA, Record Group 59, Department of State File No. 611.814/6-250.

35. Memorandum of Conversation headed "Israeli Readiness to Negotiate a Treaty of Friendship, Commerce and Navigation," dated April 25, 1950, NARA, Record Group 59, Department of State File No. 611.84A4/4-2550.

36. Memorandum by Winthrop Brown, dated February 13, 1950, NARA, Record Group 59, Department of State File No. 611.004/3-850.

in the event of expropriation."[37] The "dilemma" was to decide when it was in the public interest to conclude a "partial treaty" rather than no treaty at all.[38]

In deciding whether to make a particular modification sought by another country, the State Department considered the effect that the modification would have on the long-term development of international investment law. For example, during discussions with the head of the U.S. mission in Beirut concerning the negotiation of an FCN treaty with Lebanon, the State Department explained that it would abandon one of the major principles of the treaty only with the "greatest reluctance" because, were it to do so, "the possibility of obtaining the acceptance of that principle by other nations might thereby be considerably weakened."[39] Eight years later, when Germany sought to remove a particular MFN treatment provision on the ground that national treatment would be enough, the State Department responded that it was

> decidedly interested in the precedent value of a United States-German treaty. Countries in other parts of the world often look to the United States and Western Europe to set the pattern and the norm in treaty relations. A particular wording or provision may have its chief immediate value, therefore, not so much because it plays at the moment an essential role in the bilateral relations of countries in the North Atlantic community, but because unless the latter are prepared to subscribe to it in the treaties among themselves other countries where it is needed for demonstrably practical reasons may be disposed to resist it on the ground that it implies singling them out for unusual and suspicious demands. In the opinion of the Department of State, Germany has an interest, as well as the United States, in establishing the rule of law and of decent treatment for the alien and his property throughout the world; and thus presumably shares the United States interest in achieving a bilateral treaty which can be held up as a model of enlightenment for others to follow. The Department of State adds that it has sought to draft a treaty which incorporates sound principles and equity, good generally for countries great and small, weak or powerful, in all parts of the world—something which it can in good conscience propose equally and indiscriminately to most countries everywhere. It is believed that this is the most efficacious approach to realizing not only the immediate objective of protection for

37. National Advisory Council Document 1868 (Revised), headed "Investments in Less Developed Areas," dated December 12, 1955, NARA, Record Group 353, Records Relating to the Council on Foreign Economic Policy 1955–1961, Box 4, Folder marked "Investment in Underdeveloped Countries CFEP 511 (Folder 1)."

38. Memorandum of Conversation headed "Review of the Status of the FCN Treaty Program and Particularly the Indian Project with Especial Reference to the Problem of the Screening of Investments," dated September 26, 1950, NARA, Record Group 59, Department of State File No. 611.914/9-2650.

39. Message dated December 11, 1945, from the Department of State to the U.S. Charges d'Affaires in Beirut, NARA, Record Group 59, Department of State File No. 711.90E2/11-145.

> American interests on a bilateral basis but also the remoter objective of building toward an internationally accepted standard of treatment for the alien. These treaties are entirely mutual and the United States is asking no commitment that it is not willing itself to undertake.[40]

Similarly, when Thailand proposed deletion of a provision dealing with multiple exchange rates, on the ground that Thailand did not use multiple exchange rates, the State Department replied that "treaty pattern must be maintained if treaties are to accomplish [the] function [of] establishing good international standards."[41]

Because language in different treaties was based on a standard draft treaty, the United States also feared that changes in the language of one treaty could cast doubt on the meaning of similar language in another treaty.[42] For example, a clarification of language in one treaty might be construed as indicating that counterpart language in other treaties lacking the clarification had a different meaning. More generally, any difference in the wording of a provision from one treaty to another could be misinterpreted to indicate that the provisions had a different meaning.[43]

Just as derogations from a treaty rule could set a bad precedent, improvements in the treaty could set a good precedent. As one State Department official noted, "One of our main objectives in pursuing this treaty program is to improve the lot of aliens in all countries, including our own. We believe that to be a worthy purpose. . . . The effect of the establishment of an improved rule in a bilateral treaty reaches far beyond the two countries concerned, inasmuch as it establishes a precedent in international practice that may eventually become a generally accepted rule of international law."[44] Similarly, during negotiations with Belgium, the State Department expressed the supposition that Belgium shared the "important treaty objective . . . of joining together in building up agreed rules of the game which will set a good example for third countries in other parts of the world where American and Belgian capital may now or hereafter wish to locate."[45] The State

40. Memorandum dated November 23, 1953, Attachment to Letter dated April 29, 1954, from Carl Boehringer to the Secretary of State, NARA, Record Group 59, Department of State File No. 611.62A4/4-2954.

41. Telegram dated July 11, 1963, from the Department of State to the U.S. embassy in Bangkok, NARA, Record Group 59, Central Foreign Policy Files 1983, Box 3487, Folder marked "FT—Foreign Trade 2/1/63."

42. Telegram dated February 26, 1946, from the Department of State to the U.S. embassy in Chongqing, NARA, Record Group 59, Department of State File No. 711/932/2-2646.

43. *See, e.g.,* Memorandum headed "The Proposed Sino-American Treaty of Friendship. Commerce and Navigation," dated March 13, 1946, NARA, Record Group 59, Department of State File No. 711.932/12-2046.

44. Memorandum by Winthrop Brown dated February 13, 1950, NARA, Record Group 59, State Department File No. 611.004/3-850.

45. Instruction dated November 5, 1954, from the Department of State to the U.S. embassy in Brussels, NARA, Record Group 59, Department of State File No. 611.6554/11-554.

Department further noted that "many countries outside Europe are reluctant to commit themselves to effective treaty rules regarding the treatment of foreign private enterprise until Western European countries have shown themselves willing to subscribe to the same rules."[46]

The State Department's pragmatism included a procedural as well as a substantive element. That is, the Department never adopted a uniform procedure for negotiating FCN treaties. Rather, it sought "to adapt itself to whatever procedure may seem most expedient in a given situation."[47] In a typical case, the State Department provided the other government with a draft of the proposed treaty. After that government reviewed the draft, its representatives would meet with U.S. officials in informal sessions to discuss the purposes of the treaty, clarify any questions, identify potential issues in the negotiations, and ascertain whether a sufficient basis existed for productive negotiations. If such a basis did exist, more formal negotiations would begin. When the negotiations were held abroad, which was often the case, the ambassador and the embassy staff bore the responsibility for conducting them, subject to the instructions of the State Department. In some cases, the Department would send a treaty expert to the embassy to assist in the negotiations for a limited period of time. Any agreement reached by the embassy would be subject to State Department approval. Occasionally, negotiations were held in Washington, with the other party represented either by a visiting delegation or by embassy personnel.

Lack of Bargaining Power

As early as 1949, State Department officials were concerned that the United States lacked sufficient bargaining power to conclude a large number of FCN treaties. For example, Woodbury Willoughby, the associate chief of the Division of Commercial Policy, observed in March of that year, "The extent to which an FCN treaty is a vehicle through which significant modifications of established policy usually can be effected is quite limited. Our bargaining power is principally good will, as the United States does not actually 'give' very much in one of these documents. In the main, these treaties serve to prevent a future worsening of a present status quo."[48] Two months later, an internal State Department report made a similar observation.[49] By 1951, Assistant Legal Adviser Stanley Metzger

46. Ibid.

47. Department of State Instruction A-100 to the U.S. embassy in Brussels, dated December 13, 1954, NARA, Record Group 59, Department of State File No. 611.554/12-1354.

48. Memorandum dated March 17, 1949, from Woodbury Willoughby to Jack B. Tate, NARA, Record Group 59, Department of State File No. 611.41D2/3-1749. *See also* Memorandum of Conversation headed "Addition to FCN Treaties of Provision on Government-Owned Patents," dated November 21, 1951, NARA, Record Group 59, Department of State File No. 611.944/11-2151.

49. *Current Economic Developments,* May 2, 1949, page 2, NARA, Record Group 59, Department of State Lot Files.

had concluded that the United States had "virtually no bargaining power in an FCN negotiation."[50] The reasons were several.

First, because the United States under its Constitution treated foreign investors very well, and FCN treaty obligations provided foreign investors with little more than the protections guaranteed by the Constitution,[51] other countries recognized that the treaty would grant them little protection beyond that which they already enjoyed.[52] For example, in discussing the proposed FCN treaty with the Soviet Union, officials in the Division of Commercial Policy had noted that one important benefit that such a treaty could provide for U.S. corporations was that it would grant them the right to sue in Soviet courts, although Soviet corporations already possessed that right with respect to U.S. courts.[53] One of the "relatively few positive real advantages" that other countries gained through the conclusion of an FCN treaty was the resulting eligibility of their nationals for treaty trader visas and, after 1952, treaty investor visas.[54]

Second, in any event, most other countries were not in a position to export capital to the United States and thus had little need to gain additional access to, or protection in, the U.S. economy.[55] John King Fairbank observed in 1948 that,

50. Memorandum of Conversation headed "Addition to FCN Treaties of Provision on Government-Owned Patents," dated November 21, 1951, NARA, Record Group 59, Department of State File No. 611.944/11-2151.

51. Indeed, John Coyle has shown that, beginning in the 1940s, aliens increasingly relied on the U.S. Constitution rather than an FCN treaty to challenge U.S. laws that discriminated against them, because the protections they might otherwise have sought from an FCN treaty were available under the Constitution. *See* John F. Coyle, "The Treaty of Friendship, Commerce and Navigation in the Modern Era," 51 *Columbia Journal of Transnational Law* 302 (2013).

52. *Current Economic Developments,* May 2, 1949, page 2, NARA, Record Group 59, Department of State Lot Files; Memorandum of Conversation headed "Addition to FCN Treaties of Provision on Government-Owned Patents," dated November 21, 1951, NARA, Record Group 59, Department of State File No. 611.944/11-2151; Wilson, *United States Commercial Treaties,* page 8. *See also* Memorandum headed "First Meeting to Consider a Tentative Draft Treaty of Friendship, Commerce and Navigation between the United States and Brazil Held October 31, 1945," NARA, Record Group 59, Department of State File No. 711.322/4-2346.

53. Memorandum headed "The Third Meeting to Consider a Tentative Draft Treaty of Friendship, Commerce and Navigation between the United States and the U.S.S.R. Held May 24, 1945," NARA, Record Group 59, Department of State File No. 711.612.

54. Memorandum by Vernon Setser, dated April 15, 1954, NARA, Record Group 59, Department of State Lot Files, Walter Hollis Papers, Folder marked "Treaty Investor Visas."

55. Memorandum by Charles H. Sullivan headed "Entry of Foreign Investors into the United States under Treaties of Friendship, Commerce and Navigation," dated November 23, 1949, NARA, Record Group 59, Department of State File No. 611.004/5-350. *See also* Memorandum headed "First Meeting to Consider a Tentative Draft Treaty of Friendship, Commerce and Navigation between the United States and Brazil Held October 31, 1945," NARA, Record Group 59, Department of State File No. 711.322/4-2346.

when the United States and China signed their FCN treaty, "its egalitarian provisions were viewed by cynics as an open door for American commercial exploitation of China, with no bar to similar exploitation of the United States—providing China had the wherewithal."[56]

Third, the treaty was long and complex. Long treaties include more provisions that can become the subject of disagreement, although during the Eisenhower years the United States concluded a number of treaties in which the parties agreed simply to omit various provisions that had become the subject of difficulty, including in the case of France, Belgium, and Luxembourg, for example, the key commercial provisions, and, in the case of France and Pakistan, the navigation provisions. Long and complex treaties also can tax the negotiating capacity of other countries. The Egyptian negotiators, for example, complained in 1946 about the "all inclusive nature" of the treaty[57] and blamed the "comprehensive character" of the treaty for Egyptian delays in commenting on the U.S. proposed draft.[58] Three years later, Egyptian prime minister Ibrahim Abdel Hadi Pasha told U.S. embassy officials that he had been "appalled" when he first saw the length and complexity of the standard draft treaty, that he had not been able in the intervening years to study it sufficiently, and that he could not support such a treaty in Parliament.[59] During ultimately unsuccessful negotiations in 1950, an Argentine official observed that "no attempt should have been made to incorporate so many elements in an agreement primarily designed to encourage and protect foreign investment."[60] In 1951, Assistant Legal Adviser Stanley Metzger warned that the standard draft was "burdened close to the breaking point" and that the addition of any new provisions would render it "even less negotiable" than it already was.[61] Even where negotiations were successful, the length and complexity of the treaty was often an impediment. Iran initially paid little attention to the standard draft treaty when it was proposed for negotiation, but was willing to proceed on the basis of the shortened form of the treaty, whereas the

56. John King Fairbank, *The United States and China* (Cambridge, MA: Harvard University Press, 1948), page 328.

57. Despatch dated November 25, 1946, from the U.S. embassy in Cairo to the Department of State, NARA, Record Group 59, Department of State File No. 611.8331/11-2546.

58. Telegram dated February 12, 1947, from the U.S. embassy in Cairo to the Department of State, NARA, Record Group 59, Department of State File No. 611.8331/2-1247.

59. Airgram dated March 12, 1949, from the U.S. embassy in Cairo to the Department of State, NARA, Record Group 59, Department of State File No. 711.832/3-1249.

60. Despatch dated May 10, 1950, from the U.S. embassy in Buenos Aires to the Department of State, NARA, Record Group 59, Department of State File No. 611.354/5-1050.

61. Memorandum of Conversation headed "Addition to FCN Treaties of Provision on Government-Owned Patents," dated November 21, 1951, NARA, Record Group 59, Department of State File No. 611.944/11-2151.

sultan of Muscat and Oman believed that even the short form was too long and complex.[62]

Particularly after the reconceptualization of the FCN treaties as investment treaties in 1949, the United States had hoped that other countries would be induced to sign FCN treaties by the expectation of attracting U.S. investment.[63] In some instances, the fact that the treaty might stimulate inward investment was an important consideration in prompting another country to negotiate an FCN treaty.[64] The prospect of increased investment, however, was not sufficient to generate the large number of treaties for which the United States was hoping.

One reason was that, in the years following the war, many countries were fearful of U.S. economic domination and wanted to retain the discretion to restrict the entry of U.S. capital.[65] The FCN treaty program thus met "considerable opposition from less developed countries, particularly those just emerging from colonial status."[66] Such countries feared that their resources would be depleted by foreign investors without adequate benefit to their economies.[67] More generally, countries recently emerging from colonialism feared that an FCN treaty would replace the political imperialism of colonialism with an economic imperialism.[68]

Another fear was that an FCN treaty that opened the economy to U.S. investment would expose local businesses to disastrous competition. This fear was

62. The discussion of the length and complexity of the treaty in these negotiations is described in Chapter 7 in the sections on the negotiation of FCN treaties with Iran and the sultanate of Muscat and Oman.

63. *Current Economic Developments,* May 2, 1949, NARA, Record Group 59, Department of State Lot Files.

64. As discussed in Chapter 6, the desire to attract U.S. investment was an important reason that Israel decided to negotiate an FCN treaty and that Italy decided to negotiate a supplemental agreement to the FCN treaty that it had already concluded. As discussed in Chapter 7, the desire to attract U.S. investment was also an important consideration in the negotiations with Nicaragua, France, and Belgium.

65. Ibid., *Current Economic Developments,* May 2, 1949, NARA, Record Group 59, Department of State Lot Files.

66. National Advisory Council Document 1868 (Revised) headed "Investments in Less Developed Areas," dated December 12, 1955, NARA, Record Group 353, Records Relating to the Council on Foreign Economic Policy 1955–1961, Box 4, Folder marked "Investment in Underdeveloped Countries CFEP 511 (Folder 1)."

67. Ibid.; NAC Staff Document No. 740, Program for Obtaining Treaty Assurances to Protect United States Citizens and Property and Promote United States Private Investment in Foreign Countries, NARA, Record Group 353, Records Relating to the Council on Foreign Economic Policy 1955–1961, Box 4, Folder marked "Investment in Underdeveloped Countries CFEP 511 (Folder 2)."

68. Ibid.; NAC Staff Document No. 740. *See also* Telegram dated August 2, 1950, from the U.S. embassy in New Delhi to the Department of State, NARA, Record Group 59, Department of State File No. 611.914/8-250.

especially strong where local business had achieved stability, often through cartels that ensured controlled production at a high profit.[69]

Resistance to concluding an FCN treaty also stemmed from those philosophically opposed to liberalism, whether economic nationalists or socialists. As an NAC report noted in 1955,

> For the most part, the attitudes foreign governments have shown towards the treaty are conditioned by economic nationalism. Wherever strongly nationalistic economic ideas have become well-entrenched, unsympathetic and even hostile attitudes have been manifested towards the standard treaty provisions and the liberal principles on which they are based. This hostility has been met in countries sympathetic to free enterprise as well as those inclined towards more collective forms of economic life.[70]

As the NAC report further noted, in socialist countries, the opposition was not simply to foreign investment, but to "free enterprise as such."[71]

Summarizing the situation, the same NAC report noted that the United States had encountered hostility toward the conclusion of FCN treaties "most frequently" in four groups of countries: those recently emerged from colonial status, "underdeveloped" countries, countries where private enterprise was highly protectionist, and "countries committed to or strongly influenced by socialism or statism."[72] Unspoken was the fact that this list comprised the great majority of countries in the world.

Thus, the investment-related provisions of the FCN treaties often impeded, rather than promoted, the successful negotiation of an FCN treaty. By the early 1950s, the State Department had found that the investment provisions were the most difficult provisions in the FCN treaties on which to reach agreement with other countries.[73]

The principal objection was to the provision on national treatment,[74] especially the requirement of national treatment with respect to establishment.[75] Many countries

69. NAC Staff Document No. 740, Program for Obtaining Treaty Assurances to Protect United States Citizens and Property and Promote United States Private Investment in Foreign Countries, NARA, Record Group 353, Records Relating to the Council on Foreign Economic Policy 1955–1961, Box 4, Folder marked "Investment in Underdeveloped Countries CFEP 511 (Folder 2)."

70. Ibid.

71. Ibid.

72. Ibid.

73. Wilson, *United States Commercial Treaties*, page 21; Herman Walker Jr., "Treaties for the Advancement and Protection of Foreign Investment: Present United States Practice," 5 *American Journal of Comparative Law* 229 (1956).

74. Memorandum headed "Status of Present Program for Negotiating Treaties of Friendship, Commerce and Navigation," dated March 10, 1950, NARA, Record Group 59, Department of State File No. 611.004/3-2250; Memorandum headed "Present Status of Program for Negotiating Treaties of Friendship, Commerce and Navigation Treaties," dated December 1, 1952, NARA, Record Group 59, Department of State File No. 611.004/3-453.

75. NAC Staff Document No. 740, Program for Obtaining Treaty Assurances to Protect United States Citizens and Property and Promote United States Private Investment in Foreign

refused to grant U.S. investors the right to establish investments in their territory on the same basis as their own investors because of "fear of undue American influence in their economies."[76] The concern in particular was that U.S. investors either would colonize important sectors of the economy or would drain the economy of foreign exchange through large withdrawals of earnings and capital.[77]

In some cases, potential treaty parties feared not U.S. investors, but third country investors, typically investors from other countries in the same region.[78] Granting national treatment to U.S. investors would require treaty parties, in accordance with the MFN treatment provisions in their treaties with other countries, to grant national treatment to investors of those other countries.[79] Thus, for example, the French feared Spanish and Italian penetration of their economies. The Philippines feared the Chinese, the Irish feared the British, the Greeks feared the Italians, the Danes feared the Germans, and the Uruguayans feared the Argentines.[80] The Pakistanis feared the Japanese,[81] the Thais feared the Chinese,[82] and the Iranians feared the Soviet Union.[83] The Austrians feared the Soviet

Countries, NARA, Record Group 353, Records Relating to the Council on Foreign Economic Policy 1955–1961, Box 4, Folder marked "Investment in Underdeveloped Countries CFEP 511 (Folder 2)"; Memorandum headed "Present Status of Program for Negotiating Treaties of Friendship, Commerce and Navigation Treaties," dated December 1, 1952, NARA, Record Group 59, Department of State File No. 611.004/3-453.

76. *Current Economic Developments,* May 2, 1949, NARA, Record Group 59, Department of State Lot Files.

77. Ibid.; Memorandum headed "Present Status of Program for Negotiating Treaties of Friendship, Commerce and Navigation Treaties," dated December 1, 1952, NARA, Record Group 59, Department of State File No. 611.004/3-453.

78. Memorandum headed "Status of Present Program for Negotiating Treaties of Friendship, Commerce and Navigation," dated March 10, 1950, NARA, Record Group 59, Department of State File No. 611.004/3-2250; Memorandum headed "Present Status of Program for Negotiating Treaties of Friendship, Commerce and Navigation Treaties," dated December 1, 1952, NARA, Record Group 59, Department of State File No. 611.004/3-453; NAC Staff Document No. 740, Program for Obtaining Treaty Assurances to Protect United States Citizens and Property and Promote United States Private Investment in Foreign Countries, NARA, Record Group 353, Records Relating to the Council on Foreign Economic Policy 1955–1961, Box 4, Folder marked "Investment in Underdeveloped Countries CFEP 511 (Folder 2)."

79. *Current Economic Developments,* May 2, 1949, NARA, Record Group 59, Department of State Lot Files.

80. Ibid.

81. Telegram dated December 7, 1954, from the U.S. embassy in Karachi to the Department of State, NARA, Record Group 59, Department of State File No. 611.90D4/12-754.

82. Despatch dated August 19, 1960, from the U.S. embassy in Bangkok to the Department of State, NARA, Record Group 59, Department of State File No. 611.9242/8-1960.

83. Statement of Thorsten Kalijarvi, Deputy Assistant Secretary of State for Economic Affairs, *Commercial Treaties with Iran, Nicaragua and the Netherlands,* Exec. Rept. No. 8, 84th Cong. 2d Sess. (1956).

Union[84] and the Germans.[85] The Egyptians feared the British, the Greeks, and the Italians.[86] The Vietnamese feared the Chinese, the Japanese, and the French.[87]

The provisions on expropriation and exchange controls also presented "a substantial degree of negotiating difficulty."[88] Exchange controls were "an almost universal problem."[89] Countries feared that the burden of servicing foreign investment would deplete their foreign exchange reserves. The expropriation provision sometimes presented a problem because countries did not wish to be held to "a high standard of compensation."[90] These difficulties were exacerbated by the national treatment obligation. U.S. investors, if entitled by the national treatment provision to invest in another country, could rely upon the currency transfer rights granted by the treaty to withdraw the returns on the investment or proceeds from the liquidation of the investment and thereby drain the host country of foreign exchange reserves. At the same time, provisions requiring compensation for expropriation would prevent a country from regaining local control over assets acquired by U.S. investors who had exercised their right of establishment, unless that country paid compensation to the foreign investor, which the country might not be able to afford. Payment of compensation could drain the country of needed foreign exchange, but the provision on exchange controls protected the

84. Despatch dated March 20, 1958, from the U.S. embassy in Vienna to the Department of State, NARA, Record Group 59, Department of State File No. 611.634/3-2058.

85. Despatch dated May 16, 1961, from the U.S. embassy in Vienna to the Department of State, NARA, Record Group 59, Department of State File No. 611.6342/5-1661.

86. Memorandum headed "Negotiation of Treaty of Friendship, Commerce and Navigation with India," dated September 11, 1950, NARA, Record Group 59, Department of State File No. 611.911/9 1150.

87. Telegram dated May 1, 1957, from the U.S. embassy in Saigon to the Department of State, NARA, Record Group 59, Department of State File No. 611.51G4/5-157.

88. Memorandum headed "Status of Present Program for Negotiating Treaties of Friendship, Commerce and Navigation," dated March 10, 1950, NARA, Record Group 59, Department of State File No. 611.004/3-2250.

89. NAC Staff Document No. 740, Program for Obtaining Treaty Assurances to Protect United States Citizens and Property and Promote United States Private Investment in Foreign Countries, NARA, Record Group 353, Records Relating to the Council on Foreign Economic Policy 1955–1961, Box 4, Folder marked "Investment in Underdeveloped Countries CFEP 511 (Folder 2)"; Memorandum headed "Present Status of Program for Negotiating Treaties of Friendship, Commerce and Navigation Treaties," dated December 1, 1952, NARA, Record Group 59, Department of State File No. 611.004/3-453.

90. NAC Staff Document No. 740, Program for Obtaining Treaty Assurances to Protect United States Citizens and Property and Promote United States Private Investment in Foreign Countries, NARA, Record Group 353, Records Relating to the Council on Foreign Economic Policy 1955–1961, Box 4, Folder marked "Investment in Underdeveloped Countries CFEP 511 (Folder 2)." *See also* Memorandum headed "Present Status of Program for Negotiating Treaties of Friendship, Commerce and Navigation Treaties," dated December 1, 1952, NARA, Record Group 59, Department of State File No. 611.004/3-453.

expropriated investor's right to withdraw expropriation compensation, even during periods of foreign exchange stringency.

An assessment of the FCN treaty program for the NAC in December 1955 reflected the State Department's continued recognition that its bargaining power was "limited."[91] The assessment noted that particular problems arose where the United States itself was "pursuing a policy which it seeks to condemn through the treaty," notably restrictions on entry.[92]

Members of the NFTC believed that the State Department should be selective in identifying countries to which treaty negotiations would be proposed. In their view, the State Department should concentrate on negotiating with countries "willing to accept rather completely" the standard draft treaty, rather than compromising in order to conclude a larger number of treaties.[93]

Refusal to Coerce Negotiations

Despite the lack of progress, State Department officials steadfastly refused to apply pressure to other countries to conclude an FCN treaty.[94] In a message to its embassies transmitted in March 1953, the Department emphasized that FCN treaties "cannot and should not be negotiated unless there is a genuine interest" on the part of the other country.[95] The Department did not wish other countries

91. National Advisory Council Document 1868 (Revised) headed "Investments in Less Developed Areas," dated December 12, 1955, NARA, Record Group 353, Records Relating to the Council on Foreign Economic Policy 1955–1961, Box 4, Folder marked "Investment in Underdeveloped Countries CFEP 511 (Folder 1)."

92. Ibid.

93. Memorandum of Conversation headed "Meeting of NFTC Treaty Committee," dated November 10, 1954, NARA, Record Group 59, Department of State File No. 611.004/11-1054.

94. American business groups often urged the State Department to use U.S. economic power, particularly in the form of foreign assistance, to coerce other countries to conclude FCN treaties on terms deemed favorable by these groups. Some of these instances and the State Department's refusal to accede to the wishes of business groups in this regard are described in Chapter 2 in the section on the influence of the American business community and again in the section on the negotiation of the FCN treaty with China. The unsuccessful attempt on the part of business groups and some members of Congress to require the State Department to condition foreign assistance under President Truman's Point Four program on the conclusion of FCN treaties with the United States is described in Chapter 5 in the section on Point Four assistance and FCN treaties.

The discussion of the negotiation of the FCN treaty with China in Chapter 2 also describes one incident in which Willard Thorp suggested that, if a satisfactory treaty with China could not be obtained, the Department should examine the question of whether an impending loan to China should be used as bargaining leverage. Agreement on a treaty was reached five months later, and there is no evidence that the loan was used as leverage or that the idea was even discussed following Thorp's suggestion.

95. Circular Airgram headed "FCN Treaty Program of the United States," dated March 4, 1953, NARA, Record Group 59, Department of State File No. 611.004/3-453.

to regard the conclusion of an FCN treaty "to be merely a favor to the United States."[96]Rather, the Department wished other countries to understand "the mutual nature of the benefits which can accrue from such treaties."[97]

Writing in 1951, John M. Leddy, the deputy director of the Office of International Trade Policy and a member of the Commercial Policy Division from 1945 to 1949,[98] argued that "the promotion of the treaty program should not be 'aggressive' in the sense of indiscriminate pressure upon foreign governments to accept or consider our proposals. Such a method promotes antagonistic reactions abroad which are difficult to overcome."[99]

Leddy contended that the best approach was to await or to create opportunities when other countries would be amenable to accepting FCN treaty obligations rather than to pressure them to accept those obligations. "Our experience," he explained, "indicates that the most promising policy is to pursue a selective program, always prepared to exploit favorable opportunities to the utmost. . . . Perhaps our objectives could best be promoted if we should think of the treaty program not as a campaign for pressing treaties upon all countries, but as a program for seeking out or creating and exploiting favorable opportunities for the negotiation of treaties."[100]

Leddy believed that the United States should take advantage of any goodwill that it enjoyed with other countries to create conditions favorable to negotiations. He observed that "[i]t would be desirable to study the possibility of a more systematic exploitation for treaty purposes of the situations that result from action taken by the United States that is advantageous to foreign countries, *e.g.*, the making of loans, grants, technical aid arrangements, etc."[101] Leddy made clear that he was not arguing that the financial assistance be used in a coercive way, adding, "It is not suggested, of course, that an effort be made to purchase treaties by means of loans, etc. However,

96. Ibid. *See also* Letter dated January 19, 1954, from Weir M. Brown to Jack C. Corbett, NARA, Record Group 59, Department of State File No. 611.62A4/1-1954. *See also* Instruction dated May 8, 1957, from the Department of State to the U.S. embassy in Karachi, NARA, Record Group 59, Department of State File No. 611.90D4/4-2057 (conclusion of an FCN treaty should not be a "reward" for U.S. assistance).

97. Circular Airgram headed "FCN Treaty Program of the United States," dated March 4, 1953, NARA, Record Group 59, Department of State File No. 611.004/3-453. *See also* Despatch No. 2413 dated March 8, 1954, from the U.S. High Commissioner in Bonn to the Department of State, NARA, Record Group 59, Department of State File No. 611.62A4/3-854.

98. Leddy would later serve as assistant secretary of the treasury for international affairs and as U.S. ambassador to the Organization for Economic Cooperation and Development in the Kennedy administration and as assistant secretary of state for European affairs in the Johnson administration.

99. Memorandum from John M. Leddy to Willard Thorp, headed "Means for the More Effective Promotion of the F.C.N. Treaty Program," dated April 24, 1951, NARA, Record Group 59, Department of State File No. 611.004/4-2451.

100. Ibid.

101. Ibid.

the making of such concessions to foreign governments creates psychological or moral situations favorable for the initiation of treaty negotiations or their prompt conclusion."[102]

The 1955 NAC report similarly recommended that the negotiation of FCN treaties should be coordinated with other elements of foreign policy, "not in the sense of a quid pro quo" but rather to take advantage of the favorable climate created by loans or technical assistance.[103] Indeed, the report noted, an FCN treaty is "at base a treaty of friendship and is seldom if ever accepted by a foreign government purely from economic motives. Its negotiation normally flourishes when general relations are close and harmonious."[104]

Leddy believed that even striking rhetorical poses for U.S. domestic audiences could impede negotiations. He argued that "[a]ggressive propaganda in support of the treaty program either abroad or at home is not desirable. The sort of statements of purposes and aims that would appeal to practical businessmen would sound the wrong note abroad where nationalistic and communistic elements misrepresent our treaties as instruments of imperialism."[105]

State Department officials offered assurances to potential treaty parties that they should feel no obligation to conclude a treaty. For example, during negotiations with Ireland, the head of the U.S. legation in Dublin, Vinton Chapin, when discussing the critical point of disagreement between the two countries, assured the Irish prime minister that the United States "had no intention of 'putting a gun' to any Irish head to gain our point."[106]

Similarly, during negotiations with Japan, the Department instructed the U.S. mission in Tokyo to emphasize to the Japanese negotiators that, although the Department "want[ed] a good treaty or none at all, it does not wish [to] force any treaty provisions" upon the Japanese government.[107] That is, the United States would seek acceptance of U.S. proposals only "on a free-will basis."[108] As discussed below, the State Department even deferred the commencement of formal negotiations until after the peace treaty between the United States and Japan had

102. Ibid.

103. NAC Staff Document No. 740, Program for Obtaining Treaty Assurances to Protect United States Citizens and Property and Promote United States Private Investment in Foreign Countries, NARA, Record Group 353, Records Relating to the Council on Foreign Economic Policy 1955–1961, Box 4, Folder marked "Investment in Underdeveloped Countries CFEP 511 (Folder 2)."

104. Ibid.

105. Ibid.

106. Airgram dated October 28, 1948, from the U.S. legation in Dublin to the Department of State, NARA, Record Group 59, Department of State File No. 711.41D2/10-2848.

107. Airgram dated March 10, 1952, from the Department of State to the U.S. Political Adviser in Tokyo, NARA, Record Group 59, Department of State File No. 611.944/3-1052.

108. Airgram dated December 31, 1951, from the Department of State to the U.S. Political Adviser in Tokyo, NARA, Record Group 59, Department of State File No. 611.944/12-3151.

been signed, lest it appear that the United States was requiring Japan to conclude an FCN treaty as a condition precedent to conclusion of the peace treaty. Aaron Forsberg, reviewing the negotiating history of the FCN treaty with Japan, also found that "[t]he State Department did not desire to force an agreement upon an unwilling partner."[109]

The United States gave like assurances to Egypt. When a U.S. embassy official mentioned a proposed FCN treaty to Egyptian prime minister Ibrahim Abdel Hadi Pashi during an informal conversation, the prime minister complained about the length and complexity of the treaty, explained that Egypt could not agree to a treaty in that form, and expressed the hope that conclusion of the treaty was not a condition of U.S. assistance to Egypt. The embassy official immediately reassured the prime minister that no pressure should be inferred from the remark. He explained that his mentioning the treaty to the prime minister had been "entirely informal and personal," that he had mentioned the treaty because of his personal conviction that conclusion of the treaty would be a timely step in improving relations between the countries, and that he was not acting under instruction from the State Department.[110] Indeed, the Department had specifically cautioned the embassy not to exert any "undue pressure" on the Egyptian government to commence negotiations.[111]

The Department gave similar instructions to the U.S. legation in Lebanon. The United States and Lebanon had reached agreement on a treaty text in early 1950, but then the Lebanese government declined to schedule a date to sign the treaty. In January of the following year, Pro-American Lebanese recommended to U.S. officials in Beirut that the United States condition Point Four assistance on conclusion of a treaty, believing that the Lebanese government would sign the treaty rather than forgo the assistance.[112] Subsequently, U.S. legation personnel recommended to the Department that the United States link proposed economic and military aid to Lebanon with signature of the treaty,[113] but the Department instructed the legation not to do so.[114]

109. Aaron Forsberg, *America and the Japanese Miracle: The Cold War Context of Japan's Postwar Economic Revival, 1950–1960* (Chapel Hill: University of North Carolina Press, 2000), pages 175–176.

110. Airgram dated March 12, 1949, from the U.S. embassy in Cairo to the Department of State, NARA, Record Group 59, Department of State File No. 711.832/3-1249.

111. Telegram dated March 9, 1950, from the Department of State to the U.S. embassy in Cairo, NARA, Record Group 59, Department of State File No. 711.832/3-950.

112. Telegram dated January 25, 1951, from the U.S. legation in Beirut to the Department of State, NARA, Record Group 59, Department of State File No. 611.83A4/2-251.

113. Telegram dated February 25, 1952, from the U.S. legation in Beirut to the Department of State, NARA, Record Group 59, Department of State File No. 611.83A4/2-2552.

114. Telegram dated March 7, 1952, from the Department of State to the U.S. legation in Beirut, NARA, Record Group 59, Department of State File No. 611.83A4/2-2552.

State Department officials repeatedly affirmed that the United States would not pressure other countries to conclude a treaty.[115] For example, in 1949, during negotiations with Colombia, the Department cautioned the U.S. embassy in Bogota that the United States must avoid even the appearance of exerting undue pressure on other countries.[116] In 1950, Winthrop Brown, who was by then director of the State Department's Office of International Trade Policy (the successor to the Office of Economic Affairs), in writing about the status of FCN treaty negotiations with Chile, noted that "[s]everal months ago the Chilean Ambassador requested and received copies of a draft [FCN] treaty such as we then had under discussion with certain other governments, and we understand that this draft is now under study in Santiago. It is, of course, no part of the Department's policy to exert any pressure upon Chile to enter into such a treaty. . . ."[117] Brown returned to the same point later, noting, "The Chilean government is unquestionably free to reject our treaty proposals for any reason, or for no reason at all. That is its privilege as the government of a sovereign nation."[118]

The Department's refusal to exert pressure on other countries was not attributable to a general policy of avoiding the application of economic pressure in international relations. The Truman administration, for example, "had no qualms about using economic aid as a lever to force diplomatic concessions from the Soviets."[119] The United States also exerted considerable economic pressure on the British to dismantle the imperial preference system established in 1932 in response to the Smoot-Hawley tariff.[120]

Rather, the Department believed that, for an FCN treaty to be an effective basis for economic relations, it should be one into which the other party had freely entered.[121] As has been seen, the State Department did not see an FCN treaty as merely a catalog of concessions extracted, but as the reflection of a genuine

115. The State Department's refusal to pressure other countries to conclude an FCN treaty is also discussed in Chapter 2 in the section on the negotiation of the FCN treaty with China and in Chapter 7 in the sections on the negotiation of FCN treaties with the Netherlands and Belgium.

116. Memorandum by Herman Walker Jr., headed "Further Possible Provisions in Standard Draft of Treaty of Friendship, Commerce and Navigation (or Economic Development)," dated October 12, 1949, NARA, Record Group 59, Department of State Lot Files, Walter Hollis Papers, Folder marked "Commercial Treaties."

117. Memorandum by Winthrop Brown, dated February 13, 1950, NARA, Record Group 59, Department of State File No. 611.004/3-850.

118. Ibid.

119. Randall B. Woods and Howard Jones, *Dawning of the Cold War: The United States' Quest for Order* (Athens: University of Georgia Press, 1991), page 46.

120. Alan Dobson, *The Politics of the Anglo-American Economic Special Relationship, 1940–1987* (New York: St. Martin's Press, 1988), pages 60–97; Richard N. Gardner, *Sterling-Dollar Diplomacy in Current Perspective: The Origins and the Prospects of Our International Economic Order* (New York: Columbia University Press, 1980); Lloyd C. Gardner, *Economic Aspects of New Deal Diplomacy* (Madison: University of Wisconsin Press, 1964), pages 275–290.

121. Telegram dated February 16, 1948, from the Department of State to the U.S. embassy in Nanking, NARA, Record Group 59, Department of State File No. 611.9331/2-1048.

commitment to "right principle." Moreover, the Department recognized that guarantees of favorable treatment that a treaty party did not genuinely wish to make would be of little value. For example, the December 1955 NAC report noted that "[t]the United States negotiating position might be strengthened by linking other phases of foreign economic policy with these treaties; but it is questionable whether a treaty secured from a somewhat reluctant government would be of any real value."[122] As Herman Walker observed during negotiations with Belgium in 1959, a "worthwhile FCN treaty must by its nature represent [a] real and friendly meeting of minds in all parts."[123] Similarly, an internal memorandum written in 1948 addressing charges that the treaty with China was not sufficiently strong, observed that "moderate treaty commitments, based on mutuality and freely accepted, afford sounder safeguards for American interests in the long run, because such commitments are likely to be more effectively carried out than concessions which might appear to be of greater value accorded under pressure or because of temporary weakness."[124] In fact, a 1956 internal State Department memorandum noted, "extracting such treaties from reluctant governments which may be unprepared to accept the basic principles" in the treaties could pose "some danger" for U.S. nationals and companies that relied on the treaties.[125] The treaties were particularly ill-adapted to obtaining a right of entry from a country that did not wish to grant it.[126] Finally, the Department recognized that conditioning foreign assistance on the conclusion of an FCN treaty would reduce the Department's flexibility in managing U.S. foreign assistance programs.[127]

The Department's refusal to exert pressure on other countries to conclude FCN treaties was also to some degree a strategic choice. The State Department recognized that pressure could stiffen resistance and thus be

122. National Advisory Council Document 1868 (Revised) headed "Investments in Less Developed Areas," dated December 12, 1955, NARA, Record Group 353, Records Relating to the Council on Foreign Economic Policy 1955–1961, Box 4, Folder marked "Investment in Underdeveloped Countries CFEP 511 (Folder 1)."

123. Telegram dated May 20, 1959, from the U.S. embassy in Paris to the Department of State, NARA, Record Group 59, Department of State File No. 611.554/5-2059.

124. Memorandum headed "Comment upon Letter of Shanghai American Chamber of Commerce Regarding Sino-American Treaty of Friendship, Commerce and Navigation," dated April 15, 1948, NARA, Record Group 59, Department of State File No. 711.932/3-1148.

125. Memorandum headed "U.S. Investment in Less-Developed Areas," NARA, Record Group 353, Records Relating to the Council on Foreign Economic Policy 1955–1961," dated January 3, 1956, Box 4, Folder marked "Investment in Underdeveloped Countries CFEP 511 (Folder 2)."

126. Letter dated February 13, 1959, from Deputy Assistant Secretary of State W. T. M. Beale to Acting Assistant Secretary of Commerce Marshall Smith, NARA, Record Group 59, Department of State File No. 611.51G4/1-1559.

127. Memorandum headed "U.S. Investment in Less-Developed Areas," dated January 3, 1956, NARA, Record Group 353, Records Relating to the Council on Foreign Economic Policy 1955–1961, Box 4, Folder marked "Investment in Underdeveloped Countries CFEP 511 (Folder 2)."

counterproductive.[128] As the Department noted during negotiations with Egypt, pressure on the Egyptian government to conclude a treaty "might be utilized for propaganda adverse to United States interests in Egypt . . . ."[129] Indeed, the Department feared that even a refusal to grant treaty concessions sought by the other party could damage U.S. foreign relations. During negotiations with India, Department officials noted that "[a] refusal by us to go along with what is plausibly a reasonable agreement might, moreover, be regarded as reflective of something less than an entirely friendly attitude on our part toward India's aspirations to attain and maintain economic as well as political independence. This consideration would almost certainly be well exploited in the propaganda of our opponents."[130]

Refusal to Correlate Treaties with Increased Investment

Although they regarded FCN treaties as a means of promoting foreign investment, State Department officials did not claim that the conclusion of an FCN treaty alone would produce increased investment. For example, in early 1953, when sending a message to its embassies emphasizing the importance of negotiating FCN treaties, the Department commented that it was not to be expected that the conclusion of an FCN treaty would "necessarily be followed by a marked increase in American capital investment" in the territory of the other treaty party. The Department had made the same point the previous year in a telegram to the U.S. embassy in Port-au-Prince concerning the negotiation of an FCN treaty, observing that "[t]he conclusion of such a treaty *ipso facto* would not necessarily result in an increased flow of American private capital to Haiti."[131] Deputy Assistant Secretary of State Harold Linder told the Senate during hearings in 1952 that the FCN treaties "do not guarantee private investment . . . ."[132] Prior to the commencement of negotiations with South Korea, the State Department instructed its embassy in Seoul to

> avoid leading the Koreans to expect that the conclusion of such a treaty would necessarily be immediately productive of increased private United

128. *Current Economic Developments,* September 17, 1945, page 9, NARA, Record Group 59, Department of State Lot Files.

129. Letter dated March 9, 1950, from Acting Assistant Secretary of State John E. O'Gara to Ambassador Jefferson Caffrey, NARA, Record Group 59, Department of State File No. 611.744/3-950.

130. Memorandum headed "Negotiation of Treaty of Friendship, Commerce and Navigation with India," dated September 11, 1950, NARA, Record Group 59, Department of State File No. 611.914/9-1150.

131. Telegram dated June 3, 1952, from the Department of State to the U.S. embassy in Port-au-Prince, NARA, Record Group 59, Department of State File No. 611.384/6-352.

132. *Commercial Treaties,* Hearing Before a Subcommittee of the Committee on Foreign Relations, 82d Cong. 2d Sess. (1952), page 7.

> States investment. The main function of the treaty, insofar as investment is concerned, is to provide assurances that the juridical conditions affecting foreign investment are favorable and will remain so. The treaty cannot be expected to remove important investment impediments of a non-juridical character.[133]

As John M. Leddy noted in 1951, "Overemphasis upon treaties as sure means for stimulating foreign investment is not good salesmanship."[134]

In some cases, treaty negotiators from other countries themselves expressed skepticism concerning whether an FCN treaty would lead to increased investment. At times, they offered this skepticism as justification for caution in concluding a treaty with greater obligations than they were inclined to assume. For example, one of India's negotiators expressed the view that the impact of the treaty on investment flows would be "marginal." At the same time, the treaty language would provide a basis on which "private parties imagining that they had a grievance of one sort or another might make life tedious for the officials of both governments."[135] The Irish prime minister and the sultan of Muscat and Oman similarly expressed doubt that an FCN treaty would result in increased investment, and cited that doubt as a basis for resisting particular commitments.[136] At other times, however, their skepticism about the impact of the treaty led them to the conclusion that more must be done to attract investment. For example, during negotiations, the ambassador from Colombia told U.S. negotiators that "the whole purpose of the treaty [was] to encourage the investment of United States capital [in] Colombia but that the treaty alone would not suffice."[137] Thus, he said, Colombia should conclude a double taxation treaty with the United States and administer its exchange controls in ways that would not discourage foreign investment.

State Department officials did not claim that the conclusion of an FCN treaty would promote investment flows, because they believed that no such correlation

133. Instruction dated October 12, 1953, from the Department of State to the U.S. embassy in Seoul, NARA, Record Group 59, Department of State File No. 611.95B4/10-253.

134. Memorandum headed "Means for the More Effective Promotion of the F.C.N. Treaty Program," dated April 24, 1951, from John M. Leddy to Willard Thorp, NARA, Record Group 59, Department of State File No. 611.004/4-2451.

135. Memorandum of Conversation dated November 24, 1953, enclosure to Despatch No. 912 dated November 30, 1953, from the U.S. embassy in New Delhi to the Department of State, NARA, Record Group 59, Department of State File No. 611.914/11-3053.

136. The discussion with the Irish prime minister is described in Chapter 5 in the section on the negotiation of the FCN treaty with Ireland. The discussion with the sultan is described in Chapter 7 in the section on the negotiation of the FCN treaty with the sultanate of Muscat and Oman.

137. Memorandum of Conversation headed "Negotiation of Treaty of Friendship, Commerce and Navigation with Colombia: Nineteenth Meeting," dated January 18, 1951, NARA, Record Group 59, Department of State File No. 611.214/1-1851.

could be proved. "It is not feasible," Leddy observed, "to attempt to prepare statistical or other factual data to demonstrate the effectiveness of an FCN treaty in encouraging investment."[138] Seymour Rubin, the chief negotiator for the United States of the investment provisions of the ITO Charter and the assistant legal adviser for economic affairs for a portion of the 1940s, wrote in his private capacity in 1956 that there was "little evidence" to support a correlation between the conclusion of an FCN treaty and an increase in investment flows.[139]

Indeed, Department officials believed that there likely was no correlation, because an FCN treaty alone would usually be insufficient to stimulate investment flows. In the period immediately following World War II, political and economic uncertainties imposed "formidable" deterrents to investment.[140] Exchange controls were the norm, and U.S. investors suffered "sizeable losses" from expropriation.[141] Businesses also faced the new phenomenon of the "creeping expropriation," a series of regulatory measures that gradually eroded an investment's value, although the government never seized title or possession of the investment.[142] As President Truman himself observed in his 1949 message to Congress transmitting his proposed legislation to implement Point Four, "the problem of substantially increasing the flow of American capital abroad presents serious difficulties."[143] The 1955 NAC report compiled a long list of factors that inhibited outward U.S. investment, including the lack of a market in less-developed countries; insufficient earnings of foreign exchange to permit repatriation of returns on investment; state ownership of transportation and utilities; screening of

138. Memorandum headed "Means for the More Effective Promotion of the F.C.N. Treaty Program," dated April 24, 1951, from John M. Leddy to Willard Thorp, NARA, Record Group 59, Department of State File No. 611.004/4-2451.

139. Seymour J. Rubin, *Private Foreign Investment: Legal & Economic Realities* (Baltimore: Johns Hopkins Press, 1956), page 84.

140. Sir Arthur Salter, *Foreign Investment* (Princeton, NJ: Princeton University Press, 1951), page 54. Sir Arthur included on his list of formidable obstacles "memories of past losses, a shortage of United States 'equity' capital and highly remunerative opportunities of investment in domestic equities, political uncertainties in the capital-needing countries with dangers of inconvertibility and confiscation." The most thorough inventory of the obstacles to U.S. foreign investment in the late 1940s was Cleona Lewis's monumental study. Cleona Lewis, *The United States and Foreign Investment Problems* (Washington. DC: Brookings Institution, 1948), especially pages 141–168. Regulatory risks that deterred foreign investment at the end of the war are also discussed briefly in Chapter 1 above, under the heading "The Need to Promote and Regulate International Investment."

141. Mira Wilkins, *The Maturing of Multinational Enterprise: American Business Abroad from 1914 to 1970* (Cambridge, MA: Harvard University Press, 1974), page 301.

142. Ibid., page 307.

143. Harry S. Truman, "The Point 4 Program: Aid to Underdeveloped Areas," June 24, 1949, *reprinted in* Department of State, *A New Era in World Affairs: Selected Speeches and Statements of President Truman, January 20 to August 29, 1949,* Department of State Publication 3653 (Washington, DC: Government Printing Office, 1949), page 31.

foreign investment; regulatory risk, including taxes, exchange controls, devaluation and expropriation; Communist aggression; the absence of existing economic relations that build confidence; the demand in the United States for capital that crowded out developing countries; and past defaults.[144] As Herman Walker noted in an article that he published in 1956, "The factors which cause foreign investments to be made or not to be made are varied and numerous, and include those of a political, economic, social and environmental nature which are beyond the reach of treaties. A treaty is a legal instrument, dealing with rules of law; in turn, the extent to which a treaty can practicably deal even with legal conditions is limited."[145]

Accordingly, the Department noted in a 1950 publication that, "even with [treaty] protection, it is not likely that large amounts of private investment will flow to the underdeveloped world in the near future."[146] When the Senate was considering a group of FCN treaties in 1953, Secretary of Commerce Sinclair Weeks explained to the Committee chairman, Republican Senator Bourke Hickenlooper of Iowa, that "[t]hese commercial treaties can do no more, of course, than establish the standards to be applied reciprocally by the contracting governments in these matters. Various other favorable conditions must be present before individual firms will launch ventures where these assurances can come into play."[147] Similarly, the Department observed in a 1954 telegram to its embassy in Beirut that "obviously[,] no single law or treaty can assure [an] inflow [of] foreign private capital."[148] The 1955 NAC report described the problem in greater detail:

> The question is sometimes asked whether statistical or other evidence cannot be assembled to show how effective treaty provisions are in encouraging foreign private investment. The answer must be in the negative. The conditions that determine whether investment flows into a country are largely economic. Investors are concerned about the supply of needed materials, availability of labor, the nearness of markets and the possibility of their expansion—in short,

144. National Advisory Council Document 1868 (Revised) headed "Investments in Less Developed Areas," dated December 12, 1955, NARA, Record Group 353, Records Relating to the Council on Foreign Economic Policy 1955–1961, Box 4, Folder marked "Investment in Underdeveloped Countries CFEP 511 (Folder 1)."

145. Herman Walker Jr., "Treaties for the Encouragement and Protection of Foreign Investment: Present United States Practice," 5 *American Journal of Comparative Law* 229, 245 (1956).

146. Department of State, *Our Foreign Policy*, Department of State Publication 3972, (Washington, DC: Government Printing Office, 1950), page 75.

147. 99 *Congressional Record* 9312 (1953). Secretary of Commerce Charles Sawyer had made the same comment the year before. Letter dated May 12, 1952, from Secretary Charles Sawyer to Senator Tom Connally, *reprinted in Commercial Treaties,* Hearing Before a Subcommittee of the Committee on Foreign Relations, 82nd Cong. 2d Sess. (1952), page 41.

148. Telegram dated July 29, 1954, from the Department of State to the U.S. embassy in Beirut, NARA, Record Group 59, Department of State File No. 611.83A4/7-2754.

> the factors that have to do with the return on the investment. No matter how favorable a country's laws and treaties, if the economic factors are not present, investment will not flow. On the other hand, where very favorable economic opportunities offer, investors assume great risks and exercise resourcefulness to overcome unfavorable political and juridical conditions. A number of the countries that receive large amounts of American private investment have refused up to the present to negotiate treaties . . . . A country may enact favorable investment laws and maintain a favorable attitude toward foreign capital without entering into treaties on the subject. The negotiation of treaties constitutes only one method of attacking the problems that hinder international investment. Their effect, even within their limited area of application, cannot be depended upon to be immediately measurable. At best, the most that can be expected from treaties is a significant contribution to the improvement and stabilization of conditions over a long run.[149]

Ultimately, the report found, the conclusion of an FCN treaty "by no means assures that the acceding country will receive any substantial American private investment."[150] A different NAC report produced the same month noted that investment treaties "probably had only a marginal effect on the total flow of investment," at least in the short run.[151]

State Department officials also acknowledged that particular treaties were unlikely to result in increased investment flows to the other treaty parties. For example, during negotiations with India in 1950, the State Department cautioned its embassy in New Delhi that concluding a treaty with India "would give rise to Indian hopes for a volume of American private investment that does not now seem likely to materialize in any case and especially with screening of entry."[152] Two years later, faced with Indian resistance to granting a right of national treatment, the State Department declined to press for conclusion of a treaty, noting that the size of future U.S. investment in India was doubtful even if a treaty were concluded.[153] John M. Leddy observed in

149. NAC Staff Document No. 740, Program for Obtaining Treaty Assurances to Protect United States Citizens and Property and Promote United States Private Investment in Foreign Countries, NARA, Record Group 353, Records Relating to the Council on Foreign Economic Policy 1955–1961, Box 4, Folder marked "Investment in Underdeveloped Countries CFEP 511 (Folder 2)."

150. Ibid.

151. National Advisory Council Document 1868 (Revised) headed "Investments in Less Developed Areas," dated December 12, 1955, NARA, Record Group 353, Records Relating to the Council on Foreign Economic Policy 1955–1961, Box 4, Folder marked "Investment in Underdeveloped Countries CFEP 511 (Folder 1)"; *Current Economic Developments*, January 10, 1956, page 2, NARA, Record Group 59, Department of State Lot Files.

152. Telegram dated August 2, 1950, from the U.S. embassy in New Delhi to the Department of State, NARA, Record Group 59, Department of State File No. 611.914/8-250.

153. Telegram dated July 6, 1950, from the Department of State to the U.S. embassy in New Delhi, NARA, Record Group 59, Department of State File No. 611.914/5-1250.

1951 that "[t]wo of the three new treaties that have been ratified since World War II are with countries poor in natural resources, and for that and other reasons not particularly attractive to foreign investors. The treaty with China is not attractive for obvious reasons."[154]

Leddy believed that correlating investment with the "legal and institutional climates favorable to investment, such as the treaties are intended to promote, would probably be a more practical exercise" than seeking to correlate the treaties themselves with increased investment.[155] As Leddy's comment suggests, an FCN treaty was principally an instrument to promote the rule of law, which might or might not result in increased investment.

Affirming the Other Party's Existing Liberal Investment Policy

Although FCN treaties were justified as a means to improve the investment climate, State Department officials believed that concluding a treaty would be possible only if the other country genuinely wished to attract foreign investment. In a sense, then, the favorable climate must precede the treaty.[156] As the State Department noted during negotiations with Belgium, "the most propitious time to negotiate a satisfactory treaty is not usually when there is a great deal of complaint over bad treatment, since the existence of serious friction is likely to presage serious difficulties in attaining the harmonious meeting of the minds which should underlay a mutually satisfactory treaty. An FCN treaty is not primarily therapeutic in nature; and it is no accident that the word 'Friendship' is first in its title."[157] Seymour Rubin commented in 1956 that the United States was able to conclude an FCN treaty only with those countries that already had a pro-investment policy.[158]

Indeed, the purpose of the treaty was not so much to induce a party to change its policy as to incorporate into international legal obligations an already existing liberal policy.[159] As the State Department further explained during its

154. Memorandum headed "Means for the more effective promotion of the F.C.N. Treaty Program," dated April 24, 1951, from John M. Leddy to Willard Thorp, NARA, Record Group 59, Department of State File No. 611.004/4-2451.

155. Ibid.

156. Transcript of Proceedings, Meeting of Economic Consultants on Point Four Program, April 8, 1949, pages 110–111, NARA, Record Group 59, Department of State File No. 800.50T.A./4-859.

157. Instruction dated November 5, 1954, from the Department of State to the U.S. embassy in Brussels, NARA, Record Group 59, Department of State File No. 611.6554/11-554.

158. Seymour J. Rubin, *Private Foreign Investment: Legal and Economic Realities* (Baltimore: Johns Hopkins Press, 1956), page 85. *See also* David A. Baldwin, *Economic Development and American Foreign Policy, 1943-62* (Chicago: The University of Chicago Press, 1966), pages 114–115.

159. Letter dated January 19, 1954, from Weir M. Brown to Jack C. Corbett, NARA, Record Group 59, Department of State File No. 611.62A4/1-1954.

negotiations with Belgium, the treaty "serves to confirm, translate into international obligation, and place a barrier to retrogression in, a liberal regime of treatment of the alien and his interests as provided in existing law; and it serves also to orient administrative policy and future legislative policy in a liberal direction. A treaty establishes and 'firms up' a Government's basic sympathy toward, and its intentions to accord fair treatment to, the businessman and international investment and commerce."[160] Thus, President Eisenhower's Commission on Foreign Economic Policy noted in 1954 that FCN treaties "more often record the existence of a favorable environment than create it."[161]

The Confidentiality of Negotiations

The United States regarded treaty negotiations as confidential. For example, although the State Department did discuss the terms of the standard draft treaty with business groups, once the negotiation of a particular treaty began, the Department as a general matter declined to consult with those groups about specific provisions of the treaty under negotiation. In some cases, the State Department refrained from disclosing even the fact that negotiations were occurring,[162] although an embassy might be given the discretion to disclose the fact that a treaty had been proposed,[163] and the State Department realized that good public relations sometimes required informing the business community at least of the existence of negotiations.[164] The practice varied with the circumstances and the State Department occasionally would meet with a small number of selected business representatives for a confidential discussion of particular problems encountered in a negotiation.[165]

So great was the concern for confidentiality that the Department even sought to control discussion within the federal government of the specifics of the negotiations. On one occasion, for example, the State Department refused to show a

160. Instruction dated November 5, 1954, from the Department of State to the U.S. embassy in Brussels, NARA, Record Group 59, Department of State File No. 611.6554/11-554.

161. *Quoted in* Wilson, *United States Commercial Treaties*, page 21.

162. *See, e.g.*, Telegram dated September 23, 1946, from the Department of State to the U.S. embassy in Cairo, NARA, Record Group 59, Department of State File No. 711.832/9-1846.

163. Telegram dated January 21, 1948, from the Department of State to the U.S. Charge d'Affaires *ad interim* in New Delhi, NARA, Record Group 59, Department of State File No. 711.452/1-2148.

164. Memorandum by Willard Thorp headed "Consultation with Businessmen Regarding Treaties of Friendship, Commerce and Navigation," dated January 14, 1952, NARA, Record Group 59, Department of State File No. 611.964/1-1452.

165. For an example of such a discussion with representatives of the Philippine-American Chamber of Commerce and the NFTC, *see* Memorandum of Conversation "Discussion of Status of Treaty of Friendship, Commerce and Navigation between the United States and the Philippines," dated November 5, 1948, NARA, Record Group 59, Department of State File No. 711.962/11-548.

U.S. congressman a copy of the treaty text then under negotiation with India or to answer questions about that specific text, instead suggesting that the congressman examine the treaty already concluded with Italy.[166]

The confidentiality of negotiations was sometimes the subject of criticism. For example, the *Shanghai Evening Post & Mercury* published an editorial in March 1948 criticizing the secrecy in which the treaty with China was negotiated. Referring to the negotiations, the editorial observed that "a species of iron curtain descended, and no businessman, missionary or other private individual had any information as to how the negotiations were progressing or what their outcome might be."[167]

When others sought information about treaty negotiations, the Department, in declining to furnish the information, typically cited its policy of keeping treaty provisions secret until the Senate lifted the injunction of secrecy,[168] an event that would occur after the president sent the treaty to the Senate for advice and consent to ratification.[169] Maintaining the confidentiality of negotiations was defended as consistent with "diplomatic practice."[170]

The State Department believed that public discussion of a treaty during negotiations would add "greatly to negotiating difficulties."[171] The Department feared that such discussion could subject the parties to pressure from nongovernmental organizations that would increase the difficulties involved in negotiating the treaty.[172] As the Department explained during negotiations with Japan, discussion

166. Letter dated July 1, 1948, from Assistant Secretary of State Willard Thorp to U.S. Representative Emanuel Cellar, NARA, Record Group 59, Department of State File No. 711.452/6-2248.

167. Despatch dated March 17, 1948, from the U.S. consulate general in Shanghai to the Department of State, NARA, Record Group 59, Department of State File No. 711.932/3-1748.

168. Letter dated February 13, 1945, from Woodbury Willoughby to E. A. Locke Jr., NARA, Record Group 59, Department of State File No. 711.932/2-1345. *See also* letter dated March 29, 1962, from Deputy Legal Adviser Leonard C. Meeker to Smith H. Crowe Jr., NARA, Record Group 59, Department of State File No. 611.0042/3-2962; Agreed Minutes of Technical Discussions on the Proposed Treaty of Friendship, Commerce and Navigation between the United States of America and the Republic of the Philippines at Manila July 2 to August 24, 1948, Session July 2, 1948, NARA, Record Group 59, Department of State File No. 711.962/9-1448.

169. Memorandum of Conversation on Consultation with Other Government Agencies and with Business Interests in Connection with the Negotiation of Treaties of Friendship, Commerce and Navigation, dated June 29, 1948, NARA, Record Group 59, Department of State File No. 711.002/6-2948.

170. Letter dated June 5, 1953, from Assistant Legal Adviser Charles I. Bevans to William C. Freund, NARA, Record Group 59, Department of State File No. 611.004/5-1453.

171. Telegram dated July 15, 1948, from the Department of State to the U.S. embassy in Manila, NARA, Record Group 59, Department of State File No. 611.9631/7-1548.

172. *See, e.g.*, Telegram dated September 23, 1946, from the Department of State to the U.S. embassy in Cairo, NARA, Record Group 59, Department of State File No. 711.832/9-1846.

of the treaty with U.S. business interests would be impractical because it would mean that the Department effectively would be negotiating with U.S. business interests and Japan simultaneously.[173] The State Department also was concerned about pressure from those hostile to U.S. interests. It noted in 1953, in the context of possible negotiations with Indonesia, the desirability of avoiding public discussion or speculation about the proposed treaty because in the past public discussion of a possible FCN treaty in countries with a political climate similar to that in Indonesia had led to "hostile propaganda in the Communist and nationalist press" leading to delay or abandonment of negotiations.[174] Public discussion could create other problems as well. The Department believed that a government could not easily recede from a position once that position had been taken publicly,[175] with the result that public discussion could impede the making of compromises necessary to reach agreement. Even if the negotiations were successful, public discussion during negotiations might create expectations about the results of the negotiations that, as events would prove, could not be fulfilled, and that would result in opposition to a treaty that otherwise would have been supported.[176] Indeed, public discussion could arouse false fears, as well as false hopes, generating pressures that would impede agreement.[177]

Other countries generally sought to maintain the confidentiality of the negotiations as well. For example, when the secrecy of the negotiations between the United States and the Philippines was criticized in the press, the Philippines government defended maintaining the confidentiality of treaty negotiations as "a practice observed by all civilized nations."[178] After the Chinese press printed articles about the FCN treaty negotiations then in progress with the United States, the Chinese negotiators assured the U.S. negotiators that the Chinese government had released no information, and would not do so without the prior agreement of both parties.[179] At the inception of negotiations with Japan, the Japanese foreign affairs ministry

173. Airgram dated June 29, 1951, from the Department of State to the U.S. Political Adviser in Tokyo, NARA, Record Group 59, Department of State File No. 611.944/6-2951.

174. Airgram dated June 24, 1953, from the Department of State to the U.S. embassy in Jakarta, NARA, Record Group 59, Department of State File No. 611.004/5-2153.

175. Airgram dated June 29, 1951, from the Department of State to the U.S. Political Adviser in Tokyo, NARA, Record Group 59, Department of State File No. 611.944/6-2951.

176. Telegram dated January 21, 1948, from the Department of State to the U.S. Charge d'Affaires *ad interim* in New Delhi, NARA, Record Group 59, Department of State File No. 711.452/1-2148.

177. Telegram dated November 28, 1951, from the Department of State to the U.S. Political Adviser in Tokyo, NARA, Record Group 59, Department of State File No. 611.944/11-2851.

178. Telegram dated August 24, 1948, from the U.S. embassy in Manila to the Department of State, NARA, Record Group 59, Department of State File No. 711.962/8-2448.

179. Memorandum headed "The Proposed Sino-American Treaty of Friendship, Commerce and Navigation," dated June 6, 1946, NARA, Record Group 59, Department of State File No. 711.932/12-2046.

reported to the U.S. negotiators that it was "embarrassed" that the proposed Japanese draft treaty had become public, and assured the negotiators that it was "seeking [to] avoid further leaks."[180]

Rejection of Multilateral Negotiations

Although recognizing the difficulties associated with concluding FCN treaties, the State Department believed that bilateral negotiations were the only way to achieve agreement on a satisfactory treaty. The 1955 NAC report noted that

> [p]ast experience provides little ground for hope that a generally acceptable multilateral investment convention, containing a body of satisfactory provisions from the investor viewpoint, could be achieved under present circumstances. Rather, there is a danger that an international conference convened to consider such a convention would reveal, and crystallize extensive support for, doctrines which are repugnant to American businessmen and out of keeping with principles which a regime favorable to private international investment should reflect.[181]

The report observed that over the past 30 years three attempts to reach a multilateral agreement on investment had been attempted, and all three had failed. The first was a proposed League of Nations draft convention on the treatment of foreigners and foreign enterprises that had been developed in 1927 and 1928 and that was the subject of the International Conference on the Treatment of Foreigners, held in Paris from November 5 to December 5, 1929.[182] The delegations present had insisted upon so many reservations to the principles of the draft convention that the effect of adopting the convention would have been a regime less liberal than that already in existence.[183] The second was the attempt to include investment provisions in the ITO Charter. In that case,

> [t]he price of agreement was equivocation on the principle of just compensation in event of expropriation and, in general, undue emphasis on the

180. Telegram dated December 2, 1951, from the U.S. Political Adviser in Tokyo to the Department of State, NARA, Record Group 59, Department of State File No. 611.944/12-251.

181. NAC Staff Document No. 740, Program for Obtaining Treaty Assurances to Protect United States Citizens and Property and Promote United States Private Investment in Foreign Countries, NARA, Record Group 353, Records Relating to the Council on Foreign Economic Policy 1955–1961, Box 4, Folder marked "Investment in Underdeveloped Countries CFEP 511 (Folder 2)."

182. John Ward Cutler, "The Treatment of Foreigners: In Relation to the Draft Convention and Conference of 1929," 27 *American Journal of International Law* 225 (1933).

183. Memorandum dated April 9, 1947, from Vernon Setser to Woodbury Willoughby, NARA, Record Group 43, International Trade Files, Box 55, Folder marked "Investment."

> aspirations and sovereign rights of the host country at the expense of assurances to investors. These arrangements, by provoking sharp hostility within the American business community, contributed materially to the unfavorable reception which the ITO Charter met in this country . . ." [184]

The third was the 1948 Inter-American conference of Bogota, where the draft was "vitiated" by numerous reservations and the project was abandoned. [185]

The NAC report explained why these failures were "understandable."[186] The international community simply had not reached a sufficient consensus to permit the conclusion of an acceptable multilateral agreement. In the words of the report,

> Multilateral conventions tend to reflect a least-common-denominator position. A fruitful convention, therefore, presupposes a widespread consensus on applicable principles. In the investment field, this would mean a community of basic attitudes, which does not yet exist, toward such matters as the security of private property, the virtues of private enterprise and the profit system, the acceptability of alien ownership and management of important sectors of industry, and confidence that alien capital penetration does not mean "imperialism" or impairment of political sovereignty.' Countries like the United States . . . are in a minority.[187]

A separate NAC report prepared the same month noted that

> [a] multilateral investment treaty convention is occasionally suggested as a means of extending the benefits of treaty protection to investors in more countries. Such a convention might well result in a concerted formal expression of views common to many less developed countries but adverse to the interests of United States private investors abroad.[188]

Further, even among countries that shared the same principles as the United States, there were "variances in matters of detail" and an unwillingness to be

184. NAC Staff Document No. 740, Program for Obtaining Treaty Assurances to Protect United States Citizens and Property and Promote United States Private Investment in Foreign Countries, NARA, Record Group 353, Records Relating to the Council on Foreign Economic Policy 1955–1961, Box 4, Folder marked "Investment in Underdeveloped Countries CFEP 511 (Folder 2)."

185. Ibid.

186. Ibid.

187. Ibid.

188. National Advisory Council Document 1868 (Revised) headed "Investments in Less Developed Areas," dated December 12, 1955, NARA, Record Group 353, Records Relating to the Council on Foreign Economic Policy 1955–1961, Box 4, Folder marked "Investment in Underdeveloped Countries CFEP 511 (Folder 1)."

bound to continue the "fair treatment" that they already accorded.[189] An aggravating factor was that federal systems, because of their inability to control treatment accorded by political subdivisions, such as states or provinces, with respect to certain matters, needed reservations regarding such matters, which made it difficult to oppose reservations by other countries on other matters.[190]

Herman Walker, writing in his personal capacity in 1956, elaborated upon the problems. Walker noted that the development of the required consensus was impeded by the fact that "investment questions are susceptible of being regarded as touching upon sensitive issues of domestic sovereignty, internal economic policy, and national political philosophy."[191] Even where a consensus on principle existed, differences in national legal systems gave rise to divergences over details and, in a multilateral negotiation, such divergences could "accumulate into a massive total."[192] Further, the commitments that a country may be willing to undertake on a selective bilateral basis "may be considerably different" from those it is willing to undertake "indiscriminately vis-à-vis all the world."[193] Walker noted that the United States had concluded 15 FCN treaties as of that date, and it was "not easy to visualize how they might be amalgamated into a composite unit" that was equally satisfactory.[194]

An alternative to the negotiation of a multilateral convention was the preparation of a code by a nongovernmental organization, such as the "Draft Code of Fair Treatment for Foreign Investments" adopted in 1949 by the International Chamber of Commerce. The problem with this approach was determining how to constitute the group in such a way as to generate a worthwhile product while lending the product international prestige and credibility.[195] It was necessary, a 1955 NAC report noted, "to assure that on the one hand [the group] reflects homogeneity from the viewpoint of the enlightened interests of the private investor and, on the other hand, the capital-deficient countries will have confidence that their interests have been adequately taken into account."[196]

189. NAC Staff Document No. 740, Program for Obtaining Treaty Assurances to Protect United States Citizens and Property and Promote United States Private Investment in Foreign Countries, NARA, Record Group 353, Records Relating to the Council on Foreign Economic Policy 1955–1961, Box 4, Folder marked "Investment in Underdeveloped Countries CFEP 511 (Folder 2)."

190. Ibid.

191. Walker, "Treaties for the Encouragement and Protection of Foreign Investment," page 241.

192. Ibid.

193. Ibid., page 242.

194. Ibid.

195. NAC Staff Document No. 740, Program for Obtaining Treaty Assurances to Protect United States Citizens and Property and Promote United States Private Investment in Foreign Countries, NARA, Record Group 353, Records Relating to the Council on Foreign Economic Policy 1955–1961, Box 4, Folder marked "Investment in Underdeveloped Countries CFEP 511 (Folder 2)."

196. Ibid.

Given these problems, the best hope for progress still seemed to lie in the "unspectacular" process of negotiating bilateral treaties.[197] As the 1955 NAC report explained,

> Bilateral negotiation allows differential pacing and the case-by-case approach, which seems peculiarly adapted to the subject matter. The United States is able to deal with countries as each becomes ready, willing and able to entertain the necessary commitments; to exercise all the patience needed to remove fears and suspicions, clarify misunderstandings and find viable solutions to the many problems besetting the negotiations; and to prevent difficulties with individual countries from hardening into undesirable, public-aired issues and becoming allied with the individual difficulties of other countries.[198]

The State Department also believed that bilateral negotiations provided a setting in which the United States could address the fact that many of the other treaty parties wished to avoid extending the same treatment to third countries that it was extending to the United States.[199]

Persistence Yields Treaties

Although the negotiation of investment treaties on a bilateral basis seemed to be the most promising approach to securing protection for foreign investment, as of the mid-1950s, only the United States had adopted that approach. As the 1955 NAC report observed, no other country was "actively prosecuting a general program for the securing of investment treaties."[200]

Meanwhile, by the end of the Truman administration, the Department's years of persistence had begun to yield tangible results. A series of successful negotiations that began in 1950 gave the Department the opportunity to insert its new investment-related provisions into additional treaties and to refine the language of the provisions in the process.

These negotiations, like those conducted during subsequent administrations, illustrate the process by which the United States incorporated its foreign investment policy into international law. They show the State Department promoting core principles of liberal legality, while acknowledging the need of other countries to regulate their economies. The negotiations demonstrate as well the extent to which, by 1950, the investment-related provisions had become of primary importance in the negotiations.

197. Ibid.

198. Ibid.

199. Ibid.

200. Ibid.

As it happened, most of those investment-related provisions that addressed core rule of law principles, such as reasonableness, non-discrimination, security, and due process, only occasionally were at issue during the negotiations. Most other countries that were willing to negotiate FCN treaties with the United States readily accepted U.S. notions of legality as reflected in the treaties. The principal exception was the provision on exchange controls, which was often controversial, though not because other countries objected in principle to the repatriation of capital and returns, but because they feared that shortages of foreign exchange would render a commitment to repatriation oppressive or impossible to perform. In some instances, other countries objected to the expropriation provision, sometimes because they believed that they should not be obligated to pay full compensation for expropriation, but at other times because they feared their inability to permit transfer of the compensation.

The provisions that were the most controversial in the negotiations with other countries were those related to the movement of capital across borders. In particular, the two great concerns that arose repeatedly, even in the successful negotiations, were fears related to the national treatment provision, which granted entry for U.S. capital, and, as already noted, fears related to the exchange controls provision, which allowed the withdrawal of U.S. capital and earnings. Concerns about the entry of foreign personnel also arose in some cases.

NEGOTIATING AN FCN TREATY WITH GREECE

The first of the 1950 negotiations to produce a treaty was that with Greece. By early 1950, the Truman administration had provided Greece with a copy of a proposed FCN treaty and was seeking to initiate negotiations.[201] That draft reflected the FCN treaty as an investment treaty in its mature form, although its investment provisions differed little in substance from those in the FCN treaty with Ireland.

One of the most visible changes from the treaty with Ireland, a change that had already appeared in the treaty with Colombia, was that the Department had placed the guarantee of equitable treatment in the very first article, which required each party "at all times" to accord "equitable treatment" to the persons, property, enterprises, and other interests of nationals and companies of the other party. The placement of the guarantee at the beginning of the treaty indicated that the phrase "equitable treatment" referred to the general climate that the parties intended the treaty to create for investment, although the equitable treatment standard also continued to impose an obligation independent of the rest of the treaty.

Another visible change appeared in the provision on exchange controls. As in the case of the treaty with Colombia, the State Department had consolidated into one article language that in the treaty with Ireland had been scattered in the treaty text, the protocol, and the minutes of interpretation. The State Department had also refined the language. Thus, whereas the FCN treaty with Ireland had permitted exchange controls that were necessary to "deal with a stringency of foreign

201. Airgram dated February 1, 1950, from the Secretary of State to the U.S. embassy in Athens, NARA, Record Group 59, Department of State File No. 611.814/2-150.

exchange,"[202] the draft provided to the Greek government permitted exchange controls "to the extent necessary to prevent [a party's] monetary reserves from falling to a very low level or to effect a moderate increase in very low monetary reserves,"[203] language that had already appeared in the treaty with Colombia. As in the case of the treaty with Ireland (and Colombia), any such exchange controls, after assuring the availability of foreign exchange for goods and services essential to the health and welfare of its people, must make "reasonable provision" for withdrawal of expropriation compensation, capital, and returns, giving consideration to special needs for other transactions.[204]

Greece initially assured the United States that the draft presented "no serious questions."[205] In May, however, the Greek government transmitted to the U.S. embassy a counterproposal that suggested otherwise.[206] The counterproposal indicated that Greece objected to extensive commitments regarding national treatment, to the requirement that compensation be paid for expropriation, and to the obligation to allow the withdrawal of capital and earnings. The State Department feared that the disagreements on these issues of "basic treaty philosophy" might be so great that the negotiation of a treaty would not be feasible.

The Greek negotiators explained that Greece was reluctant to guarantee national treatment not because it feared U.S. investment, but because it had MFN commitments to other countries in the region, notably Italy, and that these commitments would have required that any national treatment obligation with respect to U.S. investors be extended to investors of those countries,[207] which Greece was reluctant to do.[208] Accordingly, Greece wished to base national and MFN treatment on reciprocity. The State Department insisted that the MFN treatment obligation remain unconditional.[209]

The MFN treatment obligation was particularly troubling to Greece with respect to the treaty's provision on withdrawal of funds. Greece was concerned that the United Kingdom might demand a similar right of withdrawal for British bondholders, and it simply did not have sufficient foreign exchange reserves to

202. Ireland FCN treaty, Protocol, Paragraph 8.

203. Greece FCN treaty, Article XV(2).

204. Ibid., Article XV(3).

205. Airgram dated February 1, 1950, from the Department of State to the U.S. embassy in Athens, NARA, Record Group 59, Department of State File No. 611.814/2-150.

206. Airgram dated May 11, 1950, from the U.S. embassy in Athens to the Department of State, NARA, Record Group 59, Department of State File No. 611.814/5-1150.

207. Airgram dated June 16, 1950, from the Department of State to the U.S. embassy in Athens, NARA, Record Group 59, Department of State File No. 611.814/6-250.

208. Memorandum headed "Present Status of Program for Negotiating Treaties of Friendship, Commerce and Navigation," dated March 10, 1950, NARA, Record Group 59, Department of State File No. 611.004/3-2250.

209. Memorandum headed "Memorandum on the Provisions of the Greek Counterdraft," dated July 31, 1950, NARA, Record Group 59, Department of State File No, 611.814/6-250.

allow British bondholders to withdraw their capital and earnings.[210] The Greek government proposed addressing this problem by excluding from coverage of the provision those investments that were made prior to October 16, 1944, the date of the liberation of Greece. This would allow U.S. postwar investments to be covered, while excluding the British bondholders who had invested prior to the war. The United States, however, resisted inclusion of an "arbitrary discrimination" with respect to the coverage of investment.[211] Although the arbitrary discrimination would have favored U.S. investors over British investors, it was unacceptable to the United States because it was inconsistent with the non-discrimination principle at the core of the treaty's investment provisions. As the State Department liked to say, the negotiation of the treaty was a search for "right principles" rather than merely a bargaining for concessions or an attempt to extract maximum gain.

The Greek government also was concerned that the escape clause in the exchange controls provision for "goods and services essential to the health and welfare of the people" was not broad enough.[212] It feared that the clause would be read to apply only to foreign exchange needed to prevent disease or hunger, not to keep factories operating and people employed.[213] Greece was prepared to give priority to the needs of U.S. investors, but not at the expense of the stability of the economy. It wanted an exception for exchange controls necessary for economic stability.

The disagreement on this point was not one of principle, but of semantics. The U.S. negotiators acknowledged that Greece needed to ensure that it had adequate reserves to promote full employment, but believed that the phrase "health and welfare" was broad enough to accommodate that need. The Greek negotiators replied that the term "welfare," when translated into Greek, meant only "succor to the needy" and did not have the breadth that it did in English.[214] The U.S. negotiators feared, however, that "economic stability" was a vague term susceptible of a broad interpretation that would undermine the treaty commitment.

The Greek government candidly admitted that it would not have sufficient foreign exchange reserves to allow the withdrawal of large amounts of capital for many years. Again, the U.S. negotiators were sympathetic. They explained that the treaty language required only "feasible" withdrawals of capital and that this would require such withdrawals only when Greece's external financial position reasonably permitted.[215] The Greek negotiators replied that other countries would

210. Telegram dated July 11, 1950, from the U.S. embassy in Athens to the Department of State, NARA, Record Group 59, Department of State File No. 611.814/7-1150.

211. Airgram dated September 22, 1950, from the Department of State to the U.S. embassy in Athens, NARA, Record Group 59, Department of State File No. 611.814/8-2450.

212. Telegram dated July 11, 1950, from the U.S. embassy in Athens to the Department of State, NARA, Record Group 59, Department of State File No. 611.814/7-1150.

213. Memorandum of Conversation headed "Exchange Control Provisions of Treaty of Friendship, Commerce and Navigation Now under Negotiation at Athens," dated November 17, 1950, NARA, Record Group 59, Department of State File No. 611.814/11-1750.

214. Ibid.

215. Ibid.

demand the same treatment that U.S. investors received and that other countries might not interpret the treaty language in the same way that the United States did.

Ultimately, the two parties resolved their semantic disagreement. The U.S. negotiators agreed to include a reference to the "avoidance of serious economic instability" in the escape clause, and Greece accepted the remaining treaty commitments.[216] The two countries signed the treaty on August 3, 1951.[217]

NEGOTIATING AN FCN TREATY WITH DENMARK

At the beginning of the 1950s, the United States and Denmark already had an FCN treaty in force, although the treaty was old, having been negotiated by Secretary of State Henry Clay in 1826.[218] Denmark initiated the discussions regarding a new treaty in summer 1949, when the economic counselor at the Danish embassy in Washington, Gunnar Seidenfaden, inquired about the FCN treaty negotiations with Uruguay. In response to that inquiry, the Department of State provided Seidenfaden with a copy of the substantive articles of a proposed treaty.[219]

The Danish government studied the proposed treaty for several months. In November 1949, Seidenfaden informed the State Department that the Danish government was prepared to commence the negotiation of a new FCN treaty to replace the 1826 treaty.[220] At the same time, however, Seidenfaden indicated that certain provisions of the treaty might require adjustment, including those guaranteeing national treatment for accountants, granting aliens the right to acquire real property, and limiting the imposition of exchange controls. By December, the Department of State had prepared a proposed treaty draft, which included the latest "improvements" and resembled closely the draft provided to Greece the previous August.[221] The draft was transmitted to the embassy at the end of the month[222] and delivered to the Danish government in January.[223]

216. Greece FCN treaty, Article XV(3).

217. Treaty of Friendship, Commerce and Navigation, entered into force October 13, 1954, 5 UST 1829, TIAS 3057, 224 UNTS 279.

218. Convention of Friendship, Commerce and Navigation, United States-Denmark, 1826, 8 Stat. 340, TS 65, 7 Bevans 1.

219. Airgram dated August 5, 1949, from the Department of State to the U.S. embassy in Copenhagen, NARA, Record Group 59, Department of State File No. 711.592/8-549.

220. Memorandum of Conversation dated November 3, 1949, NARA, Record Group 59, Department of State File No. 711.5992/11-349.

221. Memorandum dated December 21, 1949, from Winthrop Brown to Willard Thorp, NARA, Record Group 59, Department of State File No. 711.592/12-2149.

222. Letter dated December 30, 1949, from the Acting Assistant Secretary for Economic Affairs to the U.S. ambassador to Denmark, NARA, Record Group 59, Department of State File No. 711.592/12-3049.

223. Despatch dated January 25, 1950, from the U.S. embassy in Copenhagen to the Department of State, NARA, Record Group 59, Department of State File No. 611.594/1-2550.

The Danish government wanted to preserve certain laws that provided protection against possible American dominance of the Danish economy. As it had done in agreeing to the reservation for serious economic instability with Greece, the United States sought to accommodate the other party's concerns while preserving basic treaty principles.

First, Denmark wished to reserve the right to require that managers and directors of companies incorporated in Denmark have resided in Denmark for two years.[224] The State Department responded that the "essential treaty objective" was that U.S. investors have the power to exercise "final control" over Danish companies that they owned.[225] After examination of the Danish law, the State Department concluded that the law did not "appear . . . to frustrate the facile realization of genuine control by majority American stockholding interests."[226] The Department noted that several U.S. states had citizenship requirements with respect to corporate directors. Accordingly, language was inserted in the minutes of interpretation stating, "It is understood that either Party may consistently with the terms of this paragraph, maintain special requirements with respect to the residence or nationality of the founders, members of the boards of directors, and managing directors of companies constituted under its laws."[227]

Second, Denmark wished to preserve a Danish law requiring that incorporators be Danish citizens or residents. The treaty, however, did not require national treatment with respect to the right to organize corporations, but only a "practical and efficacious right," which would be present as long as it was "conveniently open" for U.S. investors to utilize the services of Danish citizens or residents to establish corporations.[228] Again, some U.S. states had similar laws. The Department noted with satisfaction that Danish law did not require that a majority of the stockholders have Danish nationality, which could have raised "a serious treaty problem."[229] As noted above, the United States agreed to include in the minutes of interpretation language that authorized each party to adopt "special requirements with respect to the residence or nationality of the founders, members of the boards of directors, and managing directors of companies constituted under its laws."[230]

224. Airgram dated May 3, 1950, from the U.S. embassy in Copenhagen to the Department of State, NARA, Record Group 59, Department of State File No. 611.594/5-350.

225. Airgram dated June 1, 1950, from the Department of State to the U.S. embassy in Copenhagen, NARA, Record Group 59, Department of State File No. 611.594/5-350; Airgram dated May 27, 1950, from the Department of State to the U.S. embassy in Copenhagen, NARA, Record Group 59, Department of State File No. 611.594/5-350.

226. Airgram dated August 9, 1950, from the Department of State to the U.S. embassy in Copenhagen, NARA, Record Group 59, Department of State File No. 611.954/7-1250.

227. Denmark FCN treaty, Minutes of Interpretation, *ad Article VIII, paragraph 1.*

228. Airgram dated August 9, 1950, from the Department of State to the U.S. embassy in Copenhagen, NARA, Record Group 59, Department of State File No. 611.954/7-1250.

229. Ibid.

230. Denmark FCN treaty, Minutes of Interpretation, *ad Article VIII, paragraph 1.*

Third, Denmark wished to reserve the right to prohibit foreign ownership of real property.[231] Such a reservation was necessary because the Danish Parliament was considering legislation to that effect in order to prohibit Germans from owning land on the Danish side of the border between Denmark and Germany. Denmark suggested that the treaty grant only MFN treatment with respect to this right. The Department could not grant MFN treatment with regard to ownership of land because it had granted national treatment to Argentina in an 1853 FCN treaty.[232] Thus, agreeing to MFN treatment would mean that Denmark would receive national treatment, but without reciprocity. Further, many state laws restricted alien land ownership, and the Department was unwilling to use the treaty to override those laws in the absence of reciprocity. The Department suggested that Denmark's concern regarding German ownership of land near the border could be addressed through an exception for national defense. The Danish government, however, was reluctant to adopt a rationale for the legislation linked in an obvious way to its relations with Germany because such an approach would have invited German retaliation. Ultimately, the United States agreed to language that essentially subordinated the right to own real property to local law.[233]

Fourth, Denmark wanted to preserve certain privileges for state-owned enterprises.[234] The State Department noted that the competitive equality provision of the treaty was intended to ensure that private businesses were not ruined by competition with state-subsidized enterprises. If the government wished to exclude private businesses from certain sectors of the economy, the Department explained, "the appropriate measure is expropriation with just compensation rather than the harassment of unfair government competition."[235] If Denmark already had state-owned monopolies, then they were by definition not in competition with private enterprise and no problem would arise. The Department also noted that the relevant treaty provision was limited only to commercial, manufacturing, and processing activities and did not apply in sectors such as banking, mining, communications, and transportation. Ultimately, Denmark agreed to the retention of the competitive equality provision.[236]

231. Airgram dated May 3, 1950, from the U.S. embassy in Copenhagen to the Department of State, NARA, Record Group 59, Department of State File No. 611.594/5-350.

232. Airgram dated June 1, 1950, from the Department of State to the U.S. embassy in Copenhagen, NARA, Record Group 59, Department of State File No. 611.594/5-350; Airgram dated May 27, 1950, from the Department of State to the U.S. embassy in Copenhagen, NARA, Record Group 59, Department of State File No. 611.594/5-350.

233. Denmark FCN treaty, Article IX(3).

234. Airgram dated May 3, 1950, from the U.S. embassy in Copenhagen to the Department of State, NARA, Record Group 59, Department of State File No. 611.594/5-350.

235. Airgram dated June 1, 1950, from the Department of State to the U.S. embassy in Copenhagen, NARA, Record Group 59, Department of State File No. 611.594/5-350; Airgram dated May 27, 1950, from the Department of State to the U.S. embassy in Copenhagen, NARA, Record Group 59, Department of State File No. 611.594/5-350.

236. Denmark FCN treaty, Article XVIII(2).

The greatest obstacles to the conclusion of the treaty involved Danish reluctance to grant national treatment with respect to the establishment of investment and to agree to the provision on exchange controls.[237] The national treatment provision was inconsistent with a set of long-standing Danish laws discriminating against aliens with respect to various business activities. The Department hoped to resolve these issues "without upsetting long-established Danish legislative policy" or "damaging the integrity of the Department's treaty objectives."[238] The Department acknowledged that it could not ask Denmark to repeal well-established legislation that had never hurt U.S. businesses in practice, even if its literal language seemed inconsistent with the treaty.[239] Reassured that the United States would not make an issue of the existing laws, Denmark agreed to the national treatment obligation.

The exchange controls provision presented a couple of problems. First, the Danish government wished to control the import of capital, and sought to ensure that the exchange controls provision would not preclude this.[240] In particular, the Danish government wished to ensure that exchange controls authorized by the IMF would be exempt from treaty restrictions.

The State Department replied that the purpose of the exchange controls provision was "to provide assurances that investors will receive reasonable consideration in the allocation of exchange during periods of exchange stringency when exchange restrictions are in force."[241] When it authorized a member to impose exchange controls, the IMF did not ordinarily set priorities for that member's allocation of available exchange. Thus, for example, a member acting under IMF-approved exchange restrictions could allow the use of foreign exchange to import luxuries, but not to withdraw earnings. The treaty language was intended to ensure that reasonable provision was made for the withdrawal of earnings. In the event that the IMF authorized specific restrictions, such as on earnings, then the IMF authorization would prevail. Accordingly, the treaty did not derogate from IMF commitments, but did impose restrictions in certain cases where the IMF left members with discretion.[242]

Second, the Danish government, like many other countries, was concerned that U.S. investors would withdraw an amount of funds sufficient to deplete

237. Airgram dated July 12, 1950, from the U.S. embassy in Copenhagen to the Department of State, NARA, Record Group 59, Department of State File No. 611.594/7-1250.

238. Airgram dated August 9, 1950, from the Department of State to the U.S. embassy in Copenhagen, NARA, Record Group 59, Department of State File No. 611.954/7-1250.

239. Airgram dated January 30, 1951, from the Department of State to the U.S. embassy in Copenhagen, NARA, Record Group 59, Department of State File No. 611.954/1-251.

240. Airgram dated May 3, 1950, from the U.S. embassy in Copenhagen to the Department of State, NARA, Record Group 59, Department of State File No. 611.594/5-350.

241. Airgram dated June 13, 1950, from the Department of State to the U.S. embassy in Copenhagen, NARA, Record Group 59, Department of State File No. 611.594-5350.

242. Ibid.

Danish foreign exchange reserves. The State Department believed that the treaty language with respect to withdrawals adequately protected the Danes "against the danger of dollar drains beyond what they can afford at any given point in time."[243]

The Department met the two Danish concerns about exchange controls, however, by redrafting the exchange controls provision in a way that maintained its substance but gave greater prominence to each party's right to impose exchange controls to assure the availability of foreign exchange for purchases essential to the health and welfare of the people.[244] The Department also agreed to language in the protocol that provided that nothing in Article XII(2), which limited the imposition of exchange controls, shall be construed to prevent a party from exercising necessary regulation over the inflow of capital, provided that such regulations shall not as a general rule be exercised in a manner that impairs rights under other provisions of the treaty.[245] With the issue of exchange controls resolved, the two countries signed the treaty on October 1, 1951.[246]

NEGOTIATING WITH ITALY—AGAIN

By January 1950, nearly two years after the conclusion of the FCN treaty between the United States and Italy, the Italian government was disappointed by the lack of U.S. investment in Italy. After consulting with the international business community, Italian officials concluded that the major impediment was the Italian government's restrictions on the withdrawal of dollars from Italy.[247] Accordingly, the Italian embassy proposed that the United States and Italy conclude a new agreement supplementing the 1948 FCN treaty that would include investment provisions similar to those that appeared in the FCN treaty between the United States and Uruguay.

In March, the State Department provided the embassy with a draft agreement that was based on the language of the FCN treaties with Colombia, Uruguay, and Ireland.[248] The Italian government had invited the new agreement, the

243. Airgram dated August 9, 1950, from the Department of State to the U.S. embassy in Copenhagen, NARA, Record Group 59, Department of State File No. 611.954/7-1250.

244. Airgram dated January 27, 1951, from the Department of State to the U.S. embassy in Copenhagen, NARA, Record Group 59, Department of State File No. 611.594/1-251; Denmark FCN treaty, Article XII(2).

245. Denmark FCN Treaty, Protocol, Paragraph 7.

246. Treaty of Friendship, Commerce and Navigation, with protocol and minutes of interpretation, entered into force July 30, 1961, 12 UST 908, TIAS 4797, 421 UNTS 105.

247. Memorandum of Conversation headed "Liberalization of Investment Provisions of US-Italian FCN Treaty," dated January 27, 1950, NARA, Record Group 59, Department of State File No. 611.654/1-2750.

248. Memorandum of Conversation headed "Negotiations for an Investment Agreement between the U.S. and Italy," dated March 10, 1950, NARA, Record Group 59. Department of State File No. 611.654/3-1050.

negotiations do not appear to have presented any great difficulties, and the two countries signed the agreement in September 1951.[249] The new agreement, among other things, prohibited arbitrary or discriminatory measures[250] and included a right to hire accountants and technical experts for internal purposes without regard to laws regarding qualifications for the practice of professions;[251] a guarantee of free transfer of both earnings and capital,[252] subject to an exception for periods of exchange stringency;[253] and a general consultations provision.[254]

NEGOTIATING AN FCN TREATY WITH ISRAEL

FCN treaty discussions with Israel began in April 1950, when the Israeli ambassador to the United States delivered a note to the State Department expressing an interest in concluding such a treaty.[255] The ambassador explained that Israel wished to conclude the treaty in order to encourage American investment in Israel.[256] Assistant Secretary of State George McGhee told the ambassador that the FCN treaty contained the kinds of provisions that American businesses considered necessary to warrant investing abroad.[257]

Informal discussions began almost immediately. On April 28, the State Department sent copies of its standard draft treaty to the Israeli embassy.[258] The U.S. draft proposed to Israel included a reformulated national treatment provision. In the past, the treaty required national treatment with respect to certain business and nonprofit activities. The list of covered activities, however, had led to interpretive difficulties about the exact scope of the terms.[259] Accordingly, the Department decided instead to formulate a general rule requiring national treatment with

249. Agreement Supplementing the Treaty of Friendship, Commerce and Navigation, entered into force March 2, 1961, 12 UST 131, TIAS 4685, 404 UNTS 326.

250. Agreement Supplementing Italy FCN, Article I.

251. Ibid., Article II.

252. Ibid., Article III.

253. Ibid., Article IV.

254. Ibid., Article VIII.

255. Despatch dated May 5, 1950, from the Department of State to the U.S. mission in Tel Aviv, NARA, Record Group 59, Department of State File No. 611.84A4/4-2450.

256. Memorandum of Conversation headed "Israeli Readiness to Negotiate a Treaty of Friendship, Commerce and Navigation," dated April 25, 1950, NARA, Record Group 59, Department of State File No. 611.84A4/4-2550.

257. Ibid.

258. Memorandum of Conversation headed "Negotiation of Treaty of Friendship, Commerce and Navigation with Israel," dated May 3, 1950, NARA, Record Group 59, Department of State File No. 611.84A4/5-350.

259. Ibid.

respect to the right to engage in gainful activity, followed by an exception under which the host country could deny national treatment in certain sectors of the economy.[260] This was accompanied by a rule guaranteeing national treatment with respect to acquiring personal property, again with an exception allowing each party to limit alien ownership of interests in particular types of activity provided that other rights under the treaty were not impaired.[261] A separate provision guaranteed national and MFN treatment with respect to engaging in scientific, educational, religious, and philanthropic activities.[262] This would become the approach employed in future U.S. FCN treaties. The treaty with Israel differed from later treaties, however, in that it did not include the language developed later that protected existing enterprises against new limitations on national treatment.

The two countries held a first round of informal discussions in Washington on May 3.[263] Three more sessions were held in May, at which point the two countries suspended further discussions while the Israeli embassy awaited instructions from Tel Aviv.[264]

By October, Israel was ready to begin formal negotiations.[265] It hoped to attract U.S. investment[266] and wished to conclude a treaty as expeditiously as possible, by the end of the year if possible.[267] The United States was concerned about the political implications of signing its first FCN treaty in the Near East with Israel[268] and, although it did not so inform the Israeli delegation, the State Department planned to prolong the negotiations at least until the end of the year in order to provide an opportunity to complete the negotiation of an FCN treaty with Lebanon.[269]

260. Ibid. The new language appears at Article VII.

261. Israel FCN treaty, Article IX(3). A right of national treatment with respect to the acquisition of personal property had already appeared in the treaty with Ireland, at Article VII(2).

262. Israel FCN treaty, Article VIII(3).

263. Memorandum of Conversation headed "Negotiation of Treaty of Friendship, Commerce and Navigation with Israel," dated May 3, 1950, NARA, Record Group 59, Department of State File No. 611.84A4/5-350.

264. Memorandum headed "Records of Preliminary Discussions of Treaty of Friendship, Commerce and Navigation with Israel," dated November 20, 1950, NARA, Record Group 59, Department of State File No. 611.84A4/5-1050; Memorandum of Conversation headed "FCN Treaty Negotiations with Israel," dated October 17, 1950, NARA, Record Group 59, Department of State File No. 611.84A4/10-1750.

265. Ibid.

266. Memorandum of Conversation headed "FCN Negotiations with Israel—4th Meeting," dated May 11, 1950, NARA, Record Group 59, Department of State File No. 611.84A4/5-1050.

267. Memorandum of Conversation headed "Israeli FCN Negotiations," dated October 20, 1950, NARA, Record Group 59, Department of State File No. 611.84A4/10-2050.

268. Memorandum of Conversation headed "FCN Negotiations with Israel—4th Meeting," dated May 11, 1950, NARA, Record Group 59, Department of State File No. 611.84A4/5-1050.

269. Memorandum of Conversation headed "FCN Treaty Negotiations with Israel," dated October 17, 1950, NARA, Record Group 59, Department of State File No. 611.84A4/10-1750.

The negotiations with Lebanon, however, eventually would end in failure because Lebanon objected to U.S. policy with respect to Palestine.

From the first discussions, the Israeli negotiators expressed concern about the provision on exchange controls, fearing that Israeli exchange controls might be inconsistent with the treaty. They noted that Israel already had made a special effort to address the needs of investors[270] and was allowing withdrawals by investors at the expense of other needs, including foodstuffs.[271] The Israeli government was concerned that a guarantee of free movement of capital would be disastrous for a country with limited foreign exchange reserves. Ultimately, the United States agreed to revisions to Article XII, dealing with exchange controls, including the insertion of language at Paragraph 6 of the protocol that authorized departures from certain treaty obligations during periods of exchange stringency. Satisfied that the revisions left it sufficient discretion, Israel signed the treaty with the United States on August 23, 1951.[272]

The State Department regarded the treaty with Israel as "the most satisfactory so far negotiated," a fact that the Department attributed to Israel's desire to utilize the treaty to attract U.S. investment.[273] The Department was particularly pleased by revisions in the articles relating to the right to engage in business and non-profit activities, revisions that the Department intended to incorporate in future treaties.[274]

NEGOTIATING AN FCN TREATY WITH ETHIOPIA

The State Department began to consider the negotiation of an FCN treaty with Ethiopia as early as 1946.[275] The U.S. business community in Ethiopia was small, however, and so the Department was not subject to the same pressure to conclude a treaty that existed in the case of many other countries.

Ethiopia, along with Iran and Afghanistan, was one of several "relatively small and undeveloped countries" with which the Department wished to conclude an FCN treaty, but that, in the Department's view, was not "sufficiently advanced in governmental and economic organization to be ready" to conclude a standard

270. Memorandum of Conversation headed "Treaty of Friendship, Commerce and Navigation with Israel—Third Preliminary Discussion," dated May 10, 1950, NARA, Record Group 59, Department of State File No. 611.84A4/5-1050.

271. Memorandum of Conversation headed "Israeli FCN Negotiations—2nd Meeting," dated May 8, 1950, NARA, Record Group 59, Department of State File No. 611.84A4/5-850.

272. Treaty of Friendship, Commerce and Navigation, with protocol and exchange of notes, entered into force April 3, 1954, 5 UST 550, TIAS 2948, 219 UNTS 237.

273. *Current Economic Developments*, June 25, 1951, page 4, NARA, Record Group 59, Department of State Lot Files.

274. Ibid.

275. Letter dated June 21, 1946, from Felix Cole to the Department of State, NARA, Record Group 59, Department of State Lot Files, Office of the Legal Adviser Files.

FCN treaty.[276] Thus, the Department commenced the preparation of a "short draft" for use with those less developed countries.[277]

The Department took the first steps toward the negotiation of a treaty with Ethiopia in April 1950, when Assistant Secretary of State George McGhee traveled to Addis Ababa. During the visit, McGhee "expressed to the Emperor the hope that the climate for foreign investment in Ethiopia would continue to be favorable and suggested that it might be desirable, in the interest of promoting Ethiopia's economic development and of furthering economic intercourse between the two countries, to consider the negotiation of a modern treaty of friendship and commerce."[278]

Even as McGhee was proposing a treaty, the State Department still was mulling the question of what should be in the short draft. In a message dated April 19, 1950, the Department asked the embassy in Addis Ababa "what a new treaty between the United States and Ethiopia might suitably provide."[279] The Department "suppose[d] that [the] standard draft [treaty] might need considerable abridgment and revision to adapt it to Ethiopia's circumstances."[280] On June 9, the State Department cabled the embassy that it was "anxious [to] proceed [with the] treaty project," but had not received any embassy comments in response to its April 19 message.[281]

The embassy responded on June 15. The embassy reported that "the Legal Advisor to the Ministry of Foreign Affairs believes it would be advantageous, mutually, to conclude a modern treaty of friendship and commerce."[282] The legal advisor noted that Ethiopia's existing treaties were "archaic affairs."[283] In addition, Robert D. Scott, an American advisor to the Ministry of Commerce and Industry, had advised the Ethiopian government that encouraging the flow of U.S. investment into Ethiopia would probably necessitate the conclusion of an FCN treaty between the United States and Ethiopia.[284]

276. *Current Economic Developments,* October 23, 1950, NARA, Record Group 59, Department of State Lot Files. *See also* Letter dated May 6, 1947, from Assistant Secretary of State Willard Thorp to Attorney General Tom Clark, NARA, Record Group 59, Department of State File No. 711.002/5-647.

277. *Current Economic Developments,* October 23, 1950, NARA, Record Group 59, Department of State Lot Files.

278. Despatch dated April 19, 1950, from the Department of State to the U.S. embassy in Addis Ababa, NARA, Record Group 59, Department of State File No. 611.754/4-1950.

279. Ibid.

280. Ibid.

281. Telegram dated June 9, 1950, from the Department of State to the U.S. embassy in Addis Ababa, NARA, Record Group 59, Department of State File No. 611.754/6-950.

282. Telegram dated June 15, 1950, from the U.S. embassy in Addis Ababa to the Department of State, NARA, Record Group 59, Department of State File No. 611.754/6-1550.

283. Ibid.

284. Telegram dated August 1, 1950, from the U.S, embassy in Addis Ababa to the Department of State, NARA, Record Group 59, Department of State File No. 611.754/8-150.

By summer, the State Department had developed the short draft that it needed. Through either abridging or removing provisions, the Department was able to reduce the draft to about half the length of the standard draft treaty.[285]

The State Department regarded the abridged version of the standard draft treaty that it prepared for the negotiations with Ethiopia as appropriate for countries "not very far advanced in their administrative and economic development."[286] To distinguish it from the standard draft treaty, it was titled a treaty of "Amity and Economic Relations."

Notably absent from the treaty proposed to Ethiopia were the provisions requiring that each party grant investors of the other party national treatment with respect to the right to engage in gainful activity or to acquire personal property (such as portfolio investment), although the enterprises controlled by nationals or companies of one party that were permitted in the territory of the other party were granted national treatment with respect to their "normal functions," including "normal growth."[287] The omission of the obligation of national treatment with respect to establishment reflected the State Department's recognition of Ethiopia's less developed status and its belief that Ethiopia should retain the discretion to exclude foreign investment. In transmitting the proposed treaty to the U.S. embassy in Addis Ababa on July 18, 1950, the Department explained to U.S. ambassador George R. Merrell that "[t]he Department has endeavored to abridge, and to adapt to Ethiopian circumstances, within the framework of established treaty policy, the standard draft which the Department normally uses as the basis for negotiating with most countries (for example, Uruguay, Italy and Ireland) in prosecuting its program of modernizing and extending the network of treaties of this type to which the United States is party."[288] Yet, the Department explained, "In its purpose and scope . . . the enclosed draft remains essentially like the Department's standard negotiating draft. The one significant variation in principle is that it refrains from asking commitments as to what sorts of American enterprises the Ethiopian Government is prepared to allow to become established within the country, but rather leaves Ethiopia free to determine which enterprises it desires."[289] The proposed treaty thus preserved the goal of promoting the rule of law, while abandoning much of the goal of securing access for U.S. investors.

Like China, Ethiopia had been subject to a regime of extraterritoriality.[290] France had concluded a treaty with Ethiopia in 1908 under which foreign

285. *Current Economic Developments,* October 23, 1950, NARA, Record Group 59, Department of State Lot Files.

286. Robert R. Wilson, "Access-to-Courts Provisions in United States Commercial Treaties," 47 *American Journal of International Law* 20, 45 (1953).

287. Ethiopia FCN treaty, Article VIII(5).

288. Telegram dated July 18, 1950, from the Department of State to the U.S. embassy in Addis Ababa, NARA, Record Group 59, Department of State File No. 611.754/6-1850.

289. Ibid.

290. Memorandum headed "Legal Position of Foreigners in Ethiopia," dated June 21, 1946, NARA, Record Group 59, Department of State Lot Files, Office of the Legal Adviser Files.

nationals were governed by French law in Ethiopia. Italy invaded Ethiopia in 1935 and occupied it until 1941, when a combination of British and Ethiopian forces deposed the Italian rulers. The next year, the United Kingdom and Ethiopia signed a treaty in which Ethiopia agreed that foreign nationals would be subject to the jurisdiction of special courts administered in large part, though not entirely, by British subjects. The 1942 treaty was supplanted by a 1944 treaty that continued British participation in the Ethiopian courts, but that treaty by its terms expired in December 1946, leaving foreign nationals subject entirely to the Ethiopian courts.

The U.S. embassy believed that the Ethiopian courts were seriously inadequate. Thus, the State Department puzzled over the extent to which, in light of the abolition of the extraterritorial court system, the treaty should include a provision on the administration of justice, a matter on which the Department consulted the embassy. In its July 18 response to the embassy's comments on the proposed draft treaty, the State Department noted that the embassy's comments were "helpful to the Department in its efforts to devise formulations with real meaning under Ethiopian conditions whilst avoiding sacrifice of the principle of mutuality or that of scrupulously avoiding the appearance of asking any extrality [extraterritoriality] status."[291] The Department decided to propose that the treaty require that, in cases involving Americans, at least one judge have judicial experience in other lands.

The Department was sensitive to the charge that the treaty would provide special privileges to U.S. nationals and companies. The State Department told the U.S. ambassador, "With reference to treaty stipulations calculated to safeguard Americans against the well-known inadequacies of the present Ethiopian system of justice, the Department would be reluctant, in view of the treaty's underlying purpose of fostering cordial relations between sovereign equals over an indefinite future, to propose textual provisions which might appear to demand special privileges, or cast what might be regarded as offensive aspersions."[292] Accordingly, the Department suggested that the issue of the administration of justice be addressed in a separate exchange of diplomatic notes rather than in the treaty itself.

Coincidentally, the chief negotiator for Ethiopia was an American lawyer named John Spencer, who served as an advisor to Emperor Haile Selassie on international law from 1936 to 1974.[293] In his account of his experiences in Ethiopia, written more than 30 years later, Spencer recalled that "[t]he most difficult point of negotiation was the insistence by the United States that in any trial 'American citizens shall have the right to demand that one of the judges sitting shall have had judicial experience in other lands' and that they 'shall be incarcerated only in prisons which are approved by an officer who has had experience in modern prison

291. Ibid.

292. Letter dated July 18, 1950, from Willard Thorp to Ambassador George Merrill, NARA, Record Group 59, Department of State File 611.654/6-1550.

293. John H. Spencer, *Ethiopia at Bay: A Personal Account of the Haile Selassie Years* (Algonac, MI: Reference, 1984).

administration.' "[294] Spencer explained that "[t]he fact that the language had been taken from the Anglo-Ethiopian agreement of 1944 in no way endeared the formula to the Ethiopians."[295] He portrayed the State Department as all but oblivious to the offensive nature of the language on the administration of justice, writing that, "Despite my strenuous objections on the ground that those provisions were unnecessary and disobliging, the United States insisted. So much resentment was caused that to resolve the difficulty the language was deleted from the body of the agreement and consigned to an exchange of notes. The United States in the early 1950s had only a dim awareness of the resentments which such privileges had engendered in the Third World."[296]

Spencer's recollection that the United States insisted upon the provision is consistent with the archival records. His portrait of the State Department as largely unaware of the sensitivity of the issue is not, however. As noted above, the Department's July 18, 1950, response to the embassy in Addis Ababa alluded to the sensitivity of the issue. Further, the same July 18 response indicated that, at the very moment that the State Department was forwarding its proposed treaty to Ethiopia and six months before Spencer became involved in the negotiations, the Department already had decided to embody the language relating to the administration of justice in an exchange of notes, rather than in the body of the treaty. Thus, the idea to use an exchange of notes originated with the State Department, not Spencer, and the Department explicitly told the U.S. ambassador that the use of notes was an effort to avoid offending the Ethiopian government.

The negotiations continued between the embassy and Spencer over a period of several months, without mention of the administration of justice issue. Rather, the major issue in the early negotiations was the provision on exchange controls. Ethiopia proposed a number of revisions to that provision. In particular, it sought to limit the provision to dollar investments.[297] The State Department objected to that proposal. In the view of the Department, the treaty sought "to assure investors that they [would] enjoy as much freedom in transferring their assets out of Ethiopia as is reasonably feasible."[298] The Department believed that the exceptions already contained in its proposed language gave the parties "ample latitude" to protect their foreign exchange reserves.[299] The exception proposed by Ethiopia would indicate that outward transfers might be prohibited even if Ethiopia had "generous exchange reserves," a signal that would not be conducive to encouraging

294. Ibid, pages 261–262.

295. Ibid.

296. Ibid.

297. Memorandum dated March 5, 1951, from the U.S. embassy in Addis Ababa to the Department of State, Enclosure No. 2, NARA, Record Group 59, Department of State File No. 611.754/3-551.

298. Airgram dated March 5, 1951, from the Department of State to the U.S. embassy in Addis Ababa, NARA, Record Group 59, Department of State File No. 611.754/.3-551.

299. Ibid.

private investment. In any event, the exception would be impractical to administer because an investment might have been established with a mixture of dollars and reinvested local currency. Determining whether a particular withdrawal was of principal or earnings or was related to an investment of foreign or domestic currency would be difficult, and could require complex accounting and engender disputes.

The administration of justice issue finally surfaced in the communications between the Department and the embassy on August 3, 1951. A telegram from the ambassador on that date reported that "Spencer and I drafted [the] proposed exchange of notes [regarding the] Admin[inistration of] Justice."[300] On August 7, the Department cabled the embassy proposing the inclusion of an additional sentence in the exchange of notes providing that American citizens would have the right to have cases to which they were a party removed to the Ethiopian High Court.[301]

In subsequent negotiations, Ethiopia proposed the deletion of certain language from the diplomatic notes on the administration of justice, but the telegram reporting on that deletion appears to have been lost. In any event, the State Department accepted the proposal transmitted by the embassy, provided that the additional language suggested by the Department on August 7 was included.[302] The final exchange of notes granted American citizens the right to transfer to the High Court any case to which they were a party and to demand, in any case before the High Court, that one of the judges have judicial experience in other lands, and it guaranteed that American citizens, if arrested, would be incarcerated in prisons that were approved by an officer with experience in modern prison administration. With this major issue resolved, the treaty was signed on September 7.[303] The two parties later terminated the exchange of notes relating to the administration of justice.[304]

Spencer's memoir seems to contradict the claim that the United States did not attempt to coerce other countries to negotiate FCN treaties. Spencer recalled that "[i]n 1951, before Ethiopia could concentrate on the problems of establishing the federation, she was confronted with a persistent demand by the United States that she first conclude with it a treaty of friendship and economic relations. Ethiopia was unable to obtain postponement of that undertaking. My weeks of work on it

300. Telegram dated August 3, 1951, from the U.S. embassy in Addis Ababa to the Department of State, NARA, Record Group 59, Department of State File No. 611.754/8-251.

301. Telegram dated August 7, 1951, from the Department of State to the U.S. embassy in Addis Ababa, NARA, Record Group 59, Department of State File No. 611.754/8-751.

302. Telegram dated August 31, 1951, from the Department of State to the U.S. embassy in Addis Ababa, NARA, Record Group 59, Department of State File No. 711.753/8-2351.

303. Treaty of Amity and Economic Relations, and related notes, entered into force October 8, 1953, 4 UST 2134, TIAS 2864, 206 UNTS 41.

304. Agreement Amending the Treaty of Amity and Economic Relations of September 7, 1951, entered into force May 3, 1973, 24 UST 2163, TIAS 7726.

had to be crammed in before I could fully address the more urgent problems of the federation."[305] Spencer had become involved in the negotiations in January 1951, while traveling in the United States with the Ethiopian delegation to the United Nations. During the trip, he met with four members of the State Department to discuss the proposed draft treaty, which he said that he had not yet had time to study in detail, although he had completed a first reading of it.[306] The treaty, of course, had been proposed to Ethiopia in July of the previous year. Thus, the implication that somehow the treaty needed to be negotiated in a matter of weeks is misleading, in that it already been under consideration for six months before Spencer became involved.

Further, the record suggests that much of the urgency for concluding the negotiations was attributable to the desire of the Ethiopian government to sign the treaty before the planned departure of the U.S. ambassador. On March 1, 1951, approximately eight months after the United States provided its proposed treaty to the Ethiopian foreign minister, the Ethiopian government gave the U.S. embassy a diplomatic note that read: "The Imperial Ethiopian Government have [*sic*] given the most favorable attention and study to the draft treaty of Amity and Economic Relations between Ethiopia and the United States of America. The draft, with substance, appears to be eminently reasonable and presents but few problems of any marked difficulty."[307] The note then informed the embassy of Ethiopia's desire to conclude the treaty quickly: "In view of this fortunate situation, and, in view, on the other hand, of the desire of both his Imperial Majesty and of the Imperial Ethiopian Government, as a mark of the esteem in which is held His Excellency George R. Merrell, first Ambassador of the United States of America to Ethiopia, now about to be reassigned, to sign and conclude such a treaty before his departure, the Ministry of Foreign Affairs have [*sic*] devoted their best and most urgent efforts to prepare the way for such signature. . . . ."[308]

The Ethiopian government's statement of respect for Ambassador Merrill apparently was sincere. Spencer himself described Merrill as "by far the most successful and admired of all U.S. representatives."[309] Although Ethiopian officials usually only reluctantly accepted dinner invitations from foreign missions, according to Spencer, they "gladly responded" to Merrell's.[310] Such was Merrill's stature, reported Spencer, "that even the Emperor came to dine."[311] In short,

305. Spencer, page 261.

306. Memorandum of Conversation dated January 24, 1951, NARA, Record Group 59, Department of State File No. 611.754/1-2451.

307. Telegram dated March 2, 1951, from the U.S. embassy in Addis Ababa to the Department of State, NARA, Record Group 59, Department of State File No. 611.754/3-151.

308. Ibid.

309. Spencer, *Ethiopia at Bay*, page 169.

310. Ibid.

311. Ibid.

Spencer appears to have exaggerated the pressure on the Ethiopians to conclude the treaty. The urgency was to a considerable extent self-imposed by Ethiopia. Indeed, by 1951, the United States had been contemplating an FCN treaty with Ethiopia for five years, and had waited four years before proposing the negotiation of a treaty. Further, in April 1951, State Department officials in an internal report noted that "[t]he Emperor of Ethiopia and his government are pressing for early signature" of the FCN treaty, while at the same time raising "a number of difficult technical negotiating problems" and proposing "rather extensive revisions."[312] Thus, from the perspective of the State Department, the pressure to conclude the treaty quickly originated with Ethiopia, apparently because of the desire of the Ethiopian government to conclude the treaty before the departure of Ambassador Merrill.

NEGOTIATING AN FCN TREATY WITH JAPAN

The Truman administration began the process of negotiating an FCN treaty with Japan in January 1951, when the State Department sent to the U.S. mission in Tokyo a copy of the standard draft FCN treaty then in use, as well as copies of the completed treaties with Italy, Uruguay, and Ireland.[313] The treaty would be the first FCN treaty signed by Japan after the war, and Japan expected it to serve as a model for its commercial treaties with other countries.[314] The United States and Japan had concluded an FCN treaty in 1911, but the United States had terminated that treaty in 1940.[315]

The U.S. business community in Japan expressed an interest in being kept informed of developments with respect to the treaty. In response, the Department authorized the release of copies of concluded treaties in order to educate the business community as to the features of modern FCN treaties, to preempt "ill-considered demands for unwarranted preferential treatment," and to provide the business community with an opportunity to make recommendations regarding any future treaty.[316]

The Department cautioned the U.S. mission that, although the mission should solicit the views of U.S. business interests prior to negotiation, the Department would not be able to discuss particular issues in the negotiation once it began. To do so would be impractical because it would mean that the State Department effectively would be negotiating with U.S. business interests and Japan simultaneously

312. *Current Economic Developments*, April 23, 1951, page 6, NARA, Record Group 59, Department of State Lot Files.

313. Airgram dated January 24, 1951, from the Department of State to the U.S. Political Adviser in Tokyo, NARA, Record Group 59, Department of State File No. 611.944/1-2451.

314. Ibid.

315. Letter dated June 13, 1940, from Assistant Secretary of State Jack McFall to Senator Henry Dworshak, NARA, Record Group 59, Department of State File No. 611.944/6-550.

316. Ibid.

and because a government cannot easily recede from a position once that position has been taken publicly.[317]

The Department hoped to begin negotiation of an FCN treaty with Japan as soon as a peace treaty ending the war between the two countries was concluded. Indeed, Article XII of the peace treaty explicitly contemplated the conclusion of an FCN treaty.[318] The United States did not wish, however, to commence formal negotiations until after conclusion of the peace treaty, lest it appear that the United States regarded conclusion of the FCN treaty as a condition precedent to conclusion of the peace treaty, a perception that could trigger an unfavorable public reaction in Japan.[319] The United States wanted to avoid even a perception that it had coerced the conclusion of an FCN treaty. The Department, however, was willing to begin informal "technical discussions" that could achieve considerable progress before formal negotiations began.

In July, the U.S. mission supplied the Japanese government with copies of U.S. FCN treaties with Italy, Uruguay, Ireland, and Colombia and formally asked the American Chamber of Commerce for an expression of its views.[320] The Japanese government responded that it was "favorably disposed" toward the negotiation of a new FCN treaty.[321] In August, the Japanese government provided the U.S. mission with a model FCN treaty that it had spent two years preparing and that it hoped to use as a basis for negotiations with other countries. The Japanese model had been drafted with "particular reference" to the U.S. postwar FCN treaties.[322] Thus, the Japanese believed that the negotiation of an FCN treaty with the United States would not be "too difficult" or prolonged.[323] Notably, the Japanese model omitted some of the investment-related provisions found in recent U.S. FCN treaties, but the Japanese government was "fully prepared" to discuss the inclusion of such provisions.[324]

The Department of State preferred to use the U.S. standard draft treaty as a basis for negotiations, in part because such a treaty would be familiar to the Senate and thus would more easily gain Senate approval. The Department, however, declined to insist upon the use of the U.S. standard draft treaty, and as a gesture of goodwill was prepared to negotiate on the basis of the Japanese model if the Japanese

317. Airgram dated June 29, 1951, from the Department of State to the U.S. Political Adviser in Tokyo, NARA, Record Group 59, Department of State File No. 611.944/6-2951.

318. *Current Economic Developments,* March 24, 1953, NARA, Record Group 59, Department of State Lot Files.

319. Ibid.

320. Despatch dated August 16, 1951, from the U.S. Political Adviser in Tokyo to the Department of State, NARA, Record Group 59, Department of State File No. 611.944/6-1651.

321. Ibid.

322. Ibid.

323. Ibid.

324. Ibid.

"strongly desire[d]" to do so.[325] In that event, however, the Department would propose a number of modifications to the Japanese model.

One of these modifications was the reinsertion of the standard provision on submission of disputes to the International Court of Justice, a provision that had been significantly revised in the Japanese model. The Department explained that the standard language had been included in all U.S. postwar FCN treaties concluded to date without "significant alteration," and was regarded by the Department "as an outstanding achievement of its current treaty program."[326] Further, its inclusion was "the clearest kind of indication that the treaty establishes a rule of law."[327]

By November, the Japanese government had agreed to use the U.S. standard draft treaty as the basis for negotiations.[328] Informal discussions began on December 4. The Japanese government posed a number of questions, including an inquiry regarding the meaning of the term "equitable treatment" in Article 1. The Japanese negotiators observed that the word would be very difficult to translate into Japanese.[329] They recommended deletion of the equitable treatment standard from the treaty on the ground that it "introduce[d] a new concept of general equitable treatment, the concrete application of which has not yet been established in international law."[330] They believed, accordingly, that the standard would add ambiguity to the treaty and would become the cause of controversy in applying the treaty.[331]

The State Department replied that the term was "a link" between the preamble, which declared the "equitable purposes" that the treaty was designed to serve, and the rest of the treaty.[332] The equitable principles that the two parties "undert[ook] to apply in particular places [were] spelled out by the specific terms of the provisions commencing with Article II."[333] That is, the term "equitable treatment" was a general reference to the basic principles of the treaty. The term served additional purposes. First, where more than one construction of the treaty language was

325. Despatch dated November 1, 1951, from the Department of State to the U.S. Political Adviser in Tokyo, NARA, Record Group 59, Department of State File No. 611.944/6-1651.

326. Ibid.

327. Ibid.

328. Airgram dated November 29, 1951, from the U.S. Political Adviser in Tokyo to the Department of State, NARA, Record Group 59, Department of State File No. 611.944/11-2951.

329. Despatch dated December 7, 1951, from the U.S. Political Adviser in Tokyo to the Department of State, NARA, Record Group 59, Department of State File No. 611.944/12-751.

330. Ibid.

331. Ibid.; Despatch dated August 6, 1954, from the U.S. embassy in The Hague to the Department of State, NARA, Record Group 59, Department of State File No. 611.564/8-654.

332. Airgram dated December 31, 1951, from the Department of State to the U.S. Political Adviser in Tokyo, NARA, Record Group 59, Department of State File No. 611.944/12-751.

333. Ibid.

equally possible, the construction that would lead to an equitable result was to be preferred. Second, it served as "a guiding principle in cases where the exact terms of the treaty's provisions do not afford complete and definitive guidance."[334]

The State Department acknowledged that the term "equitable" was not a precise one and that it "probably" would be invoked only in "extreme or unusual cases," because the other terms "define the normal commitments" that the parties would have undertaken.[335] Yet, the term was not "altogether novel in current international usage" and could be found in the ITO Charter and other international instruments.[336] It also was in use in the state trading provisions of recent U.S. FCN treaties where the Department had not yet been able to devise "a more precise rule."[337]

The Japanese negotiators responded by suggesting that the equitable treatment standard be incorporated into the preamble, and they continued to inquire as to the meaning of the standard.[338] The State Department explained that the standard "convey[ed] the idea of decent, fair and just."[339]

Despite that explanation, the Japanese negotiators continued to express concern about the imprecision of the term. The U.S. negotiators reported to the Department that the equitable treatment standard had consumed three or four days of discussion.[340]

During these discussions, the Japanese negotiators explained that it was difficult for the Japanese side to grasp the meaning of the words "equitable treatment," and that it would be still more difficult to apply the standard in specific cases. They noted the difficulty that the Economic Council of the League of Nations had experienced in defining the term as it appeared in Article 23(e) of the League Covenant. They said that, if the term merely was intended to express the friendly relations between the two parties, it belonged in the preamble. One of the U.S. negotiators, Jules Bassin, who was serving as legal attache to the U.S. political adviser in Tokyo, replied by paraphrasing the State Department's earlier response concerning the three purposes of the standard. Robert W. Adams, the second secretary to the U.S. political adviser and the junior member of the delegation, "suggested that the Japanese representatives think of 'equitable treatment' in terms of

334. Ibid.

335. Ibid.

336. Ibid.

337. Ibid.

338. Despatch dated January 2, 1952, from the U.S. Political Adviser in Tokyo to the Department of State, NARA, Record Group 59, Department of State File No. 611.944/1-252.

339. Airgram dated January 25, 1952, from the Department of State to the U.S. Political Adviser in Tokyo, NARA, Record Group 59. Department of State File No. 611.944/1-2552.

340. Despatch dated March 27, 1952, from the U.S. Political Adviser in Tokyo to the Department of State, NARA, Record Group 59, Department of State File No. 611.944/3-2752.

'fair, just and non-discriminatory treatment' in attempting to understand Article I, which he further defined as the 'friendship provision' of the FCN Treaty."[341]

The Japanese negotiators raised a new concern: that "'equitable treatment' might be interpreted as establishing a new standard of treatment in addition to national and most-favored-nation treatment and they questioned whether the granting of national and most-favored-nation treatment [was] not sufficient. . . ."[342] They again warned that the provision might prove to be controversial and suggested that it be deleted. Adams replied that "equitable treatment" did not establish a third standard of treatment in addition to national and MFN treatment[343] and, along with Dudley G. Singer, the commercial attache, he "urged the Japanese representatives to regard 'equitable treatment' as a guiding principle of justice under which the specific standards of national and most-favored-nation treatment are applied." [344] Adams, who was not paraphrasing instructions from the Department but offering his own interpretation of the standard, apparently denied that the equitable treatment was a "third standard in addition to" national and MFN treatment, because it actually incorporated national and MFN treatment.

The Japanese negotiators next posed two hypothetical questions concerning the application of the equitable treatment standard to particular circumstances. In response to one of these questions, the legal attache stated that an official notification involving the rights and obligations of a national or company of the United States that was made public solely in the Japanese language would not violate the standard. In response to the other, he agreed that the equitable treatment standard would not justify the imposition of discriminatory tariffs against a country on the ground that the standards of wages or of living in that country were lower than those in any third country.

After receiving the report of this extended discussion of the term "equitable treatment," the State Department authorized the U.S. mission to agree to the

341. Memorandum of Conversation headed "Informal Discussions on the United States Standard Draft Treaty of Friendship, Commerce and Navigation," dated February 25, 1952, and enclosure to Despatch dated March 27, 1952, from the U.S. Political Adviser in Tokyo to the Department of State, NARA, Record Group 59, Department of State File No. 611.944/3-2752. This appears to be the only instance during the many years of U.S. postwar FCN treaty negotiations that the standard was described in that way.

342. Ibid.

343. As noted in Chapter 8, in the section on the fair and equitable treatment standard, Robert W. Wilson, one of the principal FCN treaty negotiators during the 1940s, writing in his personal capacity, explicitly identified the fair and equitable treatment standard as a standard distinct from that of national and MFN treatment. As discussed in Chapter 8, the State Department routinely characterized the fair and equitable treatment provision as imposing an independent standard applicable to situations not adequately governed by other more specific standards of the treaty.

344. Memorandum of Conversation headed "Informal Discussions on the United States Standard Draft Treaty of Friendship, Commerce and Navigation," dated February 25, 1952, and enclosure to Despatch dated March 27, 1952, from the U.S. Political Adviser in Tokyo to the Department of State, NARA, Record Group 59, Department of State File No. 611.944/3-2752.

deletion of the standard. The Department explained that the equitable treatment standard was "merely desirable as a standard proposition, and not indispensable in the case of a particular negotiation where resistances or difficulties emerge."[345] It further noted that "[i]n view of the attitude shown by the Japanese and of the tenor of the discussion, the possibility seems open that the provision may be capable of causing more friction than benefit."[346] The Department had concluded, accordingly, that the standard might "appropriately be dropped." [347]

By November 25, 1952, a year after the Japanese agreed to use the U.S. standard draft treaty as the basis for negotiations, the extensive technical discussions had ended and Japan was ready to commence formal negotiations.[348] The most important issue in the Japanese negotiations involved Japan's desire to reserve the right to discriminate against foreign investment. Japan's foreign investment law authorized the screening of foreign investment as well as discrimination against foreign investment once established. The State Department accepted Japan's right to discriminate with respect to the establishment of investment in certain sectors of the economy, but insisted upon non-discriminatory treatment for investment once established.[349] Ultimately, the parties agreed to retain the principle of non-discrimination, but to add shipbuilding and public utilities to the list of excepted activities[350] and to omit the provision on competitive equality. They also included a new paragraph in the protocol authorizing either party to "impose restrictions on the introduction of foreign capital as may be necessary to protect its monetary reserves" as provided in the article on exchange controls.[351] The embassy urged that the discriminatory provisions in Japanese law that were inconsistent with the treaty be amended prior to submission of the treaty to the Diet, which would allow the treaty to be portrayed as consistent with existing, or already contemplated amendments to, Japanese law. If the treaty were submitted first, subsequent efforts to amend the law would be portrayed as unwarranted interferences in domestic policy.[352]

345. Airgram dated April 19, 1952, from the Department of State to the U.S. Political Adviser in Tokyo, NARA, Record Group 59, Department of State File No. 611.944/3-2752.

346. Ibid.

347. Ibid.

348. Telegram dated November 25, 1952, from the U.S. embassy in Tokyo to the Department of State, NARA, Record Group 59, Department of State File No. 611.944/11-2552.

349. Telegram dated December 2, 1952, from the U.S. embassy in Tokyo to the Department of State, NARA, Record Group 59, Department of State File No. 611.944/12-252.

350. Japan FCN treaty, Article VII(2). *See also* Protocol, Paragraph 3 (defining "public utilities).

351. Japan FCN treaty, Protocol, Paragraph 6.

352. Telegram dated December 11, 1952, from the U.S. embassy in Tokyo to the Department of State, NARA, Record Group 59, Department of State File No. 611.944/12-1152; Memorandum dated December 29, 1952, from Counselor to the Embassy Frank Waring to Ambassador

The Japanese negotiators believed that Japanese enterprises were undervalued because of an excessive reliance on credit for financing and because of currency depreciation. Thus, an alien, with a modest investment, could gain a controlling interest in Japan's leading enterprises. Accordingly, Japan sought to defer the right of U.S. investors to acquire interests in Japanese companies for a period of at least three years, by which time Japan expected that the problem of undervaluation would be remedied through recapitalization. The embassy concurred on the ground that few Americans were likely to purchase stock on the Japanese market because U.S. investors could obtain a better return on investment through time deposits in banks. Accordingly, the United States accepted a provision limiting the right of U.S. investors to purchase shares in Japanese enterprises for a period of three years.[353] With that issue resolved, the parties signed the treaty on April 2, 1953.[354]

The final text of the FCN treaty with Japan included two important new investment-related provisions. The first authorized the issuance of visas to Japanese nationals traveling to the United States to establish or manage an investment.[355] This language took advantage of a new provision of the Immigration and Nationality Act that had entered into force on December 24, 1952, providing for such visas.[356] Congress had enacted the provision in order to provide the State Department with a basis for seeking from other countries a right of U.S. investors to send managerial and technical personnel overseas to operate U.S. investments.[357] The Department could not demand such a right for U.S. investors investing abroad unless it could provide a similar right to foreign investors investing in the United States. The second was a prohibition on the application of new limitations on the right of national treatment with respect to carrying on activities in the reserved sectors to existing investments that were already engaged in such activities at the time the new limitations were adopted.[358] This marked the first time that national treatment rights were guaranteed in the reserved sectors.[359]

Robert D. Murphy, headed "Proposed Timing for Conclusion of FCN Treaty," NARA, Record Group 59, Department of State File No. 611.944/1-753.

353. Japan FCN treaty, Protocol, Paragraph 15. *See also Current Economic Developments,* March 24, 1953, NARA, Record Group 59, Department of State Lot Files.

354. Treaty of Friendship, Commerce and Navigation, protocol and exchange of notes, August 29, 1953, entered into force October 30, 1953, 4 UST 2063, TIAS 2863, 206 UNTS 143.

355. Japan FCN treaty, Article 1(1)(b).

356. *Current Economic Developments,* March 24, 1953, NARA, Record Group 59, Department of State Lot Files. The origins of this provisions are traced in more detail in Chapter 8 in the section on entry and sojourn.

357. Wilson, United States Commercial Treaties, page 42.

358. Japan FCN treaty, Article VII(2).

359. *Current Economic Developments,* March 24, 1953, pages. 1–2, NARA, Record Group 59, Department of State Lot Files.

The Department was very pleased by the results of the negotiations. It regarded the FCN treaty with Japan as "among the best of its type yet signed"[360] and characterized the national treatment guarantee as a "substantial achievement."[361]

SENATE ADVICE AND CONSENT TO RATIFICATION 1952–1953

The Senate Foreign Relations Committee held hearings on the first group of treaties concluded after 1950—that is, the treaties with Colombia, Israel, Denmark, Greece, and Ethiopia and the supplemental agreement with Italy—on May 9, 1952.[362] Deputy Assistant Secretary of State for Economic Affairs Harold F. Linder testified in favor of the treaties. Accompanying Linder were Herman Walker and Raymond Vernon, the deputy director of the Office of Economic Defense and Trade Policy, which in 1951 had become the successor to the Office of International Trade Policy. Roy Leifflen appeared on behalf of the Association of Marine Underwriters to urge inclusion in future treaties of a provision prohibiting discrimination with respect to the provision of marine insurance, a request to which the State Department would acquiesce in July.[363]

The decision of the State Department to omit from the treaty with Ethiopia the provision guaranteeing national treatment with respect to the establishment of investment prompted the NFTC to oppose Senate advice and consent to ratification of that treaty. Although he did not testify at the 1952 hearings, NFTC president William Swingle submitted a letter arguing that the less rigorous provisions of the treaty with Ethiopia would set a precedent leading to the dilution of protection for U.S. investors in future treaties.[364] Swingle's letter observed that "it seems doubtful whether, at the present stage of Ethiopia's economic development, any satisfying mutual convictions, or common ground for stipulations regarding private investment can be found. Moreover, a recent canvass of representative members of the Council has not developed any positive expression of interest in potential investment in that country. Therefore, it seems undesirable to dilute the pattern of our bilateral treaties . . . ."[365]

360. Despatch dated April 13, 1952, from the Department of State to the U.S. Political Adviser in Tokyo, NARA, Record Group 59, Department of State File No. 611.944/4-1353.

361. Memorandum dated March 23, 1953, from Mr. Young to Mr. Allison, NARA, Record Group 59, Department of State File No. 611.944/3-2353.

362. *Commercial Treaties*, Hearing Before a Subcommittee of the Committee on Foreign Relations, 82d Cong. 2d Sess. (1952).

363. Letter dated July 10, 1952, from Assistant Secretary of State Willard Thorp to Carl E. McDowell, NARA, Record Group 59, Department of State File No. 611.004/4-1652.

364. *Commercial Treaties*, Hearing Before a Subcommittee of the Committee on Foreign Relations, United States Senate, 82nd Cong. 2d Sess. (1952), page 21.

365. Letter dated May 8, 1952, from William S. Swingle to Willard R. Thorp, NARA, Record Group 59, Department of State File No. 611.004/5-852. *See also* Letter dated May 8, 1952,

The State Department defended its decision to omit the provision on national treatment. In a May 15, 1952, letter to the Committee responding to Swingle's letter, the Department enclosed a memorandum that objected to Swingle's characterization of the negotiations. As the Department explained, "This lack of commitment concerning the entry of investment capital was not, as suggested in Mr. Swingle's letter, a failure to overcome an obstacle to mutual understanding. On the contrary, it was evident that, in Ethiopia's existing circumstances, Ethiopia could not be expected to undertake treaty limitations upon her right to regulate the entry of foreign investment."[366] The Department argued that "[n]o benefit was to be gained from attempting in this treaty to force Ethiopia to accept American investment, especially as no American would likely wish to venture his capital in Ethiopia anyhow except with the express sanction of the Ethiopian government."[367] Thus, the Department did "not regard this treaty as at all 'diluting the pattern of our bilateral treaties,' as suggested in Mr. Swingle's letter. It is specially designed for a country like Ethiopia, not for a country of Western Europe."[368]

The State Department endeavored to maintain the support of the business community, particularly the NFTC. Harold Linder, the deputy assistant secretary of state for economic affairs who testified on behalf of the State Department in favor of the treaties, wrote to the NFTC, responding to its letter to the Senate Foreign Relations Committee. Linder explained that reopening a treaty that already had been concluded was a "hazardous procedure" and offered to meet with NFTC representatives "to review the present treaty situation."[369]

On June 11, 1952, several State Department officials met with Swingle.[370] These officials assured Swingle that the provisions on the right to establish investment in the treaty with Ethiopia would not be regarded as a precedent for any country "other than one in a similar political and economic status."[371] Despite the meeting, the NFTC refused to reconsider its position regarding the treaty with Ethiopia.[372]

from William S. Swingle to Senator John Sparkman, *Commercial Treaties,* Hearing Before a Subcommittee of the Committee on Foreign Relations, 82nd Cong. 2d Sess. (1952), page 21.

366. Memorandum by Herman Walker, dated May 13, 1952, NARA, Record Group 59, Department of State File No. 611.759/5-1552.

367. Ibid.

368. Ibid.

369. Letter dated May 26, 1952, from Harold S. Linder to William S. Swingle, NARA, Record Group 59, Department of State File No. 611.004/5-1352.

370. Report of Meeting in the Office of Harold F. Linder, dated June 17, 1952, NARA, Record Group 59, Department of State File No. 611.004/6-1852.

371. Ibid.

372. Letter from William S. Swingle to Harold F. Linder, dated August 1, 1952, NARA, Record Group 59, Department of State File No. 611.004/8-152.

Although the NFTC opposed Senate advice and consent to ratification of the treaty with Ethiopia, it recommended approval of the FCN treaties with Colombia, Denmark, Greece, and Israel and the supplemental treaty with Italy, provided that the parties to the treaties amended the new provision that prohibited "unreasonable or discriminatory" measures.[373] NFTC president William Swingle explained that the implication of this clause was that a state was entitled to adopt measures that impaired acquired rights as long as the measures were reasonable and non-discriminatory. He argued that "if the Government of a foreign country takes measures which would destroy or impair the rights or interests of an American national irrespective of the purposes underlying such destruction or impairment, corresponding payment should be made."[374] Thus, Swingle contended that the existing treaty language should be replaced with new language that read: "Neither Party shall take measures that would impair the rights or interests within its territories of nationals and companies of the other Party except on payment of prompt, adequate and effective compensation."[375] In the view of the NFTC, the government must fully compensate foreign investors for any loss in the value of their investment resulting from government action.

Swingle also recommended deletion of the provision imposing on each party an obligation not to "unreasonably impede nationals and companies of the other Party from obtaining on equitable terms the capital, skills, arts and technology needed for economic development." He argued that the provision should be deleted for two reasons. First, the obligation would fall principally on the United States. Second, terms such as "unreasonable" and "equitable" were too broad and obscure.

During the July 11 meeting, State Department officials explained that the Department could not adopt the NFTC's position that "compensation should be given if rights are destroyed" because the United States itself could not abide by such a rule.[376] Internal State Department deliberations concerning the provision had noted that the U.S. Constitution prohibited only unreasonable discriminations.[377] For example, the United States was not obligated to compensate a distiller for losses caused by Prohibition, a utility company for the consequences of a government-sponsored rural electrification program, or a business for losses resulting from price controls.[378] Thus, as the State Department explained in a

373. Memorandum of Conversation dated June 11, 1952, NARA, Record Group 59, Department of State File No. 611.754/6-1152; Letter dated May 8, 1952, from William S. Swingle to Senator John Sparkman, NARA, Record Group 59, Department of State File No. 611.004/5-852.

374. Letter dated May 8, 1952, from William S. Swingle to Willard R. Thorp, NARA, Record Group 59, Department of State File No. 611.004/5-852.

375. Ibid.

376. Ibid.

377. Memorandum dated November 15, 1949, from Stanley Metzger to Michael Cardozo, NARA, Record Group 59, Department of State Lot Files, Folder marked "Commercial Treaties."

378. Memorandum accompanying letter dated May 16, 1952, from Acting Assistant Secretary of State Harold Linder to Senator John Sparkman, *reprinted in Commercial Treaties,* Hearing before a Subcommittee of the Committee on Foreign Relations, 82nd Cong. 2d Sess. (1952), page 28.

memorandum submitted to the Senate Committee on Foreign Relations, "such a provision would appear to require compensation in circumstances in which the United States Government does not under the Constitution and laws of the United States pay compensation."[379] Once again, the State Department sought to conform FCN treaty obligations to U.S. constitutional principles. The State Department could not "recommend a treaty provision which would go beyond established United States policy in this connection and grant foreign nationals more favorable treatment than citizens receive in the United States."[380] Further, because treaty obligations were mutual, the United States could not ask other treaty parties to accept the NFTC's proposed language either.[381]

Meanwhile, Republican senator Bourke Hickenlooper of Iowa, at the urging of the American Bar Association and various state bar associations, raised an objection to a provision in the FCN treaties with Colombia, Denmark, Israel, and Greece that guaranteed national treatment with respect to the right to practice professions.[382] The provision prohibited discrimination on the basis of nationality, but did not exempt treaty aliens from laws relating to entry or licensure.[383] For example, Article VIII(2) of the treaty with Israel provided that "[n]ationals of either Party shall not be barred from practicing the professions within the territories of the other Party merely by reason of their alienage, but they shall be permitted to engage in professional activities therein upon compliance with the requirements regarding qualifications, residence and competence that are applicable to nationals of such other Party." Senator Hickenlooper's attention originally was drawn to the provision in the treaty with Israel.[384] Earlier U.S. postwar FCN treaties had exempted the practice of law from the national treatment provision,[385] but the treaty with Israel did not. Very quickly, Senator Hickenlooper extended his objection to the other treaties as well, although the language of the four treaties varied with respect to the particular professions to which the provision on professions applied.

Although the organized bar's objection was solely to the provision as it applied to the practice of law, Senator Hickenlooper believed that a broader reservation to national treatment was desirable to permit states to limit to U.S. citizens the practice of any profession.[386] Such state laws already existed

379. Ibid.

380. Ibid.

381. Report of Meeting in the Office of Harold F. Linder, dated June 17, 1952, NARA, Record Group 59, Department of State File No. 611.004/6-1852.

382. Circular Airgram No. 2748 dated August 25, 1952, NARA, Record Group 59, Department of State File No. 611.004/8-2552.

383. Airgram dated December 19, 1952, from the Department of State to the U.S. embassy in New Delhi, NARA, Record Group 59, Department of State File No. 611.914/11-2552.

384. *Commercial Treaties,* Hearing Before a Subcommittee of the Committee on Foreign Relations, 82nd Cong. 2d Sess. (1952), page 38.

385. *See, e.g.,* Italy FCN treaty, Article I(2)(a); Ireland FCN treaty, Article VI(1)(a).

386. Airgram dated August 27, 1952, from the Department of State to the U.S. embassy in New Delhi, NARA, Record Group 59, Department of State File No. 611.914/8-2752.

with respect to the practice of law, medicine, dentistry, and engineering, among other professions.[387] Senator Hickenlooper asserted that he had no objection to aliens' practicing a profession in the United States if permitted by state law,[388] but he objected to the use of a treaty to abrogate laws in approximately half the states that limited the practice of certain professions to U.S. citizens. He explained that he was "very much opposed to using the device of treaties . . . to destroy the constitutional prerogatives of individual States or invading to any great degree the rights of the States to legislate within their own boundaries in matters affecting themselves and their own local administration and local affairs."[389] He was also concerned that the right to practice professions would be extended to nationals of other countries through the operation of MFN provisions in other treaties.[390]

Senator Hickenlooper proposed that the Senate attach a reservation to its advice and consent to ratification that would exclude certain professions from the nondiscrimination obligation of Article VIII(2). His proposed reservation was based on language in the FCN treaty with Denmark,[391] which excluded certain professions from the provision on practice of professions. The reservation stated that Article VIII(2) "shall not extend to professions which, because they involve the performance of functions in a public capacity or in the interest of public health and safety, are State-licensed and reserved by statute or constitution exclusively to citizens of the country, and no most-favored-nation clause in the said treaty shall apply to such provisions."[392] The State Department found a reservation based on the language of the Danish FCN treaty less objectionable than one for all professions, but hoped to limit the reservation to law and perhaps medicine.[393] The professions that Senator Hickenlooper specifically contemplated in his reservation were law, medicine, and dentistry, although he noted that there might be others.[394] The State Department later interpreted the reservation to apply to accountancy as well.[395]

387. Airgram dated December 19, 1952, from the Department of State to the U.S. embassy in New Delhi, NARA, Record Group 59, Department of State File No. 611.914/11-2552.

388. 99 *Congressional Record* 9314 (1953).

389. Ibid.

390. Ibid., pages 9313–9314.

391. Memorandum headed "Status of FCN Treaty," dated June 30, 1953, NARA, Record Group 59, Department of State File No. 611.944/6-3053.

392. 99 *Congressional Record* 9313 (1953).

393. Memorandum headed "'Federal Clause' in FCN Treaties," dated June 9, 1953, NARA, Record Group 59, Department of State File No. 611.044/6-953.

394. 99 *Congressional Record* 9314 (1953).

395. Telegram dated July 27, 1953, from the Department of State to the U.S. Political Adviser in Tokyo, NARA, Record Group 59, Department of State File No. 611.944/7-2753; Airgram dated July 29, 1953, from the Department of State to the U.S. embassy in New Delhi, NARA, Record Group 59, Department of State File No. 611.914/7-2953.

The Department was offered the choice of acquiescing to the reservation or delaying Senate action until the following year.[396] It decided to object to the reservation,[397] noting that provisions on the practice of professions had appeared in U.S. treaties for the past 30 years[398] and that such provisions were to the advantage of the United States because the various states imposed "far fewer" nationality restrictions on the practice of professions than other countries.[399] The Department hoped to persuade members of the Senate that the national treatment provision was in the national interest.[400] Although the organized bar continued to object to the practice of professions provision, the organized accounting profession "strongly" supported the State Department. The American Medical Association took no position.[401] Given the controversy, the Committee deferred action on the treaties until the following year.[402]

On April 2, 1953, the United States concluded its FCN treaty with Japan. That treaty included language on the practice of professions similar to that in the treaty with Israel. Conclusion of the treaty with the practice of professions provision angered Senator Hickenlooper, who demanded that the language be removed and who denounced the State Department for concluding the treaty with language providing for national treatment with respect to the practice of professions "after having full warning" of his views in connection with the treaty with Israel.[403] On June 17, State Department officials met with Senator Hickenlooper and persuaded him to accept a treaty reservation in lieu of renegotiation of the treaty.[404]

On July 13, 1953, the Committee on Foreign Relations held a second round of hearings on the treaties deferred from 1952 (excluding the treaty

396. Memorandum of Conversation headed "FCN Treaties before Senate," dated June 30, 1952, NARA, Record Group 59, Department of State File No. 611.004/6-3052.

397. Letter dated July 11, 1952, from Vernon G. Setser to John Loftus, NARA, Record Group 59, Department of State File No. 611.914/7-1152.

398. Circular Airgram No. 2748, dated August 25, 1952, NARA, Record Group 59, Department of State File No. 611.004/8-2552.

399. Letter dated May 16, 1952, from Acting Legal Adviser Jack B. Tate to Senator John Sparkman, NARA, Record Group 59, Department of State File No. 611.84A4/5-1952, *reprinted in Commercial Treaties,* Hearing Before a Subcommittee of the Committee on Foreign Relations, 82nd Cong. 2d Sess. (1952), pages 39–40.

400. Airgram dated August 27, 1952, from the Department of State to the U.S. embassy in New Delhi, NARA, Record Group 59, Department of State File No. 611.914/8-2752.

401. Memorandum headed "'Federal Clause' in FCN Treaties," dated June 9, 1953, NARA, Record Group 59, Department of State File No. 611.044/6-953.

402. Airgram dated August 27, 1952, from the Department of State to the U.S. embassy in New Delhi, NARA, Record Group 59, Department of State File No. 611.914/8-2752.

403. Memorandum of conversation headed "Professional Clauses in Japanese Peace Treaty," dated June 5, 1953, NARA, Record Group 59, Department of State File No. 611.944/6-553.

404. Memorandum dated June 17, 1953, from Jack B. Tate to the Secretary of State, NARA, Record Group 59, Department of State File No. 611.944/6-1753.

with Colombia, which, as explained above, had been withdrawn by President Eisenhower on June 30) as well as on the treaty with Japan, a short treaty reactivating a 1923 FCN treaty with Germany, and a protocol to the 1934 FCN treaty with Finland,[405] during which Senator Hickenlooper offered the language of his proposed reservation.[406] Testifying on behalf of the State Department was Assistant Secretary of State for Economic Affairs Samuel C. Waugh, who was accompanied by Vernon G. Setser, the chief of the Economic Treaties Branch of the Commercial Policy Staff, and Stanley D. Metzger, the assistant legal adviser for economic affairs. Also testifying was Herman Phleger, the State Department legal adviser. David Whatley, a Washington, DC, attorney, testified in opposition to the provision in the treaties relating to the practice of professions, although he also believed that Senator Hickenlooper's proposed reservation was too broad. As it became clear, however, Whatley did not understand the reservation. Several minutes passed while Whatley interrogated Senator Hickenlooper concerning the meaning of the reservation, and the senator patiently explained the reservation to him.

During the 1953 hearings, the Committee inquired about the NFTC's concern that the Ethiopia treaty would set a bad precedent for future treaties. Assistant Secretary Waugh assured the Committee that the treaty with Ethiopia had not been treated as a precedent in subsequent negotiations.[407]

Despite the concerns of the NFTC regarding the treaty with Ethiopia, on July 17, 1953, the Committee on Foreign Relations voted to recommend advice and consent to ratification of all of the treaties. Four days later, on July 21, the Senate gave its advice and consent to the treaties as a group by a vote of 86-1.[408] As discussed in Chapter 8, the Senate's discussion included brief remarks by Senator Hickenlooper concerning the essential security interests exception. The only senator to vote in opposition was Democratic senator Patrick McCarran of Nevada. Senator McCarran did not participate in the debate on the treaties, and neither the Senate records nor the State Department records contains any explanation of the reasons for his opposition.

The Senate had approved previous U.S. postwar FCNs under a unanimous consent procedure, and thus the vote in 1953 was the first time since the war that members of the Senate had gone on record individually as supporting the FCN treaty program. The Department interpreted the vote as a "strong renewed endorsement" of the program.[409]

405. This treaty is described in Chapter 7 in the section on the FCN treaty with Germany.

406. *Commercial Treaties*, Hearing Before the Subcommittee of the Committee on Foreign Relations, 83rd Cong. 1st Sess. (1953).

407. Ibid., page 21.

408. 99 *Congressional Record* 9315–9316 (1953).

409. Department of State Circular Airgram dated August 6, 1953, NARA, Record Group 59, Department of State File No. 611.004/8-653.

Senator Hickenlooper did prevail with respect to the practice of professions, and Senate approval of the treaties with Denmark, Greece, Israel, and Japan was accompanied by his proposed reservation.[410] The State Department explained to other governments that the reservation was not intended to restrict the rights of aliens in the United States, but was related to a domestic political movement to limit the constitutional authority of the president to conclude treaties, reflecting dislike of the United Nations, resentment toward various wartime agreements, and opposition to the growth of the power of the federal government.[411]

INVESTMENT TREATIES AT THE END OF THE TRUMAN ADMINISTRATION

In late 1952, as it prepared to relinquish power, the Truman administration surveyed the status of the FCN treaty program after almost eight years of negotiations.[412] Since 1945, the Department had considered the negotiation of FCN treaties with 70 countries. It had signed treaties with 9 countries—China, Colombia, Denmark, Ethiopia, Greece, Ireland, Israel, Italy, and Uruguay—and was only months away from concluding negotiations with Japan. The treaties with Colombia and Uruguay, for reasons already explained, would never enter into force, but, as has been seen, the negotiations with Japan would conclude successfully early the next year. Thus, during the eight years between 1945 and 1953, the Truman administration would conclude eight FCN treaties (including the one with Japan) that would eventually enter into force.

The status of the treaty program with respect to the 62 countries with which no treaty was concluded illustrates the difficulties that the United States faced in trying to develop a comprehensive network of FCN treaties.

In the case of 16 countries, the Department had decided that circumstances were not favorable for the negotiation of an FCN treaty. Typically, the reasons were that the political situation did not allow the negotiation of an FCN treaty (Austria, Burma, Cambodia, Finland, Guatemala, Indonesia, Laos, and Vietnam), the country's economic policies were not consistent with FCN treaty commitments (Panama, Switzerland, and Thailand), or the economy was not sufficiently developed for the country to be able to agree to FCN treaty commitments (Iceland, Nepal, Saudi Arabia, and Yemen). In the case of Korea, the war

410. The Senate also attached to the treaty with Italy an understanding relating to a provision on social insurance.

411. Telegram dated July 24, 1953, from the Department of State to the U.S. Political Adviser in Tokyo, NARA, Record Group 59, Department of State File No. 611.944/7-2353; Airgram dated July 29, 1953, from the Department of State to the U.S. embassy in New Delhi, NARA, Record Group 59, Department of State File No. 611.914/7-2953.

412. Memorandum headed "Present Status of Program for Negotiating Treaties of Friendship, Commerce and Navigation Treaties," dated December 1, 1952, NARA, Record Group 59, Department of State File No. 611.004/3-453.

had precluded negotiations. The United States would eventually conclude FCN treaties with Korea and Vietnam.

In the case of 11 countries, the United States had proposed treaty negotiations, but the other country had not responded. These countries were Bolivia, Ceylon, Iran, Jordan, Libya, Luxembourg, New Zealand, Nicaragua, Norway, South Africa, and Venezuela. In the case of three other countries—Dominican Republic, Haiti, and Turkey—the other country was still reviewing the U.S. proposal. Ultimately, the United States would conclude FCN treaties with Haiti, Iran, Luxembourg, and Nicaragua, although the treaty with Haiti would never enter into force.

Fourteen countries had identified sufficiently serious objections to negotiating an FCN treaty with the United States that formal negotiations had never commenced. These countries were Afghanistan, Belgium, Canada, Chile, Cuba, Ecuador, Iraq, Mexico, Pakistan, Portugal, Spain, Sweden, Syria, and the United Kingdom. The objections varied. For example, Afghanistan, Portugal, and Syria complained about the length and complexity of the treaty. Belgium was preoccupied with forming the Benelux Union with Luxembourg and the Netherlands. Sweden and the United Kingdom did not see a sufficient need for such a treaty. Chile believed that conclusion of the treaty would cast aspersions on the Chilean legal system. Cuba and Iraq cited political opposition. Several countries, including Afghanistan, Canada, Cuba, Ecuador, Mexico, Pakistan, and Spain, cited substantive problems that precluded negotiation of the treaty. Eventually, Belgium and Pakistan would conclude an FCN treaty with the United States.

In the case of 10 countries, negotiations had begun but then had stalled. These countries were Argentina, Brazil, Costa Rica, Egypt, France, Germany, India, Lebanon, Netherlands, and the Philippines. In most cases, the negotiations stalled because of an insoluble disagreement over one or more issues. In the case of Lebanon, however, the parties had completed their negotiations, but then Lebanon declined to sign the treaty because of the situation in Palestine. In the case of the Netherlands, much of the problem was the desire of the Dutch government to coordinate negotiations with Belgium, which was not yet ready to negotiate an FCN treaty with the United States. Eventually, France, Germany, and the Netherlands would conclude an FCN treaty with the United States.

In the case of three countries—El Salvador, Honduras, and Liberia—the State Department in 1952 was still considering whether to propose a new FCN treaty to replace or supplement FCN treaties concluded with these countries during the interwar period. In the case of Peru, the United States had decided to propose negotiations, but had not yet done so. In the case of Australia and Paraguay, the Department anticipated that negotiations would begin soon. The Department could not know this in 1952, but none of the negotiations with these six countries would be successful.

Despite the lack of progress, the State Department remained committed to promoting outward foreign investment. Only days before the November 1952 election, the Department announced an investment promotion plan comprising three parts: the encouragement of conditions favorable to private investment, the identification of specific opportunities for investment, and the assembly and dissemination of background information needed by foreign investors.[413]

The reference to the second and third points reflected the increased attention to transparency in U.S. foreign investment policy. The report noted two benefits from increased transparency. First, "[t]he assembly of background information on a country by country basis will provide potential US investors with competent and reliable data as to the conditions and circumstances under which a private enterprise can be established and conducted."[414] Second, the information would also be "useful in efforts to develop a more favorable atmosphere for private enterprise, and [would] help in negotiations with the host country on specific restrictions which adversely affect domestic and foreign private capital, and in negotiation of international agreements, such as friendship, commerce, and development, investment guarantee agreements, and tax treaties."[415]

The report noted that missions should discourage the use of public funds in cases where private capital could be induced to undertake development projects. Missions were encouraged to direct the attention of host countries to the benefits of private investment in furthering national policy. At the same time, missions were cautioned to avoid creating the impression that the United States was seeking "to force US capital on unwilling customers."[416] Yet, efforts should not be suspended "simply for fear of attacks from pro-Communists."[417]

The Department asked its missions to explore "all possible means" of furthering private enterprise through technical assistance. Of particular importance were programs to facilitate private investment through advice relating to government fiscal policies and administration, and to tax, mining, and corporation laws. As this indicates, the administration was seeking through the Point Four program to facilitate legal reform that would promote capital formation.

As the era of the New Deal and the Fair Deal came to an end, the United States continued its efforts to bolster the rule of law in other countries through both the provision of technical assistance and the conclusion of treaties of friendship, commerce, and navigation.

413. *Current Economic Developments,* October 27, 1952, page 6, NARA, Record Group 59, Department of State Lot Files.

414. Ibid.

415. Ibid.

416. Ibid.

417. Ibid.

7

Negotiating the First Bilateral Investment Treaties

After the Truman Years

The election of a Republican president in November 1952 in no way diminished the support for the FCN treaty policy of the Roosevelt and Truman administrations. Within two months of Dwight Eisenhower's inauguration, the administration had decided to "intensify the encouragement and facilitation of the flow of private investment to countries outside the Communist satellite areas as a means of promoting economic well-being, social progress and stability throughout the free world."[1]

On March 4, 1953, the State Department, now headed by John Foster Dulles, sent an airgram to all of its missions except those in "iron curtain" countries, that is, those in Bucharest, Budapest, Prague, Moscow, Trieste, and Warsaw. The airgram voiced strong support for the FCN treaty program. "It is essential," the State Department told its missions, "that the negotiation of FCN treaties of the type concluded since World War II be considered an important part of any program relating to private investment."[2] After noting the language in section 516(d) of the Mutual Security Act of 1952 calling upon the State Department to "accelerate" the negotiation of FCN treaties, the Department said that the American business community attached "great importance" to treaties protecting foreign investment. American investors would be reluctant to assume the risks involved in foreign investment unless they received "reasonable assurances of fair treatment" for that investment.[3] Although it was not to be expected that conclusion of an FCN treaty would "necessarily be followed by a marked increase in American capital investment" in the territory of the other treaty party, the willingness of that party to conclude the treaty would "reflect a responsible attitude" toward

1. *Current Economic Developments*, March 24, 1953, page 3, NARA, Record Group 59, Department of State Lot Files.

2. Circular Airgram headed "FCN Treaty Program of the United States," dated March 4, 1953, NARA, Record Group 59, Department of State File No. 611.004/3-453.

3. Ibid.

foreign investment, and the treaty itself constituted "a formal expression of policy which can be the basis of confidence and the growth of sound business relationships."[4]

Accordingly, the Department proposed to "take more initiative in focusing the attention of foreign governments upon the mutual advantages inherent in FCN treaties."[5] The Department also intended to involve the Technical Cooperation Assistance (TCA) and Mutual Security Assistance (MSA) missions more closely in the effort to conclude FCN treaties. This did not mean, the Department assured the missions, that it intended to require the negotiation of an FCN treaty as the price of receiving foreign assistance. Rather, the objectives of FCN treaties were aimed at economic growth, as were the objectives of the assistance programs. The assumption underlying U.S. assistance was that the recipients of that assistance were seeking to tap all possible resources, including private investment. The Department emphasized that FCN treaties "cannot and should not be negotiated unless there is a genuine interest" on the part of the other country, but believed that much could be done to stimulate interest and understanding with respect to U.S. FCN treaties.[6] The Department did not wish other countries to regard the conclusion of an FCN treaty "to be merely a favor to the United States."[7] Rather, the Department wished other countries to understand "the mutual nature of the benefits which can accrue from such treaties."[8]

The Department attached to the airgram copies of the FCN treaties concluded with Colombia and Denmark, which it regarded as "good, representative treaties of their kind."[9] To the missions in Afghanistan, Iceland, Jordan, Libya, and Saudi Arabia, it sent a copy of the FCN treaty with Ethiopia.

The Department invited missions in those countries where active FCN treaty negotiations were not occurring to appraise the situation jointly with the TCA and MSA missions in order to identify factors both favorable and unfavorable to the negotiation of a treaty and to begin focusing more local attention on the nature, purpose, and importance of FCN treaties. Still adopting a pragmatic stance, the Department indicated that, where local policies or practices presented obstacles to negotiations, "there may be a variety of ways whereby the treaty

4. Ibid.

5. Ibid.

6. Ibid.

7. Ibid. *See also* Letter dated January 19, 1954, from Weir M. Brown to Jack C. Corbett, NARA, Record Group 59, Department of State File No. 611.62A4/1-1954.

8. Circular Airgram headed "FCN Treaty Program of the United States," dated March 4, 1953, NARA, Record Group 59, Department of State File No. 611.004/3-453. *See also* Despatch No. 2413 dated March 8, 1954, from the U.S. High Commissioner in Bonn to the Department of State, NARA, Record Group 59, Department of State File No. 611.62A4/3-854.

9. Circular Airgram headed "FCN Treaty Program of the United States," dated March 4, 1953, NARA, Record Group 59, Department of State File No. 611.004/3-453.

can be adapted to local situations without violation to its basic principles."[10] The Department noted that, in special circumstances, it might be realistic to consider the negotiation of an abridged treaty relating principally to establishment and investment, rather than a standard FCN treaty. In other words, the investment provisions were by then so important that the Department was prepared to regard the FCN treaty, if necessary, as essentially interchangeable with a treaty devoted exclusively to investment, although the complete FCN treaty remained the preferred instrument.

Later that month, the Department reported that it was intensifying its effort to promote U.S. private investment "in countries outside the Communist satellite areas as a means of promoting economic well-being, social progress and stability throughout the free world."[11] The effort consisted principally of steps to apprise foreign governments of the benefits of private foreign investment for economic development.

The Department explained in its report that the United States was "seeking balanced foreign economic development and encouraging US private investment abroad in fields which contribute to improving levels of employment and better living conditions."[12] The Department believed that U.S. investment could be particularly useful in the industrial sector of the economy.

The Department acknowledged the "public relations difficulties" in connection with encouraging U.S. private investment abroad, but believed that charges of economic imperialism should not deter U.S. efforts and that the United States should stress the mutual benefits associated with increased investment in developing countries.[13] The Department noted that the United States should encourage investment from other capital-exporting countries as well because the U.S. goal was to "encourage the productive and socially desirable use of all resources available in the free world."[14]

The Department observed that several approaches had been made to improving the investment climate abroad, including the proposed expansion of the FCN treaty program. The TCA and MSA were attempting to involve private enterprise to a greater extent in foreign assistance programs. The Department of Commerce was providing information to private businesses concerning investment opportunities abroad and general background information about the investment climate. For the past three years, the MSA had operated a clearinghouse in Western Europe that it intended to extend to the Near and Far East and to Latin America.

10. Ibid.

11. *Current Economic Developments,* March 24, 1953, NARA, Record Group 59, Department of State Lot Files.

12. Ibid.

13. Ibid.

14. Ibid.

The clearinghouse put Americans wishing to invest abroad in contact with foreign businesses. Since 1948, the MSA had operated an investment guarantee program, which was now present in 15 countries.[15] The program insured investors against the risk of loss through exchange controls or expropriation.

Unfortunately, the Department had found that conditions "highly conducive" to foreign investment rarely existed.[16] The State Department nevertheless intended to "press[] ahead" with its treaty program.[17]

NEGOTIATING AN FCN TREATY WITH GERMANY

As early as August 1950, officials of the Federal Republic of Germany had expressed interest in reapplying a 1923 FCN treaty[18] between Germany and the United States,[19] the continued effectiveness of which had been called into question by the war.[20] The United States considered the 1923 treaty to be one of the best of its kind.[21] Its provisions had been developed jointly by Secretary of State Charles Evans Hughes and Secretary of Commerce Herbert Hoover.[22] It was the first FCN treaty concluded by Germany after World War I.[23]

German officials regarded revival of the treaty as in part a propaganda measure and a gesture of goodwill, but they also hoped that it would encourage German

15. Ibid.

16. Ibid.

17. Department of State, Office of Public Affairs, *Commercial Treaty Program of the United States* (Washington, DC: Government Printing Office, 1952), *copy available at* NARA, Record Group 59, Department of State File No. 611.004/3-453.

18. Treaty of Friendship, Commerce and Consular Rights, United States-Germany, signed December 8, 1923, 44 Stat. 2132, T.S. No. 725.

19. Memorandum headed "Re-Application of the United States-German Treaty of Friendship, Commerce and Consular Rights, 1923," dated August 27, 1951, NARA, Record Group 59, Department of State File No. 611.624/8-2751.

20. Letter dated May 27, 1954, from Judson C. Jones to E. J. Spielman, NARA, Record Group 59, Department of State File No. 611.624/4-3054; Airgram dated March 10, 1952, from the Department of State to the U.S. High Commissioner in Bonn, NARA, Record Group 59, Department of State File No. 611.62A4/11-2151; Memorandum headed "FCN Treaty with Germany," dated October 29, 1954, NARA, Record Group 59, Department of State File No. 611.62A4/10-2954.

21. Memorandum dated June 8, 1951, from D. J. Porter to S. Houston Lay, Enclosure No. 4 to despatch dated June 29, 1951, from the U.S. High Commissioner in Bonn to the Department of State, NARA, Record Group 59, Department of State File No. 611.62A4/6-2951.

22. Memorandum headed "Notes on FCN Treaty," dated April 2, 1953, NARA, Record Group 59, Department of State File No. 611.62A4/4-253.

23. Ibid.

exports to the United States and thereby contribute to reducing the dollar gap.[24] The Truman administration believed that reapplication of the earlier treaty was desirable largely for political reasons.[25] The United States wanted "promptly to reestablish in as many fields as possible the position of the Federal Republic as a free and equal partner in the Western family of nations."[26]

As a condition of reviving the 1923 treaty, the United States required agreement on reservations to avoid conflicts between treaty provisions and U.S. rights as an occupying power.[27] It also wanted reapplication of the 1923 treaty to be followed by the negotiation of a modern FCN treaty.[28] Germany's reaction to the Truman administration's proposal of a new treaty was "extremely favorable."[29]

By May 1953, the United States and Germany had reached agreement on a so-called "little treaty" to reactivate the 1923 FCN treaty, and the United States reported itself ready to begin the negotiation of a modern FCN treaty.[30] Meanwhile, Germany had used the intervening time to prepare its own model FCN treaty, which the United States received in June 1953.[31]

The State Department did not consider the German model to be a suitable basis on which to conduct negotiations. Indeed, the Department did not believe that it could be revised sufficiently to constitute a suitable basis for negotiations.[32] Whereas the emphasis of the U.S. standard draft treaty was on investment

24. Memorandum headed "Re-Application of the United States-German Treaty of Friendship, Commerce and Consular Rights, 1923," dated August 27, 1951, NARA, Record Group 59, Department of State File No. 611.624/8-2751.

25. Telegram dated June 4, 1951, from the Department of State to the U.S. High Commissioner in Frankfort, NARA, Record Group 59, Department of State File No. 611.62A4/5-951; Memorandum headed "Commercial Treaty," dated May 24, 1952, NARA, Record Group 59, Department of State File No. 611,62A4/5-951.

26. Memorandum dated June 7, 1951, from G. B. Gardiner to P. S. Nevin, NARA, Record Group 59, Department of State File No. 611.62A4/6-2951.

27. Memorandum headed "Re-Application of the United States-German Treaty of Friendship, Commerce and Consular Rights, 1923," dated August 27, 1951, NARA, Record Group 59, Department of State File No. 611.624/8-2751.

28. Ibid.

29. Telegram dated April 2, 1953, from the U.S. High Commissioner in Bonn to the Department of State, NARA, Record Group 59, Department of State File No. 611.62A4/4-253. *See also* Telegram dated April 3, 1953, from the U.S. High Commissioner in Bonn to the Department of State, NARA, Record Group 59, Department of State File No. 611.62A4/4-353.

30. Airgram dated May 27, 1953, from the Department of State to the U.S. High Commissioner in Bonn, NARA, Record Group 59, Department of State File No. 611.62A4/5-653.

31. Despatch dated June 26, 1953, from the U.S. High Commissioner in Bonn to the Department of State, NARA, Record Group 59, Department of State File No. 611.62A4/6-2653.

32. Airgram A-164 dated July 28, 1953, from the Department of State to the U.S. High Commissioner in Bonn, NARA, Record Group 59, Department of State File No. 611.62A4/6-2653.

protection, and trade provisions were assigned a less significant role, the German model reversed that approach. Moreover, the U.S. standard draft treaty required national treatment, whereas the German model required only MFN treatment. In addition, the MFN treatment obligation in the German model was conditional rather than unconditional and was qualified by exceptions for local law. The German treaty had no provision authorizing treaty investor visas, addressing exchange controls, or calling for competitive equality. Disputes concerning the interpretation or application of the treaty were to be resolved through arbitration. The United States believed that any disputes not resolved through diplomacy should be submitted instead to the International Court of Justice.[33] The German model also lacked a guarantee of fair and equitable treatment and a prohibition on unreasonable or discriminatory measures. Indeed, the only provisions in the 1953 German model that would be regarded as elements of a bilateral investment treaty were, apart from the state-state arbitration provision, a provision requiring prompt and just compensation for expropriation, a provision on access to courts, and a provision requiring conditional MFN treatment, subject to local law.

The State Department thus hoped that Germany would be willing to utilize the U.S. standard draft treaty as the basis for negotiation, and expressed a willingness to modify the draft in some respects. The Department noted that "[i]n proposing its draft, of course, the Department is by no means suggesting a rigid document that it expects to be signed as presented. It is a starting-point draft from which, through negotiation and exchanges of views, a mutually satisfactory instrument can be ultimately developed."[34]

The Department believed that Germany's preference for its model as a basis for negotiations rested in part on its preference for the substantive approach of its draft, but also in part on "pride of authorship" and a desire to save "face."[35] Accordingly, the Department decided that, if necessary, it would agree to negotiate on the basis of a draft that followed the organization of the German draft, but used the language of the U.S. draft.[36] Before offering the compromise, U.S. negotiators urged acceptance of the U.S. draft as the basis for negotiation, on the grounds that the promotion of investment was now the primary purpose of the treaty, with trade addressed more appropriately by the GATT; that the basic treaty standard must be national treatment rather than MFN treatment; and that the U.S. draft was time-tested, having been refined through years of negotiations with

33. Ibid.

34. Ibid.

35. Despatch dated August 24, 1953, from the U.S. High Commissioner in Bonn to the Department of State, NARA, Record Group 59, Department of State File No. 611.62A4/8-2453.

36. Instruction dated September 11, 1953, from the Department of State to the U.S. High Commissioner in Bonn, NARA, Record Group 59, Department of State File No. 611.62A4/8-2453.

many different countries.[37] In late September, the German negotiators agreed to use the U.S. draft as the basis for negotiations.[38]

Discussions commenced in October 1953.[39] The German negotiators were "very friendly" and "eager to move forward as rapidly as possible."[40] Germany intended to negotiate as many FCN treaties as it could in the immediate future and, by April 1954, had already been approached by four other countries seeking to negotiate an FCN treaty.[41] The German government regarded the treaty with the United States as a model for its future agreements and wanted it to be "as liberal as possible."[42]

The most important problem that arose during negotiations related to exchange controls. Germany wanted to retain sole discretion to determine when to impose such controls. Germany also objected to the submission of disputes to the International Court of Justice, at least as long as the Soviet Union prevented Germany's admission to the United Nations, and proposed instead submission of disputes to a permanent mixed arbitral commission.[43] Other significant issues that arose related to Germany's desire for an exception to its MFN obligations with respect to trade to accommodate European integration,[44] Germany's objection to a provision on quantitative restrictions on trade,[45] and, more generally, German reluctance to agree to unconditional MFN treatment of investment.[46] The provision on competitive equality, as noted above, had been absent from the German model, and it would be omitted from the final treaty text as well.

37. Despatch dated September 24, 1953, from the U.S. High Commissioner in Bonn to the Department of State, NARA, Record Group 59, Department of State File No. 611.62A4/9-2453.

38. Telegram dated September 23, 1953, from the U.S. High Commissioner in Bonn to the Department of State, NARA, Record Group 59, Department of State File No. 611.62A4/9-2353.

39. Despatch dated April 15, 1954, from the U.S. High Commissioner in Bonn to the Department of State, NARA, Record Group 59, Department of State File No. 611.62A4/4-1554.

40. Letter dated October 28, 1953, from Carl H. Boehringer to Howard J. Hilton Jr., NARA, Record Group 59, Department of State File No. 611.62A4/10-2853.

41. Despatch dated April 15, 1954, from the U.S. High Commissioner in Bonn to the Department of State, NARA, Record Group 59, Department of State File No. 611.62A4/4-1554.

42. Despatch dated October 30, 1953, from the U.S. High Commissioner in Bonn to the Department of State, NARA, Record Group 59, Department of State File No. 611.62A4/4-3053. *See also* Memorandum dated September 24, 1954, by Cecil B. Lyon, NARA, Record Group 59, Department of State File No. 611.62A4/9-2454.

43. Despatch dated April 15, 1954, from the U.S. High Commissioner in Bonn to the Department of State, NARA, Record Group 59, Department of State File No. 611.62A4/4-1554

44. Memorandum dated September 24, 1954, by Cecil B. Lyon, NARA, Record Group 59, Department of State File No. 611.62A4/9-2454.

45. Despatch dated April 15, 1954, from the U.S. High Commissioner in Bonn to the Department of State, NARA, Record Group 59, Department of State File No. 611.62A4/4-1554.

46. Memorandum dated September 24, 1954, by Cecil B. Lyon, NARA, Record Group 59, Department of State File No. 611.62A4/9-2454.

By April of 1954, the German negotiators were suggesting that, although prior negotiations had occurred in Bonn, one final round of negotiations be held in Washington in the early summer, at which all remaining issues would be resolved and the treaty would be signed.[47] They were concerned, however, that such a round might end in failure, and sought assurances from the United States that agreement would be reached during the final round.[48]

The proposed dates for the final round continued to be deferred while discussions proceeded on the major issues noted above and on a variety of lesser issues. For example, the United States agreed to language in Paragraph 8 of the protocol permitting either party to require work permits, but stating that "such regulations shall be administered in a liberal fashion as to nationals of the other Party." Whereas the United States generally controlled alien employment through its immigration system, Germany did so through a work permit system. The United States also agreed to language in Paragraph 13 of the protocol exempting the activity of peddlers and itinerant artisans from the national treatment obligation.

The expropriation provision, in particular, posed two problems. First, Germany was concerned that the expropriation provision required greater compensation than did the German Constitution.[49] Second, Germany wanted explicit language requiring judicial review of the legality of expropriation and the amount of compensation, but the United States objected to treaty specification of internal procedures at that level of detail[50] and thought that a requirement that the expropriation be in accordance with due process, also included at Germany's request, conveyed the same principle.[51]

The U.S. response to the issue of European integration was that the United States encouraged European integration, but was unwilling to "sign a blank check."[52] The same issue had already arisen during negotiations with the Netherlands, and the United States had offered a proposal that granted the desired reservation, but would allow the United States to terminate MFN obligations if it concluded that the other party's participation in a European integration agreement was contrary to U.S. interests.[53]

47. Despatch dated April 15, 1954, from the U.S. High Commissioner in Bonn to the Department of State, NARA, Record Group 59, Department of State File No. 611.62A4/4-1554.

48. Telegram dated June 11, 1954, from the U.S. High Commissioner in Bonn to the Department of State, NARA, Record Group 59, Department of State File No. 611.62A4/6-1154.

49. Telegram dated August 24, 1954, from the U.S. High Commissioner in Bonn to the Department of State, NARA, Record Group 59, Department of State File No. 611.62A4/8-2454.

50. Instruction dated April 23, 1954, from the Department of State to the U.S. High Commissioner in Bonn, NARA, Record Group 59, Department of State File No. 611.62A4/3-2554.

51. Telegram dated August 24, 1954, from the U.S. High Commissioner in Bonn to the Department of State, NARA, Record Group 59, Department of State File No. 611.62A4/8-2454.

52. Memorandum headed "Memorandum on German FCN Negotiation," dated September 28, 1954, NARA, Record Group 59, Department of State File No. 611.62A4/9-2854.

53. Ibid.

The long-awaited final round of negotiations was held in Washington in October in connection with a visit to Washington by German chancellor Konrad Adenauer, who intended to sign the treaty during his visit.[54] The desire to conclude the treaty successfully during the visit motivated the parties to resolve the remaining areas of disagreement. The concern about MFN treatment was addressed by language stating that national treatment was extended by each party in consideration of national treatment extended by the other.[55] The disagreement regarding expropriation compensation was resolved when Chancellor Adenauer, in the closing days of the negotiation, made a "personal decision" to accept the U.S. language.[56] The problem of quantitative restrictions was addressed through an exchange of letters granting Germany a transitional period.[57] The problem of European integration was addressed with an unpublished exchange of letters that created no binding legal obligation and merely reflected the fact that Germany had raised the issue during negotiations.[58] Although, as already noted, the United States was prepared to provide an exception in the treaty, Germany decided that addressing the problem in legal terms was not necessary.[59] Germany's objection to the compromissory clause was addressed with new language in the treaty text stating that disputes would be submitted to arbitration or, upon the agreement of the parties, the International Court of Justice and language in the protocol providing that, after Germany became a member of the United Nations or a party to the Statute of the International Court of Justice, disputes would be submitted to the Court.[60] Germany's demand for unreviewable discretion to impose exchange controls, an

54. Memorandum dated September 24, 1954, by Cecil B. Lyon, NARA, Record Group 59, Department of State File No. 611.62A4/9-2454; Telegram dated September 24, 1954, from the U.S. High Commissioner in Bonn to the Department of State, NARA, Record Group 59, Department of State File No. 611.62A4/9-2154.

55. Germany FCN treaty, Article XXV(2). *See also* Summary Record of Third Meeting of the Working Group on Article XXVIII and First Meeting of the Working Group on Reciprocity Problems, October 23, 1954, NARA, Record Group 59, Department of State File No. 611.62A4/10-554.

56. *Current Economic Developments,* November 9, 1954, page 7, NARA, Record Group 59, Department of State Lot Files.

57. Instruction dated October 11, 1954, from the Department of State to the U.S. High Commissioner in Bonn, NARA, Record Group 59, Department of State File No. 611.62A4/10-1154.

58. Instruction CA-3372 dated November 19, 1954, from the Department of State to the U.S. High Commissioner in Bonn, NARA, Record Group 59, Department of State File No. 611.62A4/11-2954. *See also* letters dated October 29, 1954, between Chancellor Konrad Adenauer and Secretary of State John Foster Dulles, NARA, Record Group 59, Department of State File No. 611.62A4/10-2954.

59. Instruction CA-3372 dated November 19, 1954 from the Department of State to the U.S. High Commissioner in Bonn, NARA, Record Group 59, Department of State File No. 611.62A4/11-2954.

60. Germany FCN treaty, Article XXVII(2) and Protocol, Paragraph 24.

issue that both parties were concerned would wreck the negotiations, was met with extensive revisions of the article on exchange controls[61] and with a letter dated October 28, 1954, from the chair of the U.S. delegation to the chair of the German delegation stating that decisions made by either party with respect to its undertakings in the second sentence of Article XII(3) were "not appropriate for judicial review" under Article XXVII(2), the compromissory clause of the treaty.[62] The second sentence of Article XII(3) read, "Should either Party impose exchange restrictions with respect to the other Party, it will remove them as rapidly as it is able to do so considering its economic condition." The letter was not published and apparently was not shown to the Senate.[63] As a further concession, the United States also agreed to Paragraph 16 of the protocol under which "[e]ither Party may, for the protection of its currency and in the interest of servicing investments and their repatriation, make the importation of capital dependent on a license." On October 29, 1954, the treaty was signed by Chancellor Adenauer and Secretary Dulles.[64]

Despite their repeated comments that the U.S. FCN treaty would serve as a model for future treaties, the German negotiators believed that the U.S. FCN treaty was sufficiently long and complicated that departures from it would be necessary in future negotiations. In December 1954, a few weeks after the treaty was signed, Dr. Walter Becker, a German foreign service officer, told Weir Brown, a State Department official, that "probably very few countries would be able or willing to engage in treaties of the same breadth and duration" as the FCN treaty between Germany and the United States.[65] "Therefore," he predicted, future German treaties "would be 'somewhere in between' the short-term, one-year Trade and Payments Agreements, commonly signed in the past, and the long-term general treaty of principle signed with the United States."[66]

Less than five years after Becker and Brown spoke, in November 1959, Germany would sign its first bilateral investment treaty (BIT), with Pakistan.[67] Pakistan signed the BIT with Germany less than two weeks after signing an FCN treaty with the United States. The treaty between Germany and Pakistan would

61. Germany FCN treaty, Article XII and Protocol, Paragraphs 14–17.

62. Letter dated October 28, 1954, from Thorsten V. Kalijarvi to Dr. Walter Becker, NARA, Record Group 59, Department of State File No. 611.62A4/10-2854. The negotiations with respect to exchange controls are discussed in more detail in Chapter 8 in the section on the essential security interests exception.

63. There is no reference to the letter in the Senate files on the treaty, nor is a copy of the letter in those files.

64. Treaty of Friendship, Commerce and Navigation, with protocol and exchange of notes, entered into force July 14, 1956, 7 UST 1839, TIAS 3593, 273 UNTS 3.

65. Memorandum of Conversation headed "Future Activities of Federal Republic Foreign Office," dated December 16, 1954, NARA, Record Group 59, Department of State File No. 611.62A4/12-3054.

66. Ibid.

67. Treaty between the Federal Republic of Germany and Pakistan for the Promotion and Protection of Investments, signed November 25, 1959.

be limited solely to the promotion and protection of investment. As discussed in the Epilogue, its provisions would reflect virtually all of the investment-related provisions in the U.S. postwar FCN treaties.

The NFTC urged ratification of the treaty with Germany as soon as possible.[68] Despite its early concerns about the provision on unreasonable or discriminatory measures, the NFTC accepted the provision in the treaty with Germany.[69] The NFTC continued to call for a provision guaranteeing that covered property receive protection no less favorable than that required by international law and a provision granting a right of entry for technical personnel.[70] It also objected to Paragraph 9 of the protocol, stating that the MFN and national treatment provisions did not obligate either party to permit nationals and companies of the other party to carry on business in its territories without fulfilling requirements that were generally applicable by law, on the ground that this paragraph would permit Germany to screen foreign investment.[71] The State Department responded that the NFTC had misinterpreted that paragraph and that it did not authorize screening.[72] Rather, the language in the protocol referred to non-discriminatory requirements.

The Committee on Foreign Relations considered the treaty in executive session on July 19, 1955, hearing testimony from Deputy Assistant Secretary of State Thorsten Kalijarvi and then recommending advice and consent to ratification.[73] On July 27, 1955, after being assured that the treaty did not contain a provision on the practice of professions, "impair the constitutional rights of American citizens or . . . alter established Federal-State relations or enlarge Federal powers at the expense of the States," the Senate gave its advice and consent to ratification by a vote of 83-0.[74]

NEGOTIATING AN FCN TREATY WITH HAITI

In early 1952, the Haitian ambassador to the United States began to raise with Truman administration officials the possibility of negotiating an FCN treaty,[75] an

68. Letter dated July 8, 1955, from William S. Swingle to Senator Walter F. George, *reprinted in Treaty of Friendship, Commerce, and Navigation with the Federal Republic of Germany*, Exec. Rept. No. 10, 84th Cong. 1st Sess. (1955), page 9.

69. Memorandum of Conversation headed "Meeting of NFTC Treaty Committee," dated November 10, 1954, NARA, Record Group 59, Department of State File No. 611.004/11-1054.

70. Letter dated July 8, 1955, from William S. Swingle to Senator Walter F. George, *reprinted in Treaty of Friendship, Commerce, and Navigation with the Federal Republic of Germany*, Exec. Rept. No. 10, 84th Cong. 1st Sess. (1955), page 9.

71. Ibid.

72. *Treaty of Friendship, Commerce, and Navigation with the Federal Republic of Germany*, Exec. Rept. No. 10, 84th Cong. 1st Sess. (1955), page 3.

73. Ibid., pages 1–2.

74. 101 *Congressional Record* 11645 (1955).

75. Despatch dated June 3, 1952, from the Department of State to the U.S. embassy in Port-au-Prince, NARA, Record Group 59, Department of State File No. 611.384/6-352.

initiative prompted in part by the fact that Haiti was considering the negotiation of a similar treaty with France.[76] In response, the State Department transmitted a copy of its standard draft treaty to the U.S. embassy in Haiti on June 3.[77]

A month later, the Haitian ambassador provided comments on the draft, indicating that two problems in particular were that the national treatment obligation with respect to establishment and the provision on ownership of real property were inconsistent with Haitian law.[78] The State Department soon decided that it was prepared to grant exceptions to Haiti to accommodate local law provisions in both cases.[79]

Formal negotiations in Haiti began on December 17, 1952.[80] A new problem that arose almost immediately was that Haiti wanted to ensure that the rights granted to the Catholic Church under the Concordat of 1860 between Haiti and the Vatican would not be extended by the treaty to other religious organizations.[81] Haiti was also concerned that the employment provision would produce an influx of foreign specialists and was a "one-way street" because the establishment of Haitian enterprises in the United States was "highly unlikely."[82] In addition, although Haiti did not have exchange controls, it did not want the United States to sit in judgment of any decision it made to impose them in the future.[83] As the negotiations progressed, Haiti also raised additional objections to some aspects of national treatment with respect to establishment and to the competitive equality provision.[84]

Negotiations halted in February 1953, initially because the Haitian foreign minister needed to travel to the United States for medical treatment, then because of a change in the Haitian cabinet, and after that because of the cabinet's

76. Memorandum of Conversation headed "Negotiation of a Treaty of Friendship, Commerce and Navigation between Haiti and the United States," dated April 30, 1952, NARA, Record Group 59, Department of State File No. 611.384/4-3052.

77. Despatch dated June 3, 1952, from the Department of State to the U.S. embassy in Port-au-Prince, NARA, Record Group 59, Department of State File No. 611.384/6-352.

78. Memorandum of Conversation headed "Proposed Treaty of Friendship, Commerce and Navigation with Haiti," dated July 3, 1952, NARA, Record Group 59, Department of State File No. 611.384/7-352.

79. Airgram dated September 11, 1952, from the Department of State to the U.S. embassy in Port-au-Prince, NARA, Record Group 59, Department of State File No. 611.384/8-1252.

80. Despatch dated December 19, 1952, from the U.S. embassy in Port-au-Prince to the Department of State, NARA, Record Group 59, Department of State File No. 611.384/12-1952.

81. Despatch No. 418 dated December 22, 1952, from the U.S. embassy in Port-au-Prince to the Department of State, NARA, Record Group 59, Department of State File No. 611.384/12-2252.

82. Ibid.

83. Ibid.

84. Memorandum by Vernon Setser headed "Results of First Round of FCN Negotiations with Haiti," dated September 1, 1953, NARA, Record Group 59, Department of State File No. 611.384/9-153.

preoccupation with matters before the Haitian Parliament.[85] When negotiations resumed on January 6, 1955, the Haitian negotiators sought to reopen the entire treaty.[86] They explained that the Haitian official who had led the Haitian negotiating team in 1952 had exceeded his authority.[87] The Haitian government was particularly reluctant to agree to national treatment[88] because to do so would be inconsistent with Haitian law and would be politically imprudent.[89]

At the same time, however, the Haitian negotiators indicated that they wished to conclude the treaty quickly so that President Paul Magloire could sign it during a planned visit to the United States later in the month,[90] something he wished to do at least in part because of deteriorating relations between Haiti and the Dominican Republic.[91] With the Haitian president personally interested in the conclusion of a treaty, negotiations proceeded quickly and, by January 26, the two parties had reached agreement.[92]

The United States agreed to two notable modifications of its proposed treaty. One was an exception to national treatment for existing legislation relating to retail trade, and the other was the deletion of the provision guaranteeing nondiscriminatory treatment with respect to religious activities.[93] The United States also agreed to the omission of the competitive equality provision, a change to which it agreed in a number of other treaties.

Nevertheless, the effort to complete the treaty prior to President Magloire's visit to the United States failed, for two reasons. One was that the French translation of the treaty was not ready early enough, and the other was that the State Department wanted more time to reconsider the language relating to

85. Despatch No. 381 dated February 4, 1954, from the U.S. embassy in Port-au-Prince to the Department of State, NARA, Record Group 59, Department of State File No. 611.384/2-454; Memorandum headed "Possible Signature during Visit of President Magliore of Proposed Treaty of Friendship, Commerce and Navigation with Haiti," dated October 8, 1954, NARA, Record Group 59, Department of State File No. 611.384/10-854.

86. Telegram No. 126 dated January 6, 1955, from the U.S. embassy in Port-au-Prince to the Department of State, NARA, Record Group 59, Department of State File No. 611.384/1-655.

87. Despatch No. 249 dated January 6, 1955, from the U.S. embassy in Port-au-Prince to the Department of State, NARA, Record Group 59, Department of State File No. 611.384/1-655.

88. Telegram No. 126 dated January 6, 1955, from the U.S. embassy in Port-au-Prince to the Department of State, NARA, Record Group 59, Department of State File No. 611.384/1-655.

89. Despatch No. 249 dated January 6, 1955, from the U.S. embassy in Port-au-Prince to the Department of State, NARA, Record Group 59, Department of State File No. 611.384/1-655.

90. Ibid.

91. Telegram No. 162 dated January 24, 1955, from the U.S. embassy in Port-au-Prince to the Department of State, NARA, Record Group 59, Department of State File No. 611.384/1-2455.

92. Memorandum to the Secretary of State, headed "Completion of Negotiations and Signature of FCN Treaty with Haiti," dated January 26, 1955, NARA, Record Group 59, Department of State File No. 611.384/1-2655.

93. Ibid.

religious activities.[94] Specifically, language normally guaranteeing the right to hold religious services had been rephrased during negotiations as the right to participate in religious services, a change that the State Department wished to reverse[95] because Secretary of State John Foster Dulles believed that the language to which the U.S. negotiators had agreed "smacked of phraseology which the communists had used."[96] The Haitian foreign minister, however, refused to restore the original language. Rather, he would agree only to the phrase "hold in appropriate places," explaining that he wished to avoid "street corner harangues by religious groups."[97] The State Department objected to the Haitian language because of its concern about how Haiti would interpret the word "appropriate."[98] The U.S. ambassador had a "rather rough meeting" with the Haitian foreign minister, who became "quite irritated" over the issue.[99] The foreign minister nevertheless raised the issue with President Magloire, who refused to agree to the U.S. proposal.[100] At this point, the State Department informed the embassy that it could agree to delete the entire provision on religious activities.[101]

Haiti immediately accepted the U.S. proposal to delete this provision, and the two parties prepared to sign the treaty during a visit to Haiti by Vice President Richard Nixon, scheduled for March 3.[102] Within a couple of days, Vice President Nixon informed the State Department that he wished to sign the treaty personally. President Eisenhower authorized Nixon and the U.S. ambassador to sign jointly and severally,[103] and both signed the treaty on March 3 as scheduled.

Six days after the treaty was signed, State Department officials received telephone calls from a reporter for the Religious News Service, inquiring about the omission

94. Department of State Instruction A-87 dated February 1, 1955, to the U.S. embassy in Port-au-Prince, NARA, Record Group 59, Department of State File No. 611.384/2-155. On the religion clauses generally, *see* Robert R. Wilson, *United States Commercial Treaties and International Law* (New Orleans, LA: Hauser Press, 1960), pages 244–279.

95. Memorandum to the Secretary of State headed "Provisions on Religion in Proposed FCN Treaty with Haiti and Other FCN treaties," dated February 17, 1955, NARA, Record Group 59, Department of State File No. 611/384/2-1755.

96. Memorandum of Conversation headed "FCN Treaty with Haiti," dated February 23, 1955, NARA, Record Group 59, Department of State File No. 611.384/2-2355.

97. Ibid.

98. Ibid.

99. Ibid.

100. Ibid.

101. Ibid.

102. Memorandum of Conversation headed "FCN Treaty with Haiti," dated February 25, 1955, NARA, Record Group 59, Department of State File No. 611.384/2-2555.

103. Telegram No. 136 dated March 2, 1955, from the Department of State to the U.S. embassy in Port-au-Prince, NARA, Record Group 59, Department of State File No. 611.384/3-255.

of the religion clauses from the FCN treaty with Haiti.[104] On July 1, representatives of several Protestant religious organizations met with State Department officials to express their opposition to the treaty.[105] They explained that they believed that the conclusion of a treaty without the religion clauses set a precedent and signaled to other countries that the United States was willing to conclude an FCN treaty without the clauses. Within days, Protestant religious organizations, churches, and individuals began to send the Senate a continuous flood of letters and telegrams opposing Senate advice and consent to ratification. By mid-July, the Senate Foreign Relations Committee had decided, in light of the opposition, to postpone consideration of the treaty until the following year.[106] A year later, in the face of continued opposition, the Committee again decided to postpone consideration of the treaty.[107] Meanwhile, despite the fact that the Haitian Parliament had already approved the treaty, the Haitian ambassador to the United States told the Haitian desk officer at the State Department that he would be just as pleased if the Senate did not approve the treaty because he had become subject to personal criticism in Haiti for his role in negotiating the treaty by some who insisted that the Haitians were "selling their souls" to the United States.[108]

In December 1956, President Magloire lost power and fled Haiti, triggering a period of political chaos. With no regularly constituted government in place with which the treaty could be renegotiated and with the Senate unwilling to consider the treaty in the face of continued Protestant opposition,[109] on July 17, 1957, the State Department recommended to the president that he withdraw the treaty.[110] Six days later, President Eisenhower sent to the Senate a request that the treaty be withdrawn.[111] The Senate returned the treaty to the president, and it never received advice and consent to ratification.

104. Memorandum by Albert H. Gerberich headed "Interest of Press in Religion Clauses of Colombia and Haiti FCN Treaties," dated March 10, 1955, NARA, Record Group 59, Department of State File No. 611.384/3-1055.

105. Memorandum of Conversation headed "Council of Churches Protest over Omission of Religious Clauses from the FCN Treaty with Haiti," dated July 1, 1955, NARA, Record Group 59, Department of State File No. 611.384/7-155.

106. Memorandum by Henry Augustus Hoyt headed "Haitian FCN Treaty," dated July 13, 1955, NARA, Record Group 59, Department of State File No. 611.384/7-1355.

107. Instruction A-171 dated June 29, 1956, from the Department of State to the U.S. embassy in Port-au-Prince, NARA, Record Group 59, Department of State File No. 611.384/6-1556.

108. Memorandum of Conversation headed "Ambassador Zephirin Unenthusiastic about FCN Treaty," dated February 7, 1956, NARA, Record Group 59, Department of State File No. 611.384/2-756.

109. Letter dated August 12, 1957, from Charles W. Adair Jr., to Glenn L. Archer, NARA, Record Group 59, Department of State File No. 611.384/7-3057.

110. Memorandum dated July 17, 1957, from Secretary of State John Foster Dulles to President Dwight D. Eisenhower, NARA, Record Group 59, Department of State File No. 611.384/7-1757.

111. 103 *Congressional Record* 11217 (1957).

NEGOTIATING AN FCN TREATY WITH IRAN

The Truman administration submitted a draft FCN treaty to Iran informally in February 1948, but no negotiations resulted.[112] Two years later, the U.S. embassy believed that the time might be right to make another approach, but again no negotiations occurred,[113] largely because of Iranian objections to the provision requiring national treatment with respect to the right to establish investment.[114]

By summer of 1954, however, circumstances had created inducements for both parties to negotiate a treaty. The Iranian government was seeking increased treaty protection for Iranians living in the United States. In particular, Iran was concerned about Iranian businessmen in the United States who did not have immigration status to remain in the country.[115] U.S. oil companies were seeking greater protection for their investment in Iran,[116] particularly in the wake of the nationalization of the Anglo-Iranian Oil Company in 1951. Although the United Kingdom had suggested that all that would be necessary for the oil companies would be an investment protection treaty, the United States believed that to suggest a treaty limited to investment protection would offend the Iranian government.[117] Rather, the United States wished to propose an FCN treaty that would provide Iranians with improvements in their personal status in the United States, while also protecting U.S. investment in Iran.[118]

Recalling that the Iranian government had paid "scant attention" to the standard draft treaty presented in 1948, the State Department decided to propose a shortened version of the FCN treaty similar to that concluded with Ethiopia in 1951. Notably, the abridged version did not require national treatment with respect to the establishment of investment.[119] The "essential nucleus" of the treaty was the provisions requiring compensation for expropriation and national treatment of American business enterprises once established. The State Department believed that the provision on expropriation combined with the compromissory clause providing for adjudication of disputes by the International Court of Justice "should afford valuable assurances to the American oil companies and other

112. Telegram dated June 4, 1950, from the U.S. embassy in Tehran to the Department of State, NARA, Record Group 59, Department of State File No. 611.884/6-450.

113. Instruction dated June 22, 1954, from the Department of State to the U.S. embassy in Tehran, NARA, Record Group 59, Department of State File No. 611.884/6-2254.

114. Instruction dated July 23, 1954, from the Department of State to the U.S. embassy in Tehran, NARA, Record Group 59, Department of State File No. 611.884/7-2354.

115. Instruction dated June 22, 1954, from the Department of State to the U.S. embassy in Tehran, NARA, Record Group 59, Department of State File No. 611.884/6-2254.

116. Ibid.

117. Ibid.

118. Ibid.

119. Ibid.

American investors."[120] The immediate reaction of the Iranian ambassador when he saw the proposed treaty was that the abridged version "might be much more workable than the extremely detailed version which had been discussed with his Government some years ago."[121]

After reviewing the proposed treaty, the Iranian government was chiefly concerned with certain provisions that would have to be extended to the Soviet Union or other Iron Curtain countries under treaties with those countries granting them MFN treatment.[122] For example, Iran feared that the exchange controls provision would grant certain non-American investments priority in obtaining foreign exchange.[123] The possible extension of treaty benefits to the Soviet Union was not Iran's only concern, however. Iran also bristled at a treaty provision requiring a "modern standard of justice," a provision that did not appear in other U.S. FCN treaties and that could be interpreted as casting aspersions on the Iranian legal system.[124]

Iran soon proposed a number of changes, many of them related to concerns about the Soviet Union and its satellites. Iran feared that economic penetration by such countries could threaten its national independence, a fear that the State Department acknowledged to be legitimate.[125] For example, Iran wanted language in the Preamble indicating that the provisions of the treaty had been agreed on a reciprocal basis. Such language would provide grounds for refusing to extend similar rights to the Soviet Union under an MFN treaty obligation. Iran also proposed limiting treaty protection to privately-owned companies, thereby preventing Soviet enterprises from claiming protection. At the same time, however, Iran wanted a secret exchange of letters deeming all Iranian companies operating within the United States to fall within treaty protection, even if entirely financed by the Iranian government.[126]

120. Instruction dated July 23, 1954, from the Department of State to the U.S. embassy in Tehran, NARA, Record Group 59, Department of State File No. 611.884/7-2354.

121. Memorandum headed "Message of Condolence from the Shah," dated September 8, 1954, NARA, Record Group 59, Department of State File No. 611.884/9-854.

122. Telegram dated September 15, 1954, from the U.S. embassy in Tehran to the Department of State, NARA, Record Group 59, Department of State File No. 611.884/9-1554.

123. Telegram dated October 2, 1954, from the U.S. embassy in Tehran to the Department of State, NARA, Record Group 59, Department of State File No. 611.884/10-254.

124. Telegram dated September 15, 1954, from the U.S. embassy in Tehran to the Department of State, NARA, Record Group 59, Department of State File No. 611.884/9-1554; Despatch dated October 16, 1954, from the U.S. embassy in Tehran to the Department of State, NARA, Record Group 59, Department of State File No. 611.884/10-1654.

125. Statement of Thorsten V. Karlijarvi, *Commercial Treaty with Iran, Nicaragua and The Netherlands,* Hearing Before the Committee on Foreign Relations, July 3, 1956, 84th Cong. 2d Sess.(1956).

126. Despatch dated October 16, 1954, from the U.S. embassy in Tehran to the Department of State, NARA, Record Group 59, Department of State File No. 611.884/10-1654.

Some of Iran's proposed changes were directed not at denying benefits to the Soviet Union but at weakening treaty protection for U.S. nationals and companies. For example, Iran proposed that the prohibition on unreasonable or discriminatory measures be rephrased as a prohibition on unlawful or discriminatory measures. Iran also proposed rephrasing the expropriation provision to eliminate protection for "interests in property," apparently with the goal of excluding U.S. interests in the international oil consortium from treaty protection.[127] Iran had two objections to the provision on exchange controls. First, it wanted to retain sole discretion to determine whether exchange controls were warranted.[128] Second, it did not wish to make foreign exchange available to facilitate "hot money" transfers.[129] Finally, Iran wanted to delete from the compromissory clause language conferring jurisdiction on the Court to decide disputes involving the "application" of the treaty.[130]

The State Department was sympathetic to Iran's concern about MFN treatment, but to accomplish the same goal suggested alternative language referring to reciprocity.[131] The United States also agreed to place the right of entry for traders and investors on an MFN basis, in order to address Iranian concerns about Soviet penetration.[132] Regarding the concern about "hot money," the State Department explained that reasonable restrictions on capital to avoid a serious outflow of "hot money" in the form of scarce foreign exchange would not violate the exchange controls article.[133]

Otherwise, however, the United States largely objected to Iran's proposals. For example, the State Department replied that a secret exchange of letters was out of the question, both on policy grounds and because Article 102 of the U.N. Charter prohibited secret agreements.[134] U.S. negotiators noted that changing "unreasonable" to "unlawful" would destroy the effect of the provision.[135] They said that the expropriation provision was one of the most important in the treaty and that any substantial

127. Ibid.

128. Ibid.

129. Ibid.

130. Ibid.

131. Telegram dated November 1, 1954, from the U.S. embassy in Tehran to the Department of State, NARA, Record Group 59, Department of State File No. 611.884/11-154.

132. Memorandum headed "FCN Treaty with Iran," dated June 14, 1955, NARA, Record Group 59, Department of State File No. 611.884/6-1455.

133. Instruction dated November 10, 1954, from the Department of State to the U.S. embassy in Tehran, NARA, Record Group 59, Department of State File No. 611.884/11-1054; Despatch dated October 16, 1954, from the U.S. embassy in Tehran to the Department of State, NARA, Record Group 59, Department of State File No. 611.884/10-1654.

134. Telegram dated December 18, 1954, from the Department of State to the U.S. embassy in Tehran, NARA, Record Group 59, Department of State File No. 611.884/12-1854.

135. Telegram dated November 13, 1954, from the Department of State to the U.S. embassy in Tehran, NARA, Record Group 59, Department of State File No. 611.884/11-1354.

change would be very difficult for the United States to accept.[136] They noted that indirect investment contributed to Iran's development and thus the treaty should encourage it.[137] They argued that language giving each party sole discretion to determine whether to impose exchange controls was unnecessary because a party's determination would be presumed correct in the first instance, and the U.S. negotiators doubted that a dispute under the provision would arise in any event.[138] They reminded the Iranian negotiators that Iran had agreed on numerous prior occasions to compromissory clauses covering disputes relating to the application of a treaty.[139]

In December, the embassy reported that the Iranian negotiators had been highly receptive to the U.S. comments and had endeavored to accommodate U.S. views wherever possible. The embassy then expressed concern that the Department's negative reaction to so many of Iran's proposals was creating the impression that the United States was prepared to conclude a treaty only on its terms.[140] The Department held firm, however, and ultimately prevailed on each of these investment-related issues. The United States nevertheless did agree to some modifications to its proposed draft. For example, the treaty omits the provision regarding the right to utilize specialized personnel for internal purposes.

The treaty was signed on August 15, 1955.[141] Among its provisions was language terminating a 1928 treaty under which Iranian courts applied U.S. law to certain cases involving U.S. nationals.[142] In this way, the United States surrendered the last vestige of extraterritoriality in Iran.[143] The State Department noted that treaty provisions requiring prompt payment of just compensation for expropriated property and the submission of treaty disputes to the International Court of Justice represented "almost a complete reversal of the Iranian position in the [Anglo-Iranian expropriation] controversy and may repair much of the damage resulting from that dispute."[144]

136. Ibid.

137. Ibid.

138. Telegram dated January 14, 1955, from the Department of State to the U.S. embassy in Tehran, NARA, Record Group 59, Department of State File No. 611.884/1-455.

139. Telegram dated November 12, 1954, from the Department of State to the U.S. embassy in Tehran, NARA, Record Group 59, Department of State File No. 611.884/11-1254.

140. Telegram dated November 27, 1954, from the U.S. embassy in Tehran to the Department of State, NARA, Record Group 59, Department of State File No. 611.884/11-2754; Telegram dated December 17, 1954, from the U.S. embassy in Tehran to the Department of State, NARA, Record Group 59, Department of State File No. 611.884/12-1754.

141. Treaty of Amity, Economic Relations and Consular Rights, entered into force June 16, 1957, 8 UST 899, TIAS 3853, 284 UNTS 93.

142. Iran FCN treaty, Article XXII.

143. Memorandum headed "FCN Treaty with Iran," dated June 14, 1955, NARA, Record Group 59, Department of State File No. 611.884/6-1455.

144. *Current Economic Developments*, June 21, 1955, page 11, NARA, Record Group 59, Department of State Lot Files.

NEGOTIATING AN FCN TREATY WITH NICARAGUA

Truman administration officials at the State Department had a brief discussion during the summer of 1950 with the Nicaraguan embassy concerning the possibility of negotiating an FCN treaty, but no negotiations began at that time.[145] The United States waited another three years before approaching Nicaragua again.

In March 1953, the U.S. embassy in Nicaragua raised the issue and learned that Nicaragua was receptive to commencing negotiations.[146] On April 1, the State Department sent copies of its standard draft treaty to the embassy.[147] On April 28, during a tour of the Atlantic coast of Nicaragua, U.S. ambassador Thomas Whelan discussed the treaty with President Anastasio Somoza, who then directed his minister of economy to expedite negotiations.[148] The FCN treaty negotiations with Nicaragua would prove to be among the least difficult to conclude, no doubt in part because of support for the treaty by President Somoza, who hoped to attract foreign investment to Nicaragua.

On August 24, the Ministry of Economy sent the U.S. embassy a list of proposed changes to the U.S. standard draft treaty. The State Department transmitted to the embassy its comments on the Nicaraguan proposal on October 1.[149] The Department was pleased by the Nicaraguan proposal, which did not suggest any serious disagreement with the U.S. standard draft treaty.[150] Many of the changes proposed by Nicaragua were based on language that appeared in the U.S. FCN treaty with Colombia or Japan. For example, Nicaragua proposed the addition of shipbuilding and public utilities to the list of sectors reserved from national treatment with respect to the right of establishment,[151] a change from the standard draft treaty that was based on the treaty with Japan.

No further discussions occurred until September of the following year, when the Nicaraguan vice minister of the economy traveled to Washington. The vice

145. Memorandum of Conversation headed "Telephone Conversation with Alfredo Sacasa," dated August 1, 1950, NARA, Record Group 59, Department of State File No. 611.174/8-150; Memorandum of Conversation headed "Conversation with Dr. Rene Schick," dated August 31, 1950, NARA, Record Group 59, Department of State File No. 611.174/8-3150; Despatch dated March 16, 1953, from the U.S. embassy in Managua to the Department of State, NARA, Record Group 59, Department of State File No. 611.174/3-1653.

146. Despatch dated March 16, 1953, from the U.S. embassy in Managua to the Department of State, NARA, Record Group 59, Department of State File No. 611.174/3-1653.

147. Despatch dated April 1, 1953, from the Department of State to the U.S. embassy in Managua, NARA, Record Group 59, Department of State File No. 611.174/3-1653.

148. Despatch dated May 6, 1953, from the U.S. embassy in Managua to the Department of State, NARA, Record Group 59, Department of State File No. 611.174/5-653.

149. Instruction dated October 1, 1953, from the Department of State to the U.S. embassy in Managua, NARA, Record Group 59, Department of State File No. 611.174/9-153.

150. Ibid.

151. Nicargua FCN treaty, Article VII(2). *See also* Protocol, Paragraph 6.

minister told the State Department that he had "great enthusiasm" for concluding the treaty because it would constitute "an important part" of Nicaragua's program to attract foreign investment.[152] Indeed, the vice minister proposed retitling the treaty as a treaty of friendship, commerce, and investment protection.[153] The State Department resisted the name change, however, because investment promotion was unpopular in some countries.[154]

By a memorandum dated November 17, 1954, the State Department conveyed to Nicaragua its comments on the proposals made by the vice minister. Nicaragua responded to those comments the following March. In forwarding the memorandum to the State Department, the embassy noted that agreement had been reached on all issues, except Nicaragua's wish for an exception for a regional integration arrangement.[155] The negotiations had resulted in few changes to the investment provisions. One minor change of note was that the right to employ key personnel was qualified by a reservation permitting a party to enforce "laws regarding the nationality of employees, but such laws shall not prevent nationals and companies of the other Party from employing personnel regardless of nationality, who are essential to the conduct of their affairs."[156]

To resolve the issue concerning regional integration agreements, the State Department offered Nicaragua a variation of an approach already utilized in its treaties with Colombia and Germany, under which each party was authorized to terminate MFN obligations in the treaty in the event that it was dissatisfied with a regional integration agreement into which the other party entered.[157] Nicaragua objected to the U.S. approach and offered a counterproposal that narrowed the scope of the reservation, which the United States accepted,[158] thus completing the negotiations.[159]

The treaty was signed on January 21, 1956, at a ceremony at the presidential palace, with President Somoza in attendance as a witness.[160] After the ceremony, President Somoza requested that the pen used to sign the treaty be forwarded

152. Instruction dated November 1, 1954, from the Department of State to the U.S. embassy in Managua, NARA, Record Group 59, Department of State File No. 611.174/11-154.

153. Ibid.

154. Ibid.

155. Despatch dated March 4, 1955, from the U.S. embassy in Managua to the Department of State, NARA, Record Group 59, Department of State File No. 611.174/3-455.

156. Nicaragua FCN treaty, Article VIII(1).

157. Instruction dated March 3, 1955, from the Department of State to the U.S. embassy in Managua, NARA, Record Group 59, Department of State File No. 611.174/3-455.

158. Despatch dated June 22, 1955, from the U.S. embassy in Managua to the Department of State, NARA, Record Group 59, Department of State File No. 611.174/6-2255.

159. Despatch dated July 14, 1955, from the U.S. embassy in Managua to the Department of State, NARA, Record Group 59, Department of State File No. 611.174/7-1455.

160. Treaty of Friendship, Commerce and Navigation, and protocol, entered into force May 24, 1958, 9 UST 449, TIAS 4024, 367 UNTS 3.

to President Eisenhower with his compliments.[161] The embassy reported that the treaty received wide and favorable publicity from both the government and the opposition press.[162]

NEGOTIATING AN FCN TREATY WITH THE NETHERLANDS

The Truman administration proposed the negotiation of an FCN treaty with the Netherlands in 1948. The Dutch government appeared to be interested in negotiating a treaty,[163] but wished to do so in conjunction with the other Benelux countries (Belgium and Luxembourg), and those countries were not yet prepared to negotiate, resulting in continual postponements of further discussions.[164]

By February 1950, the interest of the Netherlands in negotiating a treaty appeared to have diminished greatly.[165] First, the central bank was opposed to the investment provisions, which prevented the formation of a consensus within the government in favor of the treaty. Second, the failure of the United States to achieve greater progress in negotiations with other European countries suggested to the Netherlands that sound reasons existed not to conclude a treaty and that the prudent course would be to wait until the United States had concluded treaties with neighboring countries. Ironically, the State Department believed that the economic conditions and policies prevailing in the Benelux countries made them among the most likely candidates for a successful negotiation and thus it was especially anxious to commence negotiations with the Netherlands.[166]

Dutch business groups, however, began to pressure the government to commence negotiations because they wanted to gain the benefit of the investment provisions and the treaty trader visa provision.[167] As a result, by May of 1950, the Dutch government was showing renewed interest in commencing negotiations.[168]

161. Despatch dated January 24, 1956, from the U.S. embassy in Managua to the Department of State, NARA, Record Group 59, Department of State File No. 611.174/1-2456.

162. Ibid.

163. Memorandum of Conversation headed "Proposed Treaty of Friendship, Commerce and Navigation with the Netherlands—ECA Cooperation in Expediting Initiation of Negotiations," dated March 24, 1950, NARA, Record Group 59, Department of State File No. 611.564/3-2450.

164. Memorandum of Conversation headed "Proposed Treaty of Friendship, Commerce and Navigation with the Netherlands," dated January 4, 1950, NARA, Record Group 59, Department of State File No. 611.564/1-450.

165. Memorandum of Conversation headed "Proposed Treaty of Friendship, Commerce and Navigation with the Netherlands—ECA Cooperation in Expediting Initiation of Negotiations," dated March 24, 1950, NARA, Record Group 59, Department of State File No. 611.564/3-2450.

166. Letter dated March 31, 1950, from R. N. Bissell Jr., to Clarence E. Hunter, NARA, Record Group 59, Department of State File No. 611.564/3-2450.

167. Message dated May 18, 1950, from the U.S. embassy in The Hague to the Department of State, NARA, Record Group 59, Department of State file No. 611.564/3-1850.

168. Ibid.

Coordination with the other Benelux countries remained an obstacle, however. In particular, the Belgian government preferred to delay negotiations until various problems associated with creating the Benelux economic union were resolved. Accordingly, the Netherlands proposed to commence negotiations with the United States and to include in the treaty an escape clause for provisions inconsistent with the Benelux Union,[169] an approach to which Belgium had no objection.[170] The State Department did not wish to press Belgium or Luxembourg "unduly" to negotiate a treaty, and thus was prepared to negotiate with the Netherlands alone and to grant the Netherlands the desired escape clause for Benelux obligations.[171] In August, Belgium reconsidered its decision to delay negotiations and proposed joint negotiations commencing in January,[172] a proposal that was acceptable to the United States despite the fact that it would have delayed negotiations by as much as five months.[173] As it happened, however, the Netherlands preferred to negotiate alone because it believed that its objectives, especially regarding national treatment, were different from Belgium's.[174] By September, the Netherlands and Belgium had agreed to negotiate with the United States separately, recognizing that joint negotiations would have been "hopelessly complicated" and that the Netherlands was prepared to offer national treatment, whereas Belgium was not.[175] The State Department concluded that negotiating with the two countries separately was the best approach under those circumstances.[176] In October Belgium notified the United States that it was not prepared to negotiate an FCN treaty at that time.[177]

The Dutch government became preoccupied with other tasks, including GATT negotiations, and progress toward negotiations was slow. In January 1951, the government formed an interagency working group to prepare for negotiations, assigning the

169. Message dated June 20, 1950, from the U.S. embassy in The Hague to the Department of State, NARA, Record Group 59, Department of State File No. 611.564/6-1250.

170. Message dated July 19, 1950, from the U.S. embassy in The Hague to the Department of State, NARA, Record Group 59, Department of State File No. 611.564/7-1950.

171. Airgram dated August 5, 1950, from the Department of State to the U.S. embassy in The Hague, NARA, Record Group 59, Department of State File No. 611.564/7-1950.

172. Telegram dated August 25,1950, from the U.S. embassy in Brussels to the Department of State, NARA, Record Group 59, Department of State File No. 611.564/8-2550.

173. Telegram dated August 30, 1950, from the Department of State to the U.S. embassy in Brussels, NARA, Record Group 59, Department of State File No. 611.564/8-2550.

174. Telegram dated September 14, 1950, from the U.S. embassy in The Hague to the Department of State, NARA, Record Group 59, Department of State File No. 611.564/9-1450.

175. Telegram dated September 19, 1950, from the U.S. embassy in The Hague to the Department of State, NARA, Record Group 59, Department of State File No. 611.564/9-1950.

176. Airgram dated September 25, 1950, from the Department of State to the U.S. embassy in The Hague, NARA, Record Group 59, Department of State File No. 611.564/9-1950.

177. Despatch No. 369 dated October 11, 1950, from the U.S. embassy in Brussels to the Department of State, NARA, Record Group 59, Department of State File No. 611.554/10-1150.

lead roles to an official of the Ministry of Foreign Affairs and an employee of a subsidiary of Royal Dutch Shell.[178] The working group proved unwieldly, and in November it was reduced to four persons, one of whom was a member of the legal department of Royal Dutch Shell.[179] Progress continued to be slow as the Dutch engaged in extensive interagency discussions and consultations with the other Benelux countries and worried about competition from American businesses and a drain on Dutch dollar reserves following entry into force of the treaty.[180]

By June 1952, prospects for commencement of negotiations had deteriorated. The business community's support for the treaty had weakened because of U.S. refusal to grant national treatment in certain areas, such as with respect to the acquisition of real property. The treaty appeared to offer the Netherlands little that it did not already have, while constraining its own regulatory discretion. Public opinion was critical of the economic policies of the United States, which were perceived as advocating free trade while protecting important areas of the U.S. market.[181]

The State Department responded to these discouraging reports with the observation that Dutch objections merely identified areas that needed to be addressed during negotiations.[182] The standard draft treaty was a basis for discussion, not a "take it or leave it document."[183]

In November, the Truman administration notified the Netherlands that Dutch businesses would no longer be eligible for treaty trader visas. Such visas had been granted since 1948 on a provisional basis because in theory the two countries were about to conclude an FCN treaty, a necessary condition for the issuance of the visas, but the progress of negotiations over the four years since then had been so slow that continued issuance of the visas could no longer be justified.[184]

The decision to deny treaty trader visas to Dutch merchants caught the attention of the Netherlands government, which at that point realized that an FCN treaty would in fact provide something of value that the Netherlands would not otherwise have. Three months later, the Netherlands embassy notified the State Department that it

178. Despatch dated January 11, 1951, from the U.S. embassy in The Hague to the Department of State, NARA, Record Group 59, Department of State File No. 611.564/1-1151.

179. Despatch dated November 20, 1951, from the U.S. embassy in The Hague to the Department of State, NARA, Record Group 59, Department of State File No. 611.564/11-2051.

180. Despatch dated October 15, 1951, from the U.S. embassy in The Hague to the Department of State, NARA, Record Group 59, Department of State File No. 611.564/10-1551; Memorandum of Conversation headed "Proposed Treaty of Friendship, Commerce and Navigation," dated December 6, 1951, NARA, Record Group 59, Department of State File No. 611.564/12-651.

181. Despatch dated June 19, 1952, from the U.S. embassy in The Hague to the Department of State, NARA, Record Group 59, Department of State File No. 611.564.611/6-1952.

182. Airgram dated August 8, 1952, from the Department of State to the U.S. embassy in The Hague, NARA, Record Group 59, Department of State File No. 611.564/6-1952.

183. Ibid.

184. Memorandum of Conversation headed "Termination of 3(6) Treaty Merchant Status for Netherlands Subjects," dated November 17, 1952, NARA, Record Group 59, Department of State File No. 611.564/11-1752.

was prepared to commence negotiations, and inquired whether this would permit resumption of the issuance of treaty trader visas.[185]

The Netherlands government prepared very carefully for the negotiations. The Foreign Ministry compiled 110 pages of comments on the treaty from other agencies and, by May 1953, was sending to the U.S. embassy lengthy and detailed lists of questions as well as several requests to incorporate language from the U.S. FCN treaty with Japan.[186] These comments revealed that Dutch concern about the provision on exchange controls was a major issue, as was a Dutch objection to a provision on restrictive business practices.[187] The Netherlands government also indicated that it would want a provision that applied to actions by the United States that did not violate the treaty, but that nullified or impaired the objectives of the treaty.[188]

Formal negotiations began on July 6, 1954, with a representative of Royal Dutch Shell present on the Netherlands negotiating team.[189] The Shell representative actively participated, at various points making proposals on behalf of the Dutch delegation or objecting to U.S. positions.[190] For example, at one point, he proposed an amended version of the prohibition on unreasonable or discriminatory measures, which the parties discussed at length.[191]

The negotiations revealed at least one of the concerns that lay behind the proposed prohibition on conduct that would nullify or impair the objectives of the treaty. Specifically, the Netherlands sought maximum entry privileges for its nationals and feared that U.S. immigration laws would not provide the degree of entry sought.[192]

185. Memorandum of Conversation dated February 27, 1953, headed "Talks on Treaty of Friendship, Commerce and Navigation between the U.S. and Netherlands," NARA, Record Group 59, Department of State File No. 611.564/2-2753.

186. Airgram dated May 18, 1953, from the Department of State to the U.S. embassy in The Hague, NARA, Record Group 59, Department of State File No. 611.564/5-1853.

187. Memorandum of Conversation dated March 23, 1954, NARA, Record Group 59, Department of State File No. 611.564/3-2554; Despatch dated May 26, 1954, from the U.S. embassy in The Hague to the Department of State, NARA, Record Group 59, Department of State File No. 611.564/5-2654.

188. Aide-Memoire, Enclosure #1 to despatch dated May 26, 1954, from the U.S. embassy in The Hague to the Department of State, NARA, Record Group 59, Department of State File No. 611.564/5-2654.

189. Despatch dated July 28, 1954, from the U.S. embassy in The Hague to the Department of State, NARA, Record Group 59, Department of State File No. 611.564/7-2854.

190. Despatch dated September 14, 1954, from the U.S. embassy in The Hague to the Department of State, NARA, Record Group 59, Department of State File No. 611.564/9-1454; Despatch dated February 17, 1955, from the U.S. embassy in The Hague to the Department of State, NARA, Record Group 59, Department of State File No. 611.564/2-1755.

191. Despatch dated August 3, 1954, from the U.S. embassy in The Hague to the Department of State, NARA, Record Group 59, Department of State File No. 611.654/8-354.

192. Aide-Memoire attached to despatch dated August 3, 1954, from the U.S. embassy in The Hague to the Department of State, NARA, Record Group 59, Department of State File No. 611.564/8-354.

The State Department explained that the treaty trader and treaty investor provisions of the treaties must be construed in conformity with U.S. immigration laws, but assured the Netherlands that any case-by-case determinations would be made in a sympathetic manner and that discretion would be exercised in a way that would further the objectives of the treaty.[193]

The Netherlands also continued to express concern about the breadth of the provision on exchange controls.[194] It wanted language allowing it to address the problem of "hot money" because the situation that occurred in the 1930s could recur.[195] The parties agreed to language at Paragraph 14 of the protocol under which either party "may impose restrictions on the introduction of foreign capital as may be necessary to protect its monetary reserves as provided in Article XII, paragraph 2, or to prevent serious monetary disturbances arising from speculative financial operations." Article XII(2) was the provision permitting imposition of exchange controls during periods of foreign exchange stringency.

The problem of European integration also became an important issue.[196] The United States supported European integration and was willing to exclude the Netherlands' obligations under its European integration arrangements from the MFN treatment provisions, but, unable to foresee the direction that European integration might take in the future, sought the right to terminate its MFN obligations in the event that such integration was contrary to U.S. interests. The Netherlands believed that this remedy was too harsh. It stressed that it must never be treated less favorably than other countries in any integration arrangement to which it belonged.[197] The problem was addressed with an exchange of notes accompanying signature of the treaty that permitted either party to suspend the operation of particular MFN provisions of the treaty "to the extent deemed appropriate to the situation," although the notes stated that it would be the policy of the United States in such a situation to extend to the Netherlands treatment no less favorable than that extended to other countries participating in the arrangement in question.

The Netherlands proposed additional language indicating that the essential security interests exception would be strictly construed so that it would not be abused.[198] The United States concurred that the exception should not be abused,

193. Ibid.

194. Despatch dated August 4, 1954, from the U.S. embassy in The Hague to the Department of State, NARA, Record Group 59, Department of State File No. 611.564/8-454.

195. Despatch dated August 16, 1954, from the U.S. embassy in The Hague to the Department of State, NARA, Record Group 59, Department of State File No. 611.564/8-1654.

196. Despatch dated August 17, 1954, from the U.S. embassy in The Hague to the Department of State, NARA, Record Group 59, Department of State File No. 611.564/8-1754.

197. Despatch dated February 10, 1955, from the U.S. embassy in The Hague to the Department of State, NARA, Record Group 59, Department of State File No. 611.564/2-1055.

198. Despatch dated September 15, 1954, from the U.S. embassy in The Hague to the Department of State, NARA, Record Group 59, Department of State File No. 611.564/9-1554.

but objected to any modification of the language lest it call into question the consistency of existing U.S. laws with the treaty. The United States strongly preferred retention of the existing language. Ultimately, however, it relented and the two parties agreed on the inclusion of a paragraph in the protocol that provided the clarification sought by the Netherlands, balanced by language that the United States proposed in response.[199]

A couple of issues threatened to end the negotiations. The Dutch negotiators were insistent that they could not agree to a provision limiting restrictive business practices, because Dutch competition policy was quite different from the U.S. policy embedded in the provision. Late in the negotiation, however, the United States agreed to delete the provision on restrictive business practices, removing what at the beginning of formal negotiations had been identified as the most serious impediment to completion of the treaty.[200]

The final serious issue arose from Dutch efforts to assist Royal Dutch Shell. The company strongly desired the right to acquire real estate in the United States, which the United States would not grant because some states had enacted laws prohibiting alien ownership of real property, and the State Department did not wish to use the FCN treaties to override those state laws. Indeed, it is highly unlikely that the Senate would have approved a treaty that interfered with state prerogatives regarding alien ownership of real property. In February 1955, with negotiations temporarily halted over the issue, Ernst van der Beugel, an official in the Dutch Ministry of Foreign Affairs, recommended to the Dutch cabinet that it reject the treaty over the refusal of the United States to grant national treatment with respect to the acquisition of real property.[201] The same official suggested an exchange of notes binding those portions of the treaty on which the parties had already agreed, apparently in an effort to obtain visa rights for Dutch merchants and investors, but the U.S. negotiators replied that no visa privileges could be granted without a treaty.[202] Ultimately, the Netherlands recognized that the United States could not accede to the Dutch proposal and withdrew it in March.[203] In May, the Netherlands made a further proposal that sought to accomplish the same goal through the use of a broadly worded MFN treatment obligation, but the State Department rejected that proposal as well.[204] In June,

199. Netherlands FCN treaty, Protocol, Paragraph 18. The protocol language is further discussed in Chapter 8 in the section on the essential security interests exception.

200. Despatch dated December 27, 1954, from the U.S. embassy in The Hague to the Department of State, NARA, Record Group 59, Department of State File no. 611.564/12-2754.

201. Telegram dated February 25, 1955, from the U.S. embassy in The Hague to the Department of State, NARA, Record Group 59, Department of State File No. 611.564/2-2555.

202. Ibid.

203. Despatch dated March 11, 1955, from the U.S. embassy in The Hague to the Department of State, NARA, Record Group 59, Department of State File No. 611.564/3-1155.

204. Instruction dated May 27, 1955, from the Department of State to the U.S. embassy in The Hague, NARA, Record Group 59, Department of State File No. 611.564/5-2755.

the Netherlands finally abandoned its efforts.[205] The Netherlands did persuade the United States to agree to language, at Article IX(5), that granted Dutch-controlled U.S. companies MFN treatment with respect to the acquisition of real property.[206] Apparently convinced that the United States had given all that it could, van der Beugel became an advocate for the treaty, arguing that, because the United States was one of the few countries with capital to invest, the Netherlands should encourage U.S. investment, and noting that the treaty was not a "purely unilateral affair" because the Netherlands had more investment in the United States than the United States had in the Netherlands.[207]

Almost a year later, in March 1956, as the parties prepared to sign the treaty, the Netherlands informed the United States that Belgium wanted the United States to conclude the treaty with the Benelux Union rather than with the Netherlands, although with certain amendments.[208] Belgium explained that it actually wanted the United States to conclude three identical treaties, one with each of the Benelux countries.[209] Belgium was concerned that the conclusion of a treaty between the United States and the Netherlands alone would weaken Belgium's bargaining power in its future negotiations with the United States.[210] Belgium argued that conclusion of treaties with Belgium and Luxembourg similar to the treaty with the Netherlands could be completed quickly, but that once the treaty with the Netherlands was concluded the urgency for Belgium to negotiate would diminish.[211] The Netherlands, however, decided that it wished to conclude the treaty that it had already negotiated,[212] in part to allay growing anti-American sentiment in the Netherlands.[213]

205. Despatch dated June 20, 1955, from the U.S. embassy in The Hague to the Department of State, NARA, Record Group 59, Department of State File No. 611.564/6-2055.

206. Memorandum dated February 7, 1956, from the Deputy Under Secretary of State to the Secretary of State, NARA, Record Group 59, Department of State File No. 611.564/2-756.

207. Despatch dated June 17, 1957, from the U.S. embassy in The Hague to the Department of State, NARA, Record Group 59, Department of State File No. 611.564/6-1757.

208. Telegram dated March 6, 1956, from the U.S. embassy in The Hague to the Department of State, NARA, Record Group 59, Department of State File No. 611.564/3-656.

209. Telegram dated March 7, 1956, from the U.S. embassy in Brussels to the Department of State, NARA, Record Group 59, Department of State File No. 611.564/3-756.

210. Telegram dated March 11, 1956, from the U.S. embassy in Brussels to the Department of State, NARA, Record Group 59, Department of State File No. 611.564/3-1156; Telegram dated March 13, 1956, from the U.S. embassy in Brussels to the Department of State, NARA, Record Group 59, Department of State File No. 611.564/3-1356.

211. Telegram dated March 13, 1956, from the U.S. embassy in Brussels to the Department of State, NARA, Record Group 59, Department of State File No. 611.564/3-1356.

212. Telegram dated March 15, 1956, from the U.S. embassy in The Hague to the Department of State, NARA, Record Group 59. Department of State File No. 611.564/3-1556.

213. Telegram dated March 21, 1956, from the U.S. embassy in The Hague to the Department of State, NARA, Record Group 59, Department of State File No. 611.564/3-2156.

The treaty was signed on March 27, 1956.[214] The Dutch government's press release announcing signature emphasized the availability of treaty trader and treaty investor visas and referred to the investment provisions as "[o]f great importance."[215]

When the treaty went before the States General in the Netherlands, Catholics attacked it because they argued that the religion clause gave American Catholics in the Netherlands greater rights than those possessed by Dutch Catholics.[216] To address that concern, the Netherlands government asked the United States to provide a clarification regarding the meaning of the religion clause, which the United States declined to do, citing a concern that such a clarification might create the impression that the treaty was being modified after it had received Senate approval (which had occurred the prior year) and noting that the religion clause had subjected treaties with other countries to "severe attack" in the past.[217] The Netherlands government actually was pleased by the U.S. response, which avoided creating a public record about the meaning of the provision that would need to be presented to the States General.[218] Ultimately, the Second Chamber of the States General debated the treaty before overflowing galleries, with the debate focusing on freedom of religion under the Dutch Constitution rather than the merits of the treaty, which were not discussed.[219] The treaty was approved by a vote of 120-12. The opposition votes were cast by six communists and six ultra-conservative Protestants. [220] The first chamber approved the treaty on September 3, apparently without controversy.[221]

SENATE ADVICE AND CONSENT TO RATIFICATION 1956

The Senate Foreign Relations Committee heard testimony on the treaties with Iran, Nicaragua, and the Netherlands in executive session on July 3,

214. Treaty of Friendship, Commerce and Navigation, with protocol and exchange of notes, entered into force December 5, 1957, 8 UST 2043, TIAS 3942, 285 UNTS 231.

215. Press release enclosed with despatch dated April 3, 1956, from the U.S. embassy in The Hague to the Department of State, NARA, Record Group 59, Department of State File No. 611.564/4-356.

216. Telegram dated May 7, 1957, from the U.S. embassy in The Hague to the Department of State, NARA, Record Group 59, Department of State File No. 611.564/5-757.

217. Aide-Memoire dated May 13, 1957, NARA, Record Group 59, Department of State File No. 611.564/5-1357.

218. Telegram dated May 16, 1957, from the U.S. embassy in The Hague to the Department of State, NARA, Record Group 59, Department of State File No. 611.564/5-1657.

219. Telegram dated May 15, 1957, from the U.S. embassy in The Hague to the Department of State, NARA, Record Group 59, Department of State File No. 611.564/5-1557.

220. Ibid.

221. Telegram dated September 4, 1957, from the U.S. embassy in The Hague to the Department of State, NARA, Record Group 59, Department of State File No. 611.564/9-457.

1956.[222] Although a treaty with Haiti had been concluded on March 3, 1955, as described above, by the date of the hearings the president had withdrawn that treaty from the Senate. The only witness testifying was Deputy Assistant Secretary of State for Economic Affairs Thorsten Kalijarvi, who was accompanied by Vernon Setser, the chief of the Economic Treaties Branch of the Commercial Policy Staff, and John J. Czyzak, the assistant legal adviser for economic affairs. At the conclusion of the hearing, the Committee voted to recommend Senate advice and consent to ratification of the treaties.[223] In so doing, the Committee urged the State Department to use the comprehensive form of the treaty, rather than the shortened form such as was used with Iran. At the same time, the Committee acknowledged the difficulties attendant to negotiating the longer treaty.[224]

During consideration of the treaties on the Senate floor, Democratic senator Walter F. George of Georgia, the chairman of the Committee on Foreign Relations, placed in the record a statement that the three treaties had received "vigorous support" from American business organizations. His statement also noted that the treaties contained no guarantee of national treatment with respect to the practice of professions and "no innovations which would affect State or Federal legislation."[225] Senator George was asked specifically by Republican senator John W. Bricker of Ohio whether the treaties would "set aside any of our domestic laws."[226] Senator George replied, "No, they will not; not at all." [227] Following that exchange, the Senate gave its advice and consent to ratification of the three treaties by a vote of 88-0.[228]

NEGOTIATING AN FCN TREATY WITH KOREA

On April 26, 1950, two months before the Democratic People's Republic of Korea invaded the Republic of Korea (Korea), Korean president Syngman Rhee expressed to several State Department officials an interest in negotiating an FCN treaty between Korea and the United States.[229] By that time, he had already instructed the Korean embassy in Washington to begin discussions with the Truman administration, and

222. *Commercial Treaties with Iran, Nicaragua and the Netherlands,* Hearing Before the Committee on Foreign Relations, 84th Cong. 2d Sess. (1956).

223. *Commercial Treaties with Iran, Nicaragua and the Netherlands,* Exec. Rept. No. 8, 84th Cong. 2d Sess. (1956), page 2.

224. Ibid., page 7.

225. 102 *Congressional Record* 12287 (1956).

226. Ibid., page 12288.

227. Ibid.

228. Ibid.

229. Memorandum headed "Korean-American Treaty of Friendship and Commerce," dated May 1, 1950, NARA, Record Group 59, Department of State File No. 611.95B4/6-150.

the State Department had sent its embassy in Seoul a copy of the U.S. FCN treaty with Uruguay.[230]

President Rhee said that he wanted the treaty to include an "amity" clause, by which he meant a commitment that either party would come to the aid of the other in the event of aggression by a third party.[231] State Department officials involved in the conversation with President Rhee resolved not to encourage further negotiations at that time, but did decide to prepare a draft that could be used in future negotiations with Korea.

The commencement of war on the Korean peninsula in June 1950 halted any further consideration of an FCN treaty with Korea. In March 1953, with the possibility of a truce looming, the State Department was still unwilling to negotiate a treaty, believing that the commencement of negotiations with Korea would unnecessarily complicate an already difficult political situation. The Department feared that the Korean government would use the negotiations as an opportunity to seek a guarantee of military security.[232] Further, until the war ended, an FCN treaty would not serve its intended effect in any event. [233]

On October 2, 1953, the U.S. embassy reported that President Rhee had again expressed an interest in concluding an FCN treaty with the United States. He believed that the existing treaty between the United States and Korea was obsolete and that the situation on the peninsula had stabilized sufficiently. He also noted the recent signature of an FCN treaty between the United States and Japan.[234] As it happened, the mutual defense treaty sought by Korea had been signed on October 1, thus removing the issue of military defense from the FCN treaty negotiations. On October 14, the Undersecretary of State formally authorized FCN treaty negotiations with Korea.[235] The Department transmitted to the embassy copies of the standard draft treaty and of the recently signed treaty with Japan.[236] With the issue of mutual security no longer pressing, however, Korea lost interest in the treaty, and no further discussions occurred at that time.

More than a year later, in December 1954, U.S. ambassador Ellis O. Briggs mentioned to the Korean foreign minister, Dr. Pyun Yongtee, that the FCN treaty was a pending matter between the two countries. The following day, Dr. Pyun

230. Ibid.

231. Ibid.

232. Despatch dated April 29, 1953, from the U.S. embassy in Pusan to the Department of State, NARA, Record Group 59, Department of State File No. 611.95B4/4-2953.

233. Ibid.

234. Telegram dated October 2, 1953, from the U.S. embassy in Seoul to the Department of State, NARA, Record Group 59, Department of State File No. 611.95B4/10-253.

235. Instruction dated October 19, 1953, from the Department of State to the U.S. embassy in Seoul, NARA, Record Group 59, Department of State File No. 611.95B4/10-1953.

236. Instruction dated October 12, 1953, from the Department of State to the U.S. embassy in Seoul, NARA, Record Group 59, Department of State File No. 611.95B4/10-253.

announced to the press that the United States and Korea were about to commence negotiations.[237]

Dr. Pyun soon informed Ambassador Briggs that Korea was concerned about economic domination by China and Japan.[238] Accordingly, Korea would need to adopt a "safeguard law" that the treaty must accommodate. [239] This would emerge as the most serious problem during negotiations.

On February 18, 1955, the Korean negotiators presented the U.S. negotiators with Korea's proposed draft treaty.[240] When formal negotiations began on February 21, Dr. Pyun told U.S. negotiators that the differences between the Korean and the U.S. draft treaties were based on Korean fears of Chinese and Japanese economic domination. He also said that the treaty with the United States would set the pattern for Korea's other FCN treaties,[241] a point that Korea reiterated later.[242] Particularly noteworthy among the differences was a provision proposed by Korea under which foreigners would be permitted to acquire only a minority interest in Korean companies.[243] Korea also proposed to eliminate the competitive equality provision because it believed that the government needed to play "an active role in the overall program of economic development," including the management of economic enterprises, and that the government could not afford to grant aliens the same privileges that it may give to public enterprises.[244] The State Department instructed the embassy that the principal purpose of the treaty was to encourage foreign investment and that the limitation to minority interests was therefore unacceptable.[245] Although it found the Korean desire to delete the competitive equality provision to be regrettable, the State Department ultimately would accept that change, as it did in several other treaties. A few days

237. Memorandum to the Secretary of State headed "Korean Ambassador's Visit with You This Afternoon," dated January 7, 1955, NARA, Record Group 59, Department of State File No. 611.95B4/1-755.

238. Telegram dated January 8, 1955, from the U.S. embassy in Seoul to the Department of State, NARA, Record Group 59, Department of State File No. 611.95B4/1-855.

239. Ibid.

240. Telegram dated February 18, 1955, from the U.S. embassy in Seoul to the Department of State, NARA, Record Group 59, Department of State File No. 611.95B4/2-1855.

241. Telegram dated February 22, 1955, from the U.S. embassy in Seoul to the Department of State, NARA, Record Group 59, Department of State File No. 611.95B4/2-2255.

242. Despatch dated February 28, 1955, from the U.S. embassy in Seoul to the Department of State, NARA, Record Group 59, Department of State File No. 611.95B4/2-2855.

243. Telegram dated February 23, 1955, from the Department of State to the U.S. embassy in Seoul, NARA, Record Group 59, Department of State File No. 611.95B4/2-1855.

244. Despatch dated February 28, 1955, from the U.S. embassy in Seoul to the Department of State, NARA, Record Group 59, Department of State File No. 611.95B4/2-2855.

245. Telegram dated February 23, 1955, from the Department of State to the U.S. embassy in Seoul, NARA, Record Group 59, Department of State File No. 611.95B4/2-1855.

later, the U.S. embassy in Seoul sent the Department a detailed explanation of Korea's departures from the U.S. draft.[246]

Over a period from March 28 to April 14, 1955, the embassy transmitted to the Korean government a series of four memoranda commenting on Korea's proposed changes to the U.S. draft.[247] Negotiations halted while Korean officials attempted to reach a consensus on how to respond to the U.S. comments.[248]

Meanwhile, the embassy reported on May 11 that President Rhee had become concerned about the slow progress of the negotiations. He was "very disturbed" by the fact that no treaty had yet been signed, a fact that he attributed to U.S. recalcitrance and a lack of desire to conclude a treaty with Korea.[249] President Rhee apparently feared that failure to conclude the treaty could jeopardize congressional approval of economic assistance to Korea.[250]

The delay in negotiations was relatively brief. By June 3, the State Department had agreed to accept a half-dozen of Korea's proposed changes, while Korea withdrew about 10 proposed changes as a result of the U.S. comments and suggested compromises on several other points.[251] The new U.S. ambassador, William S. B. Lacy, who had arrived only in March, recommended that the United States make one final "take it or leave it" offer, believing that this could have the effect of bringing the negotiations to an immediate successful conclusion.[252] The State Department rejected the recommendation, however, because it thought that negotiations were progressing "reasonably well" and that the parties should continue to negotiate as they had been.[253]

By this time, only a few differences between the parties remained. The treaty contained a denial of benefits provision under which companies of a party that were controlled by third-country nationals could be denied treaty protection, and Korea wanted the provision expanded so that it would apply if third-country nationals owned any stock at all in the company, permitting Korea to deny treaty protection to any company in which Japanese or Chinese investors had an interest.[254] The United States responded that it would be impossible to determine

246. Despatch dated February 28, 1955, from the U.S. embassy in Seoul to the Department of State, NARA, Record Group 59, Department of State File No. 611.95B4/2-2855.

247. Despatch dated May 11, 1955, from the U.S. embassy in Seoul to the Department of State, NARA, Record Group 59, Department of State File No. 611.95B4/5-1155.

248. Ibid.

249. Ibid.

250. Ibid.

251. Telegram dated June 3, 1955, from the U.S. embassy in Seoul to the Department of State, NARA, Record Group 59, Department of State File No. 611.95B4/6-355.

252. Ibid.

253. Memorandum headed "Status of FCN Treaty Negotiations with ROK," dated June 13, 1955, NARA, Record Group 59, Department of State File No. 611.95B4/6-1355.

254. Telegram dated September 6, 1955, from the U.S. embassy in Seoul to the Department of State, NARA, Record Group 59, Department of State File No. 611.95B4/9-655.

whether a single share of stock was owned by a third-country national.[255] Further, a significant portion of the stock of most of the larger American corporations was owned by aliens, which would deprive many U.S. companies of treaty protection.[256] Even substituting "significant interest" for "controlling interest" would not be an improvement, given the uncertain meaning of the term "significant."[257]

Korea also wanted the exchange rate applicable to transfers between the territories of the parties to be determined by agreement of the parties. The United States successfully resisted inclusion of any such language, fearing that, if it were included, U.S. investors would put "a good deal of pressure" on the State Department to negotiate a more favorable rate for each transfer.[258] Further, Korea could delay transfers merely by failing to reach agreement with the United States regarding the applicable rate.[259]

Korea wished to limit the right of foreign nationals to establish companies in Korea, although not to operate branches. The United States found this distinction illogical, particularly given that most countries actually preferred foreign subsidiaries over foreign branches because of the greater control over a company organized under host state law.[260]

Korea wished to add insurance to the list of excepted sectors. The State Department anticipated that this change would induce a "spirited reaction" from the U.S. insurance industry[261] and feared that opposition by the insurance industry could prevent Senate approval of the treaty.[262] The Department noted that, in any event, the presence of U.S. insurance companies in Korea would promote investment by other U.S. companies and contribute to the general development of the insurance industry in Korea.[263] Korea also wanted to add financial services to the list of excepted sectors. The United States responded that many activities performed by U.S. banks, such as investment banking, trade financing, and dealing in foreign exchange, would be beneficial to the Korean economy.[264]

255. Memorandum headed "Status of FCN Treaty Negotiations with ROK," dated June 13, 1955, NARA, Record Group 59, Department of State File No. 611.95B4/6-1355.

256. Instruction dated June 21, 1955, from the Department of State to the U.S. embassy in Seoul, NARA, Record Group 59, Department of State File No. 611.95B4/6-1655.

257. Ibid.

258. Memorandum headed "Status of FCN Treaty Negotiations with ROK," dated June 13, 1955, NARA, Record Group 59, Department of State File No. 611.95B4/6-1355.

259. Instruction dated June 21, 1955, from the Department of State to the U.S. embassy in Seoul, NARA, Record Group 59, Department of State File No. 611.95B4/6-1655.

260. Ibid.

261. Memorandum headed "Status of FCN Treaty Negotiations with ROK," dated June 13, 1955, NARA, Record Group 59, Department of State File No. 611.95B4/6-1355.

262. Instruction dated June 21, 1955, from the Department of State to the U.S. embassy in Seoul, NARA, Record Group 59, Department of State File No. 611.95B4/6-1655.

263. Ibid.

264. Ibid.

The Korean negotiators continued to express concern about economic penetration by Chinese and Japanese business interests, to such an extent that the embassy informed the Department in July that Korea might yield on all other issues if the United States would yield on that one issue and that, if the United States did not yield, conclusion of the treaty would not be possible.[265] Assistant Secretary of Commerce for International Affairs Marshall Smith objected to yielding on the issue,[266] asking why the United States "was in such haste" to conclude a treaty with a government that it was "virtually supporting" even while that government refused to promise non-discriminatory treatment.[267] Smith believed that yielding on the issue would set a bad precedent. The State Department replied that the United States had already permitted screening of foreign investment in treaties with Ethiopia, Iran, and Pakistan and that the treaty should not be lost over this one issue, recalling how the treaty with Haiti was lost over the religion clause.[268] State Department officials noted that Korea's position was not different from that of most of the newly independent countries in Asia, which feared colonialism and economic domination by the West.[269] They did not believe it to be good policy to take the position that other countries were "obliged" to accept foreign investment, particularly when the United States itself restricted foreign investment in some sectors of the economy.[270] Negotiations were suspended while the State and Commerce Departments debated the issue.[271]

By the end of September, the State Department's patience with the Commerce Department's objection was nearly exhausted. As it happened, however, Assistant Secretary Smith had left his position, and State Department officials decided to raise the issue with his successor. If the successor adopted Smith's position, then at least some State Department officials were prepared to authorize the embassy to accept the Korean proposal despite the objections from the Commerce Department.[272] In December, however, the Commerce Department

265. Telegram dated July 7, 1955, from the U.S. embassy in Seoul to the Department of State, NARA, Record Group 59, Department of State File No. 611.95B4/7-755.

266. Memorandum dated July 28, 1955, from Vernon Setser to Thorsten Kalijarvi, NARA, Record Group 59, Department of State File No. 611.95B4/7-2855.

267. Notes dated July 13, 1955, on Telephone Conversation between Marshall Smith and Thorsten Kalijarvi, NARA, Record Group 59, Department of State File No. 611.95B4/7-1355.

268. Ibid.

269. Memorandum headed "Commerce Department's Position Regarding the FCN Treaty Negotiation with Korea," dated August 15, 1955, NARA, Record Group 59, Department of State File No. 611.95B4/8-1555.

270. Ibid.

271. Instruction dated September 1, 1955, from the Department of State to the U.S. embassy in Seoul, NARA, Record Group 59, Department of State File No. 611.95B4/9-155.

272. Memorandum headed "Status of FCN," dated September 28, 1955, NARA, Record Group 59, Department of State File No. 611.95B4/9-2855.

relented and, after a five-month delay, the two parties were again able to resume negotiations.[273]

The United States agreed to permit Korea to exclude majority foreign ownership of Korean companies.[274] To avoid drawing attention to the exclusion of U.S. investment in the insurance and banking sectors, as Korea had proposed, the State Department suggested that the right to national treatment with respect to engaging in activities be limited to trade and manufacturing, thereby excluding insurance and banking without specifically identifying them.[275] The United States remained unable to agree, however, to Korea's proposed change in the denial of benefits provision because denying treaty protection to a company in which third-country nationals had an interest would deprive many publicly traded U.S. companies of the benefit of the treaty. The Department noted, for example, that the General Motors Corporation as a publicly traded company would be denied treaty protection, whereas the Ford Motor Company, the stock of which was held by members of the Ford family, would not. [276]

When negotiations resumed in February 1956, the United States learned that its concessions were not enough. Korea wanted to expand the denial of benefits provision to permit benefits to be denied to individuals acting on behalf of a third-country company or national.[277] The State Department said that the additional language relating to the denial of benefits provision was unnecessary, but offered to include a paragraph in the protocol clarifying that a party was not obligated to permit admission to its territory of nationals of the other party to conduct business as representatives of third countries or nationals or companies thereof in contravention of generally applicable laws.[278] The same paragraph of the protocol also would permit either party to deny benefits to a company controlled by a third country.

Korea also wanted to retain the right to screen investment in every field so as to ensure that foreign investment would not compete with domestic investment.[279] In addition, Korea wanted to add to its treaty Paragraph 6 of the protocol to the treaty with Japan, which permitted a party to impose restrictions on

273. Memorandum headed "Resumption of FCN Treaty Negotiations with Korea," dated January 19, 1956, NARA, Record Group 59, Department of State File No. 611.95B4/1-1956.

274. Instruction dated January 26, 1956, from the Department of State to the U.S. embassy in Seoul, NARA, Record Group 59, Department of State File No. 611.95B4/1-2656.

275. Ibid.

276. Ibid.

277. Despatch dated March 2, 1956, from the U.S. embassy in Seoul to the Department of State, NARA, Record Group 59. Department of State File No. 611.95B4/3-2256.

278. Telegram dated April 24, 1956, from the Department of State to the U.S. embassy in Seoul, NARA, Record Group 59, Department of State File No. 611.95B4/4-2056. The language appears at Paragraph 9.

279. Telegram dated February 14, 1956, the Department of State to the U.S. embassy in Seoul, NARA, Record Group 59, Department of State File No. 611.95B4/2-1456.

the introduction of foreign capital to protect its monetary reserves. The embassy predicted that, if the United States refused, the Korean government would characterize the refusal as a demonstration of American favoritism toward Japan over Korea.[280] Although Paragraph 6 was intended to allow a party to exclude short-term, speculative investments, the embassy believed that Korea intended to use it to exclude any investment that it did not wish to permit.[281]

The United States countered that it would agree to include Paragraph 6 from the treaty with Japan only if Korea would accept the original language of Article VII, which granted national and MFN treatment with respect to the right to engage in gainful activities and conferred the right to establish and control subsidiaries and branches, except that transport and public utilities could be added to the list of reserved activities, a concession that the United States had made earlier in the negotiations.[282] Korea replied that it would agree to the original language of Article VII (as amended by the exclusion of public utilities and transport) and accept the language proposed by the United States regarding denial of benefits, provided that the United States would agree to a proposed memorandum explaining Paragraph 6.[283] The State Department regarded the proposed memorandum, however, as essentially allowing Korea to screen all investment under the guise of protecting its monetary reserves.[284] The Department feared that the memorandum would be used to weaken the protocol language in other treaties where it appeared, and believed that, if screening were to be permitted, it should be done under a provision explicitly allowing screening rather than under the pretext of protecting monetary reserves.[285] The Department nevertheless decided that, rather than rejecting the Korean proposal, it would suggest modifications to the language of the memorandum that would enable it to accept the Korean proposal.[286] In particular, the State Department wanted to ensure that any exclusion of investment under the protocol language be "demonstrably related" to

280. Despatch dated March 2, 1956, from the U.S. embassy in Seoul to the Department of State, NARA, Record Group 59. Department of State File No. 611.95B4/3-2256.

281. Ibid.

282. Telegram dated March 30, 1956, from the Department of State to the U.S. embassy in Seoul, NARA, Record Group 59, Department of State File No. 611.95B4/3-256; Telegram dated April 17, 1956, from the Department of State to the U.S. embassy in Seoul, NARA, Record Group 59, Department of State File No. 611.95B4/4-1756.

283. Telegram dated May 31, 1956, from the U.S. embassy in Seoul to the Department of State, NARA, Record Group 59, Department of State File No. 611.95B4/5-3156; Telegram dated July 16, 1956, from the U.S. embassy in Seoul to the Department of State, NARA, Record Group 59, Department of State File No. 611.95B4/7-1656.

284. Memorandum dated June 14, 1956, headed "Status of FCN Treaty with Korea," NARA, Record Group 59, Department of State File No. 611.95B4/6-1456.

285. Telegram dated July 27, 1956, from the Department of State to the U.S. embassy in Seoul, NARA, Record Group 59, Department of State File No. 511.95B4/7-1656.

286. Ibid.

the protection of monetary reserves.[287] Korea agreed to the U.S. revision of the memorandum with one minor change, which the United States accepted, thereby apparently completing the negotiations.[288]

Meanwhile, upon further review, the State Department realized that various bits of clarifying language regarding the scope of Article VII needed to be added to the treaty.[289] The Korean negotiators strongly objected, noting the embarrassment at having to explain to others within the government why a treaty that had been concluded was now being reopened.[290] The State Department explained that the need for the clarifications had not been evident before because the scope of Article VII had been uncertain.[291] The U.S. negotiators said that they would be satisfied with a letter confirming that Article VII did not apply to the practice of professions, and the addition of a definition of the term public utilities to the protocol,[292] both of which were acceptable to Korea.[293] The result of this exchange, however, was that the United States did not obtain language limiting the transportation exception to air and water transport, and thus land transportation was excluded from the coverage of Article VII.[294] Further problems arose when congressional legislation enacted on August 1 necessitated a change in a provision on social security benefits.[295] After reviewing a copy of the legislation, the Korean negotiators accepted the change.[296]

The treaty was signed on November 28, 1956.[297] At the signing ceremony, Korean foreign minister Dr. Chung W. Cho noted the historical significance of

287. Telegram dated August 3, 1956, from the Department of State to the U.S. embassy in Seoul, NARA, Record Group 59, Department of State File No. 511.95B4/8-356.

288. Telegram dated August 10, 1956, from the Department of State to the U.S. embassy in Seoul, NARA, Record Group 59, Department of State File No. 511.95B4/8-956.

289. Ibid.

290. Telegram dated August 20, 1956, from the U.S. embassy in Seoul to the Department of State, NARA, Record Group 59, Department of State File No. 611.95B4/8-2056.

291. Telegram dated August 21, 1956, from the Department of State to the U.S. embassy in Seoul, NARA, Record Group 59, Department of State File No. 511.95B4/8-2056.

292. Ibid. The definition appears at Paragraph 5.

293. Letter dated August 24, 1956, from Edwin H. Cronk to William C. Ockey, NARA, Record Group 59, Department of State File No. 611.95B4/8-2456.

294. Memorandum to the Secretary of State dated October 29, 1956, NARA, Record Group 59, Department of State File No. 611.95B4/10-2956.

295. Telegram dated August 29, 1956, from the Department of State to the U.S. embassy in Seoul, NARA, Record Group 59, Department of State File No. 511.95B4/8-2956.

296. Telegram dated October 4, 1956, from the U.S. embassy in Seoul to the Department of State, NARA, Record Group 59, Department of State File No. 611.95B4/10-456.

297. Treaty of Friendship, Commerce and Navigation, with protocol, entered into force November 7, 1957, 8 UST 2217, TIAS 3947, 302 UNTS 281.

FCN treaties between the United States and Korea. He referred to Korea as formerly a "Hermit Kingdom" and noted that the 1882 FCN treaty between Korea and the United States was the first treaty that Korea had signed with a Western power.[298] He said that Korea had ended its tradition of isolation by signing the treaty because "she reposed a high trust in America" and then noted that, "[a]fter 36 years of foreign subjugation, it was America again that responded to our call for help."[299]

The Committee on Foreign Relations held hearings on the treaty on July 1, 1957, and received testimony from Deputy Assistant Secretary of State for Economic Affairs Thorsten Kalijarvi, who was accompanied by Charles H. Sullivan of the Trade Agreements and Treaties Division, which by 1955 was the name of the office responsible for negotiating FCN treaties. No other witness asked to be heard, and no communications favorable or unfavorable to the treaty were received by the Committee.[300] On August 8, 1957, after being assured that there was "no conflict between the treaty and State or Federal laws of the United States," the Senate gave its advice and consent to the treaty by a vote of 86-0.[301]

NEGOTIATING AN FCN TREATY WITH THE SULTANATE OF MUSCAT AND OMAN

The first FCN treaty concluded by the Eisenhower administration that did not originate with initial discussions between the other party and the Truman administration was the treaty with the sultanate of Muscat and Oman. The negotiations with the sultanate were triggered in the summer of 1956 by the desire of the Eisenhower administration to re-establish a consulate in Muscat. The sultan of Muscat and Oman, Said bin Taimur, replied that he would approve the consulate only if the United States agreed to renegotiate an existing 1833 FCN treaty.[302] The sultan wished to renegotiate the treaty because it limited his ability to impose customs duties on imports and granted extraterritorial rights to Americans in the sultanate.[303]

298. Despatch dated November 29, 1956, from the U.S. embassy in Seoul to the Department of State, NARA, Record Group 59, Department of State File No. 611.95B4/11-2956.

299. Ibid.

300. *Treaty of Friendship, Commerce and Navigation between the United States of America and the Republic of Korea*, Exec. Rept. No. 5, 85th Cong. 1st Sess. (1957), page 2.

301. 103 *Congressional Record* 13998 (1957).

302. Memorandum headed "Treaty of Friendship, Commerce and Navigation with Muscat," dated July 17, 1956, NARA, Record Group 59, Department of State File No. 611.86E1/7-1756.

303. Telegram dated June 25, 1957, from the U.S. consulate general in Dhahran to the Department of State, NARA, Record Group 59, Department of State File No. 611.86E4/6-2557; Despatch dated June 28, 1957, from the U.S. consulate general in Dhahran to the Department of State, NARA, Record Group 59, Department of State File No. 611.86E4/6-2857.

In 1951, the United Kingdom had negotiated a treaty that preserved British extraterritorial rights in the sultanate, and the State Department faced the issue of whether to seek the same treatment. It decided not to do so. By 1956, the United States had already concluded treaties with China, Ethiopia, and Iran that surrendered extraterritorial rights. In authorizing the commencement of negotiations, Assistant Secretary of State for Near Eastern, South Asian, and African Affairs George V. Allen placed a handwritten note on the authorization memorandum stating, "It's too late in the day for us to be renewing capitulatory rights anywhere. We'll be tarred by the brush of British imperialism by Nasser and everyone else. Muscat will have to modernize its courts. Once we got capitulations, we'd have the devil's own time getting the Senate ever to give them up."[304]

By the end of August 1956, the State Department had prepared a draft treaty of amity and economic relations that terminated U.S. extraterritorial rights in the sultanate.[305] Some within the Department complained that the treaty seemed "excessively long and complex."[306] The treaty, however, was similar to that negotiated with Iran, except that it guaranteed national treatment with respect to the establishment of commercial and manufacturing enterprises. Further, the proposed draft had received interagency clearance. Obtaining clearance of a different draft would have entailed considerable delay. Finally, those who favored the draft noted that any rights not gained in this treaty might not be obtainable in the future.[307] Thus, the Department decided not to revise the draft.

Despite the concern about delay, the State Department was not prepared to commence negotiations until June 1957, when it designated Walter K. Schwinn, the consul general at Dhahran, as the U.S. negotiator.[308] By then, the sultan had already expressed multiple times his eagerness to start the long-delayed negotiations.[309]

Schwinn's first audience with the sultan occurred on June 22, 1957. The sultan complained that the U.S. draft was "much too long and complicated."[310] He preferred a simple, general treaty that could be supplemented with specific

304. Memorandum headed "Treaty of Friendship, Commerce and Navigation with Muscat," dated July 17, 1956, NARA, Record Group 59, Department of State File No. 611.86E1/7-1756.

305. Memorandum dated August 29, 1956, from A. David Fritzlan to Fraser Wilkins, NARA, Record Group 59, Department of State File No. 611.86E1/8-2956.

306. Memorandum dated September 12, 1956, from David Newsom to Fraser Wilkins, NARA, Record Group 59, Department of State File No. 611.86E1/9-1256.

307. Ibid.

308. Memorandum headed "Credentials for the Negotiators of a Treaty with Muscat," dated June 8, 1957, NARA, Record Group 59, Department of State File No. 611.86E1/6-857.

309. Telegram dated May 20, 1957, from the U.S. consulate general in Dhahran to the Department of State, NARA, Record Group 59, Department of State File No. 611.86E1/5-2057.

310. Telegram dated June 25, 1957, from the U.S. consulate general in Dhahran to the Department of State, NARA, Record Group 59, Department of State File No. 611.86E4/6-2557; Despatch dated June 28, 1957, from the U.S. consulate general in Dhahran to the Department of State, NARA, Record Group 59, Department of State File No. 611.86E4/6-2857.

agreements with individual investors. He did not want to create a precedent by granting the United States more than he had granted other countries, and he did not want the treaty to restrict his legislative prerogatives.[311]

The first audience established the pattern for subsequent negotiations. The sultan, who had studied law in Bombay (without completing the program) and spoke excellent English, negotiated the treaty personally, unattended.[312] He typically brought no papers or notes to the negotiating sessions.[313] Even the foreign minister played no apparent role in the preparation or conduct of the negotiations.[314] Schwinn reported that the sultan generally did not consult his advisors, few of whom he trusted, and that the sultan governed "singlehandedly."[315] Schwinn noted that the sultan exercised absolute power and handled even trivial details of government, such as personally signing each entry visa.[316]

During a second round of negotiations in September, which had been postponed from July because of a rebellion within the country,[317] the sultan raised objections to the requirement of compensation for expropriation; the guarantee of national treatment, particularly with respect to manufacturing, which he did not wish to bring to the sultanate;[318] the compromissory clause; and the duration of the treaty. [319] He noted that the provision on exchange controls was meaningless in the case of the sultanate because the sultanate did not have its own currency.[320] The sultan assured Schwinn, however, that his mind was open about the specific provisions of the treaty.[321]

311. Telegram dated June 25, 1957, from the U.S. consulate general in Dhahran to the Department of State, NARA, Record Group 59, Department of State File No. 611.86E4/6-2557.

312. Despatch dated June 28, 1957, from the U.S. consulate general in Dhahran to the Department of State, NARA, Record Group 59, Department of State File No. 611.86E4/6-2857.

313. Despatch dated March 5, 1958, from the U.S. consulate general in Dhahran to the Department of State, NARA, Record Group 59, Department of State File No. 611.86E4/3-558.

314. Telegram dated September 29, 1957, from the U.S. consulate general in Dhahran to the Department of State, NARA, Record Group 59, Department of State File No. 611.86E4/9-2957.

315. Despatch dated June 28, 1957, from the U.S. consulate general in Dhahran to the Department of State, NARA, Record Group 59, Department of State File No. 611.86E4/6-2857.

316. Telegram dated June 25, 1957, from the U.S. consulate general in Dhahran to the Department of State, NARA, Record Group 59, Department of State File No. 611.86E4/6-2557.

317. Telegram dated July 30, 1957, from the U.S. consulate general in Dhahran to the Department of State, NARA, Record Group 59, Department of State File No. 611.86E4/7-3057.

318. Despatch dated October 2, 1957, from the U.S. consulate general in Dhahran to the Department of State, NARA, Record Group 59, Department of State File No. 611.86E4/10-257.

319. Telegram dated September 29, 1957, from the U.S. consulate general in Dhahran to the Department of State, NARA, Record Group 59, Department of State File No. 611.86E4/9-2957.

320. Despatch dated October 2, 1957, from the U.S. consulate general in Dhahran to the Department of State, NARA, Record Group 59, Department of State File No. 611.86E4/10-257.

321. Telegram dated September 29, 1957, from the U.S. consulate general in Dhahran to the Department of State, NARA, Record Group 59, Department of State File No. 611.86E4/9-2957.

U.S. bargaining power during the negotiations was particularly limited. Although the sultan wished to eliminate a limitation on customs duties imposed by the 1833 treaty, trade with the United States was so small that the revenue involved was negligible. The sultan also wished to eliminate U.S. extraterritorial rights, but few Americans resided in the sultanate and they were well behaved, giving no occasion for the assertion of extraterritorial rights. In any event, without a consulate, no one with the authority to exercise the extraterritorial rights was in the sultanate.[322] The sultan recognized his superior bargaining power, noting that the United States needed the treaty more than he did because of the U.S. desire to reopen its consulate. [323]

In an effort to demonstrate the value of the treaty to the sultanate, the State Department instructed Schwinn to emphasize that U.S. investors would want to have treaty protection before investing in the sultanate, but the sultan was unpersuaded by this argument. He believed that, if oil was discovered in the sultanate, U.S. investors would invest even without a treaty.[324] Indeed, Saudi Arabia was doing quite well without a treaty.[325] If oil was not discovered, then no amount of treaty assurances would attract U.S investment. The paucity of U.S. investment in the sultanate up to that point buttressed this argument.[326] The sultan noted that he was not seeking to encourage foreign investors to invest and that, if they did not like the investment climate, they did not have to come.[327] If oil was discovered, then he would consider at that time a provision on expropriation, but, until then, the benefit of such a provision was not worth the limit on his freedom.[328]

Further, few of his subjects had dealings with or in the United States, and those who did were already receiving satisfactory treatment from the United States.[329] At one point, when Schwinn noted that certain provisions of the treaty protected against arbitrary and capricious treatment, the sultan responded, "Yes, but you never do such things, so why should I worry?"[330]

The sultan was averse to committing himself to anything that would limit his power of absolute rule until some specific benefit to himself and his subjects was demonstrated, nor did he wish to undertake commitments that might interfere with his application of sharia law.[331] The sultan was particularly concerned about

322. Despatch dated October 2, 1957, from the U.S. consulate general in Dhahran to the Department of State, NARA, Record Group 59, Department of State File No. 611.86E4/10-257.

323. Ibid.

324. Ibid.

325. Ibid.

326. Ibid.

327. Ibid.

328. Ibid.

329. Ibid.

330. Ibid.

331. Ibid.

a complex agreement, the language of which might have hidden meanings that he could not discern when agreeing to the language.[332] Finally, he recognized that any commitments that he made might be claimed by third countries under MFN treatment provisions in their treaties with the sultanate.[333]

The sultan was especially adamant about not accepting the compromissory clause. Any form of dispute settlement involving a third party was equally objectionable. He believed that it was wrong to enter into a treaty with the assumption that disputes would arise and that, if a dispute did arise that could not be resolved between the parties, they should terminate the treaty.[334] He also proposed that the treaty's initial term be 7 rather than 10 years because events were moving quickly and, in 7 years, the treaty might well need to be revised, and he might be inclined to agree to more at that point.[335]

By March 1958, the parties had reached agreement on everything except the compromissory clause.[336] The United States agreed to exclude manufacturing (but not commercial activity) from the obligation of national treatment with respect to establishment, given that manufacturing in Muscat was likely to be minimal and foreign,[337] and it agreed to the seven-year term for the treaty.[338] The sultan agreed to the prompt payment of just and effective compensation for expropriated property[339] and to an abbreviated provision on exchange controls that permitted such controls when "shortages of foreign exchange may require" and that prohibited the application of exchange controls in a manner that would influence disadvantageously the competitive position of the commerce, transport, or investments of the other party in comparison with the commerce, transport, or investments of any third country.[340]

No progress was made with respect to the compromissory clause. The sultan knew little about the International Court of Justice, and he was unwilling to permit a third party to interfere in matters he considered his responsibility.[341] His

332. Ibid.

333. Ibid.

334. Ibid.

335. Ibid.

336. Despatch dated March 5, 1958, from the U.S. consulate general in Dhahran to the Department of State, NARA, Record Group 59, Department of State File No. 611.86E4/3-558.

337. Instruction A-30 dated November 27, 1957, from the Department of State to the U.S. consulate general in Dhahran, NARA, Record Group 59, Department of State File No. 611.86E4/10-257.

338. Ibid.

339. Muscat and Oman FCN treaty, Article IV(2).

340. Ibid., Article IX.

341. Despatch dated March 5, 1958, from the U.S. consulate general in Dhahran to the Department of State, NARA, Record Group 59, Department of State File No. 611.86E4/3-558;

resistance to third-party dispute resolution also stemmed from dissatisfaction with the result of the arbitration of a dispute with Saudi Arabia over the Buraimi Oasis.[342] The sultan continued to suggest that, in the event of a dispute that could not be resolved bilaterally, the parties should simply terminate the treaty. This approach would create an inducement for the parties to reach a settlement.[343]

The sultan had been cordial throughout the negotiations. On the final day of the negotiations, he set up a tripod and, using a camera with a timer, he took photographs of himself with the U.S. negotiators at the negotiating table.[344] The sultan also requested military and economic assistance as well as technical assistance under Point Four.[345]

Within a few weeks of the end of the final round of negotiations, the State Department decided to capitulate on the compromissory clause. The Department was persuaded that the sultan would never agree to it, and decided that a treaty without the clause would still provide more protection for Americans than they currently had. A treaty to curb capricious exercises of power was especially important with a country governed by an absolute ruler. Signing the treaty would also permit reopening the consulate. The Department believed that the circumstances of the sultanate were such that omission of the compromissory clause would not set a precedent applicable to other treaties.[346]

On May 7, final agreement was reached.[347] The sultan then departed for an extended visit to London, requiring that signature be postponed for a time. The treaty eventually was signed on December 28, 1958.[348]

Signature of the treaty elicited criticism from some in the region who disputed the sultan's authority outside the city of Muscat and thus objected to any reference to Oman in the treaty. From Damascus, the imam of Oman accused

Telegram dated March 3, 1958, from the U.S. consulate general in Dhahran to the Department of State, NARA, Record Group 59, Department of State File No. 611.86E4/3-358.

342. *Treaty of Amity, Economic Relations and Consular Rights with the Sultan of Muscat and Oman*, Exec. Rept. No. 1, 86th Cong. 1st Sess. (1959), page 3.

343. Despatch dated March 5, 1958, from the U.S. consulate general in Dhahran to the Department of State, NARA, Record Group 59, Department of State File No. 611.86E4/3-558; Telegram dated March 3, 1958, from the U.S. consulate general in Dhahran to the Department of State, NARA, Record Group 59, Department of State File No. 611.86E4/3-358.

344. Despatch dated March 4, 1958, from the U.S. consulate general in Dhahran to the Department of State, NARA, Record Group 59, Department of State File No. 611.86E4/3-558.

345. Ibid.; Despatch dated March 6, 1958, from the U.S. consulate general in Dhahran to the Department of State, NARA, Record Group 59, Department of State File No. 611.86E4/3-658.

346. Memorandum dated March 24, 1958, headed "Compromissory Clause in Treaty with Muscat," NARA, Record Group 59, Department of State File No. 611.86E4/3-2158.

347. Telegram dated May 12, 1958, from the U.S. consulate in Aden to the Department of State, NARA, Record Group 59, Department of State File No. 611.86E41/5-1258.

348. Treaty of Amity, Economic Relations and Consular Rights, and protocol, entered into force June 11, 1960, 11 UST 1835, TIAS 4530, 380 UNTS 181.

the United States of violating the U.N. Charter and interfering in the internal affairs of Oman.[349] The government of Saudi Arabia, which had been supporting Omani rebel forces seeking to oust the sultan, accused the United States of supporting British aggression against the Kingdom of Saudi Arabia.[350] The Saudi protest, however, appeared to be largely for the record.[351] The United States responded that the term "Muscat and Oman" had been used since the beginning of the twentieth century as the way to designate the sultan's realm, that the United States had used that designation in its 1833 FCN treaty with the sultanate, and that the new treaty did not reflect a change in U.S. policy with respect to the area.[352] The Saudi government accepted the U.S. response as an assurance that the treaty did not imply any U.S. position on boundary disputes in the region, and the embassy anticipated that the Saudi government would abandon its protest.[353]

The only U.S. business interest with a "direct interest" in the sultanate was a subsidiary of Cities Service Company engaged in oil exploration.[354] In addition, certain U.S. petroleum companies held interests in the Iraq Petroleum Company, which had "a rather extensive concession" in the sultanate.[355] The NFTC, because of the small amount of U.S. investment in the sultanate, decided neither to support nor to oppose the treaty, but urged that it not be treated as a precedent for future FCN treaties because of its omission of several provisions typically found in the standard draft FCN treaty.[356] On May 4, 1959, Cities Service Company wrote to the chairman of the Senate Foreign Relations Committee, Democratic senator J. William Fulbright of Arkansas, noted that it was engaged in oil drilling in Dhofar; and urged that the Senate give expedited consideration to the treaty.[357]

The Committee on Foreign Relations held hearings on the treaty on April 9, 1959, during which it heard testimony from Deputy Assistant Secretary of

349. Despatch dated March 4, 1959, from the U.S. consulate general in Dhahran to the Department of State, NARA, Record Group 59, Department of State File No. 611.86E4/3-459.

350. Telegram dated April 18, 1959, from the U.S. embassy in Jidda to the Department of State, NARA, Record Group 59, Department of State File No. 611.86E4/4-1859.

351. Ibid.

352. Instruction dated May 21, 1959, from the Department of State to the U.S. embassy in Jidda, NARA, Record Group 59, Department of State File No. 611.86E4/5-2159.

353. Despatch dated June 9, 1959, from the U.S. embassy in Jidda to the Department of State, NARA, Record Group 59, Department of State File No. 611.86E4/6-959.

354. Senate Foreign Relations Committee Staff Memorandum dated April 6, 1959, NARA, Record Group 46, File No. SEN86B-B7.

355. Statement of Charles H. Sullivan, Transcript of Hearing Before Committee on Foreign Relations, April 7, 1959, NARA, Record Group 46, File No. SEN86B-B7.

356. Letter dated April 6, 1959, from William S. Swingle to Senator J.W. Fulbright, NARA, Record Group 46, File No. SEN86B-B7.

357. Letter dated May 4, 1959, from Marvin B. Weaver to Senator J.W. Fulbright, NARA, Record Group 46, File No. SEN86B-B7.

State for Economic Affairs W. T. M. Beale,[358] who was accompanied by Charles H. Sullivan of the Division of Commercial Policy and Treaties (at that point the name of the office responsible for negotiating FCN treaties) and David D. Newsom, the officer in charge of the State Department's Office of Arabian Peninsula Affairs. That same date, taking note that the sultanate "may be rich in oil" and that the Soviet Union was seeking to gain influence in the Arab world, the Committee recommended Senate advice and consent to ratification.[359] The Senate considered the treaty on April 28, 1959, at which time Senator Fulbright alluded to the controversy over the extent of the sultan's authority over areas beyond the city of Muscat.[360] Following his remarks on the subject, the Senate gave its advice and consent to the treaty by a vote of 89-0.[361]

The new U.S. consul was appointed in March 1959, a month before the Senate took action on the treaty.[362] He was received by the sultan on May 6, a little more than a week after the Senate gave its advice and consent. Because of administrative problems involved in establishing the consulate in Muscat, a city of only about 5,000 inhabitants, the State Department decided that the consul would reside for a time in Aden.[363] Indeed, because of the extreme heat in Muscat, the lack of suitable facilities, and inadequate public utilities, the State Department long had anticipated that the consul would reside elsewhere.[364]

NEGOTIATING AN FCN TREATY WITH PAKISTAN

Pakistan was yet another country that the Truman administration approached in 1950 to inquire about negotiating an FCN treaty. The Pakistani government spent several months giving "a very careful scrutiny" to the draft proposed by the United States.[365] As part of this process, the Pakistani government, on November 8, 1950, gave the embassy a counterdraft that proposed a number of changes to the U.S. standard draft treaty. By December, Pakistani officials had informed the U.S. embassy that it was unwilling to guarantee national treatment

358. *Treaty of Amity, Economic Relations and Consular Rights with the Sultan of Muscat and Oman*, Exec. Rept. No. 1, 86th Cong. 1st Sess. (1959), page 1.

359. Ibid., page 3.

360. 105 *Congressional Record* 16914 (1959).

361. Ibid., page 16915.

362. Enclosure 1 to despatch dated May 15, 1959, from the U.S. consulate in Aden to the Department of State, NARA, Record Group 59, Department of State File No. 611.86E4/5-1559.

363. Despatch dated May 15, 1959, from the U.S. consulate in Aden to the Department of State, NARA, Record Group 59, Department of State File No. 611.86E4/5-1559.

364. Memorandum dated February 22, 1958, from Stuart W. Rockwell, NARA, Record Group 59, Department of State File No. 611.86E1/2-2258.

365. Despatch dated October 4, 1950, from the Department of State to the U.S. embassy in Karachi, NARA, Record Group 59, Department of State File No. 611.90D4/10-450.

to U.S. nationals and companies because that would constitute preferential treatment, inasmuch as Pakistan had not guaranteed more than MFN treatment to any other country.[366] Further, Pakistan feared economic exploitation by large foreign companies.[367] That said, Pakistan would welcome foreign enterprises in some fields, notably manufacturing.[368]

In September 1951, Vernon Setser traveled to Karachi to conduct exploratory discussions and to prepare for formal negotiations. The Pakistani negotiators continued to resist national treatment with respect to entry. They suggested that the United States compile a list of activities with respect to which national treatment was sought, to which the U.S. negotiators replied that Pakistan should prepare a list of activities with respect to which Pakistan was unprepared to grant national treatment.[369] Pakistan wished in particular to subsidize inefficient local businesses so that they could compete with foreign enterprises.[370] The Pakistani minister of commerce explained that Pakistan wished to "spoon feed" Pakistani industry, but not healthy American enterprises.[371] Pakistan also wanted to encourage the employment of Pakistanis in high managerial positions, and wanted foreign enterprises to hire Pakistanis in cases where they had equal qualifications.[372] Finally, the Pakistani negotiators noted that the provision on exchange controls did not reflect the Pakistani situation because Pakistan had no dollar reserves and earned very few dollars.[373]

The U.S. negotiators replied that omitting national treatment with respect to engaging in commercial activity as Pakistan had proposed would be unacceptable to the United States. Apart from the practical difficulty of distinguishing commercial from industrial activity, the State Department said that such an omission would invite opposition from business groups that would probably result in rejection of the treaty.[374]

366. Despatch dated December 4, 1950, from the U.S. embassy in Karachi to the Department of State, NARA, Record Group 59, Department of State File No. 611.90D4/12-450.

367. Memorandum of Conversation dated September 5, 1951, NARA, Record Group 59, Department of State File No. 611.90D4/9-1451.

368. Ibid.

369. Memorandum of Conversation dated September 11, 1951, NARA, Record Group 59, Department of State File No. 611.90D4/9-1451.

370. Ibid.

371. Memorandum of Conversation dated September 12, 1951, NARA, Record Group 59, Department of State File No. 611.90D4/9-1451.

372. Memorandum of Conversation dated September 7, 1951, NARA, Record Group 59, Department of State File No. 611.90D4/9-1451.

373. Memorandum of Conversation dated September 10, 1951, NARA, Record Group 59, Department of State File No. 611.90D4/9-1451.

374. Memorandum of Conversation dated September 8, 1951, NARA, Record Group 59, Department of State File No. 611.90D4/9-1451.

The discussions halted following Setser's visit because of the impasse over national treatment. A year later, in September 1952, the embassy sent the State Department a telegram stating that the embassy believed that an opportunity existed to conclude a treaty within the next few weeks, but that the embassy needed a list of all changes to the standard draft treaty made during negotiations with India.[375] The Department replied that the United States had agreed, in the negotiations with India, to delete the provision on national treatment with respect to entry as well as the provisions on commerce and navigation, so that the treaty was limited to matters of establishment and investment.[376] The treaty with India, however, was not near conclusion (and never would be concluded). In any event, the embassy's optimism was misplaced and no further negotiations occurred in 1952.

In April 1953, Mohammed Ali Bogra, then serving as Pakistan's ambassador to the United States, was recalled to Pakistan and appointed prime minister. He promptly told a *New York Times* reporter that Pakistan intended to begin FCN treaty negotiations with the United States the following month.[377] In response, the State Department immediately forwarded the latest version of the standard draft treaty to the embassy.[378] Again, however, the optimism was misplaced. The new prime minister heard rumors that his appointment had been dictated by the United States as a condition of Pakistan's receiving a wheat loan. The fact that some believed the rumors dictated that he move cautiously.[379]

More than a year later, in September 1954, the Pakistani government notified the United States that a visit by the prime minister to the United States would be an excellent opportunity to conclude the treaty.[380] Pakistan informed the United States of the changes that it sought in the treaty, including those to preserve its discretion to exclude aliens from engaging in business, a discretion that Pakistan wanted because it feared the entry of Japanese businesses.[381] Pakistan also wished to remove language in the protocol protecting indirectly held interests against uncompensated expropriation, fearing that Pakistanis would use it as a means of obtaining compensation

375. Telegram dated September 20, 1952, from the U.S. embassy in Karachi to the Department of State, NARA, Record Group 59, Department of State File No. 611.90D4/9-2052.

376. Telegram dated September 22, 1952, from the Department of State to the U.S. embassy in Karachi, NARA, Record Group 59, Department of State File No. 611.90D4/9-2052.

377. Telegram dated April 28, 1953, from the U.S. embassy in Karachi to the Department of State, NARA, Record Group 59, Department of State File No. 611.90D4/4-2853.

378. Ibid.

379. Telegram dated May 9, 1953, from the U.S. embassy in Karachi to the Department of State, NARA, Record Group 59, Department of State File No. 611.90D4/5-953.

380. Telegram dated September 16, 1954, from the Department of State to the U.S. embassy in Karachi, NARA, Record Group 59, Department of State File No. 611.90D4/9-1654.

381. Despatch dated September 20, 1954, from the U.S. embassy in Karachi to the Department of State, NARA, Record Group 59, Department of State File No. 611.90D4/9-2054.

from Pakistan.[382] The State Department accepted most of the Pakistani proposals in substance and believed that conclusion of the treaty was possible.[383]

Once more, the Department was too optimistic. Before the month had ended, a former minister of commerce denounced the proposed treaty, saying that it would result in the colonization of Pakistan by the United States.[384] These remarks triggered more criticism of the treaty in the press.[385] The prime minister began to reconsider his plan to sign the treaty while in the United States.[386] The embassy suggested that, in view of growing political instability in Pakistan, the treaty should be concluded quickly.[387]

The two parties worked diligently to resolve their remaining differences. The Pakistani negotiators noted that Pakistan intended to conclude more FCN treaties, using the foundation laid in the treaty with the United States, and thus Pakistan was unwilling to make commitments to the United States unless it was prepared to make the same commitments to other countries.[388] It did not appear, however, that any pending issue would prevent conclusion of the treaty. When an impasse was reached over a navigation-related issued, the United States proposed deleting the provisions on navigation,[389] a proposal to which Pakistan agreed, resulting in the retitling of the treaty as one of friendship and commerce. Similarly, when Pakistan was unwilling to guarantee that foreign banks would be permitted to operate branches for international operations, the United States agreed to omit the sentence conferring such a guarantee.[390] By February 1955, the negotiations had been completed.[391]

382. Ibid.

383. Telegram dated October 1, 1954, from the Department of State to the U.S. embassy in Karachi, NARA, Record Group 59, Department of State File No. 611.90D4/9-2054.

384. Telegram dated September 24, 1954, from the U.S. embassy in Karachi to the Department of State, NARA, Record Group 59, Department of State File No. 611.90D4/9-2454.

385. Ibid.; Despatch dated September 25, 1954, from the U.S. embassy in Karachi to the Department of State, NARA, Record Group 59, Department of File State No. 611.90D4/9-2554.

386. Telegram dated October 8, 1954, from the Department of State to the U.S. embassy in Karachi, NARA, Record Group 59, Department of State File No. 611.90D4/9-2054.

387. Telegram dated October 9, 1954, from the U.S. embassy in Karachi to the Department of State, NARA, Record Group 59, Department of State File No. 611.90D4/10-954.

388. Telegram dated December 7, 1954, from the U.S. embassy in Karachi to the Department of State, NARA, Record Group 59, Department of State File No. 611.90D4/12-754.

389. Telegram dated December 17, 1954, from the Department of State to the U.S. embassy in Karachi, NARA, Record Group 59, Department of State File No. 611.90D4/12-1454.

390. Telegram dated February 2, 1955, from the U.S. embassy in Karachi to the Department of State, NARA, Record Group 59, Department of State File No. 611.90D4/2-255.

391. Telegram dated February 21, 1955, from the U.S. embassy in Karachi to the Department of State, NARA, Record Group 59, Department of State File No. 611.90D4/2-2155.

Then new problems arose. The treaty required approval by the Pakistani cabinet, which was preoccupied with the budget and political problems.[392] In July, the cabinet decided that, because Pakistan had recently adhered to a pact with Iraq and Turkey, consideration of the FCN treaty should be postponed. The Pakistani government explained that to approve both treaties at about the same time would be "an excessive dose of vitamin pills."[393] Some cabinet members believed that Pakistan should not push an alignment toward the West too fast given Pakistan's internal political problems.[394]

The postponement was costly. A month after the cabinet decided to postpone consideration, Prime Minister Bogra left office. The new prime minister, Chaudhry Mohammed Ali, objected to the national treatment provision of the treaty, casting doubt on whether the treaty would be signed.[395] He explained that signing a treaty granting the United States national treatment would stimulate anti-American sentiment in Pakistan, thereby damaging relations between the two countries; would make it more difficult for Pakistan to continue to extend the national treatment that it already provided in practice; and would create problems for his government in the forthcoming elections.[396] Signature of the treaty would need to be postponed until after the election.[397] The State Department notified the embassy that removal of the national treatment obligation was not acceptable.[398] If it were removed, Pakistan would still gain national treatment because of the MFN provision of the treaty, but the United States would not.[399]

Elections in September brought a new government to power, and the State Department believed that the change in government might create an opportunity to conclude the treaty.[400] Once more, the Department was overly optimistic.

392. Telegram dated March 25, 1955, from the U.S. embassy in Karachi to the Department of State, NARA, Record Group 59, Department of State File No. 611.90D4/3-2555.

393. Telegram dated July 1, 1955, from the U.S. embassy in Karachi to the Department of State, NARA, Record Group 59, Department of State File No. 611.90D4/7-155.

394. Telegram dated July 23, 1955, from the U.S. embassy in Karachi to the Department of State, NARA, Record Group 59, Department of State File No. 611.90D4/7-2355.

395. Telegram dated April 2, 1956, from the U.S. embassy in Karachi to the Department of State, NARA, Record Group 59, Department of State File No. 611.90D4/4-256; Telegram dated May 18, 1956, from the U.S. embassy in Karachi to the Department of State, NARA, Record Group 59, Department of State File No. 611.90D4/5-1856.

396. Telegram dated June 25, 1956, from the U.S. embassy in Karachi to the Department of State, NARA, Record Group 59, Department of State File No. 611.90D4/6-2556.

397. Ibid.

398. Telegram dated April 25, 1956, from the Department of State to the U.S. embassy in Karachi, NARA, Record Group 59, Department of State File No. 611.90D4/4-2556.

399. Ibid.; Instruction dated July 5, 1956, from the Department of State to the U.S. embassy in Karachi, NARA, Record Group 59, Department of State File No. 611.90D4/7-556.

400. Memorandum headed "U.S.-Pakistan FCN Treaty—subject for discussion with Finance Minister at Sept. 27 meeting," dated September 25, 1956, and NARA, Record Group 59, Department of State File No. 611.90D4/9-2656.

The new government proposed a reservation that would allow exceptions to national treatment to promote the economic interests of a party's nationals or companies.[401] The State Department rejected Pakistan's proposal and instructed the embassy that, if Pakistan could not accept a national treatment obligation, then the treaty would need to wait until Pakistan recognized the benefits of the treaty.[402]

Meanwhile, a growing dispute with India over the province of Kashmir caused the Pakistani government to seek closer ties to the United States. The prime minister believed that the treaty could be promoted within Pakistan as a way of gaining U.S. support for Pakistan.[403] At the very moment, however, that the prime minister began to demonstrate an interest in promoting the treaty, the embassy developed doubts. The embassy commented to the State Department that the treaty was unlikely to stimulate foreign investment in Pakistan, but could embarrass the government and arouse charges that the United States was seeking to dominate Pakistan.[404] The Department, for its part, was disturbed by the report that the prime minister wished to promote the treaty as a way of creating closer ties to the United States. The Department told the embassy that it would be "especially undesirable to urge acceptance of the treaty by Pakistan as a public gesture to the United States . . . or, in any sense, as a reward for U.S. cooperation with or assistance for Pakistan."[405] The Department also did not wish that the treaty be pressed in a manner that would embarrass the Pakistani government.[406] Rather, the Department explained, it had proposed a treaty only after receiving high level assurances that the proposal would be welcome. The Department had never sought a "dominating position" for American interests in Pakistan, as borne out by the modifications to the proposed treaty made during negotiations.[407] If the embassy believed that further discussion of the treaty was likely to become an irritant in relations between the two countries, then it should not pursue the matter further.[408]

A breakthrough came in August 1958 when the Pakistani government signaled that it could accept the language on national treatment from the U.S. FCN treaty

401. Despatch dated October 5, 1956, from the U.S. embassy in Karachi to the Department of State, NARA, Record Group 59, Department of State File No. 611.90D4/10-556.

402. Telegram dated November 6, 1956, from the Department of State to the U.S. embassy in Karachi, NARA, Record Group 59, Department of State File No. 611.90D4/11-556.

403. Telegram dated February 10, 1957, from the U.S. embassy in Karachi to the Department of State, NARA, Record Group 59, Department of State File No. 611.90D4/2-1057.

404. Despatch dated April 20, 1957, from the U.S. embassy in Karachi to the Department of State, NARA, Record Group 59, Department of State File No. 611.90D4/4-2057.

405. Instruction dated May 8, 1957, from the Department of State to the U.S. embassy in Karachi, NARA, Record Group 59, Department of State File No. 611.90D4/4-2057.

406. Ibid.

407. Ibid.

408. Ibid.

with Iran in place of the language then in the draft treaty with Pakistan.[409] That language required national treatment of enterprises for gain once established, but only MFN treatment with respect to the right of establishment.[410] National treatment would be guaranteed with respect to engaging in scientific, educational, religious, and philanthropic activities[411] and with respect to the acquisition of personal property (which would include interests in companies).[412] The United States immediately accepted the Pakistani proposal, but by then both parties had minor changes that they wanted to make to the text to which they had previously agreed. Sensing an opportunity finally to conclude the treaty, both parties appeared motivated to resolve the new issues. Further, in October, a military coup brought to power a new government that wanted to strengthen the private sector and thus supported the treaty.[413]

Months passed as the parties continued to raise and resolve minor issues. A year after the coup, Minister of Commerce (and future prime minister) Zulfikar Ali Bhutto announced that he would be traveling to the United States and hoped to sign the treaty during his visit.[414] Pakistani officials worked hard to reach an agreement so that Bhutto could sign it in Washington. The embassy warned the State Department that, if the treaty was not signed during the Bhutto visit, new problems could arise.[415] The necessary approvals were obtained, allowing Bhutto and Secretary of State Christian Herter to sign the treaty on November 12, 1959.[416]

NEGOTIATING AN FCN TREATY WITH FRANCE

The Roosevelt administration engaged in FCN treaty negotiations with France prior to the war, and these negotiations were resumed after liberation. They were suspended in 1948, however, because French fears about competing with U.S. business precluded agreement on the investment protection provisions of the treaty.[417]

409. Airgram dated August 5, 1958, from the U.S. embassy in Karachi to the Department of State, NARA, Record Group 59, Department of State File No. 611.90D4/8-558.

410. Pakistan FCN treaty, Article VII.

411. Ibid., Article VIII(2).

412. Ibid., Article IX(3).

413. Despatch dated April 2, 1959, from the U.S. embassy in Karachi to the Department of State, NARA, Record Group 59, Department of State File No. 611.90D4/4-259.

414. Telegram dated October 12, 1959, from the U.S. embassy in Karachi to the Department of State, NARA, Record Group 59, Department of State File No. 611.90D4/10-1259.

415. Despatch dated October 23, 1959, from the U.S. embassy in Karachi to the Department of State, NARA, Record Group 59, Department of State File No. 611.90D4/10-2359.

416. Treaty of Friendship and Commerce, and protocol, entered into force February 12, 1961, 12 UST 110, TIAS 4683, 404 UNTS 259.

417. Memorandum headed "Proposed FCN Treaty with France," dated February 21, 1950, NARA, Record Group 59, Department of State File No. 611.514/2-2150; Memorandum headed

In June 1953, the French government made inquiries about the treaty.[418] Any further discussions at that time ended in September 1953, when Ambassador Douglas Dillon, who would later serve as secretary of the treasury during the Kennedy and Johnson administrations, sent a lengthy telegram to the State Department opposing the negotiation of an FCN treaty.[419] Ambassador Dillon argued that the treaty would accord U.S. nationals and capital in France no more rights than they already enjoyed. Neither would the French gain any additional benefits in the United States. The absence of a treaty did not constitute a significant barrier to U.S. investment in France. At the same time, submission of the treaty to the French Parliament would provoke attacks upon further entry of U.S. capital into France, threatening the favorable treatment already enjoyed by U.S. businesses and perhaps undermining other U.S. diplomatic objectives in France. The treaty would be opposed by communist and socialist members of Parliament and by spokesmen for French business interests concerned about U.S. competition, and its ultimate approval would not be assured. Even if the treaty were approved, the debate would damage the investment climate and thus defeat one of the principal objectives of the treaty. The treaty admittedly would have the effect of inhibiting French modification of the existing favorable investment climate, but Ambassador Dillon believed that, if the French government abandoned its favorable attitude toward U.S. investment, the essential premise on which the treaty was based would have been removed anyway.

Despite the embassy's view that the treaty would be of little benefit to U.S. business and that negotiations might actually harm the investment climate, the American Chamber of Commerce periodically approached the embassy to urge conclusion of a treaty, which the Chamber regarded as "highly desirable" and believed "could not help but increase American investments in France."[420] In 1958, after the Chamber of Commerce approached the French government about the negotiation of a treaty, the French government raised the issue with the embassy. By this time, Dillon was no longer the ambassador and Herman Walker, who had previously served as one of the principal negotiators of FCN treaties,

"Draft FCN Treaty Proposed by Department as Basis for Possible Negotiation with France," dated June 8, 1953, NARA, Record Group 59, Department of State File No. 611.514/6-853; Memorandum of Conversation dated October 29, 1958, headed "FCN Treaty Negotiation between US and France," NARA, Record Group 59, Department of State File No. 611.514/10-2958.

418. Memorandum headed "Draft FCN Treaty Proposed by Department as Basis for Possible Negotiation with France," dated June 8, 1953, NARA, Record Group 59, Department of State File No. 611.514/6-853.

419. Despatch dated September 30, 1953, from the U.S. embassy in Paris to the Department of State, NARA, Record Group 59, Department of State File No. 611.514/9-3053.

420. Despatch dated August 5, 1957, from the U.S. embassy in Paris to the Department of State, NARA, Record Group 59, Department of State File No. 611.514/8-557; Memorandum of Conversation dated October 29, 1958, headed "FCN Treaty Negotiation between US and France," NARA, Record Group 59, Department of State File No. 611.514/10-2958.

was serving as first secretary of the embassy, which meant that the embassy was well staffed to conduct the negotiations.[421] Walker believed that the successful negotiation of FCN treaties with other European countries, particularly Belgium, would improve the probability of a successful negotiation with France.[422]

In January 1959, the French ambassador to the United States met with Dillon who, by then, was serving as undersecretary of state, to propose resumption of negotiations.[423] The French government had observed that the rate of U.S. investment in the other Common Market countries that had concluded FCN treaties with the United States was higher than in France, which did not have a treaty with the United States.[424] The French were also motivated by the insistence of the American business community upon the conclusion of a treaty.[425]

Ironically, while the negotiations in 1948 had failed because of French objections to the investment provisions, the French now proposed to conclude a treaty that omitted many of the provisions not directly related to investment in order to expedite the negotiation.[426] The embassy preferred to negotiate a complete treaty because it saw the treaty as a comprehensive charter for general economic relations, but believed that an exception should be made because the investment provisions were of vital importance, trade was governed by the GATT, and the United States had already agreed to omit trade provisions from other FCN treaties.[427] Undersecretary Dillon told the French ambassador that the United States preferred a complete treaty, but would be flexible about the French desire to omit certain articles.[428] The embassy asked for authorization to tell the French government that the United States was prepared immediately to omit all of the commercial articles because trying

421. Memorandum of Conversation headed "FCN Treaty Negotiation between US and France," dated October 29, 1958, NARA, Record Group 59, Department of State File No. 611.514/10-2958.

422. Despatch dated August 5, 1957, from the U.S. embassy in Paris to the Department of State, NARA, Record Group 59, Department of State File No. 611.514/8-557.

423. Memorandum of Conversation dated January 13, 1959, NARA, Record Group 59, Department of State File No. 611.514/1-1359.

424. Memorandum dated January 12, 1959, from W. T. M. Beale to Douglas Dillon, NARA, Record Group 59, Department of State File No. 611.514/1-1259.

425. Ibid.

426. Memorandum of Conversation dated January 13, 1959, NARA, Record Group 59, Department of State File No. 611.514/1-1359; Telegram dated January 14, 1959, from the Department of State to the U.S. embassy in Paris, NARA, Record Group 59, Department of State File No. 611.514/1-1459.

427. Memorandum dated January 12, 1959, from W. T. M. Beale to Douglas Dillon, NARA, Record Group 59, Department of State File No. 611.514/1-1259.

428. Telegram dated January 14, 1959, from the Department of State to the U.S. embassy in Paris, NARA, Record Group 59, Department of State File No. 611.514/1-1459.

to negotiate them if France was reluctant to do so would serve no purpose.[429] The State Department concurred.[430] As a result, the treaty was retitled as a "Convention on Establishment and Navigation."[431] Near the end of the negotiations, the parties would also delete the navigation provisions because of their inability to reach agreement on those provisions, resulting in a "Convention on Establishment."[432]

In March, France produced a counterdraft that was "strikingly similar" to the U.S. standard draft treaty.[433] The French counterdraft, however, largely omitted the MFN treatment obligation in places where, in the U.S. draft, it appeared in tandem with national treatment.[434] The French negotiators explained that MFN treatment obligations could conflict with France's commitments under the Rome treaty. The French counterdraft added the production of electricity to the sectors in which the parties reserved the right to deny national treatment with respect to establishment, and omitted the provision on competitive equality. It also omitted treaty protection of nonprofit organizations and thus defined "company" to include only entities organized for profit.[435] Finally, it did not contain the language that appeared in the standard draft treaty requiring national and MFN treatment with respect to taking enterprises into public ownership or placing them under public control.

Formal negotiations began on March 19, 1959. The U.S. negotiators accepted the French counterdraft as the basis for negotiations. Although the ultimate success of the negotiations never appeared in doubt, the negotiators needed to resolve numerous issues. For example, France used work permits to control foreign workers whereas the United States used visas, and this difference in approach necessitated finding language that provided equivalent benefits to both countries. One of the French negotiators conceded that access to a country as large and rich as the United States meant more than American access to a country the size of France.[436] The problem was solved with a joint declaration, annexed to the treaty, stating that the two parties had "the intention of facilitating, to the greatest extent possible and on a basis of real and effective reciprocity," the establishment of nationals

429. Telegram dated January 15, 1959, from the U.S. embassy in Paris to the Department of State, NARA, Record Group 59, Department of State File No. 611.514/1-1559.

430. Ibid.

431. Despatch dated May 20, 1959, from the U.S. embassy in Paris to the Department of State, NARA, Record Group 59, Department of State File No. 611.514/5-2059.

432. Despatch dated July 15, 1959, from the U.S. embassy in Paris to the Department of State, NARA, Record Group 59, Department of State File No. 611.514/7-1559.

433. Despatch dated March 9, 1959, from the U.S. embassy in Paris to the Department of State, NARA, Record Group 59, Department of State File No. 611.514/3-959.

434. Ibid.

435. France FCN Treaty, Article XIV(4).

436. Despatch dated April 29, 1959, from the U.S. embassy in Paris to the Department of State, NARA, Record Group 59, Department of State File No. 611.514/4-2959.

who were not eligible for a treaty trader or treaty investor visa and, in particular, of qualified personnel indispensable to enterprises created by nationals or companies of one party in the territory of the other party. Consequently, the two parties "consider[ed] that they should reciprocally exercise the greatest possible liberality consistent with their national laws" with respect to entry and sojourn and with respect to establishment, "effective reciprocity being understood by them as pertaining globally to the whole of the two systems of regulation." The parties also included a lengthy paragraph in the protocol that preserved French laws on access to occupations, provided that entry rights were not impaired.[437] The French wanted to use the seat test for corporate nationality, but the United States objected because it had enacted tax laws to encourage foreign investment, and some companies seeking the tax benefit may have located their principal establishments overseas, which meant that the French proposal would deprive these companies of treaty protection, an undesirable result.[438] Regarding nonprofits, the United States proposed a compromise, accepted by France, in which their juridical personality would be recognized and they would have a right of access to courts.[439]

One problem echoed the difficulties that the State Department had encountered with the Senate in 1952 with respect to the provision relating to the practice of the professions. A French law prohibited accountants from operating in France in the absence of a reciprocity convention. The French feared that the politically powerful accounting profession would object to the provision in Article VIII(2) that permitted the use of technical experts for internal purposes, citing the French law. The lead French negotiator appreciated the reasons for the treaty provision and wanted to preserve it, but in a way that would provide him with a response to criticism from the accountants. He proposed deletion from the treaty provision of the reference to audits and the addition of language to the protocol to make clear that accounting was covered by that provision pending conclusion of a reciprocity convention,[440] a proposal that the United States accepted.[441] The French negotiator understood that there was no realistic prospect for the conclusion of such a convention in the foreseeable future. He explained, however, that "the way to deal with this subject was to present . . . the accountants with a definite decision rather than to await advance consent, just as one handles a 'certain kind of beautiful woman.'"[442]

437. France FCN treaty, Protocol, Paragraph 2.

438. Instruction dated May 13, 1959, from the Department of State to the U.S. embassy in Paris, NARA, Record Group 59, Department of State File No. 611.514/4-2959.

439. Despatch dated May 4, 1959, from the U.S. embassy in Paris to the Department of State, NARA, Record Group 59, Department of State File No. 611.514/4-2959; Despatch dated May 11, 1959, from the U.S. embassy in Paris to the Department of State, NARA, Record Group 59, Department of State File No. 611.514/5-1159. *See* France FCN Treaty, Article XIV(6).

440. Airgram dated July 11, 1959, from the U.S. embassy in Paris to the Department of State, NARA, Record Group 59, Department of State File No. 611.514/7-1159.

441. France FCN treaty, Protocol, Paragraph 9.

442. Airgram dated July 15, 1959, from the U.S. embassy in Paris to the Department of State, NARA, Record Group 59, Department of State File No. 611.514/7-1559.

By May, the negotiators were increasingly looking at stylistic issues. In that context, the French negotiators proposed a reorganization and redrafting of several provisions in the treaty. They were troubled by the prohibition on unreasonable or discriminatory measures, because French law did not include a concept analogous to the American concept of reasonableness.[443] The French negotiators thus wished to omit the requirement of reasonableness.[444] The solution lay in the realization by the French that reasonableness, as the Americans understood the term, was also required by the fair and equitable treatment standard, which was phrased in the French counterdraft as "equitable" treatment. On that basis, the French proposed that the term "unreasonable" be omitted, a proposal to which the U.S. negotiators agreed.[445] The reorganization also involved merging two separation provisions, one requiring the most constant protection and security of aliens and the other requiring the most constant protection and security of alien property, into a single provision requiring both, which was placed in Article I with the equitable treatment standard. The term "most constant protection and security" was rephrased because the French believed that the U.S. language implied strict liability. The French negotiators explained:

> The Treaty sets forth a cumulation of three distinct rules that stand on their own, unqualified by the national treatment standard. First, there is the rule of equitable treatment in Article I. This covers, *inter alia,* all that "reasonable" in the American sense is intended to cover in [the prohibition on unreasonable or discriminatory measures.] Secondly, there is the provision for [full legal and judicial protection] in the second part of Article I. This puts each Party under the responsibility of having laws and a system of protection that will assure the safety and security of the treaty-alien and his belongings. Third, there is the rule of non-discrimination in Article VI, paragraph 1 [Article IV(1) of the final treaty text], that contains the M-F-N as well as the N-T concept. Thus, there is assured equity, non-discrimination and the orderly protection of a responsible body of law and administration, which comprise all the assurances conceived to be sought by the U.S.[446]

In June, the embassy cabled the State Department to urge the Department to regard favorably the French position on the remaining issues.[447] The embassy

443. Ibid.; Despatch dated July 17, 1959, from the U.S. embassy in Paris to the Department of State, NARA, Record Group 59, Department of State File No. 611.514/7-1759; Despatch dated November 27, 1956, from the U.S. embassy in Brussels to the Department of State, NARA, Record Group 59, Department of State File No. 611.554/11-2756 (referring to Belgian law).

444. Airgram dated May 14, 1959, from the U.S. embassy in Paris to the Department of State, NARA, Record Group 59, Department of State File No. 611.514/5-1459.

445. Ibid.

446. Ibid.

447. Telegram dated June 23, 1959, from the U.S. embassy in Paris to the Department of State, NARA, Record Group 59, Department of State File No. 611.514/6-2359.

explained that the French negotiating team had responded "remarkably well" to the U.S. position regarding the content of the treaty.[448] The French attitude during negotiations had been "constructive and helpful," which the embassy attributed to the fact that French officials, including President Charles DeGaulle, "favor[ed] increased US investments in France for political as well as economic reasons."[449] Further, the French Foreign Office had defended the agreements reached with the U.S. negotiators "with vigor and skill" against critics within the French government.[450] The embassy noted the concessions made by the French, including national treatment and a provision on exchange controls,[451] among others. It observed that the tide was running with the United States and recommended that the United States conclude the treaty before the tide ebbed. It also recommended that the United States recognize the constructive spirit shown by the French negotiators and respond in an equally constructive way.[452]

By July, the embassy sensed that the momentum in favor of the treaty had passed its peak and that experts within the French government were having second thoughts, particularly about preserving France's right to screen investments.[453] France wanted especially to preserve the right to exclude investments that it thought would have an adverse impact on its balance of payments.[454] When France proposed a revision of the provision on exchange controls to make this right explicit, the embassy urged the State Department to accept it because further discussion was unlikely to lead to better language, and further delay was likely to result in a deterioration of the treaty.[455] The embassy observed that France regarded the proposed screening provision as a "small price for an array of commitments more far-reaching than France has undertaken to any country during contemporary history."[456] Seeking to conclude the treaty quickly, the United States proposed, and France agreed, that the navigation provisions, which had

448. Ibid.

449. Ibid.

450. Ibid.

451. Paragraph 3 of the article on exchange controls was revised to avoid use of the word "reasonable," which the French negotiators found "indefinite and unsatisfactory." Despatch dated July 17, 1959, from the U.S. embassy in Paris to the Department of State, NARA, Record Group 59, Department of State File No. 611.514/7-1759.

452. Telegram dated June 23, 1959, from the U.S. embassy in Paris to the Department of State, NARA, Record Group 59, Department of State File No. 611.514/6-2359.

453. Despatch dated July 15, 1959, from the U.S. embassy in Paris to the Department of State, NARA, Record Group 59, Department of State File No. 611.514/7-1559.

454. Airgram dated July 12, 1959 from the U.S. embassy in Paris to the Department of State, NARA, Record Group 59, Department of State File No. 611.514/7-1259.

455. Ibid.

456. Ibid.

provoked disagreement, be deleted.[457] The United States also accepted the French proposal on exchange controls, eliminating the last major issue. Thus, under Article X(3), the two parties agreed to "make every effort to accord, in the greatest possible measure, to nationals and companies of the other High Contracting Party the opportunity to make investments and to repatriate the proceeds of the liquidation thereof." Under Paragraph 15 of the protocol, the phrase "in the greatest possible measure" in Article X(3) "shall be understood to refer to the conditions cited in" Article X(2), specifically, the conditions in which monetary reserves were falling to, or had reached, a very low level. Paragraph 14 of the protocol added that either party "with a view to protecting its currency or facilitating the servicing of the proceeds of investments and the repatriation of capital, may subject to authorization the making of investments by foreign nationals and companies," language that was inspired by Paragraph 16 of the protocol to the treaty with Germany.

The treaty was signed on November 27, 1959.[458] During the signing ceremony, the U.S. ambassador noted that the 1778 FCN treaty between France and the United States was the first treaty of any kind signed by the United States.[459]

SENATE ADVICE AND CONSENT TO RATIFICATION 1960

Hearings on the treaties with France and Pakistan were held on June 21, 1960, with testimony received from Deputy Assistant Secretary of State Edwin M. Martin.[460] As discussed in Chapter 8, Martin's testimony included a noteworthy exchange on the application of MFN treatment provisions to a compromissory clause.[461] Following that testimony, the Committee recommended Senate advice and consent to ratification.[462]

The Senate considered both treaties on August 17. Democratic senator J. William Fulbright of Arkansas, the chairman of the Foreign Relations Committee, placed in the record excerpts from the report on the treaties recording an assurance from the State Department that the treaties "do not alter established Federal-State relations or enlarge Federal powers at the expense of the states."[463]

457. Despatch dated July 15, 1959, from the U.S. embassy in Paris to the Department of State, NARA, Record Group 59, Department of State File No. 611.514/7-1559.

458. Convention of Establishment, protocol and declaration, entered into force December 21, 1960, 11 UST 2398, TIAS 4625, 401 UNTS 75.

459. Despatch dated November 27, 1959, from the U.S. embassy in Paris to the Department of State, NARA, Record Group 59, Department of State File No. 611.514/11-2759.

460. *Treaty of Friendship and Commerce with Pakistan and Convention on Establishment with France*, Exec. Rept. No. 12, 86th Cong. 2d Sess. (1960), page 3.

461. The discussion appears in the section on MFN treatment.

462. Ibid., page 4.

463. 106 *Congressional Record* 16562 (1960).

The NFTC continued to lament the conclusion of treaties without a right of establishment, but did not oppose the treaty with Pakistan.[464] Thus, Senator Fulbright was able to report that the NFTC supported the treaty with France and expressed no opposition to the treaty with Pakistan.[465]

Senator Fulbright also addressed the scope of the compromissory clause. He noted that some of his colleagues "may be interested in whether these treaties waive the so-called Connally reservation. The answer is that, like most of our other commercial treaties, they do. Under [the compromissory clauses of the treaties], the treaty parties agree to submit disputes to the International Court of Justice that have not been settled through the normal diplomatic processes."[466] Senator Fulbright noted that "[t]his provision, on balance, becomes more of an advantage to the United States, whose businessmen can be expected to engage in many more transactions than the businessmen of the other treaty parties."[467]

A vote on the treaties was deferred in order to determine whether the Republican members of the Committee wished to speak on the treaties. When debate resumed, Democratic senator Richard Russell of Georgia asked whether the treaties had a termination date, to which Senator Fulbright responded that the treaties could be terminated by either party after 10 years.[468] Democratic senator Strom Thurmond of South Carolina asked for confirmation that any disputes under the treaty would be decided by the International Court of Justice, that a party to the treaty "would not have the right to use its own judgment if it saw fit," and that the parties would be bound by the court's determination.[469] Senator Fulbright confirmed this understanding. Democratic senator Mike Mansfield of Montana then asked for confirmation that no dispute under any of the postwar FCN treaties had been submitted to the International Court of Justice, which Senator Fulbright also confirmed. Democratic senator Dennis Chavez of New Mexico asked whether the Connally Amendment applied to the treaties, to which Senator Fulbright responded that it would not apply to disputes arising under the treaty. Senator Chavez then stated his understanding, based on Senator Fulbright's explanation, that the treaties were not affected by the Connally Amendment. Democratic senator Herman Talmadge of Georgia asked whether the treaty would prevent the imposition of tariffs or quotas on textile imports, to which Senator Fulbright responded in the negative. Following this discussion, the Senate gave advice and consent to ratification of both treaties by a vote of 94-1.[470]

464. Letter dated June 20, 1960, from John Quirk to Senator J. W. Fulbright, NARA, Record Group 46, File No. SEN86B-B8.

465. 106 *Congressional Record* 16562 (1960).

466. Ibid.

467. Ibid.

468. 106 *Congressional Record* 15418 (1960).

469. Ibid. This exchange is discussed in more detail in Chapter 8 in the section on the compromissory clause.

470. Ibid.

The sole negative vote was cast by Senator Chavez, who, it can be inferred from his question, objected to the fact that the Connally Amendment did not apply to the treaty and that the International Court of Justice, therefore, would have sole power to determine whether a dispute arising under the treaty was within the jurisdiction of the court.

NEGOTIATING AN FCN TREATY WITH BELGIUM

The Truman administration first approached Belgium concerning the negotiation of an FCN treaty in 1948. The State Department initially gave a greater priority to negotiations with the Netherlands because the U.S. 1875 FCN treaty with Belgium was more comprehensive than the 1852 FCN treaty with the Netherlands.[471] Because of the existence of the Benelux Union, however, Dutch officials expressed a "strong interest" in seeing similar negotiations between the United States and Belgium,[472] and thus State Department officials concluded that simultaneous negotiations with Belgium would facilitate the discussions already underway with the Netherlands.[473] In addition, the State Department wished to obtain acceptance by European countries of the liberal principles embodied in the treaty, and thought that adherence to such principles by "leading commercial and colonial states" was "especially desirable."[474]

Belgium was receptive in principle to the proposal, but wanted to coordinate with the Netherlands the negotiation of the commercial and navigation provisions.[475] Belgium further proposed deleting the investment-related provisions from the treaty, because it did not wish to set a precedent for including such provisions in a commercial treaty. To do so could lead to demands from other countries to include in their commercial treaties with Belgium concessions on investment matters that Belgium was willing to make to the United States, but not to other countries. Belgium particularly was concerned that such concessions, if included in the FCN treaty, would be obtained by other countries through the operation of the MFN treatment provision in its other commercial treaties.[476] In November, Belgium formally accepted the U.S. offer to negotiate an FCN treaty and proposed that the United States negotiate treaties with Belgium and the Netherlands

471. Memorandum of Conversation headed "Proposed Commercial Treaty with Belgium," dated June 24, 1948, NARA, Record Group 59, Department of State File No. 711.552/6-2448.

472. Ibid.

473. Memorandum dated July 6, 1948, to Willard Thorp, NARA, Record Group 59, Department of State File No. 711.552/7-648.

474. Despatch dated July 8, 1948, from the Department of State to the U.S. embassy in Brussels, NARA, Record Group 59, Department of State File No. 711.552/7-648.

475. Telegram dated October 1, 1948, from the U.S. embassy in Brussels to the Department of State, NARA, Record Group 59, Department of State File No. 711.552/10-148.

476. Airgram dated November 5, 1948, from the U.S. embassy in Brussels to the Department of State, NARA, Record Group 59, Department of State File No. 711.552/11-548.

that were identical, at least as far as the "economic clauses" were concerned.[477] Belgium noted that this would be its first postwar FCN treaty, that it would need to prepare thoroughly before commencing negotiations, and that it was preoccupied with work related to the GATT, the Benelux Union, and the Organization for European Economic Cooperation. Accordingly, Belgium proposed that negotiations be deferred until the following March.[478]

The negotiations did not begin in the spring of 1949 as planned. In June of that year, elections brought the Christian Social Party to power in Belgium, resulting in further delay while the new government was formed.[479] The new government examined the proposed treaty carefully[480] and, by the summer of 1950, appeared ready to begin, with the Netherlands, joint negotiations of the treaty with the United States.[481] By September, Belgium and the Netherlands had decided that, in fact, the two countries should negotiate separately because of the complications involved in joint negotiations.[482] On October 6, Belgium informed the United States that it had decided not to negotiate an FCN treaty with the United States at that time, either separately or in tandem with the Netherlands.[483] The Belgian government believed that such negotiations were premature in light of remaining problems relating to the economic union with the Netherlands and the need to further harmonize Belgian laws relating to the economic activities of aliens with the laws of Luxembourg on the same subject.[484] Belgium did propose to send an observer to the negotiations between the United States and the Netherlands, to which the Netherlands agreed.[485] The Belgian government did not see a treaty as urgent and was prepared to let the Netherlands take the lead,[486] although the State

477. Airgram dated November 24, 1948, from the U.S. embassy in Brussels to the Department of State, NARA, Record Group 59, Department of State File No. 711.552/11-2448.

478. Airgram A-887 dated November 5, 1948, from the U.S. embassy in Brussels to the Department of State, NARA, Record Group 59, Department of State File No. 711.552/11-548.

479. Telegram dated August 4, 1949, from the U.S. embassy in Brussels to the Department of State, NARA, Record Group 59, Department of State File No. 711.552/8-449.

480. Memorandum of Conversation headed "FCN Treaty with Belgium," dated April 12, 1950, NARA, Record Group 59, Department of State File No. 611.554/4-1250; Telegram dated June 26, 1950, from the U.S. embassy in Brussels to the Department of State, NARA, Record Group 59, Department of State File No. 611.564/6-2650.

481. Telegram dated August 25, 1950, from the U.S. embassy in Brussels to the Department of State, NARA, Record Group 59, Department of State File No. 611.564/8-2550.

482. Telegram dated September 19, 1950, from the U.S. embassy in The Hague to the Department of State, NARA, Record Group 59, Department of State File No. 611.564/9-1950.

483. Despatch No. 369 dated October 11, 1950, from the U.S. embassy in Brussels to the Department of State, NARA, Record Group 59, Department of State File No. 611.554/10-1150.

484. Ibid.

485. Ibid.

486. Memorandum of Conversation headed "Proposed Treaty of Friendship, Commerce and Navigation with the Netherlands—ECA Cooperation in Expediting Initiation of Negotiations," dated March 24, 1950, NARA, Record Group 59, Department of State File No. 611.564/3-2450.

Department perceived that Belgium had acquiesced to the negotiations between the United States and the Netherlands "rather grudgingly."[487]

Some four years later, in September 1954, U.S. embassy officials asked the director general of the Belgian ministry of foreign commerce whether his office was interested in the subject of investment, and learned that the Belgian government was studying several ideas to promote inward foreign investment.[488] The following November, State Department officials took advantage of a visit by a Belgian official to explain the value of an FCN treaty in creating a favorable investment climate and to report on the progress of the U.S. negotiations with the Netherlands.[489] This prompted Belgian embassy officials to inform the State Department that they were going to recommend resumption of the FCN treaty negotiations.[490] By December, the U.S. embassy saw "strong evidence" that Belgium wanted to commence negotiations.[491] The Belgian government had already reviewed the U.S. standard draft treaty and probably would "wish to move ahead rapidly" with the treaty.[492] A U.S. embassy official told an official in the Belgian ministry of foreign commerce that the provisions to improve the investment climate were the most important provisions in the treaty, to which the latter agreed.[493]

By the beginning of 1955, with negotiations between the United States and the Netherlands well advanced, Belgium was ready to commence negotiations with the United States.[494] Discussions began on February 24.[495]

The discussions progressed slowly at first because of disagreement within the Belgian government concerning the content of the treaty. More than a year after discussions began, in May 1956, Belgium presented the United States with a counterdraft that proposed numerous changes to the U.S. draft. The Belgian government had experienced "considerable difficulty" in reaching

487. *Current Economic Developments*, February 28, 1961, page 12, NARA, Record Group 59, Department of State Lot Files.

488. Memorandum of Conversation headed "Investment and FCN Treaty," dated September 29, 1954, NARA, Record Group 59, Department of State File No. 611.6554/9-2954.

489. Instruction dated November 5, 1954, from the Department of State to the U.S. embassy in Brussels, NARA, Record Group 59, Department of State File No. 611.6554/11-554.

490. Ibid.

491. Despatch dated December 4, 1954, from the U.S. embassy in Brussels to the Department of State, NARA, Record Group 59, Department of State File No. 611.6554/12-454.

492. Ibid.

493. Memorandum of Conversation dated November 30, 1954, attached to despatch dated December 4, 1954, from the U.S. embassy in Brussels to the Department of State, NARA, Record Group 59, Department of State File No. 611.6554/12-454.

494. Despatch dated January 12, 1955, from the U.S. embassy in Brussels to the Department of State, NARA, Record Group 59, Department of State File No. 611.6554/1-1255.

495. Despatch dated March 4, 1955, from the U.S. embassy in Brussels to the Department of State, NARA, Record Group 59, Department of State File No. 611.6554/3-455.

internal agreement on the counterdraft.[496] The counterdraft reflected "principally an effort to get on with the negotiation in the face of certain fears and hesitations on the part of other Belgian Ministries."[497] The United States accepted the counterdraft as the basis for negotiations.[498]

Formal negotiations began on July 31, 1956, and continued for almost five years, during the course of which three different U.S. ambassadors served in Brussels and each side had three different lead negotiators.[499] Much of the early discussion focused on the trade provisions,[500] on which agreement proved very difficult to reach.

When the parties began to address the investment provisions, they encountered a number of problems arising from differences between the U.S. and Belgian legal systems. For example, the Belgian Constitution required payment of compensation in advance of expropriation, whereas the United States believed that such a rule would be stricter than the requirement of the U.S. Constitution.[501] Conferring greater rights on Belgian investors in the United States than Americans had in the United States under the U.S. Constitution could raise an "insuperable obstacle" to Senate approval of the treaty.[502] The State Department recommended that the issue be resolved by omitting the sentence that elaborated upon when payment must be made and to rely on the formula of prompt, just and, effective, which was already in the treaty and which established the rule. The sentence to be omitted merely amplified the rule and did not add measurably to it.[503] Belgium, however, wished to retain the sentence.[504] Ultimately, the parties compromised by modifying the sentence to read that "adequate provision shall have been made not later than the time of taking for the determination and payment [of compensation]."[505]

496. Despatch dated May 3, 1956, from the U.S. embassy in Brussels to the Department of State, NARA, Record Group 59, Department of State File No. 611.6554/5-356.

497. Ibid.

498. *Current Economic Developments*, February 28, 1961, page 12, NARA, Record Group 59, Department of State Lot Files.

499. Despatch dated August 3, 1956, from the U.S. embassy in Brussels to the Department of State, NARA, Record Group 59, Department of State File No. 611.554/8-356; Ambassador's Accompanying Remarks on Occasion of Signing F.C.N. Treaty, enclosure to despatch dated February 23, 1961, from the U.S. embassy in Brussels to the Department of State, NARA, Record Group 59, Department of State File No. 611.554/2-2361.

500. Despatch dated August 3, 1956, from the U.S. embassy in Brussels to the Department of State, NARA, Record Group 59, Department of State File No. 611.554/8-356.

501. Instruction dated January 24, 1957, from the Department of State to the U.S. embassy in Brussels, NARA, Record Group 59, Department of State File No. 611.554/11-2156.

502. Ibid.

503. Ibid.

504. Despatch dated April 4, 1957, from the U.S. embassy in Brussels to the Department of State, NARA, Record Group 59, Department of State File No. 611.6554/4-457.

505. Belgium FCN treaty, Article 4(3).

Similarly, the negotiations regarding exchange controls confronted the problem that the U.S. standard draft treaty language required the host country to make "reasonable provision" for withdrawals by investors. The term "reasonable," however, did not have the same meaning in the Belgian legal system as it did in the United States.[506] The Belgian negotiators also believed that the phrase "essential to the health and welfare of its people" was a criterion that would be too difficult to apply in practice.[507] The parties resolved these problems with the exchange controls provision by redrafting the provision to eliminate the troubling language. The reference to "reasonable provision" became a reference to "provision to the fullest extent practicable in light of the level of the monetary reserves and its balance of payments."[508] In the view of the United States, the actual availability of foreign exchange should be the decisive criterion.[509] The phrase "essential to the health and welfare of its people" was shortened to "essential."[510]

Belgium wanted to use the seat test to determine corporate nationality, whereas the United States wanted to use the place of incorporation test.[511] Belgium also wanted to reserve the right to deny recognition to a company of the other party if the purpose of the company was contrary to *l'ordre public*, such as in the case of a company formed to conduct gambling operations.[512] The United States strongly preferred the place of incorporation test as a matter of policy[513] and objected to the public order exception on the ground that public policy differed from state to state, which might mean that a Belgian corporation would be recognized in some states and not others.[514] Ultimately, the parties compromised by adopting, at Article 6(3), the place of incorporation test, but with an exception permitting denial of recognition of the nationality and juridical status of a company the charter of which was inconsistent with the public policy of the denying party.[515]

506. Instruction dated April 25, 1957, from the Department of State to the U.S. embassy in Brussels, NARA, Record Group 59, Department of State File No. 611.554/4-857.

507. Despatch dated August 6, 1956, from the U.S. embassy in Brussels to the Department of State, NARA, Record Group 59, Department of State File No. 611.6554/8-656.

508. Belgium FCN treaty, Article 10(3).

509. Instruction dated April 25, 1957, from the Department of State to the U.S. embassy in Brussels, NARA, Record Group 59, Department of State File No. 611.554/4-857.

510. Belgium FCN treaty, Article 10(3).

511. Instruction dated March 25, 1957, from the Department of State to the U.S. embassy in Brussels, NARA, Record Group 59, Department of State File No. 611.554/2-157.

512. Ibid.; Despatch dated April 5, 1957, from the U.S. embassy in Brussels to the Department of State, NARA, Record Group 59, Department of State File No. 611.554/4-557.

513. The basis for this policy is explained in Chapter 8 in the section on the definition of the term "companies."

514. Instruction dated March 25, 1957, from the Department of State to the U.S. embassy in Brussels, NARA, Record Group 59, Department of State File No. 611.554/2-157.

515. Instruction A-224 dated April 18, 1957, from the Department of State to the U.S. embassy in Brussels, NARA, Record Group 59, Department of State File No. 611.554/4-557; Instruction

Further, under language in Paragraph 8 of the protocol, application of the public policy exception must be in accordance with national treatment. Finally, Paragraph 9 of the protocol provided that a company of the United States would not be recognized as such by Belgium if its "main establishment" was in Belgium.

Whereas the United States used its immigration laws to control the supply of alien workers in its territory, Belgium used a work permit system instead.[516] The parties inserted in Paragraph 5 of the protocol a reservation to allow continued use of the Belgian work permit system, even on a discriminatory basis.[517] Belgium wanted to ensure that it would be allowed to give preference to Common Market countries with respect to the issuance of work permits.[518] The United States acknowledged that it too was unable to grant MFN treatment with respect to the immigration and employment of aliens.[519]

Language excluding the practice of professions from national treatment posed problems because, in Belgium, the term "profession" had a much broader meaning than in the United States.[520] At the same time, Belgium did wish to retain the right to exclude aliens from certain occupations.[521] The two parties ultimately agreed on two separate protocol provisions. Paragraph 6 excluded from the national treatment obligation professions that involved the performance of functions in a public capacity or in the interests of public health and safety, were state-licensed, and were reserved to nationals. Paragraph 7 excluded the activity of peddlers and itinerant artisans.

Belgium objected to the treaty language under which U.S. nationals and companies would receive in Belgium treatment with respect to the acquisition of real property that was only as favorable as that accorded by the state in which

A-189 dated April 29, 1959, from the Department of State to the U.S. embassy in Brussels, NARA, Record Group 59, Department of State File No. 611.554/4-359; Instruction dated July 3, 1957, from the Department of State to the U.S. embassy in Brussels, NARA, Record Group 59, Department of State File No. 611.554/6-1257.

516. Memorandum of Conversation headed "Treaty of Friendship, Commerce and Navigation – Belgian Counterdraft," dated June 27 and 29, 1956, NARA, Record Group 59, Department of State File No. 611.564/6-2956.

517. Letter dated June 20, 1961, from Assistant Secretary of State Brooks Hays to Senator J. W. Fulbright, NARA, Record Group 59, Department of State File No. 611.5542/6-561.

518. Despatch dated October 6, 1960, from the U.S. embassy in Brussels to the Department of State, NARA, Record Group 59, Department of State File No. 611.6554/10-660; Instruction dated May 6, 1959, from the Department of State to the U.S. embassy in Brussels, NARA, Record Group 59, Department of State File No. 611.564/4-3059.

519. Despatch dated October 6, 1960, from the U.S. embassy in Brussels to the Department of State, NARA, Record Group 59, Department of State File No. 611.6554/10-660.

520. Despatch dated February 1, 1957, from the U.S. embassy in Brussels to the Department of State, NARA, Record Group 59, Department of State File No. 611.6554/2-157.

521. Instruction dated February 11, 1957, from the Department of State to the U.S. embassy in Brussels, NARA, Record Group 59, Department of State File No. 611.554/2-157.

the national was domiciled or the company was constituted. Belgium's own law required it to grant national treatment with respect to acquiring real estate, and it did not wish to grant, in the treaty, "official recognition" to the discriminatory policy of the United States.[522] Ultimately, the parties resolved the issue by deleting the provision on the acquisition of real property.

The two countries also faced the problem of an exception for European integration arrangements. Although the United States supported the Common Market and wished it "every success," it was unwilling to "sign a 'blank check'" with respect to future Belgian derogations from MFN treatment.[523] Accordingly, the United States proposed the same solution that it proposed to several other countries, including the Netherlands[524] and France,[525] that is, a provision permitting either party to terminate its MFN obligations with respect to trade. Such an act would leave the national treatment provisions intact and, in fact, the United States regarded the treaty's assurances of national treatment of foreign investment as one of the best available means of protection against possible harmful effects from European integration.[526]

In April 1959, the parties agreed to eliminate the commercial articles of the treaty, thereby removing most of the remaining issues.[527] As a consequence of eliminating the commercial provisions, the treaty was retitled as a treaty of friendship, establishment, and navigation. A month later, disagreement over a provision on restrictive business practices was also resolved by eliminating the provision, the United States having concluded that a genuine basis for agreement on the provision simply did not exist.[528]

Despite the resolution of the remaining major issues in spring 1959, signature of the treaty was delayed while the parties discussed minor points[529] and while Belgium prepared a new draft incorporating the changes to which the parties had

522. Despatch dated April 3, 1959, from the U.S. embassy in Brussels to the Department of State, NARA, Record Group 59, Department of State File No. 611.6554/4-359.

523. Despatch dated April 8, 1957, from the U.S. embassy in Brussels to the Department of State, NARA, Record Group 59, Department of State File No. 611.6554/4-857.

524. Despatch dated April 3, 1957, from the U.S. embassy in Brussels to the Department of State, NARA, Record Group 59, Department of State File No. 611.554/4-357; Despatch dated April 30, 1957, from the U.S. embassy in Brussels to the Department of State, NARA, Record Group 59, Department of State File No. 611.6554/4-3057.

525. Instruction dated January 29, 1960, from the Department of State to the U.S. embassy in Brussels, NARA, Record Group 59, Department of State File No. 611.5542/1-2960.

526. Instruction dated January 19, 1959, from the Department of State to the U.S. embassy in Brussels, NARA, Record Group 59, Department of State File No. 611.5542/12-1259.

527. Telegram dated April 30, 1959, from the U.S. embassy in Brussels to the Department of State, NARA, Record Group 59, Department of State File No. 611.554/4-3059.

528. Telegram dated May 20, 1959, from the U.S. embassy in Paris to the Department of State, NARA, Record Group 59, Department of State File No. 611.554/5-2059.

529. Despatch dated December 31, 1959, from the U.S. embassy in Brussels to the Department of State, NARA, Record Group 59, Department of State File No. 611.554/12-3159.

agreed.[530] When Belgium finally produced the new draft in September 1960, the United States discovered that references to MFN treatment had been deleted throughout the treaty, because of Belgium's concerns that MFN obligations with respect to the right of establishment might conflict with the Rome treaty.[531]

Taking account of the progress in the negotiations to date, the State Department decided to phrase its qualms about the changes as technical questions and urged retention of the MFN treatment obligation in the exchange controls provision and in a provision on commercial travelers.[532] Belgium acquiesced with respect to the exchange controls provision,[533] although it regarded such an obligation as superfluous given that its exchange controls had never been based on nationality.[534]

The parties signed the treaty on February 21, 1961,[535] at a time when the world economy had changed considerably since the signing of the first U.S. postwar FCN treaty 15 years before. At the ceremony, U.S. ambassador William A. M. Burden noted that the United States was "having difficulties" with its balance of payments.[536] He observed that the United States had been aided in its economic development in the past by foreign investment from Europe, and that newly elected president John F. Kennedy had only recently commented that European investment in the United States would provide "one important means of helping to redress" the current difficulties.[537] Ambassador Burden closed his remarks by expressing the hope that Belgian investors would consider investing in the United States.

NEGOTIATING AN FCN TREATY WITH VIETNAM

Following the creation of the Southeast Asia Treaty Organization (SEATO) in September 1954, the Eisenhower administration sought to promote closer economic relations between SEATO members and Cambodia, Laos, and the Republic

530. Despatch dated September 16, 1960, from the U.S. embassy in Brussels to the Department of State, NARA, Record Group 59, Department of State File No. 611.554/9-1650.

531. Ibid.; Memorandum of Conversation headed "FCN Treaty Negotiations with Belgium," dated January 18, 1960, NARA, Record Group 59, Department of State File No. 611.554/1-1860.

532. Instruction dated October 20, 1960, from the Department of State to the U.S. embassy in Brussels, NARA, Record Group 59, Department of State File No. 611.554/9-1660.

533. Telegram dated October 3, 1960, from the U.S. embassy in Brussels to the Department of State, NARA, Record Group 59, Department of State File No. 611.554/10-360.

534. Despatch dated October 6, 1960, from the U.S. embassy in Brussels to the Department of State, NARA, Record Group 59, Department of State File No. 611.6554/10-660.

535. Treaty of Friendship, Establishment and Navigation, entered into force October 3, 1963, 14 UST 1284, TIAS 5432, 480 UNTS 149.

536. Ambassador's Accompanying Remarks on Occasion of Signing F.C.N. Treaty, enclosure to despatch dated February 23, 1961, from the U.S. embassy in Brussels to the Department of State, NARA, Record Group 59, Department of State File No. 611.554/2-2361.

537. Ibid.

of Vietnam (Vietnam).[538] By early 1955, the State Department was considering the negotiation of FCN treaties with those three countries both for economic reasons and as evidence of their newly gained independence.[539] The Department sent a copy of the standard draft treaty to the embassy in each country.

The initial reaction of the U.S. embassy in Saigon was that a treaty with Vietnam would be inadvisable because of French sensitivities about U.S. intentions in Vietnam.[540] By summer 1956, however, the embassy had decided that the negotiation of an FCN treaty with Vietnam would be "highly constructive."[541] Indeed, the Vietnamese government informed the embassy in late summer that it was considering the adoption of a foreign investment law and asked the embassy's opinion about the law. The embassy responded that U.S. investors "might be encouraged" if Vietnam entered into an FCN treaty with the United States.[542]

The State Department decided to propose a treaty based on the U.S. FCN treaty with Iran.[543] That is, the Department intended to use the "short form" of the treaty drafted for use with "underdeveloped countries" where negotiation of the longer form was "extremely difficult."[544] The draft sent to Vietnam, however, included a guarantee of national treatment with respect to the establishment of business enterprises, a provision that the State Department regarded as "particularly important."[545] Vietnam responded by requesting copies of other U.S. FCN treaties.[546]

By January, the Vietnamese government had reviewed the proposed draft treaty and sent its comments on the treaty to the U.S. embassy.[547] The United States

538. Telegram dated February 15, 1955, from the Department of State to the U.S. embassies in Saigon, Phnom Penh, and Vientiane, NARA, Record Group 59, Department of State File No. 611.51G4/2-1555.

539. Ibid.

540. Telegram dated February 19, 1955, from the U.S. embassy in Saigon to the Department of State, NARA, Record Group 59, Department of State File No. 611.51G4/2-1955.

541. Memorandum to the Secretary of State dated August 31, 1956, NARA, Record Group 59, Department of State File No. 611.51G4/8-3156.

542. Memorandum headed "Proposed Treaty of Friendship, Commerce, and Navigation with Viet-Nam," dated September 4, 1956, NARA, Record Group 59, Department of State File No. 611.51G4/9-456.

543. Memorandum to the Secretary of State dated August 31, 1956, NARA, Record Group 59, Department of State File No. 611.51G4/8-3156.

544. Memorandum from Eli Maurer dated September 7, 1956, NARA, Record Group 59, Department of State File No. 611.51G4/8-3156.

545. Instruction dated October 18, 1956, from the Department of State to the U.S. embassy in Saigon, NARA, Record Group 59, Department of State File No. 611.51G4/10-1656.

546. Telegram dated October 16, 1956, from the U.S. embassy in Saigon to the Department of State, NARA, Record Group 59, Department of State File No. 611.51G4/10-1656.

547. Telegram dated January 21, 1957, from the U.S. embassy in Saigon to the Department of State, NARA, Record Group 59, Department of State File No. 611.51G4/1-2157.

replied to these comments through the embassy and, by April, Vietnam regarded most of the issues that it had raised as having been resolved by U.S. clarifications, believed that formal negotiations would not be necessary, and suggested that the treaty be signed during an imminent visit to the United States by President Ngo Dinh Diem.[548]

The two countries, however, soon encountered a major disagreement over the right of establishment. Vietnam had enacted a decree directed at Chinese inhabitants that excluded aliens from 11 occupations, and the embassy understood that Vietnam wished to preserve the right to keep the decree in force.[549] The embassy believed that decree covered principally small retail trade, rice processing, and transportation, occupations that were of little interest to U.S. nationals, although the scope of some of the occupations was not clear.[550] Subsequently, the Vietnamese government clarified that it was not proposing to exclude Americans from occupations covered by the decree, but, rather it wished to exclude them from certain occupations that had a security aspect.[551] A French ordinance enacted in 1933 had closed these trades to persons of "Europeanistatus," a term that included Americans.[552] Vietnam thus sought a specific national security exception for the right of establishment, but the embassy explained that such an exception might detract from the general exception for essential security interests.[553] The State Department believed that some of the occupations covered by the 1933 ordinance, such as hotel manager and radio manufacturer, were fields in which foreign investment would be beneficial.[554] In early May, Vietnam proposed that the provision guaranteeing national treatment with respect to establishment be deleted entirely because it did not wish to be obligated by MFN provisions in other treaties to extend national treatment to nationals of certain third countries, notably China, Japan, and France.[555] The State Department responded that this proposal introduced a "most serious new problem" that would require

548. Despatch dated March 30, 1957, from the U.S. embassy in Saigon to the Department of State, NARA, Record Group 59, Department of State File No. 611.51G4/3-3057; Telegram dated April 11, 1957, from the U.S. embassy in Saigon to the Department of State, NARA, Record Group 59, Department of State File No. 611.51G4/4-1157.

549. Telegram dated January 21, 1957, from the U.S. embassy in Saigon to the Department of State, NARA, Record Group 59, Department of State File No. 611.51G4/1-2157.

550. Instruction dated February 13, 1957, from the Department of State to the U.S. embassy in Saigon, NARA, Record Group 59, Department of State File No. 611.51G4/1-2157.

551. Telegram dated April 20, 1957, from the U.S. embassy in Saigon to the Department of State, NARA, Record Group 59, Department of State File No. 611.51G4/4-2057.

552. Ibid.

553. Ibid.

554. Telegram dated April 22, 1957, from the Department of State to the U.S. embassy in Saigon, NARA, Record Group 59, Department of State File No. 611.51G4/4-2057.

555. Telegram dated May 1, 1957, from the U.S. embassy in Saigon to the Department of State, NARA, Record Group 59, Department of State File No. 611.51G4/5-157.

extensive consideration and that signature during Diem's visit was now no longer possible.[556] A particular concern was the precedent that this would set in the region.[557] The embassy commented that national treatment was the "very heart" of the treaty and that a compromise on the issue would destroy the primary benefit to be gained from the treaty.[558]

Discussion of the issue of national treatment continued intermittently for more than a year and a half. The Vietnamese government understood that an MFN obligation would obtain national treatment for Vietnamese nationals and companies in the United States and thus, from its perspective, a national treatment obligation benefitted only the United States. Vietnam wanted to retain the freedom to add to the list of occupations from which Americans were excluded and to avoid granting to the United States a right of national treatment that third countries would obtain through MFN provisions in other treaties.[559]

By January 1959, the embassy had reappraised the situation. Noting that the United States had signed other FCN treaties without national treatment with respect to establishment, the embassy saw "no great harm" in deleting the provisions regarding that right.[560] Given that Vietnamese opposition to national treatment had only stiffened with time, the embassy believed that the policy against national treatment with respect to establishment was embraced at the highest levels. In reaction to a suggestion that the issue be raised with President Diem, the embassy speculated that he might well back his negotiators. If the United States was not going to be successful in obtaining national treatment with respect to establishment, the embassy thought it better for the United Stated to graciously concede the issue rather than appear to capitulate in the face of determined opposition.[561] The embassy observed that there was no point in forcing Vietnam to accept foreign investment that it did not want, and that a treaty without a right of establishment was more advantageous than no treaty at all.[562]

On March 30, the State Department cabled its authorization to delete the provision on national treatment with respect to the establishment of business enterprises,[563] although the treaty would continue to require national (and MFN)

556. Ibid.

557. Ibid.

558. Despatch dated December 30, 1957, from the U.S. embassy in Saigon to the Department of State, NARA, Record Group 59, Department of State File No. 611.51G4/12-3057.

559. Telegram dated June 13, 1958, from the U.S. embassy in Saigon to the Department of State, NARA, Record Group 59, Department of State File No. 611.51G4/6-1358.

560. Despatch dated January 15, 1959, from the U.S. embassy in Saigon to the Department of State, NARA, Record Group 59, Department of State File No. 611.51G4/1-1559.

561. Ibid.

562. Ibid.

563. Instruction dated March 30, 1959, from the Department of State to the U.S. embassy in Saigon, NARA, Record Group 59, Department of State File No. 611.51G4/1-1559.

treatment of such enterprises, once established, with respect to conducting their activities.[564] In explaining its decision, the State Department observed that continued insistence on national treatment with respect to entry would serve no useful purpose, inasmuch as treaties were not well adapted for creating a right of establishment in a developing country that was not yet willing to grant the right. At the same time, concluding the treaty without the right would be "politically advantageous" and would provide protection for those Americans who did choose to engage in business in Vietnam. The Department also noted that recent expropriations had generated strong pressure from business groups for greater treaty protection for private property and that, if the State Department did not show progress in negotiating such treaties, it could expect a strong expression of dissatisfaction from Congress.[565]

The resolution of this major issue permitted the parties to turn their attention to a few minor issues that had been deferred pending resolution of the crucial national treatment issue. For example, from the beginning of the negotiations, Vietnam had sought additional language clarifying the right of a party to impose exchange controls.[566] After the U.S. concession on establishment, the parties began a lengthy discussion of a possible interpretive note or exchange of letters that would provide Vietnam with the reassurance it sought,[567] although ultimately the parties concluded the treaty without agreeing to any such note or exchange of letters. In addition, the State Department discovered some technical problems in the treaty language that required resolution.[568] The parties also endeavored to translate the text into Vietnamese.

In September 1960, a key Vietnamese official involved in the negotiations left Vietnam for an assignment in Rome, after which the treaty lay dormant.[569] On February 13, 1961, however, the State Department received a telegram from the embassy reporting that Vietnam was prepared to sign the treaty.[570] Vietnam was holding national elections in April and the Diem administration believed that

564. Vietnam FCN treaty, Article V(1).

565. Letter dated February 13, 1959, from Deputy Assistant Secretary of State W. T. M. Beale to Acting Assistant Secretary of Commerce Marshall Smith, NARA, Record Group 59, Department of State File No. 611.51G4/1-1559.

566. Telegram dated January 21, 1957, from the U.S. embassy in Saigon to the Department of State, NARA, Record Group 59, Department of State File No. 611.51G4/1-2157.

567. *See, e.g.,* Telegram dated September 8, 1959, from the U.S. embassy in Saigon to the Department of State, NARA, Record Group 59, Department of State File No. 611.51G4/9-859; Airgram dated September 8, 1959, from the U.S. embassy in Saigon to the Department of State, NARA, Record Group 59, Department of State File No. 611.51G4/9-859.

568. *See* Instruction dated August 12, 1959, from the Department of State to the U.S. embassy in Saigon, NARA, Record Group 59, Department of State File No. 611.51G4/7-2759.

569. Letter dated December 22, 1960, from Joseph Rosa to Vernon Setser, NARA, Record Group 59, Department of State File No. 611.51K4/12-2260.

570. Memorandum headed "How Authorization for Signature of the U.S.-Viet-Nam Commercial Treaty Was Expedited," dated April 6, 1961, NARA, Record Group 59, Department of State File No. 611.51K4/4-661.

signature of a treaty with the United States would give it a political advantage in the election.[571] Further, less than four weeks before, the inauguration of President John F. Kennedy had returned the Democrats to the White House after an absence of eight years. The Diem government wanted to see whether the Kennedy administration would reaffirm U.S. support for Vietnam by signing the treaty.[572]

Because of bureaucratic delay, more than three weeks passed before the document authorizing signature of the treaty reached the secretary of state and was signed. The full power was immediately dispatched to the White House. President Kennedy signed the full power on the left side of the page and, when the document was returned to the State Department, an official in the Office of the Secretary returned it to the White House, believing that the document had been signed in the wrong place and was invalid. The White House staff refused to resubmit it to the president. An attorney in the State Department Office of the Legal Adviser, attempting to locate the full power, learned of the controversy over the signature and informed the Office of the Secretary that the document was valid whether signed on the left, on the right, or in the middle. A day later, on March 17, the Department authorized the ambassador to sign the treaty.[573] The treaty was signed on April 3, a week before the elections.[574]

SENATE ADVICE AND CONSENT TO RATIFICATION 1961

The Committee on Foreign Relations considered the treaties with Belgium and Vietnam in executive session on August 23, 1961, at which time it heard testimony from Deputy Assistant Secretary of State Peyton Kerr and then recommended advice and consent to ratification.[575] During Senate deliberations on September 11, the issues addressed were similar to those discussed during Senate consideration of FCN treaties concluded earlier. First, Democratic senator J. William Fulbright of Arkansas, the chairman of the Senate Foreign Relations Committee, assured the Senate that the two treaties were "based on existing precedents and introduce[d] no new commitments that raise[d] problems as to their effects upon domestic law."[576] Second, Republican senator Alexander Wiley of Wisconsin placed in the record a memorandum regarding the relationship

571. Ibid.; Telegram dated February 10, 1961, from the U.S. embassy in Saigon to the Department of State, NARA, Record Group 59, Department of State File No. 611.51K42/2-1061.

572. Telegram dated February 10, 1961, from the U.S. embassy in Saigon to the Department of State, NARA, Record Group 59, Department of State File No. 611.51K42/2-1061.

573. Memorandum headed "How Authorization for Signature of the U.S.-Viet-Nam Commercial Treaty Was Expedited," dated April 6, 1961, NARA, Record Group 59, Department of State File No. 611.51K4/4-661.

574. Treaty of Amity and Economic Relations, entered into force November 30, 1961, 12 UST 1703, TIAS 4890, 424 UNTS 137.

575. *Commercial Treaties with Belgium and Vietnam*, Exec. Rept. No. 9, 87th Cong. 1st Sess. (1961), page 3.

576. 107 *Congressional Record* 18878 (1961).

between the treaties and the Connally Amendment.[577] The memorandum noted that, under these two treaties, "if any dispute regarding any provision of these conventions arises as between the parties, and if such dispute is not satisfactorily settled by other means, the dispute shall be submitted to the International Court of Justice."[578] The memorandum noted that the Court would determine whether it had jurisdiction. As the memorandum further explained, the compromissory clause thus had the effect of waiving the Connally Amendment because it permitted the Court, rather than the United States, to determine whether the Court had jurisdiction, although only with respect to "the limited category of disputes" that might arise under an FCN treaty.[579] The memorandum observed that Senator Connally himself had been consulted in 1946 when the first postwar FCN treaty, with China, had been signed and that the senator had not objected to the inclusion of such a compromissory clause in the FCN treaties. Following this discussion, the Senate gave its advice and consent to ratification of both treaties by a vote of 83-0.[580]

NEGOTIATING AN FCN TREATY WITH LUXEMBOURG

The Truman administration approached Luxembourg as early as 1949 about the negotiation of an FCN treaty, but the latter did not wish to negotiate until Belgium and the Netherlands were ready to negotiate.[581] By 1956, the Netherlands had concluded its treaty and Belgium was in negotiations with the United States. Luxembourg elected to await the conclusion of the negotiations with Belgium so that it would have the Belgian treaty as a guide and indicated a desire to observe the negotiations with Belgium,[582] a request to which the United States had no objection.[583] Luxembourg appeared to be interested primarily in harmonizing its policies with Belgium's.[584] That is, Luxembourg was willing to negotiate a treaty if, but only if, Belgium did so.[585]

577. Ibid.

578. Ibid., page 18879.

579. Ibid.

580. Ibid., page 18898.

581. Telegram dated March 22, 1956, from the U.S. embassy in Luxembourg to the Department of State, NARA, Record Group 59, Department of State File No. 611.50A4/3-2256.

582. Ibid.

583. Instruction dated April 20, 1956, from the Department of State to the U.S. embassy in Luxembourg, NARA, Record Group 59, Department of State File No. 611.50A4/3-2256.

584. Telegram dated March 7, 1956, from the U.S. embassy in Luxembourg to the Department of State, NARA, Record Group 59, Department of State File No. 611.50A4/3-756; Telegram dated March 22, 1956, from the U.S. embassy in Luxembourg to the Department of State, NARA, Record Group 59, Department of State File No. 611.50A4/3-2256.

585. Telegram dated March 7, 1956, from the U.S. embassy in Luxembourg to the Department of State, NARA, Record Group 59, Department of State File No. 611.504A4/3-756.

Belgium signed its treaty with the United States on February 21, 1961. In June, the U.S ambassador notified the Luxembourgian foreign minister that the United States was prepared to negotiate a treaty. The foreign minister replied that Luxembourg was ready to negotiate as well.[586]

The parties agreed to use the treaty with Belgium as the basis for negotiations.[587] Thus, the treaty with Luxembourg would be identical to the treaty with Belgium unless the parties agreed to a modification. Accordingly, like the treaty with Belgium, it omitted the commercial provisions and was titled as a "Treaty of Friendship, Establishment and Navigation." The United States proposed a number of minor modifications to the Belgian treaty to eliminate some changes to the standard draft treaty to which it had reluctantly agreed in its negotiations with Belgium.[588] For example, the treaty with Luxembourg does not include the modification with respect to the recognition of the juridical status and nationality of companies.

Presumably because Luxembourg wanted only to harmonize its treaty with Belgium's, the negotiations appear to have presented no serious problems. The parties signed the treaty on February 23, 1962.[589] In concluding the treaty, the United States completed what it described as "an almost uniform network of legal rules governing economic relations" between the United States and the European Community.[590]

The Committee on Foreign Relations held hearings on the treaty on September 7, 1962, at which time Acting Assistant Secretary of State Philip Trezise testified in support of the treaty.[591] Later the same day, the Committee recommended advice and consent to ratification.[592]

The Senate considered the treaty on September 19, 1962. Democratic senator John Sparkman of Alabama, the acting chairman of the Senate Foreign Relations Committee, noted that the treaty was reciprocal and did not contain any provision that might "seriously impair or infringe upon the domestic laws of the United States."[593] He also drew the attention of the Senate to the compromissory clause, but noted that this did not amount to a "general waiver" of the Connally

586. Telegram dated June 13, 1961, from the U.S. embassy in Luxembourg to the Department of State, NARA, Record Group 59, Department of State File No. 611.504A4/6-1361.

587. Instruction dated August 3, 1961, from the Department of State to the U.S. embassy in Luxembourg, NARA, Record Group 59, Department of State File No. 611.50A42/8-361.

588. Ibid.

589. Treaty of Friendship, Establishment and Navigation, and protocol, entered into force March 28, 1963, 14 UST 251, TIAS 5306, 474 UNTS 3.

590. *Current Economic Developments*, February 28, 1961, page 11, NARA, Record Group 59, Department of State Lot Files. The State Department offered this description in reference to the treaty negotiations with Belgium.

591. *Treaty of Friendship, Establishment and Navigation between the United States of America and the Grand Duchy of Luxembourg*, Exec. Rept. No. 7, 87th Cong. 2d Sess. (1962), page 2.

592. Ibid.

593. 108 *Congressional Record* 19880 (1962).

Amendment. Following this brief explanation, the Senate gave advice and consent to ratification of the treaty by a vote of 86-0.[594]

NEGOTIATING AN FCN TREATY WITH TOGO

In May 1962, the U.S. embassy in Togo suggested that goodwill resulting from a recent visit to the United States by the Togolese Olympic team created a propitious moment for negotiating an FCN treaty.[595] The following month, Acting Secretary of State George W. Ball authorized the negotiation of the treaty.[596] In recommending that authorization be granted, Undersecretary G. Griffith Johnson noted that the negotiation of such a treaty would be consistent with the Foreign Assistance Act of 1961, which provided that the president shall "accelerate a program for negotiating treaties of commerce and trade . . . which shall include provisions to encourage and facilitate the flow of private investment to, and its equitable treatment in, friendly countries and areas participating in programs under this Act."[597] The treaty would be modeled after that recently concluded with Vietnam.

The negotiating history that has survived is sparse. The few existing documents indicate that Togo wished to organize the treaty into three sections—establishment provisions, commercial provisions, and general provisions—a proposal that the United States successfully resisted on the ground that some provisions could fall within more than one of these sections, and that the placement of a provision under a particular heading could cause a court to misinterpret the scope or meaning of the provision.[598] Togo also wished to retitle the treaty as an "economic cooperation agreement," a proposal that the United States also successfully resisted on the ground that this title was usually applied to treaties involving loans or technical assistance and that a title different from that used in similar treaties might imply that the treaty was different in substance and perhaps inferior in some way.[599]

594. Ibid.; Senate Voting Record No. 192, dated September 19, 1962, NARA, Record Group 46, File No. SEN87B-B10.

595. Airgram A-197 dated May 18, 1962, from the U.S. embassy in Lome to the Department of State, NARA, Record Group 59, Department of State File No. 611.70d42/5-1862.

596. Memorandum dated June 14, 1962, from Under Secretary G. Griffith Johnson to Acting Secretary George W. Ball, NARA, Record Group 59, Department of State File No. 611.70d4/6-1462.

597. Act of September 4, 1961, Pub. L. No. 87-195, section 601(b), 75 Stat. 424, 438.

598. Airgram dated May 19, 1965, from the Department of State to the U.S. embassy in Lome, NARA, Record Group 59, Central Foreign Policy Files 1964-66, Box 1037, Folder marked "FT Foreign Trade, Togo, 1/1/64."

599. Ibid; Telegram dated July 19, 1965, from the Department of State to the U.S. embassy in Lome, NARA, Record Group 59, Central Foreign Policy Files 1964-66, Box 1037, Folder marked "FT Foreign Trade, Togo, 1/1/64."

As the U.S. embassy noted in its report on the negotiations, "relatively few" changes to the draft proposed by the United States were made.[600] Notable changes included the omission of MFN treatment with respect to the right of establishment and of the competitive equality provision.

The United States and Togo signed the FCN treaty on February 8, 1966.[601] Although the United States was seeking to negotiate FCN treaties during the 1960s with other countries of sub-Saharan Africa, including Cameroon, Chad, Gabon, Ghana, Ivory Coast, Kenya, Nigeria, Somali Republic, Tanzania, Uganda, and Zambia, the treaty with Togo was the first to be concluded with a newly independent African state. President Lyndon Johnson, in transmitting the treaty to the Senate, noted that it was "another important step by the United States in implementing its policy of extending and modernizing its commercial treaty structure and of establishing conditions favorable to foreign investment."[602] None of the negotiations with the other sub-Saharan African countries was successful.

The Committee on Foreign Relations considered the treaty in executive session on September 22, 1966, at which time Deputy Assistant Secretary of State for African Affairs William C. Trimble testified in support of the treaty, after which the Committee recommended the treaty for advice and consent.[603] On September 28, the Senate gave its advice and consent to ratification without debate by a vote of 64-0.[604]

NEGOTIATING AN FCN TREATY WITH THAILAND

In November 1959, the U.S. ambassador to Thailand proposed the negotiation of an FCN treaty and gave the Thai foreign minister copies of the proposed treaty of amity and economic relations,[605] the short form treaty similar to that concluded with Ethiopia, Iran, and Muscat and Oman and that was in an advanced stage of negotiation with Vietnam.[606] This commenced a lengthy process of detailed study of the treaty within the Thai government and the beginning of informal discussions between the U.S. embassy and the Thai

600. Enclosure 3 to Airgram A-101 dated May 9, 1969, from the U.S. embassy in Abidjan to the Department of State, NARA, Record Group 59, Central Foreign Policy Files, 1967–1969, Box 975, Folder marked "FT 4, 4/1/68."

601. Treaty of Amity and Economic Relations, entered into force February 5, 1967, 18 UST 1, TIAS 6193, 680 UNTS 159.

602. Letter of Transmittal dated May 23, 1966, from the President to the Senate, *Treaty with the Togolese Republic,* Executive E, 89th Cong. 2d Sess. (1966), page 1.

603. *Treaty of Amity and Economic Relations with Togo,* Exec. Rept. No. 8, 89th Cong. 2d Sess. (1966)), page 2.

604. 112 *Congressional Record* 24242 (1966).

605. Airgram dated July 6, 1960, from the U.S. embassy in Bangkok to the Department of State, NARA, Record Group 59, Department of State File No. 611.9242/7-660.

606. Instruction A-6 dated July 18, 1960, from the Department of State to the U.S. embassy in Bangkok, NARA, Record Group 59, Department of State File No. 611.9242/7-660.

government.[607] It soon emerged that Thailand's greatest concern was that China would demand similar privileges to those granted to the United States under the treaty.[608]

After more than two years of study, in February 1962, Thailand responded to the U.S. proposal by presenting the United States with a counterdraft.[609] Thailand hoped that the treaty with the United States would serve as a model for its future treaties.[610]

Negotiations began on October 22, 1962, and were spirited.[611] One of the principal Thai negotiators held doctorates from both Oxford and Harvard and a law degree from the Sorbonne, while the other was trained as a barrister at the Inns of Court in London.[612]

The United States and Thailand encountered serious disagreement over the trade provisions. In particular, Thailand wished to include an exception to the MFN treatment obligation for a regional association for economic development (specifically, an association with the Philippines and Malaya), arguing that regional cooperation was a practice that originated with the Monroe Doctrine.[613] The United States objected to the exception based on its long-standing policy to reduce or eliminate trade preferences.[614] The dispute over the trade provisions triggered special passion, with one of the principal Thai negotiators asserting that the treaty was an "unequal" treaty "which would have been less odious in the nineteenth century."[615]

Other issues arose as well. Thailand objected to the exchange controls provision, wanting an assurance that the language permitting the allocation of foreign exchange for the health and welfare of the people included the use of foreign exchange to assure financial stability and economic development, and expressing

607. Despatch 669 dated June 12, 1961, from the U.S. embassy in Bangkok to the Department of State, NARA, Record Group 59, Department of State File No. 611.9242/6-1261.

608. Ibid.; Despatch dated August 19, 1960, from the U.S. embassy in Bangkok to the Department of State, NARA, Record Group 59, Department of State File No. 611.9242/8-1960.

609. Telegram dated October 8, 1962, from the Department of State to the U.S. embassy in Bangkok, NARA, Record Group 59, Department of State File No. 611.9242/10-862.

610. Summary Minutes of the Treaty of Amity and Economic Relations Negotiations, January 16 and 17 and February 21, 1963, NARA, Record Group 59, Central Foreign Policy Files 1963, Box 3487, Folder marked "FT—Foreign Trade 2/1/63"; Despatch dated August 19, 1960, from the U.S. embassy in Bangkok to the Department of State, NARA, Record Group 59, Department of State File No. 611.9242/8-1960.

611. Summary Minutes of the Treaty of Amity and Economic Relations Negotiations, January 16 and 17 and February 21, 1963, NARA, Record Group 59, Central Foreign Policy Files 1963, Box 3487, Folder marked "FT—Foreign Trade 2/1/63."

612. Ibid.

613. Ibid.

614. Ibid.

615. Ibid.

the view that the requirement of a "just and reasonable" rate was too abstract.[616] Thailand did not believe that it was sufficiently developed to be able to give prior public notice of proposed quantitative restrictions, and the Thai negotiators observed that it would be "un-Thai" for the government to undertake an obligation that it knew that it could not meet.[617] Thailand also objected to the competitive equality provision and to the expropriation provision, saying that it did not wish to be obligated to pay full compensation, and noting that foreign investors were not compelled to invest in Thailand.[618] Finally, Thailand objected to the submission of disputes to the International Court of Justice because of dissatisfaction with the Court's decision in the *Case concerning the Temple of Preah Vihear*[619] the prior year.[620] So strong were Thai objections to the compromissory clause that the embassy believed that that issue could jeopardize the entire treaty.[621]

In June 1963, the discussion turned to the religion clauses of the treaty. The Thai negotiators inquired whether the clause permitting freedom of conscience would permit a Thai man to practice polygamy in the United States or whether polygamy would fall within the treaty's exception reserving to either the party the right to exclude aliens on grounds related to public morals.[622] The State Department replied that the practice of polygamy did not fall within the freedom of conscience and that, in any event, laws prohibiting polygamy would fall within the public morals exception.[623] It noted that the U.S. Constitution, despite its "strictly worded" protections for religious freedom, had been interpreted to permit reasonable regulation of religious activities.[624] The goal of the treaty was to prevent unreasonable interference with religious freedom.[625] The Thai negotiators responded with some (perhaps feigned) umbrage at the U.S. suggestion that

616. Ibid.

617. Ibid.

618. Ibid.

619. (Cambodia v. Thailand), 1962 I. C. J. Rep. 6.

620. Summary Minutes of the Treaty of Amity and Economic Relations Negotiations, January 16 and 17 and February 21, 1963, NARA, Record Group 59, Central Foreign Policy Files 1963, Box 3487, Folder marked "FT—Foreign Trade 2/1/63."

621. Ibid.

622. Telegram dated June 8, 1963, from the U.S. embassy in Bangkok to the Department of State, NARA, Record Group 59, Central Foreign Policy Files 1963, Box 3487, Folder marked "FT—Foreign Trade 2/1/63."

623. Telegram dated June 10, 1963, from the Department of State to the U.S. embassy in Bangkok, NARA, Record Group 59, Central Foreign Policy Files 1963, Box 3487, Folder marked "FT—Foreign Trade 2/1/63."

624. Ibid.

625. Ibid. *See also* Telegram June 27, 1963, from the Department of State to the U.S. embassy in Bangkok, Central Foreign Policy Files 1963, Box 3487, Folder marked "FT—Foreign Trade 2/1/63."

polygamy was immoral.[626] The Thai negotiators were sophisticated men who had deliberately chosen the example of polygamy knowing that it would be provocative. Their objective in raising the issue of polygamy was to convince the United States of the necessity for an exception to the religion clauses for local laws.

The following month, the Thai negotiators tossed onto the negotiating table what the embassy described as a "blockbuster" proposal.[627] Under this proposal, nationals of either party would have the right to engage in religious or matrimonial activities regardless of race, sex, creed, or color. The Thai negotiators denied that the proposal was related to polygamy and said that it was directed at U.S. anti-miscegenation laws, noting that some years prior the daughter of the Thai prime minister was denied a license to marry a U.S. naval officer in Virginia because of that state's ban on marriage between whites and non-whites. The State Department objected to the phrase "regardless of race, sex, creed or color."[628] The Department noted that although many believed that the U.S. Supreme Court would hold that anti-miscegenation laws were unconstitutional, as indeed it did four years later,[629] the Court had not yet ruled on the validity of these laws. Thus, the reference to matrimonial rights would raise serious difficulties relating to the relationship between the federal and state governments, which was always a matter of concern to the Senate when considering a treaty.[630]

Ultimately, the United States accepted language subordinating the right of private and public worship, but not liberty of conscience, to local law.[631] The disagreement regarding exchange controls was resolved by two exchanges of notes at the time of the exchange of instruments of ratification, one of which confirmed that a party was not precluded from applying restrictions on transfers to the extent necessary to ensure the financial stability and economic development of the country and the other of which declared that, if either party believed that the rate applied in a multiple exchange rate system was not just and reasonable, the rate would be determined after consultations between the parties. Thailand did not obtain an exception to MFN treatment with respect to trade for regional

626. Telegram dated June 18, 1963, from the U.S. embassy in Bangkok to the Department of State, NARA, Record Group 59, Central Foreign Policy Files 1963, Box 3487, Folder marked "FT—Foreign Trade 2/1/63."

627. Telegram dated July 19, 1963, from the U.S. embassy in Bangkok to the Department of State, NARA, Record Group 59, Central Foreign Policy Files 1963, Box 3487, Folder marked "FT—Foreign Trade 2/1/63."

628. Telegram dated August 21, 1963, from the Department of State to the U.S. embassy in Bangkok, Record Group 59, Central Foreign Policy Files 1963, Box 3487, Folder marked "FT—Foreign Trade 2/1/63."

629. *Loving v. Virginia,* 388 U.S. 1 (1967).

630. Telegram dated August 21, 1963, from the Department of State to the U.S. embassy in Bangkok, Record Group 59, Central Foreign Policy Files 1963, Box 3487, Folder marked "FT—Foreign Trade 2/1/63."

631. Thailand FCN treaty, Article I(3).

economic cooperation agreements, but did obtain one for a customs union or free trade area or an interim agreement leading to a customs union or free trade area. The language describing the compensation owed for expropriation was revised to read "just compensation in accordance with the principles of international law." The United States agreed to delete the requirement of prior public notice of quantitative restrictions and the competitive equality provision, the embassy noting with respect to the latter that there was "no point in attempting to force on Thailand a provision which could become a continuing source of friction." [632] The compromissory clause was modified so that disputes would be submitted to arbitration rather than to the International Court of Justice.

The parties signed the treaty on May 29, 1966,[633] a date deliberately chosen by the Thai government because it was the 110th anniversary of the signing of the 1856 Treaty of Peace, Friendship, Commerce, and Navigation between the two countries.[634] At the signing ceremony, Thai foreign minister Thanat Khoman noted that the first FCN treaty between the United States and Thailand was negotiated in 1833 by Edmond Roberts on behalf of President Andrew Jackson and was the first treaty signed by the United States with an Asian nation. Roberts would subsequently travel to the Middle East, where he would negotiate the first FCN treaty between the United States and the sultanate of Muscat and Oman. The Thai foreign minister further noted that, in 1920, Woodrow Wilson had decided that the United States would become the first country to surrender extraterritorial rights in Thailand, leading to the conclusion of another FCN treaty between the two countries that same year. This 1966 FCN treaty between the United States and Thailand would be the last FCN treaty ever concluded by the United States and the end of a treaty series that the Continental Congress had initiated in 1776.

The Committee on Foreign Relations held a hearing on the treaty on July 18, 1967, at which Department of State Legal Adviser Leonard C. Meeker testified in support of the treaty.[635] On August 22, the Committee recommended Senate advice and consent to ratification.[636] The Senate gave its advice and consent to ratification of the treaty without debate on September 11 by a vote of 69-0.[637]

632. Summary Minutes of the Treaty of Amity and Economic Relations Negotiations, January 16 and 17 and February 21, 1963, NARA, Record Group 59, Central Foreign Policy Files 1963, Box 3487, Folder marked "FT—Foreign Trade 2/1/63."

633. Treaty of Amity and Economic Relations, entered into force June 8, 1968, 19 UST 5843, TIAS 6540, 652 UNTS 253.

634. Telegram dated May 3, 1966, from the U.S. embassy in Bangkok to the Department of State, NARA, Record Group 59, Central Foreign Policy Files, 1964-66, Box 771, Folder marked, "E 1/1/64 Thai-U.S."

635. *Commercial Treaty with Thailand*, Exec. Rept. No. 14, 90th Cong. 1st Sess. (1967), page 2.

636. Ibid.

637. 113 *Congressional Record* 25063 (1967).

CONTINUITY IN THE KENNEDY, JOHNSON, NIXON, AND FORD ADMINISTRATIONS

All of the FCN treaties concluded during the Eisenhower administration, with one exception, were with countries that had begun treaty discussions with the United States during the Truman administration, although in some cases formal negotiations had not yet begun. The one exception was the treaty with the sultanate of Muscat and Oman, which, as has been seen, was negotiated not at the instance of the United States, but at the instance of the sultan, who wanted to replace the existing treaty and demanded a new one as the price of opening a U.S. consulate in the sultanate.

The Eisenhower administration did seek to expand the geographic reach of the program, particularly into Southeast Asia, a region where it had not been feasible to negotiate an FCN treaty during the Truman years. The Eisenhower administration attempted to negotiate treaties with Cambodia, Laos, Vietnam, and Thailand and succeeded with the latter two, although the treaty with Vietnam would not be signed until after the inauguration of President Kennedy, while the negotiation of the treaty with Thailand would not be completed until the administration of Lyndon Baines Johnson.

The fact that the Eisenhower administration's contribution was chiefly to complete the discussions begun by the Truman administration nicely symbolizes the continuity in FCN treaty policy between the two administrations. The continuity was genuine. The standard draft FCN treaty was well settled by the time Dwight Eisenhower took the oath of office, although it would continue to evolve in small ways.[638] Moreover, the negotiating history reveals no change, after the inauguration of the Republican president, in treaty policy or even in the way in which the treaties were described. As discussed in the Introduction, the State Department continued to refer to the treaties as instruments of liberalism, based on U.S. constitutional and legal principles.

The fact that the Eisenhower administration's contribution was chiefly to complete the discussions begun by the Truman administration also nicely demonstrates the difficulty experienced by the United States in finding new treaty partners. For the most part those countries that had been unwilling to consider the negotiation of an FCN treaty with the Truman administration remained unwilling thereafter. That is, the list of countries willing to consider seriously the conclusion of an FCN treaty with the United States grew only slightly after Truman left the White House. The United States continued to conclude FCN treaties for as long as it did principally because several treaties required many years to conclude, with the result that discussions that began during the Truman administration sometimes continued into the Eisenhower or even the Kennedy administrations. The Eisenhower administration commenced ultimately successful negotiations

638. *See, e.g.*, Instruction dated November 10, 1953, from the Department of State to the U.S. embassy in The Hague, NARA, Record Group 59, Department of State File No. 611.564/10-2253.

with the sultanate of Muscat and Oman and with Vietnam in 1956, and with Thailand in 1959, but otherwise its successful negotiations were limited to countries that had begun treaty discussions during the Truman years.

The election of John F. Kennedy to the presidency in 1960 returned the party of Roosevelt and Truman to the White House and, as might be expected, the Kennedy administration continued the FCN treaty policy begun by Roosevelt and Truman. The Democratic Congress was in agreement and, when it enacted the landmark Foreign Assistance Act of 1961, it again included a directive that the president "accelerate a program of negotiating treaties for commerce and trade . . . which shall include provisions to encourage and facilitate the flow of investment to, and its equitable treatment in, friendly countries and areas participating in programs under this Act."[639]

Acceleration of the program, however, proved to be an unrealistic goal. The Kennedy administration did attempt to extend the treaty network into sub-Saharan Africa,[640] which the Truman administration had sought unsuccessfully to do in 1948, when it commenced discussions with South Africa. Despite discussions with numerous countries in Africa, however, the Kennedy administration would initiate its only successful negotiation with an African country in 1962, when it began discussions with Togo.

Indeed, the Kennedy administration would be the last to initiate a successful FCN treaty negotiation with any country. It would sign the already negotiated treaty with Vietnam, complete the negotiation of the treaty with Belgium, and conduct much of the negotiations with Thailand. It would launch and successfully conclude a negotiation with Luxembourg that had been deferred from the Truman administration (pending conclusion of treaties with the Netherlands and Belgium) and would also launch the negotiation with Togo, which would not be completed until 1966, during the Johnson administration. Following the assassination of President Kennedy, the Johnson administration completed the negotiation of the treaties with Togo and Thailand and conducted discussions or negotiations with a number of countries, particularly in Africa,[641] although it would initiate no successful negotiations.

FCN treaty discussions with other countries continued into the presidencies of Richard M. Nixon and Gerald R. Ford. The Philippines, for example, which was one of the first countries to engage in FCN treaty discussions with the United States at the end of the war, was again negotiating with the United States in the 1970s. Throughout the 10-year period from 1966 to 1976, the United States would continue its efforts to extend its FCN treaty series without a single successful negotiation. As late as 1976, for example, the Ford administration was seeking to initiate FCN treaty negotiations with Senegal. The U.S. postwar FCN treaty

639. Act of September 4, 1961, Pub. L. No. 87-195, section 601(b), 75 Stat. 424, 438.

640. Eric V. Youngquist, "United States Commercial Treaties: Their Role in Foreign Economic Policy," 2 *Studies in Law and Economic Development* 72, 85 (1967).

641. Ibid.

program, however, was largely exhausted well before that 10-year period. As indicated above, if one sets aside countries that were in FCN treaty discussions (even if not formal negotiations) with the Truman administration, the only successful negotiations that began after 1956 were with Thailand in 1959 and Togo in 1962.

During the more than 30-year lifespan of the U.S. postwar FCN treaty program, the international economy changed dramatically. The treaty program began at a time when Europe, devastated by the war, lacked both a manufacturing capacity to produce its own goods and dollars to purchase American goods. The United States government encouraged outward investment to provide not only Europe, but the developing countries of Africa, Asia, and Latin America, with dollars needed for reconstruction or development and to purchase the U.S. manufacturing surplus. By 1950, however, U.S. military expenditures abroad were so large that, despite a continuing (though shrinking) positive balance of trade, the United States was experiencing a negative balance of payments.[642] In 1958, the balance of payments deficit surged to almost $3.5 billion.[643] Thus, the Kennedy administration inherited a balance of payments deficit of "considerable gravity,"[644] which the United States would struggle unsuccessfully to address throughout the 1960s. By the end of the 1960s, the dollar gap of the late 1940s was a dollar glut.[645]

Despite the end of the dollar gap that had justified U.S. promotion of outward investment in the years immediately following the war, at the time when the U.S. FCN treaties were reconceived as investment treaties, U.S. policy with respect to those treaties never changed. The United States continued to believe that the FCN treaties embodied "right principles" founded on U.S. constitutional and legal principles and the regulated system of free enterprise of New Deal liberalism. These were principles to which, the United States believed, countries should adhere, despite changes in their economic circumstances. Chapter 8 explicates those principles.

642. "The United States Balance of Payments, 1946–1960," *Federal Reserve Bank of St. Louis Monthly Review*, Vol. 3, March 1961, pages 2–9.

643. Ibid.

644. "The United States and New Crossroads in World Economy," Address by Assistant Secretary of State Edwin M. Martin, December 29, 1960, *Department of State Bulletin*, Volume 44, No. 1125, January 16, 1961, page 75.

645. Barry Eichengreen, "From Benign Neglect to Malignant Preoccupation: U.S. Balance of Payments Policy in the 1960s," in George L. Perry and James Tobin, eds., *Economic Events, Ideas, and Policies: The 1960s and After* (Washington, DC: Brookings Institution Press, 2000), pages 185–229.

8

The International Law of Foreign Investment in the FCN Treaties

The American goal of concluding a series of investment treaties that would project New Deal liberalism, particularly the New Deal's understanding of liberal legality, onto the international plane found concrete expression in the investment-related provisions of the U.S. postwar FCN treaties. It is these provisions that best reflect the concept of legality embodied in the treaties.

The model for the concept of legality embodied in the treaties was U.S. constitutional and legal principles, which generally applied (with exceptions related to the establishment of investment) to foreign investors in the same way that they applied to U.S. investors. That is, the United States was seeking largely to assure for U.S. investors abroad the same treatment already provided to foreign (and domestic) investors in the United States under existing U.S. law and policy. As the National Advisory Council noted in 1955, "The aim has been to assure one's own citizens, when they ventured abroad, a right to approximately the same standards of treatment they received at home."[1]

Thus, the United States was not asking other countries to make any commitment that it was itself not prepared to make. As President Truman would tell Congress in 1949, when negotiating FCN treaties, "we do not, of course, ask privileges for American capital greater than those . . . we ourselves grant in this country."[2] The following year, Assistant Secretary of State Willard Thorp made the same point during his testimony in support of the FCN treaties with Uruguay

1. NAC Staff Document No. 740, Program for Obtaining Treaty Assurances to Protect United States Citizens and Property and Promote United States Private Investment in Foreign Countries, NARA, Record Group 353, Records Relating to the Council on Foreign Economic Policy 1955–1961, Box 4, Folder marked "Investment in Underdeveloped Countries CFEP 511 (Folder 2)."

2. Harry S. Truman, "The Point 4 Program: Aid to Underdeveloped Areas," June 24, 1949, *reprinted in* Department of State, *A New Era in World Affairs: Selected Speeches and Statements of President Truman, January 20 to August 29, 1949*, Department of State Publication 3653 (Washington, DC: Government Printing Office, 1949), page 32.

and Ireland when he said that "we have to ourselves give the same privileges to other countries that we are asking from them."[3]

This principle was repeatedly affirmed by the United States in statements noting that the obligations of the treaty were mutual. As described in Chapter 5, at the time the FCN treaties were reconceptualized as investment treaties, the United States inserted language into the preamble that referred to the treaties as "arrangements encouraging mutually beneficial investments, promoting mutually advantageous commercial intercourse, and otherwise establishing mutual rights and privileges . . . ." Internal State Department correspondence noted in 1954 that "[t]hese treaties are entirely mutual and the United States is asking no commitment that it is not willing itself to undertake."[4] This echoed earlier internal correspondence where Assistant Legal Adviser Stanley Metzger observed that "FCN treaties must be reciprocal."[5] The same point was made outside the Department. For example, when it informed the British government of its intent to negotiate an FCN treaty with China in 1945, the State Department explained that "[t]he principle of mutuality is applied throughout the treaty."[6] Similarly, U.S. negotiators told their German counterparts that "mutuality is the sole basis upon which it is possible to negotiate. . . ."[7] The State Department described the FCN treaties to the president as "based on the principle of mutuality."[8] It noted in a 1952 publication that "these treaties are not one-sided. They are drawn up in mutual terms; and rights assured to Americans in foreign countries are assured in like manner to foreigners in this country."[9] The Senate had the same understanding. Republican senator Bourke Hickenlooper of Iowa told his colleagues in

3. Transcript of Executive Session, Committee on Foreign Relations, May 4, 1950, NARA, Record Group 46, File No. SEN81B-B7.

4. Memorandum dated November 23, 1953, attached to letter dated April 29, 1954, from Carl Boehringer to the Secretary of State, NARA, Record Group 59, Department of State File No. 611.62A4/4-2954.

5. Memorandum headed "Mr. Walker's Memorandum of October 12 re Possible Revisions in Standard FCN Treaties," from Stanley D. Metzger to Michael H. Cardozo, dated November 15, 1949, NARA, Record Group 59, Department of State Lot Files, Walter Hollis Papers.

6. Memorandum headed "Draft Treaty of Friendship, Commerce and Navigation Presented to the Chinese Government on April 2, 1945," dated May 24, 1945, NARA, Record Group 59, Department of State File No. 711.932/5-2445.

7. Despatch dated October 2, 1953, from the U.S. High Commissioner in Bonn to the Department of State, NARA, Record Group 59, Department of State File No. 611.62A4/10-253.

8. Letter dated January 12, 1950, from Secretary of State Dean Acheson to President Harry S. Truman, NARA, Record Group 59, Department of State File No. 611.334/1-1250.

9. Department of State, Office of Public Affairs, *Commercial Treaty Program of the United States* (Washington, DC: Government Printing Office, 1952), *copy available at* NARA, Record Group 59, Department of State File No. 611.004/3-453. *See also* Testimony of Deputy Assistant Secretary of State Harold Linder, *Commercial Treaties*, Hearing Before a Subcommittee of the Committee on Foreign Relations, 82d Cong. 2d Sess. (1952), page 6.

the Senate that the FCN treaties were "based upon the principle of mutuality."[10] Herman Walker wrote in his private capacity in 1958 that "the treaties must be mutual in their provisions, with the consequence that they can in general contain only such commitments as the United States itself is prepared to undertake."[11]

This mutuality meant that the United States did not ask other countries to make commitments inconsistent with U.S. law and policy. For example, the 1955 NAC report observed that, although the United States wished to obtain unrestricted entry for its outward investment, because the treaties were mutual any provisions on entry must be subject to U.S. laws.[12] That is, the United States could not ask for national treatment in sectors of the economy where it did not grant national treatment to aliens.[13] As a different NAC report observed that same year, "There seems to be no possibility of negotiating treaties of this type upon any other basis that that of substantial mutuality. This means that no treaty provision can be more advanced in promoting private investment than the generality of U.S. laws and policies."[14] As Deputy Assistant Secretary of State Harold Linder explained during Senate hearings in 1952, "In undertaking treaty commitments that would formally confirm to foreigners a substantial body of rights in the United States, the Department of State has exercised great care to frame provisions that would be in conformity with federal law."[15]

Thus, the United States was not seeking through its postwar FCN treaties to provide greater protection for foreign investment in the United States than was already provided to U.S. (and foreign) investment under existing U.S. law and policy. Indeed, the State Department told the German FCN treaty negotiators that it was "out of the question" for the Department to submit to the Senate a treaty containing a privilege for foreign nationals not available in the United States in like situations to U.S. nationals.[16] Similarly, it told the Belgian negotiators that conferring greater rights on Belgian investors in the United States than

10. 99 *Congressional Record* 9312 (1953).

11. Herman Walker Jr., "The Post-War Commercial Treaty Program of the United States," 73 *Political Science Quarterly* 57, 78 (1958).

12. National Advisory Council Document 1868 (Revised) headed "Investments in Less Developed Areas," dated December 12, 1955, NARA, Record Group 353, Records Relating to the Council on Foreign Economic Policy 1955–1961, Box 4, Folder marked "Investment in Underdeveloped Countries CFEP 511 (Folder 1)."

13. Memorandum headed "Draft Treaty of Friendship, Commerce and Navigation with China," dated August 24, 1945, NARA, Record Group 59, Department of State File No. 711.932/8-2445.

14. NAC Staff Document No. 740, Program for Obtaining Treaty Assurances to Protect United States Citizens and Property and Promote United States Private Investment in Foreign Countries, NARA, Record Group 353, Records Relating to the Council on Foreign Economic Policy 1955–1961, Box 4, Folder marked "Investment in Underdeveloped Countries CFEP 511 (Folder 2)."

15. *Commercial Treaties*, Hearing Before a Subcommittee of the Committee on Foreign Relations, 82d Cong. 2d Sess. (1952), page 6.

16. Despatch No. 2413 dated March 8, 1954, from the U.S. High Commissioner in Bonn to the Department of State, NARA, Record Group 59, Department of State File No. 611.62A4/3-854.

Americans had in the United States under the Constitution could raise an "insuperable obstacle" to Senate approval of the treaty.[17] The State Department told the Senate Foreign Relations Committee in 1952 that it could not "recommend a treaty provision which would go beyond established United States policy . . . and grant foreign nationals more favorable treatment than citizens receive in the United States."[18] Foreign investors would receive no greater substantive rights under the FCN treaties than U.S. investors had under U.S. law, particularly U.S. constitutional principles.[19]

The treaties were instruments in which the United States promised to provide foreign investment with the treatment that it already provided to foreign and domestic investment in the United States, while seeking the same treatment for U.S. investment abroad. Accordingly, the United States would not demand treatment inconsistent with existing U.S. law and policy, which already provided in the United States the investment climate that the United States sought to create abroad through the treaties.

The mutuality of treaty obligations was the principal basis on which the State Department resisted demands by the business community for more stringent treaty obligations. The United States would not demand more than it already gave.

That fact, in turn, was the source of one of the principal weaknesses in U.S. bargaining power. Apart from treaty investor visas, permission to use unlicensed professionals for internal purposes and consent to the jurisdiction of the International Court of Justice, the United States did not offer in its investment-related provisions more than foreign investors already had under U.S. law and policy. As Woodbury Willoughby noted in March 1949, the United States did not "actually 'give' very much" in an FCN treaty. [20]

This chapter describes the investment protections that the U.S. postwar FCN treaties were intended to provide. Such a discussion could justifiably cover the entire treaty.[21] Herman Walker once wrote that "[i]n a real sense . . . the FCN treaty as a whole *is* an investment treaty; not a mosaic which

17. Instruction dated January 24, 1957, from the Department of State to the U.S. embassy in Brussels, NARA, Record Group 59, Department of State File No. 611.554/11-2156.

18. Memorandum accompanying letter dated May 16, 1952, from Acting Assistant Secretary of State Harold Linder to Senator John Sparkman, *reprinted in Commercial Treaties,* Hearing Before a Subcommittee of the Committee on Foreign Relations, 82nd Cong. 2d Sess. (1952), page 28.

19. The section below on the fair and equitable treatment standard describes how the State Department rejected recommendations from the Commerce Department's Business Advisory Council because those recommendations would have modified the FCN treaties to give foreign investors greater rights than U.S. investors received under the Constitution.

20. Memorandum dated March 17, 1949, from Woodbury Willoughby to Jack Tate, NARA, Record Group 59, Department of State File No. 611.41D2/3-1749. *See also* Memorandum of Conversation dated November 21, 1951, headed "Addition to FCN Treaties of Provision on Government-Owned Patents," NARA, Record Group 59, Department of State File No. 611.944/11-2151. The lack of U.S. bargaining power is discussed further in Chapter 6.

21. Chapter 5 described the process by which the FCN treaties were reconceived as investment treaties, during which even the guarantees of noneconomic rights were newly reconceived as

merely contains discrete investment segments. It regards and treats investment as a process inextricably woven into the fabric of human affairs generally; and its premise is that investment is inadequately dealt with unless set in the total 'climate' in which it is to exist."[22] Walker thus believed that all of the provisions of the FCN treaties could be considered investment-related, because all of them contributed in various ways to creating a favorable environment for foreign investors, a belief shared by others within the State Department.[23] Indeed, for almost 30 years after it reconceived the FCN treaties as investment treaties, the State Department resisted suggestions that the standard draft treaty be stripped of its trade and navigation provisions to facilitate the conclusion of more treaties, believing that these provisions also contributed to a favorable investment climate.

That said, however, when the Truman administration contemplated in 1949 the drafting of a treaty concerned solely with investment, it included in its proposed treaty only a small number of the provisions found in the FCN treaties.[24] These same provisions have successors in later bilateral investment treaties concluded by the United States and nearly every other country in the world. These are the provisions that eventually were recognized by the international community as the core of an investment treaty, and it is these provisions, rather than the whole of the treaty, that are the subject of this chapter.

In its investment provisions, the United States sought, first and foremost, security for investment. The single most important provision in this regard was the provision requiring prompt, just, and effective compensation for expropriation, a provision that largely replicated protection provided to investors in the United States by the takings clause of the Fifth Amendment to the U.S. Constitution. Security was also provided by the provision guaranteeing most constant protection and security to covered investors and their property, a provision that the State Department regarded as codifying a well-established principle of customary international law, which the Supreme Court has held to be part of U.S. law.[25] A third provision concerned with the security of investment was the provision on exchange controls, which prevented a host state from using exchange controls to deprive an investor of the use of its investment and earnings. This provision had no analog in U.S. law because the United States, as a matter of policy, did not impose exchange controls, and so no protection from them was necessary in the

investment-related. Note especially the discussion in the section headed "Contemplating a New Investment Treaty."

22. Herman Walker Jr., "Treaties for the Encouragement and Protection of Foreign Investment: Present United States Practice," 5 *American Journal of Comparative Law* 229, 244 (1956).

23. Memorandum dated April 7, 1947, from Joseph Coppock to Paul Nitze, NARA, Record Group 43, International Trade Files, Box 55, Folder marked "Investment."

24. This conception of the U.S. postwar FCN treaties is further discussed in Chapter 5, under the heading "Contemplating a New Investment Treaty."

25. *The Paquete Habana*, 175 U.S. 677 (1900).

United States. Thus, the security sought for U.S. investors abroad was equivalent to the security that foreign investors already received in the United States.

Second, the United States sought non-discriminatory treatment of foreign investors. The requirement of non-discrimination was embodied in the guarantees of national and MFN treatment, in the prohibition on unreasonable or discriminatory measures, and in the judicial access provision. These provisions, in general, guaranteed protection that was similar to that accorded to foreign investors in the United States by the equal protection and due process clauses of the Fifth and Fourteenth Amendments to the U.S. Constitution.[26] A competitive equality provision, which also reflected the norm of non-discrimination, precluded government subsidies to state-owned enterprises competing with private enterprises in the manufacturing and trading sectors of the economy, but the provision was crafted narrowly so that it was not expected to apply to any U.S. program, and thus similarly did not confer on foreign investors better treatment than they already received under U.S. law.

Third, the United States sought a guarantee that host state regulations of investment would be reasonable. This guarantee was embodied most explicitly in the prohibition on unreasonable or discriminatory measures. That prohibition provided protection similar to that accorded to foreign investors and their investments in the United States by the equal protection, due process, and contract clauses of the Constitution.

Fourth, the United States sought a guarantee of due process. This guarantee was embodied in the judicial access provision, which technically provided in most cases for non-discrimination with respect to access to courts, but nevertheless was a means of obtaining at least some due process rights for U.S. investors. The norm of due process also was embodied in the provision in which the parties consented to adjudication by the International Court of Justice of disputes involving the interpretation or application of the treaty. Due process is a right guaranteed to foreign investors in the United States by the due process clauses of the Constitution.

The fair and equitable treatment provision embodied all of these principles, but was intended to impose an independent standard applicable to situations where fair and equitable treatment was denied, even though the host state's action did not violate any of the other provisions of the treaty. When the State Department discussed the kinds of host state conduct to which this provision would apply, it most often referred to conduct that was unreasonable or discriminatory, although, as will be seen below, this did not exhaust the meaning of the provision.

An entry and sojourn provision, which reflected the norm of access, granted entry rights to foreign investors, but only to the extent consistent with

26. Herman Walker explicitly analogized the national and MFN treatment provisions to the concept of the "equal protection of the laws," language drawn from the equal protection clause of the Fourteenth Amendment. Herman Walker Jr., "Modern Treaties of Friendship, Commerce and Navigation," 42 *Minnesota Law Review* 805, 811 (1958). U.S. negotiators sometimes drew the same analogy during negotiations. *See, e.g.*, Memorandum headed "Proposed Sino-American Treaty of Friendship, Commerce and Navigation," dated March 16, 1946, NARA, Record Group 59, Department of State File No. 711.932/12-2046.

U.S. immigration laws. It thus did not provide foreign investors with any greater rights than those offered by U.S. law, but only enabled them to receive one of the benefits of that law. Access was also provided by treaty provisions that guaranteed national and MFN treatment with respect to the right to engage in various business and nonprofit activities, in other words, a right of non-discrimination with respect to the establishment of investment.

The FCN treaties contained two provisions on employment. One guaranteed to foreign investors the right to hire certain managerial and technical personnel of their choice, but subject to the immigration and licensure laws of the host country. The provision was intended to address host state laws that required foreign investment to grant a hiring preference to indigenous personnel. Thus, this provision, in practical effect, was another one directed at discrimination by the host state. The other employment provision permitted foreign owned enterprises to utilize expatriate technical and professional personnel on a temporary basis to perform work solely for internal use, such as an audit. This provision arguably provided foreign investors in the United States with a limited exception to local licensure laws, but the exception was so limited in scope and duration that the State Department presumably regarded any intrusion on U.S. regulations as de minimis. Moreover, as will be seen, the purpose of this provision was actually to enable U.S. companies doing business abroad to comply with U.S. regulatory laws and thus it was intended to further, rather than to derogate from, the application of U.S. legal principles.

In short, the investment-related provisions of the U.S. postwar FCN treaties largely guaranteed to U.S. investors abroad the same protection that U.S. and foreign investors received in the United States under the Fifth and Fourteenth Amendments to the U.S. Constitution and under the contract clause. The treaties did in some ways go beyond these constitutional protections, such as by guaranteeing certain rights available under customary international law and providing a limited protection against exchange controls that was actually less robust than that afforded as a matter of policy in the United States. Again, however, any substantive protections essentially replicated the treatment that foreign investors already received under existing U.S. law and policy. The treaty provisions were self-executing in the United States and thus did not require the enactment of implementing legislation.[27]

As was seen in Chapter 6, the United States did not regard these protections as concessions granted by other countries, but as reflections of "right principles" that both countries had already embraced. The State Department believed that these principles had been tested in the United States, where they had provided the protections for investors necessary to build the most productive economy in the world, while also permitting federal and state governments to regulate economic activity in the public interest.

27. Despatch dated April 16, 1959, from the U.S. embassy in Paris to the Department of State, NARA, Record Group 59, Department of State File No. 611.514/4-1659.

Indeed, consistent with New Deal liberalism, FCN treaty provisions pervasively recognized the legitimate need of the state to regulate, subject to restrictions similar to those embodied in the U.S. Constitution. For example, provisions guaranteeing reasonable treatment allowed any regulation as long as it was reasonably related to a legitimate state objective. Provisions guaranteeing non-discriminatory treatment allowed the host state to regulate investors and investment, provided only that any distinctions in the regulations were not arbitrary or based on nationality. The provision requiring national treatment with respect to the establishment of investment permitted any restriction on establishment that was non-discriminatory, and allowed the parties to impose even discriminatory restrictions in various sectors of the economy identified in the treaty or in those sectors that were closed to private enterprise entirely. In some cases, the United States accepted more sweeping exceptions, such as for balance of payments considerations, or agreed to eliminate the provision on national treatment with respect to establishment entirely. The judicial access provision prohibited only measures that were discriminatory or inconsistent with due process. The expropriation provision applied only to regulations that deprived the owner of the effective use of the property and, even so, permitted takings of private investment that were in the public interest and accompanied by the prompt payment of just and effective compensation. The exchange controls provision permitted exchange controls during times of foreign exchange stringency, allowed the host state to give priority to the health and welfare of its people in allocating foreign exchange, and, even after that priority was given, required only reasonable provision for withdrawal of foreign capital and earnings, giving consideration to special needs for other transactions. The provision on entry and sojourn was subject to U.S. immigration law. The entire treaty was subject to an exception for measures necessary to protect a party's essential security interests. To a very great extent, the host country that refrained from the adoption of unreasonable or discriminatory measures, the uncompensated expropriation of foreign investment, and the imposition of exchange controls except when required by foreign exchange stringency; that accorded due process; and that exercised due diligence to protect foreign investment was unlikely to be charged with a violation of the investment provisions of the treaty. Again, the treaty largely reflected basic norms of liberal legality—security of property, reasonableness (i.e., nonarbitrariness), non-discrimination, and due process. Herman Walker in 1958 described the FCN treaty program as one "in which must be reconciled the need for positive, universally tenable rules of law, with the equal need for moderation and a spirit of accommodation within a distinctive framework of basic purpose."[28]

The State Department repeatedly spoke of the FCN treaties as a means of promoting the rule of law, that is, of promoting liberal legality. The United States hoped that the treaties would promote the rule of law not only within the territory of the treaty parties, but throughout the world. This was expected to occur in two ways.

28. Walker, "Modern Treaties," page 810.

The first was by creating precedents that other countries would follow in drafting their own treaties. As Vernon Setser noted, "The effect of the establishment of an improved rule in a bilateral treaty reaches far beyond the two countries concerned, inasmuch as it establishes a precedent in international practice that may eventually become a generally accepted rule of international law."[29] During negotiations with Belgium, for example, the U.S. negotiators observed that no need existed for a provision on compensation for expropriation of indirect interests between the United States and Belgium because both countries provided compensation under their domestic law, "but the United States wanted to build up in these treaties a body of precedent tending to establish this as an international legal rule, with an eye on countries which do not acknowledge an obligation to pay just compensation to their nationals."[30]

The second was by producing, through adjudication or arbitration of disputes arising under the treaties, a body of case law that would further develop international law. As the State Department explained during negotiations with Austria, decisions of the International Court of Justice "contribute to the building up of a body of case law of value in the development of international law."[31] Indeed, it was largely to the decisions of tribunals that the United States looked when ascertaining the content of the international law relating to foreign investment. When asked during negotiations with India what was meant by treatment "required by international law," U.S. negotiators "referred to the large body of case law on this subject that had been produced by international judicial agencies," such as the rule requiring the exercise of due diligence to protect alien owned property during riot or insurrection.[32] The State Department described rights under international law as those "commonly recognized by international tribunals and in diplomatic correspondence in matters of protection."[33] After India questioned the existence of principles of international law relevant to investment protection, the Department replied, "For the fact of the existence of the international law standard and its nature, there is material in the writings of publicists and in the reports of international adjudications; e.g., decisions of international claims

29. Memorandum headed "Reaction of the Chilean Government to the Department's Proposals for the Negotiation of a Treaty of Friendship, Commerce and Navigation," by Vernon Setser, dated February 13, 1950, NARA, Record Group 59, Department of State File No. 611.004/3-850.

30. Despatch dated April 5, 1957, from the U.S. embassy in Brussels to the Department of State, NARA, Record Group 59, Department of State File No. 611.554/4-557.

31. Department of State Instruction A-313 dated March 20, 1958, from the Department of State to the U.S. embassy in Vienna, NARA, Record Group 59, Department of State File No. 611.634/3-458.

32. Minutes of Discussions of Draft Treaty of Friendship, Commerce and Navigation between the United States and India, August 5, 1949, NARA, Record Group 59, Department of State File No. 711.452/9-2149.

33. Airgram A-27 dated January 31, 1949, from the Department of State to the U.S. embassy in New Delhi, NARA, Record Group 59, Department of State File No. 711.452/1-2849.

commissions involving the U.S., and European and American states."[34] As an example, the Department cited the *Factory at Chorzow* case, which required full compensation for expropriation,[35] a rule supported by decisions of numerous international tribunals.[36] Writing in his personal capacity about the development of rules of customary international law, Robert Wilson, a principal FCN treaty negotiator during the 1940s, observed that "the rule can either be found and applied by arbitrators or declared not to exist in a form that would justify the tribunal's holding the respondent state to compliance with it."[37] Indeed, Wilson observed, "It has been said that so-called customary law is often not so much the product of state practice as it is the product of tribunals."[38] The advantage of such a system, Wilson noted, was the ability of tribunals to adapt rules to particular situations "in a changing milieu."[39] By way of illustration, he cited the concept of denial of justice, which was widely understood to exist, though questions regarding "the particular manner of application" were "the subject of wide disagreement."[40]

The State Department recognized a tension between the investment protection provisions, which essentially embodied rule of law norms, and the establishment provisions, which embodied the norm of access and reflected the system of free enterprise. This tension emerged, for example, during negotiations with India, which wanted a more sweeping reservation with respect to the right of establishment than the United States wished to include. Unless the United States was prepared to compromise on the right of establishment, it would be unable to obtain a treaty to protect U.S. property in India. In addressing this tension, State Department officials noted that the "fundamental purpose" of FCN treaties was to provide "bases for the diplomatic and juridical protection of American interests abroad. Regardless of any policy for the stimulation of foreign investments, the Government has a duty to place itself in the best position possible for protecting its citizens abroad."[41] Thousands of Americans lived in India, and millions of dollars were invested there. For that reason, a treaty to protect those already in

34. Telegram No. 108 dated August 18, 1952, from the Department of State to the U.S. embassy in New Delhi, NARA, Record Group 59, Department of State File No. 711.914/8-1852.

35. Ibid.

36. Telegram dated February 12, 1952, from the Department of State to the U.S. embassy in New Delhi, NARA, Record Group 59, Department of State File No. 611.914/2-752.

37. Robert R. Wilson, *The International Law Standard in Treaties of the United States* (Cambridge, MA: Harvard University Press, 1953), page 6.

38. Ibid., page 7.

39. Ibid.

40. Ibid.

41. Memorandum headed "Negotiation of Treaty of Friendship, Commerce and Navigation with India," dated September 11, 1950, NARA, Record Group 59, Department of State File No. 611.914/9-1150.

India was desirable, even if it had only a limited right of establishment.[42] In short, the State Department's primary goal in concluding FCN treaties was to gain the protection of the rule of law for U.S. interests abroad. It was prepared to compromise on the right of establishment in order to gain such protection. Indeed, before the Cold War intervened, the State Department was prepared to negotiate a treaty with the Soviet Union, which had abolished free enterprise, and throughout the duration of the treaty program it made compromises on the right of establishment. As Herman Walker noted in 1958, "Probably the most important purpose a treaty is designed to serve . . . is the protection of persons, property and other acquired interests from ill-usage and spoliation."[43] Provisions on entry were of secondary importance. The treaty promoted the system of free enterprise, but that goal was subordinate to the goal of promoting the rule of law.

An extensive record of the negotiating history of the U.S. postwar FCN treaties documents and elaborates upon this basic summary of the content of the investment-related provisions. The following pages draw upon that negotiating history to describe the ways in which the United States understood these provisions and explained them to potential treaty parties.

COMPANIES PROTECTED BY THE TREATY

When it inaugurated its postwar FCN treaty program in the mid-1940s, the State Department considered the extension of investment protection to juridical entities to be "perhaps the most striking advance" in the U.S. postwar FCN treaty program.[44] Prior to the war, the FCN treaties "either were silent concerning the applicability of their provisions to corporations and other associations, or provided in only a limited way for such entities."[45] From the beginning, FCN treaties had been concerned with protecting the rights of persons.[46] Treaty protection applied to "nationals,"[47] "citizens," or "subjects"—terms that generally

42. Ibid.

43. Walker, "Modern Treaties," page 822.

44. Testimony of Deputy Assistant Secretary of State Harold Linder, *Commercial Treaties*, Hearing Before a Subcommittee of the Committee on Foreign Relations, 82nd Cong. 2d Sess. (1952), page 4. A State Department publication described the extension of protection to companies as "the most significant advance" in the U.S. postwar FCN treaties. Department of State, Office of Public Affairs, *Commercial Treaty Program of the United States* (Washington, DC: Government Printing Office, 1952), *copy available at* NARA, Record Group 59, Department of State File No. 611.004/3-453.

45. Herman Walker Jr., "Provisions on Companies in United States Commercial Treaties," 50 *American Journal of International Law* 373 (1956).

46. Ibid.

47. The U.S. postwar FCN treaties used the term "nationals," which is broader than the term "citizens." Harry C. Hawkins, *Commercial Treaties & Agreements: Principles & Practice* (New York: Rinehart, 1951), page 3. For example, in the case of the United States, natives of American Samoa are nationals but not citizens.

were not intended to apply to companies, unless they expressly otherwise provided.[48] For example, in a 1933 exchange with Switzerland, the United States had argued that the word "citizen" used in an 1850 treaty between the two countries did not include corporations.[49] Not until 1911, when the United States concluded an FCN treaty with Japan, did the treaties begin regularly to provide some form of protection to companies. That treaty, at Article VII, granted corporations and associations organized under the laws of one party the right of access to the courts of the other party. Subsequent FCN treaties concluded prior to the 1940s also granted to nationals of a party MFN treatment with respect to the right to organize corporations.[50]

In its postwar FCN treaties, the United States decided that juridical entities should receive the same treaty protection as natural persons.[51] This change recognized the fact that most foreign investment was held through corporations. As U.S. negotiators explained in 1955 during negotiations with Belgium, extending protection to companies "represented the great step forward which the U.S. had taken in its post-World War II treaty program, as compared with previous policy; and was done in recognition of the dominant role which corporate capital plays in international investment."[52] Because most foreign investment was held by companies, an FCN treaty that failed to protect companies would not achieve its goal of protecting foreign investment. [53] As a result, provisions that previously had protected the rights of nationals were drafted to apply to "nationals and companies" of a party. Treaty protection thus applied to those entities that fell within the term "companies."

Definition of the Term "Companies"

The term "companies" was intended to embrace all juridical entities.[54] To make that clear, the State Department incorporated a definition of the term "companies" into its standard draft treaty. For example, Article XXII(3) of the 1955 standard draft treaty defined the term "companies" to mean "corporations, partnerships, companies and other associations, whether or not with limited liability and whether or not for pecuniary profit." This sentence was designed to be

48. Walker, "Provisions on Companies in United States Commercial Treaties," pages 377–378. For a review of the State Department's views on specific treaties, *see* III Green Hackworth, *Digest of International Law* (Washington, DC: Government Printing Office, 1942), pages 429–434.

49. Hawkins, *Commercial Treaties & Agreements*, page 5.

50. Walker, "Provisions on Companies," page 387.

51. Ibid., page 380.

52. Despatch No. 914 dated March 11, 1955, from the U.S. embassy in Brussels to the Department of State, NARA, Record Group 59, Department of State File No. 611.554/3-1155.

53. Walker, "Provisions on Companies," 50 *American Journal of International Law* 373, 385 (1956).

54. Ibid., page 380. Walker used the term "artificial persons" rather than "juridical entities."

"a comprehensive description of juridical entities."[55] That is, it "comprehend[ed] 'juridical persons' generally," with the term "other associations" intended to function as a "catch-all."[56] Early U.S. postwar FCN treaties had used the term "corporations and associations,"[57] which was intended to have the same scope.

The FCN treaties protected companies only if they possessed the nationality of a treaty party. A company's nationality was determined by its place of incorporation.[58] For example, the second sentence of Article XXII(3) of the 1955 standard draft treaty stated that "[c]ompanies constituted under the applicable laws and regulations within the territories of either Party shall be deemed companies thereof and shall have their juridical status recognized within the territories of the other Party." In some treaties, the United States used the word "organize" rather than "constitute," but the two terms had the same meaning.[59] A company had the nationality of the country where it was chartered, even if it conducted its business entirely in another country and its only contact with the place of incorporation was the issuance of the charter.[60]

Although it sometimes had used other tests before the war, [61] the United States decided at the end of World War II that the place of incorporation test would be the sole test for determining the nationality of juridical persons.[62] The United

55. Despatch No. 2307 dated February 23, 1954, from the U.S. High Commissioner in Bonn to the Department of State, NARA, Record Group 59, Department of State File No. 611.62A4/2-2354.

56. Instruction A-144 dated November 27, 1953, from the Department of State to the U.S. embassy in The Hague, NARA, Record Group 59, Department of State File No. 611.554/10-2953.

57. *See, e.g.*, China FCN treaty, Article III(1); Italy FCN treaty, Article II(1).

58. Memorandum concerning Draft Treaty of Friendship, Commerce and Navigation, For Use of the Embassy, NARA, Record Group 59, Department of State File No. 711.932/2-1645; Ninth Meeting to Consider a Tentative Draft Treaty of Friendship, Commerce and Navigation between the United States and Brazil, Held November 27, 1945, NARA, Record Group 59, Department of State File No. 711.322/4-2346; Memorandum to the American Mission at Beirut for Use in Negotiating Treaty of Friendship, Commerce and Navigation between the United States and the Lebanese Republic, NARA, Record Group 59, Department of State File No. 711.90E2/7-346; Airgram dated February 10, 1949, from the Department of State to the U.S. embassy in New Delhi, NARA, Record Group 59, Department of State File No. 711.452/2-1049.

59. Airgram dated June 1, 1950, from the Department of State to the U.S. embassy in Copenhagen, NARA, Department of State File No. 611.594/5-350.

60. Airgram dated February 10, 1949, from the Department of State to the U.S. embassy in New Delhi, NARA, Record Group 59, Department of State File No. 711.452/2-1049; Memorandum to the American Mission at Beirut for Use in Negotiating Treaty of Friendship, Commerce and Navigation between the United States and the Lebanese Republic, enclosure with message dated July 3, 1946, from the Department of State to the U.S. mission in Beirut, NARA, Record Group 59, Department of State File No. 711.90E2/7-346.

61. Walker, "Provisions on Companies," page 381.

62. Airgram dated July 3, 1953, from the Department of State to the U.S. embassy in The Hague, NARA, Record Group 59, Department of State File No. 611.564/6-1553.

States believed that the place of incorporation test had the virtues of simplicity and ease of determination. The test also paid deference to the laws of the country to which the company owed its existence. Further, the United States believed that the place of incorporation test made the determination of corporate nationality analogous to the determination of the nationality of natural persons,[63] goods, and ships.[64] More generally, the United States believed that the test contributed to "good order" in the law of juridical status.[65]

In some cases, the other party sought to use the seat test, to which the United States invariably objected.[66] The United States believed that the seat test introduced uncertainty because the test was unknown in U.S. practice, and in Europe the practice was not uniform, in some cases designating a company's "center of administration" as its seat and in other cases designating its "center of exploitation" as the seat.[67] The place of incorporation test avoided this confusion. The United States also believed that ascribing nationality on the basis of a company's seat would be analogous to ascribing nationality to a natural person on the basis of that person's residence.[68]

The latter part of the second sentence of the 1955 standard draft treaty quoted above required that each party recognize the juridical status of companies constituted under the laws of the other party. The United States wanted a company's juridical status to be recognized by the other party so that the company could collect debts, protect its patents, enforce contracts, and otherwise protect its rights.[69] The provision of the treaty requiring a party to recognize the juridical status of a company of the other party did not obligate the first party to permit the company

63. Instruction A-165 dated December 21, 1953, from the Department of State to the U.S. embassy in The Hague, NARA, Record Group 59, Department of State File No. 511.564/12-2153; Instruction A-201 dated March 25, 1957, from the Department of State to the U.S. embassy in Brussels, NARA, Record Group 59, Department of State File No. 611.554/2-157.

64. Walker, "Provisions on Companies," page 381.

65. Instruction A-165 dated December 21, 1953, from the Department of State to the U.S. embassy in The Hague, NARA, Record Group 59, Department of State File No. 511.564/12-2153; Instruction A-201 dated March 25, 1957, from the Department of State to the U.S. embassy in Brussels, NARA, Record Group 59, Department of State File No. 611.554/2-157.

66. Instruction A-189 dated April 29, 1959, from the Department of State to the U.S. embassy in Brussels, NARA, Record Group 59, Department of State File No. 611.554/4-359.

67. Instruction A-165 dated December 21, 1953, from the Department of State to the U.S. embassy in The Hague, NARA, Record Group 59, Department of State File No. 511.564/12-2153; Instruction A-201 dated March 25, 1957, from the Department of State to the U.S. embassy in Brussels, NARA, Record Group 59, Department of State File No. 611.554/2-157; Walker, "Provisions on Companies," pages 381–382.

68. Instruction A-201 dated March 25, 1957, from the Department of State to the U.S. embassy in Brussels, NARA, Record Group 59, Department of State File No. 611.554/2-157.

69. Telegram dated November 9, 1954, from the Department of State to the U.S. embassy in Tehran, NARA, Record Group 59, Department of State File No. 611.884/11-954.

to conduct business in its territory.[70] That is, recognition of juridical status did not imply permission to engage in the activities for which the company was organized.[71] Rather, any right to conduct business in the territory of a party would be based on other provisions of the treaty.

Denial of Benefits

The United States recognized that the place of incorporation test was subject to "abuse." Such abuse could occur, for example, where a third-country national incorporated a company under the laws of a treaty party in order to gain treaty benefits,[72] a practice that the United States regarded as a form of "free riding."[73] The United States had "no interest whatever in assuring any rights to any third country alien."[74]

To prevent "free riding" by third country nationals, the United States inserted into its FCN treaties a denial of benefits provision. For example, Article XXI(1)(e) of the 1955 standard draft treaty provided that "[t]he present treaty shall not preclude the application of measures . . . denying to any company in the ownership or direction of which nationals of any third country or countries have directly or indirectly the controlling interest, the advantages of the present Treaty, except with respect to recognition of juridical status and with respect to access to courts." In effect, a party reserved the right to substitute a place of control test for a place of incorporation test in cases where a company was controlled by third-country nationals.[75]

Such a limitation on free riding was "considered a desirable and necessary limitation, in view of the broad rights for corporations" in the treaty.[76] The denial of benefits

70. Despatch No. 2307 dated February 23, 1954, from the U.S. High Commissioner in Bonn to the Department of State, NARA, Record Group 59, Department of State File No. 611.62A4/2-2354.

71. Telegram dated August 3, 1949, from the Department of State to the U.S. embassy in Montevideo, NARA, Record Group 59, Department of State File No. 711.332/7-2249.

72. Instruction dated April 1, 1955, from the Department of State to the U.S. embassy in Seoul, NARA, Record Group 59, Department of State File No. 611.95B4/2-2855; Instruction A-201 dated March 25, 1957, from the Department of State to the U.S. embassy in Brussels, NARA, Record Group 59, Department of State File No. 611.554/2-157.

73. Instruction dated April 1, 1955, from the Department of State to the U.S. embassy in Seoul, NARA, Record Group 59, Department of State File No. 611.95B4/2-2855; Despatch dated August 6, 1954, from the U.S. embassy in The Hague to the Department of State, NARA, Record Group 59, Department of State File No. 611.564/8-654; Walker, "Provisions on Companies," page 388.

74. Instruction A-147 dated January 26, 1956, from the Department of State to the U.S. embassy in Seoul, NARA, Record Group 59, Department of State File No. 611.95B4/1-2656.

75. Harry C. Hawkins noted that historically the most common instances of this had occurred during a time of war when a majority of a corporation's shareholders were enemy nationals. Hawkins, *Commercial Treaties & Agreements*, page 4.

76. Memorandum to the Embassy at Chungking for Use in Negotiating Treaty of Friendship, Commerce and Navigation, NARA, Record Group 59, Department of State File No. 711.932/

provision also served the security interests of the United States by permitting a denial of benefits to companies controlled by nationals of hostile third countries.[77]

The denial of benefits provision did not *ipso facto* deny benefits to companies controlled by third-country nationals, but merely permitted a treaty party to do so if it chose.[78] In the words of the State Department,

> the denial of benefits provision states merely a latent power which each Party reserves to itself with respect to companies of the other, rather than a basic self-operative rule of the treaty. It allows each Party, to the extent that it may so choose, to "pierce the corporate veil," but does not require that this be done. The reservation is not expected normally to be invoked or used by either Party in a manner which will impede the companies of the other Party from freely going about their business; but it is a precautionary stipulation included mainly to allow a Party in case of need to prevent third-country interests from getting a "free ride" through the medium of a dummy or "front" corporation chartered under the laws of the other Party.[79]

Similarly, the existence of the provision did not indicate that the United States itself would always deny benefits. Assistant Legal Adviser Stanley Metzger explained in 1953 that the Department of State did not undertake in FCN treaties "to prescribe what policies the States or the Federal Government should or should not follow with respect to third-country controlled corporations, but is merely concerned with assuring that the treaties do not interfere with policies that the competent organs of government wish to formulate and enforce."[80] Thus, the denial of benefits clause preserved to the states and the federal government "the same freedom of action as they have in the absence of the treaty, to deal as they see fit with such corporations. That is, the clause makes it clear that such corporations cannot claim treaty rights as against domestic legislation now or hereafter enacted."[81]

2-1645; Memorandum to the American Mission at Beirut for Use in Negotiating Treaty of Friendship, Commerce and Navigation between the United States and the Lebanese Republic, enclosure with airgram dated July 3, 1946, from the Department of State to the U.S. mission in Beirut, NARA, Record Group 59, Department of State File No. 711.90E2/7-346.

77. Memorandum headed "Meeting with the Argentine Delegation to Discuss FCN Treaty," dated April 4, 1950, NARA, Record Group 59, Department of State File No. 611.354/4-450; Hawkins, *Commercial Treaties & Agreements*, page 4.

78. Walker, "Provisions on Companies," page 388.

79. Instruction A-144 dated November 27, 1953, from the Department of State to the U.S. embassy in The Hague, NARA, Record Group 59, Department of State File No. 611.564/10-2953. *See also* Instruction A-165 dated December 21, 1953, from the Department of State to the U.S. embassy in The Hague, NARA, Record Group 59, Department of State File No. 511.564/12-2153.

80. Letter from Assistant Legal Adviser Stanley Metzger to James W. Gould, dated February 27, 1953, NARA, Record Group 59, Department of State Lot Files, Walter Hollis Papers, Folder marked "FCN Ireland."

81. Ibid.

The denial of benefits provision granted to the denying party "broad latitude" to interpret the word "controlling,"[82] which could include any means of legal control.[83] The provision permitted the denying party to "look behind the superficialities in order to find the real control as well as the interests on whose behalf, or for whose actual benefit, the control was exercised."[84] In the typical case, the term "controlling interest" would mean those to whom "the majority of the board of directors were beholden. Ordinarily, this would be the group owning 51 percent of the common stock."[85] The possibility existed, however, that stockholders owning a small share could "exercise domination," such as where stock was widely held.[86] For this reason, the treaty used the word "controlling" rather than the word "majority."[87] The "essential treaty objective" was that, in the case of a company incorporated in the United States, U.S. nationals have "final control"[88]

During negotiations with the Netherlands, the question arose as to where the burden of proof lay. The State Department responded that the denying party

82. Telegram dated February 2, 1955, from the U.S. embassy in The Hague to the Department of State, NARA, Record Group 59, Department of State File No. 611.564/2-255; Despatch dated February 14, 1955, from the U.S. embassy in The Hague to the Department of State, NARA, Record Group 59, Department of State File No. 611.564/2-255.

83. Memorandum of Conversation dated July 8, 1947, NARA, Record Group 59, Department of State File No. 711.962/7-847.

84. Despatch dated September 8, 1954, from the U.S. embassy in The Hague to the Department of State, NARA, Record Group 59, Department of State File No. 611.564/9-854; Telegram dated February 2, 1955, from the U.S. embassy in The Hague to the Department of State, NARA, Record Group 59, Department of State File No. 611.564/2-255; Despatch dated February 14, 1955, from the U.S. embassy in The Hague to the Department of State, NARA, Record Group 59, Department of State File No. 611.564/2-255.

85. Despatch dated February 17, 1954, from the U.S. High Commissioner in Bonn to the Department of State, NARA, Record Group 59, Department of State File No. 611.62A4/2-1754. *See also* Airgram dated July 1, 1953, from the Department of State to the U.S. embassy in The Hague, NARA, Record Group 59, Department of State File No. 611.564/5-153; Instruction A-144 dated November 27, 1953, from the Department of State to the U.S. embassy in The Hague, NARA, Record Group 59, Department of State File No. 611.564/10-2953.

86. Despatch dated February 17, 1954, from the U.S. High Commissioner in Bonn to the Department of State, NARA, Record Group 59, Department of State File No. 611.62A4/2-1754. *See also* Airgram dated July 1, 1953, from the Department of State to the U.S. embassy in The Hague, NARA, Record Group 59, Department of State File No. 611.564/5-153; Instruction A-144 dated November 27, 1953, from the Department of State to the U.S. embassy in The Hague, NARA, Record Group 59, Department of State File No. 611.564/10-2953.

87. Despatch dated February 17, 1954, from the U.S. High Commissioner in Bonn to the Department of State, NARA, Record Group 59, Department of State File No. 611.62A4/2-1754. *See also* Instruction A-144 dated November 27, 1953, from the Department of State to the U.S. embassy in The Hague, NARA, Record Group 59, Department of State File No. 611.564/10-2953.

88. Airgram dated June 1, 1950, from the Department of State to the U.S. embassy in Copenhagen, NARA, Record Group 59, Department of State File No. 611.594/5-350.

is free to require the company to present reasonable proof that the company is entitled to treaty protection, in the event that such party wishes to invoke the reservation.[89]

The denial of benefits provision included an exception to ensure that even a third-country controlled company would have two rights—the right to have its juridical existence recognized by the denying party and the right of access to the courts of the denying party. These rights were necessary to permit a putatively third-country controlled company to challenge any charges of illegality and, in particular, to establish that it in fact was not a third-country controlled company.[90]

The denial of benefits provision "aroused much criticism" from the investor community.[91] One objection was that U.S. investors in a U.S. company would lose treaty protection for their interests in a company if third-country investors obtained a controlling interest in that company.[92] That concern was addressed to a limited extent by Paragraph 3 of the protocol to the 1955 standard draft treaty, which protected the interests of nationals and companies of one treaty party in property expropriated by the other treaty party notwithstanding the exercise of the denial of benefits provision with respect to the company that owned the property.[93] Another objection to the provision was that it was difficult for the management of a company to ascertain the extent of alien ownership of shares in the company.[94] The State Department retained the provision despite the criticism, believing that, as already noted, the provision was necessary in light of the expanded protections for corporations inserted into the postwar FCN treaties[95]

89. Instruction A-144 dated November 27, 1953, from the Department of State to the U.S. embassy in The Hague, NARA, Record Group 59, Department of State File No. 611.564/ 10-2953.

90. Instruction A-201 dated March 25, 1957, from the Department of State to the U.S. embassy in Brussels, NARA, Record Group 59, Department of State File No. 611.554/2-157.

91. Memorandum headed "Short Draft: List of Pending Questions Involving Possible Revisions," dated January, 1948, NARA, Record Group 59, Department of State Lot Files, Walter Hollis Papers.

92. Eleventh Meeting to Consider a Tentative Draft Treaty of Friendship, Commerce and Navigation between the United States and Brazil, Held December 3, 1945, NARA, Record Group 59, Department of State File No. 711.322/4-2346; Twenty-Ninth Meeting to Consider a Tentative Draft Treaty of Friendship, Commerce and Navigation between the United States and Brazil, Held January 21, 1946, NARA, Record Group 59, Department of State File No. 711.322/4-2346.

93. Instruction A-165 dated December 21, 1953, from the Department of State to the U.S. embassy in The Hague, NARA, Record Group 59, Department of State File No. 611.564/12-2153; Despatch dated August 6, 1954, from the U.S. embassy in The Hague to the Department of State, NARA, Record Group 59, Department of State File No. 611.564/8-654.

94. Memorandum of Conversation dated April 6, 1949, NARA, Record Group 59, Department of State File No. 611.0031/4-549.

95. Twenty-Sixth Meeting to Consider a Tentative Draft Treaty of Friendship, Commerce and Navigation between the United States and Brazil, Held January 14, 1946, NARA, Record Group 59, Department of State File No. 711.322/4-2346.

and that the exceptions for recognition of juridical status and access to courts at least partially addressed the criticism.[96]

During negotiations, the Netherlands sought language indicating that any disabilities resulting from the exercise of the denial of benefits provision would be removed as soon as control by nationals of a treaty party had been established. The United States objected to the inclusion of the proposed language on the ground that such a result was axiomatic and that the proposed wording was therefore unnecessary.[97]

Korea sought to broaden the provision to permit a denial of benefits to companies in which third-country nationals held any interest at all because it wished to exclude from treaty protection any U.S. company in which Japanese or Chinese investors owned any stock. The United States objected because ascertaining whether a third-country national owned a single share of stock in a company would be impossible in many cases and because such a change in the provision would deprive many U.S. companies of treaty protection.[98] Korea amended its proposal so that benefits could be denied to a company in which foreign nationals owned a significant interest, but the United States objected to this proposal as well because it would exclude many publicly traded U.S. companies from treaty protection and because the term "significant" was too uncertain.[99] Ultimately, the United States resolved this issue by agreeing to language in Paragraph 9 of the protocol under which treaty benefits could be denied to any company if any third country or if companies of any third country had the controlling interest and that clarified that the treaty would not require a party to grant entry to undesired third-country nationals.[100]

FAIR AND EQUITABLE TREATMENT

The U.S. postwar FCN treaties required each party to accord fair and equitable treatment to nationals and companies of the other party and to their property. For example, Article I of the 1955 standard draft treaty provided that "[e]ach Party shall at all times accord fair and equitable treatment to the nationals

96. Memorandum headed "Short Draft: List of Pending Questions Involving Possible Revisions," dated January, 1948, and NARA, Record Group 59, Department of State Lot Files, Walter Hollis Papers.

97. Despatch dated September 15, 1954, from the U.S. embassy in The Hague to the Department of State, NARA, Record Group 59, Department of State File No. 611.564/9-1554.

98. Memorandum headed "Status of FCN Treaty Negotiations with ROK," dated June 13, 1955, NARA, Record Group 59, Department of State File No. 611.95B4/5-1355; Instruction dated June 21, 1955, from the Department of State to the U.S. embassy in Seoul, NARA, Record Group 59, Department of State File No. 611.95B4/6-1655.

99. Instruction A-147 dated January 26, 1956, from the Department of State to the U.S. embassy in Seoul, NARA, Record Group 59, Department of State File No. 611.95B4/1-2656.

100. Memorandum headed "Treaty of Friendship, Commerce, and Navigation with Korea—Action under Sec. 5.5, Circular 175," dated October 29, 1956, NARA, Record Group 59, Department of State File No. 611.95B4/10-2956.

and companies of the other Party, and to their property, enterprises and other interests."

The term "fair and equitable" had a long history in U.S. foreign economic policy. Benjamin Franklin, while serving as minister to France, famously commented in 1778 that "[c]ommerce among nations, as between private persons, should be fair and equitable, by equivalent exchanges and mutual supplies."[101] The term was not limited to trade relations. It was used in the 1790s, for example, during an arbitration between the United States and Great Britain to refer to the requirement that compensation be paid for the taking of property.[102]

By the early years of the twentieth century, the term was in increasingly common use. For example, Article 23(e) of the 1919 Covenant of the League of Nations required members of the League to "make provision to secure and maintain ... equitable treatment for the commerce of all members of the League."[103]

The term also was used to refer to the type of treatment that foreign investment should receive from the host state, particularly in cases of expropriation. For example, after Spain seized U.S. petroleum interests in the 1920s, the U.S. ambassador informed the Spanish government on May 31, 1928, that the United States expected "fair and equitable treatment of the interests involved."[104] When Mexico expropriated properties owned by American companies, Secretary of State Cordell Hull issued a statement to the press on March 30, 1938, in which he said that the United States was seeking compensation for the properties and expressed the hope that a fair and equitable solution would be found.[105] On August 14, 1939, Acting Secretary of State Sumner Welles issued another statement to the press reporting that Mexican government officials and representatives of the oil companies were conducting discussions in an effort to reach a "fair and equitable

101. Letter to James Lovell, dated "Paris, July 22, 1778," *quoted in* John Bigelow, *The Life of Benjamin Franklin*, Vol. II (Philadelphia: J.B. Lippincott, 1875), page 443. This quotation appears as "Commerce among nations should be fair and equitable" on the façade of the Herbert C. Hoover Building (which houses the Department of Commerce) in Washington, DC. I am grateful to Dan Price for drawing my attention to the quotation on the facade.

102. *Betsey Case* (1797), John Bassett Moore, I *History and Digest of the Arbitrations to Which the U.S. Has Been a Party* (Washington: Government Printing Office, 1898), page 326 (Opinion of Lord Chancellor Loughborough: "there might exist a fair and equitable claim upon the King's treasury under the provisions of the treaty for complete compensation for the losses sustained by such condemnation.")

103. 13 *American Journal of International Law Supplement* 128 (1919). The origins of this language in the Covenant are traced in Mona Pinchis, "The Ancestry of 'Equitable Treatment' in Trade: Lessons from the League of Nations during the Inter-War Period," 15 *The Journal of World Investment and Trade* 13–72 (2014).

104. Department of State, *Papers Relating to the Foreign Relations of the United States 1928*, Vol. III (Washington: Government Printing Office, 1943), page 865.

105. Green Hackworth, *Digest of International Law*, Vol. III (Washington, DC: Government Printing Office, 1942), page 661.

agreement."[106] After Spain seized American interests in the National Telephone Company of Spain, also in the 1930s, Welles told the Spanish ambassador on April 16, 1940, that the United States "considered that a fair and equitable solution of the telephone controversy was of fundamental importance . . . ."[107]

By 1945, the year when the United States began the negotiation of its first postwar FCN treaty, the State Department already regarded "fair and equitable" treatment as a general descriptor of the treatment required by the treaty. For example, in a December 1945 letter to the U.S. chargé d'affaires in Beirut describing the purpose of an FCN treaty, the State Department explained that a "principal objective" of U.S. foreign policy was "achieving fairness and equity in economic relations between states."[108] The ECEFP in January of that year had called for "nondiscriminatory and just" treatment of foreign investment.[109]

The term made its first appearances in the U.S. postwar FCN treaties not as a general descriptor of the treatment required by the treaty, but in specific contexts that were not explicitly linked to investment protection. The term appeared in the first U.S. postwar FCN treaty, that with China, in several places. First, Article XIX required each party to provide fair and equitable treatment to the nationals, corporations, and associations and commerce of the other party with respect to the imposition of exchange controls. Second, Article XX(1) required that any state trading companies accord fair and equitable treatment with respect to purchases and sales. Third, Article XX(2) required each party to accord fair and equitable treatment to the nationals, corporations, associations, and commerce of the other party in awarding concessions and other contracts and in purchasing supplies. These latter two provisions had antecedents in the U.S. reciprocal trade agreements, which also applied the fair and equitable treatment standard in the antecedent provisions.[110]

The drafters appear to have used the term initially in situations where the United States wanted to impose some restriction on the conduct of the other party, but was unable to formulate a more precise rule.[111] As is discussed below in the section on exchange controls, the United States over time refined the exchange controls provision to include much more specific language and, at that point, it deleted the requirement of fair and equitable treatment in favor of the more specific language. Similarly,

106. "Expropriation of American-Owned Oil Properties in Mexico," Statement by Acting Secretary Welles, *Department of State Bulletin*, Vol. I, Number 8, August 19, 1939, pages 131–132.

107. Department of State, *Foreign Relations of the United States Diplomatic Papers* 1940 (Washington: Government Printing Office, 1955), Vol. III, page 873.

108. Letter dated December 11, 1945, from the Secretary of State to the U.S. Charge d'Affaires in Beirut, NARA, Record Group 59, Department of State File No. 711.90E2/11-145.

109. *See* Chapter 1.

110. *See, e.g.*, Reciprocal Trade Agreement between the United States of America and Mexico, *signed* December 23, 1942, 57 Stat. 833, 9 Bevans 1109, Article V.

111. *See* Airgram dated December 31, 1951, from the Department of State to the U.S. Political Adviser in Tokyo, NARA, Record Group 59, Department of State File No. 611.944/12-751.

by the time it concluded its treaty with Ireland, the United States had developed more precise language that required that state-established monopolies and public agencies make their purchases and sales in accordance with commercial considerations[112] and, at that point, it deleted the reference to fair and equitable treatment from the provision addressing state trading. By contrast, the United States was not able to develop a more precise rule with respect to the awarding of concessions and contracts and the purchasing of supplies, and thus the requirement of fair and equitable treatment remained in the provision addressing those matters.

In using the term "fair and equitable treatment" in these early provisions, the United States recognized that the term "may not be susceptible of precise definition."[113] Indeed, the State Department noted that the term, at least in the context of the provision on concessions, had been "derided by some of the more hard-headed businessmen."[114]

In preparing a proposed FCN treaty for negotiation with the Soviet Union in 1945, State Department officials observed that the meaning of the requirement to provide fair and equitable treatment with respect to exchange controls was explained in the succeeding paragraphs.[115] The provision, however, stated a "general principle" that would apply even if the succeeding paragraphs were excluded or redrafted.[116] That is, it imposed an obligation independent of the obligations imposed by other paragraphs of the treaty.

As noted above, by the 1940s, the State Department already used the term "fair treatment" or "fair and equitable treatment" as a general descriptor of the kind of treatment that it believed governments should accord to foreign investment.[117] As described in Chapter 1, by May 1946, the Foreign Investment Policy Committee's draft policy statement on foreign investment had called for intergovernmental cooperation to ensure "just and equitable" treatment of foreign

112. *See, e.g.,* Ireland FCN treaty, Article XIV(1). This remained the approach. *See, e.g.,* Korea FCN treaty, Article XVII(1).

113. Memorandum dated March 28, 1947, from Vernon Setser to Seymour Rubin, NARA, Record Group 59, Department of State Lot Files, Walter Hollis Papers. *See also* Airgram dated December 31, 1951, from the Department of State to the U.S. Political Adviser in Tokyo, NARA, Record Group 59, Department of State File No. 611.944/12-751.

114. Memorandum headed "Screening Problem in the Projected FCN Treaty with India," dated October 31, 1950, NARA, Record Group 59, Department of State File No. 611.914/11-250.

115. Memorandum headed "The Twenty-Fourth Meeting to Consider a Tentative Draft Treaty of Friendship, Commerce and Navigation between the United States and the U.S.S.R. Held October 18, 1945, NARA, Record Group 59, Department of State File No. 711.612. *See also* Memorandum to the American Mission at Beirut for Use in Negotiating Treaty of Friendship, Commerce and Navigation between the United States and the Lebanese Republic, enclosure with airgram dated July 3, 1946, from the Department of State to the U.S. mission in Beirut, NARA, Record Group 59, Department of State File No. 711.90E2/7-346.

116. Memorandum headed "The Twenty-Fourth Meeting to Consider a Tentative Draft Treaty of Friendship, Commerce and Navigation between the United States and the U.S.S.R. Held October 18, 1945, NARA, Record Group 59, State Department File No. 711.612.

117. *See also* Chapters 1, 3, and 4.

investment. By August 1947, the Committee's draft policy statement called for "fair, equitable and nondiscriminatory" treatment of investment. Meanwhile, as described in Chapter 3, the United States had sponsored the inclusion in the ITO Charter in September 1946 of language authorizing the ITO to recommend treaties for the "just and equitable" treatment of investment, language that would appear in the ITO Charter adopted in Havana. The investment code proposed by the Foreign Investment Policy Committee for inclusion in the Charter in Geneva in May 1947 and the investment proposal drafted by the Geneva delegation that same month both had used the term "fair and equitable treatment" to describe the kind of treatment sought in the Charter for foreign investment, although that language did not survive the ITO Charter negotiations. Thus, by mid-1948, the Foreign Investment Policy Committee had been using the term "just and equitable" for more than two years and the term "fair and equitable" for about a year to describe the investment climate desired by the United States, and the United States had succeeded in incorporating the term "just and equitable treatment" into the Havana Charter.

When it undertook in 1948 to develop an "investment clause" for inclusion in the FCN treaties, the State Department incorporated into its standard draft treaty, as part of that investment clause, language providing that "Each Party shall at all times accord equitable treatment to the capital of nationals and companies of the other Party."[118] The drafting of the investment clause in 1948 was the moment at which the term "equitable treatment" first appeared in the U.S. FCN treaties as a general descriptor of the treatment required with respect to foreign investment. By 1950, the State Department had moved the obligation to Article I and rephrased it as a requirement that the parties accord equitable treatment "to the persons, property, enterprises and other interests of nationals and companies of other Party." That same year, when the State Department undertook to prepare a short form of the FCN treaty for negotiations with Ethiopia, Afghanistan, and other less developed countries, it used the term "fair and equitable treatment" rather than "equitable treatment." For example, Article VIII(1) of the treaty with Ethiopia, which was concluded in 1951 and was the first treaty to be based on the short form, provided that "Each High Contracting Party shall at all times accord fair and equitable treatment to nationals and companies of the other High Contracting Party, and to their property and enterprises."

During the first formal FCN treaty negotiating session with Germany, held in October 1953, the German negotiators observed that Article I, requiring each party to provide "equitable treatment" to the persons, property, enterprises, and other interests of nationals and companies of the other party, was unnecessarily brief, indeed "naked."[119] They suggested that the term "equitable treatment" be replaced with the term "fair and equitable treatment." They explained that "fair and equitable" treatment would permit a smooth German translation. The phrase

118. Ireland FCN treaty, Article V.

119. Despatch dated October 6, 1953, from the U.S. High Commissioner in Bonn to the Department of State, NARA, Record Group 59, Department of State File No. 611.62A4/10-653.

"gerechte und billige" was an "inseparable" German expression and the equivalent of "fair and equitable."[120] The United States accepted this proposal.[121]

By 1955, the State Department had incorporated the term "fair and equitable treatment" into its standard draft treaty, although treaties concluded after 1955 often used the term "equitable treatment," for various reasons, including the fact that many of these treaties were based on earlier models or on counterdrafts proposed by the other party. The standard short draft of the treaty continued to use "fair and equitable treatment," and that is typically the term used in the treaties based on the short draft.[122]

Nothing in the negotiating history of the ITO Charter or the FCN treaties indicates that the United States understood the term "fair and equitable treatment" to have a different meaning than the term "equitable treatment." The terms "equitable treatment" and "fair and equitable treatment" were used interchangeably.[123] For example, the State Department described the requirement of "equitable treatment" in the Uruguay FCN treaty as a requirement of "fair" treatment.[124] In general, treaties based on the standard draft treaty used "equitable treatment" whereas those based on the short form used "fair and equitable treatment," although this practice was not invariable.

The fair and equitable treatment provision, such as the one that appeared in Article I of the 1955 standard draft treaty, played three roles in the U.S. postwar FCN treaties. Each of these roles was related to the others.[125]

A first role was to impose an independent standard of treatment on the parties applicable to situations not adequately governed by the other more specific provisions of the treaty. That is, it was "a guiding principle to which resort may be had in

120. Ibid.

121. Despatch dated February 26, 1954, from the U.S. High Commissioner in Bonn to the Department of State, NARA, Record Group 59, Department of State File No. 611.62A4/2-2654.

122. *See* Iran FCN treaty, Art. IV(1); Muscat and Oman FCN treaty, Art. IV(1); Vietnam FCN treaty, Art. IV(1); Togo FCN treaty, Art. IV(1); Thailand FCN treaty, Art. III(1).

123. *See, e.g.,* Robert R. Wilson, *United States Commercial Treaties and International Law* (New Orleans, LA: Hauser Press, 1960), page 120.

124. Summary of Provisions of the United States-Uruguay Treaty of Friendship, Commerce and Economic Development, signed November 23, 1949, *reprinted in Treaty of Friendship, Commerce and Economic Development with the Oriental Republic of Uruguay,* Exec. Rept. No. 5, 81st Cong. 2d Sess. (1950).

125. Instruction dated October 30, 1953, from the Department of State to the U.S. High Commissioner in Bonn, NARA, Record Group 59, Department of State File No. 611.62A4/10-653; Memorandum dated November 4, 1953, attached to letter dated April 29, 1954, from Carl H. Boehringer to the Secretary of State, NARA, Record Group 59, Department of State File No. 611.62A4/4-2954. *See also* despatch dated February 8, 1952, from the Department of State to the U.S. embassy in New Delhi, NARA, Record Group 50, Department of State File No. 611.914/2-852; Airgram dated December 31, 1951, from the Department of State to the U.S. Political Adviser in Tokyo, NARA, Record Group 59, Department of State File No. 611.944/12-751.

situations where no specific rule of the treaty is applicable or in reference to which the specific rules of the treaty do not provide an adequate standard of treatment."[126]

For example, during negotiations with the sultanate of Muscat and Oman, the State Department prepared an explanatory memorandum that addressed as a unit the paragraph that included the fair and equitable treatment standard and the prohibition on unreasonable and discriminatory measures, without distinguishing between the two obligations. The Department explained that the paragraph "should prove substantially useful . . . in resisting certain types of measures sometimes imposed to the detriment of alien interests. A case in point would be where a government imposes an excessive corporation tax, ostensibly based on a classification according to assets or income, but actually falling on one or two alien corporations, as the only ones coming within that classification."[127]

The State Department reiterated on multiple occasions that this was one of the roles of the fair and equitable treatment standard. During negotiations with Belgium, it explained that the purpose of the fair and equitable treatment standard was "to establish a blanket rule of equitable treatment to be applicable in cases or situations which may not happen to be covered by more specific provisions elsewhere in the treaty"[128] During negotiations with India, the State Department explained that the provision "provides a general guidance as to the treatment to be accorded where more specific rules are lacking or insufficient."[129] In reporting to the Senate on the FCN treaty with Uruguay, the State Department explained that the provision "sets forth the general principle of fair treatment for foreign enterprises, and . . . should be of special value with respect to situations not otherwise specifically covered by the treaty."[130] Of the three roles of the fair and equitable treatment standard, the United States believed that providing an independent standard of protection was "perhaps the major justification for the Article."[131]

126. Instruction dated October 30, 1953, from the Department of State to the U.S. High Commissioner in Bonn, NARA, Record Group 59, Department of State File No. 611.62A4/10-653.

127. Memorandum headed "Explanation of Certain Provisions of U.S. Proposals for Treaty of Amity and Economic Relations with Muscat," enclosure to instruction dated April 17, 1957, from the Department of State to the U.S. consulate general in Dhahran, NARA, Record Group 59, Department of State File No. 611.86E1/4-1757.

128. Instruction dated August 10, 1956, from the Department of State to the U.S. embassy in Brussels, NARA, Record Group 59, Department of State File No. 611.554/8-1056.

129. Despatch dated February 8, 1952, from the Department of State to the U.S. embassy in New Delhi, NARA, Record Group 59, Department of State File No. 611.914/2-852.

130. Summary of Provisions of the United States-Uruguay Treaty of Friendship, Commerce and Economic Development, signed November 23, 1949, *reprinted in Treaty of Friendship, Commerce and Economic Development with the Oriental Republic of Uruguay*, Exec. Rept. No. 5, 81st Cong. 2d Sess. (1950).

131. Instruction dated October 30, 1953, from the Department of State to the U.S. High Commissioner in Bonn, NARA, Record Group 59, Department of State File No. 611.62A4/10-653.

This role reflected the State Department's practice of using the concepts of fair treatment or equitable treatment as a reference to the overall investment climate desired. For example, the State Department explained in a 1947 letter to the Baldwin Piano Company that the FCN treaty with Italy was "designed primarily to assure equitable treatment to American nationals, corporations, and associations engaged in various legitimate activities in Italy. . . ."[132] A 1949 memorandum written by Assistant Secretary of State Willard Thorp explained that "[t]he principal demand of private investors is for adequate assurances from foreign governments of fair treatment for their investments."[133] He added that obtaining such assurances was the purpose of the FCN treaty program. U.S. negotiators explained during negotiations with Greece in 1950 that the "basic objective" of the treaty was to ensure "equal and equitable treatment for the nationals and companies of either Party in the conduct of their ordinary pursuits within the territories of the other Party."[134] Writing about FCN treaties in his personal capacity in 1951, Harry Hawkins observed that "[f]oreign capital will not enter a country unless it has some assurance that it will receive fair treatment. . . ."[135] He continued, "If the underdeveloped countries are desirous of developing their resources and raising their living standards with the help of foreign capital, they must be willing to give basic guarantees of fair treatment to an investor. . . ."[136] The State Department told its embassy in Port-au-Prince in 1952 that an FCN treaty "would establish what amounts to a code of fair treatment" for American enterprises.[137] Or, as the Department explained in 1954 during negotiations with Belgium, "A treaty establishes and 'firms up' a Government's basic sympathy toward, and its intentions to accord fair treatment to, the businessman and international investment and commerce."[138] A 1955 NAC report noted that "[t]his policy has not been one of seeking special privileges. The object has been rather to obtain assurances of fair and equitable treatment that would place American business enterprises, goods and vessels generally on a plane of competitive equality with

132. Letter dated May 23, 1947, from Ben T. Moore, NARA, Record Group 59, Department of State File No. 611.6531/5-647.

133. Memorandum by Willard Thorp headed "Balancing U.S. Trade at a High Level," dated September 26, 1949, NARA, Record Group 59, Bureau of Economic Affairs, Office of Economic Defense and Trade Policy, Subject Files, 1944–1952, Box 42, Folder marked "Investment Policy 1947–1949."

134. Telegram 794 dated November 21, 1950, from the U.S. embassy in Athens to the Department of State, NARA, Record Group 59, Department of State File No. 611.814/11-2150.

135. Hawkins, *Commercial Treaties & Agreements*, page 16.

136. Ibid., page 29.

137. Telegram dated June 3, 1952, from the Department of State to the U.S. embassy in Port-au-Prince, NARA, Record Group 59, Department of State File No. 611.384/6-352.

138. Instruction dated November 5, 1954, from the Department of State to the U.S. embassy in Brussels, NARA, Record Group 59, Department of State File No. 611.6554/11-554.

their counterparts in foreign countries."[139] During negotiations with Korea in 1956, the State Department noted that the "general treaty purpose" was to "assure equitable treatment [of] investors."[140] When signing the FCN treaty with France in 1959, U.S. ambassador Amory Houghton explained that the treaty reflected "one of the constants that should prevail in relations between friendly nations," and that constant was "the principle of fair treatment toward the individual, his property and his legitimate interests."[141] Congress used those concepts similarly. For example, the 1950 Act for International Development implementing the Point Four program called for "fair and reasonable" treatment of investment and the Mutual Security Act of 1954 and the Foreign Assistance Act of 1961 both directed the president to accelerate the negotiation of FCN treaties that would encourage "equitable treatment" of investment.[142] The United States wanted fair and equitable treatment for its investment abroad, and this provision of the treaty required that it be accorded.

In its second role, the fair and equitable treatment provision was "calculated to form a link between the Preamble and the main body of the treaty and as such to emphasize the broad scope of the treaty and to characterize in summary language the purpose of fair dealing underlying its more detailed provisions."[143] Fair and equitable treatment, in other words, was a term that encapsulated the basic principles embodied in the other articles of the treaty. It described in summary form the treatment provided by the entire treaty. Thus, the United States explained, this article "had a 'preambular flavor'" although, as noted above, it "also laid the foundation for equitable dealing with issues inadequately covered in the treaty."[144]

Finally, the provision was intended "to suggest a general policy of liberal, rather than of narrow[,] construction of the provisions of the treaty."[145] Where more than one construction of the treaty language was equally possible, the

139. NAC Staff Document No. 740, Program for Obtaining Treaty Assurances to Protect United States Citizens and Property and Promote United States Private Investment in Foreign Countries, NARA, Record Group 353, Records Relating to the Council on Foreign Economic Policy 1955–1961, Box 4, Folder marked "Investment in Underdeveloped Countries CFEP 511 (Folder 2)."

140. Telegram dated August 3, 1956, from the Department of State to the U.S. embassy in Seoul, NARA, Record Group 59, Department of State File No. 611.95B4/8-356.

141. Enclosure 1 to despatch dated November 27, 1959, from the U.S. embassy in Paris to the Department of State, NARA, Record Group 59, Department of State File No. 611.514/11-2759.

142. The first two measures are discussed in Chapter 5, while the last is discussed in Chapter 7.

143. Instruction dated October 30, 1953, from the Department of State to the U.S. High Commissioner in Bonn, NARA, Record Group 59, Department of State File No. 611.62A4/10-653; Despatch dated February 8, 1952, from the Department of State to the U.S. embassy in New Delhi, NARA, Record Group 59, Department of State File No. 611.914/2-852.

144. Despatch dated February 26, 1954, from the U.S. High Commissioner in Bonn to the Department of State, NARA, Record Group 59, Department of State File No. 611.62A4/2-2654.

145. Instruction dated October 30, 1953, from the Department of State to the U.S. High Commissioner in Bonn, NARA, Record Group 59, Department of State File No. 611.62A4/

construction that would lead to an equitable result was to be preferred.[146] That is, it provided an interpretive principle for the remaining provisions of the treaty. The State Department further explained that "the principles contained in Article I were not designed to alter subsequent treaty provisions, but had the effect of indicating that a liberal policy of interpretation was to be followed in applying the latter."[147]

The State Department never attempted to describe exhaustively what treatment was required by the fair and equitable treatment standard. Indeed, as noted above, in the context of a provision on state trading, the Department noted that "[t]he phrase 'fair and equitable treatment' may not be susceptible of precise definition."[148]

The lack of precision occasionally caused difficulties during negotiations. For example, the equitable treatment standard was eliminated from the FCN treaty with Japan in part because of the difficulty of translating the standard satisfactorily into Japanese, but also because of "the Japanese desire to have only very precise provisions."[149] The Department acknowledged during those negotiations that the term "equitable" was not a precise one and, in an effort to persuade the Japanese negotiators to accept the term, had ventured the suggestion that it "probably" would be invoked only in "extreme or unusual cases," because the other terms "define the normal commitments" that the parties have undertaken.[150] The reference to extreme cases, however, was not typical of how the Department described the fair and equitable treatment provision. Rather, as has been seen, the Department repeatedly referred to the provision as one that would provide protection whenever other more specific provisions did not apply.

The fair and equitable treatment provision encompassed the treatment required by the more specific provisions of the treaty and thus included the principles underlying those more specific provisions, such as reasonableness, non-discrimination, security, and due process, but it provided protection where the

10-653. *See also* Despatch dated February 26, 1954, from the U.S. High Commissioner in Bonn to the Department of State, NARA, Record Group 59, Department of State File No. 611.62A4/2-2654.

146. Airgram dated December 31, 1951, from the Department of State to the U.S. Political Adviser in Tokyo, NARA, Record Group 59, Department of State File No. 611.944/12-751.

147. Despatch dated February 26, 1954, from the U.S. High Commissioner in Bonn to the Department of State, NARA, Record Group 59, Department of State File No. 611.62A4/2-2654.

148. Memorandum dated March 28, 1947, from Vernon G. Setzer to Seymour J. Rubin, NARA, Record Group 59 NARA, Record Group 59, Department of State Lot Files, Walter Hollis Papers.

149. Despatch dated August 6, 1954, from the U.S. embassy in The Hague to the Department of State, NARA, Record Group 59, Department of State File No. 511.564/8-654. The concerns of the Japanese negotiators, and the efforts by the U.S. negotiators to allay those concerns, are discussed in much greater detail in Chapter 6 in the section on the negotiation of the treaty with Japan.

150. Ibid.

more specific provisions were not adequate. Indeed, this was its most important purpose.

In explaining the meaning of the fair and equitable treatment provision, the State Department relied upon the ordinary meaning of the language itself. For example, when the Japanese negotiators asked for an explanation of the term "equitable" treatment, the United States replied that the term "conveys the idea of decent, fair and just."[151] As signaled by the preambular role of the provision, its meaning was also indicated by its context, that is, by the principles underlying the other more detailed provisions of the treaty that followed it.

The fair and equitable treatment standard quite clearly included protection against unreasonable or discriminatory treatment.[152] For example, in 1949, the Commerce Department's Business Advisory Council recommended the inclusion of new language in the treaty that would prohibit burdens on foreign investment that increased with the scale of the investment, if such burdens were unreasonable or discriminatory.[153] The State Department rejected the recommendation, with a memorandum from the Office of the Legal Adviser explaining that the requirement of equitable treatment "encompasses" a prohibition on unreasonable and discriminatory classifications.[154] In other words, the memorandum added, "an unreasonable classification cannot be deemed to be 'equitable treatment.'" The memorandum further explained that, even if language such as that sought by the Business Advisory Council were included, the language would need to prohibit the unreasonable discrimination, not the disproportionate burden. The reason was that "a reasonable classification may impose disproportionate burdens in the United States without running afoul of any constitutional prohibition."[155] That is, the Office of the Legal Adviser equated the requirement of equitable treatment with U.S. constitutional norms. It was, as the memorandum explained, "the unreasonableness of the classification in view of all the facts and circumstances that is the issue; once that hurdle is passed, any disproportionate injury flowing therefrom becomes *damnum absque injurie*."[156]

151. Airgram dated January 25, 1952, from the Department of State to the U.S. Political Adviser in Tokyo, NARA, Record Group 59, Department of State File No. 611.944/1-252.

152. As shown in Chapter 3, when discussing the concept of fair and equitable treatment during the ITO Charter negotiations, the United States linked it to norms of reasonableness and non-discrimination, although the concept was not limited to those norms. As shown in Chapter 5, when drafting a proposed treaty dedicated solely to investment in 1949, the United States again linked the concept of "equitable treatment" to reasonableness and non-discrimination.

153. Memorandum by Herman Walker Jr. headed "Further Possible Revisions in Standard Draft of Treaty of Friendship, Commerce and Navigation (or Economic Development)," dated October 12, 1949, NARA, Record Group 59, Department of State Lot Files, Walter Hollis Papers.

154. Memorandum headed "Mr. Walker's Memorandum of October 12 re Possible Revisions in Standard FCN Treaties," from Stanley D. Metzger to Michael H. Cardozo, dated November 15, 1949, NARA, Record Group 59, Department of State Lot Files, Walter Hollis Papers.

155. Ibid.

156. Ibid.

During negotiations with the sultanate of Muscat and Oman, the State Department explained that the paragraph containing both the fair and equitable treatment provision and the prohibition on unreasonable or discriminatory measures "constitutes an undertaking to observe standards of elementary fairness and justice in the treatment of United States economic interests in Muscat. It does not prescribe a specific or detailed course of action in any given case. It merely seeks to assure that whatever course of action adopted does not involve arbitrary or capricious measures to harass a business enterprise or impede or prevent its enjoyment of a right or privilege to which it is entitled under Muscati law or through a grant or concession from the Sultan."[157] In this instruction, the Department made no effort to distinguish the requirement of fair and equitable treatment from the prohibition on unreasonable or discriminatory measures, signaling the extent of the overlap between the two provisions. During negotiations with Ethiopia, the Department noted that the fair and equitable treatment provision "allows flexible adaptation to varying circumstances and [could] embarrass [Ethiopia] only if [it] wished deliberately [to] exclude [Americans] or arbitrarily discriminate against them."[158]

During negotiations with France, the French negotiators asserted that the fair and equitable treatment standard "cover[ed], *inter alia*, all that 'reasonable' in the American sense is intended to cover in" the provision on unreasonable and discriminatory measures.[159] That is, the French negotiators suggested that the fair and equitable treatment standard prohibited treatment that was unreasonable, although the use of the phrase "*inter alia*" reflected their understanding that the standard required more than that. The U.S. negotiators accepted this interpretation.[160] When the treaty was signed, the press release issued by the French government stated that the treaty required equitable treatment, which, "on the whole," would be national treatment, reflecting the fact that the French proposal, accepted by the United States, did not equate fair and equitable treatment solely with reasonableness, and presumed that the fair and equitable treatment included a requirement of non-discrimination as well.[161]

The State Department's understanding of the fair and equitable treatment provision as embracing a norm of non-discrimination is fully consistent with its understanding of what fair and equitable treatment meant in the context of the more specific provisions of the treaty where the standard appeared, particularly

157. Instruction dated November 27, 1957, from the Department of State to the U.S. consulate general in Dhahran, NARA, Record Group 59, Department of State File No. 611.86E4/10-257.

158. Telegram dated September 4, 1951, from the Department of State to the U.S. embassy in Addis Ababa, NARA, Record Group 59, Department of State File No. 611.754/9-151.

159. Despatch dated May 14, 1959, from the U.S. embassy in Paris to the Department of State, NARA, Record Group 59, Department of State File No. 611.514/5-1459.

160. Ibid.

161. Despatch dated August 19, 1959, from the U.S. embassy in Paris to the Department of State, NARA, Record Group 59, Department of State File No. 611.514/8-1959.

in the early postwar treaties. For example, as noted above, the requirement of fair and equitable treatment with respect to exchange controls that appeared in early treaties, such as the proposed treaty with the Soviet Union, was elucidated in the paragraphs that followed, and these succeeding paragraphs generally imposed various more specific obligations of non-discrimination. Similarly, State Department officials regarded the obligation of fair and equitable treatment with respect to purchases by state trading companies as providing a basis for protection against discrimination.[162] State Department officials also regarded the obligation of fair and equitable treatment with respect to government purchases and the awarding of concessions as embracing the right of non-discrimination.[163] Indeed, Herman Walker specifically described the fair and equitable treatment standard in that context as an "adaptation" of the MFN treatment provision.[164] During negotiations with China, the State Department contemplated substituting "fair and equitable treatment" for MFN treatment in a provision relating to the right of treaty aliens to engage in commercial activity.[165]

The State Department on occasion explicitly linked fair and equitable treatment with either national treatment or MFN treatment. For example, during negotiations with Pakistan, the State Department described the obligation of MFN treatment with respect to engaging in gainful activity as an obligation to provide "fair and equitable consideration" to U.S. enterprises as compared with the consideration offered to enterprises of third countries.[166] As described in Chapter 3, during the ITO Charter negotiations, the State Department explained to the U.S. delegation in Geneva that the Department's proposal for an investment code had addressed national treatment through the language calling for fair and equitable treatment.[167]

During the negotiations with Germany, the State Department offered an illustration of a situation to which the fair and equitable treatment provision might apply: "For example, a given governmental measure may technically comply with the legal rule of national treatment, yet be so arbitrary and so burdensome in its impact on the foreigner as to be grossly unjust. A process of superficially objective

162. Memorandum dated March 28, 1947, from Vernon G. Setzer to Seymour J. Rubin, NARA, Record Group 59 NARA, Record Group 59, Department of State Lot Files, Walter Hollis Papers.

163. Memorandum headed "The Twenty-Fifth Meeting to Consider a Tentative Draft Treaty of Friendship, Commerce and Navigation between the United States and the U.S.S.R. Held October 23, 1945," NARA, Record Group 59, State Department File No.711.612.

164. Walker, "Treaties for the Encouragement and Protection of Foreign Investment," page 239.

165. Telegram dated March 2, 1946, from the Department of State to the U.S. embassy in Chongqing, NARA, Record Group 59, Department of State File No. 711.932/3-236.

166. Telegram dated July 7, 1959, from the Department of State to the U.S. embassy in Karachi, NARA, Record Group 59, Department of State File No. 611.90D4/6-2559.

167. Copy dated July 15, 1947, of May 24, 1947, telegram from the Department of State to the U.S. delegation in Geneva, NARA, Record Group 43, International Trade Files, Box 38, Folder marked "FIP Documents."

'classification' is one device available, in certain situations, for singling out the foreigner for harassment without breaching the letter of the national treatment rule."[168] In this particular illustration, the State Department referred to a measure that was "grossly unjust," but such extreme language was rare. In any event, this illustration was merely an example of a measure that would violate the standard. Gross injustice was sufficient, but, as suggested by the absence of similar language in other diplomatic correspondence, it was not necessary to constitute a violation of the fair and equitable treatment standard.

For example, during Senate hearings on a group of FCN treaties in 1952, the State Department explained that the prohibition on unreasonable or discriminatory measures "serve[d] a useful purpose in that it affords one more ground . . . for contesting foreign actions which appear to be injurious to American interests. A given measure of a foreign government might, for example, be fully consistent with the national treatment or most-favored-nation treatment rules of the treaty, and also short of expropriation, but yet arbitrary and unreasonable as it affected some vested American interest in the country concerned."[169] The Department told the Senate that, in such a case, the only other treaty ground that would provide a basis for protest would be the fair and equitable treatment provision, again signaling the overlap between the requirement of fair and equitable treatment and the prohibition on unreasonable or discriminatory measures.

Similarly, some years later, after the Organization for Economic Cooperation and Development adopted its 1967 Draft Convention on the Protection of Foreign Property, the United States within the month sent a diplomatic note to Canada alleging a violation of the fair and equitable treatment standard of that Convention.[170] The basis of the alleged violation was a Canadian increase in postal rates that fell disproportionately on magazines published in Canada but owned by U.S. nationals. The United States asserted that the fair and equitable treatment obligation in the Draft Convention included an obligation of national treatment.[171] At no point did the United States assert that the change in postal rates was "grossly unjust." Rather, it argued that a denial of national treatment to

168. Instruction dated October 30, 1953, from the Department of State to the U.S. High Commissioner in Bonn, NARA, Record Group 59, Department of State File No. 611.62A4/10-653.

169. Memorandum accompanying letter dated May 16, 1952, from Acting Assistant Secretary of State Harold Linder to Senator John Sparkman, NARA, Record Group 59, Department of State File No. 611.214/5-1652, *reprinted in Commercial Treaties,* Hearing Before a Subcommittee of the Committee on Foreign Relations, 82nd Cong. 2d Sess. (1952), page 28.

170. Telegram dated October 28, 1967, from the Department of State to the U.S. embassy in Ottawa, NARA, Record Group 59, Records Relating to Economic Matters 1953–1975, Box 13, Folder marked "FN 9 Foreign Property Convention 1967."

171. Ibid.; Memorandum by Bureau of European Affairs, dated October 26, 1967, NARA, Record Group 59, Records Relating to Economic Matters 1953–1975, Box 13, Folder marked "FN 9 Foreign Property Convention 1967."

an established foreign-owned subsidiary was "inconsistent with the concept of fair treatment under the rule of law."[172]

Although the State Department often referred to fair and equitable treatment as prohibiting arbitrary or discriminatory treatment, as shown above, the standard had a broader application.[173] Robert Wilson, a principal FCN treaty negotiator in the 1940s, identified it as an independent standard that could be distinguished from national treatment, MFN treatment, reasonable treatment, or the international minimum standard of treatment. He wrote in his private capacity in 1956 that "[w]hile most-favored-nation treatment and national treatment have figured most prominently in this type of treaty, other standards, such as reciprocity, the international law standard, 'equitable,' and even 'fair' and 'reasonable' treatment have found mention in them."[174] Wilson regarded the standard as being related, at least in part, to the security of investment. For example, in writing about expropriation, Wilson casually referred to "fair and equitable compensation," a term that he appeared to use interchangeably with "just and adequate compensation" in the succeeding sentence.[175] As shown above, the State Department in its diplomatic practice also used the term fair and equitable treatment when referring to the obligation to pay compensation for expropriation. More generally, Wilson believed that terms such as "just" and "equitable" reflected the concept of legality, that is, the principle that state power is limited by the rule of law.[176] As discussed in Chapter 4, Assistant Legal Adviser Sy Rubin, writing in his personal capacity after the Havana Conference, linked fairness to norms of reasonableness and security, while a State Department briefing memorandum also prepared after the Havana Conference treated "fair treatment" as a general term that included all of the investment-related obligations under the Charter. As discussed above, the State Department used the terms "fair treatment" and "fair and equitable treatment" to describe the treatment of investment required by the FCN treaty as a whole.

The fair and equitable treatment standard applied to the nationals and companies of a party, as well as to their property, enterprises, and other interests. The State Department, in choosing the words "persons, property, enterprises and

172. Memorandum by Bureau of European Affairs, dated October 26, 1967, NARA, Record Group 59, Records Relating to Economic Matters 1953–1975, Box 13, Folder marked "FN 9 Foreign Property Convention 1967"; Telegram dated October 28, 1967, from the Department of State to the U.S. embassy in Ottawa, NARA, Record Group 59, Records Relating to Economic Matters 1953–1975, Box 13, Folder marked "FN 9 Foreign Property Convention 1967."

173. In addition to the discussion throughout this Chapter, recall the discussion in Chapter 3 of the evolution of the term "fair and equitable treatment" during the ITO Charter negotiations and the discussion in Chapter 5 of the concept of "equitable treatment" during the drafting of a proposed treaty dedicated solely to investment.

174. Robert R. Wilson, "A Decade of New Commercial Treaties," 50 *American Journal of International Law* 927, 928 (1956).

175. Robert R. Wilson, "Property-Protection Provisions in United States Commercial Treaties," 45 *American Journal of International Law* 83, 87 (1951).

176. Wilson, *United States Commercial Treaties and International Law*, pages 321–322.

other interests of nationals and companies," explained that it "had in mind broad coverage encompassing the entire range of the treaty, for it is not believed that there is any topic alluded to in the treaty which is not referrable [*sic*] to one or more of the words of this recitation, liberally construed."[177]

In short, the fair and equitable treatment standard imposed an independent obligation on treaty parties that provided a basis for challenging the legality of host state treatment in situations where the other, more precise provisions of the treaty did not apply. These other, more precise provisions addressed the problems most commonly encountered by foreign investors—such as exchange controls, expropriation, and discriminatory treatment—and thus the State Department anticipated that most claims of a treaty violation would arise under them. Yet, the purpose of the treaty was to create an environment of fair and equitable treatment for covered investments, and such an environment included more than that which was required by these other, more specific provisions. The standard thus provided a residual basis for a claim where host state treatment was not fair and equitable, although the treatment did not violate any other provision of the treaty. The State Department conceded that the standard was not susceptible of precise definition. The other provisions of the treaty, however, were included within the concept of fair and equitable treatment, and thus the standard contained the principles reflected in those other provisions, although, again, it was not limited to the specific obligations imposed by those provisions. When it sought to provide illustrations of the kinds of circumstances in which the fair and equitable treatment standard might be invoked as the basis for a claim, the State Department indicated that the standard prohibited unreasonable (i.e., arbitrary) treatment, and it prohibited discriminatory treatment that was based on nationality or an arbitrary classification. The Department's illustrations rarely, if ever, went beyond those circumstances. State Department officials with responsibility for the negotiation of the U.S. postwar FCN treaties, when writing in their personal capacities, sometimes noted the importance of the security of investment as an element of fair and equitable treatment. Yet, the principle of security included within the fair and equitable treatment standard did not protect investment against all harm. Rather, the security guaranteed by that standard, like the protection against unreasonable or discriminatory treatment,[178] extended no farther than the protection provided by U.S. law and policy, particularly U.S. constitutional law. For example, the principle would not protect rights created by an obligation, such as a contract, where the obligation was in derogation of the state's

177. Instruction dated October 30, 1953, from the Department of State to the U.S. High Commissioner in Bonn, NARA, Record Group 59, Department of State File No. 611.62A4/10-653.

178. The circumscription of the scope of the unreasonable or discriminatory measures provision by U.S. constitutional norms is discussed in the section below on that provision. Note, as well, the Office of the Legal Adviser's response to the Busines Advisory Council's proposed revision of the provision, discussed above, in which the Office rejected any change that would extend the scope of the provision beyond the prohibitions imposed by the U.S. Constitution.

reserved powers.[179] As was seen above, when it invoked the fair and equitable treatment standard to protect the security of investment in diplomatic practice, the United States typically did so in a context where the investment had been expropriated without just compensation, contrary to U.S. constitutional principles. In addition to imposing an independent obligation on the treaty parties, the fair and equitable treatment standard also provided a principle for interpreting the other provisions of the treaties. More specifically, the provision signaled that, in cases of doubt, the other provisions should be interpreted in such a way as to produce a fair and equitable result.

MOST CONSTANT PROTECTION AND SECURITY

The U.S. postwar FCN treaties retained a long-standing provision of U.S. FCN treaty practice requiring each party to provide the "most constant protection and security" to the property of nationals of the other party.[180] For example, Article I of the 1934 U.S. FCN treaty with Finland had provided that "[t]he nationals of each High Contracting Party shall receive within the territory of the other, upon submitting to conditions imposed upon its nationals, the most constant protection and security for their persons and property, and shall enjoy in this respect that degree of protection that is required by international law."

The U.S. postwar treaties made three noteworthy changes to the provision. First, they extended the protection to the property of companies. Second, they placed the protection of persons and property in separate provisions of the treaty. Third, as described in the next section below, they typically omitted from the property protection provision the reference to international law that had appeared in the interwar treaties.

The changes in the language occurred in stages. In the earliest U.S. postwar FCN treaties, a single provision of the treaty guaranteed the most constant protection and security for both nationals and their property and specified that they receive the protection required by international law.[181] During the revision of the treaty in 1948–1949, the protection for persons was separated from the protection for property, resulting in the extension of the most constant protection and security provision to the property of companies as well as the property of nationals. For example, Article II(1) of the FCN treaty with Ireland provided that "Nationals of either Party within the territories of the other Party . . . shall receive the most constant protection and security, in no case less than that required by international law." Article VIII(1) of

179. Memorandum from Vernon Setser to John Czyzak dated May 16, 1958, NARA, Record Group 59, Department of State File No. 611.004/5-1658. *See also* Stanley D. Metzger, "Multilateral Conventions for the Protection of Private Foreign Investment," 9 *Journal of Public Law* 133, 138 (1960). The reserved powers doctrine was described briefly in the Introduction in the section on Legal Liberalism.

180. The early history and meaning of this provision is traced in Wilson, "Property-Protection Provisions," 45 *American Journal of International Law* 83 (1951).

181. *See* China FCN treaty, Article VI(1); Italy FCN treaty, Article V(1); Ireland FCN treaty, Article II(1).

that same treaty provided that "Property of nationals and companies of either Party shall receive the most constant protection and security within the territories of the other Party, in no case less than that required by international law." After the conclusion of the treaty with Ireland, however, the standard U.S. practice became to omit the reference to international law from the provision relating to property,[182] although it remained in the provision relating to nationals.[183]

Typical of the language used in the postwar treaties is Article VI(1) of the 1955 standard draft treaty, which provided that "[p]roperty of nationals and companies of either Party shall receive the most constant protection and security within the territories of the other Party." The most constant protection and security provision applied to interests in property that were less than full ownership.[184] Like the fair and equitable treatment standard, it was "a residual basis for treaty protection in situations not expressly or adequately covered by the more detailed stipulations of the treaty."[185]

The phrase "most constant protection and security" was "time-honored treaty language."[186] Although some countries objected that they could not accept the language if it would require strict liability,[187] the United States assured them that it required "due diligence" rather than strict liability.[188] The United States regarded the standard as declaratory of customary international law.[189] That said, as discussed below in the section on treatment in accordance with international law, the United States feared that expressly linking the standard to customary international law in the treaty could weaken it, given the uncertainties about the content of customary law. For that reason, the State Department omitted the reference to international law from the provision relating to the protection of property.

182. *See, e.g.*, Israel FCN treaty, Article VI(1); Greece FCN treaty, Article VII(1); Denmark FCN treaty, Article VI(1).

183. *See, e.g.*, Israel FCN treaty, Article III(1); Denmark FCN treaty, Article III(1). The phrase was omitted from the corresponding provision of the FCN treaty with Greece, Article IV(1), but that was exceptional in FCN treaties concluded after 1948.

184. Instruction dated October 29, 1956, from the Department of State to the U.S. embassy in Brussels, NARA, Record Group 59, Department of State File No. 611.554/10-1156.

185. Airgram dated December 31, 1951, from the Department of State to the U.S. Political Adviser in Tokyo, NARA, Record Group 59, Department of State File No. 611.944/12-3151.

186. Telegram dated August 28, 1951, from the Department of State to the U.S. embassy in Addis Ababa, NARA, Record Group 59, Department of State File No. 611.754/8-2451.

187. Telegram dated August 23, 1951, from the U.S. embassy in Addis Ababa to the Department of State, NARA, Record Group 59, Department of State File No. 611.754/8-2351; Despatch dated May 11, 1959, from the U.S. embassy in Paris to the Department of State, NARA, Record Group 59, Department of State File No. 611.514/5-1159.

188. Telegram dated August 28, 1951, from the Department of State to the U.S. embassy in Addis Ababa, NARA, Record Group 59, Department of State File No. 611.754/8-2451.

189. Ibid.; Memorandum headed "The Eighth Meeting to Consider a Tentative Draft Treaty of Friendship, Commerce and Navigation between the United States and the U.S.S.R. Held June 28, 1945," NARA, Record Group 59, State Department File No. 711.612; Instruction A-194 dated June 12, 1961, from the Department of State to the U.S. embassy in Bangkok, NARA,

TREATMENT IN ACCORDANCE WITH INTERNATIONAL LAW

The United States believed that customary international law imposed obligations on states with respect to the treatment of foreign investment, and some of the provisions of the FCN treaties were regarded as declaratory of international law.[190] As indicated in the preceding section, the FCN treaty with Ireland, adopting the language of the standard draft FCN treaty in use at the time, required that each party provide the property of nationals and companies of the other party with protection no less than that required by international law. Like other U.S. postwar FCN treaties, it also required each party to provide nationals of the other party with protection no less than that required by international law.

During the revision of the standard draft treaty that occurred in 1948–1949, the reference to treatment in accordance with international law was removed from the provision requiring most constant protection and security for property, an omission about which the NFTC routinely complained.[191] The State Department decided to omit the language, after extended internal discussion, because of fears within the Department that disputes concerning the substance of international law[192] would weaken the treaty.[193] U.S. nationals and companies would be entitled to the protection of customary law even without a reference to international law in the treaty[194] and some provisions of the treaty guaranteed protection beyond that required by international law.[195]

Record Group 59, Department of State File No. 611.9242/6-1261; Airgram dated December 31, 1951, from the Department of State to the U.S. Political Adviser in Tokyo, NARA, Record Group 59, Department of State File No. 611.944/12-3151.

190. Memorandum of Conversation headed "Critique by Le/T of the 'Further Revised Draft of Short Treaty', Previously Submitted for Its Review," among Charles Bevans, Vernon Setser, Charles Sullivan, and Herman Walker, dated March 10, 1947, NARA, Record Group 59, Department of State Lot Files, Walter Hollis Papers.

191. *See, e.g.*, Letter dated March 6, 1950, from Eugene P. Thomas to Senator Tom Connally, NARA, Record Group 59, Department of State File No. 611.334/3-650.

192. For example, during negotiations, India expressed doubt concerning whether there were any international legal principles relating to the protection of alien-owned property. Telegram dated August 6, 1952, from the U.S. embassy in New Delhi to the Department of State, NARA, Record Group 59, Department of State File No. 611.914/8-652.

193. Appendix D to Report of Meeting in the Office of Harold F. Linder, headed "Critique by Le/T of the 'Further Revised Draft Short Treaty', Previously Submitted for Its Review," dated June 17, 1952, NARA, Record Group 59, Department of State File No. 611.004/6-1852; Memorandum of Conversation dated March 10, 1947, NARA, Record Group 59, Department of State Lot Files, Walter Hollis Papers.

194. Memorandum of Conversation dated March 10, 1947, NARA, Record Group 59, Department of State Lot Files, Walter Hollis Papers

195. Memorandum on Proposed Articles for Use in Drafting Treaties of Friendship, Commerce and Navigation with Particular Countries, undated, NARA, Record Group 59, Department of State Lot Files, Walter Hollis Papers.

UNREASONABLE OR DISCRIMINATORY MEASURES

The U.S. postwar FCN treaties prohibited a party from adopting any unreasonable or discriminatory measure that would impair legally acquired rights in the capital, enterprises, or intellectual property of nationals or companies of the other party. For example, Article VI(1) of the 1955 standard draft treaty provided that "[n]either Party shall take unreasonable or discriminatory measures that would impair the legally acquired rights or interests within its territories of nationals and companies of the other Party in the enterprises which they have established, in their capital, or in the skills, arts or technology which they have supplied."

This provision was unprecedented in U.S. FCN treaty practice. Its origins lay in the work of the Foreign Investment Policy Committee created in July 1945 and the ITO Charter negotiations. As described in Chapter 1, the Foreign Investment Policy Committee by August 1947 had drafted a policy statement calling for "fair, equitable and nondiscriminatory" treatment of foreign investment, a provision that remained in the policy when it was adopted by the ECEFP in June of the following year. Thus, by mid- 1947, U.S. foreign investment policy contemplated adoption of a general prohibition on discriminatory treatment of foreign investment. Meanwhile, as has been described in Chapters 3 and 4, the negotiation of the ITO Charter resulted in the drafting of a provision prohibiting members from taking unreasonable action injurious to the rights or interests of nationals of other members in the enterprise, skills, capital, arts, or technology that they had supplied, a provision that ultimately was adopted as Article 11(1)(b) of the Charter. In addition, Belgium proposed a general prohibition on the discriminatory treatment of foreign investment, although that proposal, which the United States supported, was never adopted. As described in Chapter 1, by March 1948, the Foreign Investment Policy Committee's draft policy statement had identified situations where a U.S. investor was "subject to arbitrary or unreasonable action" as a circumstance in which the State Department might make representations on behalf of the investor. Accordingly, when it revised its standard draft treaty in 1948–1949 to include what it then termed an "investment clause," the State Department included as part of that investment clause a general prohibition on unreasonable or discriminatory measures that impaired acquired rights. The provision first appeared in the treaties with Colombia, Uruguay, and Ireland, all three of which were signed but only the last of which entered into force.[196] The provision initially included a prohibition on unjustified treatment, but this language quickly disappeared from the standard draft treaty.

The United States explained that this provision "merely seeks to assure that whatever course of action adopted does not involve arbitrary or capricious measures to harass a business enterprise or impede or prevent its enjoyment of a right or privilege

196. *See, e.g.,* Ireland FCN treaty, Article V.

to which it is entitled" under law or contract.[197] Like the fair and equitable treatment standard, it was included to protect investment against certain unfavorable treatment not otherwise covered by the treaty.[198] The prohibition on discriminatory treatment encompassed denials of either national or MFN treatment.[199] At the same time, the provision was an independent treaty rule that was in no way diminished by the presence of separate guarantees of national or MFN treatment.[200] The State Department regarded the language as an explicit rejection of the Calvo doctrine because it made clear that non-discriminatory treatment by itself did not satisfy a party's obligations to a foreign national or company.[201] Measures must be reasonable as well. The reference to skills, arts, and technology acknowledged the fact that investment may include contributions of knowledge.

As described in Chapter 6, the NFTC initially was critical of this provision. Rather than understanding that the provision imposed two new restrictions on host state treatment of foreign investment that were independent of other treaty obligations, the NFTC incorrectly regarded the provision as implicitly justifying any host state conduct as long it was reasonable and non-discriminatory. The NFTC also "severely criticized" the standard for its "indefiniteness."[202]

In response to the NFTC's criticism, the State Department explained to the Senate that the provision "serve[d] a useful purpose in that it affords one more ground . . . for contesting foreign actions which appear to be injurious to American interests. A given measure of a foreign government might, for example, be fully consistent with the national treatment or most-favored-nation treatment rules of the treaty, and also short of expropriation, but yet arbitrary and unreasonable as it affected some vested American interest in the country concerned."[203] The State

197. Instruction dated November 27, 1957, from the Department of State to the U.S. consulate general in Dhahran, NARA, Record Group 59, Department of State File No. 611.86E4/10-257. *See also* Walker, "Treaties for the Encouragement and Protection of Foreign Investment," page 236.

198. Telegram No. 108 dated August 18, 1952, from the Department of State to the U.S. embassy in New Delhi, NARA., Record Group 59, Department of State File No. 711.914/8-1852.

199. Despatch dated August 3, 1954, from the U.S. embassy in The Hague to the Department of State, NARA, Record Group 59, Department of State File No. 611.564/8-354; Despatch dated September 14, 1954, from the U.S. embassy in The Hague to the Department of State, NARA, Record Group 59, Department of State File No. 611.564/9-1454.

200. Airgram dated June 23, 1953, from the Department of State to the U.S. embassy in The Hague, NARA, Record Group 59, Department of State File No. 611.564/6-553.

201. Instruction dated December 1, 1953, from the Department of State to the U.S. High Commissioner in Bonn, NARA, Record Group 59, Department of State File No. 611.62A4/11-353.

202. Telegram No. 108 dated August 18, 1952, from the Department of State to the U.S. embassy in New Delhi, NARA, Record Group 59, Department of State File No. 711.914/8-1852.

203. Memorandum accompanying letter dated May 16, 1952, from Acting Assistant Secretary of State Harold Linder to Senator John Sparkman, NARA, Record Group 59, Department of State File No. 611.214/5-1652.

Department observed that, in such a case, the only treaty ground that would provide a basis for protest would be the fair and equitable treatment provision or the prohibition on unreasonable or discriminatory measures. The Department did note, however, that the protection for American investment abroad "for the most part" rested on the more specific provisions of the treaty.[204]

During negotiations with the sultanate of Muscat and Oman, the State Department observed that a provision that included the fair and equitable treatment standard, and the prohibition on unreasonable or discriminator measures "constitutes an undertaking to observe standards of elementary fairness and justice in the treatment of United States economic interests in Muscat. It does not prescribe a specific or detailed course of action in any given case. It merely seeks to assure that whatever course of action adopted does not involve arbitrary or capricious measures to harass a business enterprise or impede or prevent its enjoyment of a right or privilege to which it is entitled under Muscati law or through a grant or concession from the Sultan."[205]

Occasionally, potential treaty parties objected that the concept of reasonableness was not sufficiently developed as a legal standard. India, for example, doubted whether the term "reasonable" had any "content."[206] France and other civil law countries also had "great difficulty" with the term "reasonable."[207] As the U.S. embassy in Paris noted in the context of the negotiation of the provision on exchange controls, the term was "not usual in the French legal vocabulary."[208] The term was, for the French, "an odd word legally, that tends to sound indefinite and unsatisfactory in terms of their penchant for legal precision in the drafting of treaty commitments."[209] During negotiations with Belgium, one of the Belgian negotiators noted that the term was "meaningless" in French.[210] The State Department explained in response to these concerns that the term "reasonable" had been given extensive judicial interpretation in the United States and meant

204. Ibid.

205. Instruction dated November 27, 1957, from the Department of State to the U.S. consulate general in Dhahran, NARA, Record Group 59, Department of State File No. 611.86E4/10-257.

206. For example, during negotiations, India expressed doubt concerning whether there were any international legal principles relating to the protection of alien-owned property. Telegram dated August 6, 1952, from the U.S. embassy in New Delhi to the Department of State, NARA, Record Group 59, Department of State File No. 611.914/8-652.

207. Airgram dated July 12, 1959, from the U.S. embassy in Paris to the Department of State, NARA, Record Group 59, Department of State File No. 611.514/7-1259.

208. Despatch dated July 17, 1959, from the U.S. embassy in Paris to the Department of State, NARA, Record Group 59, Department of State File No. 611.514/7-1759.

209. Ibid.

210. Despatch dated March 11, 1955, from the U.S. embassy in Brussels to the Department of State, NARA, Record Group 59, Department of State File No. 611.554/3-1155.

"whatever is deemed necessary and proper, in the judgment of rational temperate men, to accomplish a worthy object."[211]

As in the case of the fair and equitable treatment provision, the State Department described the prohibition on unreasonable or discriminatory measures as having "a preambular nature" and thus serving as "an appropriate introduction to the more specific provisions that follow."[212] The Department further explained, as in the case of the fair and equitable treatment standard, that the provision "should prove substantially useful, however, in resisting certain types of measures sometimes imposed to the detriment of alien interests. A case in point would be where a government imposes an excessive corporation tax, ostensibly based on a classification according to assets or income, but actually falling on one or two alien corporations, as the only ones coming within that classification."[213]

The provision prohibited only those measures that were unreasonable or discriminatory. The United States believed that a state must "retain latitude to impose reasonable and nondiscriminatory regulations" on property.[214] For example, the provision did not apply to seizures of contraband or distraint for nonpayment of taxes or debt.[215] Indeed, the standard was not intended to impose any greater restriction than did the U.S. Constitution. For example, as discussed in Chapter Six, during hearings in 1952 on several pending FCN treaties, the State Department objected to changes to the provision proposed by the NFTC on the ground that the NFTC proposal would have required payment of compensation in circumstances where compensation was not required by the Constitution. The Department explained that it could not recommend a treaty provision that would "grant foreign nationals more favorable treatment than citizens receive in the United States."[216] As the text explicitly states, the provision did not prohibit all unreasonable or discriminatory measures, but only those that impaired acquired

211. Memorandum of Conversation headed "Negotiation of Treaty of Friendship, Commerce and Navigation with Colombia: Twenty-First Meeting," dated April 12, 1951, NARA, Record Group 59, Department of State File No. 611.214/4-1251.

212. Memorandum headed "Explanation of Certain Provisions of U.S. Proposals for Treaty of Amity and Economic Relations with Muscat," Enclosure to Instruction dated April 17, 1957, from the Department of State to the U.S. Consulate General in Dhahran, NARA, Record Group 59, Department of State File No. 611.86E1/4-1757.

213. Ibid.

214. Despatch dated September 14, 1954, from the U.S. embassy in The Hague to the Department of State, NARA, Record Group 59, Department of State File No. 611.564/9-1454.

215. Airgram dated October 27, 1948, from the U.S. legation in Dublin to the Department of State, NARA, Record Group 59, Department of State File No. 711.41D2/10-2748. *See also* Ireland FCN treaty, Minutes of Interpretation, *Ad Article VIII, paragraph* 2.

216. Memorandum accompanying letter dated May 16, 1952, from Acting Assistant Secretary of State Harold Linder to Senator John Sparkman, *reprinted in Commercial Treaties,* Hearing before a Subcommittee of the Committee on Foreign Relations, 82nd Cong. 2d Sess. (1952), page 28. As discussed above, in the section on the fair and equitable treatment provision, the State Department also rejected a proposal from the Commerce Department's Business Advisory

rights or, as the State Department sometimes described them, "vested rights."[217] For example, after the Senate approved the Japanese FCN treaty with a reservation allowing states to deny to Japanese nationals the right to practice certain professions in the United States, including law, the Japanese government began to consider the possibility of revoking the licenses of American attorneys licensed to practice in Japan. The Department of State determined that a license to practice law was an "acquired right" protected by the prohibition on unreasonable or discriminatory measures.[218] U.S. negotiators were aware that legal systems evolve, and the provision was not intended to prevent host state governments from applying new legislation to existing investments.[219] Rather, it prohibited the application to acquired rights of measures that were unreasonable or discriminatory.

The provision protected all rights legally acquired and subject to the jurisdiction of a party, regardless of where those rights were acquired.[220] That is, the provision covered "interests of every description."[221] In particular, the term "capital" was used in the broad sense, and included property.[222] The interests, however, must have been lawfully acquired.[223]

During negotiations, the Netherlands proposed adding language to clarify that this provision applied to property acquired by a company of one party controlled by nationals or companies of the other party.[224] The United States replied that any such language was unnecessary because the meaning to that effect was clear.[225]

Council that would have extended the prohibition on unreasonable or discriminatory measures beyond the strictures of U.S. constitutional norms.

217. Despatch dated September 14, 1954, from the U.S. embassy in The Hague to the Department of State, NARA, Record Group 59, Department of State File No. 611.564/9-1454; Instruction dated July 24, 1959, from the Department of State to the U.S. embassy in Managua, NARA, Record Group 59, Department of State File No. 611.174/6-3059.

218. Telegram dated February 15, 1954, from the Department of State to the U.S. embassy in Tokyo, NARA, Department of State File No. 611.944/2-1554.

219. Meeting of the American Delegation to the Havana ITO Conference, November 18, 1947, 10:15 am to 12:25 pm, page D-11, NARA, Record Group 43, International Trade Files, Box 147, Folder marked "Trade—Briefing Sessions—Habana."

220. Despatch dated September 14, 1954, from the U.S. embassy in The Hague to the Department of State, NARA, Record Group 59, Department of State File No. 611.564/9-1454; Despatch dated May 11, 1959, from the U.S. embassy in Paris to the Department of State, NARA, Record Group 59, Department of State File No. 611.514/5-1159.

221. Airgram dated May 14, 1959, from the U.S. embassy in Paris to the Department of State, NARA, Record Group 59, Department of State File No. 611.514/5-1459.

222. Despatch dated August 3, 1954, from the U.S. embassy in The Hague to the Department of State, NARA, Record Group 59, Department of State File No. 611.564/8-354.

223. Despatch dated September 14, 1954, from the U.S. embassy in The Hague to the Department of State, NARA, Record Group 59, Department of State File No. 611.564/9-1454.

224. Ibid.

225. Ibid.

NATIONAL TREATMENT

The Scope of the National Treatment Obligation

Activities for Gain

The U.S. postwar FCN treaties guaranteed to nationals and companies of one party national treatment with respect to the right to engage in various activities in the territory of the other party, most importantly activity for gain.[226] For example, Article VII(1) of the 1955 standard draft treaty provided: "Nationals and companies of either Party shall be accorded national treatment with respect to engaging in all types of commercial, industrial, financial and other activity for gain (business activities) within the territories of the other Party, whether directly or by agent or through the medium of any form of lawful juridical entity."

The term "engaging in" referred to the entire process of starting and operating the activity. Thus, the guarantee of national treatment with respect to the right to engage in gainful activity prohibited discrimination both with respect to the right to establish a business and with respect to the treatment of the business after its establishment. It applied to nationals acting on their own behalf or as an employee of another,[227] although the United States did not believe that such a provision granted foreign nationals a right of employment with public agencies or on public works projects.[228] Nor did the language require that a private employer hire a foreign national. Rather, it would apply to legislation that excluded foreign nationals from being employed by private concerns that wished to employ them in an activity in which the treaty permitted them to engage on a national treatment basis.[229] The prohibition on discrimination reached "indirect discrimination,"

226. In the very earliest postwar treaties, national treatment with respect to engaging in activity was granted to nationals and to companies in separate articles of the treaty, reflecting the novelty of providing companies with treaty protection equivalent to that provided to nationals. *See, e.g.,* Italy FCN treaty, Articles I(2) and II(3).

227. Despatch dated November 27, 1956, from the U.S. embassy in Brussels to the Department of State, NARA, Record Group 59, Department of State File No. 611.554/11-2756; Instruction dated November 10, 1953, from the Department of State to the U.S. High Commissioner in Bonn, NARA, Record Group 59, Department of State File No. 611.62A4/11-1553.

228. Memorandum on Proposed Articles for Use in Drafting Treaties of Friendship, Commerce and Navigation with Particular Countries, undated, NARA, Record Group 59, Department of State Lot Files, Walter Hollis Papers; Letter dated December 11, 1945, from the Secretary of State to the U.S. Charges d'Affaires in Beirut, NARA, Record Group 59, Department of State File No. 711.90E2/11-145; Memorandum to the American Mission at Beirut for Use in Negotiating Treaty of Friendship, Commerce and Navigation between the United States and the Lebanese Republic, NARA, Record Group 59, Department of State File No. 711.90E2/7-346; Memorandum dated March 16, 1946, and headed "Proposed Sino-American Treaty of Friendship, Commerce and Navigation," NARA, Record Group 59, Department of State File No. 911.932/12-2046.

229. Memorandum dated March 16, 1946, and headed "Proposed Sino-American Treaty of Friendship, Commerce and Navigation," NARA, Record Group 59, Department of State File No. 911.932/12-2046.

such as in the case of facially non-discriminatory language adopted to exclude foreign nationals.[230]

This guarantee of national treatment applied only to areas of the economy open to private enterprise. That is, the treaty did not require national treatment guarantees in sectors reserved to monopolies or to state-owned enterprises,[231] although state-owned or controlled enterprises could claim the protection of the treaty.[232]

Article VII(1) was stated in "sweeping language to cover all types of private business activity, including shipping and aviation."[233] Prior to 1950, however, the obligation of national treatment applied not to all gainful activity, but only to activity in specific sectors of the economy, necessitating a discussion of the scope of these sectors. For example, Article VI(1)(a) of the treaty with Ireland guaranteed national treatment with respect to engaging in commercial, manufacturing, processing, and financial activities. One important reason to broaden the provision to include all gainful activity was to eliminate the need to draw difficult distinctions among those activities that fell within or without the specified sectors. For example, the drafters had not included the term "construction" originally because they thought that it was implied in the other terms,[234] but they added it to the standard draft treaty at the end of the 1940s as a clarification.[235]

The term "commercial" activity was used "in a fairly limited sense" to refer primarily, though not exclusively, to the buying and selling of goods and activities incidental thereto.[236] It did not refer to transportation, such as navigation or aviation, to

230. Aide-Memoire accompanying dispatch dated December 14, 1960, from the U.S. embassy in Brussels to the Department of State, NARA, Record Group 59, Department of State File No. 611.554/12-1460.

231. Memorandum headed "Memorandum on the Provisions of the Greek Counterdraft," dated July 31, 1950, NARA, Record Group 59, Department of State File No, 611.814/6-250.

232. Memorandum to the Embassy at Chungking for Use in Negotiating Treaty of Friendship, Commerce and Navigation, NARA, Record Group 59, Department of State File No. 711.932/2-1645; Memorandum to the American Mission at Beirut for Use in Negotiating Treaty of Friendship, Commerce and Navigation between the United States and the Lebanese Republic, enclosure with message dated July 3, 1946, from the Department of State to the U.S. mission in Beirut, NARA, Record Group 59, Department of State File No. 711.90E2/7-346.

233. Airgram dated June 23, 1953, from the Department of State to the U.S. embassy in The Hague, NARA, Record Group 59, Department of State File No. 611.564/6-553.

234. Ibid.

235. Memorandum of Conversation headed "Treaty of Friendship, Commerce and Navigation with Israel—Second Preliminary Discussion," dated May 8, 1950, NARA, Record Group 59, Department of State File No. 611.84A4/5-850. That sector is referenced in the treaty with Greece at Article XII(1).

236. Memorandum headed "Memorandum on the Provisions of the Greek Counterdraft," dated July 31, 1950, NARA, Record Group 59, Department of State File No, 611.814/6-250; Airgram dated August 9, 1950, from the Department of State to the U.S. embassy in Copenhagen, NARA, Record Group 59, Department of State File No. 611.594/7-1250; Instruction dated July 31, 1958, from the Department of State to the U.S. consulate general in Dhahram, NARA, Record

communications, or to public utilities.[237] The Department, always cognizant of the relationship between treaty obligation and U.S. constitutional norms, often noted that it regarded the term "commercial" as narrower than the scope of activity that could be regulated under the commerce clause of the U.S. Constitution.[238] A broader interpretation would conflict with U.S. laws related to shipping, broadcasting, aviation, banking, and other activities. Although the State Department commonly referred to commercial activity as the buying and selling of goods, during negotiation of the treaty with the sultanate of Muscat and Oman the Department proposed a definition that referred merely to buying and selling and activities incidental thereto, without any specific reference to goods.[239]

The State Department understood the term "commercial" to include the business of insurance.[240] Indeed, when it was suggested that the standard draft FCN treaty be amended to make this meaning explicit, the State Department was concerned that adding the term "insurance" to future treaties would cast doubt on whether it was covered in existing treaties.[241]

The term "processing" referred to "manipulation short of manufacturing," and included activities such as printing and dyeing.[242] In later treaties, the terms

Group 59, Department of State File No. 611.86E4/7-3158. *See also* Ireland FCN treaty, Minutes of Interpretation, *Ad Article VI;* Denmark FCN treaty, Minutes of Interpretation, *ad Articles VII and VIII.*

237. Airgram dated August 9, 1950, from the Department of State to the U.S. embassy in Copenhagen, NARA, Record Group 59, Department of State File No. 611.594/7-1250. *See also* Ireland FCN treaty, Minutes of Interpretation *Ad Article VI*; Denmark FCN treaty, Minutes of Interpretation, *ad Articles VII and VIII* (mentioning only navigation and aviation).

238. *See, e.g.,* Airgram dated February 3, 1949, from the Department of State to the U.S. legation in Dublin, NARA, Record Group 59, Department of State File No. 711.41D2/12-1748; Instruction dated July 31, 1958, from the Department of State to the U.S. consulate general in Dhahram, NARA, Record Group 59, Department of State File No. 611.86E4/7-3158.

239. Instruction dated July 31, 1958, from the Department of State to the U.S. consulate general in Dhahram, NARA, Record Group 59, Department of State File No. 611.86E4/7-3158.

240. Memorandum from Vernon G. Setser to Woodbury Willoughby, dated November 4, 1946, NARA, Record Group 59, Department of State File No. 711.002/11-336; Telegram dated March 9, 1946, from the Department of State to the U.S. embassy in Chongqing, NARA, Record Group 59, Department of State File No. 711.932/3-946. These sources indicate that insurance was also included in the reference to "financial" activities.

241. Memorandum from Vernon G. Setser to Woodbury Willoughby, dated November 4, 1946, NARA, Record Group 59, Department of State File No. 711.002/11-336; Memorandum of Conversation, headed "Comments by Commerce on Philippine Draft Treaty," dated May 14, 1946, NARA, Record Group 59, Department of State File No. 611.9631/5-1446.

242. Memorandum concerning Draft Treaty of Friendship, Commerce and Navigation, For Use of the Embassy, NARA, Record Group 59, Department of State File No. 711.932/2-1645; Memorandum to the American Mission at Beirut for Use in Negotiating Treaty of Friendship, Commerce and Navigation between the United States and the Lebanese Republic, NARA, Record Group 59, Department of State File No. 711.90E2/7-346.

"manufacturing" and "processing" were replaced with the term "industrial." Industrial activity included the development of mineral resources.[243]

The practice of the professions was an area with respect to which the obligations of the treaties changed. The early U.S. postwar FCN treaties granted national treatment with respect to the right to practice the professions, with various exceptions.[244] During the revision of the standard draft treaty in 1948–1949, the right of national treatment was expanded to apply to engagement in any gainful activity, except certain specified ones, and the professions did not fall within those exceptions. Additional language specifically addressing the professions provided that "[n]ationals of either Party shall not be barred from practicing the professions within the territories of the other Party merely by reason of their alienage; but they shall be permitted to engage in professional activities therein upon compliance with the requirements regarding qualifications, residence and competence that are applicable to nationals of such other party."[245] Thus, the right of national treatment was explicitly extended to the practice of all professions, including law. Although the general national treatment obligation by its terms would seem to have applied to the professions, the United States regarded the more specific language as providing the treaty rule with respect to the practice of professions. The Senate objected to that provision on the ground that it interfered with state prerogatives to regulate the professions, leading to its removal from later FCN treaties.[246] By removing the specific provision on the practice of professions, the United States did not intend to broaden the general national treatment provision with respect to engaging in gainful activity so as to include that subject.[247] Indeed, new language was inserted into the standard draft treaty

243. Enclosure 8 to despatch dated March 5, 1958, from the U.S. consulate general in Dhahran to the Department of State, NARA, Record Group 59, Department of State File No. 611.86E4/3-558.

244. The treaty with China, at Article II(2), granted national treatment with respect to "every profession not reserved exclusively to nationals of the country." This meant that a party could exclude aliens from a profession entirely but could not otherwise deny national treatment. Telegram dated March 27, 1945, from the Department of State to the U.S. embassy in Chongqing, NARA, Record Group 59, Department of State File No. 711.932/3-2145. The treaty with Italy, at Article I(2), granted national treatment with respect to engaging in professional activities except the practice of law. The treaty with Ireland, at Article VI(1)(a), also granted national treatment with respect to engaging in all professional activities, except the practice of law. The treaty with Greece, at Article XII(1), exempted law, dentistry, and pharmacy from the right of national treatment.

245. Israel FCN treaty, Article VIII(2).

246. The Senate's action is discussed in Chapter 6 in the section headed "Senate Advice and Consent to Ratification 1952–1953."

247. Despatch dated September 8, 1954, from the U.S. embassy in The Hague to the Department of State, NARA, Record Group 59, Department of State File No. 611.564/9-854; Despatch dated August 3, 1954, from the U.S. embassy in The Hague to the Department of State, NARA, Record Group 59, Department of State File No. 611.564/8-354.

to state explicitly that Article VII(1) did not apply to the practice of professions. For example, Paragraph 4 of the protocol to the 1955 standard draft stated that "[t]he activities referred to in Article VII, paragraph 1, do not include the practice of professions."

Despite the "sweeping language" in Article VII(1) after 1950, the United States itself was not prepared to grant national treatment with respect to the right to engage in every form of gainful activity. Federal and state laws restricted in various ways the right of aliens to engage in certain business activities, and the State Department did not intend to use the FCN treaties to eliminate these restrictions.

Accordingly, treaties that granted national treatment with respect to engaging in gainful activity also included a second paragraph that created exceptions to the subject matter of the national treatment obligation. For example, Article VII(2) of the 1955 standard draft treaty stated that "[e]ach Party reserves the right to limit the extent to which aliens may establish, acquire interests in, or carry on enterprises engaged within its territories in communications, air or water transport, the performance of trust functions, banking involving depository functions, or the exploitation of land or other natural resources." The State Department believed that the essential security interests exception would be sufficient to justify any other necessary exceptions to the national treatment obligation.[248] The limitations on national treatment permitted by the treaty might include a complete prohibition on the establishment of investment or lesser limitations, such as a permission to establish an investment accompanied by conditions on the operation of that investment.

Treaty negotiations provided some clarification of the scope of these exceptions. The term "communications" included radio and television broadcasting in addition to telephone and telegraph services.[249] The term "transportation" included air and water transport.[250] The treaty thus guaranteed no right for the aircraft of one party to enter the airspace of the other party, although aircraft and freight in the territory of a party would be protected as property.[251] Air and water

248. Airgram dated June 1, 1950, from the Department of State to U.S. embassy in Copenhagen, NARA, Department of State File No. 611.594/5-350.

249. Germany FCN treaty, Protocol, Paragraph 11. *See also* Memorandum attached to letter dated April 29, 1954, from Carl H. Boehringer to the Secretary of State, NARA, Record Group 59, Department of State File No. 611.62A4/4-2954; Instruction dated November 10, 1953, from the Department of State to the U.S. High Commissioner in Bonn, NARA, Record Group 59, Department of State File No. 611.62A4/11-1553.

250. Memorandum attached to letter dated April 29, 1954, from Carl H. Boehringer to the Secretary of State, NARA, Record Group 59, Department of State File No. 611.62A4/4-2954; Instruction dated November 10, 1953, from the Department of State to the U.S. High Commissioner in Bonn, NARA, Record Group 59, Department of State File No. 611.62A4/11-1553.

251. Agreed Minutes of Technical Discussions on the Proposed Treaty of Friendship, Commerce and Navigation between the United States of America and the Republic of the Philippines at Manila July 2 to August 24, 1948, Session of July 21, 1948, NARA, Record Group 59, Department of State File No. 711.962/9-1448.

transport, in turn, included inland transportation.[252] The exception for banking was limited to depository functions, meaning the acceptance of deposits from the public at large,[253] because such functions involved "other people's money" and thus were subject to strict measures of regulation.[254] The exploitation of land and natural resources included, but was not limited to, mining, agriculture, fishing, and the development of water power.[255] It did not include manufacturing, processing, or commercial activities involving agricultural or mineral products.[256]

Although the State Department did not invite the other party in a negotiation to add sectors to the excepted list, it was prepared to consider a proposal by the other party to add more sectors, although it sought to ensure that at a minimum national treatment with respect to the right to engage in commercial and manufacturing activities would be guaranteed.[257] Thus, for example, a few treaties added public utilities to the list of excepted sectors. The term "public utility enterprises" was defined in Paragraph 3 of the protocol to the treaty with Japan to include "enterprises engaged in furnishing communications services, water supplies, transportation by bus, truck or rail, or in manufacturing and distributing gas or electricity, to the general public."[258] It was defined in Paragraph 5 of the protocol to the treaty with Korea to "include enterprises engaged in furnishing water supplies or in manufacturing and distributing gas or electricity, to the general public."

The State Department sought in negotiations to minimize the extent of the protectionism that lay behind these exceptions. It characterized restrictions on

252. Despatch dated March 16, 1954, from the U.S. High Commissioner in Bonn to the Department of State, NARA, Record Group 59, Department of State File No. 62A4/3-1654; Instruction dated November 10, 1953, from the Department of State to the U.S. High Commissioner in Bonn, NARA, Record Group 59, Department of State File No. 611.62A4/11-1553.

253. Despatch dated March 16, 1954, from the U.S. High Commissioner in Bonn to the Department of State, NARA, Record Group 59, Department of State File No. 611.62A4/3-1654; Instruction dated November 10, 1953, from the Department of State to the U.S. High Commissioner in Bonn, NARA, Record Group 59, Department of State File No. 611.62A4/11-1553.

254. Memorandum attached to letter dated April 29, 1954, from Carl H. Boehringer to the Secretary of State, NARA, Record Group 59, Department of State File No. 611.62A4/4-2954; Instruction dated November 10, 1953, from the Department of State to the U.S. High Commissioner in Bonn, NARA, Record Group 59, Department of State File No. 611.62A4/11-1553.

255. Instruction dated October 27, 1958, from the Department of State to the U.S. embassy in Saigon, NARA, Record Group 59, Department of State File No. 611.51G4/10-958.

256. Ibid.

257. Instruction dated April 5, 1955, from the Department of State to the U.S. embassy in Seoul, NARA, Record Group 59, Department of State File No. 611.95B4/2-2855.

258. A virtually identical definition appears in Paragraph 6 of the protocol to the treaty with Nicaragua.

establishment in the listed sectors of the economy as common to other countries,[259] and noted that U.S. restrictions on alien participation in these sectors were limited. As the State Department explained during its negotiations with South Korea,

> Paragraph 2 of the U.S. draft enumerates a number of important exceptions to the general principle set forth in paragraph one. The fields of activity listed in paragraph 2 are widely regarded as sensitive from the standpoint of important national interests, and alien participation therein is subject to restrictions in many countries. Although there are legislative restrictions on such participation in the United States, aliens are by no means completely barred from engaging in the listed activities. Communications are included in the exception merely because Federal law limits alien participation in radio broadcasting to a minority interest in American corporations. A similar restriction is in effect with respect to air and water transport. In the field of banking, State laws and administrative policy are such that it would be difficult to give a general assurance that aliens could establish banks to do a deposit business, although alien banks have been and may be established in certain instances. There are no restrictions upon aliens with respect to engaging in commercial or investment banking that does not involve the taking of deposits. The exploitation of land and other natural resources is included in the exception for two reasons. First, the Federal Power Act authorizes the licensing of only American citizens and corporations to develop water power sites on streams under Federal jurisdiction, although aliens may acquire stock in or even control of American corporations holding licenses. Second, a few of the States (less than a dozen) still have laws seriously restricting the acquisition of land by aliens; and a number accord citizens more favorable treatment than aliens with respect to the issuance of hunting and fishing licenses.[260]

The treaties included certain exceptions to the exceptions, thereby creating a right to engage in specified activities even within the excepted sectors. First, the United States recognized the need to engage in services related to international operations, and sought to promote such services through treaty protection.[261]

259. *See, e.g.*, Memorandum of Conversation headed "Negotiation of Treaty of Friendship, Commerce and Navigation with Costa Rica: First Meeting," dated June 25, 1951, NARA, Record Group 59, Department of State File No. 611.184/6-2551; Airgram dated September 18, 1958, from the Department of State to the U.S. embassy in Saigon, NARA, Record Group 59, Department of State File No. 611.51G4/8-2758.

260. Instruction dated April 5, 1955, from the Department of State to the U.S. embassy in Seoul, NARA, Record Group 59, Department of State File No. 611.95B4/2-2855.

261. Instruction dated November 10, 1953, from the Department of State to the U.S. High Commissioner in Bonn, NARA, Record Group 59, Department of State File No. 611.62A4/11-1553.

Thus, Article VII(2) of the 1955 standard draft treaty provided that "neither Party shall deny to transportation, communications and banking companies of the other Party the right to maintain branches and agencies, in conformity with applicable laws and regulations, to perform functions necessary for essentially international operations in which they engage." The purpose of this sentence was "to assure Americans [the] right [to] maintain offices [to] carry on international operations as distinguished [from] activities within [the] territories" of the other country.[262] That is, it ensured that "the reservation of the first sentence should not be applied in a manner that the operations of international banks, shipping, airlines, etc., companies could be frustrated."[263] Under this provision, a U.S. bank might establish an office overseas to receive funds for deposit in the U.S. bank.[264] Or, an alien operating an international shipping line, although not allowed to engage in internal or coastal shipping, would be permitted to maintain an agency to sell tickets for the receipt or delivery of freight.[265]

Second, the treaties protected existing enterprises against the effect of new exceptions to national treatment. For example, Article VII(2) of the 1955 standard draft treaty provided that "new limitations imposed by either Party upon the extent to which aliens are accorded national treatment, with respect to carrying on such activities within its territories, shall not be applied as against enterprises which are engaged in such activities therein at the time such new limitations are adopted and which are owned or controlled by nationals of the other Party." This provision thus protected whatever right to national treatment the enterprise enjoyed at the time the new limitations were adopted. It provided protection for "vested rights" in addition to that provided by the unreasonable or discriminatory measures provision.[266] During negotiations with France, the parties confirmed that each of them was free to modify existing regulations as long as they were not made more burdensome for foreign enterprises already engaged in the reserved activities.[267]

262. Telegram dated February 4, 1955, from the Department of State to the U.S. embassy in Karachi, NARA, Record Group 59, Department of State File No. 611.90D4/2-255.

263. Despatch dated March 16, 1954, from the U.S. High Commissioner in Bonn to the Department of State, NARA, Record Group 59, Department of State File No. 62A4/3-1654.

264. Instruction dated November 10, 1953, from the Department of State to the U.S. High Commissioner in Bonn, NARA, Record Group 59, Department of State File No. 611.62A4/11-1553; Instruction dated January 15, 1958, from the Department of State to the U.S. embassy in Vienna, NARA, Record Group 59, Department of State File No. 611.634/12-1357.

265. Telegram dated February 4, 1955, from the Department of State to the U.S. embassy in Karachi, NARA, Record Group 59, Department of State File No. 611.90D4/2-255; Instruction dated January 15, 1958, from the Department of State to the U.S. embassy in Vienna, NARA, Record Group 59, Department of State File No. 611.634/12-1357.

266. Letter dated July 17, 1953, from Vernon Setser to the Second Secretary to the Embassy of Japan, NARA, Record Group 59, Department of State File No. 611.944/7-753.

267. Despatch dated May 28, 1959, from the U.S. embassy in Paris to the Department of State, NARA, Record Group 59, Department of State File No. 611.514/5-2859.

Not-for-Profit Activities

The U.S. postwar FCN treaties included an entirely separate provision that guaranteed national and MFN treatment with respect to engaging in certain activities that were not for profit.[268] For example, Article VIII(2) of the 1955 standard draft treaty provided that "[n]ationals and companies of either Party shall be accorded national treatment and most-favored-nation treatment with respect to engaging in scientific, educational, religious and philanthropic activities within the territories of the other Party, and shall be accorded the right to form associations for that purpose under the laws of such other Party." The reference to "laws" referred to the laws relating to the organization of non-profit entities and was not meant to subordinate the right in this sentence to local law. In the early U.S. postwar FCN treaties, the right to engage in non-profit activities was included in the same provision as the right to engage in activities for gain.[269]

The State Department believed that "[t]he categories stipulated in the treaty are regarded as being so broad in scope that they encompass every worthwhile type of non-profit association that is entitled to treaty protection . . . ."[270] Belgium complained that charitable organizations were not adequately covered, but the State Department believed that charitable organizations were "fully covered by the term 'philanthropic'."[271] As it explained, the term "philanthropic" extended "broadly to efforts to promote the welfare of one's fellow men," whereas charitable efforts related "rather narrowly to efforts for the immediate relief of human need or suffering" and thus fell under philanthropy.[272] The right to engage in educational activities did not imply a waiver of non-discriminatory academic qualifications.

This provision explicitly excluded the right to engage in political activities. For example, Article VIII(2) of the 1955 standard draft treaty stated that "[n]othing in the present Treaty shall be deemed to grant or imply any right to engage in political activities." This exception applied to political parties and to front organizations operating ostensibly for nonpolitical purposes.[273] Nothing would bar the government from "piercing the front" and determining the true nature of the organization's activities.[274] Under that exception, each party "reserve[d] full freedom of action."[275] The State Department noted that the security exception was

268. In the earliest U.S. postwar FCN treaties, activity for gain and non-profit activity were treated in the same provision. *See, e.g.*, Italy FCN treaty, Articles I(2) and II(3).

269. *See, e.g.*, Italy FCN treaty, Articles I(2) and II(1).

270. Instruction dated November 1, 1956, from the Department of State to the U.S. embassy in Brussels, NARA, Record Group 59, Department of State File No. 611.554/10-1156.

271. Ibid.

272. Ibid.

273. Ibid.

274. Ibid.

275. Ibid.

likely to apply as well if the organization's activities were "at all dangerous."[276] Although not expressly so stated, the right to engage in non-profit activities did not apply to social clubs either.[277]

Acquiring Personal Property

An entirely separate article of the treaty guaranteed national and MFN treatment with respect to the right to acquire personal property. For example, Article IX(3) of the 1955 standard draft treaty provided, "Nationals and companies of either Party shall be accorded within the territories of the other Party national treatment and most-favored-nation treatment with respect to acquiring, by purchase, lease, or otherwise, and with respect to owning and possessing, personal property of all kinds, both tangible and intangible." This language ensured that nationals and companies of a party would receive national (and MFN) treatment with respect to the making of portfolio investment. The concern was that the right to engage in a particular activity might be read so as not to include the right to invest in a company engaged in that activity.

This provision was subject to a reservation to permit a party to restrict ownership of shares in enterprises in certain sensitive sectors of the economy and another reservation to preserve state laws restricting alien ownership of dangerous items, such as guns, explosives, poisons, or narcotics.[278] Thus, for example, Article IX(3) of the 1955 standard draft treaty further provided that "either Party may impose restrictions on alien ownership of materials dangerous from the standpoint of public safety and alien ownership of interests in enterprises carrying on particular types of activity, but only to the extent that this can be done without impairing the rights and privileges secured by Article VII [relating to national and MFN treatment with respect to engaging in gainful activity] or by other provisions of the present Treaty." In addition, Article VII(2), which, as noted above, authorized each party to reserve the right to limit the extent to which aliens were permitted to engage in activities in specified reserved sectors, also authorized each party to reserve the right to limit the extent to which aliens could "acquire interests in" enterprises engaged in activities in the reserved sectors.

Policy Considerations

The United States sought to define clearly the subject matter to which the national treatment obligation applied so that the parties could visualize their commitments and know whether they were in a position to undertake the obligation.[279]

276. Ibid.

277. Ibid.

278. Ireland FCN treaty, Minutes of Interpretation, *Ad Article VII, paragraph 2.*

279. Airgram dated December 31, 1951, from the Department of State to the U.S. Political Adviser in Tokyo, NARA, Department of State File No. 611.944/12-3151.

For this reason, nowhere did the treaty confer on nationals or companies of a party the right to national treatment in all matters. Rather, the national treatment obligation was always with respect to a particular subject matter.

Obtaining national treatment was a "cardinal objective" of the FCN treaties.[280] Along with the requirement of prompt, just, and effective compensation for expropriation, the national treatment provision was one of the two most important provisions in the treaty.[281] The State Department explained during negotiations with Egypt that the purpose of the national treatment provision was "to open up in each country a broad field of activities in which nationals and companies of the other may freely participate without discrimination."[282] U.S. FCN treaties prior to the war had subordinated the right of national treatment to local law and, in any event, had granted it only to nationals, not to companies.[283]

The State Department sometimes referred to the provision that guaranteed the right of national treatment with respect to engaging in gainful activity as the "heart of the treaty."[284] Although the United States could accept some derogations from the principle, it could not accept a complete abandonment of it[285] National treatment was indispensable.[286] Although the United States in most cases sought for its investors the right of national treatment with respect to the establishment

280. Memorandum headed "Memorandum on the Provisions of the Greek Counterdraft," dated July 31, 1950, NARA, Record Group 59, Department of State File No, 611.814/6-250.

281. National Advisory Council Document 1868 (Revised) headed "Investments in Less Developed Areas," dated December 12, 1955, NARA, Record Group 353, Records Relating to the Council on Foreign Economic Policy 1955-1961, Box 4, Folder marked "Investment in Underdeveloped Countries CFEP 511 (Folder 1)."

282. Department of State Airgram A-265 dated December 11, 1951, to the U.S. embassy in Cairo, NARA, Record Group 59, Department of State File No. 611.744/11-351.

283. *See, e.g.,* Treaty of Friendship. Commerce, and Consular Rights, United States-Finland, February 13, 1934, Article I, 49 Stat. 2659, TS 868, 4 UST 2047, TIAS 2861.

284. Airgram dated January 7, 1952, from the Department of State to the U.S. Political Adviser in Tokyo, NARA, Record Group 59, Department of State File No. 611.944/12-1751; Airgram dated June 1, 1950, from Department of State to U.S. embassy in Copenhagen, NARA, Record Group 59, Department of State File No. 611.594/5-350; Memorandum headed "Memorandum on the Provisions of the Greek Counterdraft," dated July 31, 1950, NARA, Record Group 59, Department of State File No, 611.814/6-250; Instruction dated November 10, 1953, from the Department of State to the U.S. High Commissioner in Bonn, NARA, Record Group 59, Department of State File No. 611.62A4/10-1553; Summary of Provisions of the United States-Uruguay Treaty of Friendship, Commerce and Economic Development, signed November 23, 1949, *reprinted in Treaty of Friendship, Commerce and Economic Development with the Oriental Republic of Uruguay*, Exec. Rept. No. 5, 81st Cong. 2d Sess. (1950); Memorandum headed "Third Meeting with Indian Officials regarding Proposed Treaty of Friendship, Commerce and Navigation," dated September 2, 1948, NARA, Record Group 59, Department of State File No. 711.452/9-2948.

285. Memorandum headed "Memorandum on the Provisions of the Greek Counterdraft," dated July 31, 1950, NARA, Record Group 59, Department of State File No. 611.814/6-250.

286. Instruction dated November 27, 1957, from the Department of State to the U.S. consulate general in Dhahran, NARA, Record Group 59, Department of State File No. 611.86E4/10-257.

of investment, the State Department was prepared in some cases to forgo that right.[287] The "really vital treaty rule" was that guaranteeing national treatment with respect to investment following its establishment,[288] and this was the principle with respect to which the Department would not compromise.[289]

The national treatment provision was one that the United States particularly identified with economic liberalism, that is, with the system of free enterprise. As the State Department explained during negotiations with the sultanate of Muscat and Oman, "the aim here is to provide to the greatest extent possible for the enjoyment of business rights on the basis of free enterprise principles."[290] During negotiations with Germany, the State Department explained that the provision on national treatment with respect to engaging in gainful activity was aimed "at establishing a body of rules deemed to be sound and equitable for generally all countries with enlightened concepts of law and a belief in free enterprise."[291] During negotiations with Vietnam, the State Department referred to that provision as "a forthright endorsement of the principle of free enterprise."[292]

Herman Walker a principal negotiator of U.S. postwar FCN treaties, explained in a 1948 memorandum the justification for the national treatment obligations:

> The principal objective of the United States Government contained in its proposals governing what are often termed "establishment" matters is to effect a

287. Memorandum headed "Screening Problem in the Projected FCN Treaty with India," dated October 31, 1950, NARA, Record Group 59, Department of State File No. 611.914/11-250; Letter dated October 13, 1950, from John M. Leddy to Ambassador Loy W. Henderson, NARA, Record Group 59, Department of State File No. 611.914/8-250; Memorandum headed "Negotiation of Treaty of Friendship, Commerce and Navigation with India," dated September 11, 1950, NARA, Record Group 59, Department of State File No. 611.914/9-1150.

288. Memorandum headed "Screening Problem in the Projected FCN Treaty with India," dated October 31, 1950, NARA, Record Group 59, Department of State File No. 611.914/11-250.

289. Memorandum headed "Screening: FCN Treaty with India—E Meeting," dated March 31, 1950, NARA, Record Group 59, Department of State File No. 611.914/3-3150. Of course, the right of national treatment with respect to engaging in gainful activity did not apply to every sector of the economy and was subject to the national security exceptions and thus, to that extent, the United States did compromise, although these were limitations on national treatment that, for the most part, the United States itself wanted.

290. Memorandum headed "Explanation of Certain Provisions of U.S. Proposals for Treaty of Amity and Economic Relations with Muscat," dated April 17, 1947, and enclosure to instruction dated April 17, 1957, from the Department of State to the U.S. consulate general in Dhahran, NARA, Record Group 59, Department of State File No. 611.86E1/4-1757.

291. Instruction dated November 10, 1953, from the Department of State to the U.S. High Commissioner in Bonn, NARA, Record Group 59, Department of State File No. 611.62A4/10-1553.

292. Airgram dated September 18, 1958, from the Department of State to the U.S. embassy in Saigon, NARA, Record Group 59, Department of State File No. 611.51G4/8-2758.

> basis for national treatment, that is, the recognition of equality of treatment within each country of the nationals of both. This policy is predicated upon the conviction that a regime of equality in the ordinary affairs of life is conducive to free intercourse between nations, to the release of human initiative for the improvement of living conditions, and to guarantee the liberty and freedom of the individual. The application of this policy to the realm of industrial enterprise has particular justifications of its own. It is the opinion of the United States Government that the development of productive facilities and economic enterprises, which are so necessary to the well-being and prosperity of nations, is dependent upon the existence of assurances which will enable private capital of one country to venture investments in the territory of another. . . . In consequence, the United States Government desires to establish such assurances in the faith and conviction that what it seeks is not merely in the selfish interests of capital. The benefits are fully mutual, for an investment made in productive enterprises is an addition to the employment, well-being and prosperity of the country where made, and increases the diversity of capital sources which are available to that country.[293]

When Ethiopia proposed a rule of MFN treatment alone rather than national treatment, the State Department explained that "[n]ational treatment of U.S. enterprises, or MFN treatment if more favorable than national treatment, is fundamental in [the Department's] treaty policy. Nothing less, in [the Department's] view, would contribute to [the] objective of encouraging private investment for economic development. An MFN provision alone would permit almost any kind of discriminatory treatment of alien enterprises."[294]

Similarly, when the sultan of Muscat and Oman proposed substituting MFN treatment for national treatment, the State Department objected, explaining,

> If the US enterprise were the only alien enterprise of its type operating in Muscat, recourse to MFN treatment would be useless, for there would be no other enterprise the treatment of which could be held as constituting the treatment of the most-favored-nation. The field would therefore be open to all manner of discrimination against the United States firm without infringement of the treaty.[295]

The State Department saw a direct link between non-discrimination and security, and regarded both as part of the concept of "fair treatment." As the

293. Aide-Memoire drafted by Herman Walker, dated October 20, 1948, NARA, Record Group 59, Department of State File No. 711.41D2/10-2048.

294. Airgram A-55 dated March 27, 1951, from the Department of State to the U.S. embassy in Addis Ababa, NARA, Record Group 59, Department of State File No. 611.754/2-551.

295. Instruction dated November 27, 1957, from the Department of State to the U.S. consulate general in Dhahran, NARA, Record Group 59, Department of State File No. 611.86E4/10-257.

Department commented during negotiations with the sultanate of Muscat and Oman, the guarantee of national treatment was

> vitally related to the security of the investment enterprise. There can be little security for a business enterprise if it lacks assurance that it will be free from unfair or discriminatory treatment after it has established itself in a country. Even the most liberal privileges of entry tend to become meaningless unless there is certainty about the nature of the treatment to be encountered after entry. Without such certainty, it would be difficult, if not impossible, to carry on ordinary operations with any degree of confidence, to make further investment decisions or to realize the full benefit, both for investor and country of investment, of the undertaking.[296]

The business community placed great importance on the right of establishment. The only instances where organized business interests (other than those in a specific sector of the economy) opposed, or failed to support, advice and consent to ratification of an FCN treaty occurred where they believed that the treaty lacked a sufficient right of establishment.[297] For example, during negotiations with India, business representatives informed the State Department that they would prefer no treaty at all to a treaty that lacked a right of national treatment with respect to establishment.[298] American business groups in China opposed Senate approval of the treaty with China because they did not believe that it guaranteed sufficient establishment rights to companies. Similarly, the NFTC opposed Senate advice and consent to the treaty with Ethiopia because it lacked a right of establishment, and refused to endorse the treaty with Ireland because it contained an exception to national treatment with respect to establishment.[299] It also declined to endorse both the treaty with Pakistan because the treaty lacked a right of national treatment with respect to establishment[300] and the treaty with the sultanate of Muscat and Oman because the treaty lacked several provisions common to U.S. postwar FCN treaties, including the standard provision on establishment.[301]

296. Ibid.

297. *See, e.g.*, Memorandum from Winthrop Brown to Will Clayton, dated November 5, 1946, NARA, Record Group 59, Department of State File No. 711.002/11-546.

298. Telegram dated July 6, 1950, from the Department of State to the U.S. embassy in New Delhi, NARA, Record Group 59, Department of State File No. 611.914/5-1250.

299. The refusal to endorse the treaty with Ireland is described in Chapter 5 in the section headed "Senate Advice and Consent to Ratification 1950." The opposition to the treaty with Ethiopia is described in Chapter 6 in the section headed "Senate Advice and Consent to Ratification 1952–1953."

300. The refusal to endorse the treaty with Pakistan is described in Chapter 7 in the section headed "Senate Advice and Consent to Ratification 1960."

301. The refusal to endorse the treaty with the sultanate of Muscat and Oman is described in Chapter 7 in the section on the negotiation of the treaty with the sultanate. The treaty did

As discussed in Chapter 6,[302] national treatment with respect to the right of establishment was the most difficult provision of the treaty on which to gain agreement. The State Department recognized that other states had a legitimate right to refuse a right of establishment.[303] That is, "everyone concede[d]" that the right to screen foreign investment was "an attribute of sovereignty."[304] Woodbury Willoughby observed in a March 1949 memorandum to State Department legal adviser Jack Tate that "[t]here is tenable opinion to the effect that we have no more right to insist upon unlimited and unregulated entry of capital than the other country has to insist upon unlimited entry of persons . . . ."[305] Indeed, during internal discussions in 1945 concerning a possible FCN treaty with Brazil, State Department officials commented that, although Brazil needed capital, it also needed "to be on guard against the improper exploitation of its economy by any foreign country."[306] The United States itself discriminated against aliens in particular sectors of the economy and did not wish to agree to non-discriminatory treatment in those areas, a situation that provided other countries with a basis on which to insist upon a right to discriminate in sectors of the economy that they regarded as sensitive.[307]

Further, the State Department believed that there was "no useful purpose to be served, from the point of view either of the prudent investor or of harmonious international relations, in attempting to use these treaties as a vehicle for forcing countries to agree to allow investments that they do not want."[308] It would be "unwise" for U.S. capital to enter a country on the basis of treaty rights unless the government of that country "clearly welcomed" the investment and entry was

guarantee national treatment with respect to the establishment of trading activities, but not with respect to other gainful activities.

302. The discussion appears in the section on U.S. negotiating strategy.

303. Airgram dated November 23, 1948, from the U.S. embassy in Paris to the Department of State, NARA, Record Group 59, Department of State File No. 711.41D2/11-2348.

304. Memorandum headed "Screening Problem in the Projected FCN Treaty with India," dated October 31, 1950, NARA, Record Group 59, Department of State File No. 611.914/11-250.

305. Memorandum from Woodbury Willoughby to Jack B. Tate, dated March 17, 1949, NARA, Record Group 59, Department of State File No. 611.41D2/3-1749.

306. Memorandum headed "Tenth Meeting to Consider a Tentative Draft Treaty of Friendship, Commerce and Navigation between the United States and Brazil Held November 29, 1945," NARA, Record Group 59, Department of State File No. 711.322/4-2346.

307. NAC Staff Document No. 740, Program for Obtaining Treaty Assurances to Protect United States Citizens and Property and Promote United States Private Investment in Foreign Countries, NARA, Record Group 353, Records Relating to the Council on Foreign Economic Policy 1955–1961, Box 4, Folder marked "Investment in Underdeveloped Countries CFEP 511 (Folder 2)."

308. Walker, "Modern Treaties," page 819. *See also* Instruction dated March 30, 1959, from the Department of State to the U.S. embassy in Saigon, NARA, Record Group 59, Department of State File No. 611.51G4/1-1559.

on conditions agreeable to that government.[309] Insistence upon a right of screening when a country did not wish to grant it would only exacerbate fears that the United States was seeking to engage in "imperialistic exploitation" of the other treaty party.[310] Thus, the aim was "to attain as much clarification of the country's intended policies as may be practicable and, especially, to guarantee duly established investors against subsequent discrimination."[311]

The State Department believed that even the NFTC understood that no country should be pressured to accept unwanted investment. A 1950 State Department memorandum noted, with respect to the NFTC, that "their great objection to screening was grounded less upon a feeling that capital should be guaranteed the right to force itself into a country against the country's wishes, than upon a fear lest the screening process be vitiated by capriciousness, high-handedness, inequity, and even downright corruption and skullduggery."[312]

From a practical perspective, State Department officials realized that a refusal to compromise with respect to provisions on entry would result only in the conclusion of fewer treaties. As was noted in an internal memorandum written in 1950 in connection with the negotiations with India, "A number of countries with which we should like to make treaties have adopted policies for the selective admission of foreign investments. There is little possibility that we can, in connection with treaty negotiations, induce these countries to abandon these policies. If we expect to make treaties with them, we shall have to accommodate our treaty provisions to these policies to a considerable extent."[313]

Accordingly, the United States was prepared to agree to certain general exceptions to national treatment with respect to establishment, as well as exceptions tailored to the circumstances of each country.[314] The standard draft treaty permitted screening in those areas specified in the treaty, in those areas that were closed to private enterprise entirely, in those areas in which the essential security interests exception applied, and in those areas where the screening was conducted on a non-discriminatory basis.

309. Memorandum headed "Negotiation of Treaty of Friendship, Commerce and Navigation with India," dated September 11, 1950, NARA, Record Group 59, Department of State File No. 611.914/9-1150.

310. Ibid.

311. Walker, "Modern Treaties," page 819.

312. Memorandum headed "Screening Problem in the Projected FCN Treaty with India," dated October 31, 1950, NARA, Record Group 59, Department of State File No. 611.914/11-250.

313. Ibid.

314. Airgram dated November 23, 1948, from the U.S. embassy in Paris to the Department of State, NARA, Record Group 59, Department of State File No. 711.41D2/11-2348. For example, the United States agreed in its treaty with Ireland to an exception for Ireland's Control of Manufactures Act. The discussions of the individual negotiations with other treaty parties in Chapters 2, 5, 6, and 7 contain other examples.

If it believed that the circumstances so warranted, the United States would not even propose that a treaty include an obligation of national treatment with respect to the right of establishment. For example, when it undertook to negotiate an FCN treaty with Ethiopia, the State Department prepared a shortened version of the treaty, which it titled a "Treaty of Amity and Economic Relations," and that did not require national treatment with respect to the establishment of business activity, although the treaty did require national treatment of that activity once it was established. In other instances, such as in the case of the treaty with Vietnam, the United States initially sought national treatment with respect to the establishment of business activity, but then agreed to a treaty without it.

Several countries were concerned that particular investments might result in a loss of foreign exchange. Because Article VII included an implied right of entry for capital incidental to engaging in the activities protected by that article,[315] these countries sought language reserving the right to exclude investments when necessary to protect their foreign exchange reserves. As discussed in Chapter 1, the United States recognized in the postwar world that countries would need to retain some discretion to regulate international capital movements, and it agreed in several instances to include the language sought. For example, Paragraph 6 of the protocol to the treaty with Japan and Paragraph 7 of the protocol to the treaty with Korea provided that "[e]ach Party may impose restrictions on the introduction of foreign capital as may be necessary to protect its monetary reserves as provided in Article XII, paragraph 2." Article XII(2) was the provision authorizing exchange controls to prevent a party's monetary reserves from falling to a very low level or to effect a moderate increase in very low monetary reserves. Paragraph 16 of the protocol to the treaty with Germany provided that "[e]ither Party may, for the protection of its currency and in the interest of servicing investments and providing for their repatriation, make the importation of capital dependent on a license." Paragraph 14 of the protocol to the treaty with France provided that "[e]ither High Contracting Party, with a view to protecting its currency or facilitating the servicing of the proceeds of investments and the repatriation of capital, may subject to authorization the making of investments by foreign nationals and companies."

Denmark was concerned that the exchange control article could be interpreted to preclude restrictions on restrictions on entry to protect foreign exchange reserves, and wanted language clarifying that such would not be the case. Accordingly, Paragraph 7 of the protocol to the treaty with Denmark provided that nothing in Article XII(2) shall be construed to prevent a party from exercising necessary regulation over the inflow of capital, "provided that such regulation shall not as a general rule be exercised in a manner" that impairs rights under Article VII, Article VIII, or other provisions of the treaty. Thus, the language in

315. Memorandum of Conversation dated March 4, 1952, NARA, Record Group 59, Department of State File No. 611.944/4-3052. *See also* Despatch dated August 4, 1954, from the U.S. embassy in The Hague to the Department of State, NARA, Record Group 59, Department of State File No. 611.564/8-454.

the treaty with Denmark was more in the nature of a clarification of Article XII than a reservation of rights under Article VII.

The Netherlands was also concerned that the article on exchange controls would be interpreted to prevent restrictions on entry of capital necessary to protect foreign exchange reserves, and expressed an additional concern about retaining the power to regulate "hot money." The United States responded that the implied obligation in Article VII to allow the "free import of investment capital did not carry the implication that instable 'speculative' money (in the invidious sense) had to be permitted to enter."[316] The State Department also had explained during negotiations with Iran that reasonable restrictions on capital to avoid a serious outflow of "hot money" in the form of scarce foreign exchange would not violate the exchange controls article.[317] Ultimately, however, the United States and the Netherlands agreed to include Paragraph 14 of the protocol to the treaty, which provided that "[e]ither Party may impose restrictions on the introduction of foreign capital as may be necessary to protect its monetary reserves as provided in Article XII, paragraph 2, or to prevent serious monetary disturbances arising from speculative financial operations."

The Nature of the National Treatment Obligation

The term "national treatment" was a defined term in the FCN treaties. For example, Article XXII(1) of the 1955 standard draft treaty defined "national treatment" to mean "treatment accorded within the territories of a Party upon terms no less favorable than the treatment accorded therein, in like situations, to nationals, companies, products, vessels or other objects, as the case may be, of such Party." Although the definition did not appear in the treaties with China and Italy, the State Department inserted a definition into the standard draft treaty during the 1948–1949 revision.

The prohibition on discrimination applied not only to measures that drew distinctions of nationality on their face, but to measures that employed neutral distinctions that were a pretext for discrimination. For example, a law that imposed a language requirement might constitute a violation of the prohibition on discrimination.[318]

During negotiations, the United States explained that "national treatment" did not mean identical treatment,[319] but treatment that "in sum and substance is

316. Ibid.

317. Instruction dated November 10, 1954, from the Department of State to the U.S. embassy in Tehran, NARA, Record Group 59, Department of State File No. 611.884/11-1054; Despatch dated October 16, 1954, from the U.S. embassy in Tehran to the Department of State, NARA, Record Group 59, Department of State File No. 611.884/10-1654.

318. Despatch dated December 14, 1960, from the U.S. embassy in Brussels to the Department of State, NARA, Record Group 59, Department of State File No. 611.5542/12-1460.

319. Telegram dated February 19, 1952, from the Department of State to the U.S. embassy in New Delhi, NARA, Record Group 59, Department of State File No. 611.914/2-752.

'no less favorable' (or no more burdensome)."[320] Put another way, it did not mean treatment that was the same, but rather treatment that was at least equal.[321]

Further, national treatment was required only "in like situations," a limitation that the United States considered an "important part of the concept of national treatment."[322] The principle was that an alien could not be discriminated against because he or she was an alien, but national treatment did not provide an alien with immunity from laws to which nationals were subject.[323] Discrimination was permissible if based on an "objective principle" rather than nationality. [324]

For example, a host state might justifiably offer inducements to a local company exploiting mineral deposits in a remote mountainous location that it did not offer to a foreign investor operating in a more favorably located area.[325] Paragraph 16 of the protocol to the treaty with France permitted the use of "[r]esidence criteria" in determining whether nationals or companies were in like situations.

Similarly, a host state might have been justified in imposing special obligations on foreign-owned insurance companies to ensure that they did not use their foreign status to evade their financial responsibilities to their policyholders.[326] Thus, the minutes of interpretation for the FCN treaty with Denmark stated, "It is understand too that either Party may, consistently with the terms and intent of the Treaty, apply special requirements to alien insurance companies with a view to assuring that such companies maintain standards of accountability and solvency comparable to those required of like domestic companies, so long as such requirements do not have the effect of discrimination in substance against such alien companies."[327] Other treaties included similar language in their protocols.[328] As the State Department noted during negotiations with Germany, "In the field of insurance, it is considered legitimate to require reasonable bond of alien companies, so as to assure that there will be within the jurisdiction realizable assets

320. Airgram dated January 30, 1951, from the Department of State to the U.S. embassy in Copenhagen, NARA, Record Group 59, Department of State File No. 611.594/1-251.

321. Letter dated January 13, 1950, from John Parke Young to Walter A. Chudson, NARA, Record Group 59, Department of State File No. 611.334/1-1350.

322. Instruction dated June 21, 1955, from the Department of State to the U.S. embassy in Seoul, NARA, Record Group 59, Department of State File No. 611.95B4/6-1655.

323. Airgram dated July 3, 1954, from the Department of State to the U.S. embassy in The Hague, NARA, Record Group 59, Department of State File No. 611.564/6-1553.

324. Telegram dated February 19, 1952, from the Department of State to the U.S. embassy in New Delhi, NARA, Record Group 59, Department of State File No. 611.914/2-752.

325. Ibid.

326. Airgram dated January 30, 1951, from the Department of State to the U.S. embassy in Copenhagen, NARA, Department of State File No. 611.594/1-251.

327. Denmark FCN treaty, Minutes of Interpretation, *ad Article VII, paragraph 1.*

328. Netherlands FCN treaty, Protocol, Paragraph 9; Germany FCN treaty, Protocol, Paragraph 9; France FCN treaty, Protocol, Paragraph 8.

to back their obligations to policy holders; domestic companies are not required to post the same bond because they already have reachable assets within the jurisdiction." German bonding requirements would not violate the treaty if "reasonable according to accepted insurance standards"[329] and not imposed to put an alien in an "unequal competitive position."[330] Indeed, the United States had similar laws in order to "equilibrate" foreign insurance companies with domestic companies.[331]

Following the conclusion of the FCN treaty with Colombia, in an effort to eliminate opposition to the treaty by the Catholic Church in Colombia, the Colombian ambassador proposed to the State Department that the two countries agree that national treatment with respect to engaging in religious activities meant that American Catholics would be entitled to the same treatment in Colombia as Colombian Catholics, while American Protestants would be entitled to the same treatment in Colombia as Colombian Protestants. Assistant Legal Adviser Stanley Metzger commented that, in the event that a dispute involving this provision were presented to the International Court of Justice, Colombia "would have a respectable case before the Court, based upon the proposition that national treatment means merely that a country shall not afford inferior treatment on the basis of the alienage of the foreign national."[332] That is, if Colombia imposed disabilities on American Protestants like those imposed on Colombian Protestants, the discrimination would be on the basis of religion rather than nationality. Metzger observed that the United States could not agree to such an interpretation in advance because to do so would mean that the United States had knowingly acquiesced in a religious preference, contrary at least to the spirit of the First Amendment to the U.S. Constitution.

The term "like situations" did not mean "identical situations." During negotiations, Belgium proposed that the word "like" be replaced with the word "identical." The United States rejected this proposal, observing that "[i]f the alien must be in 'identical' situation with the citizen, the result might well be the denial of treaty protection on narrow technical grounds, for the occurrence of identical conditions, in any literal sense, would be virtually impossible. The normal and reasonable canon is similarity, not exactitude . . . ."[333]

Early versions of the provision requiring national and MFN treatment with respect to engaging in business activities specified that the treatment was to be

329. Memorandum attached to letter dated April 29, 1954, from Carl H. Boehringer to the Secretary of State, NARA, Record Group 59, Department of State File No. 611.62A4/4-2954.

330. Despatch dated September 9, 1954, from the U.S. embassy in The Hague to the Department of State, NARA, Record Group 59, Department of State File No. 611.564/9-954.

331. Ibid.

332. Memorandum by Stanley Metzger dated February 18, 1953, NARA, Record Group 59, Department of State File No. 611.214/2-1853.

333. Instruction dated June 21, 1957, from the Department of State to the U.S. embassy in Brussels, NARA, Record Group 59, Department of State File No. 611.554/6-2157.

"in conformity with the applicable laws and regulations." This phrase, which appeared for example in the FCN treaty with Italy, was not intended as a derogation from the national or MFN treatment standards.[334] The phrase meant in the case of national treatment that the laws and regulations were not to be more burdensome on U.S. nationals in Italy than on Italian nationals. In the case of MFN treatment, it meant that the laws and regulations were not to be more burdensome on U.S. nationals in Italy than on nationals of any third country.[335] Thus, the term "applicable laws and regulations" referred to laws applicable to nationals and companies generally, not solely to aliens or alien-owned companies.[336] By 1947, the Department considered the phrase to be an obsolete usage and, beginning with the FCN treaties with Ireland and Uruguay, sought to eliminate it from future treaties because it was superfluous and because it was susceptible of misinterpretation as permitting discriminatory legislation in derogation of treaty rights.[337]

Special Formalities

As noted above, national treatment did not require identical treatment but rather treatment that was equal in substance. Nevertheless, to ensure that the treaty did not preclude a party from imposing certain discriminatory requirements that did not impair the substance of the right of national treatment, at the time that

334. Airgram dated December 21, 1950, from the Department of State to the U.S. embassy in Athens, NARA, Record Group 59, Department of State File No. 611.814/11-2150; Telegram dated December 19, 1947, from the Department of State to the U.S. embassy in Rome, NARA, Record Group 59, Department of State File No. 711.652/12-1547. *See also* Memorandum to the American Mission at Beirut for Use in Negotiating Treaty of Friendship, Commerce and Navigation Between the United States and the Lebanese Republic, enclosure with airgram dated July 3, 1946, from the Department of State to the U.S. mission in Beirut, NARA, Record Group 59, Department of State File No. 711.90E2/7-346; Telegram dated May 11, 1945, from the Department of State to the U.S. embassy in Chongqing, NARA, Record Group 59, Department of State File No. 711.932/5-1145.

335. Telegram dated December 19, 1947, from the Department of State to the U.S. embassy in Rome, NARA, Record Group 59, Department of State File No. 711.652/12-1547.

336. Memorandum to the Embassy at Chungking for Use in Negotiating Treaty of Friendship, Commerce and Navigation, NARA, Record Group 59, Department of State File No. 711.932/2-1645; Memorandum to the American Mission at Beirut for Use in Negotiating Treaty of Friendship, Commerce and Navigation between the United States and the Lebanese Republic, NARA, Record Group 59, Department of State File No. 711.90E2/7-346.

337. Airgram dated December 21, 1950, from the Department of State to the U.S. embassy in Athens, NARA, Record Group 59, Department of State File No. 611.814/11-2150; Memorandum by Herman Walker Jr., headed "On the Elimination of the Proviso 'In Conformity with Applicable Laws and Regulations,'" dated February 5, 1947, NARA, Record Group 59, Department of State Lot Files, Walter Hollis Papers, Folder marked "Investment Treaties"; Telegram A-399 dated December 21, 1950, from the Department of State to the U.S. embassy in Athens, NARA, Record Group 59, Department of State File No. 611.814/11-2150; Telegram dated March 27, 1951, from the Department of State to the U.S. embassy in Addis Ababa, NARA, Record Group 59, Department of State File No. 611.754/3-552.

it revised the national treatment obligation to apply to activities for gain other than those in the excepted sectors, the State Department incorporated into the standard draft treaty a "special formalities" provision allowing the parties to impose "special formalities" in connection with the establishment of investment. For example, Article VII(3) of the 1955 standard draft treaty provided that "[t]he provisions of paragraph 1 of the present Article shall not prevent either Party from prescribing special formalities in connection with the establishment of alien-controlled enterprises within its territories; but such formalities may not impair the substance of the rights set forth in said paragraph."

The State Department declined "to hazard a formal definition of the phrase 'special formalities.'"[338] Rather, the Department believed it "preferable to state the idea envisaged in comprehensible general terms and to let interpretation evolve on a case-by-cases basis. It might be said, however, that paragraph 3 was included on the theory that while the treaty should be firm as to the core principle of non-discrimination set forth in paragraph 1, it ought for very practical reasons to allow a degree of tolerance at the periphery with respect to matters of detail that in relation to the main objective are of only trivial consequence."[339] The Department selected the word "formalities" to indicate that such requirements could not interfere with the right of establishment in substance.[340] In particular, such requirements should not put a treaty alien at a competitive disadvantage relative to a national.[341]

This special formalities provision permitted, for example, state laws requiring articles of incorporation to be signed by a citizen.[342] The State Department explained that such a requirement "is in effect a mere technicality which in no way actually hampers aliens from freely taking out corporation charters in that country, for citizens willing to act as signers are readily procurable."[343] The treaty obligation was satisfied if local law granted a "practicable and efficacious right" to establish a company.[344] The provision also permitted state laws requiring that

338. Memorandum attached to letter dated April 29, 1954, from Carl H. Boehringer to the Secretary of State, NARA, Record Group 59, Department of State File No. 611.62A4/4-2954.

339. Ibid.

340. Airgram dated April 7, 1951, from the Department of State to the U.S. embassy in Athens, NARA, Record Group 59, Department of State File No. 611.814/3-951.

341. Despatch dated March 16, 1954, from the U.S. High Commissioner in Bonn to the Department of State, NARA, Record Group 59, Department of State File No. 62A4/3-1654; Instruction dated November 10, 1953, from the Department of State to the U.S. High Commissioner in Bonn, NARA, Record Group 59, Department of State File No. 611.62A4/11-1553.

342. Ibid.

343. Memorandum attached to letter dated April 29, 1954, from Carl H. Boehringer to the Secretary of State, NARA, Record Group 59, Department of State File No. 611.62A4/4-2954.

344. Airgram A-39 dated August 9, 1950, from the Department of State to the U.S. embassy in Copenhagen, NARA, Record Group 59, Department of State File No. 611.594/7-1250. The

a specified number or percentage of citizens be on a corporation's board of directors, as long as the controlling stock could be held by treaty aliens, and members of the board could be chosen by treaty aliens and were fully subject to their control.[345] In the view of the State Department, "These provisions do not act to interfere, as a matter of practice, with the organization of domestic subsidiaries by foreign companies."[346] Thus, the minutes of interpretation of the FCN treaty with Denmark stated, "It is understood that either Party may[,] consistently with the terms of [the national treatment obligation with respect to establishment], maintain special requirements with respect to the residence or nationality of the founders, members of the boards of directors, and managing directors of companies constituted under its laws."[347] The essential treaty objective was that U.S. investors have "final control" over companies that they owned.[348]

The special formalities provision also permitted regulations requiring the licensing of foreign investment, provided that such licenses were "granted automatically and as a matter of course" in the case of covered investors.[349] As the State Department explained during negotiations with Germany, "The treaty would remove from the licensing authorities the special discretion they would otherwise have, in the case of Americans, and preclude the interposition of frustrating complications, burdens and delays in connection with the licensing process; but the German authorities would be entitled to maintain the outward form of the licensing procedure."[350]

discussion of this provision during negotiations with Denmark is further described in Chapter 6 in the section on the negotiation of the FCN treaty with Denmark.

345. Despatch dated March 16, 1954, from the U.S. High Commissioner in Bonn to the Department of State, NARA, Record Group 59, Department of State File No. 62A4/3-1654; Instruction dated November 10, 1953, from the Department of State to the U.S. High Commissioner in Bonn, NARA, Record Group 59, Department of State File No. 611.62A4/11-1553; Airgram A-39 dated August 9, 1950, from the Department of State to the U.S. embassy in Copenhagen, NARA, Record Group 59, Department of State File No. 611.594/7-1250.

346. Informal Survey of Legal Provisions Affecting Foreign Investment in the United States, Attachment to airgram dated March 13, 1963, from the Department of State to the U.S. embassy in Brussels, NARA, Record Group 59, Central Foreign Policy File 1963, Box 3450, File marked "Finance FN 1 General Policy Plans."

347. 99 *Congressional Record* 9328 (1953).

348. Airgram dated June 1, 1950, from the Department of State to the U.S. embassy in Copenhagen, NARA, Record Group 59, Department of State File No. 611.594/5-350; Airgram dated May 27, 1950, from the Department of State to the U.S. embassy in Copenhagen, NARA, Record Group 59, Department of State File No. 611.594/5-350.

349. Instruction dated November 12, 1953, from the Department of State to the U.S. High Commissioner in Bonn, NARA, Record Group 59, Department of State File No. 611.62A4/10-1553; Memorandum attached to letter dated April 29, 1954, from Carl H. Boehringer to the Secretary of State, NARA, Record Group 59, Department of State File No. 611.62A4/4-2954.

350. Instruction dated November 12, 1953, from the Department of State to the U.S. High Commissioner in Bonn, NARA, Record Group 59, Department of State File No. 611.62A4/10-1553.

German negotiators were concerned that the language of the special formalities provision might not be broad enough to cover the provisions of German law relating to the organization, administration, and capital requirements of companies in Germany.[351] U.S. negotiators replied that, as long as the German laws were consistent with national treatment, reference to them in the special formalities provision was not necessary. Further, based on the German explanation of the laws, it appeared to the U.S. negotiators that the language sought by the Germans amounted to saying no more than "white is white" and that the presence of such language would raise the question of why similar reiterations did not appear with respect to other such matters.[352] The German negotiators did not dispute any of these points, but stated merely that German public opinion would require the inclusion of language in the protocol to address the matter.[353] Ultimately, the parties included, at Paragraph 9 of the protocol, a sentence stating that "[t]he provisions of Article VII do not obligate either Party to permit nationals and companies of the other Party to carry on business in its territories without fulfilling the requirements which are generally applicable by law."

National Treatment in a Federal System

A national treatment obligation is ambiguous in the case of a federal system, such as that which governs the United States. In such a system, individual states might discriminate against out-of-state companies. The ambiguity in the national treatment obligation is with respect to whether a discriminating state is required to give a company of the other party the treatment accorded to its own companies or merely the treatment accorded to companies of the other states.

The United States chose the latter approach in its postwar FCN treaties. The treaties guaranteed that each of the states would provide companies of the other party treatment no less favorable than that accorded to out-of-state U.S. companies. For example, California would be required to treat companies covered by an FCN treaty no less favorably than it treated companies incorporated in any of the other states in the union, but it would not be required to treat them as favorably as it treated companies incorporated under California law.

Accordingly, Article XXII(4) of the 1955 standard draft treaty provided, "National treatment accorded under the provisions of the present Treaty to companies of [the other treaty party], shall in any State, Territory or possession of the United States of America, be the treatment accorded therein to companies created or organized in other States, Territories and possessions of the United States of America." All

351. Instruction dated October 11, 1954, from the Department of State to the U.S. High Commissioner in Bonn, NARA, Record Group 59, Department of State File No. 611.62A4/10-1154.

352. Ibid.

353. Ibid.

out-of-state companies were regarded as "foreign," whether incorporated under the laws of another state of the United States or under the laws of a different country.[354]

The State Department variously described this approach as "patently fair,"[355] "completely fair and warranted,"[356] and "fair and equitable."[357] First, the treaty provided a foreign company with the same treatment as "the bulk of its competitors."[358] To treat alien companies the same as companies of the state would be inequitable because it would favor alien companies over the "great mass" of their American competitors.[359] In fact, providing foreign companies with a guarantee of treatment better than that accorded to most U.S. companies would create "a patently untenable situation."[360] Second, U.S. constitutional provisions greatly limited the extent to which states could discriminate against out-of-state companies.[361] Third, although some discrimination was permitted, U.S. companies had learned to accommodate instances of discrimination against out-of-state

354. Walker , "Provisions on Companies in United States Commercial Treaties," page 390; Walker, "Modern Treaties," page 818; Walker, "Treaties for the Encouragement and Protection of Foreign Investment," page 233.

355. Airgram dated January 27, 1951, from the Department of State to the U.S. embassy in Copenhagen, NARA, Record Group 59, Department of State File No. 611.594/1-251.

356. Despatch dated February 23, 1954, from the U.S. High Commissioner in Bonn to the Department of State, NARA, Record Group 59, Department of State File No. 611.62A4/2-2354.

357. Instruction dated November 13, 1957, from the Department of State to the U.S. embassy in Brussels, NARA, Record Group 59, Department of State File No. 611.554/10-1757; Memorandum of Conversation headed "Informal Discussion with Member of Philippine Embassy of Treatment Accorded by Various States to Out-of-State Corporations," dated September 23, 1947, NARA, Record Group 59, Department of State File No. 711.962/9-2347.

358. Despatch dated February 23, 1954, from the U.S. High Commissioner in Bonn to the Department of State, NARA, Record Group 59, Department of State File No. 611.62A4/2-2354; Instruction dated November 13, 1957, from the Department of State to the U.S. embassy in Brussels, NARA, Record Group 59, Department of State File No. 611.554/10-1757; Airgram dated July 3, 1953, from the Department of State to the U.S. embassy in The Hague, NARA, Record Group 59, Department of State File No. 611.564/6-1553; Instruction dated December 22, 1953, from the Department of State to the U.S. High Commissioner in Bonn, NARA, Record Group 59, Department of State File No. 611.62A4/11-3053; Walker, "Provisions on Companies in United States Commercial Treaties," page 390.

359. Memorandum by Herman Walker Jr., dated September 3, 1947, NARA, Record Group 59, Department of State Lot Files, Walter Hollis Papers.

360. Despatch dated February 23, 1954, from the U.S. High Commissioner in Bonn to the Department of State, NARA, Record Group 59, Department of State File No. 611.62A4/2-2354; Instruction dated November 13, 1957, from the Department of State to the U.S. embassy in Brussels, NARA, Record Group 59, Department of State File No. 611.554/10-1757.

361. Memorandum by Herman Walker Jr., dated September 3, 1947, NARA, Record Group 59, Department of State Lot Files, Walter Hollis Papers; Airgram dated July 3, 1953, from the Department of State to the U.S. embassy in The Hague, NARA, Record Group 59, Department of State File No. 611.564/6-1553; Telegram dated February 16, 1946, from the Department of State to the U.S. embassy in Chongqing, NARA, Record Group 59, Department of State File

companies, as could foreign companies.[362] Indeed, as a practical matter, U.S. companies were not "materially inconvenienced" by state discrimination against out-of-state companies.[363] Rather, many U.S. companies were organized on a national basis and crossed borders freely.[364] As evidence, the State Department cited the fact that many U.S. companies chose to incorporate in Delaware, notwithstanding that they might have little or no business in Delaware, because their status as an out-of-state Delaware corporation caused them few problems when doing business in any of the other states. Fourth, in some cases, out-of-state incorporation was a positive advantage because out-of-state corporations received more favorable tax treatment[365] or because of other reasons.[366] Fifth, where an alien company perceived that it was disadvantaged by the rule, the treaty granted it the right to organize a domestic corporation in the state where it wished to conduct its business.[367] Finally, even if the State Department were to agree to a different rule, the treaty might well be rejected by the Senate because of the interference with state prerogatives.[368]

No. 711.932/2-646; Walker, "Provisions on Companies in United States Commercial Treaties," page 390.

362. Airgram dated January 27, 1951, from the Department of State to the U.S. embassy in Copenhagen, NARA, Record Group 59, Department of State File No. 611.594/1-251.

363. Ibid.; Instruction dated November 13, 1957, from the Department of State to the U.S. embassy in Brussels, NARA, Record Group 59, Department of State File No. 611.554/10-1757.

364. Instruction dated November 13, 1957, from the Department of State to the U.S. embassy in Brussels, NARA, Record Group 59, Department of State File No. 611.554/10-1757; Airgram dated July 3, 1953, from the Department of State to the U.S. embassy in The Hague, NARA, Record Group 59, Department of State File No. 611.564/6-1553; Memorandum by Herman Walker Jr., dated September 3, 1947, NARA, Record Group 59, Department of State Lot Files, Walter Hollis Papers; Instruction dated December 22, 1953, from the Department of State to the U.S. High Commissioner in Bonn, NARA, Record Group 59, Department of State File No. 611.62A4/11-3053; Walker, "Provisions on Companies in United States Commercial Treaties," page 390.

365. Despatch dated February 23, 1954, from the U.S. High Commissioner in Bonn to the Department of State, NARA, Record Group 59, Department of State File No. 611.62A4/2-2354; Instruction dated December 22, 1953, form the Department of State to the U.S. High Commissioner in Bonn, NARA, Record Group 59, Department of State File No. 611.62A4/11-3053; Airgram dated July 3, 1953, from the Department of State to the U.S. embassy in The Hague, NARA, Record Group 59, Department of State File No. 611.564/6-1553; Memorandum of Conversation headed "Informal Discussion with Member of Philippine Embassy of Treatment Accorded by Various States to Out-of-State Corporations," dated September 23, 1947, NARA, Record Group 59, Department of State File No. 711.962/9-2347.

366. Memorandum by Herman Walker Jr., dated September 3, 1947, NARA, Record Group 59, Department of State Lot Files, Walter Hollis Papers.

367. Walker, "Provisions on Companies in United States Commercial Treaties," page 390.

368. Instruction dated November 13, 1957, from the Department of State to the U.S. embassy in Brussels, NARA, Record Group 59, Department of State File No. 611.554/10-1757; Instruction

This provision encountered objections in several negotiations because other countries believed that their companies would not be receiving truly reciprocal treatment in the United States, but the United States refused to modify the provision. The treaty with France included language in the protocol that permitted France, in according national treatment to a U.S. national or company, to accord treatment analogous to that accorded by the state in which the U.S. national or company was domiciled.[369]

During negotiations with Brazil, the State Department recognized that the provision could place the United States in an awkward position. Brazil drew a distinction between the rights of native-born Brazilians and the rights of naturalized Brazilians, and the State Department feared that Brazil would want to offer U.S. nationals only the treatment accorded the latter. Any U.S. demand for the most favorable treatment received by any Brazilian national would appear inconsistent in principle with the provision on the treatment of out-of-state companies.[370]

Right to Organize and Control, and National Treatment of, Subsidiaries

Foreign investors often choose to operate through an entity incorporated under the laws of the country where the operations are conducted. Accordingly, as a corollary to granting covered foreign nationals and companies national treatment with respect to the right to engage in gainful activity, the treaty guaranteed to those nationals and companies the right to establish branches, organize subsidiaries, and retain control of the enterprises that they established. For example, Article VII(1) of the 1955 standard draft treaty provided that "such nationals and companies shall be permitted within such territories: (a) to establish and maintain branches, agencies, offices, factories and other establishments appropriate to the conduct of their business; (b) to organize companies under the general company law of such other Party, and to acquire majority interests in companies of such other Party; and (c) to control and manage enterprises which they have established or acquired."

dated December 22, 1953, from the Department of State to the U.S. High Commissioner in Bonn, NARA, Record Group 59, Department of State File No. 611.62A4/11-3053.

369. France FCN treaty, Protocol, Paragraph 10.

370. Memorandum headed "Sixth Meeting to Consider a Tentative Draft Treaty of Friendship, Commerce and Navigation between the United States and Brazil, Held November 16, 1945," NARA, Record Group 59, Department of State File No. 711.322/4-2346; Memorandum headed "Seventh Meeting to Consider a Tentative Draft Treaty of Friendship, Commerce and Navigation between the United States and Brazil, Held November 20, 1945," NARA, Record Group 59, Department of State File No. 711.322/4-2346; Memorandum headed "Eighth Meeting to Consider a Tentative Draft Treaty of Friendship, Commerce and Navigation between the United States and Brazil, Held November 23, 1945," NARA, Record Group 59, Department of State File No. 711.322/4-2346.

The meaning of this provision was amplified during negotiations. The United States agreed that the word "organize" could be replaced with the word "constitute."[371] The word "enterprise" referred to "a business entity or undertaking irrespective of the particular form it has for legal purposes."[372]

The FCN treaty with the Netherlands, at Article VII, included language explicitly clarifying that the right to organize companies could be exercised "either directly or indirectly through one or more intermediaries," a principle that was implicit in the other treaties. Further, the language of the provision did not prohibit laws requiring local participation in the corporation, such as through minority ownership of stock, as long as the alien retained control.

This provision did not require national treatment, but it did require an effective, practicable right approximating national treatment in substance.[373] In organizing a company, the national or company must comply with relevant domestic legislation,[374] provided that such legislation was not discriminatory or arbitrary.[375]

The treaty also guaranteed that each party would accord national treatment to enterprises controlled by nationals and companies of the other party.[376] For example, Article VII(1) of the 1955 standard draft treaty provided that "enterprises which they control, whether in the form of individual proprietorships, companies or otherwise, shall in all that relates to the conduct of the activities thereof, be accorded treatment no less favorable than that accorded like enterprises controlled by nationals and companies of such other Party." Although this sentence did not use the term "national treatment," it was understood to require national treatment as that term was defined in Article XXII(2) of the 1955 standard draft

371. Airgram dated June 1, 1950, from Department of State to the U.S. embassy in Copenhagen, NARA, Department of State File No. 611.594/5-350; Airgram dated May 27, 1950, from the Department of State to the U.S. embassy in Copenhagen, NARA, Record Group 59, Department of State File No. 611.594/5-350.

372. Airgram dated July 1, 1953, from the Department of State to the U.S. embassy in The Hague, NARA, Record Group 59, Department of State File No. 611.564/7-153.

373. Airgram dated June 1, 1950, from the Department of State to the U.S. embassy in Copenhagen, NARA, Record Group 59, Department of State File No. 611.594/5-350; Airgram dated May 27, 1950, from the Department of State to the U.S. embassy in Copenhagen, NARA, Record Group 59, Department of State File No. 611.594/5-350.

374. Airgram dated June 1, 1950, from the Department of State to the U.S. embassy in Copenhagen, NARA, Record Group 59, Department of State File No. 611.594/5-350; Airgram dated May 27, 1950, from the Department of State to the U.S. embassy in Copenhagen, NARA, Record Group 59, Department of State File No. 611.594/5-350.

375. Airgram A-55 dated March 27, 1951, from the Department of State to the U.S. embassy in Addis Ababa, NARA, Record Group 59, Department of State File No. 611.754/2-551.

376. Memorandum headed "Proposed Sino-American Treaty of Friendship, Commerce and Navigation," dated March 16, 1946, NARA, Record Group 59, Department of State File No. 711.932/12-2046; Walker, "Treaties for the Encouragement and Protection of Foreign Investment," page 233.

treaty, discussed above.[377] This provision was exceptional in that it granted to a company organized under the laws of a party, and thus possessing the nationality of that party, treaty rights against that same party, notwithstanding the general rule that a state may not intervene on behalf of a corporation against the corporation's own government.[378] The justification for protection was based on the economic interests of the investor's state rather than the legal relationship between the subsidiary and the state exercising protection.[379]

MOST FAVORED NATION TREATMENT

The U.S. postwar FCN treaties also guaranteed to nationals and companies of a party most-favored-nation (MFN) treatment by the other party with respect to engaging in activities for gain and certain non-profit activities. Such a guarantee had appeared in U.S. FCN treaties prior to the war, although it conferred rights only on nationals, not companies.[380] In cases where both national and MFN treatment were guaranteed in the postwar treaties, the beneficiary was entitled to whichever was more favorable in that case.

The standard draft treaty varied over time with respect to the placement of the national and MFN treatment obligations relative to each other in the treaty text. In the 1955 standard draft treaty, for example, the obligation to provide MFN treatment with respect to engaging in gainful activity was imposed in a separate paragraph that cross-referenced the paragraph that imposed the obligation to provide national treatment. Specifically, Article VII(4) of the 1955 standard draft treaty provided, "Nationals and companies of either Party, as well as enterprises controlled by such nationals and companies, shall in any event be accorded most-favored-nation treatment with reference to the matters treated in the present article." Those matters were those related to national treatment with respect to engaging in gainful activity. As the language of Article VII(4) indicates, enterprises organized under the law of a party, if controlled by nationals and companies of the other party, also were entitled to MFN treatment by the first party.

The MFN treatment obligation with respect to engaging in gainful activity was broader than the national treatment obligation with respect to such activity because it applied even to those sectors of the economy with respect to which the parties had reserved the right to deny national treatment. The reservations did not apply to MFN treatment

The obligation to provide MFN treatment with respect to engaging in certain non-profit activities was imposed by the 1955 standard draft treaty in the same

377. Airgram dated June 23, 1953, from the Department of State to the U.S. embassy in The Hague, NARA, Record Group 59, Department of State File No. 611.564/6-553.

378. Walker, "Provisions on Companies in United States Commercial Treaties," page 389 note 74; Walker "Treaties for the Encouragement and Protection of Foreign Investment," page 233.

379. Walker "Treaties for the Encouragement and Protection of Foreign Investment," page 233.

380. *See, e.g.,* Treaty of Friendship. Commerce, and Consular Rights, United States-Finland, February 13, 1934, Article I, 49 Stat. 2659, TS 868, 4 UST 2047, TIAS 2861.

sentence as the obligation to provide national treatment with respect to engaging in those activities. Specifically, Article VIII(2) of the 1955 standard draft treaty provided that "[n]ationals and companies of either Party shall be accorded national treatment and most-favored-nation treatment with respect to engaging in scientific, educational, religious and philanthropic activities within the territories of the other Party, and shall be accorded the right to form associations for that purpose under the laws of such other Party."

An entirely separate article of the treaty guaranteed national and MFN treatment with respect to the right to acquire personal property. For example, Article IX(3) of the 1955 standard draft treaty provided, "Nationals and companies of either Party shall be accorded within the territories of the other Party national treatment and most-favored-nation treatment with respect to acquiring, by purchase, lease, or otherwise, and with respect to owning and possessing, personal property of all kinds, both tangible and intangible." This language ensured that nationals and companies of a party would receive MFN (and national) treatment with respect to the making of portfolio investment. The concern was that the right to engage in a particular activity might be read so as not to include the right to invest in a company engaged in that activity.

The provision on acquiring personal property was subject to a reservation to permit a party to restrict ownership of shares in enterprises in certain sensitive sectors of the economy and another reservation to preserve state laws restricting alien ownership of dangerous items, such as guns, explosives, poisons, or narcotics.[381] Thus, for example, Article IX(3) of the 1955 standard draft treaty further provided that "either Party may impose restrictions on alien ownership of materials dangerous from the standpoint of public safety and alien ownership of interests in enterprises carrying on particular types of activity, but only to the extent that this can be done without impairing the rights and privileges secured by Article VII or by other provisions of the present Treaty."

As in the case of national treatment, the standard draft treaty did not guarantee nationals and companies of a party MFN treatment with respect to all matters, but only with respect to specific subject matters. The United States believed that specifying MFN treatment in that way allowed each party to form a clearer impression of the commitments that it was undertaking.[382]

Indeed, the United States did not wish to grant MFN treatment generally. For example, during negotiations, the Netherlands proposed that the treaty be amended to guarantee MFN treatment with regard to any matter covered by the treaty.[383] The United States objected because that would have resulted in the granting of national treatment with respect to the right to acquire real property, a commitment that the

381. Ireland FCN treaty, Minutes of Interpretation, *Ad Article VII, paragraph 2.*

382. Instruction dated May 27, 1955, from the Department of State to the U.S. embassy in The Hague, NARA, Record Group 59, Department of State File No. 611.564/5-2155.

383. Ibid.

United States could not make without creating an inconsistency with the laws of several states.[384]

Further, so that the treaty would not provide greater rights than the Mineral Lands Leasing Act (which prohibited a foreign national from owning stock in a corporation engaged in mining on the public domain unless U.S. nationals received like treatment from the state of nationality of the foreign national),[385] the U.S. postwar FCN treaties permitted a party to require that the right to engage in mining on the public domain be dependent on reciprocity.[386] For example, Paragraph 5 of the protocol of the 1955 standard draft treaty provided that "[w]ith reference to Article VII, paragraph 4, either Party may require that rights to engage in mining on the public domain shall be dependent on reciprocity." The term "mining" included the exploration for and exploitation of mineral resources,[387] such as petroleum.[388]

MFN treatment was a defined term in the treaty. For example, Article XXII(2) of the 1955 standard draft treaty defined MFN treatment as "treatment accorded within the territories of a Party upon terms no less favorable that the treatment accorded therein, in like situations, to nationals, companies, products, vessels or other objects, as the case may be, of any third country."

The operation of the MFN treatment provision was rarely discussed during negotiations. The general subject of MFN treatment arose frequently, but virtually always in a context in which the other potential treaty party was expressing the concern that MFN commitments that it had made or would be making in other treaties with other countries would require it to extend to those other countries commitments that the United States wished it to make in the FCN treaty,

384. Ibid.

385. 30 U.S.C 181 (2006). *See* Memorandum headed "Tenth Meeting to Consider a Tentative Draft Treaty of Friendship, Commerce and Navigation Between the United States and Brazil Held November 29, 1945," NARA, Record Group 59, Department of State File No. 711.322/4-2346.

386. For a survey of U.S. FCN treaty practice relating to mineral lands, *see* Robert R. Wilson, "Natural-Resources Provisions in United States Commercial Treaties," 48 *American Journal of International Law* 355 (1954). Wilson observed that he had made the same point in at least four earlier publications. Ibid., page 356, note 5.

387. Memorandum to the Embassy at Chungking for Use in Negotiating Treaty of Friendship, Commerce and Navigation, NARA, Record Group 59, Department of State File No. 711.932/2-1645.

388. Despatch dated September 8, 1954, from the U.S. embassy in The Hague to the Department of State, NARA, Record Group 59, Department of State File No. 611.564/9-854; Memorandum to the Embassy at Chungking for Use in Negotiating Treaty of Friendship, Commerce and Navigation, NARA, Record Group 59, Department of State File No. 711.932/2-1645; Memorandum to the American Mission at Beirut for Use in Negotiating Treaty of Friendship, Commerce and Navigation between the United States and the Lebanese Republic, enclosure with airgram dated July 3, 1946, from the Department of State to the U.S. mission in Beirut, NARA, Record Group 59, Department of State File No. 711.90E2/7-346.

most especially the commitment of national treatment.[389] The negotiators from other potential treaty parties commonly would tell U.S. negotiators that they were willing to make certain commitments to the United States, but did not wish to extend them to other countries, particularly when those other countries had not reciprocated as the United States had.[390]

State Department officials recognized that, as a general matter, the national treatment obligation provided the stronger standard of protection.[391] As noted above, national treatment repeatedly was described as the "heart of the treaty." In an earlier time when treaties granting extraterritorial rights were in force, MFN treatment meant privileged treatment and thus was sometimes preferable to national treatment.[392] Extraterritoriality, however, was increasingly rare.

The meaning of MFN treatment did arise during negotiations with Pakistan. The Pakistani negotiators asked whether the MFN treatment obligation would be violated in a situation in which a U.S. investor and a Belgian investor both submitted identical applications for a permit to build a factory, only one permit could be issued, and Pakistan granted the permit to the Belgian investor. The State Department replied that the MFN provision would require only that the selection be based on "reasonable economic criteria that afford equality of opportunity" and that the U.S. investor receive "fair and equitable consideration."[393]

One aspect of MFN treatment that was discussed during Senate hearings on the FCN treaty with Pakistan concerned the question whether the MFN treatment provision of another treaty would extend the U.S. consent to the jurisdiction of the International Court of Justice under the FCN treaty to include disputes under the other treaty. Such a discussion was, technically, a discussion of the scope of the MFN treatment provisions of other treaties, not the FCN treaty, but the State Department's view was so categorical that it would seem to apply to the MFN treatment provisions of the FCN treaties as well.

The question arose because, in the latter part of the 1950s, some members of the Senate expressed the concern that the consent to the jurisdiction of the Court in the FCN treaties was inconsistent with the policy of the Connally Amendment to the U.S. consent to the Court's jurisdiction under the optional clause. The optional clause, which is Article 36(2) of the Statute of the International Court of Justice, provides that the parties to the statute may at any time declare that they

389. *See, e.g.,* Summary of Exploratory Discussions on American Proposal of a Draft Commercial Treaty [with China], NARA, Record Group 59, Department of State File No. 611.9331/8-1745.

390. Memorandum headed "Reciprocity Problem," dated September 24, 1954, NARA, Record Group 59, Department of State File No. 611.62A4/9-2754; Instruction dated November 10, 1953, from the Department of State to the U.S. High Commissioner in Bonn, NARA, Record Group 59, Department of State File No. 611.62A4/11-1553. This problem is also discussed in Chapter 6 in the section on U.S. negotiating strategy.

391. Hawkins, *Commercial Treaties & Agreements,* page 12.

392. Ibid.; Walker, "Modern Treaties," page 811.

393. Telegram dated June 25, 1959, from the U.S. embassy in Karachi to the Department of State, NARA, Record Group 59, Department of State File No. 611.90D4/6-2559.

"recognize as compulsory *ipso facto* and without special agreement, in relation to any other state accepting the same obligation, the jurisdiction of the Court" with respect to certain types of legal disputes. The Connally Amendment stated that the U.S. declaration accepting the Court's jurisdiction under the optional clause shall not apply to "disputes with regard to matters which are essentially within the domestic jurisdiction of the United States as determined by the United States of America." Senator Connally's contribution to the language of the U.S. declaration was to add the words "as determined by the United States of America," language that was understood to render the reservation "self-judging," meaning that the United States had sole discretion to determine whether the reservation applied.[394] Some senators questioned whether the consent to the Court's jurisdiction in the FCN treaties included at least some matters within the domestic jurisdiction of the United States. If so, then the treaties would be inconsistent with the policy of the Connally Amendment.

The State Department initially met this concern by emphasizing that consent was to disputes concerning the interpretation or application of the treaty and that such disputes would most often involve U.S. claims against the other party rather than the reverse. During the hearings on the treaties with France and Pakistan, Deputy Assistant Secretary of State Edwin Martin conceded that the compromissory clause of the treaty amounted to a limited "waiver" of the Connally Amendment, but noted that it was limited solely to issues arising under the treaty. This prompted Republican senator Bourke Hickenlooper of Iowa to ask, though not in the most artful fashion, whether other countries might assert that MFN provisions in their treaties with the United States permitted them to invoke the consent to the Court's jurisdiction in a U.S. FCN treaty. Senator Hickenlooper's unspoken concern was that, if so, U.S. consent to the Court's jurisdiction would not be limited in practice to issues arising only under the FCN treaty with Pakistan. That is, he was concerned that disputes arising under other treaties might be submitted to the Court by countries that were party to those other treaties and that were claiming under the MFN treatment provision of those other treaties the right to the benefit of the U.S. consent to the Court's jurisdiction in an FCN treaty. This could broaden considerably the exception to the Connally Amendment.

Martin referred the question to John J. Czyzak, the assistant legal adviser for economic affairs. Czyzak replied that no country could use an MFN provision in any treaty to avail itself of the U.S. consent to the Court's jurisdiction in the treaty with Pakistan or, presumably, any other FCN treaty. Here is the exchange:

> SENATOR HICKENLOOPER. Just one question.
>
> Do you interpret this provision, paragraph 2 of Article 23, let's say, of the Pakistan Treaty we have just been talking about, which refers disputes under certain circumstances to the International Court of Justice unless other

394. Arthur Larson, "The Facts, the Law and the Connally Amendment," 10 *Duke Law Journal* 74, 75 (1961).

means are devised, to be affected in any way by the most favored nation clause?

* * *

MR. MARTIN. I would prefer to have my legal adviser answer this question, if I might, sir.

MR. CZYZAK. The answer is no to Senator Hickenlooper's question.

The provision stands on its own and is not picked up by any most favored nation clause in any other treaty.

SENATOR HICKENLOOPER. It affects no other treaty?

MR. CZYZAK. No, sir.

SENATOR HICKENLOOPER. And there can be no way it can affect any other treaty?

MR. CZYAZK. That is correct.

SENATOR HICKENLOOPER. It is specifically limited to this treaty.

MR. CZYAZK. That is correct.[395]

The State Department did not say that the answer depended on the scope of the MFN treaty provision that another country might invoke. Rather, the State Department responded that no MFN treaty provision in any other treaty could permit another country to invoke U.S. consent in an FCN treaty to the jurisdiction of the International Court of Justice. In short, the State Department's understanding of the compromissory clause in the FCN treaties was that it constituted consent only to disputes arising under the treaty in which it appeared and could not, by operation of an MFN provision, be expanded to constitute consent to disputes arising under any other treaty. This was the understanding that it conveyed to the Senate.

EXPROPRIATION

Overview

The United States considered the provision on expropriation to be one of the two or three most important ones in the entire treaty.[396] So important was the provision that "if its principal substance [could] not be obtained, the Department

395. Transcript of hearing held before Committee on Foreign Relations, June 21, 1960, pages 38–39, NARA, Record Group 46, File No. SEN86B-B8.

396. National Advisory Council Document 1868 (Revised) headed "Investments in Less Developed Areas," dated December 12, 1955, NARA, Record Group 353, Records Relating to the Council on Foreign Economic Policy 1955–1961, Box 4, Folder marked "Investment in Underdeveloped Countries CFEP 511 (Folder 1)"; Memorandum headed "First Meeting for Discussion of U.S. Draft Treaty of Amity and Economic Relations, April 16, 1969," NARA, Record Group 59, Central Foreign Policy Files 1967–1969, Box 975, Folder marked "FT 4 4/1/68"; Memorandum headed "Explanation of Certain Provisions of U.S. Proposals for Treaty

would [have] probably prefer[red] not to make a treaty."[397] The provision was "basic to the structure of security and assurances which it [was] the object of the treaty to erect."[398] Moreover, the American business community was more interested in this provision than any other in the treaty.[399] Vernon Setser, the chief of the Economic Treaties Branch of the Commercial Policy Staff, the office with responsibility at that time for negotiating FCN treaties, noted in 1956 that "[t]he standard language with regard to the taking of property is regarded pretty much as a fetish here, and there is greater difficulty authorizing changes in the text than in almost any other provision of the treaty."[400]

Nowhere in the treaty was the link between its investment provisions and U.S. constitutional law more visible. The rule set forth in the treaty was "taken straight out of the U.S. Constitution and constitutional jurisprudence."[401] The Department thought the provision "fine enough to proclaim from the house-tops."[402] Further, the takings provision should be interpreted in light of U.S. constitutional principles.[403]

The expropriation provision was not intended to prevent expropriations. The United States believed that sovereign states had the right to expropriate property,

of Amity and Economic Relations with Muscat," enclosure to instruction dated April 17, 1957, from the Department of State to the U.S. consulate general in Dhahran, NARA, Record Group 59, Department of State File No. 611.86E1/4-1757.

397. Memorandum headed "Explanation of Certain Provisions of U.S. Proposals for Treaty of Amity and Economic Relations with Muscat," enclosure to instruction dated April 17, 1957, from the Department of State to the U.S. consulate general in Dhahran, NARA, Record Group 59, Department of State File No. 611.86E1/4-1757. *See also* Memorandum headed "Memorandum on the Provisions of the Greek Counterdraft," dated July 31, 1950, NARA, Record Group 59, Department of State File No, 611.814/6-250; Airgram dated May 7, 1952, from the Department of State to the U.S. Political Adviser in Tokyo, NARA, Record Group 59, Department of State File No. 611.944/4-2352.

398. Memorandum headed "Memorandum on the Provisions of the Greek Counterdraft," dated July 31, 1950, NARA, Record Group 59, Department of State File No, 611.814/6-250.

399. Minutes of the First Meeting of the Working Group on Article V, Paragraph 4 & Protocol 3, October 12, 1954, NARA, Record Group 59, Department of State File No. 611.62A4/10-554; Instruction dated October 18, 1954, from the Department of State to the U.S. High Commissioner in Bonn, NARA, Record Group 59, Department of State File No. 611.62A4/10-1854.

400. Letter dated August 9, 1956, from Vernon Setser to Woodbury Willoughby, NARA, Record Group 59, Department of State Lot Files, Walter Hollis Papers, Folder marked "Austrian FCN."

401. Memorandum headed "Memorandum on the Provisions of the Greek Counterdraft," dated July 31, 1950, NARA, Record Group 59, Department of State File No. 611.814/6-250. *See also* Despatch dated August 6, 1954, from the U.S. embassy in The Hague to the Department of State, NARA, Record Group 59, Department of State File No. 611.564/8-654.

402. Memorandum dated July 31, 1950, headed "Memorandum on the Provisions of the Greek Counterdraft," NARA, Record Group 59, Department of State File No. 611.814/6-250.

403. Despatch dated March 8, 1954, from the U.S. High Commissioner in Bonn to the Department of State, NARA, Record Group 59, Department of State File No. 611.62A4/3-854.

including property owned by aliens. As the State Department explained during negotiations with Germany,

> In principle the Department believes that a treaty should not attempt to prohibit either Government from taking and using whatever private property it may deem necessary to have for paramount reasons of public convenience and necessity in whatever needful contingencies may materialize. To write in such prohibitions would, in the Department's opinion, infringe more on the prerogatives of sovereignty than the treaty ought to attempt, and introduce a futile element of rigidity into an instrument that ought to be sufficiently flexible to permit it to endure in full force and effect over a long period of time.[404]

The Department further noted that the state's power to expropriate was recognized in the U.S. Constitution as well as the constitution of every one of its states.[405]

Expropriation was consistent with the treaty, however, only if certain conditions were met.[406] In particular, the expropriation must be for a public purpose, non-discriminatory, and accompanied by prompt, just, and effective compensation.[407] For example, Article VI(3) of the 1955 standard draft treaty provided that "[p]roperty of nationals and companies of either Party shall not be taken within the territories of the other Party except for a public purpose, nor shall it be taken without the prompt payment of just compensation." The obligation of effectiveness appeared explicitly in Article VI(3) of the 1955 standard draft treaty, which provided that "[s]uch compensation shall be in an effectively realizable form and shall represent the full equivalent of the property taken; and adequate provision shall have been made at or prior to the time of taking for the determination and payment thereof." The non-discrimination obligation appeared at Article VI(4) of the 1955 standard draft treaty, which provided that "[n]ationals and companies of either Party shall in no case be accorded, within the territories of the other Party, less than national and most-favored-nation treatment with respect to the matters set forth in" the paragraphs dealing with compensation for expropriation (and search of premises).[408]

404. Instruction dated October 26, 1953, from the Department of State to the U.S. High Commissioner in Bonn. NARA, Record Group 59, Department of State File No. 611.62A4/10-653.

405. Instruction dated November 27, 1957, from the Department of State to the U.S. consulate general in Dhahran, NARA, Record Group 59, Department of State File No. 611.86E4/10-257.

406. Ibid.

407. Ibid.; Statement of Leonard C. Meeker, Legal Adviser, Department of State, *Commercial Treaty with Thailand*, Senate Exec. Rept. No. 14, 90th Cong. 1st Sess. (1967). *See also* Statement of Deputy Assistant Secretary Harold F. Linder, *Commercial Treaties*, Hearing Before a Subcommittee of the Committee on Foreign Relations, 82d Cong. 2d Sess. (1952), page 8.

408. The draft on file in the National Archives refers to "Paragraphs 2 and 4 of the present article," but the reference to Paragraph 4 is clearly an error because, otherwise, Paragraph 4 is

The obligation of prompt, just, and effective compensation in the U.S. postwar FCN treaties was equated with the obligation of "prompt, adequate and effective" compensation, which the United States regarded as a requirement of customary international law,[409] and, in fact, the FCN treaty with Uruguay, at Article VIII, used the phrase "prompt, adequate and effective." The State Department believed that the word "just" in itself likely implied "prompt" and "effective," but endeavored to include all three terms because the omission of any of them might give rise to an inference that the parties omitted the term in order to indicate a lesser standard of protection.[410] The requirement of prompt, just, and effective compensation was an "elementary rule" of international law.[411]

The United States attached "great importance" to the language requiring full equivalency and an effectively realizable form.[412] Nevertheless, when Dutch negotiators complained that the phrase "full equivalent" was redundant, the United States agreed to omit the word "full" on that basis,[413] a change that was also made for the

cross-referencing itself. Inspection of the texts of the treaties that were negotiated on the basis of the 1955 standard draft treaty confirms that the intended reference was to Paragraph 3, dealing with compensation for expropriation.

409. *See* Statement Submitted by Assistant Secretary of Commerce Thomas C. Blaisdell Jr. to the Senate Committee on Foreign Relations in Support of Commercial Treaties with Ireland and Uruguay, May 4, 1950, NARA, Record Group 46, File No. SEN81B-B7.

410. Telegram dated April 11, 1952, from the Department of State to the U.S. embassy in New Delhi, NARA, Record Group 59, Department of State File No. 611.914/4-252.

411. Memorandum headed "Memorandum on the Provisions of the Greek Counterdraft," dated July 31, 1950, NARA, Record Group 59, Department of State File No, 611.814/6-250; Statement of Leonard C. Meeker, Legal Adviser, Department of State, *Commercial Treaty with Thailand*, Senate Exec. Rept. No. 14, 90th Cong. 1st Sess. (1967). *See also* Telegram dated February 12, 1952, from the Department of State to the U.S. embassy in New Delhi, NARA, Record Group 59, Department of State File No. 611.914/2-752; Memorandum from Stanley D. Metzger to Michael H. Cardozo headed "Mr. Walker's Memorandum of October 12 re possible revisions in Standard FCN Treaties," dated November 15, 1949, NARA, Record Group 59, Department of State Lot Files, Walter Hollis Papers; Airgram A-365 dated June 16, 1950, from the Department of State to the U.S. embassy in Athens, NARA, Record Group 59, Department of State File No. 611.814/6-250; Instruction A-194 dated June 12, 1961, from the Department of State to the U.S. embassy in Bangkok, NARA, Record Group 59, Department of State File No. 611.9242/6-1261; Memorandum headed "Eleventh Meeting to Consider a Tentative Draft Treaty of Friendship, Commerce and Navigation between the United States and Brazil, Held December 3, 1945," NARA, Record Group 59, Department of State File No. 711.322/4-2346; Airgram dated May 7, 1952, from the Department of State to the U.S. Political Adviser in Tokyo, NARA, Record Group 59, Department of State File No. 611.944/4-2352; Memorandum to the Embassy at Chungking for Use in Negotiating Treaty of Friendship, Commerce and Navigation, NARA, Record Group 59, Department of State File No. 711.932/2-1645.

412. Memorandum headed "First Meeting for Discussion of U.S. Draft Treaty of Amity and Economic Relations, April 16, 1969," NARA, Record Group 59, Central Foreign Policy Files 1967–1969, Box 975, Folder marked "FT 4 4/1/68."

413. Despatch dated February 15, 1955, from the U.S. embassy in The Hague to the Department of State, NARA, Record Group 59, Department of State File No. 611.564/2-1555.

same reasons in the FCN treaties with Germany and Israel.[414] The requirement of "adequate provision" meant that there must be "effectual procedural arrangements, along with substantive rules consistent with the spirit of the paragraph," for the determination and payment of compensation.[415]

An expropriation provision had appeared in U.S. FCN treaties prior to the war, although it applied only to the property of nationals, not companies, and imposed only two conditions on expropriation: due process and payment of just compensation. For example, Article I of the 1934 FCN treaty with Finland provided that the property of nationals "shall not be taken without due process of law and without payment of just compensation." Thus, the U.S. postwar FCN treaties extended the protection of the provision to the property of companies and added the express conditions that payment be prompt and effective, while omitting express reference to the requirement of due process.

Scope of the Provision

The word "taken" was utilized because it was part of U.S constitutional jurisprudence.[416] It was synonymous with the term "expropriated."[417] The treaty provision also applied to nationalizations and to "the assuming of state control under some other rubric."[418] In short, the treaty applied to all forms of takings.[419]

The United States regarded the application of the expropriation provision to nationalizations to be a matter of "extreme importance."[420] It resisted, however, attempts by other countries to add the word "nationalization" to the provision,

414. Despatch dated March 8, 1954, from the U.S. High Commissioner in Bonn to the Department of State, NARA, Record Group 59, Department of State File No. 611.62A4/3-854; Memorandum headed "Negotiation of Treaty of Friendship, Commerce and Navigation with Israel," dated November 20, 1950, NARA, Record Group 59, Department of State File No. 611.84A4/11-2050.

415. Minutes of Discussions of Draft Treaty of Friendship, Commerce and Navigation between the United States and India, August 5, 1949, NARA, Record Group 59, Department of State File No. 711.452/9-2149.

416. Airgram dated May 7, 1952, from the Department of State to the U.S. Political Adviser in Tokyo, NARA, Record Group 59, Department of State File No. 611.944/4-2352; Memorandum attached to letter dated April 29, 1954, from Carl H. Boehringer to the Secretary of State, NARA, Record Group 59, Department of State File No. 611.62A4/4-2954.

417. Memorandum of Conversation dated February 29, 1952, NARA, Record Group 59, Department of State File No. 611.944/4-2352.

418. Memorandum headed "Memorandum on the Provisions of the Greek Counterdraft," dated July 31, 1950, NARA, Record Group 59, Department of State File No, 611.814/6-250.

419. Instruction dated February 1, 1957, from the Department of State to the U.S. embassy in Saigon, NARA, Record Group 59, Department of State File No. 611.51G4/1-2157; Despatch dated March 30, 1957, from the U.S. embassy in Saigon to the Department of State, NARA, Record Group 59, Department of State File No. 611.51G4/3-2057.

420. Despatch dated May 14, 1959, from the U.S. embassy in Paris to the Department of State, NARA, Record Group 59, Department of State File No. 611.514/5-1459.

because of a concern that treaties that did not include the additional word would be regarded as having a narrower scope of application than those that did.[421] Nevertheless, the United States did agree in the treaty with France to include language at Paragraph 5 of the protocol stating that "the term 'expropriated . . . for a public purpose' extend[ed], *inter alia,* to nationalizations."

The expropriation provision applied to both direct expropriations and indirect expropriations. As the State Department noted on repeated occasion, the word "taken" had its source in U.S. constitutional law, where it applied to both direct and indirect expropriations.[422] For example, it applied to situations where the government deprived the owner of property of the "effective use" of that property.[423] In such cases, the property owner could recover compensation in the United States under the Tucker Act.[424]

The expropriation provision also applied to "creeping expropriations," which the State Department described as the gradual displacement of private enterprise through state action. Although the term is often applied to the consequences of a series of regulatory acts, the State Department recognized that it could also occur through government spending in the form of subsidies to state enterprises in competition with private enterprise. The United States believed that, if the government wished to preempt private activity in a particular sector of the economy, it should expropriate existing actors and compensate them, rather than gradually ruining them through subsidized competition.[425]

The United States distinguished between a taking and a tortious interference with property. It confirmed that "tort cases would be handled as such, and would not be considered as expropriation. . . ."[426] The demarcation between a taking and a tort "tended to follow the reasoning that a permanent loss of the right of enjoyment of a property constituted a 'taking', whereas a one-time or temporary damage was considered a tort."[427]

421. Despatch dated May 20, 1959, from the U.S. embassy in Paris to the Department of State, NARA, Record Group 59, Department of State File No. 611.514/5-2059.

422. Memorandum attached to letter dated April 29, 1954, from Carl H. Boehringer to the Secretary of State, NARA, Record Group 59, Department of State File No. 611.62A4/4-2954.

423. Despatch dated August 6, 1954, from the U.S. embassy in The Hague to the Department of State, NARA, Record Group 59, Department of State File No. 611.564/8-654.

424. Ibid. The Tucker Act is a waiver of sovereign immunity for certain claims, including claims based on the Constitution. *See* 28 U.S.C. § 1491 (2006).

425. Telegram dated November 14, 1952, from the Department of State to the U.S. embassy in Japan, NARA, Record Group 59, Department of State File No. 611.944/11-1452; Airgram dated June 1, 1950, from the Department of State to the U.S. embassy in Copenhagen, NARA, Record Group 59, Department of State File No. 611.594/5-350. The U.S. postwar FCN treaties also embodied this principle in the competitive equality provision, discussed below.

426. Despatch dated September 8, 1954, from the U.S. embassy in The Hague to the Department of State, NARA, Record Group 59, Department of State File No. 611.564/9-854.

427. Despatch dated March 8, 1954, from the U.S. High Commissioner in Bonn to the Department of State, NARA, Record Group 59, Department of State File No. 611.62A4/3-854.

The United States recognized that property is held subject to the right of the state to regulate it. Thus, "restrictions on the use of property under a valid zoning ordinance in the United States were not considered a 'taking' of property."[428] Further, "the same could be said of other instances in which the value or the profitability of a property right might be affected by legitimate and commonly-recognized government regulations, such as reasonable fixing of public utility rates, price-fixing during and following the war, the obligation to construct and open roadway facilities under subdivision control ordinances, and limitations on the height and character of buildings in a city."[429]

During negotiations, Germany sought to add the words "or otherwise restricted" after "taken," a proposal to which the United States objected with this explanation:

> Insertion of the words "or otherwise restricted" after "taken" appears to imply a greater commitment than the United States is prepared to undertake. Discriminatory restrictions on property being already precluded elsewhere in the draft treaty, the apparent effect of this insertion would be to prohibit all kinds of non-discriminatory restrictions on property except on payment of compensation to the alien property owner even in cases where payment is not normally made, or expected to be made, to anyone. A municipal zoning ordinance prohibiting the erection of a factory in a residential zone, or an apartment house in a zone reserved to single-family houses, is a restriction on property and a restriction, moreover, which can greatly affect the market value and income-producing potentialities of a tract of land. But compensation is not paid to the owners affected by a valid zoning ordinance; and the Department observes that it does not readily perceive why a treaty exception should be made in favor of German property owners in United States municipalities (or *mutatis mutandis*, American owners in Germany).
>
> Many other types of legitimate restrictions that do not give rise to compensation can be cited: for example, a restriction on the use of certain properties, or properties in certain areas, for the sale of alcoholic beverages; restrictions on the rates a utility company may charge, or on the areas in which it must or may not furnish services; regulations relating to the conservation of soil and water, and afforestation, in rural areas *et cetera*. . . . . Having stated the foregoing objection to the insertion regarding "restrictions", the Department may well add that the word "taken" has been chosen to convey the idea that the standard rule on compensation is aimed to cover more than outright physical seizures. The word is borrowed from United States constitutional jurisprudence, where it covers indirect deprivations of

428. Despatch dated September 8, 1954, from the U.S. embassy in The Hague to the Department of State, NARA, Record Group 59, Department of State File No. 611.564/9-854.

429. Ibid.

property of the so-called "Tucker Act" type as well as direct expropriation proper.[430]

Conditions Imposed—Public Purpose

The reference to "public purpose" was "intended to ensure that basically the power of the state could not be used merely for the selfish benefit of a private individual, not linked with the general public interest."[431] The term was not to have a narrower scope than the same term in the U.S. Constitution because it was not U.S. policy to use the FCN treaty to narrow the sovereign discretion afforded by the Constitution.[432]

As examples of the concept of 'public purpose," U.S. negotiators "cited the railway and utility companies in the United States, which had been able to have property expropriated on their behalf although they constituted private and not state enterprises; and associations of farmers who could have land expropriated on which to construct drainage ditches in swampy areas, with the result of improving the productivity of their farms."[433] U.S. and German negotiators alike mentioned the expropriation of land for housing developments as a further illustration of a taking for a public purpose.[434]

During negotiations, Germany sought to substitute "overriding reasons of public welfare" for "a public purpose." The United States objected, explaining that

> [s]ubstituting "overriding reasons of public welfare" for "a public purpose" appears to the Department of State to be an unnecessary refinement. If "overriding reasons of public welfare" means more than "public purpose", it would appear to constitute a latent source of fruitless friction over particular judgments as to whether this or that taking is or is not dictated by "overriding" reasons. If a Government determines to take a given property for plausible reasons which it considers to be in the public interest, and not for the mere benefit of private interests, it is very doubtful whether anything useful is to be gained by

430. Memorandum attached to letter dated April 29, 1954, from Carl H. Boehringer to the Secretary of State, NARA, Record Group 59, Department of State File No. 611.62A4/4-2954.

431. Despatch dated March 8, 1954, from the U.S. High Commissioner in Bonn to the Department of State, NARA, Record Group 59, Department of State File No. 611.62A4/3-854. *See also* Minutes of Discussions of Draft Treaty of Friendship, Commerce and Navigation between the United States and India, August 5, 1949, NARA, Record Group 59, Department of State File No. 711.452/9-2149.

432. Memorandum of Conversation headed "Gulf Oil Co. Interest in Treaty Provisions for Preventing Expropriation of U.S. Citizens," dated September 28, 1956, NARA, Record Group 59, Department of State File No. 611.004/9-2856.

433. Despatch dated March 8, 1954, from the U.S. High Commissioner in Bonn to the Department of State, NARA, Record Group 59, Department of State File No. 611.62A4/3-854.

434. Ibid.

> subjecting that decision to treaty challenge on the ground that it was not really dictated by unavoidable force of circumstance. The important objective on which the treaty might usefully concentrate is assurance of proper compensation *if* there is a taking.[435]

The United States did agree, however, in negotiations with the Netherlands to change "public purpose" to "public interest."[436] The treaties with Greece, Germany, Belgium, and Luxembourg used the term "public benefit."[437] The language in the treaty with Nicaragua was changed to read "for public purposes and reasons of social utility as defined by law."[438]

Conditions Imposed—Prompt Payment

The requirement of prompt payment did "not necessarily mean instantaneous" payment.[439] Rather, it required the "exercise of diligence."[440] More specifically, it required the expropriating state "diligently to prosecute such orderly and nondilatory procedures as may be established reasonably to assure correct compensation and safeguard all interests concerned."[441] Thus, payment "would be considered to be prompt if there were no lack of diligence in prosecuting the procedures that would eventuate in effective and final settlement, although

435. Memorandum attached to letter dated April 29, 1954, from Carl H. Boehringer to the Secretary of State, NARA, Record Group 59, Department of State File No. 611.62A4/4-2954.

436. Netherlands FCN treaty, Article VI(4).

437. Greece FCN treaty, Article VII(3); Germany FCN treaty, Article V(4); Belgium FCN treaty, Article 4(3); Luxembourg FCN treaty, Article IV(3).

438. Nicaragua FCN treaty, Article VI(4).

439. Telegram dated September 26, 1947, from the Department of State to the U.S. embassy in Rome, NARA, Record Group 59, Department of State File No. 711.652/9-2047; Memorandum of Conversation headed "Negotiation of Treaty of Friendship, Commerce and Navigation with Israel—4th Meeting," dated March 13, 1951, NARA, Record Group 59, Department of State File No. 611.84A4/3-1351; Agreed Minutes of Technical Discussions on the Proposed Treaty of Friendship, Commerce and Navigation between the United States of America and the Republic of the Philippines at Manila July 2 to August 24, 1948, NARA, Record Group 59, Department of State File No. 711.962/9-1448.

440. Memorandum of Conversation headed "Negotiation of Treaty of Friendship, Commerce and Navigation with Israel—4th Meeting," dated March 13, 1951, NARA, Record Group 59, Department of State File No. 611.84A4/3-1351.

441. Telegram dated September 26, 1947, from the Department of State to the U.S. embassy in Rome, NARA, Record Group 59, Department of State File No. 711.652/9-2047. *See also* Telegram dated July 28, 1948, from the Department of State to the U.S. embassy in Manila, NARA, Record Group 59, Department of State File No. 711.962/7-2348; Despatch dated August 6, 1954, from the U.S. embassy in The Hague to the Department of State, NARA, Record Group 59, Department of State File No. 611.564/8-654.

a time lapse of one or more years might occur before these procedures could be completed."[442] In the FCN treaties with Germany and Vietnam, the phrase "without unnecessary delay" was substituted for "prompt.[443]

The word "prompt" was "a relative term and had to be understood of [*sic*] the light of normal practical procedures."[444] The United States was "careful to indicate that there [was] no talismanic number of months or years involved."[445] U.S. negotiators noted that the receipt of compensation for an indirect expropriation in the United States often necessitated the prosecution of a claim under the Tucker Act.[446] In such a case, "the concept of promptness was met if a steady and diligent effort had been made throughout all phases of the case to ascertain the amount justly due and to make payment to the owner."[447] The same test would be applied to condemnation proceedings.

The treaty elaborated upon the meaning of promptness when it specified, at Article VI(3) of the 1955 standard draft treaty, for example, that "adequate provision shall have been made at or prior to the time of taking for the determination and payment thereof." This language indicated that a government should expropriate only after it had adequately planned in advance for just and prompt payment and knew "where the money was coming from."[448]

During negotiations, France proposed that the treaty require that the amount of compensation be determined no later than the time of taking. The United States objected because the amount of compensation was sometimes determined in the United States by court proceedings that occurred after the taking.[449] Further, in some cases the factors relevant to determining the amount of compensation might

442. Despatch dated March 8, 1954, from the U.S. High Commissioner in Bonn to the Department of State, NARA, Record Group 59, Department of State File No. 611.62A4/3-854.

443. Telegram dated April 20, 1957, from the Department of State to the U.S. embassy in Saigon, NARA, Record Group 59, Department of State File No. 611.51G4/4-2057.

444. Despatch dated March 8, 1954, from the U.S. High Commissioner in Bonn to the Department of State, NARA, Record Group 59, Department of State File No. 611.62A4/3-854.

445. Stanley D. Metzger, "Property in International Law," 50 *Virginia Journal of International Law* 594, 603 (1964).

446. Despatch dated March 8, 1954, from the U.S. High Commissioner in Bonn to the Department of State, NARA, Record Group 59, Department of State File No. 611.62A4/3-854.

447. Ibid. *See also* Despatch dated August 6, 1954, from the U.S. embassy in The Hague to the Department of State, NARA, Record Group 59, Department of State File No. 611.564/8-654.

448. Despatch dated March 8, 1954, from the U.S. High Commissioner in Bonn to the Department of State, NARA, Record Group 59, Department of State File No. 611.62A4/3-854. *See also* Statement of Deputy Assistant Secretary of State Harold Linder, *Commercial Treaties*, Hearing Before a Subcommittee of the Committee on Foreign Relations, 82nd Cong. 2d Sess. (1952), page 8.

449. Despatch dated May 14, 1959, from the U.S. embassy in Paris to the Department of State, NARA, Record Group 59, Department of State File No. 611.514/5-1459.

not be known until after the taking had occurred.[450] Ultimately, the parties agreed to language requiring that "adequate provision for the determination and payment of compensation" be made no later than the time of taking.[451] Subsequently, Belgium proposed that payment be made prior to expropriation, and the parties agreed to language similar to that in the treaty with France.[452]

Similarly, in 1949, the Commerce Department's Business Advisory Council proposed the addition of language that would require payment of compensation prior to a taking. The State Department rejected this proposal on the ground that it imposed an obligation greater than that imposed by the U.S. Constitution.[453]

Conditions Imposed—Just and Effective Compensation

Just compensation required payment of the "full equivalent" of the property taken.[454] The word "equivalent" meant "the fair market value of the property taken, measured as of the time of the taking."[455] It required placing the expropriated investor in the same position as it occupied before the expropriation occurred.[456] The expropriating state must pay interest from the date of taking

450. Instruction dated October 29, 1956, from the Department of State to the U.S. embassy in Brussels, NARA, Record Group 59, Department of State File No. 611.554/10-1156; Airgram dated September 11, 1952, from the Department of State to the U.S. embassy in Port-au-Prince, NARA, Record Group 59, Department of State File No. 611.382/8-1252.

451. France FCN treaty, Article IV(3).

452. Belgium FCN treaty, Article 4(3).

453. Memorandum from Stanley D. Metzger to Michael H. Cardozo headed "Mr. Walker's Memorandum of October 12 re Possible Revisions in Standard FCN Treaties," dated November 15, 1949, NARA, Record Group 59, Department of State Lot Files, Walter Hollis Papers.

454. Memorandum of Conversation dated February 29, 1952, NARA, Record Group 59, Department of State File No. 611.944/4-2352. Harry Hawkins described this as the "worth" of the property. Hawkins, *Commercial Treaties & Agreements*, page 24.

455. Minutes of the First Meeting of the Working Group on Article V, Paragraph 4 & Protocol 3, October 12, 1954, NARA, Record Group 59, Department of State File No. 611.62A4/10-554; Instruction dated October 18, 1954, from the Department of State to the U.S. High Commissioner in Bonn, NARA, Record Group 59, Department of State File No. 611.62A4/10-1854. *See also* Instruction dated November 27, 1975, from the Department of State to the U.S. consulate general in Dhahran, NARA, Record Group 59, Department of State File No. 611.86E4/10-257; Statement of the Office of the Legal Adviser—May 16, 1952, *reprinted in Commercial Treaties,* Hearing Before a Subcommittee of the Committee on Foreign Relations, 82nd Cong. 2d Sess. (1952), page 12.

456. Airgram dated April 11, 1949, from the Department of State to the U.S. embassy in New Delhi, NARA, Record Group 59, Department of State File No. 711.452/4-1149; Memorandum headed "The Eighth Meeting to Consider a Tentative Draft Treaty of Friendship, Commerce and Navigation between the United States and the U.S.S.R. Held June 28, 1945," NARA, Record Group 59, Department of State File No. 711.612; Memorandum to the Embassy at Chungking for Use in Negotiating Treaty of Friendship, Commerce and Navigation, NARA, Record Group 59, Department of State File No. 711.932/2-1645.

until the date of payment.[457] In the view of the United States, this was both the international law standard as expressed in the *Factory at Chorzow*[458] case, among other cases,[459] and the standard required by U.S. law.[460] As the United States explained to Germany, "in a day when the inviolability of private property was becoming less and less respected, we were particularly concerned to preserve it by fixing the principle of full compensation in the Treaty."[461] Disagreements over the amount of compensation, like other disputes involving the interpretation or application of the treaty, were justiciable.[462]

The purpose of the requirement that payment be in an effectively realizable form was "to 'make the owner whole.' To give him the wherewithal to earn his livelihood as before, insofar as could be possible in an expropriation situation."[463] The phrase was intended to ensure that compensation would be given "in cash or readily negotiable media and not in long-term bonds, promissory notes or similar forms of payment."[464] This would ensure that compensation was not

457. Wilson, *International Law Standard*, page 98.

458. *Factory at Chorzow*, P.C.I.J., Ser. A, No. 17, pp. 4, 27. *See* Memorandum to the Embassy at Chungking for Use in Negotiating Treaty of Friendship, Commerce and Navigation, NARA, Record Group 59, Department of State File No. 711.932/2-1645; Memorandum to the American Mission at Beirut for Use in Negotiating Treaty of Friendship, Commerce and Navigation between the United States and the Lebanese Republic, enclosure with airgram dated July 3, 1946, from the Department of State to the U.S. mission in Beirut, NARA, Record Group 59, Department of State File No. 711.90E2/7-346; Telegram No. 108 dated August 18, 1952, from the Department of State to the U.S. embassy in New Delhi, NARA., Record Group 59, Department of State File No. 711.914/8-1852.

459. Telegram dated February 12, 1952, from the Department of State to the U.S. embassy in New Delhi, NARA, Record Group 59, Department of State File No. 611.914/2-752.

460. Minutes of the First Meeting of the Working Group on Article V, Paragraph 4 & Protocol 3, October 12, 1954, NARA, Record Group 59, Department of State File No. 611.62A4/10-554; Instruction dated October 18, 1954, from the Department of State to the U.S. High Commissioner in Bonn, NARA, Record Group 59, Department of State File No. 611.62A4/10-1854. *See also* Memorandum headed "The Eighth Meeting to Consider a Tentative Draft Treaty of Friendship, Commerce and Navigation between the United States and the U.S.S.R. Held June 28, 1945," NARA, Record Group 59, State Department File No. 711.612; Memorandum headed "Eleventh Meeting to Consider a Tentative Draft Treaty of Friendship, Commerce and Navigation between the United States and Brazil, Held December 3, 1945," NARA, Record Group 59, Department of State File No. 711.322/4-2346.

461. Despatch dated September 17, 1954, from the U.S. High Commissioner in Bonn to the Department of State, NARA, Record Group 59, Department of State File No. 611.62A4/9-1754.

462. Instruction dated November 27, 1975, from the Department of State to the U.S. consulate general in Dhahran, NARA, Record Group 59, Department of State File No. 611.86E4/10-257.

463. Minutes of the First Meeting of the Working Group on Article V, Paragraph 4 & Protocol 3, October 12, 1954, NARA, Record Group 59, Department of State File No. 611.62A4/10-554.

464. Memorandum of Conversation headed "Negotiation of Treaty of Friendship, Commerce and Navigation with Colombia: Ninth Meeting," dated June 29, 1950, NARA, Record Group 59, Department of State File No. 611.214/6-2950.

illusory.[465] Freezing the compensation in a blocked account would not meet the test.[466] Similarly, payment in long-term nonnegotiable bonds would not be considered "effectively realizable" compensation.[467] Harry Hawkins, writing in his personal capacity, described the requirement that compensation be effective as a requirement that compensation be convertible into the currency of the investor's country.[468] Indeed, the early U.S. postwar FCN treaties had explicitly required that compensation be paid in the currency of the property owner's country at the most favorable exchange rate applicable at the time of taking.[469] Utilizing the exchange rate at the time of taking protected the expropriated owner against the risk of currency depreciation that, in effect, would deprive the owner of just and effective compensation.[470]

Compensation "in kind" was not necessarily precluded, as long as the investor was "made whole,"[471] that is, as long as the compensation met the requirements of the expropriation provision, including the requirement of an effectively realizable form.[472] For example, during negotiations, Japan explained that its law provided in some cases for in-kind compensation. Land taken by the government might be replaced with other land. The United States responded that this would satisfy the requirement that compensation be effectively realizable provided that the substituted land was a form of compensation acceptable to the investor or was readily

465. Minutes of Discussions of Draft Treaty of Friendship, Commerce and Navigation between the United States and India, August 5, 1949, NARA, Record Group 59, Department of State File No. 711.452/9-2149; Agreed Minutes of Technical Discussions on the Proposed Treaty of Friendship, Commerce and Navigation between the United States of America and the Republic of the Philippines at Manila July 2 to August 24, 1948, Session of July 9, 1948, NARA, Record Group 59, Department of State File No. 711.962/9-1448.

466. Minutes of the First Meeting of the Working Group on Article V, Paragraph 4 & Protocol 3, October 12, 1954, NARA, Record Group 59, Department of State File No. 611.62A4/10-554.

467. Despatch dated March 8, 1954, from the U.S. High Commissioner in Bonn to the Department of State, NARA, Record Group 59, Department of State File No. 611.62A4/3-854.

468. Hawkins, *Commercial Treaties & Agreements*, page 24.

469. China FCN treaty, Article VI(2); Italy FCN treaty, Article V(2). The treaty with Ireland, at Article VIII(2), guaranteed the right to the currency of the investor's own country at a "just and reasonable" rate of exchange.

470. Telegram dated October 7, 1947, from the Department of State to the U.S. embassy in Rome, NARA, Record Group 59, Department of State File No. 711.652/10-147; Telegram dated October 24, 1947, from the Department of State to the U.S. embassy in Rome, NARA, Record Group 59, Department of State File No. 711.652/10-947.

471. Airgram dated December 31, 1951, from the Department of State to the U.S. Political Adviser in Tokyo, NARA, Record Group 59, Department of State File No. 611.944/12-3151.

472. Despatch dated March 8, 1954, from the U.S. High Commissioner in Bonn to the Department of State, NARA, Record Group 59, Department of State File No. 611.62A4/3-854. *See also* Memorandum of Conversation dated February 29, 1952, NARA, Record Group 59, Department of State File No. 611.944/4-2352.

marketable.[473] Similarly, the State Department explained during negotiations with the Philippines that the treaty "does not prescribe [the] form of compensation. Such compensation could be in forms other than cash payments provided requirements of promptness and effectiveness were met."[474] For example, these requirements could be met by payment in government bonds, assuming that such bonds could be sold at a price that permitted the recipient to obtain the full economic value of the expropriated property. Other forms of payment that might meet treaty requirements included transferring real estate, productive facilities, or shares of stock.[475]

In some cases, prompt payment in an effectively realizable form could be impeded by a shortage of foreign exchange. For this reason, during negotiations, the Philippine government sought an understanding that the treaty did not impose any obligation to make foreign exchange available for the withdrawal of expropriation compensation. The State Department refused to agree. It explained that it was "strongly of [the] opinion" that an expropriating government should provide the means for withdrawing compensation.[476] In the words of the Department, "Simple justice requires this."[477] The Department went on to say that, if a government is unwilling to permit withdrawal of compensation, it should not expropriate.[478]

The exchange controls provision, however, authorized restrictions on transfers during times of foreign exchange stringency.[479] Such exchange controls might restrict the transfer of expropriation compensation. The United States believed, though that "a country certainly should not undertake expropriation schemes unless it could see its way clear to make reasonable provision for conversion and withdrawal of the compensation."[480] As discussed below in the section on exchange controls, the U.S. postwar FCN treaties required a party that imposed exchange controls during a period of foreign exchange stringency nevertheless to make reasonable provision for the transfer of expropriation compensation.

473. Memorandum dated December 24, 1952, from Counselor to Embassy Frank Waring to Ambassador Murphy, NARA, Record Group 59, Department of State File No. 611.944/1-753.

474. Telegram dated August 18, 1948, from the Department of State to the U.S. embassy in Manila, NARA, Record Group 59, Department of State File No. 711.962/8-348.

475. Ibid.

476. Ibid.

477. Ibid.

478. Ibid.

479. Airgram dated March 27, 1951, from the Department of State to the U.S. embassy in Athens, NARA, Record Group 59, Department of State File No. 611.814/3-251.

480. Minutes of the First Meeting of the Working Group on Article V, Paragraph 4 & Protocol 3, October 12, 1954, NARA, Record Group 59, Department of State File No. 611.62A4/10-554. *See also* Instruction dated November 10, 1954, from the Department of State to the U.S. embassy in Tehran, NARA, Record Group 59, Department of State File No. 611.884/11-1054.

Conditions Imposed—Non-discrimination

The U.S. postwar FCN treaties also guaranteed national and MFN treatment with respect to expropriation, as noted above. As a general rule, the expropriation of property solely of investors of a particular nationality would violate the non-discrimination obligations of the treaty.[481] In exceptional cases, however, a state could seize property only of a certain type, such as coastal lands in a designated area or land needed for the construction of a highway, railroad, dam, or bridge, even if the property happened to be owned only by investors of a particular nationality, provided that the selection of property to be taken was not based on nationality.[482]

Conditions Imposed—Due Process

U.S. FCN treaties negotiated during the period between World War I and World War II generally required that an expropriation be in accordance with due process.[483] That requirement also appeared in the postwar treaties with China[484] and Italy.[485] For reasons that do not appear in the historical record, that language was omitted when the standard draft treaty was revised in 1948–1949. In any event, the United States believed that the requirement that any expropriation be in accordance with due process of law was declaratory of customary international law.[486]

Although it deleted the language explicitly requiring due process from the standard draft treaty, the United States did not object to the inclusion of such language if another country so requested. For example, during negotiations, Germany proposed the addition of language requiring that any expropriation be "in accordance with due process of law," a proposal to which the United States agreed.[487] The requirement of due process also appeared in Article III(2) of the FCN treaty with Thailand.

481. Memorandum of Conversation dated February 29, 1952, NARA, Record Group 59, Department of State File No. 611.944/4-2352. *See also* Statement of Deputy Assistant Secretary of State Harold Linder, *Commercial Treaties,* Hearing Before a Subcommittee of the Committee on Foreign Relations, 82nd Cong. 2d Sess. (1952), page 8.

482. Statement of Deputy Assistant Secretary of State Harold Linder, *Commercial Treaties,* Hearing Before a Subcommittee of the Committee on Foreign Relations, 82nd Cong. 2d Sess. (1952), page 8.

483. *See, e.g.,* Treaty of Friendship. Commerce, and Consular Rights, United States-Finland, February 13, 1934, Article I, 49 Stat. 2659, TS 868, 4 UST 2047, TIAS 2861.

484. China FCN treaty, Article VI(2).

485. Italy FCN treaty, Article V(2).

486. Memorandum to the Embassy at Chungking for Use in Negotiating Treaty of Friendship, Commerce and Navigation, NARA, Record Group 59, Department of State File No. 711.932/2-1645.

487. Germany FCN treaty, Article V(4). *See also* Instruction dated October 26, 1953, from the Department of State to the U.S. High Commissioner in Bonn, NARA, Record Group 59, Department of State File No. 611.62A4/10-653.

The requirement of due process "necessarily implies, inter alia, the right of an aggrieved person to contest before a court of law both the legality of the taking and the adequacy of the compensation."[488] The United States also understood this language to require that the expropriation be consistent with the law of the party conducting the expropriation.[489] In addition, "the procedures must be regular, they must not be arbitrary, [and] they must afford a suitable opportunity for the furnishing of evidence [and] presenting testimony." [490] Similarly, the State Department observed, with respect to the due process obligation in the 1923 FCN treaty with Germany, that "[t]his stipulation will operate to secure protection against arbitrary and unjust treatment in any particular in which the Government of a country does not accord its own nationals as liberal treatment as that which is recognized by international law."[491] As this implies, the due process obligation required that the expropriating state satisfy the due process standard established by international law.[492]

Non-discriminatory Treatment of Investment in Local Enterprises

The U.S. postwar FCN treaties explicitly required that enterprises in which a national or company of a party had a substantial interest receive national and MFN treatment with respect to any nationalization program implemented by the other party. For example, Article VI(4) of the 1955 standard draft treaty provided that "enterprises in which nationals and companies of either Party have a substantial interest shall be accorded, within the territories of the other Party, not less than national treatment and most-favored-nation treatment in all matters relating to the taking of privately owned enterprises into public ownership and to the placing of such enterprises under public control."

This sentence of the treaty guaranteed non-discriminatory treatment to the enterprise, as opposed to the national or company that had invested in the enterprise. The term "enterprise," which was not defined in the treaty, was regarded as "much broader" than the term "company" and included a "business undertaking

488. Telegram dated August 24, 1954, from the U.S. High Commissioner in Bonn to the Department of State, NARA, Record Group 59, Department of State File No. 611.62A4/8-2454.

489. Memorandum headed "The Eighth Meeting to Consider a Tentative Draft Treaty of Friendship, Commerce and Navigation between the United States and the U.S.S.R. Held June 28, 1945," NARA, Record Group 59, State Department File No. 711.612.

490. Statement of Leonard C. Meeker, Legal Adviser to the Department of State, *Commercial Treaty with Thailand*, Senate Exec. Rept. No. 14, 90th Cong. 1st Sess. (1967).

491. The memorandum is quoted in Wilson, *United States Commercial Treaties and International Law*, pages 114–115.

492. Wilson, "Property-Protection Provisions," 45 *American Journal of International Law* 83 (1951); Wilson, *International Law Standard*, page 101.

in the large and popular sense, regardless of juridical form . . . ."[493] Thus, the provision protected entities that were not chartered by either of the parties.[494] This sentence was directed in particular at nationalization programs that emerged after World War II.[495] Notably, the sentence referred to public ownership and public control, the latter indicating situations where the alien retained legal title but the state assumed control.[496]

The term "substantial interest" was intended to exclude petty interests.[497] It could refer, however, to an interest as little as 2 percent, especially if this were a controlling interest. [498] That said, however, the term "substantial interest" did not necessarily refer to a controlling interest, particularly as the word "control" was used elsewhere in the treaty.[499] The substantial interest could be one held indirectly, that is, through intermediate companies.[500]

Protection of Indirect Interests

A protocol to the standard draft FCN treaty ensured that the expropriation provision would apply to property held directly or indirectly. For example, Paragraph 3 of the protocol to the 1955 standard draft treaty provided that "[t]he provisions of Article VI, paragraph 3, providing for the payment of compensation shall extend to interests held directly or indirectly by nationals and companies of either Party in property which is taken within the territories of the other Party."

The purpose of this provision was to ensure that compensation in accordance with the standards set by the treaty was paid for all interests held by nationals and companies of one party in property expropriated by the other party.[501] In particular, it prevented an uncompensated loss due to expropriation "merely because of the accident

493. Airgram dated July 23, 1952, from the Department of State to the U.S. embassy in Tokyo, NARA, Record Group 59, Department of State File No. 611.944/6-1952.

494. Walker, "Provisions on Companies," page 89.

495. Despatch dated August 3, 1954, from the U.S. embassy in The Hague to the Department of State, NARA, Record Group 59, Department of State File No. 611.564/8-354.

496. Airgram dated June 23, 1953, from the Department of State to the U.S. embassy in The Hague, NARA, Record Group 59, Department of State File No. 611.564/6-553.

497. Memorandum of Conversation headed "Negotiation of Treaty of Friendship, Commerce and Navigation with Israel," dated November 20, 1950, NARA, Record Group 59, Department of State File No. 611.84A4/11-2050.

498. Ibid.

499. Airgram dated July 1, 1953, from the Department of State to the U.S. embassy in The Hague, NARA, Record Group 59, Department of State File No. 611.564/5-153.

500. Despatch dated August 6, 1954, from the U.S. embassy in The Hague to the Department of State, NARA, Record Group 59, Department of State File No. 611.564/8-654.

501. Instruction dated March 27, 1957, from the Department of State to the U.S. embassy in Brussels, NARA, Record Group 59, Department of State File No. 611.554/2-157.

of indirect interest (e.g., ownership of minority shares) in property held by nationals of the other treaty partner."[502] Accordingly, if the Greek government were to expropriate a Greek company, it would be required to compensate U.S. investors to the extent of their interest in the company.[503] Such U.S. investors might be the ultimate owners of the expropriated company through a Greek subsidiary or they might have minority interests in it held through a third-country corporation. In either case, compensation would be required.[504] Or, property in the United States that was owned by an Argentine company that in turn was owned by a Dutch company would be protected by this provision of the U.S. FCN treaty with the Netherlands.[505]

Such a requirement, in the Department's view, was part of international law and would apply regardless of whether it was stated in the treaty.[506] The language thus was in the nature of a clarification.[507] The inclusion of this provision was a reaction to postwar European nationalization programs during which foreign corporations in which Americans held indirect interests had been expropriated.[508] The provision protected the investments of the "ultimate party in interest"[509] and protected those interests "however fractional or intermediately held such interests may be."[510] Thus, the interests need not be substantial[511] and were compensable regardless of the amount.[512]

The phrase "interests held directly or indirectly" was "intended to extend to every type of right or interest in property which is capable of being enjoyed as

502. Ibid.

503. Airgram dated March 30, 1951, from the Department of State to the U.S. embassy in Athens, NARA, Record Group 59, Department of State File No. 611.814/3-251; Telegram dated October 4, 1954, from the Department of State to the U.S. embassy in Karachi, NARA, Record Group 59, Department of State File No. 611.90D4/9-2054 (using same example but involving Pakistan).

504. Ibid. *See also* Despatch dated August 6, 1954, from the U.S. embassy in The Hague to the Department of State, NARA, Record Group 59, Department of State File No. 611.564/8-654.

505. Despatch dated August 6, 1954, from the U.S. embassy in The Hague to the Department of State, NARA, Record Group 59, Department of State File No. 611.564/8-654.

506. Airgram dated March 30, 1951, from the Department of State to the U.S. embassy in Athens, NARA, Record Group 59, Department of State File No. 611.814/3-251.

507. Telegram dated October 4, 1954, from the Department of State to the U.S. embassy in Karachi, NARA, Record Group 59, Department of State File No. 611.90D4/9-2054.

508. Telegram dated September 3, 1948, from the Department of State to the U.S. embassy in Manila, NARA, Record Group 59, Department of State File No. 711.962/8-648.

509. Walker, "Provisions on Companies," page 388.

510. Ibid.

511. Airgram dated June 23, 1953, from the Department of State to the U.S. embassy in The Hague, NARA, Record Group 59, Department of State File No. 611.564/6-553.

512. Ibid.

such, and upon which it is practicable to place a monetary value."[513] The phrase "include[d] not only rights of ownership, but rights of possession, use and enjoyment; it include[d] a leasehold interest, easements, contracts, franchises, and other tangible and intangible property rights."[514]

This provision particularly troubled the Philippines. The Philippine negotiators asked whether this provision would mean that the Philippine government would be the guarantor of payment to an American, by a Philippine corporation in which he had invested, of the proportionate amount due him following expropriation of such corporation's property by the Philippine government and payment by that government of just compensation to the corporation.[515] The State Department said in response that the provision was not intended to require double payment or to change the usual procedure in cases of expropriation of corporate property whereby payment would be made only to the corporation holding title to the property without the government's interesting itself in the direct payment to each stockholder. The purpose of the provision was to protect minority stockholders in the event that compensation was denied.[516]

EXCHANGE CONTROLS

Apart from the article on national treatment with respect to engaging in gainful activity, the most difficult article in the U.S. postwar FCN treaties on which to gain agreement was the one on exchange controls. Several countries sought language in the treaty under which they would have retained sole discretion to determine whether exchange controls that they adopted were consistent with treaty obligations, proposals to which the United States invariably objected.[517]

The State Department explained the policy underlying the exchange controls provision as follows:

> In formulating [the] exchange control [article], [the United States] started from the principle, acknowledged in postwar, multilateral agreements widely accepted by [the] nations of world, that freedom of exchange is

513. Memorandum of Conversation headed "Informal Discussion of the United States Standard Draft Treaty of Friendship, Commerce and Navigation," dated April 15, 1952, NARA, Record Group 59, State Department File No. 611.944/5-652.

514. Ibid.

515. Agreed Minutes of Technical Discussions on the Proposed Treaty of Friendship Commerce and Navigation between the United States of America and the Republic of the Philippines at Manila July 2 to August 24, 1948, NARA, Record Group 59, Department of State File No. 711.962/9-1448.

516. Memorandum of Conversation headed "Proposed Treaty of Friendship, Commerce and Navigation between the United States of America and the Republic of the Philippines," dated October 19, 1948, NARA, Record Group 59, Department of State File No. 711.962/3-249.

517. Some of these negotiations are discussed below in the section on the essential security interests exception.

> fundamentally desirable. [The United States] believes that a country with no exchange problem and possessing adequate supplies of [foreign exchange should] not restrict exchange transactions. [The United States] recognizes, however, as do the multilateral arrangements, that special circumstances may constrain a country to impose restrictions on earnings. Accordingly, [the] treaty seeks to provide that exchange transactions be permitted on as liberal basis as circumstances allow, specifying reasonable criteria for determining when a [government] may impose restrictions and [the] extent to which restrictions shall be applied.[518]

More specifically, the provision sought to assure investors that they would receive "reasonable consideration in the allocation of exchange during periods of exchange stringency when exchange restrictions are in force."[519] In short, the exchange controls provision sought balance. As Deputy Assistant Secretary of State Harold Linder explained in 1952, "Many foreign countries have a genuine need to protect their limited foreign-exchange reserves in order to insure that the highest-priority needs of their economy are met. At the same time, there is a real need for liberal provisions on withdrawals of earnings that will afford a proper protection to investors. We have sought to achieve a fair balance between the two factors."[520]

The United States believed that "[t]he ability of an investor to withdraw his capital is a paramount consideration in investment planning, and a treaty intended to encourage investment cannot neglect the subject."[521] As the State Department explained in 1951, "An important aim of the article [on exchange controls] is to encourage foreign investment. The Article therefore seeks to provide assurances to investors regarding the kind of treatment they may expect over the years with respect to the transfer of their capital and earnings."[522] Other countries understood, even as they resisted this provision, that the inability of foreign investors to repatriate capital and earnings was one of the principal barriers to U.S. investment in their countries.[523] Indeed, as noted in Chapter 5, the NAC believed that in the postwar world exchange controls were the chief obstacle to the flow of international capital.

518. Telegram dated March 15, 1952, from the Department of State to the U.S. embassy in New Delhi, NARA, Record Group 59, Department of State File No. 611.914/2-752.

519. Airgram dated May 3, 1950, from the U.S. embassy in Copenhagen to the Department of State, NARA, Record Group 59, Department of State File No. 611.594/5-350.

520. *Commercial Treaties*, Hearing Before a Subcommittee of the Committee on Foreign Relations, 82d Cong. 2d Sess. (1952), page 5.

521. Airgram dated April 28, 1953, from the Department of State to the U.S. embassy in New Delhi, NARA, Record Group 59, Department of State File No. 611.914/4-2853.

522. Telegram dated January 29, 1951, from the Department of State to the U.S. embassy in Karachi, NARA, Record Group 59, Department of State File No. 611.90D4/12-450.

523. Despatch dated January 11, 1954, from the U.S. High Commissioner in Bonn to the Department of State, NARA, Record Group 59, Department of State File No. 611.62A4/1-1154.

Nothing in the exchange controls article required a party to ensure that foreign exchange was available, unless the government controlled the purchase and sale of foreign exchange.[524] Rather, it obligated a party only to permit withdrawals, under the conditions specified, when exchange was available.[525]

Although the FCN treaties permitted exchange controls under specified circumstances, U.S. policy regarded them as undesirable. In the words of an exchange of notes between the United States and Germany, "It is also understood [that] in the implementation of Article XII each Party will be guided by the principle that exchange restrictions interfere with a multilateral system of payments and hamper the growth of production and world trade, and that accordingly their elimination is a major objective of economic policy." Or, as the State Department explained during negotiations with Pakistan, "The treaty seeks to provide that transfers be permitted on as liberal a basis as the foreign exchange position makes possible. Thus if a country has no exchange problem and possesses adequate supplies of foreign exchange, the United States believes it should not restrict transfers."[526]

U.S. FCN treaties concluded prior to the war generally did not include a provision on exchange controls.[527] The exchange controls provision of the first U.S. postwar FCN treaty, with China, required fair and equitable treatment with respect to exchange controls and imposed various obligations of non-discriminatory treatment with respect to transfers.[528] The United States recognized at the end of World War II that many countries had very limited foreign exchange and that it would need to accommodate that fact. Indeed, State Department officials even debated whether provisions protecting the right to transfer capital should be included in every proposed FCN treaty, and the earliest FCN treaties focused in that regard on ensuring a right to transfer, with respect to investment, only of expropriation compensation and proceeds from the sale of real estate where the alien was not permitted to own the property.[529] As described in Chapter 2, in 1949, the State Department devised a new exchange controls provision that protected the right to transfer both capital and returns, but with language that permitted restrictions during periods of exchange

524. Telegram dated May 17, 1950, from the Department of State to the U.S. legation in Beirut, NARA, Record Group 59. Department of State File No. 611.83A4/5-1750.

525. Telegram dated March 24, 1950, the Department of State to the U.S. legation in Beirut, NARA, Record Group 59, Department of State File No. 611.83A4/3-2450.

526. Telegram dated January 29, 1951, from the Department of State to the U.S. embassy in Karachi, NARA, Record Group 59, Department of State File No. 611.90D4/12-450.

527. *But see* Treaty of Friendship, Commerce and Navigation between the United States of America and the Republic of Liberia, August 8, 1938, Article X, 54 Stat. 1739, T.S. No. 956, 9 Bevans 595.

528. China FCN treaty, Article XIX.

529. Memorandum of Conversation headed "Exchange Control Provisions in Commercial Treaties," dated July 13, 1946, NARA, Record Group 43, International Trade Files, Box 61, Folder marked "Nationalization."

stringency. The Department decided that, because the provision had included adequate flexibility for countries with low foreign exchange reserves, it would seek inclusion of the provision in every FCN treaty. This new exchange controls provision in its final form included five separate obligations.

National and MFN Treatment

First, the provision guaranteed nationals and companies of a party national and MFN treatment with respect to the transfer of funds. For example, Article XII(1) of the 1955 standard draft treaty provided that "[n]ationals and companies of either Party shall be accorded by the other Party national treatment and most-favored-nation treatment with respect to payment, remittances and transfers of funds or financial instruments between the territories of the two Parties as well as between the territory of such other Party and of any third country."

This language, in effect, guaranteed equality of access to a currency.[530] As the State Department explained during negotiations with Germany, it addressed the rights of nationals and companies "under whatever exchange control system may be in effect."[531] Thus, for example, the MFN obligation "would mean that an American would in similarity of circumstances have the same access to francs as a Frenchman or Swede, but it would not require that dollars would be as available as francs to everyone."[532] The provision was "not concerned with rules regarding currencies as such and therefore [did] not preclude differential treatment of different currencies."[533] It would also not preclude differential treatment of persons based on residence, as opposed to nationality.[534] Paragraph 13 of the protocol to the treaty with the Netherlands explicitly clarified that this provision was "designed only to preclude discrimination on the ground of nationality and does not, for instance, preclude different treatment of different currencies or the application of residence requirements." Similarly, Paragraph 8 of the protocol to the treaty with

530. Airgram from Department of State to the U.S. embassy in Tokyo dated June 17, 1952, NARA, Record Group 59, Department of State File No. 611.944/5-2152; Memorandum of Conversation dated March 13, 1952, NARA, Record Group 59, Department of State File No. 611.944/4-3052.

531. Telegram dated September 1, 1954, from the Department of State to the High Commissioner in Bonn, NARA, Record Group 59, Department of State File No. 611.62A4/9-154; Instruction dated November 16, 1953, from the Department of State to the U.S. High Commissioner in Bonn, NARA, Record Group 59, Department of State File No. 611.62A4/11-1653.

532. Ibid.

533. Telegram dated September 1, 1954, from the Department of State to the High Commissioner in Bonn, NARA, Record Group 59, Department of State File No. 611.62A4/9-154. *See also* Telegram dated January 17, 1955, from the Department of State to the U.S. embassy in Karachi, NARA, Record Group 59, Department of State File No. 611.90D4/1-1755; Telegram dated July 7, 1959, from the Department of State to the U.S. embassy in Karachi, NARA, Record Group 59, Department of State File No. 611.90D4/6-2559.

534. Despatch dated August 4, 1954, from the U.S. embassy in The Hague to the Department of State, NARA, Record Group 59, Department of State File No. 611.564/8-454.

Pakistan stated that this provision had "only in view to preclude discrimination on the ground of nationality of persons and companies and does not, for instance, preclude special arrangements providing more favorable treatment for transactions in certain currencies than for transaction in other currencies for balance-of-payments reasons, or the application of residence requirements." Paragraph 13 of the protocol to the treaty with France stated that this provision "shall not preclude differing treatment from being applied to different currencies, as may be required by the state of the balance of payments of either High Contracting Party." Paragraph 11 of the protocol to the treaty with Belgium and Paragraph 8 of the protocol to the treaty with Luxembourg provided that the provision was "designed only to preclude discriminations on the ground of nationality but does not, for instance, preclude different treatment based on residence requirements." The national and MFN treatment obligations applied only to nationals and companies "in like situations" with their comparators, and thus these clarifications were best seen as merely elaborations upon the concept of being "in like situations."[535]

The United States sought an MFN treatment commitment with respect to exchange controls because this was an area in which aliens might enjoy greater rights than nationals.[536] Indeed, as the United States recognized, an inadequacy in the national treatment standard in this context was that investors of the home state would not have the same need for foreign exchange as foreign investors.[537] Further, neither non-discrimination obligation prevented a party from imposing stringent, albeit non-discriminatory, exchange controls.[538]

Restriction on Imposition of Exchange Controls

The second obligation was intended to limit the use of exchange controls. It prohibited "exchange restrictions," except to prevent monetary reserves from falling to very low levels or to raise reserves moderately from very low levels. For example, Article XII(2) of the 1955 standard draft treaty provided that "[n]either Party shall impose exchange restrictions as defined in paragraph 5 of the present Article except to the extent necessary to prevent its monetary reserves from falling to a very low level or to effect a moderate increase in very low monetary reserves." This

535. Despatch dated August 4, 1954, from the U.S. embassy in The Hague to the Department of State, NARA, Record Group 59, Department of State File No. 611.564/8-454; Despatch dated May 27, 1959, from the U.S. embassy in Paris to the Department of State, NARA, Record Group 59, Department of State File No. 611.514/5-2559. *See also* Telegram dated July 7, 1959, from the Department of State to the U.S. embassy in Karachi, NARA, Record Group 59, Department of State File No. 611.90D4/6-2559.

536. Despatch dated April 14, 1959, from the U.S. embassy in Paris to the Department of State, NARA, Record Group 59, Department of State File No. 611.514/4-1459.

537. Hawkins, *Commercial Treaties & Agreements*, page 27.

538. Ibid.

language was modeled after Article XII of the GATT, because the United States wanted to utilize an "international standard rather than to invent a novel and unprecedented standard."[539] The United States anticipated that it would interpret the concept of low reserves in the same way that the GATT would.[540]

The term "exchange restrictions" was defined in Article XII(5) of the 1955 standard draft treaty to include "all restrictions, regulations, charges, taxes, or other requirements imposed by either Party which burden or interfere with payments, remittances, or transfers of funds or of financial instruments between the territories of the two Parties." The definition thus was a broad one. Some of the early U.S. postwar FCN treaties included language that illustrated the broad application of the exchange controls provision in those treaties. For example, Article XVII(1) of the treaty with Ireland applied the exchange control article to "all international payments and transfers of funds effected through the medium of currencies, securities, bank deposits, dealing in foreign exchange or other financial arrangements."

The term "monetary reserves" was used in the "generally accepted sense of the term," that is, as it was used in Article XII(2)(a)(i) of the GATT and Article XIX of the IMF Articles of Agreement.[541] The State Department explained that it referred to "gold and foreign exchange holdings which are in effectively usable form for the country's balance of payments needs. Consideration would thus be given to the nature of the particular currencies held and their usefulness for the country's particular balance-of-payments requirements."[542]

Several potential treaty parties expressed the concern that treaty restrictions on a party's right to implement exchange controls were contrary to the IMF Articles of Agreement. The United States agreed that all measures taken by either party should be consistent with the IMF articles and with decisions made by the IMF.[543] The IMF was "paramount" in the field of exchange controls.[544] At the same time, however, where the IMF left discretion to its members, bilateral commitments were permissible.[545] The FCN treaty addressed only matters that the

539. Despatch dated February 10, 1954, from the U.S. High Commissioner in Bonn to the Department of State, NARA, Record Group 59, Department of State File No. 611.62A4/2-1054.

540. Ibid.

541. Airgram dated July 6, 1953, from the Department of State to the U.S. embassy in The Hague, NARA, Record Group 59, Department of State File No. 611.564/6-1553.

542. Instruction dated December 22, 1953, from the Department of State to the U.S. High Commissioner in Bonn, NARA, Record Group 59, Department of State File No. 611.62A4/11.2453.

543. Despatch dated March 5, 1954, from the U.S. High Commissioner in Bonn to the Department of State, NARA, Record Group 59, Department of State File No. 611.62A4/3-554.

544. Despatch dated February 10, 1954, from the U.S. High Commissioner in Bonn to the Department of State, NARA, Record Group 59, Department of State File No. 611.62A4/2-1054.

545. Despatch dated March 5, 1954, from the U.S. High Commissioner in Bonn to the Department of State, NARA, Record Group 59, Department of State File No. 611.62A4/3-554;

IMF left to the discretion of its members.[546] To make this clear, Article XII(2) of the 1955 standard draft treaty stated, "It is understood that the provisions of the present Article do not alter the obligations either Party may have to the International Monetary Fund or preclude imposition of particular restrictions whenever the Fund specifically authorizes or requests a Party to impose such particular restrictions."

Article XII(2) was not intended to authorize restrictions on the entry of capital, even during periods of exchange stringency,[547] but neither did it prohibit them. The United States agreed to clarifying language in the protocol to the Danish FCN treaty stating that nothing in Article XII(2) shall be construed to prevent a party from exercising necessary regulation over the inflow of capital, provided that such regulations shall not as a general rule be exercised in a manner that impairs rights under other provisions of the treaty.[548] The proviso in the Danish treaty language was an important limitation because Article VII (as it was numbered in the 1955 standard draft treaty) implicitly required the parties to permit the entry of capital incidental to engaging in the activities protected by that article.[549] That is, Article VII, rather than Article XII, addressed the entry of capital. As discussed above in the section on national treatment, the United States agreed in several treaties to permit restrictions on entry to protect foreign exchange reserves, notwithstanding Article VII.

During negotiations, the Dutch expressed a concern about the importation of "hot money" or speculative investments. The United States explained that Paragraph 3 (discussed in the next section) addressed only restrictions on outward transfers, not inflows.[550] Further, the implied obligation in Article VII to allow the "free import of investment capital did not carry the implication that instable 'speculative' money (in the invidious sense) had to be permitted to enter."[551] The

Despatch dated August 4, 1954, from the U.S. embassy in The Hague to the Department of State, NARA, Record Group 59, Department of State File No. 611.564/3-454.

546. Instruction dated December 22, 1953, from the Department of State to the U.S. High Commissioner in Bonn, NARA, Record Group 59, Department of State File No. 611.62A4/11-2453.

547. Airgram dated May 3, 1950, from the U.S. embassy in Copenhagen to the Department of State, NARA, Record Group 59, Department of State File No. 611.594/5-350; Airgram dated June 13, 1950, from the Department of State to the U.S. embassy in Copenhagen, NARA, Record Group 59, Department of State File No. 611.594/5-350.

548. Denmark FCN Treaty, Protocol, Paragraph 7.

549. Memorandum of Conversation dated March 4, 1952, NARA, Record Group 59, Department of State File No. 611.944/4-3052. *See also* Despatch dated August 4, 1954, from the U.S. embassy in The Hague to the Department of State, NARA, Record Group 59, Department of State File No. 611.564/8-454.

550. Despatch dated August 4, 1954, from the U.S. embassy in The Hague to the Department of State, NARA, Record Group 59, Department of State File No. 611.564/8-454.

551. Ibid.

Dutch negotiators believed that Article XII(2) could be interpreted to apply to capital inflows, and thus some reservation regarding hot money was necessary. Accordingly, Paragraph 14 of the protocol to the treaty with the Netherlands provided that "[e]ither Party may impose restrictions on the introduction of foreign capital as may be necessary to protect its monetary reserves as provided in Article XII, paragraph 2, or to prevent serious monetary disturbances arising from speculative financial operations." The Dutch negotiators assured the U.S. negotiators that the Netherlands would resort to restrictions on "hot money" only in "very extreme and exceptional circumstances."[552] The State Department also explained during negotiations with Iran that reasonable restrictions on capital to avoid a serious outflow of "hot money" in the form of scarce foreign exchange would not violate the exchange controls article.[553]

Allocation of Foreign Exchange Reserves under Exchange Controls

A third obligation regulated the way that a treaty party allocated foreign exchange reserves during a period when exchange controls were in place. In essence, the treaty required that a party, after assuring the availability of foreign exchange needed for the health and welfare of its people, make reasonable provision for the withdrawal of funds by investors for various enumerated purposes, taking into account special needs for other transactions. For example, Article XII(3) of the 1955 standard draft treaty provided that

> [i]f either Party imposes exchange restrictions in accordance with paragraph 2 of the present Article, it shall after making whatever provision may be necessary to assure the availability of foreign exchange for goods and services essential to the health and welfare of its people, make reasonable provision for the withdrawal, in foreign exchange in the currency of the other Party, of (a) the compensation referred to in Article VI, paragraph 3, (b) earnings, whether in the form of salaries, interest, dividends, commissions[,] royalties, payments for technical services, or otherwise, (c) amounts for amortization of loans, depreciation of direct investments, and capital transfers, giving consideration to special needs for other transactions.

The language of the provision indicated that the investor's access to foreign exchange was subordinate to the host country's need for foreign exchange to

552. Despatch dated August 16, 1954, from the U.S. embassy in The Hague to the Department of State, NARA, Record Group 59, Department of State File No. 611.564/8-1654.

553. Instruction dated November 10, 1954, from the Department of State to the U.S. embassy in Tehran, NARA, Record Group 59, Department of State File No. 611.884/11-1054; Despatch dated October 16, 1954, from the U.S. embassy in Tehran to the Department of State, NARA, Record Group 59, Department of State File No. 611.884/10-1654.

acquire goods and services essential to the health and welfare of its people. As the State Department explained during negotiations with Pakistan,

> If a country . . . lacks adequate supplies of foreign exchange, the treaty provides ample latitude for the imposition of such exchange restrictions as may be needed. A country, according to the treaty, retains the right to impose whatever exchange restrictions may be required to meet or prevent an exchange stringency and to assure the availability of foreign exchange for goods and services essential to the health and welfare of its people.[554]

The word "welfare" had a "broad meaning" and was used with reference to a country's "general well-being, including the necessities and minimum comforts for the maintenance of an adequate standard of living."[555]

Even after making allowance for essential services and imports, it would not be feasible to give investors "absolute priority" over others.[556] The United States understood that "[s]ome flexibility has to be retained to meet other perfectly proper and legitimate claims for a fair share of the limited exchange available during a stringency period."[557] The solution was to require "reasonable provision" for certain withdrawals, while also permitting use of foreign exchange for "special needs for other transactions."[558]

The provision for "special needs" was intended to permit transfers that may not qualify as essential to the health and welfare of the people but that nevertheless constituted "legitimate claims for a fair share of the limited exchange available during a stringency period."[559] Examples included transfers for student or cultural exchange programs, a small inheritance, dues for an international organization[560] or the cost of operating diplomatic missions.[561] The United States would expect, however, that a

554. Telegram dated January 29, 1951, from the Department of State to the U.S. embassy in Karachi, NARA, Record Group 59, Department of State File No. 611.90D4/12-450.

555. Memorandum of Conversation dated May 8, 1952, headed "Informal Discussion of United States Standard Draft Treaty of Friendship, Commerce and Navigation," NARA, Record Group 59, Department of State File No. 611.944/5-2152.

556. Ibid.

557. Ibid.

558. Ibid.

559. Airgram dated June 17, 1952, from the Department of State to the U.S. embassy in Tokyo, NARA, Record Group 59, Department of State File No. 611.944/5-2152. *See also* Telegram dated March 15, 1952, from the Department of State to the U.S. embassy in New Delhi, NARA, Record Group 59, Department of State File No. 611.914/2-752.

560. Airgram dated June 17, 1952, from the Department of State to the U.S. embassy in Tokyo, NARA, Record Group 59, Department of State File No. 611.944/5-2152.

561. Telegram dated March 15, 1952, from the Department of State to the U.S. embassy in New Delhi, NARA, Record Group 59, Department of State File No. 611.914/2-752; Instruction

treaty party would not grant exchange freely for luxury imports while denying it for the transfer of earnings.[562]

The reference to "reasonable provision" meant reasonable in light of a country's balance of payments position.[563] That is, reasonable provision gave "latitude to impose whatever restrictions upon the transfer of capital may be necessary and proper in the light of the position of their monetary reserves."[564] For example, this might mean that transfers for current transactions received more liberal treatment than capital transfers[565] or that imported capital would be given priority over domestic capital.[566] During very severe circumstances, "drastic restrictions"[567] or even a moratorium on withdrawals might be reasonable.[568] The term "reasonable" meant "whatever is deemed necessary and proper, in the judgment of rational temperate men, to accomplish a worthy object."[569] At the same time, however, the United States wished to assure "maximum feasible privileges to investor interests, after allowance is made for the monetary reserve considerations of paragraph 2 and the need for financing essential services and imports."[570]

dated November 10, 1954, from the Department of State to the U.S. embassy in Tehran, NARA, Record Group 59, Department of State File No. 611.884/11-1054; Airgram from Department of State to U.S. embassy in Tokyo dated June 17, 1952, NARA, Record Group 59, Department of State File No. 611.944/5-2152.

562. Telegram dated March 15, 1952, from the Department of State to the U.S. embassy in New Delhi, NARA, Record Group 59, Department of State File No. 611.914/2-752. *See also* Instruction dated July 23, 1954, from the Department of State to the U.S. embassy in Tehran, NARA, Record Group 59, Department of State File No. 611.884/7-2354.

563. Instruction dated February 6, 1956, from the Department of State to the U.S. embassy in Saigon, NARA, Record Group 59, Department of State File No. 611.51G4/1-2157.

564. Airgram A-811 dated June 6, 1951, from the Department of State to the U.S. embassy in Athens, NARA, Record Group 59, Department of State File No. 611.814/5-1051.

565. Ibid.

566. Memorandum of Conversation headed "Negotiation of Treaty of Friendship, Commerce and Navigation with Colombia: Twenty-First Meeting," dated April 12, 1951, NARA, Record Group 59, Department of State File No. 611.214/4-1251.

567. Telegram dated May 29, 1963, from the Department of State to the U.S. embassy in Bangkok, NARA, Record Group 59, Central Foreign Policy Files 1963, Box 3487, Folder marked "FT- Foreign Trade 1963."

568. Telegram dated October 29, 1952, from Department of State to the U.S. embassy in Cairo, NARA, Record Group 59, Department of State File No. 611.744/10-852; Telegram dated August 23, 1949, from the Department of State to the U.S. embassy in New Delhi, NARA, Record Group 59, Department of State File No. 711.452/8-2049.

569. Memorandum of Conversation headed "Negotiation of Treaty of Friendship, Commerce and Navigation with Colombia: Twenty-First Meeting," dated April 12, 1951, NARA, Record Group 59, Department of State File No. 611.214/4-1251.

570. Airgram from Department of State to the U.S. embassy in Tokyo dated June 17, 1952, NARA, Record Group 59, Department of State File No. 611.944/5-2152.

The specific recitals marked "a" through "c," "though entitled to particular weight," were "not to the exclusion of all other legitimate claims upon available exchange."[571] Although the three lettered paragraphs did not "establish an order of priorities, they did indicate a certain order of emphasis" and "it was no accident that the reference to capital transfers was placed at the end of the recitation."[572] The reference to compensation under Article VI(3)(a) was one to compensation for expropriation.

The obligation imposed by Article XII(3) particularly triggered concerns that the treaty was inconsistent with IMF obligations. The State Department observed in response that, as noted above, Article XII(2) explicitly provided that the article on exchange controls did not alter a party's obligations to the IMF or preclude the imposition of any restrictions specifically authorized by the IMF. Rather, Article XII(3) applied where the IMF left discretion to a party. For example, as the State Department repeatedly explained, the IMF in many cases authorized exchange controls but left to the member the question of how to allocate the use of available foreign exchange. In the absence of a bilateral commitment such as appeared in the FCN treaties, a host state might, for instance, authorize the use of foreign exchange to import luxury items but not to service capital, such as through withdrawal of earnings, dividends, or interest.[573] The FCN treaty allowed essential imports, but also required reasonable provision for the withdrawal of earnings and capital. If the IMF authorized restrictions on specific uses of foreign exchange, however, then the FCN provision permitted those restrictions.[574]

The United States regarded Paragraph 3 as the most important paragraph in the article on exchange controls. It was the "heart and essence" of the article.[575] The object of the paragraph was to ensure for the investor a "fair break."[576]

Of all of the provisions of the article on exchange controls, Paragraph 3 engendered by far the most controversy. Other countries anticipated having exchange controls for a period of years and were concerned about limitations placed upon their

571. Ibid.

572. Despatch dated August 16, 1954, from the U.S. embassy in The Hague to the Department of State, NARA, Record Group 59, Department of State File No. 611.564/8-1654.

573. Airgram dated May 3, 1950, from the U.S. embassy in Copenhagen to the Department of State, NARA, Record Group 59, Department of State File No. 611.594/5-350; Instruction dated December 22, 1953, from the Department of State to the U.S. High Commissioner in Bonn, NARA, Record Group 59, Department of State File No. 611.62A4/11.2453; Telegram dated February 4, 1954, from the Department of State to the U.S. embassy in The Hague, NARA, Record Group 59, Department of State File No. 611.564/1-2754; Letter dated February 15, 1954, from Jack C. Corbett to Weir M. Brown, NARA, Record Group 59, Department of State File No. 611.62A4/1-1954. The discussion of this concern during the negotiations with Denmark is described in Chapter 6 in the section on the negotiation of the FCN treaty with Denmark.

574. Airgram dated May 3, 1950, from the U.S. embassy in Copenhagen to the Department of State, NARA, Record Group 59, Department of State File No. 611.594/5-350.

575. Despatch dated February 10, 1954, from the U.S. High Commissioner in Bonn to the Department of State, NARA, Record Group 59, Department of State File No. 611.62A4/2-1054.

576. Ibid.

use of scarce foreign exchange during the years when exchange controls would be in force. The United States believed that Paragraph 3 reflected an attempt to "strike a fair balance" among competing considerations "in an extremely complex matter."[577]

Restriction Regarding Multiple Exchange Rates

Article XII(3) imposed a fourth obligation, applicable to situations where a country utilized multiple exchange rates. In such a situation, the treaty required the use of a rate that was approved by the IMF or, if there was no such rate, a rate that was just and reasonable. In the words of the 1955 standard draft treaty, "If more than one rate of exchange is in force, the rate applicable to such withdrawal shall be a rate which is specifically approved by the International Monetary Fund for such transactions or, in the absence of a rate so approved, an effective rate which, inclusive of any taxes or surcharges on exchange transfers, is just and reasonable." The phrase "specifically approved" referred to a specific decision made by the Fund, not discretion a country had under the IMF articles.[578]

The purpose behind this provision was to ensure that a multiple rate system did not result in "inequitable" treatment of U.S. investors,[579] that is, to assure that a withdrawal was not blocked or made "excessively costly" by the application of an "unfair" rate in a multiple rate system.[580] Experience had shown that multiple rates could be used as a form of exchange controls.[581] The United States believed that it was "virtually impossible" to identify an exchange rate that would be equitable over a period of years, and thus the treaty specified only that a "just and reasonable" rate be used. [582]

Some countries objected to the phrase "just and reasonable" on the ground that it was not sufficiently definite. The State Department denied that the term was indefinite. It explained that "[i]t is comparable to standards used in the U.S. by judicial and regulatory bodies in rulings on such matters as utility rates and earnings and produces satisfactory results. [A j]ust and reasonable rate may

577. Airgram from Department of State to U.S. embassy in Tokyo dated June 17, 1952, NARA, Record Group 59, Department of State File No. 611.944/5-2152.

578. Instruction dated November 10, 1954, from the Department of State to the U.S. embassy in Tehran, NARA, Record Group 59, Department of State File No. 611.884/11-1054.

579. Instruction W-153 dated April 13, 1962, from the Department of State to the U.S. embassy in Bangkok, NARA, Record Group 59, Department of State File No. 611.9242/2-1562.

580. Telegram 1762 dated May 29, 1963, from the Department of State to the U.S. embassy in Bangkok, NARA, Record Group 59, Central Foreign Policy File 1963, Box 3487, Folder marked "FT—Foreign Trade 2/1/63."

581. Despatch dated December 22, 1953, from the U.S. High Commissioner in Bonn to the Department of State, NARA, Record Group 59, Department of State File No. 511.62A4/12-2253.

582. Telegram dated March 15, 1952, from the Department of State to the U.S. embassy in New Delhi, NARA, Record Group 59, Department of State File No. 611.914/2-752; Message air pouched from the Department of State to the U.S. mission in Karachi, NARA, Record Group 59, Department of State File No. 611.90D4/12-450.

be described as [the] rate impartial and informed men after taking account [of] all pertinent facts would regard as fair and equitable to all concerned. [The p] rovision does not imply rights only for those transferring funds but also for the country needing to conserve exchange."[583] The United States regarded the provision as important in "view [of the] history [of] use [of] managed rate systems [in] certain countries since 1930 so as [to] seriously injure [the] interests [of] foreign investors."[584] In response to the suggestion that the treaty specify a market rate instead, the State Department replied that the market does not necessarily provide a reasonable exchange rate for particular transactions, noting that "there may be a very narrow market for capital transactions which provides [a] highly depreciated exchange rate that is inequitable for nonresidents desiring [to] repatriate their investments."[585]

Avoidance of Arbitrary Discrimination or Unnecessary Harm

A fifth obligation prohibited exchange controls that were unnecessarily detrimental or arbitrarily discriminatory to the interests of nationals and companies of the other party. For example, Paragraph XII(4) of the 1955 standard draft treaty provided that "[e]xchange restrictions shall not be imposed by either Party in a manner unnecessarily detrimental or arbitrarily discriminatory to the claims, investments, transport, trade, and other interests of nationals and companies of the other Party, nor to the competitive position thereof." A counterpart to Paragraph 4 had appeared in the U.S. postwar FCN treaties, dating back to the treaty with China.

This paragraph was intended to ensure that exchange controls were applied only to protect foreign exchange reserves during periods of stringency rather than for protectionist or arbitrary reasons. That is, exchange controls should not be administered so as to favor the importation of a product from a third country over the importation of a like product from the other treaty party.[586] The United States thus acknowledged that a country might adopt exchange controls that discriminated against the dollar, but wanted assurances that any such restrictions would

583. Telegram 1762 dated May 29, 1963, from the Department of State to the U.S. embassy in Bangkok, NARA, Record Group 59, Central Foreign Policy File 1963, Box 3487, Folder marked "FT—Foreign Trade 2/1/63."

584. Telegram dated July 11, 1963, from the Department of State to the U.S. embassy in Bangkok, NARA, Record Group 59, Central Foreign Policy File 1963, Box 3487, Folder marked "FT—Foreign Trade 2/1/63."

585. Telegram 1762 dated May 29, 1963, from the Department of State to the U.S. embassy in Bangkok, NARA, Record Group 59, Central Foreign Policy File 1963, Box 3487, Folder marked "FT—Foreign Trade 2/1/63."

586. Memorandum headed "Preliminary Discussion of Proposed United States—Philippine Treaty of Friendship, Commerce and Navigation," dated June 16, 1947, NARA, Record Group 59, Department of State File No. 711.962/6-1647.

not be adopted unnecessarily or administered in an arbitrary way.[587] For example, if a country had abundant reserves of British pounds and not dollars, it could allow freer access to pounds than to dollars.[588] The FCN treaty, in any event, did not interfere with a party's decision with respect to how much of any one currency to maintain.[589]

This paragraph also addressed other aspects of the administration of exchange controls. For example, during negotiations with Japan, the two countries agreed that this paragraph might apply to the situation where a country simultaneously reduced the convertibility of funds in one sector of the economy, while increasing convertibility in another sector.[590] It might also apply to a situation where stricter exchange controls were applied to affect accumulated earnings that an investor had been entitled to transfer, but had not yet transferred.[591]

These examples did not exhaust the uses of Paragraph 4. The paragraph stated a general principle, the application of which would have to be determined on a case-by-case basis.[592] The purpose of the paragraph "was not to freeze a previous competitive position among private enterprises, but to preclude, among other things, arbitrary action by the government of either Party that would hamper or prevent the enterprise of the other Party from competing on equal terms with the enterprise of third countries."[593] Thus, the provision did not guarantee the maintenance of a historical share of the market, but only the opportunity to compete.

587. Telegram dated September 1, 1954, from the Department of State to the U.S. High Commissioner in Bonn, NARA, Record Group 59, Department of State File No. 611.62A4/9-154; Airgram from Department of State to U.S. embassy in Tokyo dated June 17, 1952, NARA, Department of State File No. 611.944/5-2152; Memorandum of Conversation dated March 13, 1952, NARA, Record Group 59, Department of State File No. 611.944/4-3052; Memorandum of Conversation headed "Negotiations concerning Proposed United States-Philippines Treaty of Friendship, Commerce and Navigation, Eighth Meeting," dated September 3, 1947, NARA, Record Group 59, Department of State File No. 711.962/9-347.

588. Airgram from Department of State to U.S. embassy in Tokyo dated June 17, 1952, NARA, Record Group 59, Department of State File No. 611.944/5-2152; Memorandum of Conversation dated March 13, 1952, NARA, Record Group 59, Department of State File No. 611.944/4-3052.

589. Despatch dated November 24, 1953, from the U.S. High Commissioner in Bonn to the Department of State, NARA, Record Group 59, Department of State File No. 611.62A4/11-2453.

590. Memorandum of Conversation dated March 13, 1952, Enclosure No. 3 to dispatch dated April 30, 1952, from the U.S. Political Adviser in Tokyo to the Department of State, NARA, Record Group 59, Department of State File No. 611.944/4-3052.

591. Ibid.

592. Memorandum of Conversation headed "Negotiations concerning Proposed United States-Philippines Treaty of Friendship, Commerce and Navigation, Eighth Meeting," dated September 3, 1947, NARA, Record Group 59, Department of State File No. 711.962/9-347.

593. Ibid.

Sole Article on Exchange Controls

The article on exchange controls contained a carefully balanced set of provisions, a balance that could have been disrupted by the application of other treaty provisions to the subject of exchange controls. Accordingly, the United States intended and routinely told other treaty parties that the exchange controls article of the treaty, such as Article XII of the 1955 standard draft treaty, was the sole article of the treaty applicable to the subject of exchange controls.[594] Indeed, Article XII(6) of the treaty with the Netherlands and Article 10(6) of the treaty with Belgium included explicit language to this effect. Charges on transfers relating to imports and exports were addressed by another article, such as Article XIV of the 1955 standard draft treaty, which dealt in general with the entry of goods.[595] As noted above, Article VII of the 1955 standard draft accorded rights with respect to the entry of capital.

EMPLOYMENT

Right to Employ Key Personnel

A problem commonly encountered by U.S. companies doing business abroad was the lack of qualified indigenous personnel to perform managerial and technical tasks. The U.S. postwar FCN treaties thus included a provision guaranteeing to U.S. nationals and companies the right to employ expatriates in certain positions. For example, Article VIII(1) of the 1955 standard draft treaty provided that "[n]ationals and companies of either Party shall be permitted to engage, within the territories of the other Party, accountants and other technical experts, executive personnel, attorneys, agents and other specialists of their choice." The word "engage" was used rather than "employ" to avoid a narrow technical meaning that could exclude such arrangements as an attorney-client relationship.[596]

A counterpart provision had appeared in some U.S. FCN treaties concluded prior to the war. For example, Article I of the 1934 FCN treaty with Finland

594. Instruction dated July 8, 1954, from the Department of State to the U.S. High Commissioner in Bonn, NARA, Record Group 59, Department of State File No. 611. 62A4/3-2354; Despatch dated March 23, 1954, from the U.S. High Commissioner in Bonn to the Department of State, NARA, Record Group 59, Department of State File No. 611.62A4/3-2354; Minutes of the Third Meeting of the Working Group on Article XII, October 11, 1954, NARA, Record Group 59, Department of State File No. 611.62A4/10-554; Telegram dated February 4, 1954, from the Department of State to the U.S. embassy in The Hague, NARA, Record Group 59, Department of State File No. 611.564/1-2754; Despatch dated September 15, 1954, from the U.S. embassy in The Hague to the Department of State, NARA, Record Group 59, Department of State File No. 611.564/9-1554.

595. Telegram dated February 4, 1954, from the Department of State to the U.S. embassy in The Hague, NARA, Record Group 59, Department of State File No. 611.564/1-2754.

596. Telegram A-400 dated December 21, 1950, from the Department of State to the U.S. embassy in Athens, NARA, Record Group 59, Department of State File No. 611.814/11-2150.

provided that nationals, when engaging in certain treaty-protected activities, "shall be permitted . . . to appoint representatives, agents or employees of their choice, subject to the local laws in relation to the immigration of aliens."[597] As this indicates, prior to the war the employment provision granted rights only to nationals, not companies.

Early U.S. postwar FCN treaties guaranteed the right "to employ agents and employees of their choice, regardless of nationality."[598] The reference to "employees and agents" was broad language that was similar to that which appeared in the treaties prior to the war. In contrast to the prewar treaties, the postwar treaties extended the right to companies.[599] The phrase "regardless of nationality" was considered words of emphasis that could be removed without affecting the meaning of the sentence.[600] The phrase was removed from the standard draft treaty after the conclusion of the treaty with Italy.

In the late 1940s, the NFTC urged that the State Department obtain for American businesses operating overseas the right to employ U.S. nationals for the performance of managerial or technical functions in particular.[601] Foreign companies doing business in the United States typically did not experience difficulty finding qualified indigenous personnel to employ, but American businesses overseas often did have such difficulty. In many countries, indigenous personnel with the necessary managerial or technical expertise were in short supply, a circumstance that inhibited the foreign investment that the United States was seeking to promote.[602] Accordingly, during the process of revising the standard draft in 1948–1949, the State Department modified the language of the provision to refer explicitly to technical experts and executive personnel, rather than to all agents and employees.

The main purpose of this provision was to prevent the host state from "dictating" or "arbitrarily circumscribing" whom the employer might hire from among those "available and qualified for employment."[603] The provision provided some

597. Treaty of Friendship. Commerce, and Consular Rights, United States-Finland, February 13, 1934, 49 Stat. 2659, TS 868, 4 UST 2047, TIAS 2861.

598. Italy FCN treaty, Article I(2)(c). *See also* China FCN treaty, Articles II(2) and III(3).

599. Italy FCN treaty, Article II(2); China FCN treaty, Article III(3).

600. Despatch dated August 16, 1954, from the U.S. embassy in The Hague to the Department of State, NARA, Record Group 59, Department of State File. 611.564/8-1654.

601. Letter dated April 23, 1951, from William S. Swingle to Senator Tom Connally, NARA, Record Group 59, Department of State File No. 611.004/4-2351; Letter dated June 1, 1948, from E. P. Thomas to Senator Arthur Vandenberg, NARA, Record Group 59, Department of State File No. 611.004/5-350.

602. Memorandum by Charles H. Sullivan headed "Entry of Foreign Investors into the United States under Treaties of Friendship, Commerce and Navigation," dated November 23, 1949, NARA, Record Group 59, State Department File No. 611.004/5-350.

603. Memorandum headed "Memorandum on the Provisions of the Greek Counterdraft," dated July 31, 1950, NARA, Record Group 59, Department of State File No, 611.814/6-250; Despatch

assurance against harassment regarding the employment of executive and highly specialized personnel, including in some cases experienced foremen.[604]

The employment provision was "an elaboration of the principles of control and management set forth in Article VII, and [was] corollary thereto by emphasizing the freedom of management to make its own choices about personnel."[605] The object of the provision was to enable the employer to achieve high production standards, not to encourage hiring U.S. workers.[606] Indeed, the State Department noted that achieving lower labor costs and the aversion of Americans to living abroad dictated the fullest utilization of local personnel in many cases.[607]

The provision was directed in particular at the imposition of "percentile" legislation, that is, legislation requiring that a certain percentage of a company's employees be indigenous personnel.[608] Such legislation created problems for the foreign investor where it was applied to foreclose the employment of foreign nationals even where qualified indigenous employees were not available.[609] The United States, however, did not object to laws requiring the hiring of indigenous workers as long as U.S. enterprises could employ essential personnel without regard to nationality.[610] The right to employ the attorneys of one's choice, in particular, was important to enjoyment of the right of judicial access.

During negotiations, the French expressed the concern that the U.S. language "included everybody, even the charwoman."[611] In fact, however, the provision did

dated July 28, 1954, from the U.S. embassy in The Hague to the Department of State, NARA, Record Group 59, Department of State File No. 611.564/7-2854; Despatch No. 914 dated March 11, 1955, from the U.S. embassy in Brussels to the Department of State, NARA, Record Group 59, Department of State File No. 611.554/3-1155.

604. Telegram dated November 27, 1954, from the Department of State to the U.S. embassy in Karachi, NARA, Record Group 59, Department of State File No. 611.90D4/11-2754.

605. Despatch dated March 18, 1954, from the U.S. High Commissioner in Bonn to the Department of State, NARA, Record Group 59, Department of State File No. 611.62A4/3-1854.

606. Telegram dated November 27, 1954, from the Department of State to the U.S. embassy in Karachi, NARA, Record Group 59, Department of State File No. 611.90D4/11-2754.

607. Ibid.

608. Despatch dated March 18, 1954, from the U.S. High Commissioner in Bonn to the Department of State, NARA, Record Group 59, Department of State File No. 611.62A4/3-1854; Despatch dated July 14, 1954, from the U.S. embassy in The Hague to the Department of State, NARA, Record Group 59, Department of State File No. 611.564/7-1454; Despatch dated August 16, 1954, from the U.S. embassy in The Hague to the Department of State, NARA, Record Group 59, Department of State File No. 611.564/8-1654.

609. Despatch dated August 16, 1954, from the U.S. embassy in The Hague to the Department of State, NARA, Record Group 59, Department of State File No. 611.564/8-1654.

610. Telegram dated October 15, 1954, from the Department of State to the U.S. embassy in Karachi, NARA, Record Group 59, Department of State File No. 611.90D4/10-1454.

611. Despatch dated May 11, 1959, from the U.S. embassy in Paris to the Department of State, NARA, Record Group 59, Department of State File No. 611.514/5-1159.

not apply to the great mass of workers.[612] The term "executive" personnel, referred to "top-level" and "key" personnel.[613] It included, but was not limited to, directors and managers, and applied to all of the "higher employees" of a company.[614] The word "attorney" included an attorney in fact as well as an attorney at law[615] and the term could be deleted because the word "agent" was sufficient.[616]

The provision was not intended to derogate from immigration or licensure laws [617] or citizenship requirements.[618] That is, the United States was not using the treaty to gain entry for anyone other than those covered by the treaty investor or treaty trader provisions.[619] Thus, the employment provision did not authorize employment contrary to the conditions imposed on entry.[620] Similarly, the provision did not preclude "suitable regulation" of occupational qualifications, wages, and other common features of the employment regulations.[621] It gave freedom of choice as among persons lawfully present in the country and occupationally qualified under the local law.[622] Indeed, the FCN treaty with Greece made this explicit by adding the words "among those

612. Ibid.

613. Despatch date August 16, 1954, from the U.S. embassy in The Hague to the Department of State, NARA, Record Group 59, Department of State File No. 611.564/8-1654.

614. Memorandum of Conversation dated May 21, 1952, enclosure 4 to despatch dated May 21, 1952, from the U.S. embassy in Tokyo to the Department of State, NARA, Record Group 59, Department of State File No. 944/5-2152.

615. Telegram A-400 dated December 21, 1950, from the Department of State to the U.S. embassy in Athens, NARA, Record Group 59, Department of State File No. 611.814/11-2150; Despatch dated August 16, 1954, from the U.S. embassy in The Hague to the Department of State, NARA, Record Group 59, Department of State File No. 611.564/8-1654.

616. Airgram A-55 dated March 27, 1951, from the Department of State to the U.S. embassy in Addis Ababa, NARA, Record Group 59, Department of State File No. 611.754/2-551.

617. Airgram dated June 1, 1950, from Department of State to U.S. embassy in Denmark, NARA, Record Group 59, Department of State File No. 611.594/5-350.

618. Instruction A-306 dated March 18, 1958, from the Department of State to the U.S. embassy in Vienna, NARA, Record Group 59, Department of State File No. 611.634/3-458.

619. Despatch dated April 13, 1959, from the U.S. embassy in Paris to the Department of State, NARA, Record Group 59, Department of State File No. 611.514/4-1359; Despatch dated April 13, 1959, from the U.S. embassy in Paris to the Department of State, NARA, Record Group 59, Department of State File No. 611.514/4-1359.

620. Despatch dated May 20, 1959, from the U.S. embassy in Paris to the Department of State, NARA, Record Group 59, Department of State File No. 611.564/5-2059.

621. Memorandum headed "Memorandum on the Provisions of the Greek Counterdraft," dated July 31, 1950, NARA, Record Group 59, Department of State File No. 611.814/6-250.

622. Despatch No. 914 dated March 11, 1955, from the U.S. embassy in Brussels to the Department of State, NARA, Record Group 59, Department of State File No. 611.554/3-1155; Despatch dated August 16, 1954, from the U.S. embassy in The Hague to the Department of

legally in the country and eligible to work."[623] Similarly, Paragraph 11 of the protocol to the treaty with the Netherlands provided that this provision "shall not be construed to affect the right of the Netherlands to require that aliens may not be employed in the Netherlands unless the appropriate permits have been granted," although regulations relating to the issuance of such permits "shall be applied in a liberal fashion." Article VI(1) of the treaty with France stated that "these persons must fulfil the conditions necessary to the exercise of their calling under the applicable legislation."

Right to Employ Professional Personnel for Internal Purposes

As part of the 1948–1949 revision of the standard draft treaty, the State Department inserted a separate sentence that permitted foreign investors, solely for the internal use of the investors or their enterprises, to hire professionals who did not meet local licensure requirements. For example, the second sentence of Article VIII(1) of the 1955 standard draft treaty provided that "such nationals and companies shall be permitted to engage accountants and other technical experts regardless of the extent to which they may have qualified for the practice of a profession within the territories of such other Party, for the particular purpose of making examinations, audits and technical investigations for, and rendering reports to, such nationals and companies in connection with the planning and operation of their enterprises, and enterprises in which they have a financial interest, within such territories."

This second sentence was incorporated into the standard draft treaty at the recommendation of the Securities and Exchange Commission (SEC) so that American accountants could provide reports that satisfied SEC requirements. Under this sentence, a company desiring to market securities in the United States would have the right to employ accountants familiar with U.S. legislation to prepare reports for submission to the SEC.[624]

State, NARA, Record Group 59, Department of State File No. 611.564/8-1654; Despatch dated March 18, 1954, from the U.S. High Commissioner in Bonn to the Department of State, NARA, Record Group 59, Department of State File No. 611.62A4/3-1854; Despatch dated July 14, 1954, from the U.S. embassy in The Hague to the Department of State, NARA, Record Group 59, Department of State File No. 611.564/7-1454; Telegram A-400 dated December 21, 1950, from the Department of State to the U.S. embassy in Athens, NARA, Record Group 59, Department of State File No. 611.814/11-2150; Instruction A-306 dated March 18, 1958, from the Department of State to the U.S. embassy in Vienna, NARA, Record Group 59, Department of State File No. 611.634/3-458; Despatch dated April 13, 1959, from the U.S. embassy in Paris to the Department of State, NARA, Record Group 59, Department of State File No. 611.514/4-1359.

623. Greece FCN treaty, Article XII(4).

624. Instruction A-306 dated March 18, 1958, from the Department of State to the U.S. embassy in Vienna, NARA, Record Group 59, Department of State File No. 611.634/3-458.

The sentence waived professional qualification requirements in the cases specified. Such cases involved temporary jobs requiring special skills, such as knowledge of U.S. law and accounting methods, for internal management purposes.

The sentence did not create a right to engage in the general practice of a profession in the host country.[625] Indeed, a provision on the right to practice professions that appeared in early U.S. postwar FCN treaties was eliminated after 1953 because the Senate objected to the provision on the ground that it interfered with the prerogative of states to regulate the professions.[626] Thereafter, the U.S. FCN treaties provided no right to practice a profession, apart from the limited right in Article VIII(1).

The Structure of the Employment Provision

The two sentences of Article VIII(1) were linked by the word "moreover." The word was "a convenient connective, and ha[d] no special substantive significance."[627]

Article VIII dealt with the right of the employer to hire certain personnel.[628] Article VII addressed the right of the employee to be hired and the right of the employer to hire on a national treatment and MFN treatment basis.[629]

ENTRY AND SOJOURN

The right of investors to employ managerial and technical personnel of their choice, which was guaranteed by the employment provision, was "illusory" in many countries because indigenous personnel were not available and expatriates could not gain entry.[630] Accordingly, the NFTC urged the State Department to incorporate into the FCN treaties language that would guarantee a right of entry for investors and their personnel,[631] similar to language dating from the 1920s

625. Memorandum dated December 15, 1953, attachment to message dated April 29, 1954, from Carl Boehringer to the Secretary of State, NARA, Record Group 59, Department of State File No. 611.62A4/4-2954; Despatch dated October 19, 1953, from the U.S. High Commissioner in Bonn to the Department of State, NARA, Record Group 59, Department of State File No. 611.62A4/10-1953.

626. Despatch dated August 16, 1954, from the U.S. embassy in The Hague to the Department of State, NARA, Record Group 59, Department of State File No. 611.564/8-1654.

627. Despatch dated March 18, 1954, from the U.S. High Commissioner in Bonn to the Department of State, NARA, Record Group 59, Department of State File No. 611.62A4/3-1854.

628. Despatch dated August 16, 1954, from the U.S. embassy in The Hague to the Department of State, NARA, Record Group 59, Department of State File No. 611.564/8-1654.

629. Ibid.

630. Letter dated June 1, 1948, from E. P. Thomas to Senator Arthur Vandenberg, NARA, Record Group 59, Department of State File No. 611.004/5-350.

631. Ibid.

that authorized the issuance of visas for merchants, known as "treaty trader" or "treaty merchant" visas.[632]

The State Department regarded FCN treaties as an appropriate vehicle for obtaining such a right because of the "direct relation" that these treaties bore to the promotion of foreign investment.[633] The Department noted that

> [t]he primary objective of [FCN] treaties has always been to establish broad general principles under which economic relations between the United States and various other countries are conducted. At first they dealt principally with commercial matters but in response to the need to promote private investment abroad their scope has been expanded in the direction of securing broader rights for American investors in foreign countries, particularly in the establishment, control and management of business enterprises. In view of the direct relation they now bear to the promotion of foreign investments, these treaties would appear to be the proper instruments in which to embody assurances as to the right of entry and sojourn to be enjoyed by American investors in foreign countries.[634]

Gaining entry rights for American investors abroad necessitated as a practical matter that the United States grant reciprocal rights to foreign investors seeking to enter the United States.[635] The State Department, however, was unwilling to include such a right in an FCN treaty in the absence of prior congressional authorization.[636]

In 1951, the Department proposed legislation to authorize the issuance of "treaty investor" visas for aliens seeking to enter the United States to develop or direct an enterprise in which they had invested or were in the process of investing a substantial amount of capital.[637] The State Department's proposed legislation was offered as an amendment to SB 716, a comprehensive immigration bill proposed on January 29, 1951, by Democratic senator Patrick McCarran of Nevada, legislation that would become the Immigration and Nationality Act of 1952.[638]

632. *See generally* Robert Wilson, "'Treaty-Merchant' Clauses in Commercial Treaties of the United States," 44 *American Journal of International Law* 145 (1950); Green Hackworth, *Digest of International Law,* Vol. III (Washington, DC: Government Printing Office, 1942), pages 768–776.

633. Memorandum by Charles H. Sullivan headed "Entry of Foreign Investors into the United States under Treaties of Friendship, Commerce and Navigation," dated November 23, 1949, NARA, Record Group 59, State Department File No. 611.004/5-350.

634. Ibid.

635. Ibid.

636. Letter dated February 7, 1951, from Winthrop Brown to Austin Foster, NARA, Record Group 59, Department of State File No. 611.004/2-751.

637. Ibid.

638. Ibid.

The NFTC endorsed the legislation, arguing that, without entry rights for their personnel, "American business enterprises will continue to labor under a serious disability in foreign countries and may well be deterred from making new investments in areas where vitally needed."[639]

The text of the Department's amendment was drafted by a Senate subcommittee and did not explicitly refer to managerial or technical personnel,[640] although an NFTC representative testifying at the hearing on the legislation had recommended the inclusion of such language.[641] The State Department believed, however, that a "liberal administration" of the law would permit the issuance of visas to such persons.[642]

The 1952 Immigration and Nationality Act became effective on December 24, 1952.[643] Thereafter, the State Department incorporated into its proposed FCN treaties language that would authorize the issuance of visas for nationals of treaty parties who were investing or seeking to invest a substantial amount of capital. For example, Article II(1) of the 1955 standard draft treaty provided that "[n]ationals of either Party shall, subject to the laws relating to the entry and sojourn of aliens, be permitted to enter the territories of the other Party, to travel therein freely, and to reside at places of their choice. Nationals of either Party shall in particular be permitted to enter the territories of the other Party and to remain therein: . . . (b) for the purpose of developing and directing the operations of an enterprise in which they have invested, or which they are actively in the process of investing, a substantial amount of capital."

This entry and sojourn provision did not eliminate the requirement of a visa for entry.[644] Rather, the effect of Article II(1) in U.S. law was to satisfy a statutory requirement under which an alien was able to obtain a treaty investor visa authorized by the 1952 legislation only if he or she was a national of a country with an FCN treaty with the United States that included such a provision.[645] As indicated by

639. Letter dated April 23, 1951, from William S. Swingle to Senator Tom Connally, NARA, Record Group 59, Department of State File No. 611.004/2-751.

640. Letter dated February 7, 1951, from Winthrop Brown to Austin Foster, NARA, Record Group 59, Department of State File No. 611.004/2-751.

641. Wilson, "'Treaty-Investor' Clauses," page 369.

642. Letter dated February 7, 1951, from Director of the Office of International Trade Policy Winthrop Brown to Austin Foster, Chairman of the Treaty Committee of the National Foreign Trade Council, NARA, Record Group 59, Department of State File No. 611.004/2-751.

643. Instruction dated November 2, 1953, from the Department of State to the U.S. High Commissioner in Bonn, NARA, Record Group 59, Department of State File No. 611.62A4/10-653.

644. Enclosure 1 to airgram dated May 3, 1950, from the U.S. embassy in Copenhagen to the Department of State, NARA, Record Group 59, Department of State File No. 611.594/5-350; Airgram dated May 27, 1950, from the Department of State to the U.S. embassy in Copenhagen, NARA, Record Group 59, Department of State File No. 611.594/5-350.

645. Despatch dated March 8, 1954, from the U.S. High Commissioner in Bonn to the Department of State, NARA, Record Group 59, Department of State File No. 611.62A4/3-854.

the language from the 1955 standard draft treaty quoted above, the treaty provision was subject to U.S. immigration laws.[646] Thus, entry rights accorded by the entry and sojourn provision were no broader than those accorded by U.S. law.[647] Treaty investor visas could be granted, however, to aliens from countries the immigration quotas of which were already exhausted.[648]

The treaty investor was entitled to an indefinite stay as long as the status of a treaty investor was maintained.[649] The treaty provided not only for a right of entry, but a right of physical access to the business enterprise.[650] Treaty investor visas entitled the spouse and children of an investor to gain entry.[651] To clarify this, Paragraph 1 of the protocol to the treaty with Germany provided that the spouse and unmarried children of a person permitted entry under a treaty investor visa "shall also be permitted entry if accompanying him or following to join him." Paragraph 2(d) of the protocol to the treaty with France stated that the benefit of entry for a treaty investor extended "to his spouse and minor unmarried children who accompany or next follow to join him."

In addition, under a liberal interpretation of U.S. immigration laws adopted in 1954, treaty investor visas were also available for those "acting in a responsible capacity on behalf of" investors of the same nationality.[652] The State Department and the Immigration and Naturalization Service (INS) recognized that Congress's intent was to facilitate private investment and that most investment was corporate investment.[653] Indeed, as an internal State Department memorandum written in

646. Instruction dated February 6, 1957, from the Department of State to the U.S. embassy in Saigon, NARA, Record Group 59, Department of State File No. 611.51G4/1-2157.

647. Memorandum headed "Explanation of Certain Provisions of U.S. Proposals for Treaty of Amity and Economic Relations with Muscat," enclosure to instruction dated April 17, 1957, from the Department of State to the U.S. consulate general in Dhahran, NARA, Record Group 59, Department of State File No. 611.86E1/4-1757.

648. Ibid.

649. Instruction dated January 21, 1954, from the Department of State to the U.S. High Commissioner in Bonn, NARA, Record Group 59, Department of State File No. 611.62A4/1-854; Memorandum headed "Explanation of Certain Provisions of U.S. Proposals for Treaty of Amity and Economic Relations with Muscat," enclosure to instruction dated April 17, 1957, from the Department of State to the U.S. consulate general in Dhahran, NARA, Record Group 59, Department of State File No. 611.86E1/4-1757.

650. Instruction dated April 17, 1959, from the Department of State to the U.S. embassy in Karachi, NARA, Record Group 59, Department of State File No. 611.90D4/4-259.

651. Despatch dated June 18, 1959, from the U.S. embassy in Paris to the Department of State, NARA, Record Group 59, Department of State File No. 611.514/6-1859.

652. Aide-Memorie attached to despatch dated August 3, 1954, from the U.S. embassy in The Hague to the Department of State, NARA, Record Group 59, Department of State File No. 611.564/8-354; Telegram dated January 21, 1955, from the Department of State to the U.S. embassy in Tehran, NARA, Record Group 59, Department of State File No. 611.884/1-2155.

653. Instruction dated April 17, 1959, from the Department of State to the U.S. embassy in Karachi, NARA, Record Group 59, Department of State File No. 611.90D4/4-259.

1954 observed, "investment is not limited to the interest of the owner of the funds, which is often at most a passive one. It comprehends also the very real and active interest of those responsible for the management of the capital and its transformation into a going economic enterprise. The holders of this interest are for the most part agents or employees, particularly if the principal is a corporation, but their role in the complicated mechanics of modern direct investment is probably more vital, because of their executive or managerial contribution, and their stake in the success of the enterprise as great as that of the inactive financier."[654] Accordingly, the INS issued regulations authorizing treaty investor visas for responsible representatives of an investor.[655] Otherwise, the treaty investor provision might be limited only to those who were investing their own capital.

These INS regulations prompted the inclusion of a new paragraph in the protocol. For example, Paragraph 1 of the protocol to the 1955 standard draft treaty provided that "[t]he provisions of Article II, paragraph 1(b), shall be construed as extending to persons who represent nationals and companies of the same nationality which have invested or are actively in the process of investing a substantial amount of capital in an enterprise in the territories of the other Party, and who are employed by such nationals and companies in a responsible capacity." The term "responsible capacity" referred to persons "responsible for the policy-making decisions affecting control and management."[656] Such language merely clarified, as had always been the intent, that the treaty investor provision applied to corporate investors and to responsible employees as well as to principals.[657]

To be eligible for a treaty investor visa, a person must be an investor, or employed by an investor, who has invested or is in the process of investing a substantial amount of capital. The requirement that the amount be "substantial" was intended to ensure that the provision was not used to circumvent U.S. immigration laws. As the State Department explained,

> The clause initially was proposed with the view of encouraging the international flow of investment capital. Specifically, the intent was to further this objective by facilitating through treaties the entry and indefinite sojourn of persons who wish to engage in worthwhile investment activities in this country but were eligible only for temporary business visitor's visas because their activities did not constitute international trade within the meaning of clause (a) relating to treaty traders. In developing the investor clause and

654. Memorandum of Conversation headed "Granting of Treaty Investor Visas to Responsible Employees of Corporate Investors," dated May 18, 1954, NARA, Record Group 59, Department of State Lot Files, Walter Hollis Papers, Folder marked "Treaty Investor Visas."

655. Instruction dated April 17, 1959, from the Department of State to the U.S. embassy in Karachi, NARA, Record Group 59, Department of State File No. 611.90D4/4-259.

656. Ibid.

657. Instruction dated August 10, 1956, from the Department of State to the U.S. embassy in Brussels, NARA, Record Group 59, Department of State File No. 611.554/8-1056.

> obtaining its acceptance by the appropriate Congressional bodies, particular attention was given to assuring that the clause, if enacted into law, would not become a device to permit individual aliens to circumvent other provisions of the immigration laws. The concern was basically that the investment on which the granting of treaty investor status was based would be genuine and significant. Possibilities of abuse were foreseen through fictitious or dummy operations, small individual investments (e.g., in overcrowded segments of the petty retail trade) cloaking an attempt to evade the quota, and speculative ventures undertaken as a pretext for gaining entry for other purposes
>
> So far as the Department is aware, the specification by Congress of criteria for eligibility to treaty investor status was influenced mainly and perhaps exclusively by considerations of preventing abuse or evasion of the immigration laws.
>
> Substantiality of investment may be viewed in light of this aim; and similarly such corollary tests as the actuality and the enduring character of the investment. So far as is known, Congress did not frame the treaty investor section of the Immigration and Nationality Act with the intention of discouraging particular types of investment or of excluding small investments. What constitutes a substantial amount of investment is a relative matter, depending upon the pattern of investment, the prevailing type of organization and other conditions within the industry in which the individual investment is made. One factor would be whether the size and character of the investment are such as reasonably to require the immediate personal attention of the owner or controller. Size alone, measured in monetary terms, would not necessarily be the decisive factor. A relatively small commitment in terms of dollars might constitute a substantial investment if made in an enterprise engaged in certain technical processes serving a limited market, and where the ratio of necessary technology and skill to capital is high, as, for example, in the grinding of special types of optical lenses or the cutting of diamonds. On the other hand, the substantiality of an investment consisting solely of an inconsequential fractional interest in a large and heavily capitalized enterprise would obviously be open to question under clause (b). Similarly, the investment of a small sum in a common small-scale occupation (e.g., a corner grocery or filling station, a one-man general farm) suggests that the prospective "investor" be considered ineligible under clause (b), as he properly should be seeking entry as an immigrant under the quota.[658]

The entry and sojourn provision was subject to an exception for measures necessary to maintain public order and protect public health, safety, and morals. For example, Article II(4) of the 1955 standard draft treaty stated that "[t]he provisions

658. Instruction dated October 30, 1953, from the Department of State to the U.S. High Commissioner in Bonn, NARA, Record Group 59, Department of State File No. 611.62A4/10-653.

of the present Article shall be subject to the right of either Party to apply measures that are necessary to maintain public order and to protect the public health, morals and safety." This exception, although seemingly unnecessary because the treaty investor provision was subject to the immigration laws of each party, was included to provide a more specific textual basis for monitoring the activities of aliens[659] and for excluding those who were personally undesirable.[660]

The term "public order" referred to the peace and tranquility of the community[661] and was similar to "safety."[662] The term "safety" included "order."[663] The term "public morals" was a less precise concept than "public order," but "public morals" might cover cases involving obscene literature, traffic in narcotics, or the like, where no disturbance of "public order" was involved.[664] Like other treaty provisions, the entry and sojourn provision was also subject to the general exception for measures necessary to protect a party's essential security interests. The term "security" differed from "safety" in that the latter term was considered narrower and "overlap[ed] to some extent considerations of public order."[665] The former term "involve[d] considerations of national defense."[666]

The State Department recognized that the entry and sojourn provision would provide greater benefits to the United States than to other countries because few

659. In some early U.S. postwar FCN treaties, the language explicitly referred to conducting "reasonable surveillance" of the movement of aliens. *See, e.g.*, Italy FCN treaty, Article I(4); Greece FCN treaty, Article II(4).

660. Ireland FCN treaty, Minutes of Interpretation, *Ad Article I, paragraph* 3; Airgram dated May 27, 1950, from the Department of State to the U.S. embassy in Copenhagen, NARA, Record Group 59, Department of State File No. 611.594/5-350; Despatch dated March 8, 1954, from the U.S. High Commissioner in Bonn to the Department of State, NARA, Record Group 59, Department of State File No. 611.62A4/3-854; Instruction dated November 2, 1953, from the Department of State to the U.S. High Commissioner in Bonn, NARA, Record Group 59, Department of State File No. 611.62A4/10-653; Despatch dated April 4, 1957, from the U.S. embassy in Brussels, to the Department of State, NARA, Record Group 59, Department of State File No. 611.554/4-45. *See* section 212 of the Immigration and Nationality Act of 1952, 66 Stat. 182, 8 U.S.C. § 1182 (2012).

661. Airgram dated March 30, 1951, from the Department of State to the U.S. embassy in Athens, NARA, Record Group 59, Department of State File No. 611.814/3-251.

662. Memorandum of Conversation headed "Negotiation of Treaty of Friendship, Commerce and Navigation with Israel," dated November 20, 1950, NARA, Record Group 59, Department of State File No. 611.84A4/11-2050.

663. Memorandum headed "Memorandum on the Provisions of the Greek Counterdraft," dated July 31, 1950, NARA, Record Group 59, Department of State File No, 611.814/6-250.

664. Despatch dated June 11, 1954, from the U.S. High Commissioner in Bonn to the Department of State, NARA, Record Group 59, Department of State File No. 611.62A4/6-1154.

665. Memorandum of Conversation headed "Negotiation of Treaty of Friendship, Commerce and Navigation with Israel," dated November 20, 1950, NARA, Record Group 59, Department of State File No. 611.84A4/11-2050.

666. Ibid.

foreign countries had capital to export.[667] Experience suggested that, because of competition in the U.S. market from domestic enterprises, foreign companies were unlikely to attempt to establish themselves in the U.S. market unless they manufactured products already in high demand in the United States and currently supplied through imports. Thus, the Department anticipated that the number of aliens who would gain admission under the provision would be small.[668] This provision nevertheless did provide an important inducement to the negotiation of an FCN treaty in some instances, such as in the cases of Iran and the Netherlands.[669]

The entry and sojourn provision was the sole provision of the treaty that created entry rights.[670] As a special provision of the treaty, it prevailed over other more general provisions.[671] For example, the employment provision created no entry rights for those persons whose employment was protected by that provision.[672]

JUDICIAL ACCESS

The U.S. postwar FCN treaties guaranteed that nationals and companies of a party would receive non-discriminatory treatment with respect to access to the courts of the other party.[673] For example, Article V(1) of the 1955 standard draft treaty provided that "[n]ationals and companies of either Party shall be accorded national and most-favored-nation treatment with respect to access to the courts of justice and to administrative tribunals and agencies within the territories of the other Party, in all degrees of jurisdiction, both in pursuit and in defense of their rights."

A judicial access provision had appeared in U.S. FCN treaties prior to the war. For example, Article I of the 1934 U.S. FCN treaty with Finland provided that "[t]he nationals of each High Contracting Party shall enjoy freedom of access to the courts of justice of the other on conforming to the local laws, as well as for the prosecution as for the defense of their rights, and in all degrees of jurisdiction

667. Memorandum by Charles H. Sullivan headed "Entry of Foreign Investors in the United States under Treaties of Friendship, Commerce and Navigation," dated November 23, 1949, NARA, Record Group 59, State Department File No. 611.004/5-350.

668. Ibid.

669. This aspect of these negotiations is discussed further in Chapter 7 in the sections on the negotiations with Iran and the Netherlands.

670. Memorandum headed "Explanation of Certain Provisions of U.S. Proposals for Treaty of Amity and Economic Relations with Muscat," enclosure to instruction dated April 17, 1957, from the Department of State to the U.S. consulate general in Dhahran, NARA, Record Group 59, Department of State File No. 611.86E1/4-1757.

671. Instruction dated February 6, 1957, from the Department of State to the U.S. embassy in Saigon, NARA, Record Group 59, Department of State File No. 611.51G4/1-2157.

672. Ibid.

673. The early history of the judicial access provision in U.S. FCN treaty practice is traced in Robert R. Wilson, "Access-to-Courts Provisions in United States Commercial Treaties," 47 *American Journal of International Law*, 20 (1953).

established by law."[674] Thus, the language used prior to the war was phrased in absolute terms, rather than as a right of non-discrimination. Robert Wilson, one of the principal negotiators of U.S. FCN treaties in the mid-1940s, on one occasion suggested that the provisions on access to courts "may . . . possibly" be declaratory of customary law.[675] He later expressed the belief that customary law "supplie[d] the broad proposition" that "aliens should have access to courts," but did not "set out specific procedural requirements which states must meet in order to discharge their legal duty to aliens."[676] Thus, "[b]ilateral treaties afford[ed] a convenient means of supplying the additional assurances desired."[677]

The judicial access provision applied "to all forms of jurisdiction exercised by" the local courts[678] and included the right to initiate actions as well as to defend them.[679] The right of access, however, did not waive requirements for security for costs or for judgments.[680] At the same time, a provision in the protocol clarified that the right of national and MFN treatment extended to security for costs and for judgments as well as to legal aid. For example, Paragraph 2 of the protocol to the 1955 standard draft treaty provided that "[t]he term 'access' as used in Article V, paragraph 1, comprehends, among other things, legal aid and security for costs and judgment."

A further sentence guaranteed that companies of one party not engaged in activities in the territory of the other party nevertheless would have access to courts without a requirement of domestication. For example, Article V(1) of the 1955 standard draft treaty stated that it was understood that "companies of either Party not engaged in activities within the territories of the other Party shall enjoy such access therein without any requirement of registration or domestication." The intent of this sentence was to "assure that corporations of one party that are not doing business within the jurisdiction of the other may sue in the latter's court for such purposes as the protection of patents or trade mark rights or for the collection of debt without having to go through the expensive and time-consuming procedures of registration, etc., that are required of corporations intending to engage in actual business operations there."[681]

674. Treaty of Friendship. Commerce, and Consular Rights, United States-Finland, February 13, 1934, 49 Stat. 2659, TS 868, 4 UST 2047, TIAS 2861.

675. Wilson, *International Law Standard*, page 94.

676. Wilson, *United States Commercial Treaties and International Law*, page 322.

677. Ibid.

678. Despatch dated October 22, 1953, from the U.S. High Commissioner in Bonn to the Department of State, NARA, Record Group 59, Department of State File No. 611.62A4/10-2253.

679. Instruction dated August 21, 1956, from the Department of State to the U.S. embassy in Brussels, NARA, Record Group 59, Department of State File No. 611.554/8-2156.

680. Memorandum of Conversation headed "Treaty of Friendship, Commerce and Navigation with Israel—First Preliminary Discussion," dated May 3, 1950, NARA, Record Group 59, Department of State File No. 611.84A4/5-350.

681. Memorandum headed "Explanation of Certain Provisions of United States Proposals for Treaty of Amity and Economic Relations with Muscat," enclosure to instruction dated April 17,

Several treaties included language guaranteeing an absolute right of access to courts, in addition to the right of non-discrimination already mentioned. These were the early postwar treaties with China and Italy, which were more heavily influenced by U.S. prewar treaty practice than the later FCN treaties, and the treaties based on the short form of the standard draft treaty that was used with certain developing countries, where the United States was sometimes more concerned about inadequacies in the judicial system. As the State Department explained during negotiations with the sultanate of Muscat and Oman, the absolute right of free access was added to the short form of the standard draft treaty "as a safeguard against the possibility that national treatment might be rendered valueless as a standard by harsh and arbitrary requirements imposed on the nationals of the country."[682] Thus, for example, the treaties with Ethiopia, the sultanate of Muscat and Oman, Vietnam, Togo, and Thailand provided that nationals and companies of one party "shall have free access to the courts of justice and administrative agencies" within the territories of the other party.[683] The treaties with China, Italy, and Iran used the term "freedom of access."[684] The treaty with Iran added the further explanatory phrase "to the end that prompt and impartial justice be done."[685]

Further, the treaties based on the short form of the standard draft treaty, again reflecting the greater concern at times about the adequacy of the courts in the countries with which this form of the treaty was used, also required each party to ensure that the "lawful contractual rights" of nationals and companies of the other party were "afforded effective means of enforcement, in conformity with the applicable laws."[686]

COMPETITIVE EQUALITY

The U.S. postwar FCN treaties included a competitive equality provision that was intended to protect foreign investment from unfair competition by

1957, from the Department of State to the U.S. consulate general in Dhahran, NARA, Record Group 59, Department of State File No. 611.86E1/4-1757. *See also* Telegram dated March 2, 1946, from the Department of State to the U.S. embassy in Chongqing, NARA, Record Group 59, Department of State File No. 711.932/3-236.

682. Memorandum headed "Explanation of Certain Provisions of United States Proposals for Treaty of Amity and Economic Relations with Muscat," enclosure to instruction dated April 17, 1957, from the Department of State to the U.S. consulate general in Dhahran, NARA, Record Group 59, Department of State File No. 611.86E1/4-1757.

683. Ethiopia FCN treaty, Article VII(1); Muscat and Oman FCN treaty, Article III(2); Vietnam FCN treaty, Article II(2); Togo FCN treaty, Article III(2); Thailand FCN treaty, Article II(2).

684. China FCN treaty, Article VI(4); Italy FCN treaty, Article V(4); Iran FCN treaty, Article III(2).

685. Iran FCN treaty, Article III(2).

686. Ethiopia FCN treaty, Article VIII(1); Iran FCN treaty, Article VI(1); Vietnam FCN treaty, Article VI(1); Togo FCN treaty, Article VI(1); Thailand FCN treaty, Article III(1).

state-subsidized enterprises.[687] As noted in Article XVIII(2) of the 1955 standard draft treaty, "The parties recognize[d] that conditions of competitive equality should be maintained in situations in which publicly owned or controlled trading or manufacturing enterprises of either Party engage in competition, within the territories thereof, with privately owned or controlled enterprises of nationals or companies of the other Party." Although the provision first appeared in the treaty with Italy,[688] at the suggestion of business interests, the language that appeared in the early treaties was reformulated during negotiations with Greece[689] and that reformulation, with modest changes, became the typical language that appeared, for example, in the 1955 standard draft treaty.

To foster conditions of competitive equality, the treaties required that special economic advantages, such as subsidies or tax exemptions, accorded to state enterprises also be accorded to private enterprises in competition with them. For example, Article XVIII(2) of the 1955 standard treaty draft provided, "Accordingly, such private enterprises shall, in such situations, be entitled to the benefit of any special advantages of an economic nature accorded such public enterprises, whether in the form of subsidies, tax exemptions or otherwise."

This provision was one place in the treaty where foreign-controlled private enterprises were entitled to treatment as favorable as that accorded to the host state's public enterprises. Indeed, this provision potentially guaranteed to foreign-controlled private enterprises more favorable treatment than that accorded to private enterprises controlled by domestic investors.

The United States believed that this provision represented "nothing more than a minimum assurance to private enterprise of fair and equitable competition from public enterprises."[690] More specifically, it was intended to prevent a particular form of indirect expropriation, one that occurred through unfair subsidization of a state-owned competitor. As the United States explained during negotiations with Belgium,

> Some countries have sought to obtain the effect of nationalization by establishing government-controlled enterprises which, because of the competitive advantage derived from state subsidization, could run competing privately owned business enterprises into bankruptcy. Such a process of "creeping confiscation" could enable the government to take over private property without the necessity for following the normal process for expropriation with the payment of just compensation.[691]

687. Instruction dated October 1, 1953, from the Department of State to the U.S. embassy in Managua, NARA, Record Group 59, Department of State File No. 611.174/9-153.

688. *See* Italy FCN treaty, Protocol, Paragraph 2.

689. *See* Greece FCN treaty, Article XIV(2).

690. Instruction dated April 1, 1955, from the Department of State to the U.S. embassy in Seoul, NARA, Record Group 59, Department of State File No. 611.95B4/2-2855.

691. Instruction dated June 21, 1957, from the Department of State to the U.S. embassy in Brussels, NARA, Record Group 59, Department of State File No. 611.554/6-2157. *See also*

The State Department further explained during negotiations with Nicaragua,

> If the government wishes to engage in a normal business pursuit alongside private firms in the same line of business, it should not take advantage of special favors and privileges to the detriment of the private interests. Otherwise it is in position to run the private firms helplessly into bankruptcy. If the government's objective is to occupy a given line to the exclusion of private interests, the proper procedure is expropriation of established enterprises with payment of just compensation.[692]

The competitive equality provision did not prevent the state from nationalizing a sector of the economy or from creating a government monopoly.[693] Rather, it applied to the situation where the state chose to "engage" in competition with private enterprise.[694] Thus, where private enterprise made the choice to compete with an already established state enterprise, the provision would not apply.[695]

Further, the provision applied only to state enterprises in the trading and manufacturing sectors, because these were fields traditionally occupied by private enterprise.[696] The United States believed that, if a government chose

Airgram dated December 26, 1962, from the Department of State to the U.S. embassy in Bangkok, NARA, Record Group 59, Department of State File No. 611.9242/11-1462.

692. Instruction dated October 1, 1953, from the Department of State to the U.S. embassy in Managua, NARA, Record Group 59, Department of State File No. 611.174/9-153. *See also* Instruction dated April 1, 1955, from the Department of State to the U.S. embassy in Seoul, NARA, Record Group 59, Department of State File No. 611.95B4/2-2855; Instruction dated November 6, 1957, from the Department of State to the U.S. embassy in Brussels, NARA, Record Group 59, Department of State File No. 611.554/10-1757; Airgram dated June 1, 1950, from the Department of State to the U.S. embassy in Copenhagen, NARA, Record Group 59, Department of State File No. 611.594/5-350; Airgram dated May 27, 1950, from the Department of State to the U.S. embassy in Copenhagen, NARA, Record Group 59, Department of State File No. 611.594/5-350; Summary Minutes of the Treaty of Amity and Economic Relations Negotiations, January 16 and 17, and February 21, 1963, NARA, Record Group 59, Central Foreign Policy File 1963, Box 3487, File marked " FT—Foreign Trade 2/1/63."

693. Instruction dated October 1, 1953, from the Department of State to the U.S. embassy in Managua, NARA, Record Group 59, Department of State File No. 611.174/9-153. *See also* Instruction dated April 1, 1955, from the Department of State to the U.S. embassy in Seoul, NARA, Record Group 59, Department of State File No. 611.95B4/2-2855; Summary Minutes of the Treaty of Amity and Economic Relations Negotiations, January 16 and 17, and February 21, 1963, NARA, Record Group 59, Central Foreign Policy File 1963, Box 3487, File marked "FT—Foreign Trade 2/1/63."

694. Instruction dated October 1, 1953, from the Department of State to the U.S. embassy in Managua, NARA, Record Group 59, Department of State File No. 611.174/9-153.

695. *See* Airgram dated June 1, 1950, from the Department of State to the U.S. embassy in Copenhagen, NARA, Record Group 59, Department of State File No. 611.594/5-350; Airgram dated May 27, 1950, from the Department of State to the U.S. embassy in Copenhagen, NARA, Record Group 59, Department of State File No. 611.594/5-350.

696. Ibid. *See also* Instruction dated April 1, 1955, from the Department of State to the U.S. embassy in Seoul, NARA, Record Group 59, Department of State File No. 611.95B4/

to enter those traditionally private sectors of the economy, "it is only reasonable that it do so on the same terms as its private competitors."[697] Other sectors, such as finance, communication, and transportation, were not affected by the provision.[698]

Finally, even within the trading and manufacturing sectors, two exceptions existed. As provided in Article XVIII(2) of the 1955 standard draft treaty, "The foregoing rule shall not apply, however, to special advantages given in connection with: (a) manufacturing goods for government use, or supplying goods and services to the Government for government use; or (b) supplying at prices substantially below competitive prices, the needs of particular population groups for essential goods and services not otherwise practically obtainable by such groups." The State Department explained that these exceptions permitted the state to engage in activities such as the operation of a government printing office, the production of license plates, slum clearance, and the provision of low income housing or school lunches for the poor.[699]

The competitive equality provision frequently encountered opposition in negotiations. Although it always attempted to persuade the other party to accept the provision, the United States regarded the provision as "experimental" and agreed to its deletion in a number of instances, such as in the case of treaties with Colombia, Japan, Haiti, Korea, Germany, Ethiopia, France, Togo, and Thailand. The treaty with the Netherlands, at Article XVIII(1), included a special exception permitting either party to make "special concessions in aid of state-owned enterprises as it deems necessary during periods of economic crisis, especially to relieve unemployment."

TRANSPARENCY

The U.S. postwar FCN treaties included a provision that was intended to improve the transparency of trade regulations and that was based on language in the reciprocal trade agreements.[700] Although it was not an investment provision, it

2-2855; Instruction dated November 6, 1957, from the Department of State to the U.S. embassy in Brussels, NARA, Record Group 59, Department of State File No. 611.554/10-1757.

697. Instruction date November 6, 1957, from the Department of State to the U.S. embassy in Brussels, NARA, Record Group 59, Department of State File No. 611.554/10-157.

698. Instruction dated October 1, 1953, from the Department of State to the U.S. embassy in Managua, NARA, Record Group 59, Department of State File No. 611.174/9-153.

699. Ibid. *See also* Instruction dated April 1, 1955, from the Department of State to the U.S. embassy in Seoul, NARA, Record Group 59, Department of State File No. 611.95B4/2-2855; Instruction dated June 21, 1957, from the Department of State to the U.S. embassy in Brussels, NARA, Record Group 59, Department of State File No. 611.554/6-2157; Instruction dated November 6, 1957, from the Department of State to the U.S. embassy in Brussels, NARA, Record Group 59, Department of State File No. 611.554/10-1757.

700. *See, e.g.*, Reciprocal Trade Agreement between the United States of America and Mexico, *signed* December 23, 1942, 57 Stat. 833, 9 Bevans 1109, Article VI.

provided a model for transparency provisions in later U.S. bilateral investment treaties, and thus merits brief attention.

The provision imposed three obligations. First, it required prompt publication of certain trade-related laws. For example, Article XV(1) of the 1955 standard draft treaty provided that "[e]ach Party shall promptly publish laws, regulations and administrative rulings of general application" pertaining to certain trade-related matters.

The word "promptly" meant "with reasonable speed" or "without unnecessary delay."[701] The phrase "administrative ruling of general applicability" referred to "decisions or holdings of binding force enunciated by competent authority in concrete cases . . . such as interpretations of ambiguous portions of law or regulation in particular factual situations."[702] The phrase "general applicability" limited the publication requirement "to rulings that establish significant determinations applicable equally to all like cases, and that are of general public interest as a governing precedent."[703] For example, a ruling that whale meat was dutiable as a fish product would be published if applicable to whale meat as a class, but a finding that a particular consignment was falsely labeled would not be a ruling of general applicability, unless it set significant new standards for determining the falsity of labels.[704] Language that appeared in the minutes of interpretation of the treaty with Ireland explained that the provision was intended to require publication "to enable traders to have the information they legitimately need in order that they may plan their business with foresight."[705] Thus, the provision did not apply to rulings "having to do merely with the internal functioning of the public administration."[706]

Second, the transparency provision delayed the effective date of many trade-related laws. For example, Article XV(1) of the 1955 standard draft treaty provided further that, "[a]s a general matter, new administrative requirements or restrictions affecting imports, with the exception of those imposed on sanitary grounds or for reasons of public safety, shall not go into effect before the expiration of 30 days after publication, or alternatively, shall not apply to products en route at time of publication." This language provided protection against sudden unanticipated changes in the law. A party that regarded 30 days' notice as too demanding was permitted to choose instead to exempt from the change in the law products already en route. The language delaying the effective date of trade-related laws

701. Instruction dated February 15, 1962, from the Department of State to the U.S. embassy in Bangkok, NARA, Record Group 59, Department of State File No. 611.9242/2-1562; Airgram dated November 14, 1962, from the U.S. embassy in Bangkok to the Department of State, NARA, Record Group 59, Department of State File No. 611.9242/11-1462.

702. Letter dated February 13, 1951, from Herman Walker to Semah Hyman, NARA, Record Group 59, Department of State File No. 611.84A4/2-551.

703. Ibid.

704. Ibid.

705. Ireland FCN treaty, minutes of interpretation, *Ad Article XIII, paragraph 1.*

706. Ibid.

did not appear in the early U.S. postwar FCN treaties with China, Italy, Ireland, and Ethiopia. The United States agreed to omit the language from the treaty with Israel[707] and Germany,[708] although the matter was addressed by an exchange of notes in the treaty with Germany. The treaty with the Netherlands specified "a reasonable time, in light of the circumstances."[709] Some of the later treaties merely required that the parties refrain from enforcing new requirements until after public notice, which was the approach taken in the short form of the standard draft treaty, upon which several of the later treaties were based.[710]

Some treaty parties resisted inclusion of Article XV(1) because of the administrative burden that it imposed.[711] Pakistan insisted upon modification of the provision because its policy was not to publicize quotas during severe exchange crises, fearing that publication would cause hoarding, speculation, and price increases.[712]

Third, the treaty required each party to establish an appellate procedure with jurisdiction over customs matters. For example, Article XV(2) of the 1955 standard draft treaty required that a party provide an "appeals procedure" under which nationals, companies, and importers of the other party could obtain "prompt and impartial review, and correction when warranted, of administrative action related to customs matters . . . ." The reference to an "appeals procedure" referred to "redress from a higher or independent authority."[713]

Although the United States never incorporated into the standard draft treaty a parallel provision for investment-related laws or procedures, State Department officials did occasionally demonstrate their belief in the importance of transparency with respect to foreign investment law and policy. As described in Chapter 3, the proposed investment code for the ITO Charter drafted by John Parke Young's working group included provisions on transparency, as did the investment proposals offered by the U.S. delegation during the ITO Charter negotiations in

707. Israel FCN treaty, Article XV(1).

708. Germany FCN treaty, Article XV(1).

709. Netherlands FCN treaty, Article XV(1).

710. *See, e.g.,* Iran FCN treaty, Article IX(1); Vietnam FCN treaty, Article X(1); Togo FCN treaty, Article X(1); Thailand FCN treaty, Article IX(1).

711. *See, e.g.,* Memorandum headed "Fifth Meeting with Indian Officials Regarding Proposed Treaty of Friendship, Commerce and Navigation," dated October 22, 1948, NARA, Record Group 59, Department of State File No. 711.452/10-2248; Memorandum of Conversation dated May 19, 1948, enclosure no. 2 to despatch no. 146 dated May 24, 1948, from the U.S. legation in Dublin to the Department of State, NARA, Record Group 59, Department of State File No. 711.41D2/5-2448.

712. *Current Economic Developments*, November 24, 1959, page 16, NARA, Record Group 59, Department of State Lot Files.

713. Letter dated February 13, 1951, from Herman Walker to Semah Hyman, NARA, Record Group 59, Department of State File No. 611.84A4/2-551.

Geneva. Chapter 6 also described the increased attention to transparency as a way to promote outward investment at the end of the Truman administration.

The importance of transparency was sometimes discussed during FCN treaty negotiations. For example, when India insisted on retaining the right to screen investment, the United States proposed an exchange of notes that would impose some restriction on the process by which permission to establish investment was granted. The proposed notes stated that "the procedures for entertaining applications for such permission will be as simple, expeditious and unified as possible [and] the principles by which the authorities are governed from time to time in reaching decisions on such applications will be announced in order that interested persons may become acquainted with them."[714]

In a letter to U.S. ambassador Loy W. Henderson, John M. Leddy explained the nature of the transparency that the United States believed that treaty parties should provide. In a proper investment climate, screening, he explained, would be conducted "according to a policy, and not capriciously" and investors would "insofar as practicable know what the rules of the game are."[715] Further, "India would remain free to exclude or authorize enterprises for any reason whatever; but there should be a reason, and potential investors should be given some conception of what they face before they go to the trouble of seeking a permit."[716] Moreover,"[p]otential investors should know with whom they have to deal, be put to a minimum of inconvenience, form-filling and buck-passing, and be able to expect definite answers without undue delays."[717] Almost two decades later, FCN treaty negotiators noted that "[i]nvestors wanted to know where they stood when coming into a country and did not want to be exposed to the risk of arbitrary action or harassment."[718]

INTERNATIONAL PEACE AND SECURITY

The U.S. postwar FCN treaties contained an exception for measures necessary to fulfill a party's obligations for the maintenance of international peace and security. For example, Article XXI(1)(d) of the 1955 standard draft treaty provided that "[t]he present Treaty shall not preclude the application of measures . . . necessary to fulfill the obligations of a Party for the maintenance or restoration of international peace and security . . . ."

714. Memorandum headed "Suggested Redraft of India Treaty Provisions to Allow Screening," dated October 6, 1950, NARA, Record Group 59, Department of State File No. 611.914/8-250.

715. Ibid.

716. Ibid.

717. Ibid.

718. Memorandum headed "First Meeting for Discussion of U.S. Draft Treaty of Amity and Economic Relations, April 16, 1969," NARA, Record Group 59, Central Foreign Policy Files 1967–1969, Box 975, Folder marked "FT 4 4/1/68."

This exception was drafted as a reference to obligations under Chapter VII of the United Nations Charter,[719] although Robert Wilson, one of the principal negotiators of FCN treaties during the mid-1940s, understood that the provision applied to obligations undertaken in regional arrangements as well.[720] The State Department identified the action in Korea as an example of a situation to which the exception would apply.[721]

Because the U.N. Charter was a product of World War II, the exception had not appeared in U.S. treaties prior to the war. The language of the exception was based loosely on Article XXI(c) of the GATT, which in turn was based even more loosely on Article 99(1)(c) of the ITO Charter. It rarely was the subject of discussion during negotiations.

ESSENTIAL SECURITY INTERESTS

The U.S. postwar FCN treaties also included an exception for measures necessary to protect a party's essential security interests. For example, Article XXI(1)(d) of the 1955 standard draft treaty provided that "[t]he present Treaty shall not preclude the application of measures . . . necessary to protect [a party's] essential security interests."

This exception applied to both internal and external security measures.[722] The purpose and effect of the exception was "to subordinate treaty principles to [the] paramount responsibility of the state to defend itself and protect public safety."[723] The State Department explained that "[e]very legal system permits [the] state in [the] face [of] imminent peril [to] suspend assurances of [the] rights of [the] individual."[724] By way of illustration, the Department cited examples from U.S. constitutional law.

The exception authorized only those measures "demonstrably related" to essential security interests.[725] Such measures must also be reasonable. As

719. *See, e.g.,* Memorandum by Walter Hollis headed "Economic Sanctions against the Arab States and Israel," dated August 17, 1950, NARA, Record Group 59, Department of State Lot Files, Walter Hollis Papers; Memorandum to the Embassy at Chungking for Use in Negotiating Treaty of Friendship, Commerce and Navigation, NARA, Record Group 59, Department of State File No. 711.932/2-1645.

720. Wilson, *United States Commercial Treaties and International Law,* page 22.

721. Despatch dated February 17, 1954, from the U.S. High Commissioner in Bonn to the Department of State, NARA, Record Group 59, Department of State File No. 611.62A4/2-1754.

722. Telegram dated April 27, 1957, from the U.S. embassy in Saigon to the Department of State, NARA, Record Group 59, Department of State File No. 611.51G4/4-2757.

723. Telegram dated June 14, 1955, from the Department of State to the U.S. embassy in Karachi, NARA, Record Group 59, Department of State File No. 611.90D4/6-1455.

724. Ibid.

725. Telegram dated April 22, 1957, from the Department of State to the U.S. embassy in Saigon, NARA, Record Group 59, Department of State File No. 611.51G4/4-2057.

U.S. negotiators explained during negotiations with the Philippines, the exception "would seem to make it possible for either country to apply reasonable restrictions with respect to military zones."[726] At the same time, the exception was a broad one.[727]

No similar exception appeared in U.S. FCN treaties prior to the war. Such an exception had appeared, however, in some U.S. trade agreements. Article XVII of the U.S. trade agreement with Mexico, for example, provided that "[n]othing in this Agreement shall be construed to prevent the adoption or enforcement of measures . . . relating to public security or imposed for the protection of the country's essential interests in time of war or other national emergency."[728] The reference to "war" was omitted from the FCN treaties because of the postwar security arrangements envisioned in the U.N. Charter.[729]

Following the example of the U.S. trade agreements, the standard draft FCN treaty in use immediately after the war limited the exception to measures taken during time of national emergency that were necessary to protect a party's "essential interests." For example, Article XXV(1)(c) of the 1945 standard draft treaty exempted from treaty obligations measures "necessary for the protection of the essential interests of such High Contracting Party in time of national emergency." Thus, the limitation to national emergencies and the term "essential interests" appeared in the treaties with China and Italy.[730] The term "essential interests" was understood to include national security.[731]

During negotiations, the Philippines proposed that the limitation to national emergencies be expanded to include times of public necessity. The U.S. negotiators "strongly opposed" the change because of the lack of an "objective test of what constitutes 'public necessity.'"[732] The effect of incorporating this phrase thus "might be to allow either party to practice discrimination on the basis of

726. Memorandum of Conversation headed "Preliminary Discussion of United States—Philippine Treaty of Friendship, Commerce and Navigation," dated June 17, 1947, NARA, Record Group 59, Department of State File No. 711.962/6-1747.

727. Summary Minutes of the Treaty of Amity and Economic Relations Negotiations, January 16 and 17, and February 21, 1963, NARA, Record Group 59, Central Foreign Policy File 1963, Box 3487, Folder marked "FT—Foreign Trade 2/1/63."

728. Reciprocal Trade Agreement between the United States and Mexico, *signed* December 23, 1942, 57 Stat. 833, 9 Bevans 1109, Executive Agreement Series 311.

729. Memorandum concerning Draft Treaty of Friendship, Commerce and Navigation, For Use of the Embassy, NARA, Record Group 59, Department of State File No. 711.932/2-1645.

730. China FCN treaty, Article XXVI(1)(d); Italy FCN treaty, Article XXIV(1)(e).

731. Memorandum dated November 19, 1947, headed "The Proposed Lebanese-American Treaty of Friendship, Commerce and Navigation," NARA, Record Group 59, Department of State File No. 711.90E2/11-1947.

732. Telegram dated July 20, 1948, from the U.S. embassy in Manila to the Department of State, NARA, Record Group 59, Department of State File No. 711.962/7-2048.

nationality upon its own decision that there was 'public necessity.'"[733] The United States, in other words, objected to the inclusion of language that would permit either party to be the sole judge of the applicability of the exception. The United States noted that the inclusion of such language would have a "possibly undermining effect on the whole treaty."[734]

To reassure the Philippines about the adequate breadth of the term "national emergency," the U.S. negotiators observed that a national emergency "might not have regard to international situations; that a threat of uprising or an earthquake might be a national emergency."[735] The Philippine negotiators, however, were not entirely reassured. Subsequently, they proposed that the phrase "in time of national emergency" be deleted.[736] The U.S. negotiators objected that "the deletion of this restrictive phrase would make the exception so broad that it would not be acceptable."[737] They added that "national emergency as used in this subparagraph had a physical connotation, such as volcanic eruption or war."[738] It was agreed that a national emergency need not be nationwide, but could include a regional disaster or emergency.[739]

The necessity of proving objectively the applicability of the essential interests exception arose again during internal U.S. government discussions in 1946 concerning whether to initiate negotiations with Brazil. In reviewing the meaning of various treaty provisions, State Department officials noted that, even assuming that a national emergency existed, "it would still be necessary to prove that 'essential interests' require protection."[740]

The ITO Charter proposed by the United States in 1946 included an exception for measures necessary to protect a party's "essential security interests," as opposed to "essential interests," although the exception was applicable only to a

733. Agreed Minutes of Technical Discussions on the Proposed Treaty of Friendship, Commerce and Navigation between the United States of America and the Republic of the Philippines at Manila July 2 to August 24, 1948, NARA, Record Group 59, Department of State File No. 711.962/9-1448.

734. Telegram dated July 20, 1948, from the U.S. embassy in Manila to the Department of State, NARA, Record Group 59, Department of State File No. 711.962/7-2048.

735. Ibid.

736. Agreed Minutes of Technical Discussions on the Proposed Treaty of Friendship, Commerce and Navigation between the United States of America and the Republic of the Philippines at Manila July 2 to August 24, 1948, NARA, Record Group 59, Department of State File No. 711.962/9-1448.

737. Ibid.

738. Ibid.

739. Ibid.

740. Memorandum headed "Twenty-Fifth Meeting to Consider a Tentative Draft Treaty of Friendship, Commerce and Navigation between the United States and Brazil, Held January 11, 1946," NARA, Record Group 59, Department of State File No. 711.322/4-2346.

portion of the Charter. Specifically, Article 32 of the proposed Charter provided that "[n]othing in Chapter IV [relating to international trade] of this Charter shall be construed to prevent the adoption or enforcement by any Member of measures . . . in time of war or other emergency in international relations, relating to the protection of the essential security interests of a Member."[741] Article 49 included a similar exception for the chapter on commodity agreements. As discussed in Chapter 3, during the Preparatory Committee meeting in Geneva, the language of the essential security interests exception was modified in two important respects. First, the language was recast as an exception to all of the obligations of the Charter, not only those relating to trade and commodity agreements. Second, the language was revised to permit a member to take "any action which it consider[ed] necessary for the protection of its essential security interests" where such action related to fissionable materials, traffic in arms or other goods to supply a military establishment or taken in time of war, or other emergency in international relations.[742] Thus, the new language applied to any measure that the member adopting the measure considered necessary for the protection of its essential security interests, provided that other objective conditions were met, such as that the measure be taken in time of war or other emergency in international relations. This language would appear at Article 99(1)(b) of the ITO Charter and, with minor revisions, at Article XXI(b) of the GATT.

During the Geneva Preparatory Committee meeting, representatives of the armed services on the U.S. delegation sought to modify the language so that the applicability of the exception would be determined solely by the party invoking the exception, but they failed because most members of the U.S. delegation feared that other countries would abuse the exception, and believed that the modification would undermine the legally binding nature of the substantive obligations to which the exception applied—the same concerns expressed by State Department officials during FCN treaty negotiations with the Philippines.[743] The U.S. delegation decided that the application of the essential security interests exception in a treaty must not be left to the sole discretion of a treaty party. Thus, although each party had sole discretion under the ITO Charter to determine whether an action was "necessary," that discretion did not extend to determining whether the action met the other conditions of the exception, such as the condition that the action be taken in time of war or other emergency in international relations.

The State Department continued to be concerned about the possible abuse of the exception by other countries. During treaty negotiations in 1948 with Ireland, the United States proposed two modifications to the language of the

741. Department of State, *Suggested Charter for an International Trade Organization of the United Nations* (Washington, DC: Government Printing Office, 1946), page 24.

742. Article 94(b). *Draft Charter for the International Trade Organization of the United Nations*, Department of State Publication 2927, Commercial Policy Series 106 (Washington, DC, Government Printing Office, 1947), page 56.

743. This debate is described in Chapter 3 in the section headed "The Cold War Comes to Geneva."

exception that appeared in its standard draft treaty, which had already been presented to Ireland and which was serving as the basis for negotiations. First, the United States proposed that the phrase "essential interests" be modified to read "essential security interests," bringing the FCN treaty language into conformity with the language of the ITO Charter and the GATT. Second, it proposed that qualifying language limiting the exception to "times of national emergency" be deleted, a change that departed from the language of the ITO Charter and the GATT. Notably, the phrase "it considers," which had been the subject of so much debate within the U.S. delegation during the ITO Charter negotiations, was not incorporated into the treaty with Ireland or into any other FCN treaty. The State Department explained that these changes to the language of the treaty with Ireland were intended to "prevent abuse of this language by certain countries other than Ireland to which this language may be proposed,"[744] thus indicating the reason that the use of self-judging language would have been unacceptable. In any event, as a result of these changes, the language of the U.S. FCN treaty with Ireland would provide that the treaty shall not preclude the application of measures "necessary to protect [a party's] essential security interests," the language that would appear in the standard draft treaty thereafter.

The United States regarded the compromissory clause of the treaty as the ultimate preventative of abuse of the exception.[745] For example, during negotiations, the Philippine negotiators expressed the concern that the exception for measures to fulfill obligations to maintain international peace and security or necessary to protect a party's essential security interests was "rather broadly worded."[746] The U.S. negotiators responded that "disagreements as to the scope of the exception would come under the provisions of Article XXVI," which was the compromissory clause.[747] Thus, the United States understood that the International Court of Justice, rather than a party, would determine whether a measure fell within the exception.

This understanding was consistent with the U.S. understanding of FCN treaty provisions generally. On a number of occasions, other countries during negotiations sought to incorporate language into the treaty that would permit a party, rather than the International Court of Justice, to determine the applicability of some other provision of the treaty. The United States steadfastly refused to permit such language to be included.

For example, Lebanon sought a special "essential interests" exception to the right of national treatment with respect to the acquisition of real property to

744. Airgram from the Department of State to the American legation in Dublin, dated November 15, 1948, NARA, Record Group 59, Department of State File No. 711.41D2/10-2748.

745. The State Department's recognition that the compromissory clause provides protection against abuse of the exception is further discussed below in the section on the compromissory clause.

746. Memorandum of Conversation headed "Preliminary Discussion of United States—Philippine Treaty of Friendship, Commerce and Navigation," dated June 17, 1947, NARA, Record Group 59, Department of State File No. 711.962/6-1747.

747. Ibid.

preserve Lebanese legislation controlling transfers of real property to aliens and entities identified with international political movements considered contrary to Lebanese national security, the tranquility and security of Lebanon's neighbors, or Lebanon's friendly relations with members of the Arab League. Lebanon wished to make clear that it would "primarily" make the determination of what constituted its essential interests and proposed the insertion, following the reference to "essential interests," of the phrase "to be determined solely by the Lebanese Republic."[748] The United States agreed to the exception, but objected to the inclusion of the self-judging language, noting that "the reference to 'essential interests' implicitly carried within it the proposition that a nation primarily determines for itself what its essential interests are" and that the inclusion of the proposed wording could raise doubts concerning the meaning of essential interests exceptions in other treaties.[749] Further, the United States did not wish to be foreclosed from raising objections to "any determination whatsoever that Lebanon might make."[750] Lebanon abandoned its request to include the language, and the two parties agreed to include in the minutes a statement that "[t]he determination of what constitutes 'the essential interests of the Lebanese Republic' is primarily to be made by the Lebanese Republic itself, according to its own judgment and without prior consultation. The presumption is that such determination is correct and valid. However, such presumption is rebuttable; and the United States is entitled to object to any determination that seems clearly arbitrary, untenable or otherwise out of keeping with the mutual understanding of the two High Contracting Parties as to the applicability of the reservation in question. . . . "[751]

The United States during negotiations with Pakistan again objected to self-judging language. The latter country had proposed that the employment provision be amended so that the host country could determine conclusively whether an employee was essential. The United States refused to accept the change because "the technical effect would be to remove the affected provision from the treaty."[752]

When describing the essential security interests exceptions during routine discussions within the United States government, including discussions of the treaties with the Senate, the State Department never described it as self-judging or even mentioned the possibility that it might be.[753] For example, when Republican senator George Aiken of Vermont expressed a concern, during hearings on the

748. Memorandum headed "Proposed Lebanese-American Treaty of Friendship. Commerce and Navigation," dated November 21, 1947, NARA, Record Group 59, Department of State File No. 711.90E2/11-2147.

749. Ibid.

750. Ibid.

751. Ibid.

752. Telegram dated November 27, 1954, from the Department of State to the U.S. embassy in Karachi, NARA, Record Group 59, Department of State File No. 611.90D4/11-2754.

753. *See, e.g.,* Memorandum to the Embassy at Chungking for Use in Negotiating Treaty of Friendship, Commerce and Navigation, NARA, Record Group 59, Department of State File No.

FCN treaty with the sultanate of Muscat and Oman, that a provision in the treaty requiring MFN treatment with respect to the importation of products might preclude the United States from giving preference to the importation of Canadian or Venezuelan oil, Deputy Assistant Secretary of State W. T. M. Beale replied that "there would be no violation of this treaty so long as [the president's] action was taken in accordance with" the national security provision.[754] Presented with an opportunity to reassure the senator that the United States had complete discretion under the national security exception, Beale did not do so. Similarly, during hearings on the treaty with Italy, addressing concerns about the consistency of the treaty with the Trading with the Enemy Act, the State Department submitted a memorandum to the Senate stating, "It is thought that, in most instances, measures taken under the Trading with the Enemy Act would be covered by" the essential interests exception.[755] The State Department did not tell the Senate that the United States would have sole discretion to determine whether a measure fell within the exception and, in fact, the Department seemed to concede that some measures under the act would not be justifiable under the exception. In some instances, State Department officials would determine that a particular measure that the United States proposed to adopt did not fall within the exception.[756] Former FCN treaty negotiators writing in their personal capacities similarly never described the exception as self-judging.[757]

The Negotiations with Germany

The essential security interests exception was the subject of extensive discussion between the United States and Germany. U.S. negotiators explained at the beginning of the discussion that

> No precise delineation or interpretation existed for this expression [(protect . . . essential security interests)] . . . [T]he language had been drafted in such a manner as to leave a wide area of discretion to both parties in order

711.932/2-1645; Memorandum headed "Third Meeting to Consider a Tentative Draft Treaty of Friendship, Commerce and Navigation between the United States and Brazil, Held November 7, 1945," NARA, Record Group 59, Department of State File No. 711.322/4-2346; Letter dated March 18, 1957, from the Secretary of State to the President, *reprinted in Friendship, Commerce and Navigation with China,* Executive J, 80th Cong. 1st Sess. (1947).

754. Transcript of Hearing Before the Committee on Foreign Relations, April 7, 1959, pages 36–37, NARA, Record Group 46, File No. SEN86B-B7.

755. *Proposed Treaty of Friendship, Commerce and Navigation between the United States and the Italian Republic,* Hearings Before a Subcommittee of the Committee on Foreign Relations, April 30, 1948, 80th Cong. 2d Sess. (1948), page 3.

756. *See, e.g.,* Memorandum by Walter Hollis headed "Economic Sanctions Against the Arab States and Israel," dated August 17, 1950, NARA, Record Group 59, Department of State Lot Files, Walter Hollis Papers.

757. *See, e.g.,* Wilson, *United States Commercial Treaties and International Law,* pages 22–23.

> to allow for necessary action over an indefinite future. . . . [N]o serious consequences were expected from this reservation so long as the relations between both countries remained friendly . . .[758]

Thus, the exception granted the parties wide, but not sole, discretion. The State Department "stressed [that] the words 'necessary' and 'essential' had been added to emphasize that the reservation was not to be invoked in a frivolous manner."[759]

The German negotiators stated that they were glad to hear the last point, "as they did not believe a security reservation ought to be made the excuse for economic measures not genuinely based on real security considerations.[760] Thus, Germany, like the United States, feared abuse of the exception and wanted to ensure that the treaty language imposed limitations on the invocation of the exception.

The German negotiators "then asked whether the clause was justiciable." As it happened, the negotiations with Germany were occurring only a few months after the Senate had taken action on several FCN treaties concluded during the early 1950s. As discussed below in greater detail, during the Senate debate on those treaties, Republican senator Bourke Hickenlooper of Iowa, the chairman of the Committee on Foreign Relations, had made a passing reference to the importance of the essential security interests exception and the latitude that it allowed the parties. U.S. negotiators apparently were anxious to avoid taking a position that would endanger the support of Senator Hickenlooper, and drew the attention of the German negotiators to those remarks. They then declined to answer the question directly. The U.S. team "replied that offhand it knew of no international court precedents, but believed national as well as international courts would probably give very heavy weight to arguments presented by the government invoking the reservation and would have difficulty in finding a justiciable issue." Both sides then noted that they knew of no precedents on this point in the national courts of their countries, and concurred that the question would tend to be regarded as "political" rather than "legal" by the national courts. Thus, neither the United States nor Germany claimed that the exception was intended to confer nonreviewable discretion on the party invoking it. Rather, the United States speculated that national and international courts would "probably" give "very heavy weight" to the arguments of a party invoking the provision and both parties concurred that national courts in particular might well find issues raised by the exception to be nonjusticiable.[761]

Next, in response to a question from the German negotiators, the United States said that the reservation would justify a ban on the export of strategic materials. The U.S. negotiators did not say that a party would have sole discretion to

758. Despatch dated February 17, 1954, from the U.S. High Commissioner in Bonn to the Department of State, NARA, Record Group 59, Department of State File No. 611.62A4/2-1754.

759. Ibid.

760. Ibid.

761. Ibid.

determine whether the ban was within the exception. The U.S. negotiators went on to note that such a ban would not violate the treaty in any event as long as it was non-discriminatory.[762] After hearing these explanations, the German negotiators accepted the essential security interests exception.

This was not the only provision with respect to which Germany raised the issue of justiciability. The German negotiators indicated that Germany did not want to submit to arbitral review any decision that it made to impose exchange controls.[763] Thus, although the German negotiators merely inquired about the justiciability of the essential security interests exception, they sought to ensure that disputes arising under the provision on exchange controls would not be justiciable.

The United States replied, just as it did in the case of the essential security interests exception, by suggesting that legal bodies would have difficulty finding a justiciable issue under the provision on exchange controls. U.S. negotiators explained that Article XII(3), which prescribed how foreign exchange must be allocated during periods when exchange controls were in place, was "framed in terms [of] economic value judgments which cannot easily lead to [a] justiciable dispute within [the] competence [of the] legal body under Article XXII, paragraph 2 to decide."[764] Article XXII(2), of course, was the compromissory clause, which provided for the resolution of disputes concerning the interpretation or application of the treaty either by an arbitral tribunal or the International Court of Justice.

Once again emphasizing the difficulty of finding a justiciable issue under the provision on exchange controls, the State Department further explained that "[t]o be referrable [*sic*] to the Court, a dispute must be justiciable; that is, it must present a *legal* issue which is susceptible of settlement by a court of law. Assuming, as must be assumed until the contrary is clear, a good faith endeavor to carry out a treaty obligation, it is only upon an extreme set of facts indeed that a justiciable dispute could conceivably arise over paragraph 3 of Article XII, since that paragraph is framed basically in terms of value judgments and economic appraisals rather than of precise legal standards."[765]

The Department reiterated once more the difficulty of finding a justiciable issue, saying that "it is difficult to visualize as a practical matter how the Court could find a justiciable issue, within its competence to decide, over the reasoned policy judgment the German government would exercise in choosing, in a given set of economic facts and appraisal, whether to (a) devalue the currency, (b) embark on a domestic deflation, or (c) institute exchange restrictions . . . for it is not a judicial function to make economic policy judgments or to choose between tenable

762. Ibid.

763. Telegram dated September 20, 1954, from the U.S. High Commissioner in Bonn to the Department of State, NARA, Record Group 59, Department of State File No. 611.62A4/4-2054.

764. Instruction dated September 23, 1954, from the Department of State to the U.S. High Commissioner in Bonn, NARA, Record Group 59, Department of State File No. 611.62A4/9-2354.

765. Ibid. (emphasis in original).

theories as to what is the most efficacious approach to dealing with an economic problem."[766]

The German negotiators, however, still were not reassured. They proposed amending the treaty text to incorporate what they described as a "subjective" test under which each party would have the sole discretion to determine whether to impose exchange controls.[767] Specifically, Germany proposed to insert a provision that read, "Should either Party consider it necessary to impose exchange restrictions with respect to the other Party it will remove them as rapidly as it considers its economic position makes this possible."[768] The German negotiators explained that the purpose of their language was "to make the decision concerning the application and removal of exchange controls a subjective one rather than an objective one which could be the subject of arbitration."[769] The German delegation believed that the U.S, language was "too objective," and therefore proposed the insertion of the phrase "it considers."[770]

The German negotiators had gone too far. Although U.S. negotiators were willing to suggest in negotiations that certain issues might not be justiciable, they refused to incorporate language into the treaty text that would foreclose judicial review. Thus, the U.S. negotiators objected to addition of the phrase "it considers" on the ground that addition of the phrase would make the determination "unilateral" and "in effect nullify the paragraph."[771] They opposed "unnecessary linguistic departures" from the treaty text that would raise questions of interpretation.[772] They compared the discussion of the exchange controls provision with the discussion of the essential security interests exception, where the language had not been changed, while "pointing out how important [the security exception] was to the United States." [773] In other words, the United States had not insisted that the application of the essential security interests exception be within a party's sole discretion, and Germany therefore should not make the same demand with respect to the exchange controls provision. The United States insisted that the final wording of the article must allow the "tenability of [the] economic rationale motivating restrictions to be open to examination."[774] In the face of these arguments, the German negotiators agreed to omit the "subjective" test.

766. Ibid.

767. Minutes of the Second Meeting of the Working Group on Article III, NARA, Record Group 59, Department of State File No. 611.62A4/10-554.

768. Ibid.

769. Ibid.

770. Ibid.

771. Ibid.

772. Ibid.

773. Ibid.

774. Instruction dated September 23, 1954, from the Department of State to the U.S. High Commissioner in Bonn, NARA, Record Group 59, Department of State File No. 611.62A4/9-2354.

Ultimately, however, the United States agreed to a compromise whereby the chiefs of the two delegations exchanged letters "of explanation" that were not to be ratified as part of the treaty[775] and that were not shown to the U.S. Senate or otherwise made publicly available until the negotiating history of the treaty was declassified. The letters stated that a party's decisions in connection with the second sentence of Article XII(3) were "not appropriate for judicial review" under the compromissory clause.[776] The United States did not believe that issues arising under Article XII(3) were inherently nonjusticiable, but rather that, given the economic value judgments required by that paragraph, justiciable issues would arise only in extreme cases.[777]

A similar discussion occurred with respect to Article XI of the treaty with Germany, dealing with matters of taxation. Article XI(4) imposed restrictions on the extent of taxation of companies and non-resident nationals of the other party. The German negotiators noted that the consequences of Article XI(4) could not be foreseen and expressed concern that controversies might arise that would be referred to the International Court of Justice. Once again, the U.S. negotiators attempted to allay German concerns by professing that yet another provision of the treaty might raise nonjusticiable issues. The United States delegation replied that "the emergence of a justiciable dispute over paragraph 4 was not easy to visualize."[778]

As the negotiations with Germany illustrate, the United States in multiple instances acknowledged that some issues arising under various provisions of the treaty might be treated by a court as nonjusticiable. It invariably refused, however, to insert into the treaty any language that would declare, or render, an issue nonjusticiable, such as language giving a party sole discretion to determine the applicability of a treaty provision.

The Negotiations with the Netherlands

The Netherlands was also concerned about abuse of the essential security interests exception. During negotiations in February 1955, a year after the negotiations with Germany, the Dutch negotiators informed the U.S. team that they intended to propose new language that "would emphasize that security measures were to be taken only in exceptional circumstances for reasons of genuinely vital concern, and were

775. Memorandum headed "Summary Record of the Third Meeting of the Working Group on Article XII," dated October 11, 1954, NARA, Record Group 59, Department of State File No. 611.62A4/10-554: Minutes of the Third Meeting of the Working Group on Article XII dated October 11, 1954, NARA, Record Group 59, Department of State File No. 611.62A4/10-554.

776. Letter dated October 28, 1954, from Thorsten V. Kalijarvi to Dr. Walter Becker, NARA, Record Group 59, Department of State File No. 611.62A4/10-2854.

777. Instruction dated September 22, 1954, from the Department of State to the U.S. High Commissioner in Bonn, NARA, Record Group 59, Department of State File No. 611.62A4/9-2354.

778. Despatch dated March 8, 1954, from the U.S. High Commissioner in Bonn to the Department of State, NARA, Record Group 59, Department of State File No. 611.62A4/3-854.

not to be prolonged any longer than the circumstances calling for them existed."[779] The Dutch negotiators said that they wanted to emphasize that the security reservation "ought to be strictly construed so as not to open it to abuses."[780]

The U.S. negotiators "indicated that they concurred in the thought that this reservation was to be used for serious reasons, and was not intended to be a loophole through which arbitrary actions would or could be taken so as to defeat the purposes of the Treaty."[781] Still recalling, however, Senator Hickenlooper's remarks from some 18 months before, they emphasized, that the presence in the Treaty of an "ample security reservation" was "deemed essential" by the United States. [782]

The U.S. negotiators then attempted to persuade the Dutch negotiators that the treaty language should be left unchanged. They "added that they could see no advantage whatsoever in trying to elaborate on the present wording, and that any attempt to elaborate on it would give rise to misapprehensions lest its scope was being narrowed to the detriment of the United States to take the measures it might consider essential or vital to national security."[783] The Senate had accepted the existing language, and thus any change could pose an obstacle to Senate advice and consent to ratification.

The U.S. negotiators explained the importance of the exception to the United States. They "stressed that there must not be the slightest implication that the United States is committing itself to abandon any of the present security controls, even though it is unlikely that these controls are actually inconsistent with any of the provisions of the Treaty as regards U.S.-Netherlands relations."[784] They "emphasized that each Party would have to determine, according to its own discretion, what was essential from the viewpoint of its security interests."[785] The Dutch negotiators "said that they did not question the proposition that each Party would have to make its own determinations, but that they wanted to lay down some 'guide posts.' "[786]

Ultimately, the U.S. negotiators agreed to draft language that would satisfy the desire of the Dutch to ensure that the exception was not abused. They proposed a draft consisting of two sentences, the first of which reflected the Dutch concern and the second of which reflected the U.S. concern. During discussion of the language, the Dutch negotiators sought to ensure that "primary emphasis" was given to the first sentence.[787] The language originally was included in minutes

779. Despatch dated September 15, 1954, from the U.S. embassy in The Hague to the Department of State, NARA, Record Group 59, Department of State File No. 611.564/9-1554.

780. Ibid.

781. Ibid.

782. Ibid.

783. Ibid.

784. Ibid.

785. Ibid.

786. Ibid.

787. Ibid.; Despatch dated February 17, 1955, from the U.S. embassy in The Hague to the Department of State, NARA, Record Group 59, Department of State File No. 611.564/2-1755.

of interpretation, but later in the negotiation the Dutch negotiators, wishing to follow the approach in the U.S. FCN treaty with Germany (where no minutes of interpretation had been used), proposed that the minutes of interpretation be abandoned and that certain items from the minutes be included in the protocol.[788] The U.S. negotiators again objected to changing the language of the treaty, preferring to leave the essential security interests exception as it appeared in the standard draft treaty. Ultimately, however, the United States "acceded to the Dutch wish on the theory that, although the first sentence represented the Dutch interest, the second sentence set forth a principle to which the Senate attached great importance, as exemplified by the floor debate accompanying the Senate vote on the eight treaties which passed July 21, 1953."[789]

The language to which the two parties eventually agreed was incorporated at Paragraph 18 of the protocol. It stated, "With reference to Article XXII, paragraph 1(d), it is understood that it is not the purpose of the security reservation to create a basis for unduly prolonged departures from any provision of the Treaty. On the other hand, each Party determines, according to its own best judgment, the measures deemed necessary to protect its essential security interests."

The language inserted by the United States into its FCN treaty with the Netherlands to the effect that "each Party determines, according to its own best judgment, the measures deemed necessary to protect its essential security interests" was similar to language used by the United States to refer to the application of various other provisions of the treaty as well. The United States commonly said that each party was authorized to determine in its own judgment whether a measure was consistent with the treaty. When the United States used this language, however, it did not mean to foreclose a challenge by one party to a determination by the other party. Rather, the United States meant merely that each party made the initial determination of whether a measure was consistent with the treaty, but that the other party was entitled to challenge that determination through consultations or adjudication before the International Court of Justice.

For example, during negotiations with India, the State Department noted that the Indian negotiators frequently had asked whose judgment would prevail in interpreting specific treaty provisions. In response, the Department explained that each Party "has [the] right to make its own initial interpretation.... Differences which may arise can, as a rule, be handled amicably through consultation. Of course, any difference which cannot be so settled may be handled under [the compromissory] provision."[790]

Similarly, during negotiations with Ethiopia, the U.S. embassy suggested to the State Department that it inform the Ethiopian government that the provisions of the treaty would not prevent Ethiopia from "building up reserves it may consider

788. Ibid.

789. Ibid.

790. Airgram A-126 dated April 11, 1949, from the Department of State to the U.S. embassy in New Delhi, NARA, Record Group 59, Department of State File No. 711.452/4-1149.

adequate for servicing its [foreign] obligations."[791] The State Department replied to the embassy that "[u]nder [the] treaty each party [would] make [its] own determination of adequacy in light of [the] treaty provisions. [The o]ther party however [would] have [the] right to question such determination. [The b]urden of proof [would] be on [the] complaining party."[792] The Department also admonished the embassy not to use the words "it may consider."[793]

As noted above, the United States and Lebanon agreed to include in the minutes of their negotiation a statement that "[t]he determination of what constitutes 'the essential interests of the Lebanese Republic' is primarily to be made by the Lebanese Republic itself, according to its own judgment and without prior consultation. The presumption is that such determination is correct and valid. However, such presumption is rebuttable; and the United States is entitled to object to any determination that seems clearly arbitrary, untenable or otherwise out of keeping with the mutual understanding of the two High Contracting Parties as to the applicability of the reservation in question. . . ."[794]

During the negotiation of the treaty with Haiti, in discussing the provision on exchange controls, the State Department explained that "each country has full primary discretion to determine whether exchange restrictions are necessary according to its own estimate of what the situation requires . . . . This is not to say, however, that the other country waives its right to question or to raise objections to the imposition of particular restrictions . . . ."[795]

During negotiations with Japan regarding the exchange controls provision, the United States explained that "[t]he presumption in treaty commitments is that each country acts to live up to its treaty obligations; but this presumption, while a strong one, is rebuttable and may be contested in the case of a particular action which the other country has good reason to believe improper."[796] Thus, for example, the adequacy of its foreign exchange reserves initially was "for each country to determine" although the determination must not be capricious and must conform to the provisions of the treaty.[797] Japan sought language in the protocol that

791. Telegram dated July 27, 1951, from the U.S. embassy in Addis Ababa to the Department of State, NARA, Record Group 59, Department of State File No. 611.754/7-2451.

792. Telegram dated July 31, 1951, from the Department of State to the U.S. embassy in Addis Ababa, NARA, Record Group 59, Department of State File No. 611.754/7-2451.

793. Ibid.

794. Memorandum headed "Proposed Lebanese-American Treaty of Friendship. Commerce and Navigation," dated November 21, 1947, NARA, Record Group 59, Department of State File No. 711.90E2/11-2147.

795. Airgram A-104 from the U.S. embassy in Port-au-Prince to the State Department, dated January 16, 1953, NARA, Record Group 59, Department of State File No. 611.384/12-2352.

796. Airgram dated May 22, 1952, from the Department of State to the U.S. Political Adviser in Tokyo, NARA, Record Group 59, Department of State File No. 611.944/4-3052.

797. Ibid.

would authorize exchange restrictions that a party "considered necessary" to protect its monetary reserves. The United States objected to the word "considered" because the word could be interpreted "to the effect that it renders all decisions and determinations of a Party immune to challenge by the other Party, no matter how arbitrary and unjustifiably adverse to the latter's interests. It [was] not the Department's purpose that any part of either Party's performance under the exchange control article should be excluded from consultation; or that it should be a matter in respect to which either Party has the unique right of determining unilaterally its definitive treaty obligations in the extreme event that a serious dispute arose over what those obligations were."[798]

During negotiations with Iran concerning Article VII, dealing with exchange controls, Iran proposed the insertion of the phrase "in its own judgment" to indicate that each party would be the sole judge of whether exchange restrictions were consistent with the treaty. As it always did, the United States objected to treaty language that would give a party sole discretion. The State Department responded that "the procedure applicable to the treaty as a whole would apply to Article VII. Each party would be free to make its own judgment whether contemplated actions on its part were consistent with the provisions of the treaty."[799] For this reason, the State Department said, the insertion of the phrase "in its own judgment" would be "superfluous."[800] Moreover, the Department added, the phrase was "undesirable in that its inclusion could be construed to imply that a country could exercise unilateral judgment to the point of excluding the right of the other party to consult."[801] The U.S. delegation went on to observe that "the other party would be free to question and consult if it considered the treaty to be improperly interpreted or applied."[802]

Egypt, during negotiations, wished to add the phrase "it considers" to the provision on exchange controls. The U.S. embassy objected that the addition of the phrase "would practically destroy the value of the provision."[803] The Egyptian negotiators explained that Egypt did not want decisions concerning its foreign exchange control policy to be made bilaterally. The U.S. negotiators replied that "it was inherent in the treaty, applicable to Article 13, but to the other articles as well, that each party has full primary discretion to make determinations according to

798. Airgram dated January 9, 1953, from the Department of State to the U.S. Political Adviser in Tokyo, NARA, Record Group 59, Department of State File No. 611.944/1-953.

799. Instruction dated November 10, 1954, from the Department of State to the U.S. embassy in Tehran, NARA, Record Group 59, Department of State File No. 611.884/11-1054.

800. Ibid.

801. Ibid.

802. Ibid.

803. Despatch dated July 16, 1951, from the U.S. embassy in Cairo to the Department of State, NARA, Record Group 59, Department of State File No. 611.744/7-1651. *See also* Memorandum attached as enclosure 1 to despatch dated March 13, 1952, from the U.S. embassy in Cairo to the Department of State, NARA, Record Group 59, Department of State File No. 611.744/3-1352.

its own best estimate of what the situation requires, in the light of the provisions of the treaty, without having to obtain the advice or consent of the other party."[804] The United States adamantly refused, however, to include self-judging language, and Egypt acquiesced.[805]

Costa Rica, during its negotiation with the United States, proposed language that would have given it sole discretion to determine whether to impose exchange controls. The State Department objected, saying that such language was superfluous because it was implicit that Costa Rica had discretion to decide whether to impose controls. U.S. negotiators added, however, that "if action taken by Costa Rica were of a kind which the United States considered to be in violation of the provisions of this paragraph, it would be entitled to seek the same remedies that it would seek in the event of a violation of any other provision of the treaty."[806] Thus, the United States refused to accept language that would give Costa Rica sole discretion.

During negotiations with Germany with respect to Article XII on exchange controls, John Parke Young explained that "in normal practice a party applies the treaty to situations that arise using its own judgment in making determinations. . . ."[807] The other party, if it disagreed with the manner in which the treaty was being applied, could require consultations. Young told the German negotiators that the United States wanted to ensure that in making its determinations a party would be "guided by certain principles" and would not act arbitrarily.[808] Young said that the United States objected to language that would render a decision "unilateral" and "in effect nullify the paragraph."[809]

Senate Deliberations

The essential security interests exception, as already noted, was discussed briefly on the Senate floor on July 21, 1953, during Senate consideration of the FCN

804. Despatch dated July 16, 1951, from the U.S. embassy in Cairo to the Department of State, NARA, Record Group 59, Department of State File No. 611.744/7-1651. *See also* Memorandum attached as enclosure 1 to despatch dated March 13, 1952, from the U.S. embassy in Cairo to the Department of State, NARA, Record Group 59, Department of State File No. 611.744/3-1352.

805. Despatch No. 2401 dated May 28, 1952, from the U.S. embassy in Cairo to the Department of State, NARA, Record Group 59, Department of State File No. 611.744/2-2852. *See also* Memorandum attached as enclosure 1 to despatch dated March 13, 1952, from the U.S. embassy in Cairo to the Department of State, NARA, Record Group 59, Department of State File No. 611.744/3-1352.

806. Memorandum headed "Negotiation of Treaty of Friendship, Commerce and Navigation with Costa Rica: First Meeting," dated June 25, 1951, NARA, Record Group 59, Department of State File No. 611.184/6-2551.

807. Minutes of the Second Meeting of the Working Group on Article III, NARA, Record Group 59, Department of State File No. 611.62A4/10-554.

808. Ibid.

809. Ibid.

treaties with Denmark, Ethiopia, Greece, Israel, and Japan and the supplemental agreement with Italy. Republican senator Bourke Hickenlooper of Iowa, the chairman of the Committee on Foreign Relations, observed that "[t]hese treaties have been formulated in such manner as to avoid any interference with or qualifications of the right of the United States to apply such security measures as it may find necessary. . . . Each of the treaties, as below indicated, contains a general reservation making it clear that nothing in the treaty shall be deemed to affect the right of either party to apply measures 'necessary to protect its essentials security interests.'. . . . I make that clear because we were especially zealous to see that these treaties in no way offended or destroyed our inherent right to make such regulations or to continue such regulations for our own internal security as we felt were justified. By the same token, the other countries have the same right."[810]

Although Senator Hickenlooper's observation in two instances that the exceptions would permit the United States to apply such measures "as it may find necessary" or "as we felt were justified" could be read to mean that he thought that the United States was the sole judge of whether a measure was necessary, it does not seem likely that such was his intended meaning. First, such an interpretation of the exception would constitute a major derogation from the compromissory clause and provide other countries with an easy way to escape any of their obligations under the treaty, and yet he noted none of these consequences. Second, on one of the three occasions when Senator Hickenlooper was describing the exception, the occasion when he was drawing the attention of the Senate to the precise language of the provision, he did not say in that instance that the exception applied to any measures that the United States considered necessary. Third, when U.S. negotiators, during negotiations with Germany and the Netherlands, referred to Senator Hickenlooper's comments, they did not say that the Senate believed that each party had sole discretion to determine the applicability of the exception, but instead spoke about the latitude afforded by the exception. In other words, the State Department did not appear to believe that Senator Hickenlooper thought that the exception was self-judging. Thus, it seems more likely that Senator Hickenlooper's use of those phrases was just his manner of speaking. He used those phrases on two occasions and not on a third occasion. The United States presumably would have no reason to apply a measure that it did *not* think was necessary or justified, and thus the only measures that he had to address in his remarks were those that the United States thought necessary or justified. No other measures needed to be excepted from treaty obligations, and so he had no reason to assure the Senate that other such measures were excepted from treaty obligations. If Senator Hickenlooper did believe that the exception was self-judging, his belief was not based on any communication from the State Department, insofar as can be ascertained, and was not consistent with how the exception was portrayed by the State Department to the Senate, to other treaty parties, or in its internal discussions.

810. 99 *Congressional Record* 9315–9316 (1953).

In any event, seven years later, during Senate consideration of the FCN treaties with France and Pakistan in 1960, the chairman of the Senate Foreign Relations Committee addressed the issue explicitly and made clear that a party's determination under any provision of an FCN treaty was in fact subject to review by the International Court of Justice. The issue arose when Democratic senator Strom Thurmond of South Carolina asked the chairman of the Senate Foreign Relations Committee, Democratic senator J. William Fulbright of Arkansas, to confirm that the two treaties contained a provision under which disputes concerning the interpretation or application of the treaties that were not settled through diplomacy would be submitted to the International Court of Justice. Senator Fulbright confirmed that understanding. Senator Thurmond then summarized the implications, noting, "In other words, the dispute would be referred to the International Court of Justice, and any party signatory to the treaty would not have the right to use its own judgment if it saw fit."[811] Senator Fulbright responded by reading the compromissory clause of the convention with France. Senator Thurmond pressed his point that the Court, not the parties themselves, would determine conclusively the interpretation and application of treaty provisions, saying, "So, the parties would be bound by the decision of the International Court of Justice. A country could not make its own decision, under this convention, if it failed to settle a dispute by normal diplomatic means."[812] Senator Fulbright concurred: "The parties are bound, under the convention, to submit the dispute to the International Court of Justice."[813] Senator Thurmond asked whether this statement applied to both treaties, and Senator Fulbright confirmed that it did. Moments later, both senators voted in favor of the resolution granting Senate advice and consent to ratification of the two treaties, a resolution that passed by a vote of 94-1.[814] Although Senator Hickenlooper was on the floor during the discussion and voted in favor of both treaties, he did not take exception to Senator Fulbright's explanation or deny that the Court had the ultimate authority to decide issues arising under the essential security interests exception. This understanding of the Court's jurisdiction was reaffirmed the following year, during Senate consideration of the FCN treaties with Belgium and Vietnam, when Republican senator Alexander Wiley of Wisconsin, just prior to a unanimous Senate vote approving both treaties, placed in the record a memorandum stating that, "if any dispute regarding any provision of these conventions arises as between the parties, and if such dispute is not satisfactorily settled by other means, the dispute shall be submitted to the International Court of Justice."[815] The memorandum identified no exceptions.

811. 106 *Congressional Record* 15418 (1960).

812. Ibid.

813. Ibid.

814. Ibid.

815. 107 *Congressional Record* 18878 (1961). These deliberations are discussed in more detail in Chapter 7 in the section on Senate advice and consent to ratification in 1961.

After some 15 years of considering FCN treaties, the Senate understood, as did the State Department, that the International Court of Justice, rather than a party, had the power to determine all questions relating to the interpretation or application of the treaty.

Application to Specific Circumstances

On a very few occasions, during negotiations, one party inquired of the other party whether a particular measure would be justified by the essential security interests exception. In no case did the United States or the other party suggest that a party would have sole discretion to make that determination. For example, as already noted above, during negotiations with the Philippines, U.S. negotiators explained that the exception "would seem to make it possible for either country to apply reasonable restrictions with respect to military zones."[816] The United States did not say that the matter was within the sole discretion of a party to determine.

Argentina inquired whether an Argentine law prohibiting aliens from owning real estate within 40 kilometers of the border would fall within the essential security interests exception. The State Department replied that a specific exception for this law should be included in the treaty because it would not normally fall within the national security exception.[817]

Dutch negotiators described a Dutch law that permitted the military authorities to seize property during a war and not make payment until after the war. The Dutch negotiators said that they believed that such an action would be justified under the essential security interests exception, but asked for the views of the United States.[818] The U.S. negotiators responded that the exception "would undoubtedly allow a certain amount of flexibility in the modalities of payment, in a war emergency; but the security reservation would not be regarded as derogating from the basic principle that compensation would be due and payable."[819]

Later, during the same negotiating session, the Dutch negotiators stated that they wished to include a provision under which enemy property seized during wartime would be returned to the owners once the "enemy taint" had been "purged."[820] The U.S. negotiators responded that the essential security interests exception "would in effect give the U.S. authorities latitude to do what they

816. Memorandum of Conversation headed "Preliminary Discussion of United States—Philippine Treaty of Friendship, Commerce and Navigation," dated June 17, 1947, NARA, Record Group 59, Department of State File No. 711.962/6-1747.

817. Memorandum headed "Discussion of U.S. Revised Draft of FCN Treaty with Argentines," dated May 8, 1950, NARA, Record Group 50, Department of State File No. 611.354/5-850.

818. Despatch dated September 8, 1954, from the U.S. embassy in The Hague to the Department of State, NARA, Record Group 59, Department of State File No. 611.564/9-854.

819. Ibid.

820. Ibid.

considered necessary in wartime on this subject."[821] They added that the vesting of enemy property "was a highly involved subject," and suggested that the issue could be pursued through other channels.[822] The Dutch negotiators replied that they did not intend to press the point further.

Japan sought a treaty reservation with respect to the provisions on exchange controls to permit measures necessary to deal with low foreign exchange reserves. Japan was concerned principally about the impact of trade on its balance of payments. One of the U.S. negotiators inquired whether the restrictions that Japan contemplated would fall within the essential security interests exception, thus, presumably, obviating the need for a separate reservation. The Japanese negotiator replied that such restrictions "might often have a national security character," but questioned whether such restrictions would always fall "clearly in this category."[823]

CONSULTATIONS

The U.S. postwar FCN treaties typically contained a provision calling upon each party to engage in consultations at the request of the other. For example, Article XXIV(1) of the 1955 standard draft treaty provided that "[e]ach Party shall accord sympathetic consideration to, and shall afford adequate opportunity for consultation regarding, such representations as the other Party may make with respect to any matter affecting the operation of the present Treaty." This language was based on Article 41 of the ITO Charter and Article XXII of the GATT, and it had an antecedent in the U.S. reciprocal trade agreements as well.[824]

The United States anticipated that disputes would arise concerning treaty obligations, but believed that they would ordinarily be resolved through diplomatic consultations between the parties. The consultations provision was "intended to preclude one country from taking umbrage because the other country wished to take up a matter respecting the treaty."[825] It was a "statement of diplomatic usage in intercourse between friendly countries."[826] Consultations provisions were useful for avoiding misunderstandings.[827]

821. Ibid.

822. Ibid.

823. Memorandum of Conversation headed "Informal Discussions on the United States Standard Draft Treaty of Friendship, Commerce and Navigation," dated April 1, 1952, NARA, Record Group 59, Department of State File No. 611.944/5-652.

824. *See, e.g.,* Reciprocal Trade Agreement between the United States of America and Mexico, *signed* December 23, 1942, 57 Stat. 833, 9 Bevans 1109.

825. Memorandum of Conversation headed "Negotiation of Treaty of Friendship, Commerce and Navigation with Israel," dated December 13, 1950, NARA, Record Group 59, Department of State File No. 611.84A4/12-1350.

826. Ibid.

827. Airgram A-175 dated January 27, 1951, from the Department of State to the U.S. embassy in Copenhagen, NARA, Record Group 59, Department of State File No. 611.594/1-251.

The United States assured other countries that the word "consultation" in no way required that the parties reach agreement.[828] The provision did not confer the power to bind or impose.[829] It meant "no more than discussion, the asking of questions, the imparting of views."[830]

COMPROMISSORY CLAUSE

The U.S. postwar FCN treaties, for the first time in U.S. FCN treaty practice, included a compromissory clause applicable to future disputes. The clause contained each party's consent to the submission of disputes to the International Court of Justice. For example, Article XXIV(2) of the 1955 standard draft treaty provided that "[a]ny dispute between the Parties as to the interpretation or application of the present Treaty, not satisfactorily adjusted by diplomacy, shall be submitted to the International Court of Justice, unless the Parties agree to settlement by some other pacific means."

The United States regarded a right of recourse to binding, third-party dispute settlement as critical to the role of the FCN treaties in promoting the rule of law. Indeed, Herman Walker believed that the acceptance of the Court's jurisdiction for the resolution of treaty disputes "may perhaps be said to rank in significance with the systematic provision of corporate rights, in signaling the outstanding advances which current treaty policy has effected over that prevailing in recent years."[831]

At the same time, however, the United States expected that resort to the Court would be a rarity. Rather, it believed that the parties ordinarily would observe their treaty obligations and that, when disputes did arise, they would be resolved through negotiation or perhaps even referral to arbitration. Adjudication before the International Court of Justice would be a last resort. Yet, it was essential to the rule of law that such a right exist.

These sentiments were expressed by the State Department on a number of occasions. For example, the Department explained during negotiations with Germany in 1953 that

> [i]t is presupposed that the treaty will operate smoothly through the normal observance of its terms by each Party. Should problems of application arise,

828. Memorandum dated July 31, 1950, headed "Memorandum on the Provisions of the Greek Counterdraft," NARA, Record Group 59, Department of State File No, 611.814/6-250.

829. Airgram dated June 14, 1950, from the Department of State to the U.S. embassy in Copenhagen, NARA, Record Group 59, Department of State File No. 611.594/5-350.

830. Memorandum headed "Memorandum on the Provisions of the Greek Counterdraft," dated July 31, 1950, NARA, Record Group 59, Department of State File No, 611.814/6-250. *See also* Memorandum of Conversation headed "Treaty of Friendship, Commerce and Navigation with Israel—Third Preliminary Discussion," dated May 10, 1950, NARA, Record Group 59, Department of State File No. 611.84A4/5-1050.

831. Walker, "Treaties for the Encouragement and Protection of Foreign Investment," page 239.

> through inadvertence or otherwise, consultations will ordinarily obviate the emergence of serious differences; and differences, should they materialize, would commonly be settled through the amiable processes of regular diplomacy. In the contingency of a real dispute, beyond the power of normal diplomacy to solve, the Parties could at the time arrange for arbitration in whatever manner the circumstances of the occasion seemed to indicate best. This, of course, is another illustration of the theory that the treaty should deal in broad principles which, as in the case of the U.S. Constitution, permits necessary adaptations, without constant amendment, to the changing conditions of an unknown future.
>
> Ultimate resort, in the rare event that all else failed, would be to the International Court. The Department has felt that treaty recognition of the ultimate role of the Court constitutes a worthwhile and appropriate contribution to building the Court's prestige, and to the development of the rule of law in international relations.[832]

Or, as the Department explained the following year, during the same negotiations,

> a treaty of this kind is carried out by each Party acting independently to observe the terms to which it has agreed; and whatever action it takes or fails to take in full awareness of the terms of the treaty, is presumed in the first instance to be correct and in compliance with its obligations, as it is presumed that each Party intends of its own volition to observe its treaty undertakings. The other Party is of course entitled to raise questions, and to ask for consultation, about actions or non-actions of the other Party which it feels may not be in keeping with the treaty. But any problems arising would ordinarily be reviewed and settled bilaterally through the normal processes of diplomacy. If, of course, an irreconcilable difference finally crystallized over the interpretation or application of the treaty, either Party would be entitled as an ultimate resort, under the terms of Article XXIV, paragraph 2, as now written, to submit the dispute for decision to the International Court, unless the Parties agreed at the time to arbitration or some other friendly procedure for settling the particular dispute.[833]

832. Airgram dated July 28, 1953, from the Department of State to the U.S. High Commissioner in Bonn, NARA, Record Group 59, Department of State File No. 611.62A4/6-2653.

833. Instruction dated September 23, 1954, from the Department of State to the U.S. High Commissioner in Bonn, NARA, Record Group 59, Department of State File No. 611.62A4/9-2354. *See also* Telegram dated January 14, 1955, from the Department of State to the U.S. embassy in Tehran, NARA, Record Group 59, Department of State File No. 611.884/1-1455; Telegram dated January 18, 1955, from the U.S. embassy in Tehran to the Department of State, NARA, Record Group 59, Department of State File No. 611.884/1-1855; Telegram dated November 27, 1954, from the Department of State to the U.S. embassy in Karachi, NARA, Record Group 59, Department of State File No. 611.90D4/11-2754.

Again, during negotiations with Germany, the United States argued that the "ideal" of final settlement by the Court was important "even though it was true that the likelihood of a case ever coming before the Court under this treaty was very remote indeed—inasmuch as differences would normally be settled by consultation and the normal processes of diplomacy or even by submission to arbitration if the two parties at the time of the dispute decided to follow that procedure."[834]

The State Department observed during negotiations with the sultanate of Muscat and Oman that the compromissory clause did not preclude other peaceful means of dispute settlement. The Department explained that the provision "emphasizes settlement through the diplomatic channel, for experience shows that almost every question will be settled by that method." It also contemplated possible recourse to good offices, conciliation, mediation, and arbitration. Referral to the Court would be "largely a matter of final resort."[835]

During negotiations with India, the State Department told the U.S. embassy in New Delhi that it was "[a]nticipated that adjustment of disputes would normally be by diplomacy or means, such as arbitration, other than submission to [the International Court of Justice.]."[836] The Department further explained that the "[l]atter would be the exceptional case." [837] Indeed, during negotiations with Austria, the Department observed that it did "not anticipate litigation under the treaty."[838]

During negotiations with Thailand, U.S. negotiators observed that the State Department's experience was that differences under an FCN treaty were "settled through diplomatic channels."[839] Referral to the International Court of Justice would be largely "a matter of final resort."[840]

During Senate debate on the FCN treaties, senators sometimes expressed the concern that the compromissory clause was inconsistent with the Connally Amendment to the U.S. consent to the Court's jurisdiction under Article 36(2) of the Statute of the Court. That amendment provided that U.S. consent did not extend to matters essentially within the domestic jurisdiction of the United States

834. Despatch dated February 23, 1954, from the U.S. High Commissioner in Bonn to the Department of State, NARA, Record Group 59, Department of State File No. 611/62A4/2-2354.

835. Instruction dated December 2, 1957, from the Department of State to the U.S. consulate general in Dhahran, NARA, Record Group 59, Department of State File No.611.86E4/10-257.

836. Telegram dated June 27, 1949, from the State Department to the U.S. embassy in New Delhi, NARA, Record Group 59, Department of State File No. 711.452/6-249.

837. Ibid.

838. Instruction A-313 dated March 20, 1958, from the Department of State to the U.S. embassy in Vienna, NARA, Record Group 59, Department of State File No. 611.634/3-458.

839. Enclosure No. 3 to airgram A-324 dated November 14, 1962, from the U.S. embassy in Bangkok to the Department of State, NARA, Record Group 59, Department of State File No. 611.9242/11-1462.

840. Instruction A-194 dated June 12, 1961, from the Department of State to the U.S. embassy in Bangkok, NARA, Record Group 59, Department of State File No. 611.9242/6-1261.

as determined by the United States. Although the compromissory clause was inconsistent with the Connally Amendment, Senator Connally himself had been consulted at the inception of the U.S. postwar FCN treaty program and expressed no opposition to the clause.[841]

Repeatedly, the State Department stressed the importance of the compromissory clause in promoting the rule of law. During negotiations with the sultanate of Muscat and Oman, it observed that the jurisdiction of the Court should be extended "as doing so tends to strengthen the rule of law in international affairs."[842] During negotiations with Japan, the Department said that the inclusion of the clause was "the clearest kind of indication that the treaty establishes a rule of law."[843] When during negotiations Austria objected to the compromissory clause, the U.S. negotiators explained, in defense of the inclusion of the clause, that "the United States is interested in furthering the rule of law between nations and had considered that in the case of a small country such as Austria it would be in Austria's own interest to be able to present its problems before the Court."[844] The Department instructed its embassy in Bangkok that the "provision for settlement of disputes in accordance with law [is] an essential factor . . . . Without it, [the] treaty with Thailand would be regarded as defective. . . ."[845]

The State Department sometimes noted that submission to the Court had practical benefits, apart from promoting the rule of law. One was that investment disputes would be removed from the political domain. As the Department explained during negotiations with the sultanate of Muscat and Oman, "the basic security of United States investments in that country requires a binding assurance that disputes affecting such investments shall have available, if needed, a forum where settlement may be had in accordance with the principles of international law and free from political pressure."[846] Similarly, during

841. This concern is discussed in greater detail in Chapter 7 in the sections on Senate advice and consent to ratification in 1961 and in this chapter in the section on MFN treatment.

842. Instruction dated December 2, 1957, from the Department of State to the U.S. consulate general in Dhahran, NARA, Record Group 59, Department of State File No.611.86E4/10-257. *See also* Airgram dated July 28, 1953, from the Department of State to the U.S. High Commissioner in Bonn, NARA, Record Group 59, Department of State File No. 611.62A4/6-2653; Instruction dated September 23, 1954, from the Department of State to the U.S. High Commissioner in Bonn, NARA, Record Group 59, Department of State File No. 611.62A4/9-2354; Undated memorandum by Herman Walker headed "Compromissory Clause," NARA, Record Group 59, Department of State File 611.62A4/9-2454.

843. Despatch dated November 1, 1951, from the Department of State to the U.S. Political Adviser in Tokyo, NARA, Record Group 59, Department of State File No. 611.944/6-1651.

844. *See, e.g.,* Despatch dated February 25, 1958, from the U.S. embassy in Vienna to the Department of State, NARA, Record Group 59, Department of State File No. 611.634/3-458.

845. Telegram dated May 22, 1963, from the Department of State to the U.S. embassy in Bangkok, NARA, Record Group 59, Central Foreign Policy Files 1963, Box 3487, Folder marked "FT-Foreign Trade 1963."

846. Instruction dated December 2, 1957, from the Department of State to the U.S. consulate general in Dhahran, NARA, Record Group 59, Department of State File No. 611.86E4/10-257.

negotiations with Germany, the State Department noted that the Senate "after serious deliberation, had taken a very significant step in approving paragraph 2 at the time of its action in the Italian and Chinese treaties, and that its attitude had undoubtedly been greatly influenced by the eminent standing of the Court as a strictly legal body, deciding issues solely on prudent juridical and non-political bases."[847]

In short, in the event of a dispute, the Court, rather than either of the parties, would decide on the basis of law how each of the provisions of the treaty would be interpreted and applied. As Robert Wilson, one of those responsible for negotiating FCN treaties during the Truman administration, noted in 1949, the compromissory clauses "assure that, in the last analysis, not each interested party for itself . . . but the principal judicial agency of the United Nations will have the role of final, authoritative interpreter of the treaty provisions."[848] On a different occasion, Wilson noted that the provisions of the treaty entrusting to the Court the role of "final, authoritative interpreter should provide safeguards against any party's arbitrary or unreasonable constructions."[849] And, on still another occasion Wilson made clear that the Court was the final interpreter of every clause of the treaty, noting, "In the final analysis, neither party to a treaty containing an unconditional compromissory clause must accept as final the other party's interpretation or application of the treaty. Interpretation and application of the establishment (as of all) provisions of the treaties become, as of right, a matter for international judges."[850]

Another benefit was that investors would receive a definitive resolution of the dispute. As the State Department noted, again during negotiations with the sultanate of Muscat and Oman, "considerations of good relations in general demand an orderly procedure for final and definitive settlement of treaty disputes. Otherwise, such disputes can drag on indefinitely, worsening in the process."[851] The Department further noted that an FCN treaty that failed to specify "a final means of dispute resolution," like one that failed to provide for dispute resolution in accordance with law, would be "defective."[852]

The United States favored resort to the International Court of Justice, in particular, because it was seeking as a matter of policy to enhance the prestige of

847. Despatch dated February 23, 1954, from the U.S. High Commissioner in Bonn to the Department of State, NARA, Record Group 59, Department of State File No. 611/62A4/2-2354.

848. Robert R. Wilson, "Postwar Commercial Treaties of the United States," 43 *American Journal of International Law* 262, 287 (1949).

849. Wilson ,"Property-Protection Provisions in United States Commercial Treaties," page 105.

850. Wilson, *United States Commercial Treaties and International Law*, page 25.

851. Instruction dated December 2, 1957, from the Department of State to the U.S. consulate general in Dhahran, NARA, Record Group 59, Department of State File No.611.86E4/10-257.

852. Ibid. *See also* Instruction A-313 dated March 20, 1958, from the Department of State to the U.S. embassy in Vienna, NARA, Record Group 59, Department of State File No. 611.634/3-458.

the Court.[853] As the Department noted, the Senate's approval of the FCN treaty with China

> was a landmark decision, as it committed the United States to acceptance of compulsory jurisdiction of the Court without reservation, for the first time in a significant context. The appearance of this clause in the FCN treaties establishes in the clearest possible manner the principle of the rule of law and of objectivity in the carrying out of treaty obligations and, moreover, it contributes to the up-building of the prestige of the Court as an arbiter of disputes between nations.[854]

Further, the State Department believed that the Court was better suited than an arbitral tribunal to resolve disputes on the basis of law. During negotiations with the sultanate of Muscat and Oman, the State Department asserted that adjudication before the Court was superior to arbitration because the Court was composed of 15 judges who were trained in the law. In addition, the Court was "not chargeable with the alleged defect of arbitration—the tendency of arbitrators to 'split the difference.'"[855] As the Department observed during the same negotiations, "If the intent of the parties is to be carried out, agreement in advance on an orderly procedure assuring a final settlement is indispensable, and in the present organization of international justice, referral to the Court is the logical method to designate."[856] In response to the sultan's concerns about the cost of adjudication, the Department noted that adjudication before the Court was less expensive than arbitration, because the parties did not bear the costs of the tribunal.[857]

During negotiations, Germany urged the use of arbitration rather than the Court. The State Department objected, explaining,

> The German proposal for an arbitration procedure is not an adequate substitute. We have opposed it, and should continue to resist it. Aside from making this treaty conspicuously different from other FCN treaties in an important particular, it suffers the following drawbacks—(1) it would be a retrograde step, returning us to pre-World War I thinking. The U.S., moreover, apparently does not have any precedent for a specific arbitration provision in any of its FCN treaties. (2) The framing of an arbitration provision involves verbosity and detail that departs from the simplicity and generality

853. Telegram dated March 15, 1950, from the Department of State to the U.S. embassy in Montevideo, NARA, Record Group 59, Department of State File No. 611.3311/3-1350.

854. Undated memorandum by Herman Walker headed "Compromissory Clause," NARA, Record Group 59, Department of State File 611.62A4/9-2454.

855. Instruction dated December 2, 1957, from the Department of State to the U.S. consulate general in Dhahran, NARA, Record Group 59, Department of State File No.611.86E4/10-257.

856. Ibid.

857. Ibid.

> which should pervade a treaty of this type. ... (3) Historically our Senate has frowned on advance commitments for automatic arbitration, and has tended to accept arbitration procedures only subject to the condition that each individual submission of a dispute be first approved by the Senate.[858]

In a few instances, the other party resisted the inclusion of its consent to the jurisdiction of the Court, for different reasons. Germany, for example, objected to the utilization of the Court because the Soviet Union had refused to permit Germany to join the United Nations.[859] Thailand had recently adjudicated the *Case concerning the Temple of Preah Vihear*[860] before the Court and was deeply disappointed by the result, making it politically impossible for the Thai government to agree to the Court's jurisdiction over any other dispute.[861] The sultan of Muscat and Oman objected in principle to the involvement of a third party in a dispute between the two treaty parties, also, at least in part, because of a disappointing experience in an international arbitration.[862] The United States responded to these objections by arguing that the provision consenting to the jurisdiction of the Court was "fundamental"[863] and "essential" to the treaty.[864]

In most cases, the United States was able to overcome objections to the Court. For example, Ireland and Japan both agreed to the compromissory clause, despite not being members of the United Nations at the time that they concluded the treaty.[865] The United States was prepared, however, if agreement on the Court's jurisdiction was simply not possible, to agree to arbitration instead.[866] For example, the United States proposed that its FCN treaty with Germany provide

858. Undated memorandum by Herman Walker headed "Compromissory Clause," NARA, Record Group 59, Department of State File 611.62A4/9-2454.

859. This discussion is further described in Chapter 7 in the section on the negotiation of the FCN treaty with Germany.

860. (Cambodia v. Thailand), 1962 I. C. J. Rep. 6.

861. This discussion is further described in Chapter 7 in the section on the negotiation of the FCN treaty with Thailand.

862. This discussion is further described in Chapter 7 in the section on the negotiation of the FCN treaty with the sultanate of Muscat and Oman.

863. Telegram dated November 12, 1954, from the Department of State to the U.S. embassy in Tehran, NARA, Record Group 59, Department of State File No. 611.884/11-1254.

864. Instruction dated December 2, 1957, from the Department of State to the U.S. consulate general in Dhahran, NARA, Record Group 59, Department of State File No.611.86E4/10-257; Telegram dated May 22, 1963, from the Department of State to the U.S. embassy in Bangkok, NARA, Record Group 59, Central Foreign Policy Files 1963, Box 3487, Folder marked "FT-Foreign Trade 1963."

865. Undated memorandum by Herman Walker headed "Compromissory Clause," NARA, Record Group 59, Department of State File 611.62A4/9-2454.

866. Telegram dated November 12, 1954, from the Department of State to the U.S. embassy in Tehran, NARA, Record Group 59, Department of State File No. 611.884/11-1254.

for arbitration until such time as Germany became a member of the United Nations, a solution that would preserve the "ideal" of submission to the Court while acknowledging Germany's political problem and that Germany ultimately accepted.[867] Similarly, the United States eventually proposed that Thailand agree to ad hoc arbitration in lieu of submission of disputes to the Court,[868] a proposal that Thailand accepted.[869] The United States was not able to overcome the objections of the sultan of Muscat and Oman, and thus the treaty with the sultanate became the only U.S. postwar FCN treaty that did not include a compromissory clause.

During negotiations, the Netherlands appeared to support the Court at least as strongly as the United States. Specifically, the Dutch negotiators proposed the addition of language that would state explicitly that either party could unilaterally submit a dispute to the Court. The United States resisted this language, not because it disagreed with the principle, but merely because it wished to preserve uniformity in the language of this provision. As reported by the U.S. embassy in The Hague, the U.S. negotiators explained that

> the Senate, in approving the compromisery [sic] clause for the first time, after much deliberation in connection with the 1946 treaty with China, had taken a most significant step; and that altogether adequate language hitherto approved by the Senate should be allowed to stand just as it is. The Dutch said that while they appreciated the Department's view in the matter and thoroughly concurred in the belief that few disputes would in actual practice ever be taken to the Court, and that it would be very rare and extraordinary, indeed, if any case were brought to the Court except on a mutual consent basis, that nevertheless they felt that the principle of the Court's ultimate jurisdiction was so important that there could never be any dispute over the proposition that a Treaty Party did have the right to go before the Court unilaterally as a final resort, if it so decided.[870]

After some discussion, the parties agreed that the matter might be addressed in the minutes of interpretation.[871] Subsequently, however, the Netherlands decided

867. Instruction dated April 16, 1954, from the Department of State to the U.S. High Commissioner in Bonn, NARA, Record Group 59, Department of State File No. 611.62A4/2-2354; Undated memorandum by Herman Walker headed "Compromissory Clause," NARA, Record Group 59, Department of State File 611.62A4/9-2454.

868. Telegram dated May 22, 1963, from the Department of State to the U.S. embassy in Bangkok, NARA, Record Group 59, Central Foreign Policy Files 1963, Box 3487, Folder marked "FT-Foreign Trade 1963."

869. Thailand FCN treaty, Article XIII(2).

870. Despatch dated August 17, 1954, from the U.S. embassy in The Hague to the Department of State, NARA, Record Group 59, Department of State File No. 611.564/8-1754.

871. Ibid.

that it wished to dispense with the minutes of interpretation by omitting some items and transferring others to the protocol.[872] The United States agreed, provided that "severe selectivity" was exercised in identifying the material to be transferred to the protocol.[873] When the parties compiled the protocol, they omitted the language with respect to unilateral submissions to the Court.

872. Memorandum headed "Status of Negotiations with Netherlands as Reported Informally by Mr. Walker in Letter of February 5, 1955," NARA, Record Group 59, Department of State File No. 611.654/2-155.

873. Despatch dated February 11, 1955, from the U.S. embassy in The Hague to the Department of State, NARA, Record Group 59, Department of State File No. 611.564/2-1155.

Thai Foreign Minister Thanat Khoman and U.S. Ambassador Graham Martin sign the FCN treaty between the United States and Thailand in Bangkok on May 29, 1966. This was the last signing ceremony in the history of the U.S. FCN treaty program.
SOURCE: Department of State News Letter, July 1966, page 18. This is a reproduction of a copy housed at the National Archives.

Epilogue

In May of 1966, as the last FCN treaty ever to be concluded by the United States awaited signature, the U.S. Senate took action that it hoped would strengthen the rule of law with respect to foreign investment. Specifically, it gave advice and consent to ratification of the Convention on the Settlement of Investments Disputes between States and Nationals of Other States, generally known as the ICSID Convention.[1] The ICSID Convention created an International Centre for Settlement of Investment Disputes (ICSID), an affiliate of the World Bank,[2] that provided rules and a facility for the arbitration of investment disputes between investors and host states.

The ICSID Convention addressed the problem that no mutually acceptable forum existed for the resolution of disputes between foreign investors and host states.[3] Investors were unwilling to submit disputes to local courts.[4] The International Chamber of Commerce (ICC) long had urged that host states consent to the arbitration of investment disputes with investors before existing arbitral organizations, such as the ICC,[5] but host countries had been unwilling to submit their disputes to private arbitral bodies.[6] The ICC, in the alternative,

1. Signed March 18, 1965, 17 UST 1270, TIAS 6090, 575 UNTS 159. The origins of ICSID are described in Antonio R. Parra, *The History of ICSID* (Oxford: Oxford University Press, 2012).

2. The World Bank consists of two organizations: the IBRD created in 1944 at the Bretton Woods conference described in Chapter 1, and the International Development Association, which provides very low-interest or interest-free loans to the poorest countries.

3. Letter of submittal dated February 7, 1966, from Acting Secretary of State George W. Ball to President Lyndon B. Johnson, *reprinted in Convention on the Settlement of Investment Disputes*, Exec. A, 89th Cong. 2d Sess. (1967).

4. Letter dated October 9, 1965, from the National Association of Manufacturers to Senator J.W. Fulbright, *reprinted in Convention on the Settlement of Investment Disputes*, Exec. Rept. No. 2, 89th Cong. 2d Sess. (1966), page 33.

5. *See, e.g., Current Economic Developments*, June 23, 1953, NARA, Record Group 59, Department of State Lot Files.

6. Letter dated October 9, 1965, from the National Association of Manufacturers to Senator J. W. Fulbright, *reprinted in Convention on the Settlement of Investment Disputes*, Exec. Rept. No. 2, 89th Cong. 2d Sess. (1966), page 33.

had proposed as early as 1947 the creation of a standing Court of Arbitration[7] or the modification of the Permanent Court of Arbitration to provide a facility for investor-state arbitration.[8] Although the U.S. postwar FCN treaties had provided for submission by the parties of investment disputes arising under the treaties to the International Court of Justice, the United States had anticipated that resort to the Court for that purpose would be rare and, in fact, as of the mid-1960s no investment dispute arising under a U.S. postwar FCN treaty had ever been submitted to the Court, confirming that the Court would be all but unavailable as a practical matter. By filling the need for a readily available procedure to resolve investment disputes, the State Department believed, the Convention would assist private investors, stimulate the flow of private investment to developing countries in need of it, and benefit foreign relations by having disputes settled directly by the investor and government involved.[9]

Two witnesses appeared before the Committee on Foreign Relations in support of the ICSID Convention, Undersecretary of the Treasury Joseph W. Barr and State Department Legal Adviser Leonard C. Meeker. Meeker presented a written statement in which he said that "[a] mechanism for impartial resolution of disputes between investors and host governments is a meaningful step toward assuring fair treatment for investor and host country alike."[10] He noted that the ICSID Convention did not provide any substantive rules regarding investment protection, but it was "anticipated that decisions through the convention's mechanism will create a significant new body of international law. Thus, international law in this area can be expected to grow as the result of this convention."[11]

Meeker explained the benefit to the United States of this development: "As the country with the greatest amount of international investment, and the greatest stake in the development and wide acceptance of international law standards regarding the protection of private property, the United States stands to gain substantially from acceptance of the convention and use of its facilities."[12] In the conclusion to his remarks, Meeker again returned to the theme that the creation of ICSID could make "a significant contribution . . . to the development of international law."[13]

7. *See* Report by ICC Committee on Foreign Investment, March 1946, NARA, Record Group 43, International Trade Files, Box 55, Folder marked "Investment."

8. *See, e.g., Current Economic Developments*, June 23, 1953, NARA, Record Group 59, Department of State Lot Files.

9. Letter of submittal dated February 7, 1966, from Acting Secretary of State George W. Ball to President Lyndon B. Johnson, *reprinted in Convention on the Settlement of Investment Disputes*, Exec. A, 89th Cong. 2d Sess. (1967).

10. *Convention on the Settlement of Investment Disputes*, Exec. A, 89th Cong. 2d Sess. (1967), page 29.

11. Ibid.

12. Ibid.

13. Ibid., page 31.

The Convention was well received. Following the testimony by Barr and Meeker, Democratic senator J. William Fulbright of Arkansas, the chairman of the Committee, observed, "I personally think it is a very good idea, and I am very strong for it."[14] On the Senate floor, just prior to the vote on the Convention, Democratic senator Wayne Morse of Oregon would assure the Senate that the Convention enjoyed the "enthusiastic support" of the Committee.[15]

Members of the Senate were particularly attracted by the role of ICSID in developing international law. Senator Morse observed during the hearings, "I will heartily support the objectives of this convention because I think this is a step in the direction really of building up the common law of international law, which is so sorely needed in the whole field of international law. We do not have enough precedents of an international common law, and arbitration awards are part and parcel of a system of international law. . . ."[16] The Committee's report on the Convention noted that the Convention was designed to stimulate the flow of international investment to less developed countries, which the Committee described as a "commendable objective."[17] The report noted that, "[i]n addition, it is reasonable to expect that a substantial body of new international law will be developed as a result of this convention. This, also, is a step in the right direction."[18] On the Senate floor, Democratic senator Vance Hartke of Indiana argued that the ICSID Convention would "lift the curtain of uncertainty" concerning the framework governing foreign investment.[19] Senator Hartke placed into the record a recent speech by Undersecretary Barr in which he had observed that "as the convention operates over a period of time, we can look forward to the emergence of a new body of case law to guide nations in both avoiding and settling investment disputes."[20]

Further, ICSID "may also serve to move investment disputes from the political to the legal arena."[21] Barr believed that "at a time of considerable sensitivity between the developed and the developing nations" this could "only be regarded as an important step forward."[22]

When the Convention came before the Senate for a vote on May 16, Senator Morse took the floor again to emphasize the contribution of the Convention to building international law. He explained that the Convention was "another opportunity for us to add further foundation stones to the erection of an international organization with

14. Ibid.

15. 112 *Congressional Record* 10122 (1966).

16. *Convention on the Settlement of Investment Disputes*, Exec. A, 89th Cong. 2d Sess. (1967), page 13.

17. Ibid., page 3.

18. Ibid.

19. 112 *Congressional Record* 9434 (1966).

20. Ibid., page 9435.

21. Ibid.

22. Ibid.

procedure for the settlement of disputes by the substitution of the rule of law. We all know that there is a great need in this country for the building of the precedents of international law."[23]

Moments later, the Senate gave advice and consent to the ratification of the Convention by a vote of 72-0.[24] Although support for the ICSID Convention was unanimous, the three senators who spoke in support of it—Senators Fulbright, Morse, and Hartke—were all Democrats whose foreign policy in the 1960s was defined by their opposition to the Vietnam War. Senator Morse, for example, had been one of only two senators who had voted in 1964 against the Gulf of Tonkin Resolution, which the Johnson administration treated as congressional authorization for the war. The very same month in which the Senate approved the ICSID Convention, Senator Fulbright delivered at Johns Hopkins University a lecture called "The Arrogance of Power," in which he criticized U.S. military intervention in Vietnam. The following year, Senator Fulbright expanded the lecture and published it in book form.[25] A year later, Senator Hartke published his book, *The American Crisis in Vietnam*,[26] in which he too condemned the war. In short, the ICSID Convention was most strongly endorsed by liberal Democrats who supported the promotion of the rule of law in international relations, that is, by those senators who were liberal internationalists in the tradition of Franklin Roosevelt's New Deal.

By 1977, when Democrat Jimmy Carter was inaugurated as president, some 15 years had passed since the initiation of a successful FCN treaty negotiation. Meanwhile, in 1959, Germany had concluded a treaty with Pakistan concerned solely with the protection of foreign investment.[27] Pakistan signed its bilateral investment treaty with Germany less than two weeks after it had signed its FCN treaty with the United States.

This first German BIT, with Pakistan, consisted largely of counterparts to the investment-related provisions in the U.S. postwar FCN treaties. Like the U.S. FCN treaties, the Germany-Pakistan BIT guaranteed both national and MFN treatment (though not with respect to the establishment of investment),[28] contained general prohibitions on discriminatory treatment,[29] guaranteed protection and security for investment[30] (which would become "full" protection and security

23. 112 *Congressional Record* 10122 (1966).

24. Ibid., page 10123.

25. J. William Fulbright, *The Arrogance of Power* (New York: Random House, 1967).

26. Vance Hartke, *The American Crisis in Vietnam* (Indianapolis, IN: Bobbs-Merrill, 1968).

27. Treaty between the Federal Republic of Germany and Pakistan for the Promotion and Protection of Investments, signed November 25, 1959.

28. Ibid, Protocol, Paragraph 2.

29. Ibid., Articles I(2) and 2.

30. Ibid., Article 3(1).

by 1961),[31] required compensation for expropriation[32] and guaranteed free transfer of capital and returns, with no balance of payments exception.[33] Disputes under the Germany-Pakistan BIT would be submitted to arbitration or, if both parties agreed, to the International Court of Justice.[34] By 1961, Germany would add the fair and equitable treatment standard to its BITs.[35] The BIT between Germany and Pakistan would also commit the parties, within one year after signing the treaty, to enter into negotiations to conclude an establishment treaty that would make provision for, among other things, entry and sojourn, engaging in business and professional activities, employment of managerial and technical staff, and access to courts.[36] Although the German treaties also drew from the Draft Convention on Investments Abroad authored by Hermann Abs and Lord Hartley Shawcross,[37] the authors of that Draft Convention explained that all but one of the substantive provisions in their Convention were derived from the U.S. postwar FCN treaties.[38]

Other European countries soon followed Germany's example. For example, between 1959 and 1966, the year that the United States concluded its last FCN treaty, Germany, France, Switzerland, the Netherlands, Italy, the Belgium-Luxembourg Economic Union, Sweden, Denmark, and Norway all inaugurated new BIT programs. By the late 1970s, more than 170 BITs had been concluded among some 65 countries.[39]

31. The evolving German practice and the practice of other European countries in the early 1960s with regard to this standard is discussed in Kenneth J. Vandevelde, *Bilateral Investment Treaties: History, Policy and Interpretation* (New York: Oxford University Press, 2010), pages 243–246.

32. Germany-Pakistan BIT, Article 3(2).

33. Ibid., Articles 4 and 6.

34. Ibid., Article 11(2).

35. The evolving German practice and the practice of other European countries in the early 1960s with regard to this standard is discussed in Vandevelde, *Bilateral Investment Treaties*, pages 195–198.

36. Germany-Pakistan BIT, Protocol, Paragraph 1.

37. 9 *Journal of Public Law* 115 (1960). The creation of the German BIT program and the origins and influence of the Abs-Shawcross Convention are described in Lauge N. Skovgaard Poulsen, *Bounded Rationality and Economic Diplomacy: The Politics of Investment Treaties in Developing Countries* (Cambridge: Cambridge University Press, 2015), pages 50–54. *See also* Rudolf Dolzer and Yun-i Kim, "Germany" in Chester Brown, ed., *Commentaries on Selected Model Investment Treaties* (Oxford: Oxford University Press, 2013), pages 292–295.

38. Ibid., pages 119–121. The provisions drawn from the U.S. postwar FCN treaties were the requirements of fair and equitable treatment, most constant protection and security, and payment of compensation for expropriation and the prohibition on unreasonable or discriminatory treatment. The new substantive provision was one requiring each party to observe undertakings with respect to investment.

39. Mark S. Bergman, "Bilateral Investment Protection Treaties: An Examination of the Evolution and Significance of the U.S. Prototype Treaty," 16 *New York University Journal of International Law and Politics* 1, 3 (1983).

The content of the other European BITs, like those of Germany, included counterparts to all but a few of the investment-related provisions of the U.S. postwar FCN treaties. These European BITs typically required MFN (and often national) treatment of investment, fair and equitable treatment, most constant protection and security, just compensation for expropriation, free transfer of capital and returns, and binding, third-party dispute settlement, and they prohibited unreasonable or discriminatory measures.[40] The European BITs also included a few provisions without precedent in the U.S. FCN treaties, including a provision requiring each party to observe any obligation into which it had entered with respect to investment, a provision addressing compensation for losses caused by war or civil disturbance, and, beginning in 1969, a provision for submission of disputes between investors and host states to arbitration before ICSID.

By the 1970s, the U.S. business community was well aware of the contrast between the successful European BIT programs and the moribund U.S. FCN treaty program. Groups such as the International Chamber of Commerce and the State Department's Advisory Committee on Transnational Enterprises recommended the initiation of a U.S. BIT program and began to pressure the State Department to emulate the European example. Members of Congress, such as Democratic senators Frank Church of Idaho (who would serve as chairman of the Committee on Foreign Relations from 1979 to 1981) and Claiborne Pell of Rhode Island (who would serve as chairman of the Committee on Foreign Relations from 1987 to 1995), similarly urged the negotiation of additional treaties to protect foreign investment. As in the case of Senate approval of the ICSID Convention, the most vocal support within the Senate for the inauguration of the BIT program came from liberal Democrats who had been early opponents of the Vietnam War and who were heirs to the liberal internationalism of the New Deal.[41]

On March 7, 1977, the State Department's legal adviser, along with the assistant secretary of state for economic affairs, jointly proposed the inauguration of a new series of U.S. BITs that would serve as the successors to the FCN treaties. The U.S. BITs, like the European BITs, would consist largely of provisions based on the investment-related ones of the U.S. postwar FCN treaties. They included successors to all of the investment-related provisions discussed in Chapter 8—provisions on national and MFN treatment, fair and equitable treatment, most constant protection and security, treatment in accordance with international law, unreasonable and discriminatory measures, just compensation for expropriation,

40. I have traced the origins of the provisions in the European bilateral investment treaties in Vandevelde, *Bilateral Investment Treaties.*

41. Senator Frank Church was one of the sponsors of the Cooper-Church Amendment and the Case-Church Amendment, which sought to end U.S. military intervention in Southeast Asia. Prior to his election to the Senate, Claiborne Pell was a foreign service officer in the State Department who participated in the 1945 San Francisco Conference that produced the United Nations Charter. His opposition to the war is described in G. Wayne Miller, *An Uncommon Man: The Life and Times of Senator Claiborne Pell* (Lebanon, NH: University Press of New England, 2011).

free transfer of investment and returns, entry and sojourn, employment of key personnel, judicial access, competitive equality, transparency, consultations, and binding, third-party settlement of disputes involving the interpretation or application of the treaty as well as exceptions for security-related measures. Thus, the treaty provisions that had implemented the foreign investment policy of the Roosevelt and Truman administrations were once again incorporated into a series of U.S. investment treaties by another Democratic administration, although by the 1970s this treaty series comprised the BITs rather than the FCN treaties.

The new U.S. BITs did include some innovations in U.S. investment treaty practice. The most important such innovation was the provision, pioneered in the European BITs, that included each party's consent to arbitration before ICSID of investment disputes with investors. This provision offered investors a much more effective means of enforcing treaty commitments than had been available under the U.S. FCN treaties. At the same time, it served the same function as the compromissory clauses of the FCN treaties in promoting the rule of law by shifting disputes from the political arena to a legal proceeding and by developing a body of precedent that elaborated the content of international investment law.

The new U.S. BITs also contained a new substantive provision taken from the European BITs, the provision requiring each party to observe any obligation into which it had entered with respect to investments. The United States, however, would reconsider its inclusion of this provision and would remove it from its model BIT in 1994. The U.S. BITs contained as well a new provision, similarly taken from the European BITs, on losses caused by war and civil disturbance, although it can be argued that this provision merely replicated protection provided by other provisions of the treaty.[42]

The new U.S. BITs did include a couple of new substantive provisions with no precedent in the European BITs. One required publication of laws relating to investment, language that was based on a provision in the FCN treaties requiring publication of certain laws relating to customs matters.[43] Another was a provision requiring each party, upon the request of the other, to provide certain information relating to investment matters. A third was a provision prohibiting performance requirements, that is, investment-related measures that affected trade, such as a requirement that an investment purchase components locally or that it export its product. The insertion of the new performance requirements provision was an effort to address a problem that became a matter of concern after the investment provisions of the FCN treaties had been developed. It reflected the policy of liberal trade that underlay the FCN treaties and was reminiscent of the U.S. practice in the era of the FCN treaties of addressing investment and trade concerns in a single instrument.

The Carter administration's 1977 decision to launch a new BIT program effectively terminated a U.S. FCN treaty program that only a few months before

42. *See* Kenneth J. Vandevelde, *U.S. International Investment Agreements* (New York: Oxford University Press, 2009), pages 432–433.

43. This provision is discussed in Chapter 8 in the section on transparency.

had commemorated the 200th anniversary of its launching by the Continental Congress. Thereafter, when another country approached the United States to inquire about negotiating an FCN treaty, the U.S. response was to propose the negotiation of a BIT instead.

The inauguration of the BIT program reinvigorated the foreign investment policy represented by the FCN treaties. Freed from the cumbersome and complicated context of the FCN treaties in which they had been for so long encased, the investment-related provisions in the BITs proved acceptable to a wide range of countries and, by the early 1980s, the United States was again successfully concluding bilateral treaties for the protection of foreign investment.

The U.S. postwar FCN treaties, however, were the first bilateral investment treaties concluded by the United States or any other country, and they established the foundation on which would be built in the last half of the twentieth century the contemporary international law of foreign investment. Those involved in negotiating the U.S. postwar FCN treaties regarded this as precisely their goal. Herman Walker, a principal negotiator of the U.S. postwar FCN treaties, when evaluating the treaty program in 1956, observed that "[q]uantitatively, the group of treaties concluded to date between the United States and like-minded countries since World War II measure perhaps but a modest accomplishment; qualitatively, moreover, shortcomings in the degree of completeness with which they meet all conceivable company requirements are doubtless detectable."[44] Nevertheless, Walker continued, "they mark a definite advance in an area in which progress through multilateral agreements has so far been lacking."[45] Further, "[t]he growth of this pattern, if and as it occurs with the accretion in time of additional examples, should be conducive to the development of international standards of practice . . . with respect to the treatment of companies."[46]

A half-century after Germany signed its BIT with Pakistan, more than 2,500 bilateral investment treaties had been concluded, with approximately 180 countries having concluded at least one such treaty.[47] When Canada, Mexico, and the United States negotiated the North American Free Trade Agreement, which was signed in 1992, they included an investment chapter that contained provisions similar to those in the U.S. BITs. In so doing, the United States reembraced the FCN treaty approach that it had abandoned only15 years before, viz. the approach of embedding investment provisions in a larger treaty that deals comprehensively with economic relations between the parties. Since the conclusion of the NAFTA,

44. Herman Walker Jr., "Provisions on Companies in United States Commercial Treaties," 50 *American Journal of International Law* 373, 393 (1956).

45. Ibid.

46. Ibid.

47. The United Nations by the end of 2008 had identified 2,676 bilateral investment treaties plus another 273 free trade agreements with investment-related provisions similar to those found in bilateral investment treaties. United Nations Conference on Trade and Development, *Recent Developments in International Investment Agreements (2008–June 2009)* (Geneva: United Nations, 2009).

hundreds of free trade agreements (FTAs) with investment chapters have been negotiated worldwide. Further, hundreds of claims have been submitted to binding arbitration under the BITs and the FTAs, and hundreds of millions of dollars in compensation have been awarded to investors. The U.S. postwar FCN treaties laid the foundation for much of the contemporary legal framework for global capitalism. The framework that they contemplated was a projection of New Deal liberalism, a framework in which free enterprise is facilitated and regulated by host state law, subject to basic rule of law principles found in the U.S. Constitution.

U.S. FCN treaty negotiators in the 1940s and 1950s did not remotely foresee the explosion in treaty negotiations that would occur at the end of the twentieth century. Theirs was a world in which foreign exchange reserves were limited, nearly every country was concerned about the impact of capital movements, fear of economic imperialism was epidemic among newly independent developing countries, New Deal liberalism was challenged by both nationalism on the right and socialism on the left and rarely could the United States expect to conclude more than one or two FCN treaties in a year.

Despite the slow pace of negotiations, the State Department persevered with its postwar FCN treaty program in an effort to extend throughout the world the principles of liberal legality found in U.S. constitutional law. The Department noted as much at the end of the Truman administration in a 1952 public policy statement on the postwar FCN treaties, where it observed that "[t]heir fundamental objectives—protection of the foreigner, maintenance of good order in everyday business affairs, mutual encouragement of economic development, strengthening the rule of law in the dealings of one nation with another—all are manifestations of friendship between nations and a practical example of how they can act together, under law, for their own and the common good."[48] In sum, said the Department, "When an American goes abroad, these treaties can be for him much the same sort of shield that the Constitution is at home."[49]

48. Department of State, Office of Public Affairs, *Commercial Treaty Program of the United States* (Washington, DC: Government Printing Office, 1952), *copy available at* NARA, Record Group 59, Department of State File No. 611.004/3-453.

49. Ibid.

Appendix

Excerpts from the 1955 Standard Draft U.S. FCN Treaty

Draft Treaty
of
Friendship, Commerce and Navigation
Between the
United States of America
and
. . . .

The United States of America and . . . . desirous of strengthening the bonds of peace and friendship traditionally existing between them and of encouraging closer economic and cultural relations between their peoples, and being cognizant of the contributions which may be made toward those ends by arrangements encouraging mutually beneficial investments, promoting mutually advantageous commercial intercourse and otherwise establishing mutual rights and privileges have resolved to conclude a Treaty of Friendship, Commerce and Navigation, based in general on the principles of national and of most-favored-nation treatment unconditionally accorded, and for that purpose have appointed as their Plenipotentiaries,

The President of the United States of America:

and

. . . .

Who, having communicated to each other their full powers found to be in due form, have agreed as follows:

ARTICLE I

Each party shall at all times accord fair and equitable treatment to the nationals and companies of the other Party, and to their property, enterprises and other interests.

ARTICLE II

1. Nationals of either Party shall, subject to the laws relating to the entry and sojourn of aliens, be permitted to enter the territories of the other Party, to travel therein freely, and to reside at places of their choice. Nationals of either Party shall in particular be permitted to enter the territories of the other Party and to remain therein: (a) for the purpose of carrying on trade between the territories of the two Parties and engaging in related commercial activities; (b) for the purpose of developing and directing the operations of an enterprise in which they have invested, or in which they are actively in the process of investing, a substantial amount of capital.
2. Nationals of either Party, within the territories of the other Party, shall enjoy freedom of conscience; and they shall be at liberty to hold religious services, both private and public, at suitable places of their choice.
3. Nationals of either Party shall be permitted, within the territories of the other Party, to gather information material for dissemination to the public, and shall enjoy freedom of transmission of such material to be used abroad for publication by the press, radio, television, motion pictures, and other means; and they shall be permitted to communicate freely with other persons inside and outside such territories by mail, telegraph, and other means open to general public use.
4. The provisions of the present Article shall be subject to the right of either Party to apply measures that are necessary to maintain public order and protect the public health, morals and safety.

ARTICLE III

1. Nationals of either Party within the territories of the other Party shall be free from molestations of every kind, and shall receive the most constant protection and security, in no case less than that required by international law.
2. If, within the territories of either Party, a national of the other Party is taken into custody, the nearest consular representative of his country shall on the demand of such national be immediately notified and shall have the right to visit and communicate with such national. Such national shall: (a) receive reasonable and humane treatment; (b) be formally and immediately informed of the accusations against him; (c) be brought to trial as promptly as is consistent with the proper preparation of his defense; and (d) enjoy all means reasonably necessary to his defense, including the services of competent counsel of his choice.

* * * *

ARTICLE V

1. Nationals and companies of either Party shall be accorded national treatment and most-favored-nation treatment with respect to access to the courts of justice and to administrative tribunals and agencies within the territories of the other Party, in all degrees of jurisdiction, both in pursuit and in defense

of their rights. It is understood that companies of either Party not engaged in activities within the territories of the other Party shall enjoy such access therein without any requirement of registration or domestication.

2. Contracts entered into between nationals and companies of either Party and nationals and companies of the other Party, that provide for the settlement by arbitration of controversies, shall not be deemed unenforceable within the territories of such other Party merely on the grounds that the place designated for the arbitration proceedings is outside such territories or that the nationality of one or more of the arbitrators is not that of such other Party. No award duly rendered pursuant to any such contract, and final and enforceable under the laws of the place where rendered, shall be deemed invalid or denied effective means of enforcement within the territories of either Party merely on the grounds that the place where such award was rendered is outside such territories or that the nationality of one or more of the arbitrators is not that of such Party.

ARTICLE VI

1. Property of nationals and companies of either Party shall receive the most constant protection and security within the territories of the other Party. Neither Party shall take unreasonable or discriminatory measures that would impair the legally acquired rights or interests within its territories of nationals and companies of the other Party in the enterprises which they have established, in their capital, or in the skills, arts or technology which they have supplied.
2. The dwellings, offices, warehouses, factories and other premises of nationals and companies of either Party located within the territories of the other Party shall not be subject to molestation or to entry without just cause. Official searches and examinations of such premises and their contents, when necessary, shall be made only according to law and with careful regard for the convenience of the occupants and the conduct of business.
3. Property of nationals and companies of either Party shall not be taken within the territories of the other Party except for a public purpose, nor shall it be taken without the prompt payment of just compensation. Such compensation shall be in effectively realizable form and shall represent the full equivalent of the property taken; and adequate provision shall have been made at or prior to the time of taking for the determination and payment thereof.
4. Nationals and companies of either Party shall in no case be accorded, within the territories of the other Party, less than national treatment and most-favored-nation treatment with respect to the matters set forth in paragraphs 2 and [3] of the present Article. Moreover, enterprises in which nationals and companies of either Party have a substantial interest shall be accorded, within the territories of the other Party, not less than national treatment and most-favored-nation treatment in all matters relating to the taking of privately owned enterprises into public ownership and to the placing of such enterprises under public control.

ARTICLE VII

1. Nationals and companies of either Party shall be accorded national treatment with respect to engaging in all types of commercial, industrial, financial and other activity for gain (business activities) within the territories of the other Party, whether directly or by agent or through the medium of any form of lawful judicial entity. Accordingly, such nationals and companies shall be permitted within such territories: (a) to establish and maintain branches, agencies, offices, factories and other establishments appropriate to the conduct of their business; (b) to organize companies under the general company laws of such other Party, and to acquire majority interests in companies of such other Party; and (c) to control and manage enterprises which they have established or acquired. Moreover, enterprises which they control, whether in the form of individual proprietorships, companies or otherwise, shall in all that relates to the conduct of the activities thereof, be accord treatment no less favorable than that accorded like enterprises controlled by nationals and companies of such other Party.
2. Each Party reserves the right to limit the extent to which aliens may establish, acquire interest in, or carry on enterprises engaged within its territories in communications, air or water transport, the performance of trust functions, banking involving depository functions, or the exploitation of land or other natural resources. However, new limitations imposed by either Party upon the extent to which aliens are accorded national treatment, with respect to carrying on such activities within its territories, shall not be applied as against enterprises which are engaged in such activities therein at the time such new limitations are adopted and which are owned or controlled by nationals and companies of the other Party. Moreover, neither Party shall deny to transportation, communications and banking companies of the other Party the right to maintain branches and agencies, in conformity with the applicable laws and regulations, to perform functions necessary for essentially internationals operations in which they engage.
3. The provisions of paragraph 1 of the present Article shall not prevent either Party from prescribing special formalities in connection with the establishment of alien-controlled enterprises within its territories; but such formalities may not impair the substance of the rights set forth in said paragraph.
4. Nationals and companies of either Party, as well as enterprises controlled by such nationals and companies, shall in any event be accorded most-favored-nation treatment with reference to the matters treated in the present Article.

ARTICLE VIII

1. Nationals and companies of either Party shall be permitted to engage, within the territories of the other Party, accountants and other technical experts, executive personnel, attorneys, agents and other specialists of their choice. Moreover, such nationals and companies shall be permitted to engage

accountants and other technical experts regardless of the extent to which they may have qualified for the practice of a profession within the territories of such other Party, for the particular purpose of making examinations, audits and technical investigations for, and rendering reports to, such nationals and companies in connection with the planning and operation of their enterprises, and enterprises in which they have a financial interest, within such territories.

2. Nationals and companies of either Party shall be accorded national treatment and most-favored-nation treatment with respect to engaging in scientific, educational, religious and philanthropic activities within the territories of the other Party, and shall be accorded the right to form associations for that purpose under the laws of such other Party. Nothing in the present Treaty shall be deemed to grant or imply any right to engage in political activities.

ARTICLE IX

1. Nationals and companies of . . . . shall be accorded, within the territories of the United States of America: (a) national treatment with request to leasing land, buildings and other real property appropriate to the conduct of activities in which they are permitted to engage pursuant to Articles VII and VIII and for residential purposes and with respect to occupying and using such property; and (b) other rights in real property permitted by the applicable laws of the States, Territories and possessions of the United States of America.
2. Nationals and companies of the United States of America shall be accorded within the territories of . . . . national treatment with respect to acquiring by purchase, lease, or otherwise, and with respect to owning, occupying and using land, buildings and other real property. However, in the case of any such national domiciled in, or any such company constituted under the laws of, any State, Territory or possession of the United States of America that accords less than national treatment to nationals and companies of . . . . in this respect, ... shall not be obligated to accord treatment more favorable in this respect than such State, Territory or possession accords to the nationals of . . . .
3. Nationals and companies of either Party shall be accorded within the territories of the other Party national treatment and most-favored-nation treatment with respect to acquiring, by purchase, lease, or otherwise, and with respect to owning and possessing, personal property of all kinds, both tangible and intangible. However, either Party may impose restrictions on alien ownership of materials dangerous from the standpoint of public safety and alien ownership of interests in enterprises carrying on particular types of activity, but only to the extent that this can be done without impairing the rights and privileges secured by Article VII or by other provisions of the present Treaty.
4. Nationals and companies of either Party shall be accorded national treatment within the territories of the other Party with respect to acquiring property of all kinds by testate or intestate succession or through judicial process. Should they because of their allegiance be ineligible to continue to

own any such property, they shall be allowed a period of at least five years in which to dispose of it.

5. Nationals and companies of either Party shall be accorded within the territories of the other Party national treatment and most-favored-nation treatment with respect to disposing of property of all kinds.

ARTICLE X

1. Nationals and companies of either Party shall be accorded, within the territories of the other Party, national treatment and most-favored-nation treatment with respect to obtaining and maintaining patents of invention, and with respect to rights in trade marks, trade names, trade labels and industrial property of every kind.
2. The Parties undertake to cooperate in furthering the interchange and use of scientific and technical knowledge, particularly in the interests of increasing productivity and improving standards of living within their respective territories.

* * * *

ARTICLE XII

1. Nationals and companies of either Party shall be accorded by the other Party national treatment and most-favored-nation treatment with respect to payments, remittances and transfers of funds or financial instruments between the territories of the two Parties as well as between the territories of such other Party and of any third country.
2. Neither Party shall impose exchange restrictions as defined in paragraph 5 of the present Article except to the extent necessary to prevent its monetary reserves from falling to a very low level or to affect a moderate increase in very low monetary reserves. It is understood that the provisions of the present Article do not alter the obligations either Party may have to the International Monetary Fund or preclude imposition of particular restrictions whenever the Fund specifically authorizes or requests a Party to impose such particular restrictions.
3. If either Party imposes exchange restrictions in accordance with paragraph 2 of the present Article, it shall, after making whatever provision may be necessary to assure the availability of foreign exchange for goods and services essential to the health and welfare of its people, make reasonable provision for the withdrawal, in foreign exchange in the currency of the other Party, of: (a) the compensation referred to in Article VI, paragraph 3, (b) earnings, whether in the form of salaries, interest, dividends, commissions[,] royalties, payments for technical services, or otherwise, (c) amounts for amortization of loans, depreciation of direct investments, and capital transfers, giving consideration to special needs for other transactions. If more than one rate of exchange is in force, the rate applicable to such withdrawal shall be a rate which is specifically

approved by the International Monetary Fund for such transactions or, in the absence of a rate so approved an effective rate which, inclusive of any taxes or surcharges on exchange transfers, is just and reasonable.

4. Exchange restrictions shall not be imposed by either Party in a manner unnecessarily detrimental or arbitrarily discriminatory to the claims, investments, transport, trade, and other interests of the nationals and companies of the other Party, nor to the competitive position thereof.
5. The term "exchange restrictions" as used in the present Article includes all restrictions, regulations, charges, taxes, or other requirements imposed by either Party which burden or interfere with payments, remittances, or transfers of funds or of financial instruments between the territories of the two Parties.

* * * *

ARTICLE XV

1. Each Party shall promptly publish laws, regulations and administrative rulings of general application pertaining to rates of duty, taxes or other charges, to the classification of articles for customs purposes, and to requirements or restrictions on imports and exports or the transfer of payments therefor, or affecting their sale, distribution or use; and shall administer such laws, regulations and rulings in a uniform, impartial and reasonable manner. As a general practice, new administrative requirements or restrictions affecting imports, with the exception of those imposed on sanitary grounds or for reasons of public safety, shall not go into effect before the expiration of 30 days after publication, or alternatively, shall not apply to products en route at time of publication.
2. Each Party shall provide an appeals procedure under which nationals and companies of the other Party, and importers of products of such other Party, shall be able to obtain prompt and impartial review, and correction when warranted, of administrative action relating to customs matters, including the imposition of fines and penalties, confiscations, and rulings on questions of customs classification and valuation by the administrative authorities. Penalties imposed for infractions of the customs and shipping laws and regulations shall be merely nominal in cases resulting from clerical errors or when good faith can be demonstrated.

* * * *

ARTICLE XVII

1. Each Party undertakes (a) that enterprises owned or controlled by its Government, and that monopolies or agencies granted exclusive or special privileges within its territories, shall make their purchases and sales involving either imports or exports affecting the commerce of the other Party solely in accordance with commercial considerations, including price, quality, availability, marketability, transportation and other conditions of purchase or sale; and (b) that the nationals, companies and commerce of

such other Party shall be afforded adequate opportunity, in accordance with customary business practice, to compete for participation in such purchases and sales.

2. Each Party shall accord to the nationals, companies and commerce of the other Party fair and equitable treatment, as compared with that accorded to the nationals, companies and commerce of any third country, with respect to: (a) the governmental purchase of supplies, (b) the awarding of concessions and other government contracts, and (c) the sale of any service sold by the Government or by any monopoly or agency granted exclusive or special privileges.
3. Neither Party shall impose any measure of a discriminatory nature that hinders or prevents the importer or exporter of products of either country from obtaining marine insurance on such products in companies of either Party.

ARTICLE XVIII

1. The two Parties agree that business practices which restrain competition, limit access to markets or foster monopolistic control, and which are engaged in or made effective by one or more private or public commercial enterprises or by combination, agreement or other arrangement among such enterprises, may have harmful effects upon commerce between their respective territories. Accordingly, each Party agrees upon the request of the other Party to consult with respect to any such practices and to take such measures as it deems appropriate with a view to eliminating such harmful effects.
2. The Parties recognize that conditions of competitive equality should be maintained in situations in which publicly owned or controlled trading or manufacturing enterprises of either Party engage in competition, within the territories thereof, with privately owned and controlled enterprises of nationals and companies of the other Party. Accordingly, such private enterprises shall, in such situations, be entitled to the benefit of any special advantages of an economic nature accorded such public enterprises, whether in the nature of subsidies, tax exemptions or otherwise. The foregoing rule shall not apply, however, to special advantages given in connection with: (a) manufacturing goods for government use; or (b) supplying at prices substantially below competitive prices, the needs of particular population groups for essential goods and services not otherwise practically obtainable by such groups.
3. No enterprise of either Party, including corporations, associations, and government agencies and instrumentalities, which is publicly owned or controlled shall, if it engages in commercial, industrial, shipping or other business activities within the territories of the other Party, claim or enjoy, either for itself or for its property, immunity therein from taxation, suit, execution of judgment or other liability to which privately owned and controlled enterprises are subject therein.

* * * *

ARTICLE XXI

1. The present Treaty shall not preclude the application of measures:
   (a) regulating the importation or exportation of gold or silver;
   (b) relating to fissionable materials, to radioactive by-products of the utilization or processing thereof, or to materials that are the source of fissionable materials;
   (c) regulating the production of or traffic in arms, ammunition and implements of war, or traffic in other materials carried on directly or indirectly for the purpose of supplying a military establishment;
   (d) necessary to fulfill the obligations of a Party for the maintenance or restoration of international peace and security, or necessary to protect its essential security interests;
   (e) denying to any company in the ownership or direction of which nationals of any third country or countries have directly or indirectly the controlling interest, the advantages of the present Treaty, except with respect to recognition of juridical status and with respect to access to courts; or
   (f) regarding its national fisheries and the landing of products thereof.

* * * *

4. Nationals of either Party admitted into the territories of the other Party for limited purposes shall not enjoy rights to engage in gainful occupations in contravention of limitations expressly imposed, according to law, as a condition of their admittance.

ARTICLE XXII

1. The term "national treatment" means treatment accorded within the territories of a Party upon terms no less favorable than the treatment accorded therein, in like situations, to nationals, companies, products, vessels or other objects, as the case may be, of such Party.
2. The term "most-favored-nation treatment" means treatment accorded within the territories of a Party upon terms no less favorable than the treatment accorded therein, in like situations, to nationals, companies, products, vessels or other objects, as the case may be, of any third country.
3. As used in the present Treaty, the term "companies" means corporations, partnerships, companies and other associations, whether or not with limited liability and whether or not for pecuniary profit. Companies constituted under the applicable laws and regulations within the territories of either Party shall be deemed companies thereof and shall have their juridical status recognized within the territories of the other Party.
4. National treatment accorded under the provisions of the present Treaty to companies of . . . . shall, in any State, Territory or possession of the United States of America, be the treatment accorded therein to companies created or organized in other States, Territories, and possessions of the United States of America.

* * * *

ARTICLE XXIV

1. Each Party shall accord sympathetic consideration to, and shall afford adequate opportunity for consultation regarding, such representations as the other Party may make with respect to any matter affecting the operation of the present Treaty.
2. Any dispute between the Parties as to the interpretation or application of the present Treaty, not satisfactorily adjusted by diplomacy, shall be submitted to the International Court of Justice, unless the Parties agree to settlement by some other pacific means.

* * * *

PROTOCOL

At the time of signing the Treaty of Friendship, Commerce and Navigation between the United State of America and .... the undersigned Plenipotentiaries, duly authorized by their respective Governments, have further agreed on the following provisions, which shall be considered integral parts of the aforesaid Treaty:

1. The provisions of Article II, paragraph 1 (b), shall be construed as extending to persons who represent nationals and companies of the same nationality which have invested or are actively in the process of investing a substantial amount of capital in an enterprise in the territories of the other Party, and who are employed by such nationals and companies in a responsible capacity.
2. The term "access" as used in Article V, paragraph 1, comprehends, among other things, legal aid and security for costs and judgment.
3. The provisions of Article VI, paragraph 3, providing for the payment of compensation shall extend to interests held directly or indirectly by nationals and companies of either Party in property which is taken within the territories of the other Party.
4. The activities referred to in Article VII, paragraph 1, do not include the practice of professions.
5. With reference to Article VII, paragraph 4, either Party may require that rights to engage in mining on the public domain shall be dependent on reciprocity.
6. The provisions of Article XVII, paragraph 2 (b) and (c), and of Article XIX, paragraph 4, shall not apply to postal services.
7. The provisions of Article XXI, paragraph 2, shall apply in the case of Puerto Rico regardless of any change that may take place in its political status.

* * * *

Index

www.ingramcontent.com/pod-product-compliance
Ingram Content Group UK Ltd.
Pitfield, Milton Keynes, MK11 3LW, UK
UKHW020850150926
475595UK00003B/115

9 780190 679576